Caribbean For Dummies®
1st Edition

D0562928

Our Favorite Caribbean Beaches

The main reason most folks go to the Caribbean is to relax on the beach. And just as you can visit many different kinds of islands, you can find many different kinds of beaches to suit almost anything you want to do. Here are our favorites:

- **Bathsheba, Barbados.** Who would have thought there'd be something like this in the Caribbean? Giant boulders and crashing waves make for a perfect spot to watch the sunrise. The rocks look like they'll teeter over any minute in the pounding Atlantic surf. But they don't, and at dawn a gaggle of surfers are already out to enjoy the waves. It's not a beach for swimmers, but we like the vibe and the view. (See Chapter 15.)

- **Chenay Bay, St. Croix, U.S. Virgin Islands.** In a calm, protected bay, local moms bring their kids to splash in the placid sea along with visiting children. It's a relaxed atmosphere on the white sand beach where sea grapes and palms offer shade. The beach grill and bar is close at hand. (See Chapter 35.)

- **Condado, Puerto Rico.** One of the most famous Caribbean beaches, though not the prettiest, the Condado throbs with energy and is peopled with Ricky Martin and Jennifer Lopez lookalikes. It's a fun, happening spot. (See Chapter 31.)

- **Loblolly Beach, Anegada, British Virgin Islands.** If we were pirates, we'd blend in with the casual crew on forgotten Anegada, known for its famed Caribbean lobsters caught just offshore. You can enjoy great snorkeling while your lunch is being grilled. (See Chapter 19.)

- **Magen's Bay, St. Thomas, U.S. Virgin Islands.** This beach is the don't-miss attraction on St. Thomas. An ideal spot for swimming and sunning, this half-mile stretch is protected by two peninsulas. (See Chapter 35.)

- **Palm Beach, Aruba.** This gorgeous, palm-lined wide white strand is the quintessential Caribbean beach, plus it's clean and safe. You'll have to arrive early to snag a cabana. At the far end, you can see wind surfers guiding their colorful crafts. During the evenings, visitors go from hotel to hotel enjoying the beach parties. (See Chapter 11.)

- **Seven Mile Beach, Grand Cayman.** Okay, so it's been discovered. Despite the crowds, you can't beat this beautiful white strand for every kind of water fun. (See Chapter 23.)

- **Trunk Bay, St. John, U.S. Virgin Islands.** This beauty of a beach has been photographed more times than Cindy Crawford. Despite complaints that it's been overexposed, Trunk Bay is stunning and has great facilities. You can have a picnic on the beach, snorkel the marked trail (though much of the coral has been damaged), or just bask in the sun. (See Chapter 35.)

Two Spots to Try If You Could Care Less about the Beach

We realize that not everyone enjoys the beach, so here are some great vacation spots in the Caribbean if you hate to get sand in your shoes.

- **Blue Mountains, Jamaica.** At Strawberry Hill, high above Kingston, you'll be given heated duvets to ward off the mountain chill at night, and a fire is always lit in the elegant bar area. You can relax at the Aveda Spa, hike the coffee plantations high in the Blue Mountains, and linger over the wild flowers that dot the mountainsides. (See chapters 24 and 27.)

- **Old San Juan, Puerto Rico.** Cobblestone streets and gorgeous architecture in this colonial city remind us of Spain. The bustling art scene, great restaurants, and upscale shopping can keep you thoroughly entertained. (See chapters 28 and 31.)

Diving and Snorkeling in the Caribbean

The Caribbean yields a plethora of diving experiences: easy shore dives, great wall dives, wreck dives, night dives, and drift dives. Best of all are the incredible critters and fish that you encounter along the underwater way.

Here are some top diving spots:

- **Grand Cayman.** Here, you can mingle with the stingrays at famous Sting Ray City or enjoy unparalleled wall diving.
- **Bonaire.** A quick day trip from Aruba, this island is ringed with great shore diving sites, and the marine park is one of the better preserved in the Caribbean.
- **Puerto Rico.** You can experience the glow of a phosphorescent bay at night and explore a host of caves.
- **The British Virgin Islands.** Here, you'll find the wreck where part of the movie *The Deep* was filmed.
- **St. John, the U.S. Virgin Islands.** A fabulous underwater national park is among its treasures.

Questions to Ask Dive Operators

- **How many boats does the operator have? Are they all in good repair and currently operating?** Some Caribbean operators are weak on keeping their facilities topnotch.
- **What's the maximum number of divers per boat?** Beware of "cattle boats" where divers get herded on and off; you can easily get lost in the shuffle.
- **Is the dive operator on-site at a hotel or resort?** When you are lugging heavy gear, the last thing you want to do is hassle with extra transportation.
- **How many dives are allowed each day?** The answer will help you get a feel for whom the operation is geared.
- **If I buy a package, can I substitute dives because of personal schedule or weather changes?** In the Caribbean, you want a flexible operator who will work with you if the weather or other variables wreak havoc with your plans.
- **Who (if anyone) guides the dives?** An attentive divemaster can make all the difference between a nice dive and a superb experience. On the other hand, bored divemasters who hustle you past all the small reef life can be frustrating.
- **What is the cost per dive?**
- **Are night dives available?**
- **Are Nitrox fills available?** Nitrox is an alternative breathing gas that is becoming increasingly popular with experienced divers.
- **Is shore diving available?** Shore diving gives you much more diving freedom, so that you aren't always reliant on a boat.
- **Are rinse tanks (for cleaning your gear) and lockers (for storing your gear between dives) available?** Conveniences make a big difference in your experience, and to us these are important features a good dive operation should have.

For Dummies™: Bestselling Book Series for Beginners

 ™

References for the Rest of Us! ™

BESTSELLING BOOK SERIES

Do you find that traditional reference books are overloaded with technical details and advice you'll never use? Do you postpone important life decisions because you just don't want to deal with them? Then our *...For Dummies®* business and general reference book series is for you.

...For Dummies business and general reference books are written for those frustrated and hard-working souls who know they aren't dumb, but find that the myriad of personal and business issues and the accompanying horror stories make them feel helpless. *...For Dummies* books use a lighthearted approach, a down-to-earth style, and even cartoons and humorous icons to dispel fears and build confidence. Lighthearted but not lightweight, these books are perfect survival guides to solve your everyday personal and business problems.

> *"More than a publishing phenomenon, 'Dummies' is a sign of the times."*
>
> — The New York Times

> *"A world of detailed and authoritative information is packed into them..."*
>
> — U.S. News and World Report

> *"...you won't go wrong buying them."*
>
> — Walter Mossberg, Wall Street Journal, on IDG Books' ...For Dummies books

Already, millions of satisfied readers agree. They have made *...For Dummies* the #1 introductory level computer book series and a best-selling business book series. They have written asking for more. So, if you're looking for the best and easiest way to learn about business and other general reference topics, look to *...For Dummies* to give you a helping hand.

IDG BOOKS WORLDWIDE

1/99

Caribbean
FOR
DUMMIES®
1ST EDITION

by Echo Montgomery Garrett and Kevin Garrett

IDG
BOOKS
WORLDWIDE

IDG Books Worldwide, Inc.
An International Data Group Company

Foster City, CA ✦ Chicago, IL ✦ Indianapolis, IN ✦ New York, NY

Caribbean For Dummies™, 1st Edition

Published by
IDG Books Worldwide, Inc.
An International Data Group Company
919 E. Hillsdale Blvd.
Suite 400
Foster City, CA 94404
www.idgbooks.com (IDG Books Worldwide Web Site)
www.dummies.com (Dummies Press Web Site)

Library of Congress Control Number: 00-103379

ISBN: 0-7645-6197-9

Printed in the United States of America

10 9 8 7 6 5 4 3 2 1

1B/QR/QZ/QQ/IN

Distributed in the United States by IDG Books Worldwide, Inc.

Distributed by CDG Books Canada Inc. for Canada; by Transworld Publishers Limited in the United Kingdom; by IDG Norge Books for Norway; by IDG Sweden Books for Sweden; by IDG Books Australia Publishing Corporation Pty. Ltd. for Australia and New Zealand; by TransQuest Publishers Pte Ltd. for Singapore, Malaysia, Thailand, Indonesia, and Hong Kong; by Gotop Information Inc. for Taiwan; by ICG Muse, Inc. for Japan; by Intersoft for South Africa; by Eyrolles for France; by International Thomson Publishing for Germany, Austria and Switzerland; by Distribuidora Cuspide for Argentina; by LR International for Brazil; by Galileo Libros for Chile; by Ediciones ZETA S.C.R. Ltda. for Peru; by WS Computer Publishing Corporation, Inc., for the Philippines; by Contemporanea de Ediciones for Venezuela; by Express Computer Distributors for the Caribbean and West Indies; by Micronesia Media Distributor, Inc. for Micronesia; by Chips Computadoras S.A. de C.V. for Mexico; by Editorial Norma de Panama S.A. for Panama; by American Bookshops for Finland.

For general information on IDG Books Worldwide's books in the U.S., please call our Consumer Customer Service department at 800-762-2974. For reseller information, including discounts and premium sales, please call our Reseller Customer Service department at 800-434-3422.

For information on where to purchase IDG Books Worldwide's books outside the U.S., please contact our International Sales department at 317-572-3993 or fax 317-572-4002.

For consumer information on foreign language translations, please contact our Customer Service department at 1-800-434-3422, fax 317-572-4002, or e-mail rights@idgbooks.com.

For information on licensing foreign or domestic rights, please phone +1-650-653-7098.

For sales inquiries and special prices for bulk quantities, please contact our Order Services department at 800-434-4322 or write to the address above.

For information on using IDG Books Worldwide's books in the classroom or for ordering examination copies, please contact our Educational Sales department at 800-434-2086 or fax 317-572-4005.

For press review copies, author interviews, or other publicity information, please contact our Public Relations department at 650-653-7000 or fax 650-653-7500.

For authorization to photocopy items for corporate, personal, or educational use, please contact Copyright Clearance Center, 222 Rosewood Drive, Danvers, MA 01923, or fax 978-750-4470.

is a registered trademark under exclusive license to IDG Books Worldwide, Inc., from International Data Group, Inc.

About the Authors

Being in the Caribbean as part of their job means that Echo and Kevin Garrett get absolutely no sympathy from their friends when they are on deadline — nor from their two young sons, for that matter. Recently, when Kevin was leaving to spend eight days photographing and writing about Jamaica, he told their sons he was going away on a business trip. The eldest, Caleb, arched an eyebrow and asked, "Does this business trip involve an island?"

Indeed, the Garretts make the Caribbean their playground, having hiked, biked, snorkeled, dived, windsurfed, sailed, shopped, and dined their way through the islands over the past decade. Kevin is the author of *Fielding's Caribbean*. His articles have appeared in *Affordable Caribbean, The Atlanta Journal-Constitution, Biztravel.com, Bridal Guide, Chicago Magazine, Coastal Living, Elegant Bride, Executive Getaways, Fantastic Flyer, Great Outdoor Recreational Pages, Investor's Business Daily, Islands, Second Home* and *The Self-Employed Professional*.

He and Echo updated/wrote chapters on Aruba, Bonaire, and Curaçao for *Rum & Reggae's Caribbean 2000*. The duo also co-wrote chapters on Tennessee and Georgia for three Fodor's guide books. An award-winning photographer and member of the American Society of Media Photographers, Kevin's images (www.kevingarrett.com) have run in several of the above publications as well as *Voyages: The Romance of Cruising* (Tehabi Books), *Hemispheres, Los Angeles, Management Review, Smart Money, Southern Accents, Travel Holiday, Travel & Leisure, Weight Watchers,* and *World Trade*.

Echo worked as an editor at *McCall's* and *Venture* before going freelance in 1988, racking up credits from the *New York Times* to *Money*, where she became a contributing writer covering travel. Her stories were frequently picked up by television media, and she was interviewed on *Good Morning America* about staying safe while you travel. Her first book, *How to Make a Buck and Still Be a Decent Human Being,* was published by HarperBusiness in 1992.

Echo was a founding editor for an award-winning Web site, *BizTravel.com,* responsible for *Executive Getaways*; a contributing writer for "News For You," the best-read, front-page column in *Investor's Business Daily*; and a contributing writer covering hospitality and restaurants for *The Atlanta Business Chronicle*. She's now a regular contributor to *Business Week's* "Frontier" section. Her work has appeared in more than 50 national publications.

One of their favorite recent assignments was following in James Bond's footsteps in the Caribbean for *Coastal Living*. They stayed at Goldeneye, Ian Fleming's Jamaica estate where he wrote all 14 James Bond novels. As part of the assignment, Kevin went diving with sharks accompanied by the folks who do the shark wrangling for the Bond flicks. When they are not living a James Bond fantasy, the Garretts live in Marietta, Georgia.

ABOUT IDG BOOKS WORLDWIDE

Welcome to the world of IDG Books Worldwide.

IDG Books Worldwide, Inc., is a subsidiary of International Data Group, the world's largest publisher of computer-related information and the leading global provider of information services on information technology. IDG was founded more than 30 years ago by Patrick J. McGovern and now employs more than 9,000 people worldwide. IDG publishes more than 290 computer publications in over 75 countries. More than 90 million people read one or more IDG publications each month.

Launched in 1990, IDG Books Worldwide is today the #1 publisher of best-selling computer books in the United States. We are proud to have received eight awards from the Computer Press Association in recognition of editorial excellence and three from Computer Currents' First Annual Readers' Choice Awards. Our best-selling ...*For Dummies*® series has more than 50 million copies in print with translations in 31 languages. IDG Books Worldwide, through a joint venture with IDG's Hi-Tech Beijing, became the first U.S. publisher to publish a computer book in the People's Republic of China. In record time, IDG Books Worldwide has become the first choice for millions of readers around the world who want to learn how to better manage their businesses.

Our mission is simple: Every one of our books is designed to bring extra value and skill-building instructions to the reader. Our books are written by experts who understand and care about our readers. The knowledge base of our editorial staff comes from years of experience in publishing, education, and journalism — experience we use to produce books to carry us into the new millennium. In short, we care about books, so we attract the best people. We devote special attention to details such as audience, interior design, use of icons, and illustrations. And because we use an efficient process of authoring, editing, and desktop publishing our books electronically, we can spend more time ensuring superior content and less time on the technicalities of making books.

You can count on our commitment to deliver high-quality books at competitive prices on topics you want to read about. At IDG Books Worldwide, we continue in the IDG tradition of delivering quality for more than 30 years. You'll find no better book on a subject than one from IDG Books Worldwide.

John Kilcullen
Chairman and CEO
IDG Books Worldwide, Inc.

*Eighth Annual
Computer Press
Awards ⥲1992*

*Ninth Annual
Computer Press
Awards ⥲1993*

*Tenth Annual
Computer Press
Awards ⥲1994*

*Eleventh Annual
Computer Press
Awards ⥲1995*

IDG is the world's leading IT media, research and exposition company. Founded in 1964, IDG had 1997 revenues of $2.05 billion and has more than 9,000 employees worldwide. IDG offers the widest range of media options that reach IT buyers in 75 countries representing 95% of worldwide IT spending. IDG's diverse product and services portfolio spans six key areas including print publishing, online publishing, expositions and conferences, market research, education and training, and global marketing services. More than 90 million people read one or more of IDG's 290 magazines and newspapers, including IDG's leading global brands — Computerworld, PC World, Network World, Macworld and the Channel World family of publications. IDG Books Worldwide is one of the fastest-growing computer book publishers in the world, with more than 700 titles in 36 languages. The "...For Dummies®" series alone has more than 50 million copies in print. IDG offers online users the largest network of technology-specific Web sites around the world through IDG.net (http://www.idg.net), which comprises more than 225 targeted Web sites in 55 countries worldwide. International Data Corporation (IDC) is the world's largest provider of information technology data, analysis and consulting, with research centers in over 41 countries and more than 400 research analysts worldwide. IDG World Expo is a leading producer of more than 168 globally branded conferences and expositions in 35 countries including E3 (Electronic Entertainment Expo), Macworld Expo, ComNet, Windows World Expo, ICE (Internet Commerce Expo), Agenda, DEMO, and Spotlight. IDG's training subsidiary, ExecuTrain, is the world's largest computer training company, with more than 230 locations worldwide and 785 training courses. IDG Marketing Services helps industry-leading IT companies build international brand recognition by developing global integrated marketing programs via IDG's print, online and exposition products worldwide. Further information about the company can be found at www.idg.com.   1/26/00

Dedication

To our beloved sons, Caleb and Connor.

Authors' Acknowledgments

We'd like to express our deepest thanks to our many friends and sources who aided us in producing this book. First, of course, thanks to Suzanne Jannetta of IDG Books and Margot Weiss for her encouragement and edits. A special thanks to Larry and Jennifer Salberg for keeping our heads and hearts in the right place. Big hugs to Marcia Scaggs, Amy Mullis, Dana Hawkins, and Anne Stevens who helped keep us organized and lent a hand with our kids. Kudos to: Aruba's Doreen Boekhoudt; Frances Borden; Scott Croft, Peter Martin & Associates; Ginny Craven, Progressive Public Relations; Laura Davidson and Kristen Crowley, Laura Davidson Public Relations; Lyla Naseem, Patrice Tanaka & Company; Marcella Martinez and Mary Brennan, Martinez Public Relations; Tiffany Wentz and Shantini Ramakrishnan, Spring O'Brien Public Relations; Lisa Blau, Adams Unlimited; Julie Zirbel, Rosewood Hotels & Resorts; Alyssa Rogers, Jensen/Boga, Inc.; Marilyn Marx; Virginia Haynes Montgomery, BCN; Ingrid Stewart and Kelly Fontenelle, St. Lucia Tourist Board; Mary Jane Kolassa, YP&B; Kristen Driska, FCB; Suzanne McManus, SuperClubs; Cheryl Andrews and Kathy Vivancos, Cheryl Andrews Marketing; Roberta Garizoli, Jensen Boga Public Relations; Jason Henzell, Jake's; Teresa Mears and Hilari Dobbs, Kahn Travel Communications; Karen Weiner, Escalera Associates; Quinn & Company; Ruder-Finn; Maren Lau, Hill & Knowlton; Lou Hammond, Lou Hammond & Associates; and our buddy, David Swanson. A special hats off to Amy A. Atkinson and Luana Wheatley, Martin Public Relations.

Publisher's Acknowledgments

We're proud of this book; please register your comments through our IDG Books Worldwide Online Registration Form located at http://my2cents.dummies.com.

Some of the people who helped bring this book to market include the following:

Acquisitions, Editorial, and Media Development

Editors: Joan Friedman, Suzanne Jannetta

Senior Copy Editor: Linda S. Stark

Cartographer: John Decamillis

Editorial Manager: Christine Meloy Beck

Editorial Assistant: Carol Strickland

Production

Project Coordinator: Emily Wichlinski

Layout and Graphics: Jason Guy, Gabriele McCann, Shelley Norris, Barry Offringa, Kristin Pickett, Jill Piscitelli, Brent Savage, Kathie Schutte, Jeremey Unger, Erin Zeltner

Proofreaders: David Faust, Susan Moritz, Jeannie Smith

Indexer: Joan Griffitts

Special Help
Mary Fales

General and Administrative

IDG Books Worldwide, Inc.: John Kilcullen, CEO; Bill Barry, President and COO

IDG Books Consumer Reference Group

Business: Kathleen A. Welton, Vice President and Publisher; Kevin Thornton, Acquisitions Manager

Cooking/Gardening: Jennifer Feldman, Associate Vice President and Publisher

Education/Reference: Diane Graves Steele, Vice President and Publisher; Greg Tubach, Publishing Director

Lifestyles: Kathleen Nebenhaus, Vice President and Publisher; Tracy Boggier, Managing Editor

Pets: Dominique Devito, Associate Vice President and Publisher; Tracy Boggier, Managing Editor

Travel: Michael Spring, Vice President and Publisher; Suzanne Jannetta, Editorial Director; Brice Gosnell, Managing Editor

IDG Books Consumer Editorial Services: Kathleen Nebenhaus, Vice President and Publisher; Kristin A. Cocks, Editorial Director; Cindy Kitchel, Editorial Director

IDG Books Consumer Production: Debbie Stailey, Production Director

IDG Books Packaging: Marc J. Mikulich, Vice President, Brand Strategy and Research

Packaging and Book Design: Patty Page, Manager, Promotions Marketing

◆

The publisher would like to give special thanks to Patrick J. McGovern, without whom this book would not have been possible.

◆

Contents at a Glance

Cartoons at a Glance

By Rich Tennant

Maps at a Glance

Table of Contents

· ·

Introduction

●●

*W*e know that you've been looking for *Caribbean For Dummies*. About two minutes after we introduce ourselves to new acquaintances and tell them that we specialize in writing about the Caribbean, we inevitably get the question: Where should I go on my anniversary / honeymoon / birthday / vacation?

Of course, the shelves are groaning with guidebooks on the Caribbean, but this one is different. In *Caribbean For Dummies*, we guide you through choosing the right island for you and yours and take you on a romp that hits the high points of each. We don't try to give you an exhaustive guide to the Caribbean. Lots of other books do that (and often leave you more confused than when you started).

Indeed, we've left out a whole bunch of islands, sticking to those that are the most popular with tourists. And on the islands we do cover, we keep information pared to the basics: what you'll encounter when you land, where to stay, where to eat, and where to go to have fun while you're there.

How to Use This Book

You can use this book in three ways:

- ✔ **As a trip planner.** If you are trying to decide between two islands or more, we steer you in the right direction. Then you can skip straight to the chapters on your particular destination to plan every aspect of your trip, from packing the right stuff to getting the best deal on your resort.

- ✔ **As an island guide.** Bring this book with you to your island destination because we let you know what to expect and tell you our favorite places to go — from the best beaches to the coolest bars to the most romantic restaurants.

- ✔ **As a fun overview.** If you want to get a good feel for the Caribbean as a whole, read this book straight through because we hit all the high points.

Please be advised that travel information is subject to change at any time — and this is especially true of prices. Therefore, we suggest that you write or call ahead for confirmation when making your travel plans. The authors, editors, and publisher cannot be held responsible for the experiences of readers while traveling. Your safety is important to us, however, so we encourage you to stay alert and be aware of your surroundings. Keep a close eye on cameras, purses, and wallets, all favorite targets of thieves and pickpockets.

Conventions Used in This Book

In this book, we've listed our favorite hotels and restaurants, as well as information about special attractions on each island. As we describe each, we often include abbreviations for commonly accepted credit cards. The following list explains each abbreviation:

AE – American Express

DC – Diners Club

DISC – Discover

MC – MasterCard

V – Visa

We also include some general pricing information to help you decide where to unpack your bags or dine on the local cuisine. We've used a system of dollar signs to show a range of costs for one night in a hotel or a meal at a restaurant. Unless we say otherwise, the lodging rates are for a standard double room during high season. (Chapter 3 explains what high season is.) For restaurants, we give the price range for main courses. Check out the following table to decipher the dollar signs.

Cost	Hotel	Restaurant
$	Less than $100 per night	Less than $10
$$	$100–$150	$11–$15
$$$	$150–$225	$15–$20
$$$$	$225–$300 or so	$21–$25
$$$$$	More than $300 per night	$26 and up, up, and away

Foolish Assumptions

As we wrote this book, we made some assumptions about you and what your needs might be as a traveler. Here's what we assumed:

✔ You may be an inexperienced traveler looking for guidance about whether to take a trip to the Caribbean and how to plan a trip to specific islands.

✔ You may be an experienced traveler, but you don't have a lot of time to devote to trip planning or you don't have a lot of time to spend in the Caribbean once you get there. You want expert advice on how to maximize your time and enjoy a hassle-free trip.

    ✔ You're not looking for a book that provides every bit of information available about the Caribbean or that lists every hotel, restaurant, or attraction you could experience. Instead, you're looking for a book that focuses on the places that will give you the best or most unique experience in the Caribbean.

If you fit any of these criteria, then *Caribbean For Dummies* gives you the information you're looking for.

How This Book Is Organized

Caribbean For Dummies is divided into 11 parts. The chapters within each part cover specific topic areas in detail. Feel free to skip around; you don't have to read this book in order. It's kind of like a cafeteria: You can pick and choose what you like.

Part I: Getting Started on Your Caribbean Getaway

In this part, we tell you which islands you'll find in the Caribbean and give you comparisons and contrasts between the popular islands we cover in the book. Each Caribbean island is extremely different from the others, so you need to carefully consider which one sounds like the best fit for you. We also explain in detail the various "seasons" that are used to describe more- and less-popular times of year for people to travel to the Caribbean. We discuss what kind of prices and weather you can expect during each season. We talk about the dreaded H-word (*hurricane*) and discuss how much hurricanes should be considered in your planning — if at all. We thoroughly explain the different accommodations you'll find in the Caribbean along with all the different meal plans and what *all-inclusive* means. Finally, we give resources and tips for families, seniors, travelers with disabilities, and gay and lesbian travelers planning a Caribbean trip.

Part II: Tying Up the Loose Ends

Here we wrap up all the critical information you need in order to decide whether to use a travel agent, a packager, or the Internet when planning your trip. We give you details about which airlines will get you where and what connections you can make to get to some of the more remote areas. You'll also find a chapter that helps you create a trip budget and answers all your questions about money in the Caribbean, from the currency used on each island to what size tips you should give. We wrap up this part by addressing safety concerns, discussing whether you should rent a car, explaining travel insurance, and covering other odds and ends.

Parts III–IX: The Islands

Now we get down to the fun stuff. For each island or island group — **Aruba, Barbados,** the **British Virgin Islands, Grand Cayman, Jamaica, Puerto Rico,** and the **U.S. Virgin Islands** — we give you the scoop on the hotel scene; what you can expect when you actually land on the island (from the airport to taxi drivers); what restaurants you should consider; and, finally, where to go and what to do to squeeze the most fun possible out of your Caribbean vacation.

Part X: The Part of Tens

Every *For Dummies* book has a Part of Tens. Here we tell you what we consider the best Caribbean souvenirs and where to get them. We ruminate over the best local meals we've enjoyed in our island travels. Perhaps most importantly, we give you helpful hints to prevent you from acting too much like a tourist.

At the back of the book, we've also included a bunch of worksheets to make your travel planning easier. Among other things, you can determine your vacation budget, create specific itineraries, and keep a log of your favorite restaurants so you can hit them again next time you're in the islands. You can find these worksheets easily because they're printed on yellow paper.

Icons Used in This Book

This icon signals the most romantic restaurants, hotels, and attractions in the Caribbean. That's one of our favorite parts of our job, and we take it very seriously to personally test the romance factor.

We sparingly give resorts, restaurants, and attractions the kid-friendly icon, which indicates a place or event that children will enjoy.

This icon indicates that a specific place or activity has a special dash of local charm.

Watch for this icon to identify annoying or potentially dangerous situations, such as tourist traps, unsafe neighborhoods, rip-offs, and other things to avoid.

Attention, bargain hunters: If you're looking to save money, check out our bargain icons, sprinkled throughout the text.

The Tip icon alerts you to useful advice on how to plan and implement your trip in order to make the best use of your time and money.

Where to Go from Here

Whether you've been to the Caribbean a dozen times or have never set foot outside your hometown, we know that you'll find what you're looking for in *Caribbean For Dummies*. So sit back, relax, and enjoy your trip planning. After all, the planning part lasts a lot longer than the trip itself; why not make it part of the fun?

Part I

Getting Started on Your Caribbean Getaway

In this part . . .

*P*lanning a trip to a place that you know only as a dot on the map? You need to get a sense of where you're going before you commit to the destination. In Part I, we help you point your compass in the right direction.

First, the basics: What is each island like, and which one will mesh with your island fantasy? Next come the details — like when you want to go and what kind of hotel is likely to fit your preferences. Finally, we offer tips for travelers with special needs, so your trip can fulfill your requirements as well as your dreams.

Chapter 1

Discovering the Caribbean

· ·

· ·

*W*e certainly needed a book like this before we embarked on our first Caribbean trip, which was on our honeymoon in 1982 — a gift from Dad. At our wedding reception, just before the stroke of midnight, Dad's secretary handed us three pages of single-spaced, typewritten notes listing the items that we'd need for our trip. Our vague fantasy of the Caribbean featured a sandy beach dotted with palms and high-rise hotels equipped with discos, glitzy casinos, and piña coladas. Like most people, we just sort of lumped all islands south of Florida into this formless mass and called it the Caribbean.

After scanning the list, which advised us to bring toilet paper, peanut butter, and insect repellent, we quickly figured out that where we were going and what we'd been expecting were completely different animals. We'd packed for our Caribbean fantasy, but our surprise destination was Green Turtle Cay, a tiny island in the Bahamas with one car and a population of 400 who rarely saw tourists.

We wound up having a wonderful time, but our travel experience could have been even better if we had been prepared. The lesson? If you choose the Caribbean for your vacation, you still have decisions to make. After all, we're talking about a whole different world. So slow down, get in the island groove, and smile. The Caribbean has stolen our hearts. We bet its magic will charm yours, too.

Finding the Island(s) Right for You

If you're not sure which island you want to visit, you're in good company. Even the Caribbean's first tourist was overwhelmed by the choices. "I saw so many islands that I could hardly decide which to visit first," Christopher Columbus wrote to Spain's Queen Isabella. We know just how he felt.

Knowing that we've specialized in the Caribbean for the past eight years, our friends are always asking us where they should go. That's a little like being asked which of your children you like best — each one has something special to offer.

That sweep of aquamarine blue-on-blue sea called the Caribbean stretches nearly 2,000 miles from Cuba to South America and encompasses more than 30 different nations and a mind-boggling 7,000 islands — give or take a few. Technically, the Bahamas and the Turks and Caicos islands aren't even in the Caribbean. As for the islanders themselves, they, too, are a diverse group, representing 100 different cultures. On most Caribbean islands, the majority of the population are descendants of African slaves.

Which island is right for you depends on what you enjoy and what kind of vacation you want. For example, our best friends love shopping, glittering nightlife, the beach, and golf, so we'd send them to Aruba, Puerto Rico, Jamaica, or St. Thomas. Our tastes run toward secluded hideaways with great snorkeling, gourmet dining, and grand vistas, so whenever we get the chance, we head to the British Virgin Islands or St. John in the United States Virgin Islands.

Suffice it to say that we've never been bored anywhere we've traveled in the Caribbean. Whether you're the independent type who likes adventure and discovery, or you prefer to be pampered and veg out on the beach, there's a Caribbean island to suit you.

In this book, we give you an insider's view of some of our favorite islands. In this chapter, we hit the highlights on a whirlwind tour, leaving the wonderful history and culture of this fascinating part of the world for you to discover on your own . . . or not. Here are the Caribbean's top destinations, with the lowdown on the ins and outs of each. A quiz at the end of this chapter pulls all this information together, helping you set your sights on the island that's right for you.

Introducing Aruba

Sugar-white beaches. Splashy casinos. A stark, other-worldly, cactus-dotted landscape known as the *cunucu*, where *divi-divi* (watapana) trees have been bowed to a 45-degree angle by the constantly blowing trade winds. Think Arizona with a beach, and you've got Aruba, an independent country within the Kingdom of the Netherlands.

Located a scant 15 miles north of Venezuela, this Dutch treat has a diverse heritage. In fact, the lyrical local language, Papiamento, is laced with Spanish, Dutch, and Portuguese, as well as African, French, and Arawak Indian dialects.

Aruba is surprisingly small — popular with the package-tour crowd and cruise ships, as well as honeymooners and families — and is famed for its wide, seven-mile stretch of white-sand beach, where most of its 30 hotels are tightly packed. Aruba's tiny capital, Oranjestad — with its pastel, stucco walls topped by wedding-cake cupolas and terra-cotta roofs — makes for a nice afternoon stroll.

With more than 40 distinct nationalities represented in its population of 91,500, Aruba has some of the Caribbean's best and most varied dining options. You can look forward to an array of 100-plus restaurants from which to choose.

If you want a hassle-free, relaxing introduction to the Caribbean, Aruba should be high on your list. The hotels offer great packages, and even though Aruba is one of the more far-flung islands, you can get a direct flight from several major cities in the U.S. and Europe. What we like about Aruba is that it's easy to navigate, and the people are hospitable. Even though the island heavily relies on tourism, you can feel the locals' genuine happiness to have you, and they exude a small-town friendliness. Plus, thanks to a heavy Latin influence, the nightlife can't be beat.

However, sophisticated travelers will find little appeal on Aruba. We were disappointed to see the bland buildup along its stunning beaches. We heard that a moratorium now restricts new construction, but to our minds, the island had long ago reached the saturation point anyway. Although we had lots of fun on this island, Aruba is far from our definition of a tropical getaway.

As long as you've come this far, reserve a few days to visit Aruba's next-door neighbors: Bonaire, which offers the Caribbean's best diving and snorkeling, and Curaçao, which boasts a postcard-perfect Colonial city that looks like a mini-Amsterdam. Each island is just a brief plane or boat ride away.

Bottom line: If you want guaranteed sun, great food, plenty of activity, and a vibrant nightlife, Aruba is a good bet.

Hits

- ✔ **Lots of variety.** From gambling to windsurfing to horseback riding along the beach, Aruba delivers the fun factor.

- ✔ **Lively nightlife.** You won't feel overdressed in your designer duds on Aruba. You can try your luck at a dozen casinos, reserve a stage-side table for the productions at one of the showrooms, or dance the night away at hot spots.

- ✔ **Consistently perfect weather.** Aruba lies outside the hurricane belt. Trade winds and low humidity keep its average year-round temperature of 82° F from feeling uncomfortably hot. The island gets only 17 inches of rainfall annually.

- ✔ **Good vibes.** Cosmopolitan Arubans are friendly, and just about everyone speaks English.

But keep in mind

- ✔ **It's built up.** High-rise hotels with little island flair crowd the prime beaches.

- ✔ **Tourism reigns supreme.** Forget your Robinson Crusoe fantasy.

- ✔ **The scenery is desertlike, not lush.** This dry, cactus-dotted countryside may clash with your vision of a tropical paradise.

Visiting Aruba, Bonaire, and Curaçao: As easy as ABC

We usually don't recommend trying to visit more than one island during your trip, but the ABC islands, as Aruba, Bonaire, and Curaçao are known, offer a golden opportunity. Both Bonaire and Curaçao rank among our favorites, though for different reasons. If you're a diver or nature lover, **Bonaire** (☎ **800-BONAIRE** or Internet www.infobonaire.com/) should be a don't-miss on your itinerary. History buffs and culture hounds adore **Curaçao** (☎ **800-270-3350** or 212-683-7660; fax 212-683-9337; Internet www.curacao-tourism.com), which recently celebrated its 500th birthday on the world map. Thanks to Willemstad, its Dutch colonial capital, Curaçao has joined such sites as the Great Wall of China and the Pyramids as a UNESCO World Heritage Site.

Befriending Barbados

Steeped in English tradition and more straitlaced than some of its neighbors, Barbados has been giving the wealthy and famous the royal treatment for centuries. The easternmost of the Caribbean's Lesser Antilles chain, Barbados juts out into the Atlantic Ocean and used to serve as a gateway to the West Indies for ships coming to and from Europe and South America. As a result, its islanders got first pick of the bounty flowing into the Caribbean. The island's prosperity remains in evidence today, especially in the bustling shopping district (which we didn't find to be overly impressive or a bargain).

Known for its posh resorts from Sandy Lane to Royal Pavilion (think "Lifestyles of the Rich and Famous," and you've got the picture), Barbados offers a range of accommodations, whether you're seeking idyllic days at an intimate guesthouse or the frenetic activity of a sprawling resort. You'll receive the royal treatment from the moment you are greeted at the airport and whisked away to your hotel. You'll pay for it, too. The star treatment doesn't come cheap.

During our first afternoon, high tea by the pool seemed an oddity, but by the second day, we slipped into the spirit and joined the other guests in this tradition. We felt like we'd been ushered into some special club. Coming from the land of biggie cups and super-sized fries, choosing exactly what kind of tea to steep and savor while daintily snacking on cucumber sandwiches was amusing and endearing. We used the time to socialize with the largely older British crowd who migrate to this island year after year. Barbados naturally would feel like a second home to them, considering that it was the only Caribbean island continually under British rule for three centuries until 1966.

Another tradition to be aware of is dressing up for dinner; it's a must on Barbados. We quickly learned firsthand why Barbados has garnered international acclaim for its restaurants.

Barbados is also known for its gardens — again, the British influence. We came expecting the lush, junglelike beauty of St. Lucia or Barbados's wild cousin, Jamaica. Barbados is green, but years of use by planters have left its countryside restrained and managed.

The mood on Barbados is unmistakably civilized — so much so that we felt a little stifled and hamstrung by all the tradition. We were relieved to come upon surfers hanging out near Bathsheba. With their hip attitudes, they definitely clashed with the island's character, but they actually made us feel more at home. Barbados residents, called Bajans (pronounced *bay-johns*), cut loose only when it comes to rum. Bajans are extremely proud of the locally made rums, and several little dives around the island serve rum at all hours.

Bottom line: If your idea of paradise is the feel of an English outpost in the tropics, Barbados will be your cup of tea.

Hits

- ✔ **The dining scene.** Chefs on Barbados, unlike those on some Caribbean islands, are experimental, sophisticated, and eager to meet the challenge of demanding palates.

- ✔ **Safety.** Crime is hardly a concern on this well-heeled island.

- ✔ **Snap-to service.** You won't want for attention; you'll have help at your beck and call.

But keep in mind

- ✔ **Mind your manners.** The "have it your way" philosophy doesn't belong here — it's the Queen's rules all the way. Better polish up on what fork to use with which course.

- ✔ **Deals, deals, deals . . . not!** Rates are out-of-sight unless you're willing to look hard. Prices are high on everything from food to hotel rooms to greens fees.

- ✔ **Claustrophobia-inducing roads.** Oddly, you're likely to find busy, narrow roads right next to your room at many hotels.

Getting to Know the British Virgin Islands

Even if you've never been on a boat in your life, the British Virgin Islands will make you want to hoist a sail and swill some grog. Brace yourself for the moment when you finally glimpse Jimmy Buffett's idea of paradise. These sleepy little islands — like a giant's stepping-stones scattered across the sea — are a sailor's and water-lover's delight. You're never out of sight from the next island as you tool around on your choice of watercraft.

We're hesitant to write about how much we love the BVIs because we don't want them to change. Simply put, these exquisite, emerald-green islands will take your breath away.

Okay, okay, so getting here is a royal pain, but the extra effort is worth it. And because getting to the BVIs is neither easy nor cheap, you may feel like you have the islands all to yourself at times. You can fly into Tortola, but you'll probably need to ply the sapphire-blue Caribbean waters by water taxi or ferry to reach your hotel, villa, or guesthouse. Thankfully, you won't find any monolithic, high-rise hotels straddling the beaches here. You also won't find any rah-rah all-inclusive resorts.

Still a British colony, the BVIs — actually more than 50 islands are in the chain, though only a handful are inhabited — are remarkably undeveloped and sparsely populated, with only 18,000 inhabitants. Tourism began here in the mid-1960s when Laurence Rockefeller opened Little Dix Bay on Virgin Gorda. Like nearby St. John, much land on the BVIs is preserved in national park areas.

If you must have your MTV, shopping, golf, or a happening casino, skip the BVIs. But if you want to chill out and spend your afternoons doing nothing more stressful than napping in a hammock by the sea, the BVIs are a perfect choice.

Although we noted a touch of British formality, the vibe here is casual and fun. When you're at the beach bar, you'll be sitting alongside captains of industry, rock stars, famous actors, and colorful local characters, all gathered to sip Painkillers — a rum concoction — with their new best friends.

About the only place where you'll see much evidence of tourism is at the most famous spot on Virgin Gorda, called The Baths. There, grand granite boulders frame the most perfect blue Caribbean you could desire. Cruise ships are allowed to dock on that island, but the number of passengers they can bring each day is tightly controlled.

The BVIs we cover in this book are

- ✔ **Tortola:** The largest of the BVIs, Tortola is only 21 miles long. Its name means "turtledove" in Spanish. The BVI capital, Road Town, is here, as well as a huge marina filled with hundreds of yachts that account for half of the BVIs' "tourist beds."

- ✔ **Virgin Gorda:** Home to some of the most spectacular resorts in the BVIs, Virgin Gorda packs a world of beauty into a mere 8½ miles. It has two national parks, both great for hiking. (Gorda Peak reaches 1,500 feet.)

- ✔ **Anegada:** Although this stretch of land is within sight of the other islands, you can easily overlook the flat, sandy island that looks like a giant beach and feels like the ends of the earth.

Bottom line: Picnics on deserted beaches, sunset sails in a tiny boat, and morning walks where you don't run into another soul make the British Virgin Islands one of our favorites.

Hits

- ✔ **Sailing, sailing.** Free spirits love just drifting from one isle to the next through Sir Francis Drake Channel.

- ✔ **Eye-popping, gorgeous setting.** The Caribbean doesn't get any better than this. You can truly find that island getaway and snag your own private strand of beach.

- ✔ **Unexpected fun.** When you're at Foxy's or Bomba's beach bar, you may encounter Jimmy Buffett plucking out his latest ode to sailing or the Beach Boys jamming the night away. Honestly.

But keep in mind

- ✔ **Forget posh nightlife.** You'll need to whip up your own entertainment.

- ✔ **Transportation hassles.** Getting around can be expensive and time-consuming unless you rely on the regularly scheduled ferries.

- ✔ **Limited dining choices.** If you don't happen to like the chef at your hotel, you're cooked.

Greetings to Grand Cayman

We have to be honest up front: Unless you're a diver or a serious snorkeler, go elsewhere. You can find more island flavor in other places for a much cheaper price. The Cayman Islands, the birthplace of the Caribbean's recreational diving, rely on a good reputation for their relatively healthy reefs and dramatic wall dives with almost 200 dive sites and visibility up to 100 feet. Of the trio that makes up the Cayman Islands — Grand Cayman, Cayman Brac, and Little Cayman, just south of Cuba — Grand Cayman is the primary draw with its famed 5½-mile-long Seven Mile Beach.

So why is Grand Cayman one of the top tourist destinations in the Caribbean? Diving aside, Grand Cayman is easy to reach and easy to navigate once you're there. It's safe and sanitized in every way. It's the kind of place where you can go to sleep in your beach chair, wake up, and still have all your stuff intact. English is spoken, U.S. dollars are accepted, and, most importantly, you are made to feel welcome.

Grand Cayman's top-drawer restaurants, cool attractions like its Turtle Farm and Stingray City, tidy beaches, and a plethora of watersports make it a popular choice with families, honeymooners, and divers who are traveling with nondivers. Grand Cayman is also one of the main stops for the many cruise ships in the Caribbean.

If you crave glittery nightlife, you'll be bored on Grand Cayman; go to Puerto Rico or Aruba instead. Even though the banking industry has made this island wealthy, flashing affluence at trendy clubs or gambling it away at casinos isn't the thing here. Expect to be in the company of the old money crowd, whose idea of fun is watching the sun set from a lantern-festooned deck while celebrating happy hour at a British-style pub.

You'll find friendly, laid-back islanders who speak with a lilting brogue echoing their Scotch/Irish/Welsh heritage. They also probably have a bigger bank account than you do. About the only time a party atmosphere sets in is during Pirates Week; parades, street dances, and fireworks break out everywhere during this national event in October.

Bottom line: If you're the active type who loves water sports, gourmet food, and a dash of history, Grand Cayman is a winner.

Hits

- **Divers' heaven.** The Cayman Islands are renowned for some of the Caribbean's best diving.

- **Great dining.** Gourmet restaurants offer truly inventive island cuisine.

- **Classy, but casual.** The Cayman Islands are sophisticated and upscale islands without attitude.

- **Untrammeled isles.** Peaceful Cayman Brac and Little Cayman lie within easy reach.

But keep in mind

- **Your wallet will get hit.** The Cayman Islands are expensive, especially when it comes to food — although the island has taken the bite out of prices with discounts during the off-season in recent years.

- **Nightlife? What nightlife?** Divers tuck in early.

- **Daytrippers.** The famed beach and popular dive sites get overrun — especially when cruise ships are in port.

Jamming on Jamaica

Quintessential ladies' man Errol Flynn called Jamaica "more beautiful than any woman I've ever seen." Nobody ever comes back from Jamaica and labels the island just "nice." Jamaica stands out from the other Caribbean islands as an in-your-face kind of place. It's an assault on the senses: the continual throbbing of reggae and rock steady music that reverberates in taxis and on the streets; lush places with improbable names like Fern Gully and Bamboo Alley; the fiery taste of jerk chicken; and the plucky salesmanship of self-taught artists eking out a living in the craft markets.

Does your island fantasy include rafting a river and swimming in a blue lagoon? How about racing to the top of a waterfall, or sitting on a verandah sipping your morning coffee while overlooking the bushes from which the coffee beans were plucked? Choose your favorite sunny spot from Jamaica's 200 miles of beaches. Hike the 7,400-foot summits of the Blue Mountains. Cuddle under a heated duvet to ward off the cool mountain air at night.

Jamaica owes part of its success to the prevalence of all-inclusive resorts, which were first popularized here and have spread to several other Caribbean islands. However, these compounds have proven both a blessing and a curse. Many tourists like them because they take a lot of the guesswork out of your trip, letting you control costs up front. Unfortunately, the self-contained attractions also make it highly unlikely that you'll venture from the cushy confines of your resort and experience the real Jamaica. In turn, the lack of tourists willing to actually visit *the island* and not just an all-inclusive resort has hit restaurants and attractions hard, making Jamaicans even more desperate for your business.

We have a love/hate relationship with the island. We adore the less touristy parts and the way people quickly warm up if you are kind to them and show interest in their country. We abhor the brazen approaches of shady characters peddling drugs and prostitutes that you're likely to encounter on the beaches and outside the resorts' gates. Although the government has tried in recent years to educate the local population about how important tourists are to the economy, the message has had little effect on aggressive vendors and sometimes surly service people. On the other hand, if you are looking for local color and are genuinely interested in this beautiful country, you can make friends for life here.

The island has four main resort areas — and some up-and-coming spots — each tempting in a different way with tennis, golf, horseback riding, and water sports.

Montego Bay. Here in Mo Bay (as it's called by locals), green hills cup the blue harbor of Jamaica's No. 1 tourist destination (some might say "trap"). One of the livelier Caribbean destinations, it offers everything from duty-free shopping to craft markets to legends of witchcraft at Rose Hall, an eighteenth-century plantation Great House said to be haunted.

On the plus side, you'll find a decent selection of restaurants and nightclubs in Mo Bay, which has brought in the college spring-break crowd. But Mo Bay is big, poor, and crowded, and it lacks the fine architecture that gives St. Thomas's Charlotte Amalie its allure. If you spend your entire vacation here, you're probably going to leave feeling a little let down.

Negril. A hedonistic pulse courses through this resort area at Jamaica's western tip. Known as a counterculture escape in the 1970s (when it didn't even have electricity), this sleepy little haven had been discovered by tourists when the 1980s rolled around.

Negril has retained its funky edge and is still celebrated for its sunsets and seven miles of beach as soft as talc, but it has definitely been embraced by the masses, some coming for the clothing-optional sections of beach. The all-inclusive resorts occupy much of the fabulous beach with smaller properties tucked in between. Sunseekers looking for a little less frenzy can find it on Negril's West End, where boutique resorts hug the cliffs above a honeycomb network of caves. For a taste of what Negril used to be like, head to the southwest coach where Treasure Beach, a tiny fishing village, has been adopted by trendy, beautiful people as a hangout.

Ocho Rios. Cruise ships regularly disgorge passengers in Ochi (the local name, pronounced *oh-chee*). The tourists stampede for the shopping and then make the obligatory climb up Dunn's River Falls, where a natural stone staircase leads to the top of the 600-foot cascading water. After that trek, tourists then run the gauntlet past vendors hawking "I survived the Falls" T-shirts. Unfortunately, that experience has led many to dismiss Ochi as a kitschy town for tourists. Actually, you don't have to venture far off the well-beaten path here to see Ochi's Eden-like nature — we love the Coyaba Gardens tucked away above the city. Ocho Rios boasts some of the country's more exquisite resorts, as well as our absolute favorite all-inclusive resort, Grand Lido San Souci.

Port Antonio. Those who know and love Jamaica often pick lush and mountainous Port Antonio as the most romantic region of the country. Indeed, Port Antonio, on the northeast coast and in the foothills of the Blue Mountains, fueled Errol Flynn's passion and remains removed from the primary flurry of tourism. Rafting by torchlight on the gentle Rio Grande is the main to-do here. Although Port Antonio doesn't have the high profile of the other resort areas, stars like Johnny Depp, Glenn Close, and Robin Williams have fallen for it.

Bottom line: We're willing to overlook Jamaica's rough edges, because overall its rugged beauty delivers the quintessential Caribbean experience.

Hits

- ✔ **Choice of destinations.** Whether your pace is languid or action-packed, you can easily find a resort area to match your vacationing style.

- ✔ **Cool digs.** Accommodations range from hyperactive all-inclusive resorts, to Old World villas where butlers serve tea on silver trays, to funky cottages by the beach.

- ✔ **The breadth of natural beauty.** The variations of Jamaica's terrain are unparalleled — expansive beaches; lush jungles punctuated with waterfalls; the cool, misty Blue Mountains; and savannas that echo the African plains.

- ✔ **All-inclusive resorts.** You'll know how much your vacation will cost before you even leave home. And you won't have to think of a thing once you're there.

- ✔ **The vibrant culture.** Reggae by the late Bob Marley still rules the airwaves from Houston to Copenhagen. In tiny crafts stores and grand galleries, you'll find earthy, made-in-Jamaica items, such as wood carvings and handmade pottery.

But keep in mind

- ✔ **The most aggressive vendors in the Caribbean.** Travelers need to be cautious. Think New York City on a beach. Vendors on the beach and in the markets can be maddeningly persistent.

- ✔ **Traffic accidents.** The roadways here are in disrepair, and the island has the dubious ranking as one of the top spots for car wrecks in the world.

- ✔ **Grinding poverty.** Besides Haiti, Jamaica has the lowest standard of living in the Caribbean, and some visitors find it hard to enjoy themselves when the islanders are so obviously struggling.

- ✔ **Litter.** The natural beauty of the island is marred by trash.

- ✔ **Crime.** Unless you're a Bob Marley fanatic and want to make a pilgrimage to his house, now a museum, steer clear of Kingston, where much of Jamaica's crime occurs.

Partying on Puerto Rico

We admit it. We thought those winning commercials with stunning images of Puerto Rico challenging you to "guess where?" were too good to be true. For many years, we went to Puerto Rico just because it was the main jumping-off point for the Caribbean, but we never spent any time there. Today, just thinking about this visual feast of an island makes our hearts beat faster. Puerto Rico scores high on our list of favorite Caribbean islands for more reasons than native son Ricky Martin can shake his "bon-bon" at.

This stunner of a destination dishes out everything that your heart could desire in an island vacation — all with a steamy Latin beat. The colonial city of Old San Juan, with its well-preserved forts and narrow stone streets overhung with balconies brimming with flowers, has managed to avoid the T-shirt tackiness that mars so many of this hemisphere's port cities. Yet with its chic art galleries and incredible restaurant scene, it has gracefully bridged the gap between old and new.

Those who want high-rise hotels, a happening beach scene, high-energy discos, and frenetic casinos can find it on Condado and Isla Verde in San Juan. That's our least favorite part of the island, because it's touristy with all the things we dislike: vendors hawking tacky trinkets and little island charm.

Puerto Rico has enough natural wonders to keep you more than occupied, including one of the world's largest river caves for spelunking, extensive rain forests for hiking, bioluminescent bays and good corals for diving, and 272 miles of Atlantic and Caribbean coastline for horseback riding, swimming, surfing, and walking hand-in-hand. The island also rates well with people who love golf and deep-sea fishing. Escape artists find a more laid-back scene in Vieques and Rincon. Think of San Juan like Miami. Vieques is considered the Spanish Virgin Island.

As for accommodations, Puerto Rico arguably has the broadest range of choices in the Caribbean, from a hotel converted from a 500-year-old convent to mega-resorts with all the bells and whistles. It also yields gems called *paradores* — clean, comfortable, and reasonably priced bed-and-breakfasts (B&Bs) that must pass government inspection.

Of course, because Puerto Rico is a U.S. territory, you'll never have a problem finding English speakers — although Spanish is the dominant language of the people. To make your life as a traveler even easier, you can take the cash you're most accustomed to; the U.S. dollar is the currency in Puerto Rico.

Bottom line: Puerto Rico runs the gamut. It packs sizzle to spare with a sexy nightlife scene, but eco-hounds and sports nuts will be in paradise, as will those souls who are content to sit on the beach sipping margaritas.

Hits

- ✔ **A convenient location.** You won't have a problem getting to Puerto Rico. Almost all the airlines that service the Caribbean fly through this airport.

- ✔ **No passport, no problema.** You get the intoxicating mix of both worlds here: the exotic Latin flavor blended with the comforting familiarity of home. But if you're from the United States, you don't have to worry about a passport or changing money.

- ✔ **Living la vida loca.** Put on your designer duds and tango until the sun comes up. Puerto Ricans love the nightlife.

- ✔ **Culture club.** The art scene and intriguing history meld to bring a level of sophistication to Puerto Rico that you don't find on most of the other Caribbean islands.

But keep in mind

- ✔ **The secret's out.** Puerto Rico is a popular stop for cruise ships, and its more famous beaches (all are public) get crowded and dirty.

- ✔ **Hurricanes.** During the hurricane season, Puerto Rico regularly goes on alert.

- ✔ **Spring break and holiday crowds.** During the time that most people think about coming to the Caribbean, finding room at the inn can be almost impossible. Unlike other places, travel traffic doesn't slow down in April either, thanks to spring break and Easter celebrations.

Venturing onto the U.S. Virgin Islands

Blessed with about 300 sunny days a year, the U.S. Virgin Islands have deservedly been dubbed America's Paradise. The island group encompasses St. Thomas, St. John, and St. Croix, plus another 50 islets and cays, most of them uninhabited.

As an American territory, the USVI is a breeze for U.S. citizens to visit. English is spoken everywhere, the currency is the dollar, and you don't need a passport. The other cool thing is that you can easily and conveniently visit more than one of these beautiful islands, awash in flowers ranging from brilliantly colored bougainvillea to fragrant jasmine to the cheekily named "jump-up-and-kiss-me," which has ruby-red blossoms. And you'll want to visit more than one, because they each have such distinctive personalities. In fact, we'd highly recommend arranging your trip with several islands on the agenda. If you only have a week, though, pick two and save the third for next time.

The most populous of these islands, St. Thomas, is also one of the busier cruise ports in the Caribbean. Shoppers surge through its capital, Charlotte Amalie, scooping up jewelry, perfume, clothes, and trinkets. Eco-lovers flock to St. John, where two-thirds of the island is preserved as a national park and visitors who are in the know reserve tents in its popular campgrounds at least eight months in advance. The largest of the three, St. Croix, sometimes gets overlooked, but it's our favorite. St. Croix gives you the best of the other two. It has the beautiful architecture of Charlotte Amalie in its two towns, with a nice selection of shops and good restaurants. You can walk the streets and get a sense of history without being distracted by commercialism. St. Croix's natural beauty hasn't been swallowed up by development, either. In fact, its agricultural roots are still much in evidence.

St. Thomas. Celebrated for its duty-free shopping, gourmet restaurants, busy nightlife, golf courses, and lovely beaches, St. Thomas is by far the most cosmopolitan of the trio and the most touristy. Frenetic energy courses through busy and historic Charlotte Amalie (pronounced *ah-mahl-ya*), where jungle-thatched hills and red-tile roofed houses surround a sapphire-blue harbor punctuated with every kind of craft from sailboats to gargantuan cruise ships.

The main shopping area is limited to a few congested waterfront streets, but it's great fun for strolling. A mind-boggling number of jewelry shops clamor for your attention, giving away cheap gems to lure you in.

If you are the type who simply must feel a strong U.S. connection, no matter where you are, St. Thomas will satisfy that need. Like any heavily populated U.S. city, Charlotte Amalie battles crime and grime, but common sense precautions will suffice.

St. Thomas boasts one of the Caribbean's more famous beaches: Magens Bay, a broad, U-shaped inlet edged by a mile of sugar-white sand. Whether you crave the reliable luxury of the Ritz-Carlton or want to cook your own meals in a bare-bones condo, you can find something to suit your wallet.

St. John. Although it's a mere 15-minute ferry ride away from St. Thomas, St. John feels like another world when you step onto the dock at Cruz Bay. Nature reigns supreme on lush St. John, which was largely transformed into a national park in 1956 and boasts challenging hills ideal for hiking and turquoise waters perfect for snorkeling. On the island's north coast, the necklace of pearl-white beaches rank among the world's best, including Hawksnest, Trunk Bay (whose coral reefs have been trammeled by too many tourists of late), and Cinnamon Bay.

Although neighboring St. Thomas wins the prize for the most shops, St. John gets our vote for the most intriguing — especially those at Mongoose Junction. Almost 200 of the island's 5,000 residents put "artist" on their tax returns. You can find some real treasures here. And for such a small island, its restaurant scene is surprisingly happening with some terrific new entries. Its nightlife has a collegial feel to it.

St. John is renowned for its eco-tents, but its selection of villas is dazzling, too. Its two traditional luxury resorts — the venerable, old money Caneel Bay and newcomer Westin St. John — have plenty of fans as well. Count us among them. In other words, no matter where you stay on St. John, you'd have to be a grouch not to have fun.

St. Croix. Forty miles and a 20-minute plane hop to the south of St. Thomas, St. Croix presents a dazzling montage of scenery: powdery, white-sand beaches; cactus-dotted plains; mangrove swamps; stands of mahogany trees; and rain forests. Christiansted, the capital, remains virtually unchanged from 200 years ago when it was the centerpiece of the Danish West Indies, with waterfront arcades and an imposing ochre yellow fort at its heart. Rent a car for at least a day or two and just explore. You'll find exquisite botanical gardens, abandoned sugar mills all over the island, an artist who uses naturally fallen trees to carve island-style furniture, and Great Houses (the plantation houses from the days when sugar cane covered the island) in various stages of restoration. Another good way to see the island is by horseback or by bicycle.

Not as popular with the cruise ships, St. Croix yields more opportunities for finding your own little private strand of sand. Two miles off the northeast shore, you can rest assured of claiming uncrowded territory. Have a champagne picnic for two on the beach of uninhabited Buck Island, a wooded nature preserve administered by the U.S. National Park Service. Nearby is a coral reef that President Kennedy had declared the nation's first underwater national park.

Bottom line: In the U.S. Virgin Islands, you don't have the sheer number of islands of neighboring British Virgin Islands, but you'll find plenty to love.

Hits

- ✔ **Spectacular beaches.** All three islands have glorious ones, especially St. John. Both diving and snorkeling are generally excellent.

- ✔ **Amazing, dutyfree shopping.** The islands — St. Thomas is king of the hill — are known for bargains on liquor, crystal, china, linens, and perfumes. The duty-free allowance is $1,200 a person, twice that of other Caribbean islands.

- ✔ **They're American.** If you're coming from the United States, you'll get an easy introduction to the Caribbean.

- ✔ **Top-notch watersports and sailing.** Consistent trade winds, deep cruising waters, and dozens of safe anchorages make the USVI and neighboring British Virgin Islands a pleasure to sail or fish.

But keep in mind

- ✔ **The (sometimes) madding crowds.** The shopping area in Charlotte Amalie is claustrophobic when the cruise ships disgorge.

- ✔ **On guard.** Travelers should use caution — and taxis — around Charlotte Amalie and Christiansted at night.

- ✔ **Too much like home.** If seeing all-too-familiar fast-food joints clashes with your dream of the tropics, St. Thomas probably isn't for you. Pockets of St. Croix are industrial.

- ✔ **Hurricanes.** Within two weeks of each other in September 1995, Hurricanes Luis and Marilyn swept through the region, causing extensive damage to St. Thomas and St. John (both of which have completely rebounded). St. Croix was spared and subsequently discovered by the cruise lines that normally frequented St. Thomas.

Deciding How Many Islands Per Trip

If you've never been to the Caribbean before, the thought of visiting more than one island is probably overwhelming. But island-hopping can be surprisingly easy, depending on where you decide to go. American Airlines and Air Jamaica have generous programs that make hitting more than one island surprisingly reasonable (see Chapter 5). Or you can catch a small regional carrier for less than $100, usually.

If you know that you're going to a particular island but are interested in checking out what's nearby, see the "Hitting the Beach and Other Fun Things To Do" chapter for each destination. At the end of this chapter, we highlight easily accessible islands that you might want to visit. For more details, check the appropriate chapter, but this brief summary will get you started.

Both the British Virgin Islands and the United States Virgin Islands lend themselves beautifully to island hopping. Indeed, in the BVIs you won't be able to help yourself. With the USVI, it's a toss-up, but we recommend visiting at least two of the three. For that matter, as long as you have your passport, you can go back and forth between the BVIs and USVIs by boat or plane.

As we noted earlier in this chapter, two other Dutch islands are a short puddle jumper away from Aruba. You can either visit Bonaire or Curaçao, but we wouldn't recommend trying to cram all three into your schedule.

Both Puerto Rico and Jamaica are so large that you'll be too busy to go anywhere else. However, we must mention one foray that has enormous appeal to U.S. visitors due to the forbidden fruit appeal — a trip to neighboring Cuba from Jamaica. It's simple to arrange, but we've never tried it personally.

Hard-core divers might be lured from Grand Cayman to one of its smaller, laid-back sister islands, Little Cayman or Cayman Brac.

Visitors to Barbados should consider spending a few days on St. Lucia, which is a quick flight away but a whole different experience and one of our favorite islands for romance.

Caribbean bounty

Very few of the stunningly beautiful flowers and luscious fruits in the Caribbean are indigenous. *The Bounty's* Captain Bligh carried the breadfruit tree from Africa and coconuts from Malaysia. Bananas and plantains come from the Canary Islands, which also provided the Caribbean sugar cane. From Mexico, Central America, and South America came papaya, poinsettias, cashews, and allemanda. Tamarind and African tulip trees and many local vegetables hail from Africa. The brilliant orange flamboyant trees so common throughout the islands are Madagascar's gifts. Hawaii donated hibiscus, and Asia contributed the sweet-smelling frangipani. Mangos, now one of the more prolific fruit trees, originated in the Himalayan foothills of India.

Narrowing Your Island Choices

Now that you have a thumbnail sketch of the differences among the Caribbean islands, it's time to figure out which one you'd most like to visit. This quiz will help you determine which islands are best suited to your vacation style and interests. Here's how you do it:

Step #1: Get to know your "Rate the Islands" scorecard

Your scorecard, which you'll find at the end of this chapter, has a column for each island and a row for each category in our island-rating system. Use this scorecard to compile a rating for each of the islands based on the special-interest categories that follow. The top five islands in each category will get a predetermined 1 to 5 points, based on how suited it is to the interest or activity in that category. Five points is the highest rating, one is the lowest. If an island isn't listed, assume that it scores a zero in that particular category.

Step #2: Score the islands based on your interests and needs

Go through each category. Stop only at those categories that interest you. For example, if you're not a golfer, skip over the golf category entirely; don't plug in points for any of the islands in the "Golf" row of the scorecard. If you are into nightlife, stop at "If you want to party the night away." Insert each island's score into your scorecard.

Move on to the next category that interests you, and insert the scores into the appropriate row in your scorecard. Keep going until you've reviewed all the categories and given each island a score for each category that matters to you.

1) If you want to be in the lap of luxury . . .

Rating	Island	Why?
5 points	**Barbados**	White-glove treatment all the way at resorts fit for a king or queen.
4 points	**Jamaica**	A taste of the old Jamaica can be had — for a price — at resorts where you'll have a maid, gardener, butler, and cook to fulfill your every whim.
3 points	**Puerto Rico**	Dramatic and grand, the upscale resorts here consistently appear on lists of travelers' favorites.
2 points	**St. Thomas**	The Ritz Carlton, anyone? Need we say more?
1 point	**BVIs**	Small, luxurious resorts with entire islands all to themselves.

2) If you want to party the night away . . .

Rating	Island	Why?
5 points	**Puerto Rico**	Live Latin music, sizzling dancing, great food, and gambling combine for a continual fiesta.
4 points	**Jamaica**	Almost every night, you can find live bands playing reggae, dance hall, and the latest sounds in Negril, Mo Bay, and Ocho Rios.
3 points	**Aruba**	Most resorts tag "casino" onto their names. Plus, good discos with a heavy Latin influence and Las Vegas-style stage shows.
2 points	**Barbados**	Rum shops, discos, and late-night dining make this scene sizzle.
1 point	**St. Thomas**	The cruise ship has brought nightclubs and discos.

3) If you want to eat really well . . .

Rating	Island	Why?
5 points	**Puerto Rico**	Experimental, talented chefs — especially in Old San Juan — have made nouvelle Puerto Rican, New World, and fusion cuisine hot, hot, hot.
4 points	**Jamaica**	Whether you're paying top dollar for an elegant New Jamaican dinner at Strawberry Hill or a few dollars for jerk chicken from a roadside vendor, Jamaica offers mouth-watering variety.
3 points	**Barbados**	European chefs flock to this eastern outpost of the Caribbean.
2 points	**Aruba**	Its many nationalities, strong Dutch ties, and proximity to Central and South America make Aruba's dining scene one of the more memorable and varied in the Caribbean.

1 point	**Grand Cayman**	This wealthy, upscale island is one of the few in the Caribbean to have developed its own recognizable cuisine based around fresh seafood.

4) If you're looking for the Caribbean's most romantic beaches . . .

Rating	Island	Why?
5 points	**BVIs**	Because much of the BVIs are accessible only by boat, you can find secluded beaches on islands that you'll be sharing with only iguanas and lizards.
4 points	**St. John**	Here you'll find those powdery-white, palm-lined, near-perfect beaches you've been dreaming of — and you're likely to have them virtually to yourself.
3 points	**Puerto Rico**	You can have your own private fiesta on (almost) virgin strands on Puerto Rico's Virgin islands.
2 points	**St. Croix**	This oft-overlooked gem boasts virtually untouched stretches of sand; plus, there's always deserted Buck Island.
1 point	**Jamaica**	You may have to look a little harder for privacy, but this setting's hard to beat. Long Bay Beach is a stunner.

5) If you're watching your wallet but still want to stay on the sand . . .

Rating	Island	Why?
5 points	**Jamaica**	Many bargain hotels compete for your business here.
4 points	**Puerto Rico**	*Paradores* (B&Bs) keep costs down.
3 points	**St. Thomas**	Three words: competition, competition, competition.
2 points	**St. Croix**	Eager to grab some attention from its better known sibling islands, this one offers deals, deals, deals.
1 point	**Aruba**	So many hotels crowd the beach that prices are slashed in the summer.

6) If you want to experience the real Caribbean vibe . . .

Rating	Island	Why?
5 points	**Jamaica**	Funky reggae, strong national pride, and native arts and crafts rule.
4 points	**BVIs**	A Jimmy Buffett song come to life.
3 points	**Puerto Rico**	The Caribbean with a Latin beat

| 2 points | Barbados | Local rum shops, colorful chattel houses. |
| 1 point | St. Croix | A rural island with a funky edginess. |

7) If you want Caribbean history and culture . . .

Rating	Island	Why?
5 points	Puerto Rico	The most beautiful colonial city in the Caribbean, combined with a hot art scene.
4 points	Barbados	Three centuries as an English outpost left a strong legacy.
3 points	St. Thomas	Charlotte Amalie's colonial buildings.
2 points	St. Croix	Two Colonial Dutch cities and sugar mill ruins bring the island's past to life.
1 point	Jamaica	A fantastic history as a haven for pirates and coveted prize among the colonial superpowers.

8) If you want to tee off . . .

Rating	Island	Why?
5 points	Jamaica	Known for tricky winds, Jamaica is still tops after all these years — with courses like Half Moon and Tryall.
4 points	Puerto Rico	A range of choices, with two in the shadow of El Yunque rain forest.
3 points	Barbados	The Robert Trent Jones-designed Royal Westmoreland is a standout.
2 points	St. Croix	Guests on neighboring St. John and St. Thomas often fly over just for the golf at The Buccaneer (situated by the sea) and Carambola.
1 point	St. Thomas	President Clinton favored Mahogany Run when he was on the island.

9) If you're not getting older, just getting better . . .

Rating	Island	Why?
5 points	Puerto Rico	Easy access plus the disabilities act make Puerto Rico a piece of cake to visit.
4 points	Aruba	A is for: Always sunny, always flat, always safe, always beautiful.
3 points	Grand Cayman	Upscale, ultra-safe with a world-renowned beach, diving, and golf.
2 points	St. Thomas	Accessible for cruise ship passengers with disabilities, plus cool historical sights and great shopping.

| 1 point | Barbados | A well-manicured, easily accessible Caribbean experience with good golf, good food, good shopping, and lots of history. |

10) If you love hiking . . .

Rating	Island	Why?
5 points	St. John	Two-thirds of the island is designated as a national park, with more trails than you can shake a walking stick at.
4 points	Jamaica	The Blue Mountains, coffee country, and wildflowers.
3 points	Puerto Rico	The rain forests and jungles.
2 points	BVIs	Ups and downs on Sage Mountain provide amazing views.
1 point	Aruba	Its new national park.

11) If you're a nature lover . . .

Rating	Island	Why?
5 points	BVIs	Unpopulated and well-preserved.
4 points	St. John	Preservation was at work here long before it was hip.
3 points	Puerto Rico	El Yunque, a magnificent lush rain forest.
2 points	Jamaica	Known for bird watching, the Blue Mountains, and the crocodiles in the mangroves of the Black River.
1 point	St. Croix	Rural with a diverse landscape worth exploring.

12) If you want to check out music festivals . . .

Rating	Island	Why?
5 points	Jamaica	The reggae of native son Bob Marley is celebrated rollickingly with Reggae Sum Fest, plus Air Jamaica's Jazz and Blues Festival and Ocho Rios Jazz Festival.
4 points	Barbados	Barbados's jazz festival — Paint-It-Jazz — is worth the trip.
3 points	Puerto Rico	The Pablo Casals festival honors the great classical cellist.
2 points	St. Croix	Dig the Blues Heritage Festival here.
1 point	Aruba	Music all through its rollicking Carnival.

13) If you want to sightsee . . .

Rating	Island	Why?
5 points	**Puerto Rico**	Old San Juan.
4 points	**Jamaica**	Great Houses, waterfalls, mountains.
3 points	**Barbados**	Gardens, rock formations at Bathsheba.
2 points	**St. Thomas**	Historic Charlotte Amalie and grand vistas.
1 point	**BVIs**	The Sir Francis Drake Channel is the weekend pirate's playground.

14) If you want to go diving or snorkeling . . .

Rating	Island	Why?
5 points	**Grand Cayman**	200 marked dive sites and visibility to 100 feet.
4 points	**BVIs**	Wreck dives. So many islands, so little time.
3 points	**St. John**	Thank you, Mr. Rockefeller, for donating much of the land for this fabulous national park.
2 points	**Puerto Rico**	Night dives in a bioluminescent bay.
1 point	**St. Croix**	Underwater National Marine Park and wall diving at Cane Bay.

15) If you want an array of watersports . . .

Rating	Island	Why?
5 points	**Aruba**	A world-class destination for windsurfing.
4 points	**BVIs**	A sailor's paradise, plus surfing along Tortola.
3 points	**Puerto Rico**	From surfing to waterskiing to snorkeling, this island teems with water activities.
2 points	**St. Thomas**	Sailing capital of the Caribbean, plus snorkeling, parasailing, and deep-sea fishing.
1 point	**Barbados**	Surfers play in the rugged surf on the Atlantic side of this easternmost Caribbean island.

16) If you're craving peace and quiet . . .

Rating	Island	Why?
5 points	**BVIs**	You can get lost here.
4 points	**St. John**	Villas tucked away high on the hills overlooking the sea.
3 points	**St. Croix**	Much of the island is still rural.

2 points	**Jamaica**	It's big enough that you can get away . . . if you really want to.
1 point	**Puerto Rico**	Its Spanish Virgins.

17) If you are traveling with children . . .

Rating	Island	Why?
5 points	**Puerto Rico**	Easy to get to, and Hyatts' top-notch kids programs once you're there.
4 points	**Jamaica**	Several kid-friendly all-inclusives with wonderful staffs.
3 points	**St. Croix**	Islanders love children and children love this island.
2 points	**Aruba**	Deep discounts in the summer on family packages.
1 point	**St. Thomas**	Familiarity with great watersports and plenty of activities.

18) If you want to get there quickly . . .

Rating	Island	Why?
5 points	**Puerto Rico**	American Airlines' hub.
4 points	**Jamaica**	Air Jamaica's hub.
3 points	**St. Thomas/ St. Croix**	The dropping-off point for all three U.S. Virgin Islands.
2 points	**Barbados**	Many direct flights from New York and London, including flights on the Concorde during high season.
1 point	**Aruba**	Lots of direct air service and an easy 15-minute drive to any of its hotels.

Step #3: Tallying the scores to determine your final destination(s)

After you've reviewed the categories and plugged ratings into your scorecard, tally each island's score.

The winner — the island with the highest total score — should be your primary destination. If a second island scores high, consider splitting your time between the two islands. If a third island scores high and you have a good amount of time to spare, you may want to visit three islands. Scores really close? Flip a coin and vow to hit the one that comes in second on your next vacation.

"Rate the Islands" Scorecard

POINTS FOR:	Aruba	Barbados	British Virgin Islands	Grand Cayman	Jamaica	Puerto Rico	St. Thomas	St. John	St. Croix
1) Luxury									
2) Nightlife									
3) Great food									
4) Beaches									
5) Bargain rates									
6) Local color									
7) Caribbean culture									
8) Golf									
9) Senior appeal									
10) Hiking									
11) Natural beauty									
12) Music festivals									
13) Sightseeing									
14) Diving/snorkeling									
15) Watersports									
16) Peace and quiet									
17) Family friendly									
18) Easy access									
TOTAL SCORE:									

Chapter 2

Deciding When to Go

*W*hen most people think of the Caribbean, they think of a place where they can escape winter's chill. The truth is, the Caribbean makes a magnificent vacation destination pretty much year round. In fact, summer is one of our favorite times to visit. We enjoy the quick shower bursts followed by beautiful skies, rainbows, and gorgeous sunsets. In the broadest terms, the weather in this part of the world is tropical, warm, humid, and sometimes rainy.

In this chapter, we demystify the hotel lingo about seasons and explain the connection between the timing of your trip and the related expenses that you can expect to pay. We also give you an honest assessment of the dreaded "h" word — hurricane — and what it means for your Caribbean getaway. Finally, we tell you about the climates of the different islands and about the timing of various festivals and carnivals.

Translating the Seasons — and the Effects on Your Wallet

When you plan a trip to the Caribbean, you can expect to encounter lots of talk about seasons: *The* Season, high season, holiday season, low season, shoulder season, rainy season, and hurricane season. For a place where the leaves don't change and the temperature rarely budges more than a few degrees either direction from around 80°F, you'll hear the word *season* tossed about an awful lot.

The reason seasons matter in the Caribbean has virtually nothing to do with the weather and everything to do with your room rate. For example, published room rates for a resort may include as many as a half-dozen different prices listed for the exact same accommodations. What you'll pay all depends on exactly when you visit; timing is everything when it comes to a Caribbean vacation.

Generally, seasonal differences break down something like this, but keep in mind that there are lots of variations:

- ✔ **Holiday season (a.k.a. The Season):** December 15 to January 3.

- ✔ **High season:** January 4 to April 14.

- ✔ **Shoulder season:** April 15 to May 30 and September 1 to December 14.

- ✔ **Low season:** May 30 to August 31.

- ✔ **Hurricane season (overlaps with shoulder and low seasons):** June 1 to November 30.

Holiday season and high season

The Caribbean's high season heats up right before Christmas and lasts through mid-April. During the holiday season, referred to on the upscale islands as simply *The* Season, longtime guests often snatch up reservations for the best lodgings years in advance. At Christmas a few seasons ago, Jamaica's exclusive Round Hill even turned away James Bond — er, Pierce Brosnan, who plays the character originally conceived by author Ian Fleming at his home on Jamaica.

So if you're going to a resort on Jamaica, Barbados, or the British Virgin Islands around the holidays (where being there during *The* Season means that you've achieved a certain station in life), be prepared to make your plans well in advance.

The nicer hotels often have minimum stay requirements in effect during the holiday season and stringent cancellation policies. If you plan a trip during the holidays, make your reservations as early as possible, expect crowds, and plan to pay top dollar for everything.

The last two weeks of January sometimes provide a slight lull in the tourism, but high season shifts back into high gear in February and March, the busiest months in the Caribbean.

The forecast: If you're craving an escape and don't mind planning ahead and shelling out the bucks — rates reach their peak the last two weeks of December — this blast of sunshine is sure to cure your midwinter blues.

Shoulder season

In the shoulder seasons — late spring and the fall — prices are sometimes slightly reduced. Shoulder season is great if you want to go at a quiet time, because children are in school and few families are on the island.

There is an exception to the above rule: Between the Easter holidays and spring break, April is an extremely tough and expensive time to book a vacation on Puerto Rico. You might also have difficulties booking in Montego Bay and Negril (Jamaica) and St. Thomas (USVI) at this time.

 Some smaller resorts and restaurants close for repairs and maintenance in July, August, September, or October. So before you take an expensive taxi ride over to a top restaurant, call first to make sure it's open. You'll still need to make reservations for the most popular places anyway.

We've never found more than a few places shuttered, and lots of other options have always been available. The islands where closures could be a problem are the smaller ones like Nevis (not covered in this guide). We ran into a newlywed couple who had left The Four Seasons on Nevis to come to The Ritz-Carlton, St. Thomas, because they were so limited in their dining choices on tiny Nevis. "Everything was closed, and there wasn't anything to do," the young bride told us.

The forecast: Rate reductions of 10% to 20% beat holiday season charges, but they're not as economical as in low season. In April and May the weather barely differs from the bright sunshine of winter months, but in the early fall — especially September — you have to consider the possibility of hurricanes and tropical storms. That is, unless you've decided on Aruba, which is below the hurricane belt.

Low season

 If you come during the low season (or, as we call it, the slow season), rates drop like an anchor. Rates decrease as much as 60% in June, July, and August, making even some of the more exclusive resorts affordable. Travelers often make the assumption that because the Caribbean is so deliciously warm in the winter, it must be searingly hot in the summer. (That's not the case, but more on that in a minute.)

 Because school is out and bargains for families abound, you'll see lots of kids during low season — especially from Europe. On some islands, several hotels and resorts band together with the tourist boards during the summer months to offer amazing deals for families as well as honeymooners.

 In the last few years, the Caribbean has finally begun convincing people that it's a year-round destination. Despite that self-promotion, finding a hotel room in the low season is pretty easy. Booking your flight might not be as simple. Many nationals go home to visit during the summer — flights to Jamaica are especially full. And Europeans, who have much longer vacations than Americans, frequent the Caribbean in summer months. Reserve your flight as soon as you pick your destination.

 If there's a restaurant that you have your heart set on, call ahead so you aren't disappointed. Chefs often take their vacations in the summer months (especially August).

Tropical storms can kick up quickly in Caribbean summers, but they usually pass just as fast, leaving brilliant blue skies in their wake.

The forecast: You can get fantastic deals on rooms — how does as much as 60% off sound? — but you'll have to plan ahead for your flight (and fight to be seated with your family and friends). Don't expect everything to be open, either.

Hurricane season

Part of the Caribbean's low season dovetails with the hurricane season, which officially runs from June 1 through November 30, with September being the peak time for a hurricane to hit. Of course, the rainy season also mirrors hurricane season, though it doesn't last as long on some islands. (See Table 2-1 later in this chapter for the exact duration of the rainy season on each island.) Fortunately, in the tropics, rainstorms typically pass over rapidly.

We travel to the Caribbean all the time during hurricane season, because that's when we find great bargains. In all these years, we've only been evacuated once, and it turned out to be for nothing (luckily for St. Croix). Of course, that's no guarantee, and our good fortune certainly won't make you feel better if you're the one being sent packing by the storm.

Hurricane lingo

Because we'd never lived where hurricanes were much of a factor — Echo is from Tennessee, and Kevin hails from South Georgia — we had to take some time to catch on to all the hurricane lingo tossed around on CNN's Weather Channel (www.weather.com). Here's a rundown of what we've picked up from paying attention to the weather experts.

Hurricanes are rated by the following categories:

- ✔ **Category 5** is the most dangerous, packing winds of more than 155 mph (134 knots), which produce storm tides of more than 18 feet. That's strong enough to drive a palm frond through a coconut tree.

- ✔ **Category 4** has winds of 130 to 155 mph with a storm surge of 13 to 18 feet.

- ✔ **Category 3** has winds between 110 and 130 mph and storm surge of 9 to 12 feet.

- ✔ **Category 2** has winds from 96 to 110 mph with a storm surge of 6 to 8 feet.

- ✔ **Category 1** has winds of 74 to 95 mph with a storm surge of 4 to 5 feet.

When the weather forecasters talk about *tropical storms,* they mean a distinct circulation with winds exceeding 74 mph. Tropical storms can quickly turn into hurricanes and vice versa. As a hurricane loses strength, weathercasters define its intensity as a tropical storm.

Some Caribbean islands are better bets than others during hurricane season. Here's the rundown:

- ✔ **Aruba** lies outside the hurricane belt.

- ✔ **Grand Cayman** has had the luck of the draw for the past few years and hasn't been hit hard.

- ✔ **Jamaica's** last big hurricane was in 1987 (resulting in Echo's parents being stuck in Negril for several days).

- ✔ **The British Virgin Islands, St. Thomas,** and **St. John** were struck hard by Hurricane Marilyn in 1995. Three hurricanes skipped past these islands in 1999, causing only minor damage.

- ✔ **St. Croix,** just 40 miles away from St. Thomas, was unscathed by the most recent round of hurricanes and Hurricane Marilyn. Its last major hit was Hurricane Hugo in 1989.

- ✔ Parts of **Puerto Rico** have suffered damage in recent years.

We don't want you to be naïve about how powerful and devastating hurricanes can be. Modern tracking systems, however, allow early warnings. So, unlike the old days when islanders were caught completely unaware, guests and residents alike can have at least four or five days' notice to get ready and decide what course of action to take. Other good news: Buildings have been reconstructed with more hurricane-resistant materials, enabling resorts in recent years to bounce back more quickly when they do get hit.

If a hurricane does threaten when you're in the Caribbean, hoteliers will provide as much information as possible so you can make an informed choice as to whether to stay or go. If you decide to leave, ask your concierge to call the airport as soon as possible to get a flight out. Do not try to get a few more hours in at the pool, because flights fill up quickly.

With the popularity of the Internet, islanders are extremely aware of impending storms — much more so than even a decade ago. The best source for detailed and up-to-date information is the **National Hurricane Center's** Web site at `www.nhc.noaa.gov/`. If you want to see what hurricane seasons have been like most recently, check the site at `USAtoday.com/weather/huricane`. Finally, a great place to see what the weather experts are predicting is via the Internet at `http://typhoon.atmos.colostate.edu/forecasts`.

Here are some other good Web sites:

- ✔ **WeatherNet's** Tropical Weather is the largest collection of tropical weather Web site links. Find it at `cirrus.sprl.umich.edu/wxnet/tropical.html`.

- ✔ **Caribbean Weather Man** is based on Tortola in the BVIs and gives good information about that region, particularly for sailors. Check out `www.caribwx.ccom/cyclone.html`.

> ✔ **Caribbean Hurricane Updates** has chat rooms and local correspondents on the islands where you can get the real scoop. Check out www.2gobeach.com/hurr.htm.

When you're setting up a trip months in advance, there's no way to predict the weather. However, you can take some precautions to make sure that you're not hung out to dry. If you are traveling to an island where hurricanes sometimes hit, ask the hotel to fax you its hurricane policy in writing — just in case. Larger, more affluent properties are much more likely to give credits toward future travel.

In 1998, **SuperClubs** (☎ 877-GO-SUPER; Internet www.superclubs.com), which operates 13 properties in Jamaica, St. Lucia, The Bahamas, St. Kitts, and Brazil, introduced a *No Hurricane Guarantee*, which gives guests full reimbursement for the total value of disrupted nights and issues a voucher for a future stay for the same number of nights to be used during the same month the following year. Meanwhile, **Sandals's** (☎ 888-SANDALS or 305-284-1300; Internet www.sandals.com) *Blue Chip Hurricane Guarantee* provides guests with a replacement vacation if a hurricane directly hits a property and the all-inclusive activities are disrupted. You can take the replacement vacation at the Sandals or Beaches resort of your choice, and you also get free round-trip airfare.

Smaller properties often won't give refunds, no matter what. We strongly urge you to consider buying trip interruption/cancellation insurance, which covers everything from hurricanes to missed connections due to snowstorms snarling air traffic stateside. (See Chapter 7 for more on purchasing insurance.)

If you hear that a storm has struck the Caribbean, and your island vacation is on the horizon, don't panic. Remember that the region takes up one million square miles. Fretting over a hurricane in St. Thomas when you're going to Aruba is like someone in Chicago freaking over a tornado in Texas. Unfortunately, U.S. weather reports are often vague and inflammatory and talk about the Caribbean as one big mass.

If you're truly concerned, put in a quick call directly to your hotel — not the reservation toll-free number, which is usually in the U.S. Don't ask a general question about hurricane damage to the island. Ask specifics like:

> ✔ Do you have any water damage?
>
> ✔ How's your beach? (Sometimes an island does not have to suffer a direct hit from a hurricane to have damage to its beaches.)
>
> ✔ Are all of your facilities open? (Restaurants, bars, and watersports facilities near the beach are often likely to suffer damage.)
>
> ✔ If the property has been damaged, when will everything be back in order?

The forecast: As long as a hurricane doesn't blow in and you don't arrive in the middle of a week of rain, this season is a great time to snag terrific deals.

Weathering an Endless Summer

Aruba is the hottest Caribbean island and the one where you'll find sunshine practically guaranteed. St. Croix is the runner-up in terms of least rainfall. Aruba gets a mere 17 inches of rain a year, while Jamaica gets 78 inches. Table 2-1 shows what you can expect weather wise in nine island locations.

Table 2-1   **Weather Averages**

	Summer Temperature	Winter Temperature	Annual Rainfall	Rainiest Months	Summer Water Temperature	Winter Water Temperature
Aruba	85°F (29°C)	81°F (27°C)	17" (43 cm)	Oct–Dec	82°F (28°C)	82°F (28°C)
Barbados	82°F (28°C)	79°F (26°C)	47" (119 cm)	June–Nov	83°F (28°C)	79°F (26°C)
BVIs	86°F (30°C)	80°F (27°C)	60" (152 cm)	May–Nov	83°F (28°C)	78°F (26°C)
Grand Cayman	85°F (29°C)	75°F (24°C)	60" (152 cm)	May–Oct	84°F (29°C)	79°F (26°C)
Jamaica	85°F (29°C)	80°F (27°C)	78" (198 cm)	May–Oct	83°F (28°C)	79°F (26°C)
Puerto Rico	83°F (28°C)	77°F (25°C)	62" (157 cm)	May–Nov	83°F (28°C)	79°F (26°C)
St. Croix	84°F (29°C)	79°F (26°C)	40" (102 cm)	Aug–Oct	83°F (28°C)	79°F (26°C)
St. John	82°F (28°C)	77°F (25°C)	54" (137 cm)	Aug–Oct	83°F (28°C)	79°F (26°C)
St. Thomas	85°F (29°C)	79°F (26°C)	44" (112 cm)	Aug–Oct	83°F (28°C)	79°F (26°C)

Even on the greener islands like the Virgin Islands and Jamaica, rain showers tend to be brief. We've never once found ourselves stuck inside for an entire day because of rain. **SuperClubs** (☎ 877-GO-SUPER; Internet www.superclubs.com) has introduced a *"Jamaica Sunshine" Guarantee,* which means that for any day the sun doesn't show its face, guests are issued a credit voucher for that day's value (good for one year) toward another SuperClubs vacation.

The trade winds are always blowing in the Caribbean, keeping the temperatures pleasant. In fact, you may feel slightly cool walking on the beach at night, exploring a rain forest, hiking in the mountains, or dining in an overly air-conditioned restaurant.

The year-round average water temperature in the Caribbean is a warm 78°F or 25°C and reaches a bathlike 84°F or 29°C or so in summer. Surf conditions are localized, so if the waves or undertow are threatening on your beach, you can usually find sheltered calmer waters by taking a short walk. Ask hotel staff for recommendations.

Taking In Festivals, Carnivals, and More Fun

As you consider when to go to the Caribbean, take a look at a calendar of ever-popular festivals — from jazz to reggae to Carnival — which can complicate the business of booking flights and hotel rooms. Because these dates change and more festivals seem to crop up each year, check with the tourist board of the island you intend to visit to make sure that you won't unexpectedly run into throngs of festival-goers — or to make sure you don't miss out on the fun.

Jamaica's Jazz Festival and Sum Fest rank among the most popular events, while every Tuesday evening Aruba celebrates the Bonbini Festival at Fort Zoutman with traditional dancing and music.

The Caribbean's calendar of special events

January

In mid-January, the Barbados **"Paint It Jazz" Festival** is one of the Caribbean's premier jazz events. It's a weekend jammed with perform-ances by international artists, jazz legends, and local talent. For tickets, e-mail bdosjazz@caribsurf.com.

February

Colorful **Carnival** events whirl through Aruba's streets — kicked off by a children's parade — during a two-week period. Carnival usually occurs in February, but the dates vary from year to year. For the schedule of events, check the Web site at www.aruba.com or call ☎ 800-862-7822.

The week-long **Holetown Festival** is held at the fairgrounds in Holetown to commemorate the date in 1627 when the first European settlers arrived in Barbados. Food, carnival rides, the Royal Barbados Police Force Band, and mounted troops add to the enjoyment. For further information, call ☎ 246-430-7300.

Three weeks of opera, concerts, and theatrical performances are presented in Barbados during **Holder's Opera Season.** The open-air theater at Holder's House, St. James, seats 600, and the program has won acclaim for its productions, which have included headliner Luciano Pavarotti. For information, call ☎ 246-432-6385.

April

Dubbed the "World's Greatest Street Party," Barbados's **De Congaline Carnival** is a festive celebration of music, dance, and local arts and crafts. Held at the end of April, the highlight is the Caribbean's longest conga line. For information, contact the Barbados Tourism Authority (☎ 246-427-2623; Internet www.barbados.org).

The British Virgin Islands' **Spring Regatta** is a sailor's dream with three days of sailboat races. It attracts boating enthusiasts from around the world (☎ 284-494-3286; fax 284-494-6117; e-mail bviyc@surfbvi.com; Internet www.bvispringregatta.org).

During the Grand Cayman's colorful **Batabano Carnival,** the weekend before Easter, revelers dress up as dancing flowers and swimming stingrays. Call ☎ 345-949-5078.

May

Gospelfest in Barbados features performances by Gospel headliners from around the world. For information, contact the Barbados Tourism Authority (☎ 246-427-2623; Internet www.barbados.org).

June

If you want to see an utterly British parade spiced with island-style panache, check out the **Queen's Birthday Bash** on Grand Cayman. At the sportfishing competitions in **Million Dollar Month,** huge cash prizes are awarded, including one for a quarter of a million dollars that's given to the angler who breaks the existing Blue Marlin record. Contact the Department of Tourism at ☎ 345-949-0623; fax 345-949-4053; Internet www.caymanislands.ky.

July

Dating back to the nineteenth century, the **Crop Over Festival** in Barbados, a month-long event beginning in early July, marks the end of the sugar cane harvest with competitions, music and dancing, Bajan food, and arts and crafts. The grand finale of Crop Over is a huge carnival parade on **Kadoonment Day,** the first Monday in August, a national holiday and the biggest party day of the year; visitors are welcome to participate. Contact the Barbados Tourism Authority (☎ 246-427-2623; Internet www.barbados.org).

The British Virgin Islands' two-week **Emancipation Festival** starts at the end of July and goes into August. It also has the **HIHO Festival,** a windsurfing and sailing competition. Contact the tourist board at ☎ **284-494-3134** or on the Internet at www.bviwelcome.com.

August

Jamaica's **Sum Fest** is a reggae party that draws top names, including the late Bob Marley's children. For information call the tourist board at ☎ **876-929-9200,** e-mail jamaicatrv@aol.com, or visit the Web site at www.jamaicatravel.com.

October

The end of October in Grand Cayman sees the carnival-like atmosphere of **Pirates Week** (which really lasts 10 days and includes a mock invasion of Hog Sty Bay by a mock Blackbeard and company). Visitors and locals dress up like pirates and wenches; music, fireworks, and a variety of competitions take place island-wide. Kids participate, too. Contact the Department of Tourism at ☎ **345-949-0623;** fax 345-949-4053; Internet www.caymanislands.ky.

December

The best local *fungi* (Caribbean folk music performed with homemade instruments) bands compete at the **Scratch/Fungi Band Fiesta** on Tortola, BVI. Contact the tourist board at ☎ **284-494-3134** or visit the Web site at www.bviwelcome.com.

Chapter 3

Pillow Talk: The Caribbean's Accommodations

In This Chapter

▶ Understanding your lodging options

▶ Choosing the best facility for you

▶ Booking the best room in the house

*I*n this section, we introduce you to the Caribbean's accommodation possibilities. We give you honest descriptions and try to make sure that you don't suffer a serious mismatch between your island fantasy and the reality awaiting you on the other side of your hotel door. That way, you can return home crowing about your wonderful experience rather than the resident, not-so-pleasant surprises.

Deciding Which Kind of Accommodation Works for You

The Caribbean runs the gamut in terms of places to stay. High-end accommodations are so fancy that they include a maid, gardener, cook, laundress, and butler, all in starched uniforms, standing ready to anticipate your every whim. At the lower end of the scale, you can live your desert island fantasy in a beach hut (don't expect air-conditioning!) or in a small guesthouse for less than $75 a night. Our tastes lie somewhere in the middle of these two extremes.

Travelers to the Caribbean typically have the following options:

　✔ Hotels and resorts

　✔ All-inclusive resorts

　✔ Villas

　✔ Condominiums and timeshares

　✔ Guesthouses

Expectations and reality often clash for first-time travelers in the tropics. Life moves languidly in the Caribbean. Change comes slowly and in small increments — radically different from the instantaneous responses we expect from our point-and-click world. We feel cheated in the United States if our hotel room doesn't have at least two dataport lines, voicemail that we can personalize, and HBO on the tube. In the Caribbean, concerns are different. In the past few years, enormous battles have been waged at some of the region's finer resorts over whether to install phones and air-conditioning in the rooms at all. One general manager at a luxury resort cheerfully vowed to chase into the surf any guest caught with a cell phone.

Although all of our recommended choices in the individual island accommodations chapters are located on the beach and have air-conditioning (unless otherwise noted), understand that some of the sexiest resorts in this region have no air-conditioning, no phone, no television, no alarm clock — not even *USA Today* or *CNN*.

Hotels and resorts: A variety of options

No matter what you're looking for, you can probably find something that suits your fancy. You'll find a tremendous range of hotel and resort accommodations, from small budget places that provide a basic room with a bed and a bathroom all the way up to exclusive resorts owned and managed by some of the world's finer chains. The latest trend among Caribbean hotels is the addition of spa services and upgraded workout facilities.

On most islands, building ordinances require that structures be no taller than the tallest coconut tree. On Puerto Rico, St. Thomas, Jamaica, and Aruba, however, you can see high-rise hotels like those on Miami Beach. Chains operate the best properties on Aruba (Marriott, Hyatt, Sonesta, and Radisson), Grand Cayman (Westin, Hyatt, and soon The Ritz-Carlton), and St. Thomas (Marriott and The Ritz-Carlton). But many of the hotels listed in this book have fewer than 100 rooms, and several are considered *boutique hotels,* stylized and unique in character. We tend to favor these kinds of places.

Hotels and resorts often include meal plans and the use of facilities in their rates. Chapter 6 discusses the different meal plans. Even if a hotel or resort doesn't offer all-inclusive packages (explained in the next section), you can usually count on full use of the pool and nonmotorized watersports. However, you may have to pay for use of a lounge chair on the beach and snorkeling or other equipment.

We recommend hotels and resorts for

- Honeymooners or couples who want to focus on each other.
- Families who want programs and sitters close at hand.
- Sports lovers who want all the facilities.

- ✔ First-time visitors to the Caribbean.

- ✔ Travelers with disabilities, because these places are much more likely to have appropriate facilities.

But staying at a hotel or resort also has its drawbacks:

- ✔ Many resorts and hotels lack island atmosphere.

- ✔ You may feel obliged to spend your time on the property, because you've paid so much to be there.

- ✔ Extra expenses for meals, drinks, and watersports add up quickly, and you're likely to get a shock at checkout if you've been charging everything to your room.

All-inclusive resorts: Simplifying your vacation

The all-inclusive concept, where you shell out the dough for your vacation in advance (with no tipping allowed once you get on the island), is essentially a one-price-buys-all package that includes your hotel room, meals, drinks, and activities. All-inclusive resorts have found their niche because we all want to simplify our lives. The Caribbean's version of the concept started on Jamaica and now dominates the accommodation scene on that island. You'll run into the all-inclusive concept on Barbados, St. Thomas, and Aruba, and in a smattering of places across most of the other islands, too.

Recently, the top-tier all-inclusive resorts have been duking it out by adding more and more extras. For instance, stung by criticism in the early days that they were cheapskates when it came to food and drink, the big players all now serve premium brand alcohol and have been hiring better and better chefs for their restaurants. Now you may find yourself with half a dozen or so restaurants from which to choose — without ever leaving your resort.

Tipping tips

Many guests at all-inclusive resorts are under the mistaken impression that they do not need to tip baggage handlers at the airport and drivers who get you to and from your resort. That is not the case, and this misunderstanding has unfortunately created tension on both sides. Unless the person helping you is an employee of the resort, assume that you do need to tip.

The new battleground, however, appears to be in the spa arena. The words "& Spa" after the name of the all-inclusive resort are becoming almost as ubiquitous as the words "& Casino" after the name of almost every hotel on Aruba. Guests at many spa resorts get one or two spa treatments (full-body massages and facials are the most popular) per day included in their all-inclusive package.

We like all-inclusive resorts and have included our favorites in this book, along with several smaller boutique hotels and resorts that don't have the big advertising budgets.

The main operators of all-inclusive resorts in the Caribbean are

- ✔ **Sandals** (☎ **800-SANDALS** or 305-284-1300; fax 305-284-1336; Internet www.sandals.com), which operates nine couples-only properties and three resorts open to everyone.

- ✔ **SuperClubs** (☎ **800-GO-SUPER** or 954-925-0925; Internet www.superclubs.com), which owns numerous properties in Jamaica and a few on other islands.

- ✔ **Club Med** (☎ **800-CLUBMED**; Internet www.clubmed.com), which has a half-dozen "villages" in the Caribbean.

Each company offers packages that allow you to get married for free when you book a honeymoon with them.

 One of our favorite features of Sandals and SuperClubs is a cool program that lets you split your time between resorts within each company's range of accommodations. To us, that's the resort equivalent of ordering the fisherman's platter. You get to sample the best of everything. For example, SuperClubs allows you to book a stay at the slightly less expensive Grand Lido Sans Souci and then spend a few days of your minimum six-night stay at the more expensive Grand Lido Negril.

 What you get at an all-inclusive resort varies dramatically, and the differences can be confusing. A Web site that rates all-inclusive resorts is www.allinclusiveratings.com. It operates similarly to AAA Diamond Awards, using a ten-star rating, assigning point values to all the services and amenities. Sandals, which obviously has a vested interest, is a partner in the undertaking.

Good candidates for all-inclusive resorts are

- ✔ Honeymooners
- ✔ Families
- ✔ Inexperienced travelers
- ✔ The budget-conscious
- ✔ The super-stressed

The drawbacks to staying at an all-inclusive resort?

✔ In order to feel that you've squeezed every last penny out of your vacation, you might feel obligated to spend all your time on the property, because you've paid so much to be there.

✔ Every island is exactly the same when viewed from the cushy confines of an all-inclusive. It's tough to break away from your lounge chair. You miss what makes the island special after you've traveled so far to get there.

✔ Rah-rah activity instructors can wear on your nerves.

Villas: Vacationing with the comforts of home

Villa is a broad word in the Caribbean. Basically, it means a rental property. Properties ranging from princely digs to modest bungalows fall into this category.

A villa promises two luxuries: space and good kitchen facilities. Villas usually offer more privacy than hotels and resorts and are tucked away on gated lots with either sea or mountain views. If you like the comforts of home, a villa is the way to go. Villas are particularly popular in the Virgin Islands, Jamaica, and Puerto Rico.

Villas rent for anywhere from less than $1,000 a week all the way up to thousands of dollars a day. Three couples traveling together can easily rent a villa for a week for less than $1,000 per person. We've been amazed at how reasonably priced some drop-dead gorgeous villas are, particularly on St. John. You can also find some good deals in Jamaica. Many villas must be booked for a minimum of a week.

We recommend booking a villa through a professional management company that's responsible for renting out and maintaining the house when the owner isn't on the island. (See our recommendation in the next paragraph or look at the back of the ad sections in *Caribbean Travel & Life* or *Islands* magazines.) Renting a villa from an individual can be a little iffy, because the Caribbean has a way of taking a toll on even the finest resorts. Unless an owner is extremely diligent about upkeep, a place can quickly slip below par. You also run the risk of renting a place where the décor looks like leftovers from a yard sale. In this book, we include only villas that we've inspected personally and recently.

For the preeminent source on villas, try **Unusual Villas** (409F North Hamilton Street, Richmond, VA 23221; ☎ **800-846-7280** or 804-288-2823; fax 804-342-9016; e-mail johng@unusualvillarentals.com; Internet www.unusualvillarentals.com). Owner John Greer, who has been specializing in villas since 1992, has an award-winning Web site with more than 1,500 pages dedicated to villas. He has more than 100 villas for rent on Barbados and Jamaica. On St. Thomas, he handles rentals for about 50 villas, and he deals with a handful on other Caribbean islands as well.

So that you don't waste time and money on duplicate supplies, check with the management company about what the villa will have on hand for your use. Depending on the unit, you may be treated to a welcome platter of fresh fruit and a bottle of wine. You may find that you get access to a vehicle as part of the rental as well.

We recommend villas for

- ✔ Families.
- ✔ A group of friends. (You'd better be close, though, or you run the risk of fights over the master bedroom, which invariably has some cool feature that everyone covets.)
- ✔ Honeymooners or couples craving privacy.
- ✔ Independent travelers who want to connect with the island.

But staying at a home-away-from-home can also have a downside:

- ✔ You don't get the extensive dining facilities and other amenities of a resort.
- ✔ A villa may not offer daily maid service and other niceties (like a pool or Jacuzzi) that you consider vital to your relaxation.
- ✔ Few are located right on the beach; resorts usually snag the prime real estate.
- ✔ You definitely won't get (or be subjected to, depending on your point of view) the nightly entertainment that almost every Caribbean hotel trumpets.
- ✔ The good news is you're isolated. The bad news is you're isolated, so you'd better really like your traveling companion.
- ✔ Of all the travel options, villas are least likely to live up to their brochure promises.

Condos and timeshares: Apartment-style living

Condos and timeshares are popular options on Aruba, Grand Cayman, and the U.S. Virgin Islands (mainly St. Thomas). With these properties, you get apartment-style accommodations in a hotel setting. The amenities range greatly. At busy La Cabana on Aruba, for example, the experience isn't much different from staying at a large resort. (See Chapter 8 for a full review of the property.) The Ritz-Carlton on St. Thomas, the

Westin St. John, and the Aruba Marriott have all entered the timeshare business in recent years with units that are on the same property as their respective resorts. Prices are comparable to what you'd pay at a hotel, but you almost always have kitchen facilities.

We recommend condos and timeshares for

- ✔ Families. You can feed your kids what you want and not have to suffer disapproving looks from the honeymooners at the next table when Junior flips his soggy cereal on the floor.
- ✔ A group of friends. (You'd better be close, though, or you run the risk of fights over the master bedroom, which invariably has some cool feature that everyone covets.)
- ✔ Older couples looking for quiet.
- ✔ Long-term vacationers. Cooking your own meals is a great money-saving tactic for an extended stay on an island.
- ✔ Independent travelers who want to connect with the island and its people.

What are some drawbacks of staying at a condo or timeshare?

- ✔ All the comforts of home, plus all the work.
- ✔ Limited amenities.
- ✔ You're trusting your tropical dream to someone else's decorating taste.
- ✔ When dinner time comes, you're the staff as well as the diner.

Guesthouses: Living like a local

If you want lodging that resembles a bed-and-breakfast, guesthouses are the Caribbean's answer. In a guesthouse, only a few rooms are rented out, and the owner/manager lives on the property.

Guesthouses work well for bargain-hunters and those who like being under someone else's roof. You may get a light breakfast as part of your rate, which is usually $100 or less per night. If you plan to explore a great deal, this option may be good for you, too — you'll have a place to come home to after you satisfy your wanderlust.

We recommend guesthouses for

- ✔ Older couples who like the bed-and-breakfast concept.
- ✔ Long-term vacationers on tight budgets.
- ✔ The independent traveler who needs a home base.

Here are some of the drawbacks of staying at a guesthouse:

- ✔ You may be far from the beach, without a pool.
- ✔ The digs may not be glamorous.
- ✔ You may not get along with your host.
- ✔ Housekeeping standards vary widely.
- ✔ If there's a problem, you're stuck dealing one-on-one with the house owner.

Getting a Great Room

Somebody has to get the best room in the house; it might as well be you. This is where the reservations agent in the hotel comes in handy: He or she will actually know which rooms are the best. Let the person know of any special event you're celebrating or any concerns you have. Ask how long the walk is from your room to the beach — you may find out that it's across the road, like most of the rooms at Hyatt Regency Grand Cayman. Ask the reservations agent which room he or she would want to book for a special occasion. If you have small children, ask which room is nearest to the kids' program.

Be clear about what's important to you. For example, some of the larger rooms at Caneel Bay, an exclusive resort on St. John, are less pricey because they aren't as close to the beach. If we were traveling with our boys, we'd gladly walk the few extra steps in return for more space for the four of us.

Specify what size bed you want, or you may find yourself with two twins — especially on British islands like Barbados.

Also check to see if the hotel is in the midst of renovation; if it is, request a room away from the work site. Ask if the rooms have been refurbished recently. The salt-water air, sun, and sand wreak havoc with bedspreads and other furnishings. You want something as fresh as possible, so ask for the most recently redone rooms.

If your resort isn't air-conditioned and relies on trade winds and ceiling fans for cooling, try to get a room as close to the sea as possible. You'll get more of a breeze if you're on the second floor or higher. Corner rooms with more windows give you that much more breeze coming through. At The Ritz-Carlton in St. Thomas, for example, the suites occupy the far-end corner of the building overhanging the bluff with a view of the harbor. Although the suites are air-conditioned, you can also open the windows out to the sea, as well as the doors onto the private wraparound decks.

Many hotels now offer nonsmoking rooms; by all means ask for one if smoke bothers you. Inquire, too, about your room's proximity to any of the hotel's open-air restaurants, beach bars with steel pan bands, family pools with screaming kids, and discos blaring reggae — all sources of irritating noise that can be torture if you're a light sleeper.

If you aren't happy with your room when you arrive, talk to the front desk manager. For instance, we recently stayed at a resort where we were given a lovely room right on the beach. However, when we walked out the front door of our room, the trash receptacle for the hotel was behind a nearby wall and the smell was overpowering. If the wind hadn't shifted, we would have been in the manager's office. In a case like that, speak up. If the hotel has another room, you'll be accommodated, within reason.

For tips on saving money on your accommodations, see our list of pointers in Chapter 6.

Chapter 4

Planning Ahead for Special Travel Needs

Caribbean travel planning seems to inspire some common questions: How family-friendly are the islands? Where can couples honeymoon or even tie the knot? What discounts and privileges are available for seniors? Which islands have the best facilities for travelers with disabilities? And which put out the welcome mat for gay and lesbian travelers? If you're among those who have special needs or concerns about your Caribbean visit, read on — our discoveries can help you prepare for a delightful, rather than disappointing, getaway.

Ensuring a Fun, Safe Family Vacation

These days we're part of a growing number of families spending their summer and holiday vacations in the Caribbean. Eager to take advantage of this trend, hotels and resorts are scrambling to add facilities and services appealing to pint-sized customers. And that's not a tough task: Between the pool and the warm Caribbean Sea, the kids are already enthralled. Add in games like limbo, crab races, and reggae dance contests, and they're over the moon. And relatively new programs, which offer cultural and ecological exploration, impress parents and children both. For instance, your child could spend the morning learning from a marine biologist how to protect coral reefs.

 The last few summers we've chosen to spend our vacations at **Boscobel**, near Ocho Rios on Jamaica (see Chapter 24), but all of the islands mentioned in this book have family-friendly resorts, restaurants, and activities. Look for the Kid Friendly icon, which indicates our top choices.

Flying with kids

For us, probably the toughest part of traveling with our kids is that time-worn question, "Are we there yet?" Getting there with kids in tow is definitely not half the fun, but for most island destinations, the trip really isn't that bad. To us, it sure beats a long car trip.

Don't forget that when traveling internationally, children — babies, too — must have either a certified copy of a birth certificate (with a raised seal) or an official passport. (See Chapter 7.) Here are some other things to keep in mind when traveling with young children:

✔ Children's airfares are typically discounted 50%, but during peak season, the reduction may be as little as 33%.

✔ You can't expect many empty seats on Caribbean flights, so don't gamble on being able to seat your infant (under age 2) beside you. If you both want to be comfortable, buy a seat for your child. Ask about special children's fares.

✔ Order a kid's meal when you reserve your flight and ask about the airline's rules regarding carseats.

✔ Because Caribbean flights are so full, you'll probably have to check your child's stroller. Make sure that you label the stroller with your name and where you'll be staying on the island.

✔ Make sure that you're seated together on the plane. If you don't have boarding passes, get to the airport at least two hours early to ensure that you get seats together. Caribbean flights are usually packed, and we've seen families separated by several rows.

✔ The bulkhead, which has extra space, is in high demand, but you may get lucky if you request it early.

✔ Pack four times the amount of favorite snacks you think you'll need. Delays can be lengthy and airport food prices are sky-high. Baby wipes (even if your children are older) come in handy, too. Also bring a large bottle of water for each child — especially if you're changing planes. For babies and toddlers, bring a large supply of diapers onboard with you, too.

✔ Let your child bring some small favorite toys. But don't bring expensive electronic ones that are likely to get misplaced or stolen. (Yes, we learned that the hard way.) On islands with high poverty levels, like Jamaica, we like to bring boxes of crayons and small items that we can leave behind for island children.

✔ Do not board your plane early, even though the opportunity's offered. Why keep your little ones cooped up any longer than necessary? The only time this makes sense is if you are traveling with an infant and want to lock in your child's safety seat.

✔ To relieve painful pressure on eardrums, bring chewing gum for older children. Nurse or give babies a bottle on take-off and landing to keep their ears from hurting.

> ✔ If you rent a car, request a carseat in advance. If a hotel is arranging transportation for you, ask if the vehicle being sent will have seat belts. We've found that even family-friendly resorts often send vans and cars with nary a seat belt in sight.

Choosing a family-friendly resort

We've learned over the years that although most major resorts claim to have children's programs, the offerings differ greatly. Take a tour of the facilities before dropping off your kids. Some of the ritzier resorts accept children only at certain times of year, and then the staff's attitude may be one of tolerance rather than enthusiasm. A children's program in such a place may consist of a bored sitter stuck in a small room with several kids. We actually got a press release from one place trumpeting its new kids' "program," which consisted of setting out cookies and milk for children each evening.

Always check before you book to make sure that you're getting what you think you're getting. Here are some good questions to ask:

> ✔ What is the ratio of teachers to children?
>
> ✔ How are the ages divided?
>
> ✔ How much beach or pool time do they get — with expert supervision, of course?
>
> ✔ Where and what do the children eat?

Be sure to alert the workers to any food allergies your child has and double-check to make sure they really understand.

Some programs won't accept children who are not potty-trained. Others have skimpy or nonexistent offerings for teens. If you travel during a slow period, you may find that the kids' program hours have been cut in response to diminished numbers of participants.

Make sure to let the children's program workers know where to find you in case of an emergency. If your children sunburn easily, slather on waterproof sunscreen first thing in the morning (it takes about a half hour before it starts working), because the childcare workers probably won't have time to apply it as painstakingly as you do.

Overall, rest assured that West Indians love children. So even if your resort doesn't have a formal children's program, you can find a reliable baby-sitter through your concierge or hotel manager if you desire an evening out. Try to give at least 24 hours notice.

If your kids are older, almost all of the islands have enough adventure activities to entice even the most stubborn teen or 'tween. Of course, the watersports are terrific everywhere in the Caribbean. We especially recommend the ATV riding and hiking on Jamaica; hiking and sailing in the Virgin Islands; spelunking and surfing on Puerto Rico; and windsurfing and horseback riding in Aruba. Teens who are into scuba diving will enjoy Grand Cayman, but we've heard complaints of boredom from those who don't go for watersports. We think Barbados would be too buttoned up for teens as well.

You may want to warn teens that drug offenses are taken extremely seriously on the islands, and that if they get into trouble, they are considered guilty until proven innocent.

At family-friendly resorts, kids 12 and under usually stay and eat for free, although you may have to pay a daily fee for using the children's program. (Check when you reserve; it's usually about $30 to $80.) During the summer low season (approximately mid-April through early December), off-season rates drop anywhere from 15% to 60%. Islands that offer excellent summer specials for families include Aruba, Barbados, Grand Cayman, St. Croix, and St. Thomas. Look for the Kid Friendly icon throughout the hotel chapters.

Unfortunately, the typical kids' menu in the Caribbean is usually greasy food like burgers, fries, chicken fingers, and pizza. Fresh fruit is cheap and plentiful on most islands and makes a great snack. Just be sure to wash or peel it before your kids eat it.

For more information on traveling with kids, pick up Paris Permenter and John Bigley's book *Caribbean with Kids* (Open Road).

Saying "I Do" in the Caribbean

According to *Brides Magazine*, more and more couples are choosing to get hitched abroad. With the exception of Aruba, the Caribbean offers great options.

Almost all the larger hotels we mention in this book have on-site wedding planners, as do many of the smaller ones. Even better, basic weddings at most of the all-inclusive resorts are free. A company called **Weddings on the Move, Inc.** (☎ **800-444-6967;** fax 414-306-7100; e-mail: deb@idoweddings.com; Internet www.idoweddings.com) specializes in planning island weddings. If you prefer to handle everything yourself long distance, check out the Web sites www.TheKnot.com or www.theweddingsource.com, where you can find free listings of wedding vendors, plus advice on good wedding locations and tips on how to choose vendors.

On St. Thomas, which has many, many weddings each year, Debra Williams, founder of **Fantasia Weddings & Honeymoons** (168 Crow Bay, St. Thomas, 00802; ☎ **888-WED-USVI** or 340-777-6588; fax 340-774-8009; e-mail fantasia@islands.vi; Internet www.wedusvi.com), has been coordinating wedding services from the simplest ceremonies to lavish affairs on yachts since 1990.

For the basic legalities of a Caribbean wedding, contact the **Caribbean Tourism Organization** (☎ 212-635-9530; e-mail get2cto@dorsai.org) to request its "Weddings Requirement Chart," which tells you everything you need to know at a glance. Because the rules of a foreign wedding can change suddenly, though, call the tourist board about two months ahead of time for any last-minute updates. Generally speaking, the waiting period — if there is one — is only a day or two. The license fees range from the price of a stamp in Puerto Rico to $250 in Jamaica. Aruba doesn't allow tourist weddings unless one of you is originally from that island.

Table 4-1 gives you the scoop on island-to-island requirements for nuptials in each location.

Table 4-1		Wedding Requirements		
Country	**Fee**	**Blood Test**	**Waiting Period**	**What You Need**
Barbados	BDS $50	No	None	Passports, proof of divorce or death certificate of former spouse (if applicable), letter from the authorized officiant performing service.
BVIs	BVI $110	No	3 days	Passports or original birth certificates and photo IDs, proof (original copy) of divorce or death certificate of former spouse (if applicable).
Cayman Islands	US $200	No	None	Passports or birth certificates and photo IDs, original or certified copies of divorce decree or former spouse's death certificate (if applicable), return or ongoing ticket, proofs of entry (Cayman Islands International Immigration Department pink slips or cruise ship boarding passes), letter from authorized officiating marriage officer.
Jamaica	J $250	No	3 days (varies with programs at different hotels and resorts)	Certified copies of birth certificates that include father's name, proof of divorce or death certificate of former spouse (if applicable).

Country	Fee	Blood Test	Waiting Period	What You Need
Puerto Rico	No fee	No	Yes, within 10 days of the wedding	U.S. driver's license or passports for non-U.S. citizens. Send request in writing two months in advance to Dept. of Health, Demographic Registry Office, Box 11854, Fernandez Juncos Station, Santurce, PR 00910 (☎ 787-728-7980). Proof of divorce or death certificate of former spouse (if applicable), letter accompanying Application for Marriage stating date of visit, length of stay, preference of date if having ceremony performed by a judge.
U.S. Virgin Islands	US $150	No	8 days from the receipt of the notarized application; couples need not be on the islands when the application arrives.	Proof of divorce or death certificate of former spouse (if applicable), letter accompanying Application for Marriage stating date of visit, length of stay, preference of date if having ceremony performed by a judge.

Planning the Perfect Honeymoon

The Caribbean is a paradise for couples in search of romance. Honeymoon packages at most resorts are generous, even creative. Some all-inclusive resorts — on Jamaica in particular — are devoted exclusively to couples. The downside is that you'll be just two faces in a flock of lovebirds. In other words, don't expect anyone to go to great lengths and deliver beyond what's promised in your honeymoon package. Often, the honeymoon package is good enough, though, because you can be assured that you won't encounter conventioneers, family reunions, or young children.

If you have any special requests, fax them to the concierge about a month before your arrival; you want to give your hotel or resort plenty of time to make your dreams come true. Don't worry, they're up to the challenge. One concierge told us of a groom who requested different colored satin sheets and matching rose petals for each night of his honeymoon. The staff had to call all over the place to find king-size satin sheets in a rainbow of colors, but they did it.

Cashing In on Senior Discounts

Older people are treated with great respect in Caribbean cultures. However, you usually won't get special privileges or discounts for being over a certain age. Your best bet at getting discounts is on the front end by making reservations through a travel club for seniors.

If you're over 50, join **AARP** — the American Association of Retired Persons (601 E St. NW, Washington, DC 20049; ☎ **202-434-AARP;** Internet www.aarp.org). Always mention your AARP membership (which costs $8 a year) when you make reservations. You'll get discounts ranging from 5% to 20% on car rentals with Avis, Hertz, and National, as well as with cruises, hotels, and airlines.

 Some car rental agencies have maximum age limits; if you're over 65, you may not be able to rent with some agencies in the Caribbean.

 Many airlines, including American, United, Continental, US Airways, and TWA, offer discount programs for senior travelers (ages 62 and above), but restrictions often apply on popular Caribbean routes. Rate reductions are worth asking about whenever you book a flight.

 In some Caribbean cities, people over the age of 60 received a slightly reduced admission at theaters, museums, and other attractions, and they can often get discount fares on public transportation. Carry identification with proof of age, just in case.

Here are some more good resources for senior travelers:

- ✔ *The Mature Traveler,* a monthly 12-page newsletter on senior citizen travel, is a valuable resource. It is available by subscription ($29.95 + $2 shipping for a year) from GEM Publishing Group, Box 50400, Reno, NV 89513-0400. GEM also publishes *The Book of Deals,* a collection of more than 1,000 senior discounts on airlines, lodging, tours, and attractions around the country; it's available for $9.95 by calling ☎ **800-460-6676** or e-mailing maturetrav@aol.com.

- ✔ Another helpful publication is *101 Tips for the Mature Traveler,* available from **Grand Circle Travel** (347 Congress St., Suite 3A, Boston, MA 02210; ☎ **800-221-2610** or 617-350-7500; fax 617-350-6206; Internet www.gct.com), a travel agency specializing in vacations for seniors, including Caribbean cruises. Traveling companions must be age 13 or older.

- ✔ **SAGA International Holidays** (222 Berkeley St., Boston, MA 02116; ☎ **800-343-0273;** e-mail Sales_info@sagaholidays.com; Internet www.sagaholidays.com) offers cruises in the Caribbean for those 50 and older.

Ensuring Access for Travelers with Disabilities

Generally speaking, most of the islands in this book offer some options for travelers with disabilities. Of course, public spaces in Puerto Rico and the U.S. Virgin Islands are required by law to be wheelchair accessible, but at this writing, San Juan, St. Thomas, and St. Croix were the only Caribbean destinations serviced by wheelchair-accessible van companies.

Aruba, Barbados, Jamaica, and Grand Cayman have some wheelchair-accessible hotel and restaurant facilities, but for the most part, wheelchair-bound travelers will find accessibility still at Third World standards in the Caribbean — with the exception of San Juan, St. Thomas, and St. Croix. Mountainous St. Lucia and the British Virgin Islands present very challenging travel and lack easy access. Traveling on those islands requires going up and down lots of steps and getting on and off a variety of modes of transportation. You won't find sidewalks there, and many roads are unpaved.

The cruise industry is recognizing slowly that the needs of travelers with disabilities have been overlooked in the Caribbean. By 2001, more than 1,200 wheelchair-accessible staterooms (twice as many as in 2000) will be available on Caribbean cruise ships each week. New cruise ships typically have a larger number of wheelchair-accessible cabins than in the past. However, many of the Caribbean's ports still remain inaccessible.

Howard McCoy, R.N., is a tour operator and planner who runs **Accessible Journeys** (35 West Sellers Avenue, Ridley Park, PA 19078; ☎ 800-846-4537 or 610-521-0339; fax 610-521-6959; e-mail sales@ disabilitytravel.com; Internet www.disabilitytravel.com). The agency focuses primarily on travelers with mobility challenges and is now the largest cruise wholesaler for wheelchair vacations in the world. The company sponsors five to eight Caribbean cruise groups with guaranteed space and guaranteed departure annually.

Travelers with disabilities may want to use a travel agent who specializes in special needs trips. One of the better outfits that books Caribbean cruises is **Flying Wheels Travel** (143 West Bridge or P.O. Box 382, Owatonna, MN 55060; ☎ 800-535-6790).

Owned by individuals with mobility impairments, **Barrier Free Vacations** (Sunset Harbor, Suite 505, 236 North Derby, Ventnor, NJ 08406; ☎ 800-749-5635; e-mail barrier-free-vacations@worldnet. att.net; Internet www.barrier-free-vacations.com) provides free travel reservation services for individuals with physical disabilities and has identified barrier-free Caribbean destinations that are accessible by cruise ships.

A World of Options, a 658-page book of resources for travelers with disabilities, covers everything from biking trips to scuba outfitters. It costs $35 and is available from **Mobility International USA** (P.O. Box 10767, Eugene, OR 97440; ☎ **541-343-1284,** voice and TTY; fax 503-343-6812; Internet www.miusa.org). For information by phone, call the **Travel Information Service** at ☎ **215-456-9603** (voice) or 215-456-9602 (TTY).

Another good networking organization is run by a wheelchair-bound gentleman who became disheartened at how little information was out there. **Travelin' Talk** (P.O. Box 3534, Clarksville, TN 37043-3534; ☎ **931-552-6670;** fax 931-552-1182) produces a $35 directory for members in the international network, who exchange information on local lodgings, medical services, accessible restaurants, and other topics important to people with disabilities.

The Oxygen Traveler (☎ **937-848-7100;** fax 937-848-7949; e-mail oxygen0202@aol.com; Internet www.access-able.com/tips/oxy. html) is not a travel agancy but helps travelers who require oxygen and durable medical equipment for international and cruise travel. The company makes arrangements for transporting equipment to ships, airports, or hotels by working with travel agencies, health care providers, and the cruise line industry. Right now, the company has contacts in Aruba, Barbados, Jamaica, Puerto Rico, St. Lucia, and the United States Virgin Islands. The Oxygen Traveler may also be able to make arrangements on Tortola in the British Virgin Islands. Currently, it does not have any contacts in the Cayman Islands.

Vision-impaired travelers can contact the **American Foundation for the Blind** (11 Penn Plaza, Suite 300, New York, NY 10001; ☎ **800-232-5463**) for information on traveling with seeing-eye dogs.

Traveling to Gay- and Lesbian-Friendly Destinations

Judging from recent news stories, gay and lesbian travelers might assume that homosexuality and the Caribbean mix about as well as oil and water. In 1998, the Cayman Islands government announced that a cruise ship carrying a gay and lesbian group from the United States would be denied landing rights for its planned visit to Grand Cayman. "Careful research and prior experience has led us to conclude that we cannot count on this group to uphold the standards of appropriate behavior expected of visitors to the Cayman Islands," the Minister of Tourism wrote. What careful research and prior experience had been studied was not outlined, nor were standards of appropriate behavior in the Cayman Islands explained.

The Caribbean should not be confused with New York, London, or any other metropolis where gays and lesbians enjoy relatively open lifestyles. In much of the Caribbean, homophobic attitudes are common. Most islands, like some U.S. states, have anti-gay laws on the books. The former British colonies in particular (like Jamaica and the Cayman Islands) frown on gay and lesbian relationships.

But this is not to say that gays and lesbians cannot vacation comfortably in the Caribbean. Shortly after the Grand Cayman flap, community members from St. John welcomed with love beads a small cruise ship carrying lesbian travelers. In general, the discreet can travel virtually anywhere in the Caribbean without fear of hassle. Most hotels are indifferent to the issue. Prominent exceptions are the Sandals and SuperClubs chains and a few other all-inclusive outfits. They call themselves "couples-only" resorts but define that term in strictly male/female terms.

Puerto Rico is home to the region's most visible gay scene and features a robust nightlife in San Juan. The U.S. and British Virgin Islands, St. Barthelemy, Sint Maarten/St. Martin, Trinidad, Santo Domingo in the Dominican Republic, and even tiny Saba are other places where gays and lesbians will feel most comfortable.

A handful of Caribbean lodgings, while not necessarily gay-owned, have classified themselves as gay-friendly.

In San Juan, Puerto Rico:

- **Atlantic Beach Hotel** (☎ **888-611-6900**; fax 787-721-6917; Internet www.stormloader.com/abh/).
- **Hosteria Del Mar** (☎ **787-727-3302**).
- **L'Habitation Beach** (☎ **787-727-2499;** fax 787-727-2599; e-mail habitationbeach@msn.com).
- **Numero Uno** (☎ **787-726-5010**).

In the U.S. Virgin Islands:

- **Cormorant Beach Club Hotel,** St. Croix (☎ **800-548-4460** or 340-778-8920; e-mail vacations@cormorant-stcroix.com; Internet www.cormorant-stcroix.com/).
- **Inn at Blackbeard's Castle,** St. Thomas (☎ **800-344-5771** or 340-776-1234).
- **Maho Bay** and its sister properties, St. John (☎ **800-392-9004,** or in the New York City area 212-472-9453; e-mail mahobay@maho.org; Internet www.moho.org).
- **On the Beach,** St. Croix (☎ **800-524-2018** or 809-772-1205).

In the British Virgin Islands:

- ✔ **Fort Recovery Estates** (☎ **800-367-8455** or 284-495-4354).

- ✔ **Cooper Island Beach Club** (☎ **800-542-4624** or 413-863-3162; e-mail info@cooper-island.com; Internet www.cooper-island.com/).

In Jamaica:

- ✔ **Hotel Mocking Bird Hill** (☎ **877-364-1100;** fax 860-264-1102).

Tying Up
the Loose Ends

The 5th Wave   By Rich Tennant

"I asked for a seat near the steel drum,
but I don't see any steel drum."

In this part . . .

So you've decided which island you want to visit and what time of year to go. Now what? In this part, we give you advice for booking the trip of your dreams — either through a travel agent or on your own. We help you determine the fastest and most economic ways to travel to your destination.

We also show you how to estimate the cost of your trip and keep it within your budget. Finally, we walk you through the details you need to know in order to have a smooth travel experience, from securing the necessary paperwork to packing like a pro.

Chapter 5

Making Your Travel Arrangements

· ·

· ·

*T*raveling to your dream destination in the cheapest, most comfortable, and fastest way possible is a chief concern when you start to plan a trip. You may save a bundle if you read this chapter before making reservations the old-fashioned way.

In this chapter, we tell you whether you're wiser to do-it-yourself when booking your trip or work with a travel agent. We give you the latest tips on getting the best airfare and tell you which airlines fly to which destinations. We explain package tours, including what they mean for your wallet and what impact they have on your Caribbean experience. And, for those of you who think you'd rather float than fly, we offer some information on cruises, too.

Tapping the Talents of a Travel Agent

In recent years, the Web has made booking trips incredibly easy, so much so that you may start to wonder if you need a travel agent at all. The answer depends on you. During our travels, we've met many people who have booked their Caribbean vacations online. Armed with this book and a do-it-yourself attitude, you should have no problem going it alone. However, if you aren't Web savvy, if you like to talk over your choices with an expert, or if your trip is at all complicated (for example, you're island-hopping or making several airline connections), the safest bet is to go through a travel agent.

Getting more for your travel agent money

A few years ago, airlines and resorts slashed travel agent commissions or eliminated them altogether, throwing travel agencies into turmoil. As a result, some travel agents have begun charging customers fees, such as $10 for an airline booking or up to $100 for planning a trip. More complex trip planning may be based on an hourly fee — or you may not have to pay a penny, depending on the agency's business policy.

The agent's fee may be a small price to pay, because a savvy travel agent can save you hundreds — even thousands — of dollars. Travel agents are often aware of discounts, specials, and other promotions involving air travel, car rentals, and hotel accommodations. A *knowledgeable* agent can snag you a well-priced rental car with an upgrade and steer you to a better hotel room for about the same price as you plan to spend on an inferior place. A top-flight travel agent will also go the extra mile by finding a cheap flight that doesn't require you to change planes several times en route.

Unfortunately, you may have a hard time finding that top-flight, knowledgeable travel agent who can plan your dream vacation for much less money than you'd imagined. Many travel agents have little practical experience with the Caribbean; in fact, after you read this book, you'll know far more than most! And if your travel agent has only glimpsed the Caribbean through Web surfing and brochures, you take a gamble if you rely on his or her choices. (Believe us, we've seen Caribbean resorts use every trick in their promotional materials to make their pools look gargantuan, their landscaping impossibly lush, and their location prime seafront.) If your friends can't recommend a knowledgeable travel agent, take a look at our list of Caribbean specialists in the next section.

We hate to be cynical, but most travel agents never even see some of the best resorts. The way the average travel agent explores an island is to take a trip sponsored by a big resort operator such as Sandals. Sandals frequently brings a large group of agents in for what's called a "familiarization trip," or "fam" for short. Can you guess which resort has been named tops among travel agents worldwide for six years running? Surprise! It's Sandals.

To get the most benefit from your travel agent, do a little homework on your destination. We've already done much of the legwork for you by eliminating the peripheral attractions, substandard hotels, and blah restaurants that other guidebooks dutifully catalogue. If you have Internet access, check prices on the Web before you meet with a travel agent. (See "Booking Your Trip Online" later in this chapter for more information.) Travel agents have little incentive to spend a great deal of time researching the best schedule and fare for you now that airlines have slashed their commissions. Arming yourself with some idea of what you want and the available fares will make your meeting or e-mail session with your travel agent far more productive.

Locating Caribbean specialists

The **Caribbean Tourism Organization** provides names of its recommended travel agents at ☎ **212-635-9530** or on the Internet at www.caribtourism.com. Another source is **The Agency Coalition for Caribbean Tourism** (☎ **800-931-ACCT**), which will match you with the Caribbean travel agent nearest you. You can go online to find travel agents specializing in the Caribbean at the **Association of Retail Travel Agents** (Internet www.artaonline.com) or the **American Society of Travel Agents** (Internet www.astanet.com).

TourScan (☎ **800-962-2080** or 203-655-8091) has specialized in the Caribbean since 1987, and twice a year it compiles information on all the different packages offered by tour operators. Because tour operators often have varying prices for the exact same resort, this information makes bargain-shopping a lot easier. This agency offers the lowdown on 1,800 properties on 56 islands in the Carribean, the Bahamas, and Bermuda. The information is available by catalog or on the Internet at www.tourscan.com.

Some agencies have narrower specialties, focusing on a particular island or type of vacation. For example, **Caribbean Connection Plus Limited** (☎ **800-893-1100** or 203-261-8603) is an especially good travel agency well-versed in assembling island-hopping packages. The agency covers 47 islands in the Caribbean as well as Bermuda and the Bahamas. The no-nonsense owner knows her stuff and has been traveling to the Caribbean since 1967.

If you can get up and go at the drop of a straw hat, try **Changes in L'Attitudes** (1161 49th St. N., Suite 11, Clearwater, FL 33762; ☎ **800-330-8272** or 727-573-3536; fax 727-573-8648; Internet www.changes.com). This agency, which has specialized in the Caribbean since 1985, has a terrific Web site that connects you to tons of resorts. It also lists specials and promotions with a heavy concentration on Aruba and Jamaica. Honeymooners and sailors will find some good deals here.

If you think that you want to stay at an all-inclusive resort, **All-Inclusive Vacations** (21999 Van Buren St., Suite 6, Grand Terrace, CA 92313; ☎ **800-944-3862** or 909-824-8825; e-mail jamaica@all-inclusive.com; Internet www.no-problem.com) has specialized in discounted all-inclusive packages for Sandals and SuperClubs since 1991. Most of its deals are on St. Lucia and Jamaica. Its excellent Web site answers many common questions about all-inclusives.

For adventure (including boating, fishing, sailing, scuba diving, horseback riding, whale watching, cave exploring, windsurfing, golfing, or volcano hiking) and eco packages, talk to Wendy Swartzell at Atlanta-based **Passport to Adventure, Inc.** (☎ **770-454-7205**; fax 770-454-8486; e-mail Thetripchicks@aol.com). She and her partner Ann Lombardi have 18 years of experience under their dive belts and sometimes lead groups to the Caribbean.

If you know that you want to go to Puerto Rico, **Modern Travel** (#6 Clemenceau St. Corner of Joffre, Condado, PR 00907; ☎ **800-443-3422** or 787-721-3984; fax 787-723-5884) is an award-winning agency worth checking out.

Exploring Package Tours

Package tours are not the same thing as escorted tours, so if you're picturing something like "12 islands in 14 days" and being herded around in a group on a bus, don't worry. That's not the way anybody tours the Caribbean. (If you want that sort of trip, the closest thing would be a cruise ship that stopped at three or four ports.)

Defining our terms

Package tours are simply a way of buying your airfare and accommodations (and sometimes your car rental) at the same time at a discounted rate. For popular destinations like the Caribbean, packages are a smart way to go if you don't want to deal with a travel agent. They save you a ton of money, and they're an easy introduction to the islands.

In many cases, a package that includes airfare, hotel, and transportation to and from the airport will cost you less than you'd pay for the hotel alone if you booked it yourself. That's because packages are sold in bulk to tour operators, who resell them to the public.

Packages vary as much as the islands themselves. Some packages offer a better class of hotels than others. Some offer the same hotels for lower prices. Some offer flights on scheduled airlines, while others book charters. In some packages, your choices of accommodations and travel days may be limited. Some packages will allow you to add on just a few excursions or escorted day trips (at prices lower than you'd pay if you booked them yourself).

Finding the best deal

Each destination usually has one or two packagers that are better than the rest because they buy in even bigger bulk. The time you spend shopping around will be well rewarded.

A good place to start looking is the travel section of your local Sunday newspaper. Also check the ads in the back of national travel magazines like *Caribbean Travel & Life, Islands, Travel & Leisure, National Geographic Traveler,* and *Condé Nast Traveler.*

If you don't want to research packages on your own, **Liberty Travel** will do it for you (☎ **888-271-1586** or check local listings for a location near you; Internet www.libertytravel.com). Liberty is the sixth-largest travel agency in the United States and usually boasts a full-page ad in Sunday papers. You won't get much in the way of service, but Liberty offers a quick way to find out about several Caribbean tour packages.

Liberty books many of its Caribbean packages with American Airlines and TWA. The latter just started flying to several Caribbean islands.

Here are some packagers we like:

- ✔ **West Indies Management Company,** a Caribbean and Bermuda villa and hotel expert, represents 800 villas and 75 hotels in the region. Contact this company at ☎ **800-932-3222** or 401-849-8012; fax 401-847-6290; e-mail wimco@well.com; Internet www.wimcovillas.com.

- ✔ **Caribbean Inns, Ltd.** (☎ **800-633-7411** or 803-785-7411), which has been in business 13 years, puts together terrific honeymoon packages if you're interested in a small, intimate inn in the three- to five-star range. Contact them at P.O. Box 7411, Hilton Head Island, SC 29938; fax 803-686-7411; e-mail INNS4CARIB@aol.com; Internet www.caribbean-inns.com.

- ✔ **Island Destinations** (☎ **800-729-9799,** 888-333-1212 in the Southeast only, or 914-833-3300; fax 914-833-3318; Internet www.islanddestinations.com) is a tour operator for upscale travelers that represents some of the more exclusive properties on 15 Caribbean islands, including 19 hotels and three groups of villas. This agency sends representatives to each property annually, so that they can match clients to the best place.

- ✔ If you want to stay at a villa, try booking through **Unusual Villas** (409F North Hamilton St., Richmond, VA 23221; ☎ **800-846-7280** or 804-288-2823; fax 804-342-9016; e-mail johng@unusualvillarentals.com; Internet www.unusualvillarentals.com). This company has more than 100 villas for rent on Barbados and Jamaica, and about 50 on St. Thomas.

- ✔ For dive trips, try either **Maduro Dive Fanta-Seas** (4500 Biscayne Blvd., Suite 320, Miami, FL 33137; ☎ **800-327-6709;** fax 305-438-4220; e-mail maduro@netpoint.net; Internet www.maduro.com) or **Caribbean Dive Tours** (Johnson Ferry Road, Marietta, GA 30068; ☎ **800-404-3483** or 770-578-8028). The latter wholesales trips to dive shops across the country and also makes bookings for individual travelers.

- ✔ One of the leading Caribbean packagers for Canadian travelers is **Signature Vacations** (160 Bloor St. East, Suite 400, Toronto, Ontario, Canada M4W 1B9; ☎ **800-268-7074** or 416-967-1510; fax 416-967-1510; Internet www.signature.ca). Savvy customers from the northern United States can often save a significant amount by booking through this packager, because the U.S. dollar is stronger than the Canadian dollar. You just have to fly out of Toronto, Vancouver, or Montreal, and the savings can be significant enough to make an extra airline ticket (to head north before you go south) worth it.

Other good resources are the airlines themselves, which package their flights together with accommodations. Your options include

- ✔ **Air Jamaica Vacations** (☎ 800-LOVE-BIRD).

- ✔ **American Airlines Vacations** (☎ 800-321-2121; Internet www.aavacations.com).

- ✔ **Continental Airlines Vacations** (☎ 800-634-5555; Internet www.coolvacations.com).

- ✔ **Delta Dream Vacations** (☎ 800-755-4224, 800-872-7786, or 888-346-3619; Internet www.deltavacations.com).

- ✔ **TWA Getaway Vacations** (☎ 800-GETAWAY or 800-438-2929; Internet www.twa.com/getaway).

- ✔ **United Vacations** (☎ 800-328-6877; Internet www.unitedvacations.com).

- ✔ **US Airways Vacations** (☎ 800-455-0123).

Putting a Trip Together on Your Own

We know you're out there. The contrarian, the entrepreneur, the maverick who likes to be in control and do everything alone. After all, that's one of the main reasons you bought this book, so you could become an instant expert and make your own decisions. Well, read on. These next few sections give you all the essentials you need to blaze your own trail to the Caribbean.

Booking your flight

Getting to the Caribbean from the United States and Canada is relatively easy. With improved connections from the West Coast, many islands are seeing more visitors from that area who want to experience something other than Hawaii. With that said, you should do a few things to make sure that your flight goes smoothly.

Reserve early: Flights to the Caribbean tend to be extremely full. During the summer months islanders who live in the United States go home to visit, and during the winter months tourists are flocking to the warm weather, so seats go quickly year-round.

Stick together: When you book your tickets, make sure to request seats together for everyone in your party. If you travel with friends, or if your family members don't all have the same last name, ticketing agents definitely won't try to keep you together unless you request it. Arrive early at the airport to get boarding passes to secure your seats. We've been amazed at the number of couples (even honeymooners) and families who spend flights separated by several rows.

Get a head start: We've found that booking the earliest flight out prevents us from getting caught in the frequent air traffic jams — especially if we have to make connections in Miami or Puerto Rico, which are always congested.

The rest of this section is filled with additional tips for getting the best flight for your itinerary (at the best price).

Figuring out who flies where

For many years, American Airlines and American Eagle, which fly to more than 40 destinations in the Caribbean, dominated from their Miami and Puerto Rico hubs. However, two factors have combined to give travelers more options. Air Jamaica has made Montego Bay its hub. (Previously, almost everything was funneled through Puerto Rico.) And in 1998, American cut back on many of its nonstop flights out of the Northeast as well as on service from its San Juan hub to the Caribbean. Other carriers like Air Jamaica, Delta, TWA, United, and Continental Airlines quickly scrambled to fill the void. The bottom line is better connections and improved access.

We really like flying Air Jamaica, which has brand-new jets, friendly flight attendants, and free champagne and wine throughout the flight. The food is consistently a cut above most airline fare, too. Air Jamaica, which just celebrated its 30th year flying, was named "Best Caribbean Airline" at the most recent annual World Travel awards.

Our least favorite airline is Air ALM, which services Aruba, Bonaire, and Curaçao. Those who have flown with the Dutch airline joke that the name stands for "All Luggage Missing." Because Aruba, Bonaire, and Curaçao are all popular with divers, who frequently haul lots of expensive gear with them, ALM's baggage handling mishaps become an even bigger issue. ALM also has a bad reputation for making travelers miss their connections. We'd recommend staying away from this airline, unless you like hanging out in airports.

Following is a list of the airlines that currently service the Caribbean and where each of them flies. Please note that air service is always subject to change.

- ✔ **Air ALM** (☎ **800-327-7197** or 305-592-7646) has service from Miami to Aruba, Bonaire, and Curaçao.

- ✔ **Air Aruba** (☎ **800-882-7822** or 305-551-2400) has service from Baltimore, Newark, Philadelphia, Tampa, and Miami to Aruba.

- ✔ **Air Canada** (☎ **800-776-3000;** Internet www.aircanada.ca) flies direct from Toronto to Barbados and to Montego Bay and Kingston in Jamaica.

- ✔ **Air Jamaica** (☎ **800-523-5585;** Internet www.airjamaica.com) has more than 330 flights a week with direct service from Atlanta, Baltimore, Chicago, Fort Lauderdale, Houston, Los Angeles (daily service with ten weekly flights), Miami, Newark, New York's JFK, Orlando, Philadelphia, Phoenix, and Washington, D.C., to Montego Bay and Kingston airports. You can make connections to Barbados, Bonaire, and Grand Cayman. This airline also flies from Jamaica to Cuba, Trinidad, and Tobago, as well as from New York's JFK to Barbados (nonstop). In addition, its code-share agreement with Delta Airlines and joint-fare arrangements and compatible schedules with United help extend access to more than 150 cities in the United States.

- ✔ **American Airlines** (☎ 800-433-7300; Internet www.aa.com) and **American Eagle** (☎ 800-981-4757) service almost every destination in the Caribbean from several U.S. cities. For nonstop flights, American Airlines often can't be beat for U.S. travelers. American Eagle has 180 daily flights to and from 21 Caribbean destinations.

- ✔ **British Airways** (☎ 800-247-9297, or 0845 77 333 77 in the U.K.; Internet www.british-airways.com) flies from London to Grand Cayman as well as Kingston and Montego Bay in Jamaica.

- ✔ **BWIA West Indies Airways** (☎ 800-538-2942 or 718-520-8100) has service from New York, Miami, and Toronto to Barbados.

- ✔ **Canadian Holidays** (☎ 416-620-8050) charters from Toronto to Barbados, Grand Cayman, San Juan, and Tortola (BVI).

- ✔ **Cayman Airways** (☎ 800-422-9626 or 305-266-6760) has service from Atlanta, Houston, Miami, and Tampa to Grand Cayman.

- ✔ **Continental Airlines** (☎ 800-525-0280; Internet www.continental.com) flies nonstop daily from New York and Newark to San Juan, Grand Cayman, and Jamaica, and from Houston to Aruba.

- ✔ **Delta Airlines** (☎ 800-221-1212; Internet www.delta-air.com) has daily nonstop flights from Atlanta to Aruba, San Juan, St. Croix, and St. Thomas; from New York (JFK) to Aruba and Grand Cayman; and from Cincinnati to San Juan. Via a code-share with Air Jamaica, Delta has five weekly flights from JFK to Barbados and two weekly flights from Phoenix to Montego Bay, Jamaica.

- ✔ **Northwest World Vacations** (☎ 800-727-1111 or 612-470-1111) has scheduled service from all Northwest hubs to Jamaica and Grand Cayman.

- ✔ **Trans World Airlines** (☎ 800-221-2000; Internet www.twa.com) has service from New York and St. Louis to San Juan.

- ✔ **United Airlines** (☎ 800-241-6522; Internet www.ual.com) flies direct daily from Chicago's O'Hare to San Juan and from Washington, D.C. and Chicago to St. Thomas on the weekends in the winter months.

- ✔ **US Airways** (☎ **800-428-4322;** Internet www.usairways.com) has service from Baltimore to Grand Cayman, San Juan, St. Croix, and St. Thomas; from Charlotte to Grand Cayman, Montego Bay, San Juan, and St. Thomas; and from Philadelphia to Grand Cayman, San Juan, and St. Thomas.

- ✔ **Virgin Atlantic Airways** (☎ **800-862-8621** or 01293 747 747 from the U.K.; Internet www.virgin.com) flies to Barbados from London.

Hopping island-to-island

Island-hopping in the Caribbean is easy via the numerous small carriers servicing the islands. You can often find alternative routes to get where you want to go even if an airline says a certain itinerary is booked.

Air Jamaica (☎ **800-523-5585** or 718-830-0622), **BWIA** (☎ **800-538-2942** or 718-520-8100), and **LIAT** (☎ **268-462-0700**) all offer bargain fares that make it extremely affordable to visit more than one island. For example, with Air Jamaica's "Island Hop" package you can visit two islands for the price of one. Air Jamaica's new Eastern Caribbean Express (a.k.a. EC Express) uses Barbados as a hub and provides daily service to St. Lucia as well as half a dozen other Eastern Caribbean islands.

Apparently in response to Air Jamaica's popular island-hopping packages, **American Airlines** and **American Eagle** (☎ **800-433-7300;** Internet www.aa.com) introduced "Caribbean Explorer" fares in early 2000 for island-hopping from the San Juan hub, offering lower prices for the more segments purchased.

Here are other airlines to call if you plan to hip-hop in the Caribbean:

- ✔ **Air St. Thomas** (☎ **800-522-3084** or 340-776-2722) has service from St. Thomas to San Juan and Fajardo, and from San Juan and St. Thomas to Virgin Gorda.

- ✔ **Air ALM** (☎ **800-327-7197** or 305-592-7646) has inter-island connections from Aruba, Bonaire, and Curaçao to San Juan and Kingston (Jamaica).

- ✔ **BWIA International** (☎ **800-538-2942** or 718-520-8100) has island-hopping flights between Barbados and St. Lucia.

- ✔ **United Airlines** (☎ **800-241-6522;** Internet www.ual.com) flies from San Juan to St. Thomas and St. Croix through a code-share with Gulfstream International.

Hunting for the best airfare

Good airfares to this part of the world can disappear in the time it takes the ice in your drink to melt in the Caribbean sun. If you find a fare that sounds good, book it immediately.

Generally speaking, you're most likely to find discounted fares to the Caribbean from May through December 15, which is the low season. As for using your frequent-flyer miles on Caribbean routes, good luck! We've never been able to use our miles for Caribbean forays. "Those seats are already taken," we're always told. Our advice: Call way in advance if you want to try to apply your miles on this route.

Consolidators, also known as *bucket shops,* are a good place to check for the lowest fares. Their prices are much better than the fares you could get yourself and are often even lower than what your travel agent can come up with. You can find their ads in the small boxes at the bottom of the page in your Sunday newspaper travel section.

Two of the more reliable consolidators are **1-800-FLY-4-LESS** and **1-800-FLY-CHEAP. Council Travel** (☎ **800-226-8624;** Internet www. counciltravel.com) caters especially to young travelers ages 12 to 25. Most of its bargain-basement prices are available only to youths, students, and teachers, but some of its discounted airfares are open to adults.

If you can travel on a Tuesday, Wednesday, or Thursday, you may find cheaper flights to your destination. When you inquire about airfares, ask if you can get a cheaper rate by flying on a different day.

The best time to book your ticket is just after midnight in the middle of the week. That's when the airlines download low-priced airfares to their computers. You also have a chance to purchase cheap seats that were booked but never ticketed. Obviously, you may have trouble finding a travel agent awake at that time to help you out. To access these midnight specials, call the toll-free reservation number for the airline or research and book your flight online. The next section walks you through the steps for making travel arrangements online.

Booking Your Trip Online

Although online travel agencies, which allow you to book your trip electronically, work well for trips within North America, travelers destined for the Caribbean are likely to save time and money by using a travel agent or consolidator.

But if you want to know as much as possible about your options, the Web is a boon. Bargain hunters and spur-of-the-moment travelers, in particular, can take advantage of airlines' last-minute specials.

The top online agencies, including Travelocity and Expedia, offer an array of research tools that are valuable even if you don't book online. You can check flight schedules, hotel availability, and car rental prices.

Longing to talk to a real person

While online agencies have come a long way over the past few years, they don't always yield the best price. And if you think that you have even the slightest chance of needing follow-up services, such as itinerary changes, a travel agent who is easily reachable is still your safest bet. Though some of the online agencies employ agents who are available by phone, these sites are geared primarily for self-service. We've run into snafus trying to contact a live body when we had a problem. Let's just say customer service is still a work in progress.

Not all these sites are programmed to alert you to the big money you can save if you fly a day earlier or a day later than you initially plan. On the other hand, if you're looking for a bargain fare, you might find something online that an agent wouldn't take the time to dig up.

If you want to book your trip over the Web, don't let the fear of sending your credit card information into cyberspace hold you back. To be sure that you're in secure mode when you book online, look for a little icon of a key (in Netscape) or a padlock (in Internet Explorer) at the bottom of your Web browser. If you are truly afraid of typing in your credit card number, find a flight online and then book it by calling a toll-free reservation number or contacting your travel agent. But remember that cheap fares to the Caribbean can evaporate quickly, so don't waffle.

Do not use electronic tickets when traveling to the Caribbean. Wise travelers still insist on the old paper version for travel out of the country, especially if you're changing airlines en route. Having that paper trail can become critical if you run into cancellations or delays; you may need to have a gate agent endorse your ticket or receipt so that you can hop the next flight on another airline.

Booking on the best sites

Here's a rundown of our favorite travel booking sites, including details on the special features and frustrations of each:

1travel.com (Internet www.onetravel.com): This site offers deals on international flights, cruises, hotels, and all-inclusive resorts, such as Club Med, Sandals, and SuperClubs. onetravel.com's "Saving Alert" compiles last-minute air deals so you don't have to scroll through multiple e-mail alerts.

Arthur Frommer's Budget Travel Online (Internet www.frommers.com): You'll find indispensable travel tips, reviews, monthly vacation giveaways, and links to online booking at this site.

Best Fares (Internet www.bestfares.com): Budget guru Tom Parsons lists some great bargains on airfares, hotels, rental cars, and cruises, but the site is poorly organized. "News Desk" is a long list of hundreds of bargains, but they're not broken down into cities or even countries, so it's not easy to find what you're looking for. If you have time to wade through this site, you might find a good deal. Some material is available only to paid subscribers, who receive a magazine listing good deals and access to a club that offers a 5% discount through its travel agencies.

Cheap Tickets (Internet `www.cheaptickets.com`): This site features discounted rates on domestic and international airline tickets and hotel rooms. Sometimes discounters such as Cheap Tickets have exclusive deals that aren't available through more mainstream channels. Registration at Cheap Tickets requires inputting a credit card number before getting started, which sends potential customers to the company's toll-free number in droves.

One of the more frustrating things about the Cheap Tickets site is that it offers fare quotes for a route and later shows that this fare is not valid for your dates of travel.

Expedia (Internet `www.expedia.com`): Expedia is the "Air Tickets" link on the MSN home page. If you have a Microsoft Internet Explorer browser, you can't miss it. You can book domestic and international flights, hotels, and rental cars on this site. It offers late-breaking travel news, destination features, commentary from travel experts, and deals on cruises and vacation packages. Free registration is required for booking.

Expedia makes it easy to handle flight, hotel, and car booking on one itinerary, so it's a good place for one-stop shopping — especially important for Caribbean travelers. Expedia's hotel search offers crisp, zoomable maps to pinpoint most properties; click on the camera icon to see images of the rooms and facilities. But like many online databases, Expedia focuses on the major chains, like Hilton and Hyatt, with a skimpy selection of the unique resorts that can be half the fun of a Caribbean sojourn.

After you register, you can start booking with the "Roundtrip Fare Finder" box on the home page, which expedites the process. After selecting a flight, you can hold it until midnight the following day or purchase online. If you think you might do better through a travel agent, you'll have time to shop for a lower price.

Expedia's computer reservation system does not include all airlines.

Go4less.com (Internet `www.go4less.com`): Specializing in last-minute cruise and package deals, Go4less has some eye-popping offers. You can avoid sifting through all this material by using the search box and entering vacation type, destination, month, and price range you are willing to pay.

Last Minute Travel (Internet `www.lastminutetravel.com`): Suppliers with excess inventory distribute unsold airline seats, hotel rooms, cruises, and vacation packages through this online agency.

Moment's Notice Discount Travel Club (☎ 718-234-6295; Internet `www.moments-notice.com`): As the name suggests, Moment's Notice specializes in last-minute vacation and cruise deals. You can browse for free, but if you want to purchase a trip you have to join at a cost of $25.

Priceline.com (Internet `www.priceline.com`): Even people who aren't familiar with too many Web sites have heard about Priceline.com. Launched in 1998 with a $10 million ad campaign featuring ex-Trekkie William Shatner, Priceline lets you "name your price" for domestic and international airline tickets and hotel rooms. In other words, you select a route and dates, guarantee with a credit card, and make a bid for what you're willing to pay.

Priceline can be good for travelers who need to take off on short notice (and who are thus unable to qualify for advance purchase discounts), but there are also several disadvantages to using this service. If you overbid and one of the airlines in Priceline's database has a fare that's lower than your bid, your credit card will be automatically charged, and Priceline will pocket the difference. You can't say what time you want to fly — you have to accept any flight leaving between 6 a.m. and 10 p.m. on the dates you choose — and you may have to make one stopover. No frequent flyer miles are awarded, and tickets are nonrefundable; they also can't be exchanged for another flight. So if your plans change, you're out of luck.

Smarter Living (Internet `www.smarterliving.com`): Best known for its "one-stop shopping" e-mail dispatch of weekend deals on 20 airlines, Smarter Living also keeps you posted about last-minute bargains like cut-rate Windjammer Cruises. Smarter Living also links to a variety of airfare sites, such as `www.lowestfare.com`, `www.Cheaptickets.com`, `www.expedia.com`, and `www.travelocity.com`.

Travelocity (Internet `www.travelocity.com`): This site, which also incorporates Preview Travel, offers domestic and international flight, hotel, and rental car booking, as well as deals on cruises and vacation packages. "Air Deals" spotlights latest bargain airfares. Free (one-time) registration is required for booking.

Some have worried that Travelocity, which is owned by American Airlines' parent company AMR, directs bookings to American. But we have always been directed to the cheapest listed flight. You also get bonus frequent flyer miles for choosing one of the featured airlines.

Note to AOL Users: You can book flights, hotels, rental cars, and cruises on AOL at keyword: Travel. The booking software is provided by Travelocity/Preview Travel and is similar to the Internet site. Use the AOL "Travelers Advantage" program to earn a 5% rebate on flights, hotel rooms, and car rentals.

WebFlyer (Internet `www.webflyer.com`): The ultimate online resource for frequent flyers has an excellent last-minute air deals listing. Click on "Deal Watch" for a roundup of weekend deals on flights, hotels, and rental cars from domestic and international suppliers.

Finding last-minute fares

Airlines really don't enjoy flying with lots of empty seats. Thanks to the Internet, airlines can offer last-minute bargains to entice travelers to fill those seats. Most of those openings are announced on Tuesday or

Wednesday and are valid for travel the following weekend, but some can be booked weeks or even months in advance. You can sign up for weekly e-mail alerts at the airlines' sites or check a site that compiles lists of these bargains, such as **Smarter Living** (Internet www. smarterliving.com), which will round up all the deals and send them in one convenient weekly e-mail.

Cruising the Islands

A great way to see more than one island is on a cruise. Request a Q&A booklet from **Cruise Lines International Association** (☎ 212-921-0066; Internet www.cruising.org). Some lines that sail in the Caribbean include the following:

- ✔ **American Canadian Caribbean Line** (☎ 800-556-7450; Internet www.accl-smallships.com)
- ✔ **Carnival** (☎ 800-438-6744)
- ✔ **Club Med Cruises** (☎ 800-CLUB MED; Internet www.clubmed.com)
- ✔ **Disney** (☎ 800-939-2784)
- ✔ **Windstar** (☎ 800-258-7245; Internet www.windstarcruises.com)
- ✔ **Seabourn Cruise Line** (☎ 800-929-9595; Internet www. seabourn.com)
- ✔ **Royal Caribbean** (☎ 800-327-6700)
- ✔ **Windjammer Barefoot Cruises** (☎ 800-327-2601; Internet www. windjammer.com).

Because so many new cruise ships have come online in the last several years, you can easily find cruises at a deep discount — especially if you can wait till the last minute to make your plans. Check out the regular prices on the cruise line Web pages and then compare with the following discounters:

- ✔ **Cruises Only** (☎ 800-683-SHIP) or **The Cruise Line, Inc.** (☎ 800-777-0707) are sister companies whose specials can be booked on the Internet at www.mytravelco.com.
- ✔ **Spur-of-the-Moment Cruises** (☎ 800-343-1991; Internet www. spurof.com)

Because we could fill a large barge with information on cruising — and we have somewhat less space in this book — we suggest you check out *Cruise Vacations For Dummies,* by Fran Golden (IDG Books Worldwide, Inc.), for more help in this area.

Chapter 6

Money Matters

● ●

In This Chapter

▶ Deciding on which form of money to bring

▶ Estimating the cost of your trip

▶ Keeping a lid on the hidden expenses

▶ Cutting costs — not fun

● ●

*W*e know that money can be a delicate subject, so we've tried to make this chapter as painless as possible. We think that you'll be pleasantly surprised to know how *un*complicated money issues are when vacationing in the Caribbean. Making purchases is really no more difficult than when vacationing in, say, Las Vegas.

Planning a budget is a bit more complex. In this chapter, we also work through the basic elements of your vacation, unveiling the hidden costs that could trip you up, and show you how to cut costs without trimming your fun.

ATMs, Credit Cards, Traveler's Checks, or Cash?

Because we like to keep the hassle-factor as low as possible, we rarely change any money into local currency. The only time we make the exchange is when we're planning to use public transportation; buses sometimes accept only exact change in the local currency. With that in mind, here are our tips for making the financial end of your vacation as worry-free as possible.

Turning plastic into cash

If you do decide to exchange money, ATMs tied to U.S. banks through the Cirrus and Plus networks are easily found throughout the islands, and they give you the best exchange rates. For more details on ATM availability, you can call a staff specialist at the **PLUS system** (☎ **800-336-8472**) who will give you a list of bank chains that honor PLUS ATM cards or Visa cards at their branch ATM machines. You can also find the information online at www.visa.com/atms. Prerecorded information regarding the **CIRRUS network** can be accessed at ☎ 800-4CIRRUS or online at www.mastercard.com/atm.

Be aware that if you use an ATM on an island where the official currency is not your own, you'll receive cash in the local currency.

In addition to using your ATM card, you can also go to a local bank branch in the Caribbean and request a cash advance on your credit card. Don't forget your personal identification number (PIN) if you plan on doing so.

Giving yourself some credit

MasterCard and Visa are the most widely accepted credit cards in the Caribbean, followed by American Express. We usually each carry a different credit card in our wallets. If you travel solo, carry two just in case you hit a snag with one. We like paying with credit cards because then we have a paper trail to look at for budgeting purposes.

You can also use a credit card to get local currency from an ATM machine. The exchange rate for a cash advance on a credit card is better than you receive when exchanging currency in the banks. On the downside, interest rates for cash advances are often significantly higher than rates for credit card purchases. Also, you start paying interest on the advance the moment you receive the cash. On an airline-affiliated credit card, a cash advance does not earn frequent-flyer miles.

We've never had anything stolen on any of the islands. But if the unthinkable happens, almost every credit card company has a toll-free number you can call to get help. The credit card companies may be able to wire you a cash advance off your credit card immediately, and in many places, they can deliver an emergency credit card in a day or two. If your **Visa** card is lost or stolen, call ☎ 800-1518 (no, the number's not missing any digits) in Aruba, and ☎ 800-847-2911 in Barbados, the BVIs, Cayman Islands, Jamaica, Puerto Rico, and the USVIs. If your MasterCard is lost or stolen, call ☎ 800-1561 in Aruba, and ☎ 800-307-7309 in Barbados, the BVIs, Cayman Islands, Jamaica, Puerto Rico, and the USVIs. **American Express** cardholders and traveler's check holders should call ☎ 800-221-7282 for all money emergencies.

Your hotel's guest services can help you quickly take the appropriate steps as well. Cancel your credit cards immediately, after you've explained the problem to your hotel. Although you're unlikely to recover your lost purse or wallet, file a police report if you plan to make any claim on your home insurance policy or trip insurance policy for your losses. The companies often require a police report before they will honor any claims.

Steering clear of traveler's checks

 We don't take traveler's checks to the Caribbean, because we feel they're more trouble than they're worth on the islands. Traveler's checks are such an anachronism these days that we've even seen people on the islands have difficulties getting them cashed.

 If you do opt to carry traveler's checks, be sure to keep a record of their serial numbers (separately from the checks, of course) so you can be ensured a refund in case of theft. Also hang on to the name and toll-free number of the issuer — just in case your checks travel, as in away from your safekeeping.

Rolling in the green

 Good news: If you bring U.S. dollars on your trip, you don't need to exchange them. They are accepted throughout the Caribbean. In fact, U.S. dollars are the official currency in the Virgin Islands — even the British ones — and Puerto Rico. We describe the local currencies and the exchange rate at press time in the "Settling into" chapter for each island.

We like to bring at least $100 in small denominations to have handy for tips and another $200 cash for shopping in craft markets and paying the airport departure tax at the end of the trip. (Only cash is accepted for this tax.) Locals on poorer islands such as Jamaica prefer U.S. dollars, and you get a slight edge in craft markets if you pay in U.S. dollars. Tips in U.S. currency are often better received, too.

European and Canadian currencies are not accepted at Caribbean establishments, but you can readily exchange them into the local money at banks, currency exchange offices, or at your hotel. The rate of exchange fluctuates daily according to international monetary markets. For the most recent exchange rates on a variety of currencies, check out the Web site at www.xe.net/ucc/.

 When cashing or exchanging traveler's checks or exchanging currency, the bigger the bank the better. Beware of commercial moneychangers or facilities in airports; you can pay 10% or more in fees for each transaction.

Calculating the Cost of Your Trip

We know that thinking about how much all of this Caribbean fun is going to cost is probably the last thing you want to do. We don't want to throw a wet beach blanket on your exotic dreams, but we actually think you'll be relieved once you work through the numbers.

Budgeting for your Caribbean vacation isn't difficult, but keeping a close eye on costs is another matter. Using the worksheets at the end of the book can help you come up with an idea of your trip's approximate cost. A good way to get a handle on all costs is to start the tally from the moment you leave home. Walk yourself mentally through the trip. Begin with transportation to your nearest airport and then add the flight cost, the price of getting from the airport to your hotel, the hotel rate per day, meals (exclude these if they're included in the hotel rate), and activities, shopping, and nightlife. After you've done all that, add on another 15% to 20% for good measure.

Adding up lodging expenses

In the Caribbean, accommodation expenses are going to take the largest bite from your budget. Keep in mind that when you look at the price of an all-inclusive resort versus the price of a hotel, the all-inclusive rate appears inflated. Make sure to compare mangos to mangos, and take into account that you'll be shelling out extra for meals, drinks (many all-inclusives include premium alcohol in their rates), and activities if you're at a hotel or resort where the price covers only your room. (For more on the different types of accommodations, see Chapter 3.)

In each of the island accommodation chapters later in the book, you'll see dollar signs that indicate the price categories for lodging options. See the introduction for an explanation of those rate ranges.

Picking a rate range

Many Caribbean properties have up to a half dozen different rates during the year. Rates frequently plunge as much as 60% in the summer (low season), though the norm is more in the 20% to 40% range. The luxury resorts typically offer the biggest discounts. In this book, we let you know if a property is known for having special package deals worth asking about. (In particular, see the section on package deals in Chapter 5.)

You won't find many entries in the "dirt cheap" category in this book, because most of the places that are *that* cheap in the Caribbean we wouldn't feel comfortable sending anyone to. (Exceptions that spring to mind are Jake's on Jamaica and Hilty House on St Croix.) Low-end properties exist, but you're likely to be sharing a bathroom with strangers, and the cleanliness and service issue will be a big question mark. And, you're almost guaranteed *not* to get air-conditioning.

Many accommodations fall in the middle (still reasonable) price range, and if we mention a particular feature in the review, take that as an indication that the property had something noteworthy in that area. For example, if we mention the balconies, terraces, or nice sea views, those features are somehow a little or a lot better than similar properties on the island. (Many hotels have sea views, but those views differ significantly from place to place.)

In the high-end categories, you can expect all the extras you'd get at a four- or five-star hotel anywhere in the world. We've had gargantuan Jacuzzis in our room, fruit trays and champagne on arrival, private butler service where our suitcases were unpacked for us, and all kinds of other extravagances. The expensive hotels often throw in the full use of all workout and watersport facilities (even including lessons sometimes). You'll often find CD players and dataport phones in the room. Several hotels and resorts have added extensive business facilities so that their guests can stay connected easily.

People often wonder whether they should shell out a lot of extra money for a sea view or a big room. That decision depends on the property and your own agenda. If you will almost never be in the room anyway, why add that cost? But at some facilities, a sea view is vital to the experience. In our individual property reviews, we mention the places where the views and suites are really worth the additional expense.

Beating the rack rate

The *rack rate* is the official published rate that a hotel charges for a room. It's the rate you'd get if you walked in off the street and asked for a room for the night.

In all but the smallest accommodations, the rate you pay for a room depends on many factors, not the least of which is how you make your reservation. A travel agent may be able to negotiate a better price with certain hotels than you could get on your own. (See Chapter 5 for details.) That's because the hotel gives the agent a discount in exchange for steering business toward that hotel.

Of course, hotels are happy to charge you the rack rate, but with minimal effort and planning you can easily do better. Reserving a room through the hotel's 800 number may sometimes result in a lower rate than if you called the hotel directly. However, we've found that when it comes to the Caribbean, the people manning the central reservations number sometimes don't know about the latest deals on the island. In fact, the reservations agent is usually sitting at a desk in Florida or New Jersey and has never set foot on the island.

We strongly recommend that you make initial comparisons using the toll-free hotel reservation numbers; narrowing your choices down to three; and then e-mailing, calling, or faxing each resort directly to check the rates again. (Faxes or e-mails work best with islands like Puerto Rico and Jamaica, where the unfamiliarly accented English may be difficult to follow on the phone.) Make sure to ask about last-minute specials, and double-check to be certain that you're not missing some fantastic package that the U.S.-based reservation service hasn't been told about yet. That happens all the time. (The "Sweet Dreams: Choosing Your Hotel" worksheet at the back of the book is a handy form for keeping track of prices.)

Outsmarting the seasons

Room rates also change with the season and as occupancy rates rise
and fall. (See Chapter 2 for a full discussion of how time of year effects
hotel rates.) If a hotel is almost full, it is not likely to extend discount
rates. If it's empty, it may be willing to negotiate. With many Caribbean
hotels, you probably need to call nine months or more in advance to
get a room during the popular winter months. In summer, you can
almost always snag a deal.

Although you might feel a little like an ambulance chaser, if you're
willing to put up with some hassle, you can try to book a trip to an
island soon after a hurricane has hit. Resorts and airlines are left
scrambling for customers. Hotels are often back on track quickly, but
because of the media-induced panic, guests don't come back for weeks
or even months. The palm trees will be tattered and you may have to
put up with the sound of hammers, but the sun still shines.

If you travel with a group, consider staying in a villa. With three couples,
you can easily rent a villa for under $1,000 per person for a week.
Unusual Villas (409F North Hamilton St., Richmond, VA 23221; ☎ **800-846-7280** or 804-288-2823; fax 804-342-9016; e-mail johng@
unusualvillarentals.com; Internet www.unusualvillarentals.
com) represents a large number of properties in the Caribbean.

Tallying transportation costs

Most of the time, aside from your airfare to the Caribbean (see Chapter
5 for tips on how to decrease this particular expense), your transportation costs should be relatively low during your Caribbean stay. This is
especially true if you passed on the rental car or received a couple of
free days as part of your package deal.

Many package tours include transfers from the airport to your resort
or hotel. Several fine restaurants arrange free transportation, too; be
sure to inquire when you make a reservation. In either case, you still
need to tip the driver. See Chapter 5 for more details on booking a
package trip.

Taxi fares add up quickly, even on a less expensive island like Puerto
Rico, because attractions are often spread out. If you want to cover a
lot of ground for the best price, you're usually better off lumping most
of your touring into a single day and hiring a driver for the entire day at
a rate ranging from $60 to $100 (not including tip).

Don't plan on taking public transportation, except on Aruba and
Barbados where the bus service between the beach resort area and the
main town is quick, reliable, easy, and cheap. As much as possible, take
advantage of the free transportation offered by your hotel. If you pay
attention to schedules, you can often find a free shuttle to the nearest
place for shopping or a special beach.

Figuring dining dollars

In each of the dining chapters, we include reviews of our favorite restaurants, ranging from the pick of the high-end resort choices to local finds with rock-bottom prices. Each has dollar-sign symbols to indicate its price category; see the Introduction for an explanation of those categories.

Where, when, and what you eat in the Caribbean makes a big difference in your final vacation tab. To save money, we generally suggest signing up for some sort of dining plan at your resort. Choose whatever plan makes the most sense for you and your tastes. For example, if breakfast is the most important meal of the day to you, don't sign on for a plan that only serves a continental spread.

Investing in a dine-around plan

If you visit Aruba, Puerto Rico, St. Thomas, Jamaica, or Barbados, you probably want to try some of the good local restaurants that each island is known for. But you also want to keep costs in check, so ask if your hotel offers a dine-around plan. That way you won't get stuck in a culinary rut or shell out tons of money for food. Sandals has created its own internal dine-around plan on Jamaica. Its guests can choose from 23 restaurants at its different hotels and resorts.

Dine-around plans are not all identical, but the way they usually work is that you pay a flat fee for a certain number of gourmet meals (say three to five for the week). You then get to use your dine-around credits with the hotels/restaurants that are part of the program.

Dining at your resort

Most hotels offer a European Plan (EP), which means that no meals are included. If you see a Continental Plan (CP) listed, that means you get only a continental breakfast — juice, coffee, and some kind of bread. A Breakfast Plan (BP) signifies a full American-style breakfast. Another popular option, which leaves couples to figure out only the evening meal on their own, is the Modified American Plan (MAP), which provides two full meals daily. With the Full American Plan's (FAP's) three daily meals, that's exactly what you'll be — full. Finally, *all-inclusive* means that you get three all-you-can-eat meals a day and (often) all the alcohol you can guzzle — sometimes including premium liquors and great wines.

Dining options have greatly improved at all-inclusive resorts in the last few years because travelers have become so much more sophisticated. Now most all-inclusive dining packages feature local dishes at least one night a week, and often you can find several local specialties amidst more familiar fare.

If you have special dietary restrictions and are staying at an all-inclusive or at a resort where you've signed on for an extensive meal plan, ask the reservation agent for the executive chef's name and send a fax with your special requests about a month before you arrive. Most chefs consider pleasing their guests a point of pride, and they bend over backwards to accommodate you. However, because it can take time to order special items on the islands, you need to give chefs advance notice.

 If you go for the popular à la carte breakfast buffet, expect to pay a staggering $20 or more per person, including coffee and juice. That's *before* tipping. And unless your cash flow is extremely good, don't even think about ordering room service. For one thing, the wait is often interminable, but you also have to add a tip on top of an already pricey way to dine.

Entertaining meals outside your resort

Outside the resorts, your dining choices generally fall into two categories: expensive and cheap. Dinner entrées at nicer restaurants routinely start at around $15, and a three-course meal for two with cocktails can easily top $100 before the tip. Why so much? Many products must be brought from outside the island, and the high costs of importing are passed along to you. On some islands, even the seafood is frozen and shipped in; we've had Maine lobster more than once. If that fact bothers you, be sure to ask your server about the origin and freshness of the fish before you order.

Keep in mind also that the European connection is strong on these islands, and many of them attract some of the world's finest chefs, who consider spending time in the tropics a career perk. Although we may pay the same amount we'd pay at the best restaurants in Atlanta (and on pricey islands like Barbados and Aruba, our dinner tab may be closer to New York prices), we're legitimately getting a gourmet meal. Plus, we get the kind of killer view that is in short supply at home.

 Happily, on the other end of the payment scale, eating cheaply in the Caribbean doesn't mean risking your health the way it sometimes does in Mexico. You rarely have to be concerned about the safety of the food and water in the Caribbean. If you're willing to eat where the locals do, you can find some terrific meals for around $10.

 In terms of cheap joints, you can follow our recommendations or, if you're feeling adventurous, ask a local where to go. Don't expect much in the way of surroundings; you may sit on a plastic chair at a wobbly plastic table enlivened with plastic flowers. But you'll get to bask in the friendly Caribbean atmosphere, *limin'* (island slang for "hanging out") with the locals, and enjoying treats like jerk chicken with *bammy* (a fried Jamaican bread) or a bowl of *sopa de pollo con arroz* (Puerto Rico's answer to grandmother's chicken soup). For more authentic recommendations, see Chapter 37.

Going for do-it-yourself meals

If you plan to stay in a villa, condo, or guesthouse, you can cut costs by cooking your own meals. Some islands, like St. Thomas, now have low-price superstores where you can pick up supplies relatively cheap.

Before you lug things like salt and pepper with you, ask management to send you a list of what's already stocked in the kitchen. Remember that spices are cheaper on some islands, such as lush Jamaica.

Toasting top prices for drinks

Unless you're at an all-inclusive where drinks are part of your up-front tab or you're content to drink water, another big expense will be drinks. Paying $2 for a soda isn't uncommon, and you won't get refills without paying again. On many islands, import duties raise the prices of wines and imported beers sky-high. We've found that wines are often barely drinkable because they are improperly stored en route (sitting in the broiling tropical sun on a dock somewhere) or, once they arrive, the bottles are not kept cool enough. Save money and your taste buds by drinking local. The Caribbean is noted for its rums and beers.

If your kids don't react well to too much sugar, beware of ordering juice on the islands. Often "juices" are actually fruit drinks, made up largely of corn-syrup sweeteners rather than pure juice.

Tapping more cost-cutting tips

Here are a few more ways to trim your dining costs:

- ✔ **Fill up at the breakfast buffet** at your hotel. If you eat late and eat well, you'll eliminate the need for a big lunch, especially if all you're going to be doing is lazing on the beach.

- ✔ **Share.** Portions are often pretty hefty, and if you eat everything on your plate, you might get that way, too. At least try splitting appetizers and desserts.

- ✔ **Take advantage of happy hours** and the manager's welcoming cocktail party. There are usually free nibbles, too.

- ✔ **Forget about the lobster** (unless you're on Anegada, of course); it's the most pricey item on the menu. The freshly caught local fish is less expensive and often just as good or better.

- ✔ **Avoid your mini-bar,** or use it to stash the less expensive drinks and snacks that you buy outside your resort.

Spending wisely on activities and attractions

Of course, the two main activities in the Caribbean — swimming in that beautiful, impossibly blue sea and basking on those sandy beaches — are absolutely free. However, if you're interested in activities like scuba diving, snorkeling, windsurfing, and waterskiing, they usually cost extra.

In recent years, more and more of the all-inclusives have started offering terrific freebies like scuba and windsurfing lessons, free water-skiing, and free snorkeling gear for the week. Some even toss in a free round of golf.

Watersports

Although the charges vary slightly from island to island, we've generally found a two-tank boat dive to run around $45. Snorkeling trips vary widely in cost, but if you're going out on a boat, you'll pay at least $30; just renting snorkeling equipment at a beach usually costs about $15. Windsurfing lessons and gear will cost close to $50 an hour, and water-skiing also goes for about $50 an hour. You also need to factor in the cost of a tip if you're receiving instruction.

Tons of variables are involved in calculating the costs of deep-sea fishing, but assuming that you don't mind mingling your lines with people you haven't met before, you'll probably pay at least $75 per person, including bait, fishing license, and ice to preserve your catch.

Golf

For golf in the Caribbean, green fees run from about $70 at Jamaica's Sandals Golf and Country Club to about $130 at Aruba's Tierra Del Sol and Jamaica's Half Moon Bay. You also pay at least $12 for club rentals and a minimum of $12 for a manual golf cart. In Jamaica, you also have the quirky rule that you must have a caddy, who will of course need to be tipped. (The show makes the cost worthwhile: Your caddy carries your golf bag by balancing it sideways on his or her head.)

Sightseeing tours

You'll probably want to spend at least one day touring the island, even if you're on one like Grand Cayman where you won't find many interesting attractions. Sightseeing tours vary according to destination, duration, and extras like meals and snacks. But here's a rough estimate of cost: Expect to spend a minimum of $50 (including tip) for a half-day island tour. For a full-day, guided tour including lunch and a stop for snacks on islands like Jamaica, Barbados, and Puerto Rico (where there's lots to see), you're looking at about $80 minimum, including tip.

Stocking up on souvenirs

Shopping is the wild card. You can easily get away with buying a few inexpensive souvenirs at the craft markets, where you may pick up a hand-woven straw hat for about $15 or a small basket of spices for $7. But at the other end of the spectrum, artwork by notable Caribbean artists can go for thousands of dollars. Don't miss Old San Juan's fantastic art galleries, St. John's funky boutique shops, or Jamaica's hip art galleries. (See Chapter 36 for our favorite local souvenirs.)

If you're eager to load up on luxury items from china to perfume, duty-free shops dot the islands. However, if you intend to shop for major items like jewelry, we urge you to do some comparative pricing at home first. You may have a very hard time determining which items are truly bargains in the duty-free shops; don't be fooled by signs trumpeting terrific deals.

Tasting the nightlife

Even the smallest resorts usually roll out a reggae or steel pan band sometime during the week. Nightlife in the Caribbean runs the gamut from resort-sponsored theme nights (available on every island) to glitzy casinos (in Puerto Rico and Aruba). You can find high-class night-clubs where merengue and salsa rule (Puerto Rico and Aruba) and reggae rocks (St. Thomas), and you can enjoy Jamaica's street parties where locals mingle with visitors to the thumping beat of rock steady, reggae, and *soca* (reggae dance music).

The action on Barbados is in the rum shops, and the British Virgin Islands' funky beach bars are renowned for their rollicking impromptu parties. The best part is that the beach and street parties are free, and you'll usually only have a small cover charge ($5 to $10 a person) to gain entry into clubs. As for casinos, well, that all depends on whether you're feeling lucky.

Keeping a Lid on Hidden Expenses

A lot of visitors forget that a government tax, which ranges from 6% on Aruba to Jamaica's whopping 23%, applies to their final hotel bill. When you ask for lodging rates, clarify whether the tax is included in the quote; obviously that can make a big difference. We strongly urge you to ask the hotel for a written outline of everything that's included in the rate — faxed, if possible. We've run into people who were extremely annoyed because they thought they had a set rate, and the government tax came as a nasty surprise. The rates quoted in this book *do not* include government tax and service charges.

Tipping tips

For the most part, tipping is much the same in the Caribbean as in the rest of the world. Plan to tip 15% of the bill in a restaurant, $1 per bag to a bellhop, and $2 per night for a maid in a resort. (If your hotel is not very expensive, leave $1 a night on your pillow; leave it each day because the maids often rotate out.) Taxi drivers and tour guides get a 10% to 15% tip.

Tips are often automatically included in a bill (in European fashion). If you're in doubt, ask before you accidentally overtip. Bring along lots of small denomination bills; otherwise, you're likely to end up giving a much larger tip than the situation calls for — or, worse, stiffing someone.

Telephone traps

Making long distance calls from the Caribbean is extremely expensive. Don't ever dial direct from your hotel room, unless forking over $50 or so for a five-minute call is no big whoop to you. Also, be aware that many Caribbean hotels charge even for attempted calls, and toll-free numbers are not free in the Caribbean. (We learned that the hard way, once winding up with a $30 phone bill for making a few calls to check on our brokerage account.)

In your room, you'll usually find long-distance instructions that give you some options, but you're best off using your calling card. However, we've had problems on some islands connecting to the appropriate operator, so call the front desk at the first sign of trouble and ask the hotel operator to guide you through their particular system. Unless a call is urgent, we've found faxing much less expensive. That way, neither party has to worry about the other person's availability to answer.

Trimming Your Costs

The Caribbean delivers plenty of thrills if you get a rush out of being a savvy consumer. Following are our best money-saving tips.

- ✔ **Go off-season.** If you can travel at nonpeak times (generally May through November), you'll find hotel prices that are as much as 60% off from high season rates. But keep in mind that some resorts lower their rates more than others. Generally speaking, bargain hunters do best in Aruba, Jamaica, Puerto Rico, and USVI.

- ✔ **Travel on off days of the week.** If you can travel on a Tuesday, Wednesday, or Thursday, you may find cheaper flights to your destination. When you inquire about airfares, ask if flying on a different day will make your fare cheaper.

- ✔ **Try a package tour.** For many destinations, you can book airfare, hotel, ground transportation, and even a sightseeing tour just by making one call to a travel agent or packager, for a lot less than if you tried to cobble the trip together yourself. (See "Exploring Package Tours" in Chapter 5 for specifics.)

- ✔ **Reserve accommodations with a kitchen and do your own cooking.** If you can stomach having to wash dishes on your vacation, you save a lot of money by not eating in restaurants three times a day. Even if you only make breakfast and an occasional bag lunch, you still save in the long run. One couple we know blew $90 on a basic dinner early in their stay on Grand Cayman. Subsequently, they bought about $100 worth of groceries and ate well for the rest of the week at their condo.

- ✔ **Always ask for discount rates.** Membership in AAA, frequent-flyer plans, trade unions, AARP, or other groups may qualify you for discounted rates on plane tickets and hotel rooms.

✔ **Find out if your kids can stay in your room with you.** This is usually the norm rather than the exception in the Caribbean. A room with two double beds doesn't cost any more than one with a queen-size bed. And many hotels won't charge you extra if the additional person is pint-sized and related to you. Even if you have to pay $10 or $15 for a rollaway bed, you save big bucks by not taking two rooms. Many resorts are now offering programs that let kids stay and eat free.

✔ **Try expensive restaurants at lunch instead of dinner.** Lunch tabs are usually a fraction of what dinner costs at most top restaurants, and the menu often includes many of the same specialties.

✔ **Cut down on the souvenirs.** Does your cousin really need another T-shirt? Oddly, we've found tacky items to be fairly pricey, especially in comparison to genuine island keepsakes.

✔ **Substitute less expensive activities for pricier ones.** Waverunners can be fun, but they cost a lot to rent, and the ride doesn't last that long. You may be better off spending a few hours snorkeling instead.

✔ **At your hotel you should never make a direct-dial long-distance call from your room; send out your laundry; or exchange money.** (Many hotels consider money-changing a profit center.)

Chapter 7

Taking Care of Details

● ●

In This Chapter

▶ Getting your ID papers in order

▶ Going through customs

▶ Buying travel and medical insurance

▶ Deciding whether to rent a car

▶ Packing wisely (and lightly)

● ●

Although we can't cover everything from $\underline{A}$*ckee* (a Jamaican fruit) to $\underline{Z}$*ouk* (an African-influenced Caribbean music) in this book, we can address a few of the more important must-knows. In this chapter, we help you make sure that your passport is in order and that you have the insurance coverage you need before traveling to the Caribbean. We also help you decide whether to rent a car on the islands, and we share some tips for packing what you need without bringing along pounds of unnecessary luggage.

Embarking on the Great Paper Chase: Passports, Please

Do you need a passport to go to the Caribbean? Sounds like a simple enough question, but the answer is more complicated than you might think. If you are a U.S. or Canadian citizen, you don't need a passport to visit the U.S. Virgin Islands or Puerto Rico, because they are U.S. territories. Aruba, Barbados, the British Virgin Islands, the Cayman Islands, and Jamaica all *say* that they accept alternative identification for U.S. and Canadian citizens (for example, a hospital-issued birth certificate with a raised seal, plus a valid driver's license with a photo ID), but the rules differ slightly from island to island and are subject to change.

If you are from the United States or Canada and you don't have an up-to-date passport, you must have the following papers with you, unless you're headed to Puerto Rico or the United States Virgin Islands:

✔ Either an official certified copy of your birth certificate (if it doesn't have a raised seal, it doesn't count), or an expired passport (which can't be more than 1 to 4 years old, depending on the island).

> ✓ An official photo identification, such as a valid driver's license.
>
> ✓ A return round-trip plane ticket.

Citizens from the U.K. must have passports and return-trip tickets to visit Aruba, Barbados, the British Virgin Islands, Jamaica, Puerto Rico, St. Lucia, and the U.S. Virgin Islands. To visit the Cayman Islands, British citizens need a passport or a birth certificate and current photo ID.

U.S., U.K., and Canadian visitors don't need any special visas to enter the islands that we describe in this book. Citizens of other countries should call the tourist board of the country they want to visit to find out what documents they need to have in hand when they travel to the Caribbean.

Identifying requirements for kids

Children from the U.S. who are under age 18 need to present a passport or an official birth certificate and an official photo identification. We recommend bringing a passport photo of babies and preschool children or a current school photograph of older children and teens. If a child is traveling with only one parent or with grandparents, we also suggest bringing a notarized permission letter (with the child's photo attached) from the other parent or parents as a precaution. Be sure to authorize the person who has charge of the children to seek medical attention if the need arises. We've heard of one grandmother being turned away at the airport because she didn't have a notarized permission letter authorizing her to take her two grandsons out of the country. That situation may be rare in the Caribbean, but we're erring on the side of caution here.

Minor children from other counties, including Canada, are allowed to travel on their parent's passport. That's the most efficient way to handle the issue. However, if you're planning to bring children to the Caribbean, we suggest that you call the tourist board of the island you plan to visit and confirm any special documentation you will need for anyone under age 18.

Planning ahead for the BVIs

If you're a U.S. citizen visiting the U.S. Virgin Islands, bring your passport if you want to make the popular jaunt over to the neighboring British Virgin Islands. That thought holds true even if you're arriving by boat. Many visitors have been turned away disappointed because they forgot the required identification. You can't set foot on the BVIs — not even from a privately chartered yacht — without that all-important passport.

Please note that entry requirements are subject to change, and U.S. Customs has cracked down lately regarding what's acceptable identification when you're reentering the states. To simplify your life, we strongly urge both you and your children to get passports no matter where you're from and where you're going. If you're like us, you don't like to take any chances.

Getting a passport

Obtaining a passport in the United States, Canada, the United Kingdom, Ireland, Australia, or New Zealand carries its own respective requirements, as covered in the next sections:

U.S. citizens

If you apply for a first-time passport, you need to do so in person at one of the following locations:

- ✔ A passport office (there are 13 in the United States).
- ✔ A federal, state, or probate court.
- ✔ A major post office. (*Note:* Not all post offices accept passport applications; later in this section, we provide a number to call to find the ones that do.)

When you apply, you need to present a certified birth certificate as proof of citizenship, and you're wise to bring along your driver's license, state or military ID, and Social Security card as well. If you are a newlywed with a name change, bring a copy of your marriage certificate. You also need two identical passport-sized photos (2-x-2 inch), which can be taken at any corner photo shop. (You cannot use strip photos taken from a photo vending machine.)

For people over age 15, a passport is valid for ten years and costs $60 ($45 plus a $15 handling fee). For those age 15 and under, the passport is valid for five years and costs $40. If you're over 15 and have a valid passport that was issued within the past 12 years, you can renew it by mail and bypass the $15 handling fee. Allow plenty of time to renew your passport; processing normally takes three weeks but can take longer during busy periods (especially spring).

For general information about passports, call the **National Passport Agency** (☎ 202-647-0518). For more information on how to get a passport or to find your regional passport office, call the **National Passport Information Center** (☎ 900-225-5674). On the U.S. State Department's Web page (`www.travel.state.gov`), click on Passport Services; you can get information there and download an application. Applications are also available at many post offices and travel agencies.

We advise allowing at least eight weeks for processing when you apply for a new passport; if you're even remotely cutting it close to the full eight weeks, we recommend paying an extra $35 plus the express mail service fee to have your application expedited, which means that you can expect your passport to arrive within seven to ten working days.

If you suddenly realize that you don't have the proper documentation, and you leave on your trip in two days, all is not lost. **Passport Express** (☎ **800-362-8196** or 401-272-4612; e-mail info@passportexpress.com; Internet www.passportexpress.com) expedites U.S. passports in as little as 24 hours. You can also download U.S. passport applications and instructions from its site.

To use Passport Express, your departure date must be within three weeks. If your departure date is more than a week away, the fee is $100 + $95 in government fees; less than a week away from your departure, the fee jumps to $150 + $95 for government fees. The company's representatives walk your application through the guaranteed process and then send your passport back to you (via Federal Express) within 24 hours. Based on some of our own panic-inducing experiences, we'd use this service in a heartbeat if we found ourselves cutting it close again.

Canadian citizens

You can pick up a passport application at one of 28 regional passport offices or most travel agencies. Applications are also available from the central **Passport Office** (Department of Foreign Affairs and International Trade, Ottawa, Ont. K1A 0G3; ☎ **800-567-6868;** Internet www.dfait-maeci.gc.ca/passport). A passport is valid for five years and costs $60. Children under 16 may be included on a parent's passport if they are traveling together but need their own passport to travel unaccompanied by the parent. Applications must be accompanied by two identical passport-sized photographs and proof of Canadian citizenship. Processing takes five to ten days if you apply in person or about three weeks if you send your application by mail.

Residents of the United Kingdom

To pick up an application for a ten-year passport, visit your nearest passport office, major post office, or travel agency. You can also contact the **London Passport Office** at ☎ **0171-271-3000** or search its Web site at www.ukpa.gov.uk/ukpass/.htm. Passports are £28 for adults and £14.80 for children under age 16.

Residents of Ireland

You can apply for a ten-year passport, costing IR£45, at the **Passport Office,** Setanta Centre, Molesworth St., Dublin 2 (☎ **01-671-1633;** Internet www.irlgov.ie/iveagh). You can also apply at 1A South Mall, Cork (☎ **021-272-525**) or over the counter at most main post offices. Those under age 18 and over age 65 must apply for a IR£10 three-year passport.

Residents of Australia

Apply at your local post office or passport office or search the government Web site at www.dfat.gov.au/passports/. Passports for adults are A$128 and for those under age 18 A$64.

Residents of New Zealand

You can pick up a passport application at any travel agency or Link Centre. For more info, contact the **Passport Office,** P.O. Box 805, Wellington (☎ **0800-225-050**). Passports for adults are NZ$80 and for those under age 16 NZ$40.

Dealing with Customs and Duties

If you tote expensive camera or computer gear or expensive jewelry, don't forget to register these items with customs before you leave the country. Otherwise, upon your return you may wind up being charged a duty for them.

Unless Puerto Rico is your vacation spot, you have to go through U.S. Customs. (If you go to Puerto Rico, you can skip U.S. Customs and can bring back as much stuff as you want, except plants, fruits, and vegetables that may not be allowed on the U.S. mainland.)

What's cool about Aruba and USVI is that you pass through U.S. Customs via the islands' airports. From all other points, you have to go through stateside, which means that if you bought more than $400 worth of merchandise on your trip, you must fill out a simple form stating how much you spent on the goods you're bringing back. Save receipts from duty-free stores, just in case. Each family member can bring a whopping $1,200 worth of goods back from the U.S. Virgin Islands — double the allowable amount from the other islands.

Dressing for acceptance

Don't dress sloppily when you go to the Cayman Islands. If the customs officers think you don't look like you've got the money to bankroll your visit, they'll question you and may even demand proof that you have the bucks to lavish on your island getaway. Kevin forgot this quirky little rule on our last visit — plus, he had long hair at the time. Sure enough, he got stopped for questioning. (He was allowed in.)

Remember that until you pass through U.S. Customs, you technically do not enjoy the same rights as you do on U.S. soil. Customs officials are allowed to pull anyone out of line and even order a strip search without having any reason beyond how you look. Kevin recently cut his hair and shaved his beard, because each time we came back into the country we were faced with more and more questions from U.S. Customs officials. Maybe having a copy of this book with us next trip will help prove that we aren't just party animals looking for a good time in the islands.

Leaving keepsakes (and trouble) behind

Although the Caribbean has a reputation for being a laid-back region as far as drug use goes, in reality, marijuana (*ganja*), cocaine, and other illicit substances are just as illegal here as they are in the states. The islands have drug informants who turn people in to the authorities all the time, and the drug dogs in the airport are highly skilled at finding illegal drugs and other contraband. We've seen many people pulled out of line.

Using drugs or trying to smuggle them back are serious infractions, and in other countries you have no rights as U.S. citizens. In fact, your hometown lawyer can't even represent you unless he or she is licensed to practice in the Caribbean. Penalties are severe, prison conditions downright nasty, and you won't get bail.

Jamaica's reputation as a freewheeling place causes some people to think that they can get away with drug use on this island. In fact, that's where we've seen the strictest controls: two checkpoints with drug dogs before you get on a plane, and then another when you land. Once, while traveling, we met a woman from Texas who was on her way to visit her 19-year-old daughter in a Jamaican jail. She told us that her daughter had been caught with a small amount of marijuana at the airport and was serving an 18-month sentence.

No matter what a local tells you, you'll also get in trouble with U.S. Customs (and have your purchases confiscated) if you try to bring back any live souvenirs. Coral, sea turtle shells, and even shells from the beach are contraband.

Securing Your Investment and Safety

Basically, when it comes to having a hassle-free sojourn, you need to keep three potential problem areas in mind: insuring against loss or trip interruption, medical emergencies, and lost luggage. Here we spell out what you need, and what you can skip.

Covering your losses with travel insurance

Travel insurance falls into three categories: trip cancellation/interruption, medical, and lost luggage. If you plan an expensive Caribbean vacation or a cruise that requires you to pay most costs up front, we strongly advise you to spring for the first one.

Good trip cancellation/interruption insurance covers you in a variety of scenarios. Policies typically reimburse you for the nonrefundable components of your trip if you have to cancel — for example, if a family member gets seriously ill or your hotel is damaged by a hurricane. Refunds can also be made on the unused portion of your trip and reimbursements made on your airfare home if your trip is cut short for covered reasons. Optional add-ons for these types of policies include medical and dental expenses, tour-operator bankruptcy, and bad weather. (Weather problems don't just include hurricanes — missed connections due to winter snowstorms in the U.S. may be covered as well.)

If you plan a trip to a small boutique hotel during hurricane season, trip cancellation/interruption insurance is vital. Most small places do *not* give refunds even if the hotel is severely damaged by a hurricane. Even if you're vacationing with SuperClubs or Sandals, both of which offer generous guarantees against having your trip ruined by a hurricane (see Chapter 2), we still recommend trip interruption/cancellation insurance because so many other things can cause problems.

Insurance policies offered through cruise lines and tour operators tend to be skimpy. Compare prices and policies with one of the companies listed here and get advice from your travel agent.

Trip cancellation insurance costs average between 6% to 8% of the total value of your vacation. If you travel with more than one person, split the cost so that your names all appear on the policy. This way everyone is eligible for medical evacuation insurance (explained in the following section), in case one of you has an accident or emergency.

Following are several reputable issuers of travel insurance:

- ✔ **Access America,** 6600 W. Broad St., Richmond, VA 23230 (☎ **800-284-8300;** fax 800-346-9265).

- ✔ **Mutual of Omaha**, Mutual of Omaha Plaza, Omaha, NE 68175 (☎ **800-228-9792**).

- ✔ **Travel Guard International,** 1145 Clark St., Stevens Point, WI 54481 (☎ **800-826-1300**).

- ✔ **Travel Insured International, Inc.,** P.O. Box 280568, East Hartford, CT 06128 (☎ **800-243-3174**).

Ensuring your safety with medical coverage

Check to see if your existing health insurance covers you in the Caribbean. If you belong to an HMO, make sure that you are fully covered when away from home. If you worry that your existing policy won't be sufficient, purchase travel medical insurance (see the list of reputable issuers of travel insurance in the previous section).

If you have any serious health problems, if you're adventurous, or if you're a diver, make sure you have coverage that will pay for medical evacuation in case of an emergency, in addition to your regular insurance. **Divers Alert Network** (6 W. Colony Place, Durham, NC 27705; ☎ **800-446-2671** or 919-684-2948; e-mail dan@diversalertnetwork.com; Internet www.diversalertnetwork.org) has an excellent policy for divers that costs $35 a year plus the annual $25 membership fee. For $10 more you can cover the whole family. For emergencies worldwide, members can call collect at ☎ **800-684-8111** or 919-684-4326.

Another excellent resource for medical evacuation coverage is **International SOS Assistance** (P.O. Box 11568, Philadelphia, PA 19116; ☎ **800-523-8930** or 215-244-1500; e-mail internationalsos.com; Internet www.internationalsos.com). This agency provides evacuation to the closest medical care facility that would be equivalent to what you'd get in the U.S. For $55 per person for up to 14 days ($96 per couple or $151 per family), you're covered for air evacuation and all travel-related expenses. This insurance does not cover hospitalization or other charges related to medical care.

Insuring personal property when you hit the skyways

Forget about taking out extra insurance on your baggage. This type of insurance is expensive and difficult to collect. We urge you not to carry anything with you that is very pricey anyway. (See our section on what to pack later in this chapter.) Although our luggage has never been lost in the Caribbean, we've met plenty of fellow travelers who've been in that unenviable position. Your homeowner's insurance should cover lost or stolen luggage as part of your off-premises theft protection; check with your agent for confirmation. U.S. airlines are responsible for up to $2,500 if they lose your luggage, but when you read the fine print on your ticket, so many items are excluded — like electronics and computers — that you may have trouble collecting on the full amount. If you must carry something valuable on your trip, keep it in your carry-on bag.

Some credit cards (such as American Express and certain gold and platinum Visa and MasterCards) offer automatic flight insurance against death or dismemberment in case of an airplane crash, but only if you use that card to pay for your tickets.

Playing It Safe: Preventing Illness, Injury, and Theft

The Caribbean is generally considered an easy place to travel. You don't have to get special shots to go to the islands that we recommend, and you don't need to worry about consuming the food and water.

If you have any concerns about these issues, you can check the State Department's Web page for travel warnings at www.travel.state. gov or you can check with the Centers for Disease Control at its Web site www.cdc.gov/travel.

One of our Jamaican vacations is particularly memorable, but not because of its pleasant and relaxing properties. The first morning, weekend warrior Kevin injured his back taking advantage of waterskiing at dawn. Next, our youngest son had an allergic reaction to the corn syrup sweeteners used in many of the tropical fruit drinks. A few days later, our older son began to shake uncontrollably and had to go to the clinic. He eventually was diagnosed as being extremely dehydrated — a common problem for children at play in the cool breezes of the tropics.

Next, Kevin got an ear infection after he went diving. The last straw came on our final morning, before we had to leave for the airport. Kevin was taking a farewell dip in the waist-deep end of the pool when he stepped on a metal bristle from the pool brush, imbedding the splinter in his foot. The bartender had to pull it out. Of course, we couldn't remember when he'd last had a tetanus shot, so we took yet another trip to the clinic. We were greeted there by name.

Not one of our better trips.

Staying healthy

Clearly, vacations are not always smooth sailing when it comes to your health. Bring all your medications with you, but keep them in their original bottles so you don't run into problems with customs. Carry a prescription for more if you worry that you'll run out.

If you suffer from motion sickness, bring a remedy like Dramamine, even if you're not planning to be on a boat. You may suddenly decide that a sunset sail is irresistible. Plus, we've often found that the combination of heat and winding roads can cause problems even if we're not on the water.

If you have health insurance, bring your carrier identification card in your wallet. If you suffer from a chronic illness, talk to your doctor before taking the trip. For concerns such as allergies to medication, epilepsy, diabetes, or a heart condition, wear a Medic Alert identification tag, which will immediately alert any doctor to your condition and give him or her access to your medical records through Medic Alert's 24-hour hotline. To enroll with Medic Alert, you pay $35, which gets you a stainless steel bracelet or necklace engraved with information about your specific medical information. This effort is especially a good idea if you plan to dive or jog and likely won't have any other form of identification on you. Medic Alert charges a $15 annual fee, which is waived the first year. Contact the **Medic Alert Foundation,** 2323 Colorado Ave., Turlock, CA 95381-1009; ☎ **800-825-3785.**

If you do get sick, ask the concierge at your hotel to recommend a local doctor. You'll get a better recommendation from a concierge than from any national consortium of doctors available through a toll-free number. If you can't get a doctor to help you right away, try the emergency room at the local hospital.

Island creatures great and small

Be prepared to see lots of lizards, geckos, and iguanas. You may even find the first two in your room, but they are harmless. They eat bugs, which is good, because you'll see those also. We've rarely had any problem with mosquitoes, except on the southwest coast of Jamaica in the summertime. The stiff trade winds seem to keep them at bay. But if you're one of those unlucky people who is a mosquito magnet, bring repellent or Avon's Skin So Soft, which seems to do the trick. What we almost always find on any fresh flowers or fruit trays in our room are tiny little ants, which are harmless.

Spray children's clothes with repellent, instead of applying it directly on the skin.

Expect to see stray animals strolling in and out of even the nicer restaurants on the islands. As tempting as it is to pet and feed them, keep a safe distance from the many dogs and cats that you'll see on the islands — some heartbreakingly thin. Teach your children to do the same. We've seen youngsters get scratched and bitten when they disregarded the rules that apply back home. Rabies is rare in the Caribbean, but it does exist.

In the water, the best policy is to look but don't touch. Some marine life inhabiting these waters can inflict nasty stings. Don water shoes so that you don't step on something painful. Coral inflicts cuts that almost always become raw and infected, and you can easily damage this living organism with just the slightest touch. If you step on a sea urchin — the ocean's answer to a porcupine — its spines will deliver a painful prick. Jellyfish stings are infrequent but can also be painful. If you see what looks like a plastic baggie with tentacles floating on the water surface, move away immediately. If you are stung, don't rub the wound. Gently put baking soda on it; vinegar for a Portuguese man-of-war, which is more severe, and then remove any tentacles clinging to the spot. Barracuda and shark attacks are extremely rare. We have seen barracudas and sharks on our dives but have never felt threatened. Avoid wearing shiny jewelry in the water, which can attract them.

Water, water everywhere, but is it safe to drink?

We like to bring bottled water with us on the plane to keep hydrated en route to the Caribbean, especially if we have a long ride to our hotel after we arrive on the island.

After you arrive at your destination, follow these tips to help prevent any illnesses from drinking contaminated water:

- ✔ Tap water is safe to drink on most islands in the Caribbean.

- ✔ Never drink from a freshwater stream, no matter how tempting it looks, because the water can contain dangerous parasites.

- ✔ Drink bottled water if you're on an island after a major storm, because sewage can sometimes seep into the water supplies during such times.

Some of the ritzier island resorts provide you with bottled water at no charge if you request it, while others charge for bottled water. Before you swig those bottles in the minibar or the ice bucket, be crystal clear on whether the resort intended the bottled stuff as a freebie or not. We once wound up paying about $70 for a week's worth of bottled Evian and Perrier that we mistook as complimentary.

Protecting yourself and your valuables

In all our travels to the islands, we've never once had anything stolen or been the victim of any crime. We lived in New York City for 12 years, so we're fairly street-savvy. Our danger antennae did go up in Jamaica's craft markets (where vendors are overly aggressive); in Jamaica's airports (where drug dealers lurk); and on the beach in Negril (where drugs and sex are openly peddled). Of all the islands, we're most guarded on Jamaica, where poverty is an extreme problem. We're also on guard in the more densely populated areas of St. Thomas, Puerto Rico, and St. Croix — in descending order of concern.

What we mean by "guarded" is that we wouldn't walk about freely at night without first checking with our hotel to see if we should avoid any specific areas. We're also wary while browsing in the markets. At the same time, we like to buy on the islands, because we know that the vendors in the markets are desperately poor. Understand that bargaining is the norm in island markets, so don't be rattled at the back-and-forth. On the other hand, don't be bullied into buying something. If you aren't interested, politely and firmly say "no," and move on.

That said, even on Jamaica we never just ensconce ourselves behind the guarded gates of an all-inclusive hotel or resort and refuse to venture out. In fact, we highly recommend getting out to see the country and experience the culture. Just be smart. Don't take a stranger up on an offer to "guide" you around. Stick with guides known to your hotel.

On the islands we haven't mentioned in this section, we feel as safe as we do at home in Marietta, Georgia. But no matter which island we're on, we always exercise caution — just as we do when visiting an unfamiliar city in the U.S. Use your room or hotel safe to store any valuables. Never leave valuables lying on the beach or in a beach chair. We know that sounds obvious, but you wouldn't believe how many folks tuck their wallets in their towels and go for a stroll on the beach. Don't flash expensive baubles, cash, or credit cards.

Before you travel, make two copies of the key information pages of your passport(s), as well as your airline tickets and credit cards. On the same sheets, jot down international help line numbers to report lost or stolen cards. Leave one copy with a relative or friend back home. Keep the other copy with you — in a safe spot separate from your actual passport. Also bring two extra passport photos. If you do lose your passport or it gets stolen, the copy will help speed the replacement process. If you've brought traveler's checks, record the serial numbers and keep a copy in a safe place separate from the checks so that you can be ensured a refund in case of theft.

Scuba divers should keep a list of all equipment and their serial numbers. If your gear gets lost or stolen, file a police report immediately. Both that list and a copy of the report will be needed to collect on your insurance once you return home.

Deciding Whether to Rent a Car

When you live in a car-crazed society, you can have a hard time imagining a place where you don't necessarily need wheels. But just as you wouldn't rent a car in New York City (unless you were training to become a cabdriver), you may not want to rent a car on certain islands either.

However, renting a car is a good idea on Barbados, Puerto Rico, and St. Thomas. Puerto Rico and St. Thomas are large enough that you need your own wheels if you want to get a full flavor of the island. You'll be dealing with the big U.S.-based chains in those locations. Barbados also begs for motorized exploration, and you can rent from local companies on that island.

Rent a car for a day or so to take a tour if it's part of a package, if you're a scuba diver, or if you're staying in a villa or condo on Aruba, Grand Cayman, or St. Croix.

You don't need a car on the British Virgin Islands and St. John. Renting a car in the BVIs is really more trouble than it's worth. The main mode of transportation between the various BVIs is via boat. If you stay in a villa on St. John, you may want to rent a Jeep, but that island is small, and you can get a taxi easily.

Rent at your own risk on Jamaica. If you're the adventurous type, renting a car on Jamaica can be fun. The driving style is supposedly British, but it's best described as Third-World craziness. The country has the third-highest accident rate in the world, the roads are often in disrepair or under construction, and the police stop drivers frequently for infractions both real and imagined. See Chapter 25 for additional details.

If you determine that you want to rent a car, do so well in advance of your trip and make sure that the reservation agent faxes or mails you a confirmation, including the specifications on the car you were promised. Rental cars can be snapped up quickly during high season or during a festival or other event, so that piece of paper could become important. On more than one occasion, we've seen tired, angry people at car rental desks arguing with clerks that they had indeed reserved a car with the company. But because they had nothing to back up their claim, well, let's just say we don't think they got anywhere fast.

Because import taxes on vehicles are usually outrageous in the Caribbean, be assured that your rental car choices are going to be fairly limited. You'll probably be issued a Toyota Corolla or some other similarly small car. On many of the islands, though, Jeeps and small trucks are becoming increasingly popular with tourists. If you have dive gear or lots of watersports toys to haul around, paying a few extra dollars for a Jeep or truck probably makes sense.

Getting a good rental rate

Car rental rates vary widely in the Caribbean, from a modest $30 a day to $80 or even more. The price depends on many things, including (but not limited to) the following:

- ✔ Which island you're on.
- ✔ The size of the car.
- ✔ Whether the car has such niceties as four-wheel drive (a good idea on mountainous islands like Jamaica, St. Lucia, and St. John) and air-conditioning.
- ✔ The length of time you keep it.
- ✔ Where and when you pick it up and drop it off.
- ✔ Where you take it.

On most islands, we rent the smallest car without air-conditioning and other expensive add-ons. (We often get upgrades, but even if you don't, a smaller car is easier to navigate on the narrow roads.) However, we do pay the extra few dollars to have an automatic transmission rather than a standard. The steering wheel may be on the opposite side from what you're used to, and you drive on the left side of the street on all Caribbean islands except Puerto Rico. We figure we have enough strange factors thrown into the mix without having to think about shifting gears, too.

If you need a carseat, be sure to ask if one is available when you reserve the car; request that it be put on reserve as well. However, if you have young children, we strongly recommend that you bring your own carseat for the highest level of safety.

Generally, you don't have to worry about drop-off charges in the Caribbean. In fact, most companies are so eager for your business that they offer complimentary delivery and pick up to and from your resort. Mileage is usually unlimited. (We guess the companies figure, "How far can they go? We're surrounded by an ocean!")

Some companies offer refueling packages, which require you to pay for an entire tank of gas up front. The price is usually fairly competitive with local gas prices, which are much higher than what you find in the U.S. However, you don't get credit for any gas remaining in the tank when you return the car. If you reject this option, you pay only for the gas you use, but you have to return the vehicle with a full tank or else face charges of $3 to $4 a gallon for any shortfall. If, like us, you like to squeeze in every last second on the beach or at the pool, finding a gas station on the way to the airport and messing with lines and paying the clerk may make you miss your plane. We'd rather take advantage of the fuel purchase option.

When you ask about package deals to the Caribbean, find out if a few days' car rental is included; this perk is common, especially during the summer months. The car rental value-added feature is really a good deal, because most of the islands are small enough that you can easily see everything worth seeing in that time frame.

If you can forego air-conditioning, you can save money on your rental. Asking a few key questions could save you a mint. For example, week-end rates may be lower than weekday rates. Ask if the rate is the same for pickup Friday morning as it is Thursday night. If you're keeping the car five or more days, a weekly rate may be cheaper than the daily rate.

Don't forget to mention membership in AAA, AARP, frequent-flyer pro-grams, and trade unions. Most car rentals are worth at least 500 miles on your frequent-flyer account. Club or association memberships usu-ally entitle you to discounts ranging from 5% to 30%. Ask your travel agent to check these rates.

Internet resources make comparison shopping easier. Point your Web browser to `travel.yahoo.com/travel/` or check out `www.onetravel.com` or `www.travelocity.com`. Enter the size car you want, the city where you want to rent, and the pickup and return dates. The server returns a price. We find it somewhat difficult to get Internet resources to allow us to compare prices by changing the extras on the car, but at least you can get a general idea of the cost to expect.

You may also have to pay a nominal fee for a temporary local license. See the individual "Settling into . . ." chapter for the island you're con-sidering to learn more about car rentals.

Demystifying car renter's insurance

On top of the standard rental prices, other optional charges apply to most car rentals. The Collision Damage Waiver (CDW), which requires you to pay for damage to the car in a collision, is covered by many credit card companies. Check with your credit card company to see if you're covered before you go, so you can avoid paying this hefty fee of $10 a day and up.

When you ask your credit card company if it covers the Collision Damage Waiver (CDW), make sure to explain where you're going, because coverage is not extended to all islands. For example, American Express has suspended coverage of car rentals on Jamaica.

 The car rental companies offer additional insurance for liability (if you harm others in an accident), personal accident (it you harm yourself or your passengers), and personal effects (if your luggage is stolen from your car). If you have insurance on your car at home, you are probably covered for most of these unlikely events. A quick phone call to your insurance agent to make sure that you're covered internationally is a smart move. If your own auto insurance or credit card coverage doesn't cover you for rentals, or if you don't have auto insurance, buy the additional coverage.

Packing Like a Pro

Pros at traveling in the Caribbean try to limit themselves to carry-on baggage only, because the Miami and Puerto Rico airports have acquired a reputation for losing or misdirecting luggage. However, with rules tightening all the time about what you can carry on and Caribbean flights being full almost all the time, this advice isn't really practical anymore unless you're an expert packer or only going for four days or less.

 For international travel, most airlines are now limiting passengers to one carry-on item, excluding purses. You won't be able to bypass this rule. If you buy anything large on the islands, don't count on being able to carry it back with you on the plane. You'll either need to check your purchase (by packing it in a piece of luggage that you brought, empty, on the way to the islands) or have it shipped home.

Carrying on essential items

So what should you bring in that all-important single carry-on? Remember that it must fit in the overhead compartment or the seat in front of you. Here are our suggestions:

- ✔ Books and magazines you may want in-flight.
- ✔ Prescriptions.
- ✔ Sunglasses for when you arrive.
- ✔ Any breakable items you don't want to put in your suitcase.
- ✔ A personal headphone stereo.
- ✔ A snack in case you don't like the airline food.
- ✔ Any vital documents that you don't want to lose in your luggage (like your return tickets and passport).
- ✔ The sweater or jacket that you may need on-board. (We often find the airplanes overly cool and airline-issued blankets in short supply.)

Also put your bathing suits in your carry-on; that way if you arrive at your resort and your luggage hasn't made it yet or your room isn't ready (a frequent occurrence at large resorts during high season), you can at least relax in your suits by the pool.

Remember that children are also entitled to carry-ons. You can let older children tote backpacks and some of their own gear. If you have young children, be sure to carry diapers (also pack plenty of diapers in your suitcase, as they're expensive on the islands). Bring the light-weight umbrella stroller for toddlers and babies. Most strollers fit in the overhead compartment; larger ones may have to be checked.

Stocking your suitcase with just the right stuff

Don't bring your nicest luggage. We recommend something sturdy and hard-sided with wheels — you won't find many people-movers and moving sidewalks in the islands. Use a luggage strap that locks, which discourages pilfering and also will somewhat keep your belongings intact in case your suitcase pops open en route.

On the way to the Caribbean, put a temporary tag on your luggage listing your island hotel and phone number. Inside your luggage, tuck in your business card or tape a sheet of paper with your name and address.

When packing, start with the biggest, hardest items like shoes, then fit smaller items in and around them. Put things that could leak, like shampoo and suntan lotion, in resealable bags, away from anything that could be ruined if something seeps out.

When you pack for the Caribbean, put everything in a big pile and then automatically eliminate half. We're serious — whatever you bring, it'll be too much. Most islands are extremely casual, and you'll scarcely need much beyond your sunglasses, swimsuits, casual clothes (shorts and sundresses), sandals, and sturdy water shoes. (Pieces of coral and shells can wreak havoc on bare feet.)

Don't forget your camera and film. The latter often sells out in the hotel gift shops. And if you can find it, the sky-high price will make you swoon. We learned the hard way.

Sun survival kit

Remember to bring plenty of extra sunscreen; it's a good idea to slather it on lavishly whenever you're outside. We recommend using a water-proof one with a factor of 15 or more. For kids, we especially like the new lotions that come in fun colors. The colors fade an hour or so after they're applied, but initially they allow you to see exactly where you need more lotion.

Toting your diving gear

Don't forget your certification card (C-Card) and a logbook recording your recent dives. Good operators will want to see it before they allow you to make a boat dive or even get scuba tanks filled with air. And if you don't have a logbook, you'll likely have to take a check-out dive before you're allowed to proceed.

If you have your own fins, booties, mask, and snorkel, bring them. If you own a regulator, a buoyancy control device (an inflatable vest), a dive computer, or a wet suit or dive skin, bring those, too. You may think that you don't need the latter in the warm waters of the Caribbean, but once you get down 30 feet or so, you cool off quickly.

Bring decongestants and antihistamines with you to be sure that your nasal passages stay clear. These items are often scarce or pricey on the islands.

Women should bring a large hat or plan to buy one. (If you go to windy Aruba, you need to be able to tie it under your chin, or you'll be chasing it all over the island.) Men should bring a baseball cap or plan to buy a straw hat.

Clothing choices

Women may want to bring one or two nice dresses for evenings out or for visiting some historic churches and synagogues that don't allow shorts. Men should bring one dress shirt and one pair of long pants, which are requested at some casinos and restaurants. Jackets are required at only a handful of places on British-influenced isles like Bermuda, Jamaica, and Barbados. Even the exclusive Jamaica Inn, which has been known for decades as a place where gentlemen were expected to wear a jacket and tie for dinner, has loosened up a little and done away with the tie requirement.

Humidity can leave you drenched in sweat, so bring natural fabrics. The Caribbean is one place where we have to nix basic black by day, because it's too hot. And ditch the cowboy boots (sweltering) and expensive jewelry (which screams "rich tourist, rob me"). Yes, we've seen both faux pas; same couple.

Don't worry about ironing things. Nobody cares if you have a few wrinkles. And in the places where they do, irons are provided. The nights are generally warm and sultry, but some casinos, clubs, and restaurants — particularly on Aruba and Puerto Rico where the Latin influence has everyone scrambling for designer duds — overdo the air-conditioning, so tuck in a light jacket or sweater. Don't bring dry-clean-only items, unless they can wait until you're back in your own neighborhood.

Bring sturdy walking shoes; Kevin has river-rafting shoes that are lightweight but give great traction for rain forest treks. Also pack lightweight rain gear if you're going in the rainy season. High heels don't work on the cobblestone streets of Old San Juan or Charlotte Amalie.

Bring a few gallon-sized sealable plastic bags to pop wet swimsuits in if, like us, you like to hang by the pool until the last possible moment. Those plastic bags also come in handy when you're dealing with wet, sandy shoes.

Don't forget your driver's license if you're going to rent a car. Seniors and students should bring proof of age and status, though discounts are limited in the Caribbean.

Part III
Aruba

By Rich Tennant

The resort said it had its own beach. This must be it.

In this part . . .

1f you're thinking about basking in Aruba's warm hospitality, we share our recommendations for the best accommodations on the island. We give you the ins and outs of traveling to Aruba and exploring the sights after you arrive.

Aruban cuisine is as delicious as it is diverse, and we guide you toward the most appealing restaurants on the island. Finally, we share lots of ideas for ways to spend those lazy, sunny days — both in and out of the water.

Chapter 8

The Lowdown on Aruba's Hotel Scene

*A*ruba's best asset is its people, the friendliest in the Caribbean. They not only deal with the teeming masses, but also they handle visitors with aplomb and a smile. Their hospitality is even more refreshing when juxtaposed against the concrete and plastic world of Aruba's hotel district, which sprouted in the 1980s along the island's best beaches.

Virtually none of the lodging properties on Aruba capitalizes on the island's surreal natural beauty. Familiar U.S.-based chains, condos, and timeshares and a few small, individually owned hotels are congregated on the southwest edge of the island. The landscape looks like most of the architects watched too many reruns of the opening minutes of the old TV show *Hawaii 5-0*. Book 'em, Danno.

Aruba hosts a big share of U.S. travelers looking for an easy sun-and-sand vacation package in the Caribbean. A sprinkling of European tourists come as well, but most Europeans opt for neighboring Curaçao, which has far more architectural charm and is almost unknown to most U.S. tourists. Wealthy South Americans like Aruba for its proximity — it's only a few miles north of Venezuela — as well as its dizzying nightlife and casinos. Most of the large resorts have attached the words "& Casino" to their names in the past several years. Safe and clean, Aruba is also a consistent choice for the cruise ship lines because it lies outside the hurricane belt.

We've noticed that most visitors to Aruba fall primarily into one of two camps: honeymooners and families with children. You rarely see singles on Aruba.

Figuring Out Where You Want to Stay

While Aruba doesn't have the range of accommodation choices you'll find on islands like Puerto Rico and Jamaica — no secluded little hide-aways or unique inns — it makes up for this lack with good service and guaranteed sun. Almost all of Aruba's hotels (with more than 7,000 hotel rooms) are jammed adjacent to the wide, white sand beaches on the island's calm southwest coast. Abutting a string of high-rise resorts is Aruba's most famous and aptly named beach: Palm Beach, which is popular with North and South Americans.

Low-rise hotels (as they're called by the locals) hug **Eagle** and **Manchebo** beaches, a quieter area that appeals more to Europeans. The most tranquil and widest point of Eagle Beach is in front of one of our favorite hotels, **Bucuti Beach Resort.** Because the hotel doesn't encourage families as vacation visitors and the resort is popular with Europeans, this part of the beach is the one spot where you may see a few topless sunbathers. (However, the practice is officially frowned upon in conservative Aruba.)

You can find some timeshares and hotels slightly inland from the beach, but we don't feature any of them in this book. We figure that if you go to Aruba, you go for the beach. The savings are so negligible if you stay at an inland location that we don't think it's worth the five-minute walk. The one exception is the **Sonesta** resorts, which are downtown, adjacent to the waterfront. Sonesta has its own small island for guests, with a plethora of watersports and good facilities.

Conserving Cash

Many Aruba properties offer an all-inclusive option, but we suggest a less-restrictive plan that allows you to save some cash for Aruba's sparkling dining scene. (See Chapter 10 for information on Aruba's dine-around program, the most extensive in the Caribbean.) Of course, with so many timeshares and condos on the island, families can also use their own kitchens to save on dining out.

During the summer months for the past few years, several of Aruba's best resorts have teamed up with the active tourist board to assemble heavily discounted packages brimming with extras geared to families. The packages generally run from June 1 through September 30. For example, Aruba's "One Cool Summer" package includes free breakfast and a free stay at a resort for up to two children (11 years old and younger) staying in an adult's room; free access to the supervised children's program; a welcoming gift for each family; free kids' dinners at Aruba Gastronomic Association restaurants; a free carriage ride, sailing trip, and pony ride; and free diving. That's just a small sampling of the goodies that await.

Aruba's "One Cool Honeymoon" package is similarly generous with two dozen different freebies and discounts. This package is offered year-round. Newlyweds just need to identify themselves as honeymooners when they are making reservations and remind the hotel upon check-in that they wish to participate in the package. *Note:* Aruba is the one island where you can't tie the knot — unless of course you fall for an Aruban.

Aruba's Best Accommodations

All of our choices are air-conditioned (gotta have that luxury on the Caribbean's hottest island) and all, except the Sonesta resorts, are on Palm, Eagle, or Manchebo beaches.

The rack rates that appear for each accommodation are in U.S. dollars, and they represent the price range for a standard double room during high season (mid-December to mid-April), unless otherwise noted. Lower rates are often available during the off-season and shoulder season; see Chapter 2 for information on travel seasons.

Aruba Marriott Resort & Stellaris Casino

$$$$–$$$$$ **Palm Beach**

The name Marriott doesn't usually register on our romance meter, but this stunner is an exception. We're hard-pressed to pick our absolute favorite hotel on Aruba from this one and the two entries that follow. Opened in May 1995 before the moratorium on any new construction, this five-star high-rise resort with 411 guestrooms, including 20 suites, occupies the best spot on Palm Beach.

The Marriott is at the end of the high-rise hotel district with great views of prime Caribbean waters for windsurfing. The biggest plus here are the oversized, sun-drenched guestrooms at 500 square feet apiece with roomy 100-square-feet balconies that give you unfettered sea views. The rooms also have walk-in closets as big as ours at home. (Trust us, that's big.) Each air-conditioned room has individual climate control, telephone with voice mail, remote control TV, AM/FM alarm clock radio, in-room pay movies, hair dryer, iron/ironing board, refrigerator, in-room safe, and dual sinks. Nonsmoking and wheelchair-accessible rooms are available upon request.

Marriott's new **ManDara Spa,** opening in December 2000, will be the island's largest. Its bi-level fitness center with floor-to-ceiling windows is already one of Aruba's best. It boasts the latest equipment in a sunny, air-conditioned space near the magnificent free-form pool (one of our favorites in the Caribbean, with a popular swim-up bar looking out at the sea). The **Stellaris Casino** boasts 10,700 square feet of gaming space. The casino and a shopping mall are adjacent to the cavernous lobby — marble, tropical plants, and splashing fountains abound. Restaurants, including the new Simply Fish overlooking the beach, are a significant cut above Marriott's usual overly cautious approach to dining. (See Chapter 10 for a complete review of the resort's northern Italian restaurant, Tuscany.)

Aruba's Hotels

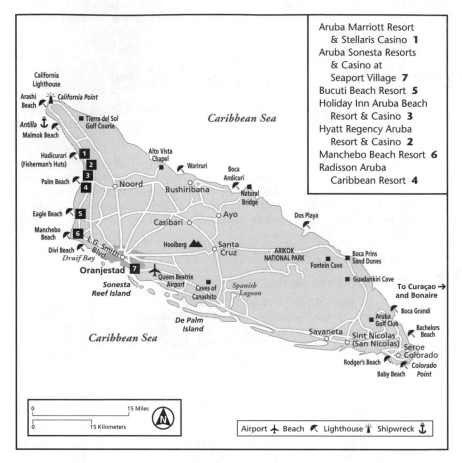

Aruba Marriott Resort
& Stellaris Casino **1**
Aruba Sonesta Resorts
& Casino at
Seaport Village **7**
Bucuti Beach Resort **5**
Holiday Inn Aruba Beach
Resort & Casino **3**
Hyatt Regency Aruba
Resort & Casino **2**
Manchebo Beach Resort **6**
Radisson Aruba
Caribbean Resort **4**

The children's program doesn't appear to be a priority here. If you've got kids, you're better off with Sonesta, Hyatt, or Holiday Inn.

L.G. Smith Blvd. 101, Palm Beach. ☎ *800-223-6388 or 297-86-9000. Fax: 297-86-0649. Internet:* www.marriott.com. *Rack rates: $300–$500 double; for MAP (two meals daily), add $50 per person per night. AE, MC, V.*

Aruba Sonesta Resorts & Casino at Seaport Village

$$$$–$$$$$ Oranjestad

Although located in the heart of Aruba's capital and convenient to its chic discos and bustling shopping areas, this luxury hotel, which is decorated throughout with a collection of tasteful island art, is good for couples and families looking for lots to do combined with a little privacy. The resort fronts a marina rather than a beach, but Sonesta cleverly turned a negative into an asset by acquiring a small private island just five minutes away by motorboat and transforming it into a lovely alternative to

Aruba's somewhat crowded beaches. You step off the elevator in the lobby to a waiting motorboat launch, which speeds you to Sonesta's island where full facilities await. All of the usual watersports are offered. One path on the island leads to the adults-only section, where hammocks beckon. Another path takes you to an area reserved for families.

The Sonesta's regular guestrooms are on the small side (crowded for families taking advantage of the good children's program) and are caught in a 1980s time warp. Go for the suites ($750–$999 in high season), if budget permits.

L.G. Smith Blvd. 9, Oranjestad. ☎ *800-766-3782 or 297-83-6000. Fax: 297-83-4389. Internet www.arubasonesta.com. Rack rates: $300–$500 double; for MAP (two meals daily), add $50 per person a night. AE, DC, MC, V.*

Bucuti Beach Resort

$$$–$$$$ Eagle Beach

If you don't feel like shelling out for one of the top-drawer hotels, this graciously managed place is a great lower-priced alternative. It's also one of the few resorts that's geared more to couples than families and has a perfect location on the widest section of pristine Eagle Beach, far from the madding crowds. Constructed in a low-slung, hacienda style, Bucuti has big, sunny rooms, all stylishly decorated in bright Caribbean colors, with handmade furnishings custom-designed for the resort. Its guestrooms meld contemporary luxury with tropical chic and come with ceiling fans, microwave ovens, mini-bars, refrigerators, and coffeemakers. All have either queen or king-size beds. There's an on-site grocery store, a place to do laundry, and a well-equipped workout area shaded under a huge palapa beach hut. The open-air, beachfront Pirate's Nest serves good food with generous portions (see Chapter 10 for more detail).

L.G. Smith Blvd. 55B (P.O. Box 1299, Eagle Beach). ☎ *800-223-1108 or 297-83-1100. Fax: 297-82-8161. E-mail:* bucuti@setarnet.aw. *Internet:* www.bucuti.com. *Rack rates: $220–$310 double; for MAP (two meals daily), add $42 per person per night. AE, MC, V.*

Holiday Inn Aruba Beach Resort & Casino

$$$ Palm Beach

This sprawling resort — which just got a multimillion-dollar facelift along with a redo of its Excelsior Casino — now boasts more than 600 guestrooms, and you need a map to figure out where everything is. This Holiday Inn is a busy place, right on a quarter mile of the island's most popular beach, but it's great for families thanks to an excellent kids' program and the fact that children 18 and under stay free. The resort has a big, shady playground, too, adjacent to a special kids' pool and the beach. The friendly staff is eager to please, and the guestrooms are unusually large and come with direct-dial phones with dataports, hair dryers, coffeemakers, iron, and ironing board.

Water lovers will appreciate **Pelican Watersports,** a Gold Palm five-star PADI (Professional Association of Diving Instructors) dive operation on-site, as well as parasailing, snorkeling, windsurfing, or boating. Or you can rent one of the floating sea mats and loll in the calm Caribbean in front of the hotel.

Altogether, this Holiday Inn boasts three restaurants and two bars. However, management apparently thinks quantity makes up for quality. Even the solicitous waitstaff can't bridge the gap between the good presentation and what the food actually tastes like. Gourmands should dismiss the all-inclusive option and consider the dine-around program (see Chapter 10). Several meal plans are available. A car rental and tour desk, concierge, and shopping arcade are all on site.

J.E. Irausquin Blvd. #230. ☎ *297-86-3600. Fax: 297-86-5165 (reservations); 297-86-3478 (guest). E-mail:* holidayinn@setarnet.aw. *Internet:* www.holidayinn-aruba.com. *Rack rates: $190 and up double. Ages 18 and under stay free in parents' room. AE, DC, MC, V.*

Hyatt Regency Aruba Resort & Casino

$$$–$$$$$ Palm Beach

Set on 12 acres fronting one of the more action-packed stretches of Palm Beach, this Mediterranean-style tropical oasis popular with families and couples centers on a three-level landscaped waterpark with a 5,000-square-foot lagoon and a two-story waterslide.

If you're the active type who wants plenty to do but hates the frantic atmosphere that plagues some resorts, this place is sure to sate your restlessness without sacrificing privacy. Although the resort has 360 rooms, you never feel overrun by other guests. We love the hacienda-feel of the open-air lobby — birds often fly by the desk. The guestrooms come with an arsenal of amenities: electronic locks, voice mail, plush carpeting, cable, hairdryers, coffeemakers, ironing boards, and juice bars. Unfortunately, the balconies are too small to enjoy. The pool area is so incredible, however, that you won't want to hang in your room anyway.

The resort has five restaurants and four bars, a lively casino, on-site shops, a health and fitness center with sauna, steam, and massage, **Red Sail Sports** — in case you want to scuba dive, jet ski, or windsurf — and aerobics on the sun deck.

J.E. Irausquin Blvd. 85. ☎ *800-233-1234 or 297-86-1234. Fax: 297-86-1682. Internet:* www.hyatt.com. *Rack rates: $210–$525 double. AE, DISC, DC, MC, V.*

Manchebo Beach Resort

$$$ Manchebo Beach

This sprawling low-rise resort with 71 rooms is located on one of Aruba's best beaches and is popular with Europeans. It has comfortable quarters with ceiling fans, direct-dial telephones, refrigerators, and in-room safes. The resort is a good choice for scuba divers and offers friendly, personal attention in a relaxed atmosphere. Manchebo hosts theme nights in one of its three restaurants and has a freshwater pool and dive shop. A casino is adjacent. Ask about discounted dive packages.

J.E. Irausquin Blvd. #55. ☎ *800-223-1109 or 297-82-3444. Fax: 297-83-2446. E-mail:* reserve@manchebobeach.com. *Rack rates: $199 double. AE, MC, V.*

Radisson Aruba Caribbean Resort

$$$$–$$$$$ Palm Beach

Following a $55 million transformation of one of Aruba's original Palm Beach resorts, the beautiful new Radisson is gunning to be top dog on the island. It opened shortly before this book went to press, and the report back from a fellow writer who shares our sensibilities was that Radisson's launch into the upscale market has raised the bar on Aruba. He heaped praise on the lush tropical landscaping and good use of colonial West Indian–style design and heavy mahogany furnishings. The grounds of the 358-room resort (including 32 suites) are laced with lagoons and waterfalls. The top two floors of the nine-story Aruba Tower are concierge floors. Guestrooms have minibars, coffeemakers, irons/ironing boards, hair dryers, make-up mirrors, and in-room safes. All rooms have balconies, but for sea views, you need to be above the fourth floor.

You could opt for lazing on the resort's 1,500-foot beach in the middle of Palm Beach or chill out in one of the two beachfront free-form swimming pools. You'll also be in the company of two whirlpools amid the tropical gardens, a casino, four restaurants (which are run-of-the-mill at this point), and a watersports center offering scuba and PADI certification. A full spa and a kids' program/center are scheduled to open in the fall of 2000. Early verdict: great for honeymooners and families.

4400 J.E. Irausquin Blvd. 81, Palm Beach. ☎ *800-333-3333, 954-359-8002, or 297-86-6555. Fax: 297-86-3260. Internet:* www.radisson.com/palmbeachaw. *Rack rates: $345–$550 double; $510–$1,850 suite. AE, DISC, DC, MC, V.*

Chapter 9

Settling into Aruba

● ●

In This Chapter

▶ Knowing what to expect when you arrive

▶ Getting around the island

▶ Discovering Aruba from A to Z

● ●

*A*ruba's declaration of independence from the Kingdom of the
Netherlands on July 1, 1986, coincided with this small island's
enthusiastic embrace of tourism as its future. Its warm, friendly
people — among the Caribbean's most highly educated, because a
quarter of the national budget is devoted to education — are known
for their hospitality. In fact, many of them study at Europe's finest hotel
schools before returning home to work in the tourism trade. In this
chapter, we help you get settled into Aruba, and we cover all those
essentials like arriving and getting around.

Arriving in Aruba

Arriving in the Caribbean just doesn't get any easier than this. Having
welcomed nearly 700,000 visitors in 1999, tiny Aruba sure knows what
it's doing. After you've gotten off the plane and whetted your appetite
with the gorgeous sunshine, you'll whisk right through customs and
passport control.

Thanks to a much-needed, $64 million expansion that tripled its
capacity, Aruba's busy, busy **Queen Beatrix International Airport**
(☎ 297-82-4800; e-mail airportaruba@setarnet.aw; Internet
www.arubaairport.com) makes a much better first impression than it
used to. It handles jumbo jets and charters that arrive from all over the
world, disgorging tourists from the U.S., South America, and Europe
amazingly well. The airport is clean, bright, and well-staffed.

You'll be immediately presented with armloads of tourist information —
all free. Pick up copies of the excellent magazines *Aruba Experience*
(☎ 297-83-4467; Internet www.aruba-experience.com) and *Aruba
Nights* (Internet www.nightspublications.com). Cheerful tourist
board representatives chirping *bon bini* (the Papiamento phrase for
"welcome") patrol the orderly lines looking for tourists to assist.

Traveling from the Airport to Your Hotel

Right after you've claimed your bags and cleared customs, you'll find spiffy taxis lined up at the curb. Courteous drivers quickly approach when you beckon. The capital of Aruba, Oranjestad, is a 5- to 10-minute ride from the airport, which costs between $5 and $8. The Aruba Marriott, an easy 20-minute, $20 ride, is the farthest hotel from the airport. The average tab runs $14 to $18 along the hotel strip. You can tip from 10% to 15% of the fare, but it's not mandatory.

Your transfer from the airport may be included in your hotel package, in which case, look for a driver holding a sign with your name or the name of your hotel on it.

If you rented a car, you can pick it up across from the airport building, along with easy-to-follow directions to your hotel.

Getting around Aruba

Because most of the hotels are lined up along the island's fabulous beaches (see Map 8-1 in Chapter 8), you may not feel the need to wander far from the hotel pool and the milky teal blue calm of the Caribbean.

You definitely don't need a car to tour downtown Oranjestad. A leisurely stroll through the picturesque town with its charming Dutch architecture is all that's required to take in the entire shebang.

On foot

The hassle-free, pristine beaches of Aruba are perfect for long walks. We've never been quite this ambitious, but you could actually walk all the way from the Marriott at the far end of Palm Beach into Oranjestad, following the beaches almost the entire way.

If you like to walk, Oranjestad is a good spot, too. Nature lovers and adventurers may want to take the easy hike around **Arikok National Park.** Ask your hotel to refer you to a guide, or contact the park at Piedra Plat 42; ☎ **297-82-8001;** fax 297-82-8961; e-mail PNA@ setarnet.aw; Internet www.arubanationalparks.com.

By bus

Aruba has a reliable public bus system that runs hourly trips between the hotels fronting Palm and Eagle beaches and Oranjestad, as well as down the coast between Oranjestad and San Nicolas. Each trip costs $1 each way, and U.S. dollars are accepted. You can pick up a current schedule at your hotel's front desk. The terminal is on Oranjestad's main drag across from the waterfront, next to the Royal Plaza shopping center.

By taxi

Fixed fares are set by the government. After midnight, you pay an additional $1 surcharge for trips. Tell the driver where you want to go before you climb in, and he or she will tell you the fare. Make sure to ask for it in U.S. dollars.

Taxis are also available for sightseeing tours; an hour-long tour for one to four people costs $25. For the **airport dispatch office,** dial ☎ **297-82-2116** or 297-82-1604. Or ask your hotel to call a taxi for you. In town, you can easily flag one by raising your hand.

By car

Car rental companies on Aruba are eager for your business, and a free day's rental is often rolled into package deals, especially during generous summer promotions. We think that renting a car for a day here — especially if it's a freebie — is a fun idea, because this island is so safe and friendly. You'll probably also get extras like free pickup and delivery. Still, during high season, call ahead and reserve.

Whether you've reserved your car ahead of time or not, look for coupons in the handy tourist guides you grabbed when you got off the plane and present them when you start the transaction. Or simply ask about any special discounts. All rental companies offer unlimited mileage; with an island measuring 19 miles long by 6 miles wide, it's a no-lose proposition. Without a coupon, expect to spend about $50 a day. Local rental car agencies are sometimes slightly less expensive. You'll mainly see Toyotas and Suzuki Samurais on the road.

Here are some of the car rental operators: **Amigo** (☎ **297-86-0502**); **Budget** (☎ **800-527-0700** or 297-82-8600); **Dollar** (☎ **297-82-2783**); **Economy Car Rental** (☎ **297-83-0200** main office or 297-88-3208 at the airport); **Happy Island Rentals** (☎ **297-87-5236**); **Hertz** (☎ **800-654-3001** or 297-82-4545); **National** (☎ **800-227-7638** or 297-82-5451; at airport and Holiday Inn); and **Toyota Rent a Car** (☎ **297-83-4832**; e-mail toyota. rentacar@setarnet.aw; Internet www.toyotacarrent-aruba.com).

Request a 4-wheel drive vehicle if you plan on touring the island's less-developed countryside, the _cunucu,_ which is kind of like Australia's Outback. The weather's hot, so don't forget air-conditioning. Really, a day's rental is all you need to tour the entire island. (But a cheaper way to accomplish the same thing is to book one of the 4x4 tours of Aruba — see Chapter 11.)

All the roads in Oranjestad and toward the hotels are well-marked and in good shape. On other parts of Aruba, though, the signage quickly dwindles down to sketchy at best, and the same goes for the roads at certain points. Think rural Arizona.

 You would think it'd be tough to get lost on such a small island, but we've even been with a few local drivers who appeared confused sometimes. Also, you may be unfamiliar with the road signs here, which use international symbols, and the European-style traffic lights. And speaking of signs, keep an eye out for one-way directionals in Oranjestad — the capital is a collection of one-way streets.

If you do rent a car, study the local rules of the road before setting out, bring a map (but feel free to ask directions), drive defensively, and remember that there are no right turns on red.

Parking is free, and traffic isn't bad. You get a few mild jam-ups in Oranjestad when people get off work or during a celebration, which, come to think of it, happens with great frequency. Aruba is safe, so if you do get lost, pull over and ask a local. Just be prepared to get directions in landmarks, rather than by street signs.

By bicycle, moped, and motorcycle

The flat terrain makes Aruba a fun place to bike or ride, but because of the ferocious intensity of the sun and wind, we recommend bicycles only for masochists or for those in good shape. Stay off Routes 1 and 2, which have busy traffic around the hotel strip and town. And take plenty of water and sunscreen.

Bicycles are available through many hotels. **Pablito Bike Rental** (☎ 297-87-8655) in Oranjestad rents mountain bikes for a full day for $12. Olympian triathlete Gert Van Vliet rents mountain bikes through his **Tri Bike Aruba** (☎ 297-85-0609) in Santa Cruz.

Motor scooters and motorcycles, which rent for $40 to $100 a day, can be found at **George's Scooter Rentals** (☎ 297-82-5975) or **Nelson Motorcycle Rentals** (☎ 297-86-6801). Motorcycle Mamas and Papas who want to go whole hog can rent Harleys at **Big Twin Aruba**, L.G. Smith Blvd. 124-A, (☎ 297-82-8660; fax 297-83-9322). Or at least have your picture taken with Big Twin's 1939 Harley Davidson Liberator.

Quick Concierge

ATMs

You'll find two ATMs at the airport. Several machines are available in town in the shopping areas: Noord Branch Palm Beach 4B; Seaport Marketplace, L.G. Smith Blvd.; Playa Linda Beach Resort, L.G. Smith Blvd. 87; Sun Plaza Building, L.G. Smith Blvd. 160. For a complete listing, look in the back of the handy guide you get at the airport.

Baby-sitters

Most hotels are happy to help you arrange baby-sitting. The average cost per hour is $10.

Banks

ABN/AMRO Bank (Caya G.F. Betico Croes 89) and Caribbean Mercantile Bank are in Oranjestad. Hours are weekdays 8 a.m. to 4 p.m. (Banks do not close for lunch in Aruba.)

Credit Cards

Major credit cards and traveler's checks (with ID) are readily accepted.

Currency Exchange

The official currency is the Aruban florin (also called the Aruban guilder), written as Af or Afl. U.S. dollars are happily accepted everywhere: U.S. $1 = Afl $1.78. You really don't need to exchange money, unless you want pocket change for soda machines or a few coins to collect, because they are cool-looking.

U.S. dollars are the only foreign currency readily accepted on Aruba; however, other monies can be easily converted at any local bank. All exchange rates are posted in the bank, or check the Internet at www.xe.net/ucc/.

Doctors

Hotels have doctors on call.

Emergencies

Call ☎ 115 (fire and ambulance).

Hospitals

Horacio Oduber Hospital, J.E. Irausquin Blvd., can be reached at ☎ 297-87-4300.

Information

You can find a tourist office in the airport. Prior to your visit, contact the **Aruba Tourism Authority** (1000 Harbor Blvd., Weehawkien, NJ 07087; ☎ 800-862-7822 or 800-TO-ARUBA in the U.S.; 416-975-1950 in Canada; 800-268-3042 in Quebec and Ontario; Internet www.aruba.com).

Language

Dutch is the official language, but Arubans also speak English and Spanish. The everyday language of the people is Papiamento. Locals often mix three or four languages in the same conversation; keep your ears tuned for some interesting exchanges, even if you can't understand what's being said.

Maps

Maps are available throughout the island and in the back of free guides.

Newspapers/Magazines

Boulevard Drug & Bookstore (☎ 297-82-7385) in the Seaport Village Mall can keep you in touch with current events, and the store sells stamps and road maps as well.

Pharmacies

For prescriptions and other needs, visit **Boulevard Drug & Bookstore** (☎ 297-82-7385) in the Seaport Village Mall.

Police

Call ☎ 100.

Post Office

If you're ambitious, you can visit the post office at 9 J. E. Irasquin Blvd., Oranjestad (☎ 297-82-1900), but your hotel's front desk can also mail your letters and postcards.

Safety

Crime is extremely rare on Aruba, which is a prosperous island. You can walk about freely, but common sense rules apply. Don't leave valuables wrapped in your towel on the beach or have your camera dangling behind you while you look at the shops along the waterfront.

Taxes

The government room tax is 7.6%, and hotels will sting you for an additional 10% service charge for room, food, and beverages. The Departure Tax is $23, plus $3.25 for those making use of the U.S. Departure terminal and, therefore, U.S. INS/Customs services in Aruba. The Departure Tax, officially referred to as the Passenger Facility Charge, is included in the airline ticket price.

Telephone

To call Aruba from the U.S., dial 011, then 297, and then the 6-digit local number.

International calls made from hotels carry heavy service charges resulting in a charge five times the normal rate. Walking or driving to a nearby SETAR teleshop is worth the time, resulting in a comparatively low cost of one U.S. dollar per minute. In your hotel room, you can find a guide that lists the codes to reach the major carriers and also alerts you to which one the hotel deals with. Or you can call your hotel oper-ator, who can usually quickly and efficiently connect you to the long-distance carrier you desire. You can reach **AT&T** at ☎ 800-462-4240; **Sprint** at ☎ 800-877-8000; and **MCI** at ☎ 800-888-8000.

Time Zone

Aruba is on Atlantic Standard time year-round, so most of the year Aruba is one hour ahead of Eastern Standard time (when it's 10 a.m. on Aruba, it's 9 a.m. in New York). When daylight saving time is in effect in the United States, clocks in Aruba and New York show the same time.

Tipping

The standard is 10% to 15% if the tip is not already included, and $1 per day for maids and $1 per bag for bellhops. Many restaurants tack on 10% to 15% service charges to their bills, so check before you leave a double tip.

Water

The water's fine to drink; it comes from a desalinization plant on the island.

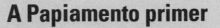

A Papiamento primer

Papiamento is the mother tongue of Arubans. The language is a lyrical blend of Spanish, African, Portuguese, Dutch, and Arawak Indian that's evolved over the island's 500-year history. It's fun to speak. Our sons quickly picked up the rhythm, delighting the natives. Here are a few phrases to try:

Welcome: *Bon bini*

How are you?: *Con ta bai?* ("bai" sounds like "bye")

I am fine: *Mi ta bon*

Thank you very much: *Masha danki* ("danki" sounds like "donkey")

Good morning: *Bon dia*

Good afternoon: *Bon tardi*

Good evening: *Bon nochi*

Beautiful: *Bunita*

Goodbye: *Ayo*

Fish: *Pisca*

Cheese: *Keshi*

Chapter 10

Dining in Aruba

● ●

In This Chapter

▶ Sampling local cuisine

▶ Saving money on meals

▶ Locating the island's best restaurants

● ●

*I*n the mood for Indonesian? How about a nice Argentinian steak? Or some sushi so fresh that it's practically swimming? You name it, you can expect it to be good here. Aruba is one of those islands where you'll really miss out if you just stick with the meals served at your all-inclusive resort. Many of the chefs on the island were trained in Europe's best hotel schools and restaurants. Some attained additional seasoning by working on cruise ships and in other hotels abroad. In other words, your palate reaps the full benefit of Aruba's melting pot.

Indeed, with more than 40 nationalities represented on this small island, finding a restaurant isn't the problem — you have more than 100 to choose from. Deciding on a restaurant is the hard part. We give you a head start in this chapter by reviewing some of our favorites.

Enjoying a Taste of Aruba

The local cuisine is a combination of Dutch and Caribbean. Dutch cuisine tends to use a lot of fine cheeses and meats with heavy sauces, and the Caribbean influence adds fresh seafood and curries. We love the result and urge you to try at least one local specialty while you're on the island, although sensitive stomachs might find local food too rich.

You'll also find a strong South American influence lending additional spice, because Aruba is so close to that part of the world. You'll have no problem getting a good steak here; the meat is imported from Argentina, which is noted for its terrific beef.

During Aruba's "One Cool Summer" celebration — May through September — the Watapana Food & Arts Festival allows you to sample specialties from several different restaurants while you browse works by local artists. Staged every Wednesday from 6 p.m. to 8:30 p.m. and located outdoors between the Allegro and Hyatt Regency on Palm Beach, the festival also features local entertainers.

Outrageous import taxes on wine render getting a decent bottle without paying sky-high prices virtually impossible. If you're a wine drinker, the excellent and more reasonably priced Chilean wines from nearby South America are your best bet. Beer drinkers are in luck: Because of the Dutch connection, Amstel and Heineken are brewed on neighboring Curaçao.

Two excellent liqueurs are brewed on the island: *Ponche crema,* which tastes kind of like eggnog, and *Coe Coe,* made from the agave plant. You'll find these two as ingredients in a number of tropical libations, lending them an Aruban spin.

Eating Out without Breaking the Bank

The local Dutch-meets-Caribbean cuisine tends to be lower-priced than other choices, but another way to save money is through the *Dine-Around Program.* This unique program allows you to purchase coupons redeemable for 3, 5, 7, or 10 meals at 20 of the island's better restaurants. The price for 3 dinners is $109; 5 for $177; 7 for $245; and 10 for $339. The meals include appetizer, main course, dessert, coffee, and service charge. Beverages are not included, and surcharges apply to some menu items. For information, call the **Aruba Gastronomic Association** (☎ **800-477-2896** or 297-86-2161; fax 297-86-2162) or **De Palm Tours** (☎ **297-82-4400;** e-mail aga@setarnet.aw; Internet www.arubadining.com).

The *VIP Gourmet Selection* ($60 per dinner per person with a minimum purchase of three dinners) lets you choose a multi-course gourmet dinner with a special menu, including service charge. For that option, you choose from Le Dome, L'Escale, Papiamento, and Valentino's. (See our reviews of L'Escale and Papiamento later in this chapter.)

Although some of the better restaurants are at the hotels, several places are worth a taxi ride. Even if you're at an all-inclusive resort, the Dine-Around Program enables you to experience other restaurants at a reasonable price instead of eating at your hotel night after night.

Refer to Chapter 6 for more budget tips and explanations of our price categories. For more on Aruba's restaurants, check out this Web site: www.arubadining.com.

Aruba's Best Restaurants

Boonoonoonoos

$$ Oranjestad   Caribbean

Boonoonoonoos (pronounced *boo-new-new-news*) is a fun surprise and fun to say. The word is Jamaican slang for "extraordinary." Tucked into a restored colonial home playfully splashed with crayon-bright Caribbean colors, this delightful restaurant has become a favorite with the lunch crowd. In addition to atmosphere, you can get a good meal here for under $10 — try the spicy pumpkin soup.

Boonoonoonoos is also an entertaining place for families with kids, and the large portions are good for sharing. Austrian chef/owner Kurt Biermanns and his Aruban wife Jacqueline deserve kudos for the sheer breadth of the Caribbean cuisine they tackle — from Jamaican jerk ribs to Cuban black beans. If you're ravenous at dinnertime, share the Carib Combo platter, a virtual culinary tour of the region that groans with 11 dishes. On some nights, local talent entertains the appreciative crowd.

Wilmelminastraat 18A, Oranjestad. ☎ *297-83-1888. Reservations recommended. Main courses: lunch $4–$15; dinner $15–$34. AE, MC, V. Open for lunch and dinner Monday through Saturday 11:30 a.m. to 11 p.m., Sunday dinner 5 p.m. to 11 p.m.*

Brisas del Mar

$$–$$$ Savanetta   Seafood/Traditional Aruban

For expertly prepared, spanking fresh seafood, splurge one night on the 20-minute, $24 cab ride to get you to this locally owned, open-air seaside restaurant. Housed in what was formerly a police station in the 1800s, this spot is now a little frayed around the edges, with fishermen's nets hanging from the ceiling and nothing special in the looks department. But we quickly forgot the plastic flowers once we tasted the fish stew and classic Aruban fish cakes *(kerri kerri)*, made from the old family recipes of diminutive proprietress Lucia Rasmijn. She pops out of the kitchen throughout the evening to mingle with her guests and delights in sharing Aruban folktales or island history with anyone who asks.

Request a table right by the water overlooking Boca San Carlo, where the local fishermen arrive daily with their catches. You can order whatever they've brought to Lucia while enjoying the sounds of the sea. On the weekends, live music brings in hordes of local families, and it's a fun place to bring your children, too.

Savanetta 22A. 20 minutes from downtown Oranjestad. ☎ *297-84-7718. Reservations required. Main courses: lunch $5–$20; dinner $10–$29. AE, MC, V. Open Tuesday through Sunday for lunch noon to 2:30 p.m and dinner nightly 6:30 p.m. to 9 p.m.*

Places for picky eaters

If your kids' favorite refrain is "Euuuw, Mom, do I have to eat that!?", try **Tony Roma's** (across from the Holiday Inn; ☎ 297-86-7427) for ribs, or **Benihana** (Sasakiweg; ☎ 297-82-6788) for good Japanese food prepared by chefs who entertain with their elaborate knife play while they prepare your dinner. Talk about playing with your food.

Chalet Suisse

$$$$ Oranjestad Swiss

We were caught off guard by the excellence of Chalet Suisse. (Okay, we confess right now that our knowledge of Swiss cuisine was nil.) The restaurant is conveniently located on Eagle Beach. Soothed by romantic lighting and an attentive waitstaff, we enjoyed such scrumptious creations as the hot "Chalet Suisse" appetizer (shrimp, crabmeat, fish, lobster, and fresh mushrooms), a peppery filet mignon "Madagascar," and a Caribbean seafood platter, which included lobster. Each dinner comes with fresh vegetables and home-baked bread. You won't leave hungry.

J. E. Irausquin Blvd. 246. ☎ 297-87-5054. Reservations recommended. Main courses: $16–$35. AE, MC, V. Open for dinner 6 p.m. to 10 p.m. Monday through Saturday.

Charlie's Bar

$–$$ San Nicolas Creole/International

On the day you head to Baby Beach or Boca Grandi, stop in at Charlie's Bar, which has been operating since 1941 and is now run by the late Charlie's grandson Charlito. Forget about the food, you're here to soak up the atmosphere. While away an afternoon with the locals, artists, sailors, musicians, and other tourists drinking Amstels and nibbling on platters of Creole calamari and jumbo shrimp, accompanied by local bread and Aruban-style french fries (fat and freshly cut). The walls are cluttered with oddities left behind — from tennis shoes to license plates. Make a point of chatting with the friendly staff; you can pick up all kinds of fascinating island trivia. Kids are welcome at this authentic Caribbean-meets-Cheers hangout.

Main Street 56, Zeppenfeldtstr 56 San Nicolas. ☎ 297-84-5086. Main courses: $18–20. No credit cards. Open for lunch and dinner Monday through Saturday 11:45 a.m. to 9:30 p.m.

Aruba's Restaurants

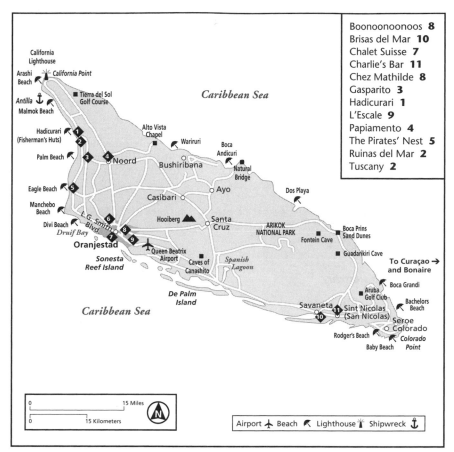

Boonoonoonoos **8**
Brisas del Mar **10**
Chalet Suisse **7**
Charlie's Bar **11**
Chez Mathilde **8**
Gasparito **3**
Hadicurari **1**
L'Escale **9**
Papiamento **4**
The Pirates' Nest **5**
Ruinas del Mar **2**
Tuscany **2**

Chez Mathilde

$$$$ Oranjestad   French

If you're going to splurge, go for it at Chez Mathilde, one of the island's best restaurants. In an elegant house built in the 1800s — one of the few fine examples remaining on the island — you can enjoy French specialties focusing on fresh local seafood and imported aged beef. We suggest starting with the rich bouillabaisse and escargots escoffier. For a main course, try the mildly flavored sole with a delicious sauce or the *tournedos au poivre* (beef fillet with a pepper sauce).

Make a reservation as soon as you're on the island and ask for a private nook in the ultra-romantic Pavilion Room, awash in tasteful beiges and decorated in Italian and French antiques. An elegant fountain serves as the tropical garden's centerpiece.

Havenstraat 23, Oranjestad. ☎ *297-83-4968. Reservations essential. Main courses: $17–$43. AE, DISC, MC, V. Open for lunch Monday through Saturday 11:30 a.m. to 2:30 p.m. and dinner nightly 6 p.m. to 11 p.m.*

Gasparito

$$ Palm Beach   Traditional Aruban

Across from the high-rise district in a traditional country house, a clever combination restaurant/art gallery turns out some of the best local cuisine around. Relax and enjoy the excellent service while sampling such favorites as *keshi yena*, a wheel of Dutch gouda cheese filled with seafood, spiced chicken, or beef. (Trust us, it tastes much better than it sounds.) You'll see why the chef frequently wins awards in Caribbean cooking competitions.

Gasparito #3, Noord, near the high-rise hotel section. ☎ *297-86-7044. Average meal price: $30. AE, MC, V. Open for dinner Monday through Saturday 5:30 p.m. to 11 p.m., Sunday lunch 11 a.m. to 4 p.m.*

Hadicurari

$ Palm Beach   Local

For years, this spot was a gathering place for local fishermen to anchor their colorful wooden boats and swap tales, but the development of the high-rise hotel district gradually encroached on their turf. Finally, the government agreed to give them this area to congregate, and it's also become an excellent casual dining spot in the heart of the action on Palm Beach.

You can walk up and get the grilled catch of the day for $6, which gets you *crioyo* sauce (Aruba's version of Creole sauce), salad, and fried plantains. You also get a choice of either *funchi* (a cornmeal polenta), *pan bati* (a traditional Aruban flat bread), french fries, or rice.

A steel pan band plays here every Saturday and Sunday from noon to 4 p.m. Have some fun dancing on the beach with a mix of locals (many middle-aged Arubans) and tourists from the surrounding hotels. Sometimes the beach party goes on until 9 in the evening.

Centro di Pesca (The Fishery Center), L. G. Smith Blvd. ☎ *297-86-0820. Main courses: $6–$15. No credit cards. Open daily for lunch noon to 4 p.m. and dinner 6 p.m. to 9:30 p.m.*

L'Escale

$$$$ Oranjestad Harbor   French

Sonesta's, home of L'Escale, deserves a spot on your hot list even if you aren't staying at the hotel. Whether you've just finished shopping downtown, feel like trying your luck in the adjoining Crystal Casino, or just want a terrific meal, book dinner here. Aruba-born Chef Calvert Cilie quit his day job at the local oil refinery to study cooking in Europe. Good career move for him and lucky for us. Using traditional French techniques, he skillfully blends local ingredients. Try any red snapper dish or the rack of lamb, or just put yourself in his capable hands and order the chef's choice. If you're in the mood to spring for a bottle of wine, L'Escale maintains one of the better selections on the island. A strolling string trio adds to the romance factor.

Request a table away from the casino by the windows overlooking the seaport.

Aruba Sonesta Resort at Seaport Village. ☎ 297-83-6000, ext. 1791. Reservations strongly suggested. Main courses: $22–$30. AE, DISC, MC, V. Open for brunch Sunday 10 a.m. to 1p.m., and dinner nightly 6:30 p.m to 9:30 p.m.

Papiamento

$$$$ Noord   Local/Continental

If you are looking for a leisurely evening on a moonlit night, Papiamento is one of our absolute favorites. You feel as though you're dining in a grand country home at this elegant, family-owned and run Dutch-style restaurant.

The traditional Aruban and continental dishes (the menu changes nightly) are served poolside amidst riotous tropical gardens dotted with large terra-cotta pots. Tiny twinkling lights are twined through palms surrounding their private manor, built in the 1860s and filled with treasured antiques from Europe and Aruba.

When Queen Beatrix is in town, she comes here for the red snapper, sizzled tableside on a hot marble stone. Chatêaubriand for two and Caribbean lobster are also winners. Don't skip dessert. The pastry chef and daughter in this talented family, Annelotte Ellis, is deservedly renowned on the island.

Romantics should ask to be seated right by the pool or at the lone special table for two tucked into a private room.

Washington 61, Oranjestad. Noord. ☎ 297-86-4544. Reservations required. Main courses: $20–$40. AE, MC, V. Open for dinner Tuesday through Sunday 6:30 p.m. to 10:30 p.m.

The Pirates' Nest

$$$ Eagle Beach   Steaks/Seafood

At first glance, the kitschiness of this hotel restaurant might be a turnoff. The grand scheme is a fake Dutch galleon designed to look as if it's sinking in the sand. But it's also open air and situated on the best part of Eagle Beach. By day, this is a fun spot to come with the kids for good sandwiches and tasty salads. By night, the twinkling lights, moonlight, and torches transform the place. Chef Kurt Hoffman specializes in fresh seafood and steaks. The best dinner deal is the five-course chef's choice for two, which includes a bottle of wine and cappuccino, coffee, or tea for $75 per couple. In the mornings, you can get a lavish champagne buffet breakfast here, too.

Bucuti Beach Resort, L. G. Smith Blvd. #55B. ☎ 297-83-1100. Reservations recommended. Main courses: champagne breakfast $11.95; dinner $30. AE, DISC, MC, V. Open daily for breakfast 7 a.m. to 11 a.m., lunch noon to 5 p.m., and dinner 6 p.m. to 10:30 p.m.

Ruinas del Mar

$$$$ Palm Beach   Continental

For the hands-down best romantic ambience, head to the Hyatt Regency's Ruinas del Mar. Built to look like the old stone gold mine ruins on the island and lit by torches and candlelight, this is an absolute stunner. Add to that the lush tropical landscaping, a lagoon complete with koi and black swans, and we're happily gazing into each other's eyes all evening.

Executive Chef George Hoek, a native Aruban, spent time at the Hyatt Regency Beaver Creek in Colorado before returning home. His signature dish is a seafood mixed grill of locally caught fish and Caribbean lobster tail. His shrimp tempura with mango tequila salsa is a winner, too.

Hyatt Regency, J. E. Irausquin Blvd. #85. ☎ 297-86-1234. Internet: www.hyatt.com. Reservations essential and resortwear requested. Main courses: $20–$33. AE, DISC, MC, V. Open daily for breakfast 7 a.m. to noon and dinner 5:30 p.m. to 10 p.m.

Tuscany

$$$$ Palm Beach   Northern Italian

When it comes to hotel dining, Tuscany, which snagged the island's best-known executive chef, Fernand "Ferry" Zievinger, takes top honors in our book. After more than a decade living in New York, we consider ourselves somewhat snobbish when it comes to Italian food, yet this upscale casual restaurant managed to exceed our expectations and then some. From generous and beautifully presented antipasto to frothy cappuccino, our meal was well worth the price. And with oil paintings of the Tuscany countryside, sparkling chandeliers, and the tinkling of a piano in the background, the place manages to be romantic — often a difficult stunt in a hotel setting.

In the Aruba Marriott, L. G. Smith Blvd. 101, Palm Beach. ☎ 297-86-9000. Reservations essential. Main courses: $20–$38. AE, MC, V. Open for dinner nightly 6 p.m. to 11 p.m.

Chapter 11

Hitting the Beach and Other Fun Things to Do

....

In This Chapter

▶ Soaking up the sun on Aruba's top beaches

▶ Diving into fun with watersports

▶ Satisfying the landlubber: Shopping and nightlife

▶ Planning some super side trips

....

*I*n this chapter, our focus is on fun. We offer plenty of suggestions for activities that help you take advantage of Aruba's chief assets: water, sand, and sun. Aruba offers watersports galore, including world-class windsurfing and wreck scuba diving. If you prefer to be on solid ground, consider driving a four-wheeler through the desert or golfing on one of the Caribbean's most unique courses.

We wind up this chapter with a look at Aruba's nightlife scene, one of the most active among all the islands in this book. And in case this day-into-night excitement is not enough to keep you busy, we explain the ABCs of island hopping in this area of the Caribbean, giving you the scoop on Aruba's neighbors: Bonaire and Curaçao.

Hitting the Beaches

Aruba's main draws are its glorious powder-white beaches (all public) and its virtually guaranteed sunshine. The glossy photos that you've probably seen are accurate — impossibly white sand juxtaposed against the calm sea's turquoise and cobalt blues. The beaches are spotless, too. Locals and hoteliers alike understand the direct correlation between trash-free beaches and your willingness to visit their island.

 When people talk about the *leeward side* of Aruba, they refer to the calmer waters of the northwest and southwest coasts, from **Arashi** down to **Baby Beach** on the southern tip. The *windward* or north side of the island spans the northeast to southeast coasts, from behind the **California Lighthouse** to **Bachelors Beach.** The windward side experiences much rougher waters and has surrealistic coral landscapes carved out by the pounding waves.

Try to get out on the beach before 10 a.m. so that you can enjoy some quality time before the sun goes into high-broil mode, which lasts from noon to 3 p.m. And don't forget to slather on that sunscreen; you are, after all, just a few degrees above the equator. Stay hydrated by drinking lots of water. (Alcoholic beverages don't help: They make you dry out faster!)

Leaning toward the leeward side

You'll find Aruba's best-known beaches — **Palm, Eagle,** and **Manchebo** — on the leeward side. The low-rise and high-rise hotel districts are located here as well. Our favorite stretch of the famed **Palm Beach** — lined by the island's finest hotels and an abundance of imported palms — lies in front of the Aruba Marriott. Despite the constantly blowing trade winds, the Caribbean's clear, blue waters are remarkably smooth and boast visibility up to 100 feet. Even children can safely play in the gentle surf here.

Anywhere along Palm Beach, you can find beach and swim-up bars, casual restaurants, and public rest rooms galore. If you decide to go for a long stroll, take along some money in case you work up a thirst.

A great place to stop and get a bite or an icy Amstel is **Hadicurari Fisheries Center,** the fishermen's co-op right on Palm Beach. By law, the food prices must be low enough that the fishermen can afford to eat here, so you can get fresh fish (caught that day) at a great price. See our review of Hadicurari in Chapter 10.

You don't have to limit yourself to the beach right in front of your hotel. On Palm Beach, which gets pretty crowded during high season, you can jockey for a position in front of the larger hotels. Competition is especially fierce for shade-providing cabanas, which are free to the public and maintained by the hotels. Expect to pay about $5 a day for a beach chair if you aren't a guest at the hotel where you want to lounge.

On **Arashi,** parts of **Eagle Beach,** and **Baby Beach,** the government provides cabanas for visitors. The quietest and widest point of Eagle Beach is in front of the **Bucuti Beach Resort.** If you aren't staying there, reserve lunch or dinner at its restaurant, **The Pirate's Nest,** and hang out at the beach before or after your meal. (See Chapter 10 for a review of the Pirate's Nest.)

On **Fisherman's Hut Beach,** littered with the battered remains of conch shells, several watersport outfitters casually but expertly give windsurfing lessons. This spot is ideal for watching the neon-colored sails of the windsurfers as they skim across the aquamarine sea. You'll think you're watching a butterfly ballet.

At night, you can safely stroll along the beaches and hotel-hop until you settle on a "theme night" — pirates, anyone? — that best fits your mood. Holiday Inn's toga parties are kitschy fun and have been popular on the island for more than two decades.

Breezing toward the windward side

On the windward side of the island, the pounding waves and wild surf crashing against odd rock formations translate into only a few beaches that are worth investigating. But some of the beaches here offer a truly unique experience. On the southeastern tip of the island, **Boca Grandi** (Big Cove) is one of the prettiest and least crowded of Aruba's beaches. Skilled windsurfers and snorkelers love this beach, but you need to be a strong swimmer to go in the water here because the undertow can be fierce. **Dos Playa** is a good place for a quiet picnic and for swimming in the waves, but you should beware of the undertow here as well.

Wariruri, found near Alto Vista, is the island's hottest surfing/body-boarding spot. Extreme sports enthusiasts also use the beach coves of **Boca Andicuri,** which is also an *advanced shore dive site,* meaning that you can wade to the dive site from the shore, instead of taking a boat. (Boca Andicuri is located near the Natural Bridge, which is described in the "Exploring Aruba" section later in this chapter.) **Alto Vista, Dos Playa,** and **Boca Grandi** are other great shore dive sites.

Terrific for families is the aptly named **Baby Beach.** Located on the southeast shore near San Nicolas, this beach makes a semicircular curve around bath-water calm, shallow waters sheltered by a promontory of rocks. You can buy cold drinks and food at the beach's concession stand, as well as rent snorkeling equipment. Baby Beach has a fun, festive vibe, thanks to the locals who adore this spot.

On **Rodger's Beach** (just up the coast from Baby), you can find slightly better facilities with showers, rest rooms, picnic tables, food vendors, and shade. Rodger's also has a shallow reef close to shore. Brave souls can venture farther out, where the coral reef offers decent snorkeling. A much greater abundance of marine life awaits in the waters surrounding either Curaçao or Bonaire. (See descriptions of these two islands later in this chapter.) You can rent snorkeling gear here for about $15 a day.

Picnicking Aruba-style

If you want to have a down-home picnic Aruba-style, try an Aruba barbeque. Every Sunday afternoon, home-style barbecue shops set up to sell a cholesterol jamboree: takeout platters groaning with slabs of ribs, chicken drumsticks and thighs, fish filets, and blood sausages, along with sides of rice, potato salad, and macaroni salad. If the hotel concierge desk can't direct you to a favorite stop, a quick drive around an Aruban neighborhood should turn up something. The average price is about 10 florins ($6).

Staying Active on Land and Sea

When you tire of soaking up the rays on the beach, Aruba offers plenty of other options for having a good time — in, on, and around the beautiful, bountiful beaches.

Putting wind in your sails

With its steady, strong trade winds (which average 15 knots year-round), Aruba is a natural location for windsurfing and one of the better places in the world to learn the sport. The calm waters off **Fisherman's Hut** (a.k.a. Hadicurari) and the beaches of **Arashi** and **Malmok** are the most popular windsurfer hangouts. Fisherman's Hut is where the annual Hi-Winds Amateur Windsurfing Competition is held. But its waters aren't so crowded that beginners feel intimidated.

When we took lessons, neither of us was much good. But the leather-tanned instructors, who all wore mirrored sunglasses (maybe so we couldn't see the laughter in their eyes) were immensely patient and skilled. Once, Echo thought her instructor was waving at her to let her know she was doing well. Actually, he was signaling her to come back in because she was headed to Venezuela. Nonetheless, we had a great time trying our hand at this sport. **Fisherman's Huts Windsurf Center** (Aruba Marriott Resort, ☎ **297-86-9000**) rents boards for $60 a day. Beginner lessons run $45 an hour and include a board.

Good news for parents with adventuresome kids: Windsurfing instruction starts for children as young as age 4. The miniaturized boards for tots are adorable.

Both **Sailboard Vacations** (☎ **800-252-1070,** stateside 617-829-8915) and **Roger's Windsurf Palace** (☎ **800-225-0102**) offer windsurfing and accommodations packages. Both are on Malmok Beach and have fully equipped shops with good instructors. This section of the beach has a little more of the surfer dude feel to it.

Dining and dancing onboard

Our favorite dinner and dance cruise combo is aboard the *Sea Star* (☎ 297-86-2010), which sails you to a waterfront marina restaurant for a candlelit meal accompanied by island music. Then it's back on the boat for merengue and salsa dance lessons. Book through **De Palm Tours** (☎ 297-82-4400) for $59.50 a person. Or reserve an evening for dirty dancing on *Tattoo* (☎ 297-86-2010), a party boat with a buffet dinner. It's $49 per person for a four-hour tour. If you're feeling frisky, wear your swimsuit under your clothes and take the plunge from the boat's rope swing.

If swinging strikes your fancy, you can also book a trip for $48 per person on the *Mi Dushi* (☎ 297-86-2010), a 78-foot Swedish sailing vessel built in 1925, which has a rope swing and specializes in four-hour guided snorkel trips crowned with a hot barbecue lunch.

Diving right in

Aruba ranks right behind Bermuda for its wreck diving. For five years running, *Rodale's Scuba Diving* magazine has rated Aruba in the top five for the Best Wreck Diving in the Caribbean/Atlantic Region category. The magazine also notes that Aruba has one of the "World's Favorite Dive Sites." *The Antilla,* a hulking German freighter that sunk off Malmok Beach during WWII, is one of the Caribbean's largest and most notable wrecks. *The California,* a wooden cargo ship that sank while trying to deliver general merchandise from Liverpool to South America, is also a popular wreck dive. (In the midst of a midnight party, the *California* crew let the ship get a little too close to the dark Aruban coast.) If you're a qualified diver interested in wreck diving, contact **De Palm Tours** (L. G. Smith Blvd. 142; ☎ 297-82-4400).

For those less enamored of making like Jacques Cousteau, Aruba has many less challenging dive and snorkeling sites where you can see manta rays, lobsters, groupers, sea fans, corals, sea turtles, and octopuses. Another option is SNUBA, which is safe and easy to learn and has recently become popular on the island. SNUBA goes beyond snorkeling; you wear a mask, but you can go beneath the surface and breathe without having to wear all the heavy diving tanks.

Family-owned **De Palm Tours** (L. G. Smith Blvd. 142; ☎ **297-82-4400 ext. 206**) offers SNUBA, diving, and snorkeling instruction and equipment. To experience SNUBA, you can pay $45 for an hour, which includes a briefing and time in the water. Introductory diving courses cost $65 for a one-tank dive. A four-hour snorkeling experience costs $22 and includes equipment. For snorkeling, De Palm ferries you out to its private island from Balashi, about ten minutes from Oranjestad. The island has full facilities with volleyball and basketball courts, a kids' playground, decent food, and a full bar. It also has one of the best-stocked gift shops in Aruba, with lots of unique items from Venezuela and other South American countries.

De Palm Tours offers a terrific family combo package for $77.50 per adult and no charge for an accompanying child. The deal includes snorkeling at De Palm Island, a tour of Aruba, and sailing and snorkeling from De Palm's *Fun Factory* catamaran.

De Palm's honeymoon package ($269 a couple) includes a sail and snorkel, a Jeep tour, and a fantasy dinner and dance cruise.

Another excellent operator, centrally located on Palm Beach between Holiday Inn and Playa Linda, is **Pelican Adventures N.V. Tours & Watersports** (P.O. Box 1194, Oranjestad; ☎ **297-87-2302;** fax 297-87-2315; e-mail pelican-aruba@setarnet.aw; Internet www.pelican-aruba.com). Pelican has a PADI Gold Palm five-star facility with custom-built dive boats and numerous dive packages. Rates run as follows: introductory scuba course, $70; PADI Open Water Certification, $350; one-tank dive, $35; two-tank dive, $55; night dive, $39.

Cruising the depths and staying dry

Okay, so it's not yellow. But it *is* a real submarine and a great solution for those who don't like the idea of diving but still want to explore the ocean depths. For $75 per person, **Atlantis Adventures** (L. G. Smith Blvd. 82; ☎ 297-83-6090) takes you on a two-hour submarine cruise. The sub plunges 150 feet below the surface off Sonesta Reef, allowing you close views of the wrecks of *Mi Dushi* (a 70-year-old wooden sailing yacht), *Morgenster* (a steel-hulled 110-foot-long ship), and several airplanes. Kids love it, as do people who wouldn't dream of diving in the water themselves. But the experience will bore divers, and if you get claustrophobic, forget it.

Other good operators include **Unique Sports of Aruba,** the third largest operator on the island (L. G. Smith Blvd. 79; ☎ 297-86-0096); **Fly 'n Dive,** which has multiple dive sites on Aruba as well as on neighboring islands (Shiribana 9-A Paradera; ☎ 297-87-8759); **Native Divers,** a husband-and-wife team that takes groups of two to six experienced divers and offers far more flexibility than other operators (Koyari 1; ☎ 297-86-4763); and **Aruba Pro Dive** (Ponton 88; ☎ 297-88-5520).

We've heard from other scuba divers that **Red Sail Sports** (L. G. Smith Blvd. 83; ☎ 297-86-1603) often dives in the same location more than once a week even though several other sites are available. We had a good experience with the same outfit on Grand Cayman but would heed this advice: Don't presume a dive operator with the same name operates in the same way on every island.

Swinging a round of golf

Aruba's deluxe hotels offer golf at the island's **Tierra del Sol** (Malmokweg; ☎ 297-86-0978; e-mail tierra.rent@setarnet.aw; Internet www.tierradelsol.com), an 18-hole championship course designed by Robert Trent Jones Jr. You can view the sea from an astounding 15 holes. Located near the California Lighthouse, this par-71, 6,811-yard course allows you to admire the rugged beauty of Aruba's northwest coast. The sights include cacti, a saltwater marsh inhabited by egrets, a bird sanctuary with rare burrowing owls, and odd rock formations.

The trade winds add an extra challenge to your swing, but Tierra del Sol is not an overly difficult course. Even beginners (like us) enjoy trying their hand at the game here. The surroundings are beautiful, and the pros have a sense of humor. (If you don't know your eight irons from your Tiger Woods, check out the club's "No Embarrassment" golf clinics.)

The $120 greens fee includes a golf cart, and club rentals are an extra $25 to $45. The golf clinic is a real bargain: $50 for a half day, which includes an excellent lunch at **Ventanas del Mar,** where floor-to-ceiling windows overlook the course.

During the low season, you can rent beautiful villas that surround the course (starting at $250 a night) and get free green and cart fees as well as access to the club swimming pool. To book a villa, contact the **Executive Office** at ☎ **297-86-7800.**

Galloping along

Aruba's desert plains are perfect for exploring by horseback. Add in the calm cowboys and good-natured horses, and even the tenderest of tenderfoots can straddle a saddle and giddyap. The stables let kids as young as age 6 take the reins.

We rode through the *cunucu* (the Papiamento word for "countryside") to Malmok Beach. After admiring the sunset, we picked our way back through cacti sentries to the stables. Another well-loved path takes you through the countryside to the Natural Pool, a romantic spot where you can take a dip.

For bookings, try **Rancho Del Campo** (☎ **297-83-8632**), **Rancho Diamari** (☎ **297-86-0239**), or **Rancho Notorious** (☎ **297-86-0508**). The average price for rides is about $25 an hour.

Exploring Aruba

If you just stick to the hotel strip, you'll think that Aruba's not much more than an overbuilt sand bar. Traveling across the island's unusual landscape or visiting its cultural attractions can paint an entirely different — and far more intriguing — tropical picture.

Traveling the cunucu by jeep

Getting there is half the fun. That phrase certainly applies to Aruba's requisite island tour. Our favorite is the pink Jeep tour provided by **Eagle Jeep Tours** (☎ **297-83-9469**). You start out at the picturesque California Lighthouse. And yes, you actually do your own driving on this tour.

Here's the rub. You follow your leader along the rugged (and dusty) north coast, so try to get as close to the front of the line as possible. The big highlight is the **Natural Bridge,** a dramatic coral structure that stretches for 100 feet and hangs 25 feet above the wild surf that created it in the first place. It's the Caribbean's highest coral structure and Aruba's most photographed site.

If you look closely as you drive through the desert, you can see wild goats and lizards. Cacti and the weird divi-divi trees (growing at a 45-degree angle because of the trade winds) are everywhere. You'll get a good view from Alto Vista chapel. The remainder of the tour takes you through **Arikok National Park,** north of the road between Boca Prins and San Fuego and bound on the east by the coastline as far as Boca Keto. There, you'll see more cacti and birds such as *shoko* (owls) and *prikichi* (the Aruban parakeet). You may also see the almost extinct Aruban rattlesnake called *cascabel*.

The park, set aside by the government in 1997 to preserve 17% of Aruba's total land mass, has recently opened a well-marked, 35-km walking trail through areas that were not easily accessible until recently. Now you can get a close look at the abandoned gold mines in the park, old farm sites from settlers' days, and Indian cave drawings. A new visitors' center opened in the summer of 2000.

Driving the rugged north coast can be a sunny, dusty trip. Bring some bottled water, sunglasses, extra sunscreen, and a bandana. Then get ready to eat some trail dust.

Taking in some Aruban culture

The **Bon Bini Festival** is held every Tuesday starting at 6:30 p.m. at small **Ft. Zoutman** (Zoutmanstraat Z/N, Oranjestad; ☎ 297-82-6099), which houses an even smaller historical museum in its tower. The festival is well worth an hour or so of your time. The folkloric dancing and music will give you a feel for Aruba's warm-hearted people and their culture. The event is joyous and homespun, perfect for families, and only $3 per person. Skip the museum, though: The faded labeling is all in Dutch.

Sizing Up the Shopping Scene

Aruba's tiny capital, Oranjestad, is a great place to stroll. Even better is the fact that its chief shopping strip, **Caya G. F. Betico Croes,** provides a whole afternoon's worth of browsing. Dutch porcelain, Dutch cheese, hand-embroidered linens, and skin creams made from the native aloe vera plant are all good buys and dutyfree.

The high-end shops are tucked into **Royal Plaza Mall,** a colorful building designed in traditional Dutch architecture, rendering it as pretty as a wedding cake. You can find some cool shops across the street at the 90-shop **Seaport Village Mall** and the 60-shop **Seaport Marketplace.** The local market is right on the waterfront, too, but there's not much to it.

Because Aruba is so close to Central and South America, those with slightly offbeat tastes like us can find unique items in the boutiques. We found a store that was selling gorgeous long *parreos* (used as wraps over swimwear) for $8 to $12 each. At home, they'd cost at least four times that amount. Echo also bought a faux tortoise-shell bag for $15 (real tortoise-shell products cannot be brought back into the United States) and a Panamanian straw hat for $18 that still win compliments every time she uses them.

Living It Up after the Sun Goes Down: Aruban Nightlife

Feeling lucky? Almost every major Aruban hotel (11 at last count) comes with a casino attached. Most offer blackjack, poker, craps, roulette, baccarat, slot machines, and an island original called Caribbean Stud Poker, invented in 1988. This high-stakes game is like blackjack but tempts players with a progressive jackpot.

The **Sonesta's Crystal Casino** (Sonesta Resort, Oranjestad) stays open all day and all night. We like it because it draws a more upscale crowd and is centrally located in downtown. It's also handy to the discos, in case we tire of blackjack. We recommend dining at **L'Escale** (see Chapter 10 for our review) in the Sonesta before you start gaming. Then wind up the evening at whichever disco is the rage at the moment.

The other casinos worth checking out are the **Alhambra Bazaar** (across from the Aruba Beach Club) and the **Royal Cabana Casino** (adjacent to La Cabana All-Suites Beach Resort & Casino). The latter is the Caribbean's largest casino, and though it's not as upscale as Sonesta's, you still won't find diehards forlornly pumping quarters into the slots like they do in Atlantic City. The Royal Cabana Casino's big claim to fame is the **Tropicana Showroom,** which has the island's longest running show, the Jewel Box Revue, featuring a group of female impersonators.

Aruba's club scene is also worth exploring. Go late — the Latin influence means the action doesn't even get started until around 11 p.m. — and dress in your best resort wear. The South Americans, especially, deck to the nines.

At press time, there were several hip joints to hit. **The Cellar** (☎ 297-82-8567), one block behind the Sonesta and located between two Benetton shops, is a trendy downtown pub that alternates between a live band and a DJ. **Mambo Jambo** (☎ 297-83-3632) in the Royal Plaza Mall is a funky Caribbean hangout that attracts locals and tourists. **La Fiesta** (☎ 297-83-5896) in the Aventura Mall is a casually hip place to dance or just be seen. **Club** (Weststraat 5; ☎ 297-93-6784) is a techno-chic inspired nightclub that has a spectacular house band playing a mix of musical styles. **Carlos 'N Charlies** (Weststraat; ☎ 297-82-0355) plays a heady mix of Latin American hits and U.S. disco favorites. But when in doubt, ask your concierge to steer you. Arubans have one thing in common with New Yorkers: They're fickle when it comes to the club scene.

Tripping Away for the Day

Although Aruba's tourism-centered attitude and offerings attract lots of attention, two nearby islands, Curaçao and Bonaire, are well worth visiting.

Seeing the colors of Curaçao

As long as you've come this far, reserve at least a day to visit Aruba's next-door-neighbor Curaçao, which boasts a colorful, postcard-perfect Colonial city along this hemisphere's deepest natural harbor.

Curaçao has many of Aruba's attributes (casinos, great restaurants, friendly people, good beaches, and good diving) as well as the prettiest city in the Caribbean with the exception of Old San Juan, which we give a whisper of an edge. Thanks to **Willemstad,** its Dutch colonial capital, which looks like a mini-Amsterdam, Curaçao recently joined such sites as the Great Wall of China and the Pyramids as a UNESCO World Heritage Site.

Curaçao also boasts the Caribbean's best aquarium, the **Curaçao Sea Aquarium** (Bapor Kibra; ☎ **599-9-461-6666;** fax 599-9-461-3671; Internet seaquarm@cura.net). The aquarium is open daily from 8:30 a.m. to 5:30 p.m. Admission is $13 for adults and $7.25 for children. Fees for the "Animal Encounters" are $57.75 for divers and $28.88 for snorkelers, but you must reserve space for these activities 24 hours in advance. Admission also gives you access to the excellent beach for the day, which features a procession of beach bars, watersports providers, and shops.

The absolute don't-miss attraction is the riveting and heartrending **Museum Kurá Hulanda** (Klipstraat 9; ☎ 599-9-462-1400; fax 599-9-462-1401; Internet www.kurahulanda.com). Open seven days from 10 a.m. to 5 p.m., admission is $6 for adults and $3 for children. The museum opened in 1999 and is named with the Papiament phrase for "Dutch courtyard." The largest and most dramatic museum chronicling the history of slavery in the Caribbean is on the site of the former Kurá Hulanda Wharf, once the most notorious slave yard in this region. The museum displays artifacts of the transatlantic slave trade dating from 1441 to 1863 as well as reconstructions and artifacts from empires of Ancient Ghana, Mali, and Songhay dating from 500 B.C. "Black by White" is a collection of more than 200 prints from France and Germany dating from 1880–1950 that depict prejudice against Africans.

De Palm Tours (L .G. Smith Blvd. 142; ☎ **297-82-4400**) offers round-trip airfare, lunch, sightseeing, and shopping on Curaçao for $235 for adults and $150 for kids 11 and under, departing every Friday at 7 a.m. and returning to Aruba at 9 p.m. The sightseeing tour on Curaçao is offered by **Taber Tours;** for more information contact Marcial Garcia at ☎ **599-9-737-6637;** e-mail Tabertrs@cura.net.

Wix Representations (P.O. Box 4207, Noord, Aruba; ☎ **297-82-0347** or 297-82-0357; fax 297-82-0307; e-mail wixtours@setarnet.aw) offers a day tour to Curaçao on Wednesdays that departs at 7 a.m. and returns about 6 p.m. The price, which includes transfers, airfare, island tour, shopping, and lunch, is $225 for adults, $185 for kids 11 and under.

For more information, contact the **Curaçao Tourist Development Bureau** (☎ **800-270-3350**) or the **Visitor Information Desk of the Curaçao Tourism Development Bureau** (☎ **599-9-461-6000** on the island or 212-683-7660 from the U.S.; fax 212-683-9337; Internet www.curacao-tourism.com).

Taking in the beauty of Bonaire

Bonaire is one of our favorite Caribbean destinations. The island is ringed by some of the Caribbean's most pristine coral reefs, thanks to conservation efforts launched a full decade before most other islands even thought about it.

Tiny Bonaire primarily attracts divers and avid snorkelers who love the easy shore diving available night and day from many sites. An especially neat dive site is located in the mangrove swamps, where you can see baby barracuda and other marine life young hiding out.

Bonaire has none of Aruba's frenetic nightlife. After long days of diving, nobody goes out partying. But if you want a few days of the Caribbean's best scuba diving, reserve part of your vacation for Bonaire. (We like the Cayman Islands, too, but for us the lack of crowds and easy shore dives make Bonaire irresistible.) Be sure to plan this side trip in the middle of your vacation, because you can't fly home within 24 hours of diving.

For information on Bonaire, call ☎ **800-BONAIRE** from the United States, or contact **Tourism Corporation Bonaire** at Kaya Lib. Simon Bolivar #12, Kralendijk, Bonaire, Netherlands Antilles; ☎ **599-717-8322**; fax 599-7-8408; e-mail tcbinfo@bonairelive.com; Internet www.infobonaire.com. If you want to make a side trip from Aruba, contact **Air ALM** (☎ **800-327-7230**). A round-trip ticket between Aruba and Bonaire should run about $100.

Part IV
Barbados

"You and your big idea to vacation at one of the lesser
known Caribbean islands! Whoever heard of St. Bronx anyway?"

In this part . . .

Before you pack your bags and head off for some royal treatment on Barbados, check out our recommendations for the best among a wide array of accommodations. We give you tips for arriving at your destination and for setting out to see the island's landscape.

On an island where food is an art form, you want to make the best of your dining experiences; our recommendations guide you to some prime choices. Finally, we show you how to live it up while the sun shines — and after it sets — with a guide to the best activities Barbados has to offer.

Chapter 12

The Lowdown on Barbados's Hotel Scene

*B*arbados's range of accommodations can't be beat. The island is home to some of the Caribbean's most over-the-top resorts, places that are luxurious to the point of absurdity. The ultra-exclusive **Sandy Lane** (closed for renovations for three years at a cost in excess of $200 million) leaps to mind. The general manager claims that guests wanted slightly larger rooms and a spa, but we were there shortly before it was shut down and everything looked good to us. Island scuttlebutt had it that Sandy Lane's wealthy Irish owners were determined to secure a position as Barbados's most exclusive property — not an easy task. We'll see if they've succeeded when the new Sandy Lane is unveiled; at press time, the reopening was expected in 2001.

Barbados has villas, classy resorts, small boutique hotels, timeshares, and a handful of all-inclusives. But you won't find big familiar-name chains. The biggest operator on Barbados, with a total of 572 luxury rooms at five different resorts, is the **Elegant Hotels Group** (☎ 800-326-6898), which owns Colony Club, Crystal Cove, Coconut Creek, Tamarind Cove, and Turtle Beach Resort.

This island is not the place for romantic secluded retreats like you find on the British Virgin Islands or Jamaica. It's also not the place to find stunning structures; most hotels have less than 100 rooms and, with few exceptions, the architects who designed them didn't go for the cutting-edge look. Most resorts have relied instead on Barbados's beautiful beaches and lush gardens to enchant visitors.

Barbados can claim some of the region's more sophisticated and charming hoteliers. Many properties are exquisitely managed with a careful eye toward making guests feel welcome. One of our favorite hosts is Hamish Watson at **Cobblers Cove.** The affable Antigua-born Watson, who now calls Barbados home, genuinely makes you feel like you're the honored guest of an English country gentleman.

Figuring Out Where You Want to Stay

Barbados is developed, so don't expect to find a little gem tucked into the edge of jungle-like growth. Most of our recommendations are in fashionable **St. James, St. Peter,** or **St. Michael** parishes. (Parishes are like counties in the U.S.) All three are on Barbados's western shore, where Caribbean waters are calm. This area is nicknamed the **Gold Coast** — supposedly for the color of the sand, but we think it's because you need a bag of gold to pay your hotel bill. The resorts here tend to be self-contained. If you stay on the Gold Coast, don't expect to walk to a nearby restaurant; two-lane Highway 1 runs along the coast, and it's too busy to safely stroll for any distance.

Hotels on the south coast in **Christ Church** parish (near Bridgetown) tend to be a bit less pricey. If you like to restaurant-hop and enjoy nightlife, we recommend staying near here. A few of our picks are on the scenic Atlantic side where the waves crash against the shoreline. Villas, private homes, and condos are available south of Bridgetown, in the Hastings-Worthing area, and along the west coast in St. James and in St. Peter.

Many of the resorts, though on good beaches, are also near busy roads. If traffic noise bothers you, make sure you ask to be booked as close to the sea as possible. Unfortunately, some truck drivers on the island apparently find it great fun to merrily toot their horns as they roll by the hotels — especially in the wee hours of the morning.

Conserving Cash

Barbados boasts exclusive properties in demand among the old-money set as well as hotels that have tapped into the European and Canadian charter market. Because of this dual demand, rates fluctuate inexplicably, which can be maddening when you're trying to plan a special vacation without breaking the bank.

Truth be told, if you're on a budget, Barbados isn't the best choice, unless you go during the summer low season. Ask for a room price for an approximate time in the distant future, and a reservationist is likely to tell you crisply, "those rates haven't been set yet," or "the rate will depend on availability." Translation: We'll charge as much as we possibly can, depending on how business shakes out. Best to have several *exact* dates in mind before you call to extract a quote.

Barbados does have some bargains, but you have to hunt for them. Try small efficiency condos where you can whip up your own meals. Or pick from a dozen or so guesthouses where you'll be treated to Bajan hospitality and traditional Bajan cooking.

Many Barbados hotels insist that you take their meal plans if you visit in winter. We find this limiting, especially because Barbados is known for having great restaurants.

You're always better off with at least a week-long package. Barbados hotel prices are geared to the longer vacation times of Europeans, not the U.S. vacationers' habit of popping onto an island for three or four days. As a result, several per-night rates listed in this chapter may curl your hair — or even shock it into dreadlocks.

Cobblers Cove is one of only four hotels in the Caribbean on the list of Relais & Chateaux properties, which are recognized for their unique hospitality and food. But the small resort also has a generous dine-around plan that allows you to sample other top restaurants.

Two-bedroom villas near the beach start at $285 a night during the summer and double that price in winter. Most include maid service, and the owner or manager can arrange for a cook to make your meals. Several villas close in September and October. Rentals are available through Barbados realtors. Among the firms to contact are

- ✔ **Alleyne, Aguilar & Altman.** Derricks, St. James. ☎ **246-432-0840.** E-mail: altman@caribsurf.com. Internet: www.aaaltman.com.

- ✔ **Jennifer Alleyne Limited.** Molyneux Plantation. ☎ **246-432-1159.** E-mail: jalleyne@caribsurf.com.

- ✔ **Bajan Services Ltd.** Gibbs Beach, St. Peter. ☎ **246-422-2618.** E-mail: bajan@caribsurf.com. Internet: www.bajanservices.com.

- ✔ **John M. Bladon & Co., Ltd.** Hastings, Christ Church. ☎ **246-426-4640.**

- ✔ **Ronald Stoute & Sons Ltd.** Sam Lord's Castle, St. Philip. ☎ **246-423-6800.** E-mail: ronstoute@caribsurf.com.

The **Barbados Tourism Authority** (☎ **246-427-2623;** fax 246-426-4080) maintains a list of apartments and rates.

In April 1999, the **Barbados Super Saver Program** (☎ **246-228-4221**) debuted as a means to beef up business in the slower summer months. It includes round-trip air on American Airlines, Air Jamaica, or BWIA, transfers in Barbados, the first night free with a minimum five-night stay, and full breakfast daily. You also get an authentic "Bajan Meet-and-Mingle Meal Event" that includes a range of daily options: high tea at the **Sunbury Plantation House;** lunch or dinner at the **Rusty Pelican Restaurant** in downtown Bridgetown; *tapas* (hors d'oeuvres) at the classy **Waterfront Café;** dinner at the traditional fish fry in **Oistins;** and a buffet lunch and Bajan "lime" at the beachfront **Weisers on the Bay.** Guests also enjoy savings on car rentals and attractions. More than 20 hotels are participating in the program, including the Accra Beach Hotel & Resort, Sam Lord's Castle Resort, Silver Rock, and Treasure Beach.

During summer, rates drop dramatically at almost all properties, and some of the more upscale resorts open their gates to families. Always ask about land-air packages.

Between Barbados's hefty room tax and the 10% surcharge, expect your final hotel bill to jump by about 25% of the subtotal.

Barbados's Hotels

Accra Beach Hotel & Resort **7**
Almond Beach Village **1**
Atlantis Hotel **13**
Bougainvillea Beach Resort **11**
Casuarina Beach Club **9**
Cobblers Cove **2**
Coral Reef Club **5**
Divi Southwinds Beach Resort **10**

Glitter Bay **3**
Royal Pavilion **3**
Sandy Beach Island Resort **8**
Silver Rock Resort **12**
Tamarind Cove Hotel **6**
Time Out at The Gap **10**
Turtle Beach **9**

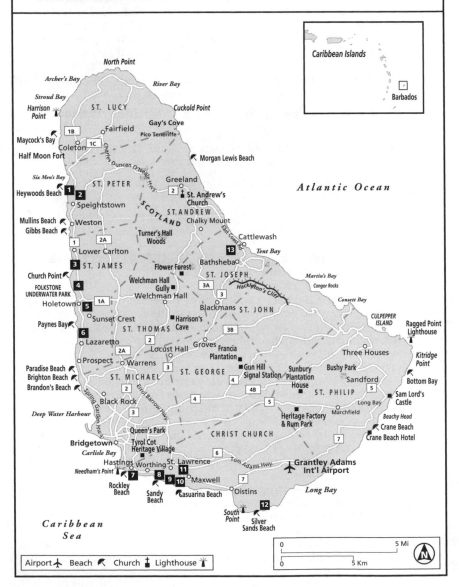

Barbados's Best Accommodations

The rack rates listed below are in U.S. dollars and are for a standard double room during high season (mid-December to mid-April), unless otherwise noted. Lower rates are often available during the off-season and shoulder season; see Chapter 2 for information on travel seasons.

Accra Beach Hotel & Resort

$$$ Rockley

Convenient to Bridgetown, this mid-range choice on the South Coast is good for families and those with disabilities. The four-story main building houses spacious rooms done in soothing pastels, and each has a balcony facing Accra Beach. Six duplex penthouse suites have ocean-view sitting rooms downstairs, refrigerators, and a spacious bedroom and huge bath with whirlpool upstairs. Each guestroom has a hair dryer. Between the hotel and its beach are a large clover-leaf-shaped pool, a snack bar, and a poolside bar. In the evening, some couples take a spin on the outdoor dance floor. Children under 12 stay free with a paying adult. A beauty salon, exercise room, squash court, and shops, including the boutique *Madison* (owned by the prime minister's wife), round out the facilities.

Hwy. 7 (Box 73W), Rockley, Christ Church, Barbados, W.I. ☎ *800-223-6510 or 246-435-8920. Fax: 246-435-6794. Internet:* www.funbarbados.com. *Rack rates: $165–$210. Meal plans available. AE, MC, V.*

Almond Beach Village

$$$$$ Heywoods

Set on a mile-long stretch of beach just north of Speightstown, this busy all-inclusive — Barbados's largest resort — is one of the island's best options for families and sports enthusiasts. Children's facilities are spacious and clean, and the Kid's Club staff is friendly to the kids.

The superior deluxe rooms or one-bedroom suites give needed extra room if you've got a big family. This is a good pick for those who like to settle into a resort and stay put. The **Family Entertainment Center** at the southern end of the sprawling, 32-acre complex is solely dedicated to families: 64 guest rooms, swimming pools, two playgrounds, a bandstand for live entertainment, and a restaurant with special selections for kids.

Rooms are in three-story buildings, and the resort is on a lovely beach. It has nine swimming pools (no, that's not a typo) and a good selection of watersports, as well as a nine-hole executive golf course, five lit tennis courts, and two squash courts.

One child under age 16 stays free when traveling with a paying single parent or two adults. All other children are charged at a rate of $50 per night per child. Almond Beach Village also has a dine-around program and provides round-trip transport to and from restaurants.

Couples looking for romance might want to try adults-only **Almond Beach Club & Spa** (Vaxhall, St. James; ☎ 800-425-6663 or 246-432-7840; fax 246-432-2115; Internet www.almondresorts.com). The 161-room hotel set on four tropical acres fronts the Caribbean and a powder-white sand beach dotted with palm and almond trees. The all-inclusive rates are $460 to $650 for a double in high season.

Heywoods, St. Peter, Barbados, W.I. ☎ 800-425-6663 or 246-422-4900. Fax: 246-422-0617. Internet: www.almondresorts.com. Rack rates: $570–$670. Rates are all-inclusive. AE, MC, V.

Atlantis Hotel

$ St. Joseph

You can lose your stress at The Atlantis, a quaint hotel on the craggy Atlantic coast overlooking **Tent Bay** and near popular surfer hangout **Bathsheba,** one of the more dramatic landmark vistas in the Caribbean. The Atlantis started as a modest family guesthouse and over decades has evolved into a small hotel. Fishermen often use the bay below the hotel. If you're looking for a tranquil spot, Atlantis is a good bet. You won't find TVs in the rooms; about the only thing to watch is the changing seascape from the few rooms with balconies. The Atlantis Hotel restaurant's daily Bajan buffet is a popular luncheon spot. Although it does have a beachfront, the water's too rough for swimming.

Tent Bay, Bathsheba, St. Joseph, Barbados, W.I. ☎ 246-433-9445. Rack rate: $75. AE.

Bougainvillea Beach Resort

$$$–$$$$$ Christ Church

This lovely beachfront resort — surrounded by lush gardens and towering palms on **Maxwell Beach** — offers a terrific value for families or for couples and friends vacationing together. You can rent a spacious time-share apartment in a four-story building by the week in high season or for a three-day minimum during off-season. The accommodations come with an in-room safe and daily maid service.

All units have a terrace or balcony with a beautiful water view or a view of the riotous gardens; three units have plunge pools. The resort has three pools; one is especially large and has a swim-up bar, and one is devoted to the kiddies. Kayaks, sunfish, boogie boards, and snorkeling gear are available for the asking. A car-rental desk and a restaurant are on-site, and several restaurants are within walking distance. A tennis court and exercise room round out the offerings.

This hotel participates in the Super Saver Program. (See the "Conserving Cash" section earlier in the chapter.)

Maxwell Coast Rd., Christ Church, Barbados, W.I. ☎ 800-223-6510, 800-988-6904, 800-742-4276, or 246-418-0990. Fax: 246-428-2524. E-mail: centralres@sunbeach. net. Internet: www.funbarbados.com. Rack Rates: $218–$480 studios and two-bedroom suites. AE, DC, MC, V. EP.

Casuarina Beach Club

$$$ St. Lawrence

Family owned and operated Casuarina Beach somehow manages to be an oasis of calm in the midst of the frenetic south coast — even though it's just four miles from Bridgetown and within walking distance of restaurants and nightlife. Casuarina is popular with families and package groups from Canada and the U.K. The Spanish-style, four-story hotel is comprised of a clutch of five buildings nestled in seven-and-a-half acres of lush tropical gardens, dotted with casuarina pines and coconut palms. Its oversized pool, perfect for doing laps, is among the accomodation's attributes. The 900-foot strand of white, powder-soft sand has plenty of inviting lounge chairs on hand for the tanning set. The hotel's restaurant and two bars are adjacent to it. The hotel also has tennis courts lit for night play and air-conditioned squash courts. All rooms and one- or two-bedroom suites have kitchenettes and large balconies. Scuba diving, golf, and other activities can be arranged. The hotel has a supervised children's playroom, and all facilities are wheelchair-accessible.

St. Lawrence Gap, Christ Church, Barbados, W.I. ☎ ***800-742-4276****, 800-223-9815, or 246-428-3600. Fax: 246-428-1970. E-mail:* casbeach@bajan.com. *Internet:* www.bajan.com. *Rack rates: $190–$205. AE, DISC, MC, V. EP, CP.*

Cobblers Cove

$$$$$ St. Peter

Built on the site of a former British fort, Cobblers Cove is adjacent to a small but pleasant crescent beach situated on a placid cove on Barbados's famed Gold Coast. This small resort, a favorite of gourmands and older European visitors, stands out as one of those comfortable places we could see ourselves returning to, year after year. It's the kind of location Kevin's grandmother — a gracious Southern grand dame who used to school him on manners "in case you dine with the Queen" — would have adored. Not quite splashy, but ripe with a cozy elegance.

Spacious suites, done up in classic English chintzes with touches of the Caribbean, are housed in two-story villas with louvered shutters that open onto a large patio or wooden balcony. Only bedrooms are air-conditioned. Suites have wide sitting areas, big bathrooms, wet bars with snacks, and kitchenettes. (Some are a bit too close to the busy highway; ask for suites 1 through 8, toward the sea.)

The centerpiece of the three-acre grounds is the pink-washed great house, which has two sun-drenched suites upstairs, the Camelot and the Colleton, each with plunge pools, king-size four-poster beds, fresh orchids, and island murals. Afternoon tea is served poolside near the clubby lounge/library. **The Terrace,** its excellent restaurant (see Chapter 14 for our review), helped snag the vaunted designation of Relais & Chateaux.

Guests get complimentary water-skiing, windsurfing, snorkeling, and sun-fish sailing (instruction included), as well as guaranteed tee times at the **Royal Westmoreland Golf Club.** A small workout room and a boutique have been added. From January to March, the atmosphere is primarily adults-only. Families will be happier at the Almond Beach Village, described earlier in this section.

Road View, Speightstown, St. Peter, Barbados, W.I. ☎ *800-890-6060 or 246-422-2291. Fax 246-422-1460. E-mail:* cobblers@caribsurf.com. *Internet:* www.barbados.org/hotels/cobblers.htm. *Rack rates: $600–$890 suite; $880–$990 Camelot/Colleton suites. For MAP (two meals daily) add $93 per person per night, including tax and service . AE, MC, V.*

Coral Reef Club

$$$$$ St. James

To give you an idea of the relaxing pace at this bastion of English elegance, afternoon tea time is about as rollicking as it gets at this small, family owned and managed resort. It has set the pace for Barbados's luxury resorts for four decades. Please don't get the idea that it's stuffy; nothing could be further from the truth. Public areas are strung along the sandy white beach adjacent to the calm, bath-like Caribbean, and small coral-stone cottages are scattered over 12 flower-filled acres. (Those farthest from the beach require a bit of a hike to the main house.)

Fresh flowers grace the spacious accommodations. Each room has a small patio and amenities such as radios and hair dryers. Junior suites have a sitting area and large private balcony or patio; cottage-style suites have an additional single bed and dressing room. We recommend splurging on the ultra-spacious luxury plantation suites, if your budget allows. Each has a private terrace and an open sundeck with a 9-x-9-foot pool.

 A beauty salon, masseuse, three tennis courts, exercise room, billiards, windsurfing, boating, and waterskiing are also available. The TV is available by request only and carries an extra charge. Guests on the Modified American Plan, which includes two full meals daily, have dining and golf privileges at Royal Westmoreland Golf Club. The adjacent Folkestone Marine Park is great for snorkelers. Another convenience is the free weekday shuttle into Bridgetown. No children under age 12 allowed.

Hwy. 1, Holetown, St. James, Barbados, W.I. ☎ *800-223-1108, 800-525-4800, or 246-422-2372. Fax: 246-422-1776. Rack rates: $540–$750 double or suite. AE, MC, V.*

Divi Southwinds Beach Resort

$$$–$$$$ St. Lawrence

This ultra-busy resort is for those who like being in the center of the action — it's steps from a sandy white beach in the heart of the restaurant district and Bajan nightlife in St. Lawrence Gap. The buildings on 20 lush acres are vanilla-plain, but it's the sort of place where you don't spend much time in the room anyway. The friendly staff goes out of its way to make sure that you're having fun. We favor taking one of the larger rooms, with a kitchenette and a balcony overlooking the gardens and pool. If you're a beach bunny, the trade-off for being right by the beach is taking a smaller, older room.

You have a choice of two restaurants, two bars, or cooking in your room. On-site you also find two pools, a beauty salon, a putting green, two lighted tennis courts, basketball, volleyball, a dive shop, and other shops. Watersports claim lots of attention.

St. Lawrence Gap, Christ Church, Barbados, W.I. ☎ *800-367-3484 or 246-428-7181. Fax: 246-428-4674. E-mail:* reserve@diviresorts.com. *Internet:* www. diviresorts.com. *Rack rates: $210–$255. AE, DC, MC, V.*

Glitter Bay

$$$$$ **Porters**

In the case of this classy resort, all that glitters is . . . everything — from the accommodating staff to the polished suites to the sparkling Caribbean. Guests won't notice the recent change in management to Fairmont Hotels & Resorts. In fact, this resort remains such a favorite with repeat guests that you have to book nearly a year in advance to get a room during high season. English shipping magnate Sir Edward Cunard built this Moorish-style stucco estate in the 1930s to resemble his palazzo in Venice. Now the great house serves as the reception area for this elegant resort amidst grand gardens that sweep to a half-mile long stretch of beach. You'll see guests waterskiing, swimming, snorkeling, and boating in the placid waters. Glitter Bay's beachside hotel restaurant deserves high marks for romance.

You can select from one- and two-bedroom suites as well as duplex penthouses. All have king-size or two twin beds, plus private balconies or terraces that are angled from the beach, so you're almost always guaranteed a view. Some have full kitchens, and all have in-room safes and mini-bars. We prefer the beach house, which contains five garden suites. The grounds feature two pools with a waterfall and footbridge.

Although Glitter Bay is more casual and family-oriented than its next-door neighbor, the Royal Pavilion, we still think that you can find better resorts on the island for children. These two sister resorts share facilities, including watersports and dining privileges. Guests enjoy privileges at **Royal Westmoreland Golf Club** (with complimentary transportation). A beauty salon, masseuse, two lighted tennis courts, exercise room, and shops are on-site.

Porters, St. James, Barbados, W.I. ☎ *800-223-1818 or 246-422-4111. Fax: 246-422-3940. Internet:* www.cphotels.ca. *Rack rates: $529–$1,199 suite. AE, DISC, DC, MC, V. EP, MAP.*

Royal Pavilion

$$$$$ Porters

This elegant Spanish mission–style resort, located next door to its sister resort (the more casual though still pricey Glitter Bay), is one of our favorites on Barbados. Like Glitter Bay, it stays almost fully booked in the winter months. The resort attracts a sophisticated clientele who want an idyllic respite with a little water fun tossed in.

The same landscape architect from Glitter Bay is responsible for Royal Pavilion's equally breathtaking grounds. Splashing fountains and riotous blossoms soothe the senses. Of the 75 suites here, 72 are oceanfront; the remaining three are ensconced in a two-story garden villa. Take one of the oceanfront, ground-floor suites (with cool marble floors and comfy king-size beds); you can walk ten steps to the sandy white beach.

Royal Pavillion shares amenities and a management company (Fairmont Hotels & Resorts) with Glitter Bay. Two lit tennis courts, nonmotorized watersports, 24-hour concierge, laundry, and limousine service are part of the eye-popping rates. Breakfast and lunch are served alfresco at the edge of the beach. Afternoon tea and dinner are in the Palm Terrace. **Royal Westmoreland Golf Club** is almost across the street. The welcome mat is yanked for children ages 12 and under. Housekeeping and the front desk could be snappier — especially at these prices.

Porters, St. James, Barbados, W.I. ☎ **800-223-1818** *or 246-422-4444. Fax: 246-422-3940. Internet:* www.cphotels.ca. *Rack rates: $679–$1,200 suite. AE, DISC, DC, MC, V.*

Sandy Beach Island Resort

$$ Worthing

One of Barbados's better values, this comfortable hotel on an excellent wide swath of beach boasts efficient and friendly staff members who want guests to have fun. The rooms — one- and two-bedroom suites with full kitchens and dining areas — sport tropical colors rather than the hotel bland palatte of many Barbados resorts. The hotel is a convenient walk to the good restaurants of St. Lawrence Gap, and the on-site **Beachfront Restaurant** serves a West Indian buffet Tuesday and Saturday nights. The hotel has a boardwalk gazebo, a roof garden, and a free-form pool with a poolside bar. The staff will help you arrange dive certification, deep sea fishing, harbor cruises, windsurfing, snorkeling, and catamaran sailing.

Worthing, Christ Church, Barbados, W.I. ☎ **800-742-4276,** *800-448-8355, 800-223-9815, 800-GO-BAJAN, or 246-435-8000. Fax: 246-435-8053. Internet:* www.funbarbados.com. *Rack rates: $130–$231. AE, DC, MC, V.*

Silver Rock Resort

$–$$$ Silver Sands

Ideal for professional windsurfers and adventure seekers, this beachfront hotel opened in January 2000. A range of beachfront, ocean-view, and garden-view accommodations are available. The hotel's open-air restaurant, **Jibboom,** serves tasty local and international dishes and has occasional theme nights.

Guests frequently take part in the Friday Night Street Party at nearby **Time Out at the Gap** (see the review later in this section). The resort has a noted windsurfing program led by world-champion windsurfer Brian Talma, and lessons are available. Other sports popular with the hard-bodies who populate this spot include scuba diving, snorkeling, boogie boards, surfing, hiking, beach volleyball, and sea kayaking. All guests receive reduced greens fees and preferential tee times at the newly opened **Barbados Golf Club,** the island's only public championship golf course.

Silver Sands, Christ Church, Barbados, W.I. ☎ *246-428-2866. Fax: 246-428-3687. E-mail:* silver@gemsbarbados.com. *Internet:* www.gemsbarbados.com. *Rack rates: $95–$250 double.*

Tamarind Cove Hotel

$$$$$ Paynes Bay

You'll think that you've taken a magic carpet ride when you encounter the Spanish Moorish architecture at Tamarind Cove. Its expansive courtyard is a visual feast with brilliantly hued bougainvillea. All 164 rooms have king-size beds, a mini-refrigerator, and a private balcony or patio facing the sea. Honeymoon suites have lavish extras such as private Jacuzzis or plunge pools. You get a smorgasbord of watersports, including water skiing, sailing, and snorkeling. And the resort has — we're not kidding — eight freshwater pools. Twice a week, Tamarind Cove hosts a candlelight dinner served directly on the hotel's magnificent stretch of white-sand beach. Set against the backdrop of waves gently breaking against the shore, enveloped by a night sky blanketed with stars, this five-course gourmet dinner is served to an intimate group of no more than 20 guests, so reserve early.

Paynes Bay, St. James, Barbados, W.I. ☎ *800-326-6898 or 246-432-1332. Fax: 246-432-6317. E-mail:* elegantna@earthlink.com. *Internet:* www.eleganthotels.com. *Rack rates: $456–822. AE, MC, V.*

Time Out at The Gap

$$ St. Lawrence Gap

This 76-room property is located opposite Dover Beach in the vibrant St. Lawrence Gap area and offers a casual, fun-filled environment near bike rentals, shops, bars, and nightclubs. The hotel's restaurant, the **Whistling Frog Sports Pub,** provides guests with pub-style dining and entertainment including billiards, darts, and a wide-screen TV for viewing sports events. It's also the setting of a Friday night party that has become quite an event. Flowers surround the hotel's free-form pool. All activities and sports can be organized through the **Out and About** shop, where an informative staff waits to assist guests with their plans. Cricket is among the unique activity choices at this place. The modest rooms have safety deposit boxes, kettles for tea, coffeemakers, irons/boards, and hair dryers.

St. Lawrence Gap, Christ Church, Barbados, W.I. ☎ *246-420-5021. Fax: 246-420-5034. E-mail:* Timeout@gemsbarbados.com. *Internet:* www.gemsbarbados.com. *Rack rates: $115–$150. AE, MC, V. EP.*

Turtle Beach

$$$$$ Christ Church

Set on a wide, 1,500-foot-long white strand of beach on the south coast, this three-story hotel opened in 1998 as the flagship of the Elegant Hotel Group. It gets its name from the sea turtles that occasionally nest on the beach — although based on our experience in the Caribbean, whenever a property lays claim to turtles, sightings quickly become a rarity. Nonetheless, this well-done, 166-suite all-inclusive is a good addition to the Barbados hotel scene. It's a good choice for the active types who love golf and the nightlife of Bridgetown, just 15 minutes away.

Included in the price, you get instruction and the equipment to participate in scuba diving, waterskiing, snorkeling, kayaking, sailing, and boogie boarding. Set in six acres of lush gardens, the hotel promises you ocean views from every suite. Tennis equipment is provided; golfers get special rates and times at **Royal Westmoreland Golf Club.** The **Kid's Club,** running daily from 9 a.m. to 9 p.m., offers games, activities, and equipment (including computers with Sega games and Internet access). Ask about the hotel's excellent children's packages, which let one child age 2 to 12 stay free in the off-season. (Additional children stay at 50% off the adult rate.)

Dover, Barbados, W.I. ☎ *800-326-6898 or 246-428-7131. Fax: 246-428-6089. Rack rates: $626–$742 suite. Rates are all-inclusive. AE, DC, MC, V.*

Chapter 13

Settling into Barbados

- -

In This Chapter

▶ Knowing what to expect when you arrive

▶ Getting around the island

▶ Discovering Barbados from A to Z

- -

Steeped in English tradition and a bit more straitlaced than some of its neighbors, Barbados has been giving the royal treatment to the wealthy and the famous for centuries. George Washington (and his younger brother) really did sleep here. You'll discover as soon as you arrive that this island knows how to provide a rich experience for visitors.

The British influence remains quite strong, in part because Barbados is the favorite island retreat of most Brits and the retirement choice of many. Most hotels serve afternoon tea, cricket is the national pastime, and patrons at some bars are as likely to order a Pimm's Cup as a rum and coke. *Bajans*, as islanders are known, partner British-style manners with a Caribbean friendliness and openness — a combination that makes travelers feel welcome and pampered.

Arriving in Barbados

This sophisticated island — which regularly hosts VIPs from the British royals to U.S. presidents, from the Rolling Stones to the Rockefellers — handles arriving guests with grace and aplomb. Expect the royal treatment from the moment you arrive, whether you're at the airport or the Barbados cruise ship terminal.

During high season when the Concorde whizzes in from New York, its streamlined, high-tech silhouette doesn't seem at all out of place at thoroughly modern **Grantley Adams International Airport,** located on the south coast about a half-hour drive from the capital of Bridgetown. You won't find crinkly, sun-bleached tourist posters taped to the walls at this immaculate airport; the surroundings are clean and orderly, and the personnel smiling and helpful.

We'd like to say that flying to this island is no sweat, but until airport renovations are complete, we concede that you might actually (gasp!) break a sweat because the arrival areas aren't yet air-conditioned. Expect that to change by 2005, when Barbados will have plunked down $70 million to ensure its airport is oh-so-right. In addition to adding air-conditioning to the customs, baggage claim, and departure lounge areas, a lot of those bucks will go to doubling the airport's dutyfree shopping area to more than 10,000 square feet.

Not to be outdone, the **Barbados Cruise Ship Terminal** was recently renovated to the tune of $6 million. Located on Bridgetown's waterfront, the terminal is now one of the Caribbean's finest.

 Going through passport control and customs is a snap. Expect a wait of five minutes or less. The neatly uniformed customs officials are crisply efficient and pleasant. If you're carrying valuables like expensive jewelry and camera equipment, don't forget to register those items with the customs officials as you're entering the country. Otherwise, you may find yourself paying an import duty on those items at the end of your stay.

The **Barbados Tourism Authority** operates welcome kiosks from 8 a.m. to 8 p.m. at both the airport and the cruise terminal (☎ **246-428-5570** and ☎ **246-426-1718,** respectively). And for those who arrive cash-poor, ATM machines are handily stationed at the kiosks.

About 500,000 people visit Barbados each year, and about half of them are cruise ship passengers. Bridgetown's **Deep Water Harbour** is on the northwest side of Carlisle Bay, and as many as eight cruise ships can dock simultaneously at its cruise ship terminal, whose interior features a faux island street scene with storefronts, brightly colored chattel houses, tropical flowers, benches, and push carts. Postal and banking facilities are also available at the terminal.

As soon as you clear customs and immigration, you can whip out your plastic. The port facility now has 18 dutyfree shops, 13 retailers, and dozens of vendors. You can also find car and bike rentals, a florist, dive shops, and a communications center with fax and telephones. Downtown Bridgetown is a half-mile (1 km) walk from the pier; a taxi costs about $3 each way.

Getting from the Airport to Your Hotel

 Presuming that your hotel knows your arrival time (make sure you provide that information when you make your reservations), a driver likely will be holding a sign (discreetly, of course) for you at baggage claim. Your resort will usually provide free transport from and to the airport. If you stay at one of the upscale resorts, the wheels sent to fetch you will be elegant. Rolls Royce or BMW, anyone?

Airport taxis aren't metered, but drivers don't gouge here. Taking advantage of visitors simply isn't done on this island.

A large sign at the airport announces the fixed rate for a taxi ride to each hotel or parish (district). You can readily pick out official taxis by the "Z" on their license plates. Rates are given in both Barbados and U.S. dollars: Count on about $28 to Speightstown, $20 to hotels on the west coast, and $10–$13 to south coast locations.

This island is a good one on which to rent a car (see the next section for more details). You can pick up your vehicle at the airport. At the same time, you need to purchase an international driver's license or Barbados driving permit, which you can pick up at a car rental kiosk or a police station for $5. Again, the rental process is a smooth one. Or if you prefer, you can request a driver with your car.

If you're doing your own driving, ask how to get to the Adams-Barrow-Cummins (ABC) Highway, which bypasses Bridgetown and saves you travel time to the west coast where most of the hotels are.

Getting Around Barbados

After you get to your hotel, you probably want to check out the island and its landscape. This section shares some sightseeing options.

By car

Our favorite way to explore Barbados is by car. The island has good (though narrow) roads, more than 800 miles of which are paved. The downside is that we have to remember to drive on the left, and most rental cars are tiny little putt-putts called *mini mokes*. Sounds like something that Austin Powers's Dr. Evil would drive. For a little more money, though, you can rent a four-wheel-drive Jeep or a convertible, which is more our speed.

To rent a car you must have an international driver's license or Barbados driving permit, obtainable at the airport, police stations, and car-rental firms for $5 with a valid driver's license.

Oddly, none of the familiar major firms offer rentals on this island, but you'll find about 30 local agencies that rent cars, jeeps, or small open-air vehicles for $50 to $90 a day (or $250 to $325 a week), depending on the vehicle and whether it has air-conditioning. (We don't think air-conditioning is necessary, but consult Chapter 2 for information on the temperature at the time you'll be visiting to see if you'd prefer to keep cool.) The rental generally includes insurance. Rental companies provide pickup and delivery service, offer unlimited mileage, and accept major credit cards. Free carseats are usually available upon request.

Gas costs about 75¢ per liter (approximately $2.75 per gallon). You can find gas stations in Bridgetown, on the main highways along the west and south coasts, and in most inland parishes. Although times vary, most stations are open daily with hours that extend into the evening; some are open 24 hours a day.

Rental agencies include the following:

- ✔ **Coconut Car Rentals.** St. Michael; ☎ **246-437-0297.**
- ✔ **Corbins Car Rentals.** St. Michael; ☎ **246-427-9531,** 246-426-8336, or 246-426-8336.
- ✔ **Courtesy Rent-A-Car.** Grantley Adams International Airport; ☎ **246-431-4160.**
- ✔ **Drive-a-Matic.** St. James; ☎ **246-422-4000.**
- ✔ **National Car Rental.** Bush Hall, St. Michael; ☎ **246-426-0603.**
- ✔ **P&S Car Rentals.** St. Michael; ☎ **246-424-2052.**
- ✔ **Sunny Isle Motors.** Worthing; ☎ **246-435-7979.**
- ✔ **Sunset Crest Rentals.** St. James; ☎ **246-432-2222.**

Take time to study a map. Otherwise, you might whiz past small signs tacked to poles at intersections that point you to most attractions. Fields and fields of tall sugar cane often obstruct views, too.

The good news: Even remote roads are in fairly good repair, though you may find potholes. Roads aren't well-lit, and they're so narrow that they make you feel like you need to suck in your breath as you pass within a whisper of oncoming cars. So we recommend starting out early in the day and trying to be home before dark.

Don't let the gorgeous scenery distract you from the road. Pedestrians and the occasional sheep often stroll into the roadway. Approach "roundabouts" (traffic circles) with caution. When someone flashes headlights at you at an intersection, it means "you first."

The speed limit, in keeping with the pace of life and the narrow roads, is 60 km/h (roughly 37 mph) on the highway, 50 km/h (about 30 mph) in the country, and 30 km/h (20 mph) in town. Remember that kilometers per hour are the norm here; a shift in mental gears can keep you out of trouble if you're accustomed to miles per hour.

In Bridgetown, parking can be difficult. Never turn your car over to a local who offers to find you a parking space for a small finder's fee. Tourists who have done so often find out the hard way that the space was illegal, which makes them the target of a ticket. Bridgetown's rush hour runs from 7:30 to 8:30 a.m. and 4:30 to 5:30 p.m.

By bus

Taking a bus in the Caribbean is not something we usually recommend, but Barbados is an exception among the islands. If you don't want to rent a car, you can explore this island easily and cheaply by relying on a bus.

Buses (☎ **246-436-6820**) are efficient, inexpensive, and plentiful. The fare is 75¢ for any one destination. Public buses require exact change. Private coaches expect correct fare but are more flexible when it comes to making change. Blue buses with a yellow stripe are public; yellow buses with a blue stripe are private. Vans, white with a burgundy stripe, are also private. Just take whichever one comes along first, public or private; they are all equally nice.

Buses depart from Bridgetown several times a day between 6 a.m. and midnight. All travel about every 20 minutes along Highway 1 (St. James Road) and Highway 7 (South Coast Main Road), as well as inland routes, and are usually packed. Small signs posted on roadside poles — saying TO CITY or OUT OF CITY, meaning the direction relative to Bridgetown — indicate the bus stops.

Flag down the bus with your hand, even if you're standing at the stop; drivers don't always stop automatically.

By taxi

Taxis aren't metered but operate according to fixed rates set by the government. They carry up to four passengers, and the fare may be shared. For short trips, the rate per mile should not exceed $1.50.

Taxi drivers are courteous and knowledgeable, and most will narrate a tour at a fixed hourly rate of $17.50 for up to three people. Be sure to settle the rate before you start off and agree on whether the payment will be in U.S. or Barbados dollars.

On a guided tour

A half- or full-day tour is a good way to get your bearings. Your hotel concierge can arrange the trip for you. An average full-day tour (five to six hours) costs about $30 to $50 per person and includes lunch and admissions to tour stops.

Family-run **Bajan Tours,** Gleayre, Locust Hall, St. George (☎ **246-437-9389**) offers eight different coach or minivan tours, including cultural, historic, ecological, and general sightseeing routings. The full-day tours include a Bajan buffet lunch at Bonita Beach Bar in Bathsheba. Prices are $40 for half-day and $56 for full-day tours (children half-price).

Sally Sheara operates **VIP Tour Services,** Hillcrest Villa, Upton, St. Michael (☎ **246-429-4617**). She drives you around in her plush, air-conditioned Mercedes-Benz and charges $160 for a 4-hour tour for four people. Additional time is billed at $40 per hour. Your choice of tours (coastal, inland, cultural, naturalist, architectural, or customized) includes stops along the way for refreshments.

L. E. Williams Tour Co. (☎ 246-427-1043) offers a 6½-hour island tour for about $50 per person. A bus picks you up between 8:30 and 9:30 a.m. and hits the highlights, including Bridgetown, the St. James beach area, and Sam Lord's Castle. You have beverages along the way, and the tours culminate with a West Indian lunch at the Atlantis Hotel in Bathsheba.

By scooter or bicycle

Scooters or bikes are a viable option for more adventurous travelers on this lush island. The roads are better than most Caribbean islands without being too challenging, and the motorists are generally subdued — especially compared with Jamaica or St. Lucia.

The rub? Finding a rental agency. Most outfits decided to close their businesses because of dwindling profits. You can call the tourist office at ☎ 246-427-2623 to gauge availability of two-wheelers.

By helicopter

Bajan Helicopters (☎ 246-431-0069) at the Bridgetown Heliport offers an eagle's-eye view of Barbados. The price per person ranges from $65 for a 20- to 25-minute "Discover Barbados" flightseeing tour to $115 for a 30- to 35-minute full "Island Tour" that makes a full circuit of the coastline.

Quick Concierge

ATMs

About 50 automated teller machines (ATMs) are available 24 hours a day at bank branches, transportation centers, shopping centers, and other convenient spots throughout the island. ATMs dispense Barbados dollars, of course.

Baby-sitters

Expect to pay $5–$15 an hour, depending on the ages and number of children. Contact your hotel for recommendations.

Banks

Major banks are the following: **Barbados National Bank** (☎ 246-431-5700); **Barclays Bank** (☎ 246-431-5151); **the Bank of Nova Scotia** (☎ 246- 431-3000); **Canadian Imperial Bank of Commerce** (☎ 246-426-0571); and **Royal Bank of Canada** (☎ 246-431-6700). All have main offices on Broad Street in Bridgetown, plus branches in Speightstown, Holetown, and various towns along the south coast. The Barbados National Bank has a branch at the airport, and Canadian Imperial Bank of Commerce has a branch at the cruise ship terminal.

Business Hours

Bridgetown offices and stores are open week-days 8:30 a.m. to 5 p.m. and Saturdays 8:30 a.m. to 1 p.m. Out-of-town locations may stay open later. Some supermarkets are open daily 8 a.m. to 6 p.m. or later. Banks are open Monday to Thursday from 8 a.m. to 3 p.m. and Friday 8 a.m. to 5 p.m.

At the airport, the Barbados National Bank is open from 8 a.m. until the last plane leaves or arrives, seven days a week, even on holidays.

Credit Cards

Major credit cards and traveler's checks are widely accepted.

Currency Exchange

At press time, the Barbados dollar (Bds$1) was tied to the U.S. dollar at the rate of Bds$1.98 to US$1. U.S. dollars are readily accepted. Be sure that you know which currency you're dealing in when making a purchase. British pounds are not accepted; the currency exchange rate fluctuates daily and is posted at banks or online at www.xe.net/ucc/.

Departure Tax

At the airport, before leaving Barbados, each passenger must pay a departure tax of $12.50 (Bds$25), payable in either currency; children 12 and under are exempt.

Doctors/Dentists

Your hotel might have a list of doctors on call. The most often recommended are Dr. J.D. Gibling (☎ 246-432-1772) or Dr. Ahmed Mohamad (☎ 246-424-8236), both of whom pay house calls to patients unable or unwilling to leave their hotel rooms. Dr. Derek Golding (Beckwith Shopping Mall, Bridgetown ☎ 246-426-3001) maintains a busy dental practice on Barbados. Everyone on his dental team received training in the United States, Britain, Canada, or New Zealand, and his practice is often open late for emergencies.

Electricity

Electric current on Barbados is 110 volts/50 cycles, U.S. standard. Hotels generally have adapters/transformers for use by travelers from countries that operate on 220-volt current.

Emergencies

In an emergency, call ☎ 211. For an ambulance, call ☎ 511; in case of fire, call ☎ 311. To report a scuba diving accident, call **Divers' Alert Network** (DAN) at ☎ 246-684-8111 or 246-684-2948. The island also has a 24-hour hyperbaric chamber (Coast Guard Defence Force, St. Ann's Fort, Garrison, St. Michael; ☎ 246-427-8819; for nonemergencies, 246-436-6185).

Hospitals

If an accident or injury requires a hospital visit, you can choose from two facilities on Barbados: **Bayview Hospital,** St. Paul's Ave., Bayville, St. Michael (☎ 246-436-5446) or **Queen Elizabeth Hospital,** Martindales Rd., St. Michael (☎ 246-436-6450).

Information

The **Barbados Tourism Authority** is on Harbour Road in Bridgetown (☎ 246-427-2623; fax 246-426-4080). Hours are 8:30 a.m. to 4:30 p.m. weekdays. Prior to your visit, contact the office of the Barbados Tourism Authority at 800 Second Avenue, 2nd Floor, New York, NY 10017 (☎ 800-221-9831; e-mail btany@ barbados.org; Internet www.barbdos. org).

Language

The Queen's English is the official language and is spoken by everyone, everywhere. An amazing 98% literacy rate is a sign of the island's sophistication. The Bajan dialect is based on Afro-Caribbean rhythms tinged with an Irish or Scottish lilt.

Maps

You can pick up a free guide just about any-where you travel across the island.

Pharmacies

We recommend **Collins Pharmacy,** Broad Street, Bridgetown (☎ 246-426-4515), open from 8 a.m. to 5 p.m.

Police

In an emergency, call ☎ **211;** otherwise call ☎ 246-430-7100.

Post Office

An airmail letter (the only direct travel method) from Barbados to the United States or Canada costs Bds$1.15 per half ounce; an airmail postcard costs Bds45¢. Letters to the United Kingdom cost Bds$1.40; postcards, Bds70¢. The main post office, in Cheapside,

Bridgetown, is open weekdays 7:30 a.m. to 5 p.m.; the Sherbourne Conference Center branch is open weekdays 8:15 a.m. to 4:30 p.m.; branches in each parish are open weekdays 8 a.m. to 3:15 p.m.

Safety

Although crime is not a major problem on Barbados, the U.S. State Department has reported an increase in crimes such as purse snatching, pickpocketing, armed robbery, and even sexual assault on women. Although this island is generally wealthy, poverty does exist here. Take normal precautions: Don't leave cash or valuables in your hotel room, beware of purse snatchers when walking, exercise caution when walking on the beach or visiting tourist attractions, and be wary of driving in isolated areas of Barbados.

When swimming, avoid stepping on black sea urchins (locally called "cobblers"), which have needle-sharp spines. They won't kill you, but their sting hurts terribly and will make you feel like you have the flu.

Beware of the little green apples that fall from the *manchineel* tree — they may look tempting, but they are poisonous to eat and toxic to the touch. Even taking shelter under the tree when it rains can give you blisters. Most manchineels are identified with signs. If you do come in contact with one, immediately wash your skin off with water, go to the nearest hotel, and have someone there phone for a physician.

Taxes

A 7.5% government tax is added to all hotel bills. A 15% VAT (value-added tax) is imposed on restaurant meals, admissions to attractions, and merchandise sales (other than dutyfree). Prices are often tax-inclusive; if not, the VAT will be added to your bill.

Telephone

Direct-dialing to the U.S., Canada, and other countries is efficient, and the cost is reasonable, but always check with your hotel to see if a surcharge awaits on the final bill. To charge your overseas call on a major credit card without incurring a surcharge, dial ☎ 800-744-2000 from any phone.

All local calls are free if placed from private telephones. From pay phones, the charge is Bds25¢ for five minutes. Prepaid phone cards, which can be used in pay phones throughout Barbados and other Caribbean islands, are sold at shops, tourist attractions, transportation centers, and other convenient outlets. For **MCI** dial ☎ 800-888-8000, for **Sprint** ☎ 800-877-4646, and for **AT&T** ☎ 800-872-2881.

Time Zone

Barbados operates on Atlantic Standard Time year-round (same as Eastern Daylight Time).

Tipping

A 10% service charge is usually added to hotel bills and restaurant checks in lieu of tipping. You can tip beyond the service charge to recognize extraordinary service. If no service charge is added, tip waiters 10%–15% and maids $1 per room per day. Tip bellhops and airport porters $1 per bag. Taxi drivers expect a 10% tip.

Water

The water on the island is plentiful and pure. It is naturally filtered through 1,000 feet of pervious coral and safe to drink from the tap.

Weather Reports

Call ☎ 246-976-2376 for current conditions.

Chapter 14

Dining in Barbados

• •

In This Chapter

▶ Sampling the local cuisine

▶ Saving money on meals

▶ Locating the island's best restaurants

• •

*B*arbados was often the first stop for ships carrying goods either from Europe or South America, so Bajans are used to having first pick of the bounty flowing into and out of the Caribbean. As a result, dining on this sophisticated island has been elevated to a fine art.

Want proof of Barbados's status in the world of cuisine? Recently, *Food & Wine,* American Express, and *Travel & Leisure* sponsored a chef exchange that saw some of New York's chic chefs trading aprons with chefs from the Barbados establishments **Coral Reef Club, Turtle Beach,** and **Carambola.** Also, many of the zippy young chefs coming out of London to make a name in the food world come to the Caribbean — chiefly Barbados and the British Virgin Islands — to hone their talents. Gone are the days when English pub grub was about the most exciting thing coming out of the United Kingdom. These chefs, often trained in France and at the finest English country estates, design experimental and fun menus.

In this chapter, we give you a heads up about what tastes you can expect to experience on Barbados, and we list our favorite restaurants to make your dining decisions easier.

Enjoying a Taste of Barbados

Interestingly enough, there's a strong culinary connection between Barbados and South Carolina, so if you're familiar with Low Country cooking, you'll have a good handle on the native cuisine of Barbados. Of course, catches from the Atlantic and Caribbean figure heavily into the menus here. Flying fish, the national bird — oops, we mean fish — leaps onto menus all over the island. Sides of rice and peas are important, as are spicy stews. Desserts are often made using fresh fruit.

Most restaurants here offer a strong taste of local flavor, even franchises like KFC. Would you believe that a side order of the Colonel's mashed potatoes here are really sweet potatoes spiked with local herbs? Even more shocking, they're stuffed into pig intestines and served with *souse* (pig's feet marinated in lime juice).

Pack your tiara and your jacket and tie for dining out on this island. On Barbados, you'll likely have the urge to dine at some swank spot at least once, and dressing up is the way it's done here. Shorts generally elicit raised eyebrows (at the least) in the evenings.

Following British custom, the waiters on this island do not bring your final bill until you signal that you're ready for it.

Barbados's Best Restaurants

Angry Annie's

$$ Holetown   Local/International

Trust us, you can't miss this place, operated by Annie and Paul Matthews from the United Kingdom. It's decorated inside and out in dayglow Caribbean pinks, blues, greens, and yellows. If the colors don't lift your spirits, you'll jump for joy with the barbecued "jump-up" ribs and chicken, spicy curries, grilled fresh fish or juicy steaks, and vegetarian favorite "Rasta pasta." Eat inside on gaily colored furniture, or — as we prefer — eat outside under the stars.

First Street, Holetown, St. James. ☎ *246-432-2119. Reservations required. Main courses: $8–$16. AE, DC, MC, V. Open for dinner from 6 p.m. to 10 p.m.*

Atlantis Hotel

$ Bathsheba   Local/Bajan

For stunning views of the crashing Atlantic surf and a great introduction to Bajan cuisine in one fell swoop — and we aren't just talking flying fish — Atlantis's Sunday spread can't be beat. Just don't get lost and show up late, or you'll lose your spot.

Sample local favorites like fried flying fish, pumpkin fritters, spinach cake, pickled breadfruit, pepper-pot stew, and okra and eggplant. Homemade coconut pie tops the dessert list.

St. Joseph. ☎ *246-433-9445. Reservations required for the Sunday buffet and the 7 p.m. dinner; reservations recommended at all other times. Main courses: Fixed-price lunch $12.50; fixed-price dinner $15.75; Sunday buffet $18.75. AE. Open for lunch daily from 11:30 a.m. to 3 p.m.; dinner daily after 7 p.m.*

Barbados's Restaurants

Angry Annie's **3**	Nico's Champagne Wine Bar
Atlantis Hotel **10**	& Restaurant **5**
Bellini's Trattoria **8**	Olives Bar & Bistro **3**
Bonito Beach Bar & Restaurant **10**	Pisces **8**
Brown Sugar **7**	Ragamuffins **3**
Carambola **4**	T.G.I. Boomers **8**
David's Place **8**	The Bagatelle Great House **9**
Edgewater Inn **10**	The Cliff **6**
Ile de France **3**	The Emerald Palm **2**
Luigi's Restaurant **8**	The Ship Inn **8**
Mango's by the Sea **1**	Waterfront Café **7**

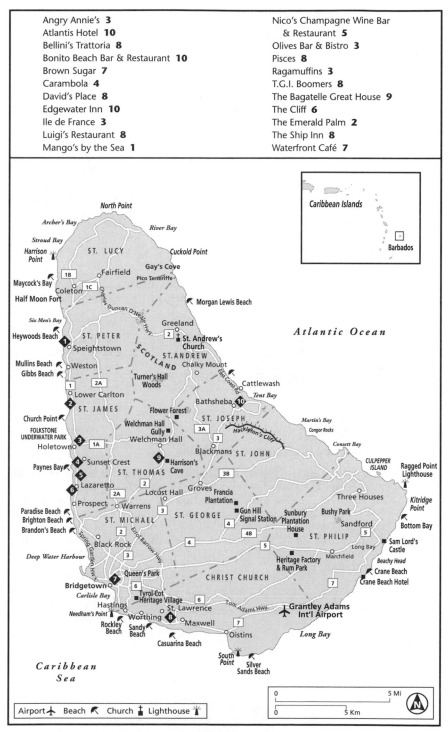

The Bagatelle Great House

$$$ St. Thomas   French/Caribbean

This restored coral-stone plantation house was built circa 1645 and is named for a 19th-century poker game, during which the property's owner staked his house. "A mere bagatelle," he shrugged, upon losing the bet.

Now both *Gourmet* and *Bon Appetit* hail this sylvan retreat as one of the island's finest and most elegant choices for French cuisine with a Caribbean flair. Candles and lanterns illuminate the dramatic archways and the ancient trees, accenting the charm of the original buildings. The service is the best we've found on Barbados.

Try the homemade duck-liver pate, deviled Caribbean crab backs, or smoked flying-fish mousse with horseradish mayonnaise. The beef Wellington Bagatelle-style is a favorite, as is the crisp roast duckling with an orange-and-brandy sauce. The local catch of the day can be prepared grilled, barbecued, or in the style of Baxters Road (that is, highly seasoned and sauteed in deep oil). A different list of homemade desserts is featured nightly. Sunday night is "Lobster Night," and during the day the international buffet is a can't-miss.

The garden terrace offers intimacy with tables for two. Upstairs, reached by an impressive double palladian staircase, are a gallery of Caribbean art, a crafts showroom, and a gift shop.

Hwy. 2A, St. Thomas. (Cut inland near Paynes Bay north of Bridgetown, three miles from both Sunset Crest and the Sandy Lane Hotel.) ☎ *246-421-6767. E-mail:* gourmand@sunbeach.net. *Internet:* www.dinebarbados.com. *Reservations required. Fixed-price dinner $45. MC, V. Open for dinner Tuesday through Sunday from 7 p.m.*

Bellini's Trattoria

$$ St. Lawrence Gap   Northern Italian

Soft Italian music and waves gently lapping beneath the Mediterranean-style veranda set the stage for informal yet romantic dining. The cuisine is classic Northern Italian with a contemporary flair. Toast the evening with a Bellini cocktail (iced champagne with a splash of fruit nectar), and start your meal with antipasto, a small gourmet pizza, or a tasty homemade pasta. Move on to the signature shrimp, veal, steak, or seafood dishes, beautifully accented with fresh herbs. How else to finish it off but with the excellent tiramisu?

Little Bay Hotel, St. Lawrence Gap, Christ Church. ☎ *246-435-7246. Fax: 246-435-8574. Main courses: $12–$23. AE, DC, MC, V. Open for dinner from 6 p.m. to 10:30 p.m.*

Bonito Beach Bar & Restaurant

$ St. Joseph   Bajan/International

When you tour the rugged east coast, plan to stop here for a lunch of Mrs. Enid Worrell's wholesome West Indian home-cooking. The view of the Atlantic from the bright and breezy second-floor dining room is the most striking aspect of the otherwise plain-Jane decor. The Bajan buffet lunch includes fried fish and baked chicken, accompanied by a selection of vegetables and salads fresh from the family garden. If your timing is right, Mrs. Worrell might have homemade cheesecake for dessert. Be sure to try the fresh fruit punch — with or without rum.

Coast Road, Bathsheba, St. Joseph. ☎ 246-433-9034. Main courses: $8–$16. No credit cards. Open from 10 a.m. to 6 p.m. daily.

Brown Sugar

$$–$$$ Bridgetown   Bajan

Hidden behind lush foliage, Brown Sugar is an alfresco restaurant in a turn-of-the-century Barbadian bungalow. Slow-turning fans hang from a latticed ceiling, and soft candlelight bathes the hanging ferns on the open veranda. Cascading water gardens add to the tranquility of this spot, across from the Grand Barbados Beach Resort. From noon to 2:30, local businesspeople come for the three-course Planter's Buffet Luncheon — featuring dishes such as cou-cou and pepper-pot stew. A grand buffet lunch is served on Sunday ($20). Conch fritters and garlic pork are especially spicy options. Dinner entrees include local black-bellied lamb and creole orange chicken. For dessert, we recommend the Bajan bread pudding with rum sauce, but other homemade treats on hand include angel food chocolate mousse cake, passion fruit or nutmeg ice cream, and lime cheesecake.

Aquatic Gap, Bay Street, St. Michael. ☎ 246-426-7684. E-mail: brownsug@caribsurf.com. *Internet:* www.brownsugarrestaurant.com. *Reservations recommended. Main courses: $14.50–$50. Lunch buffet $19 weekdays, $20 Sunday. MC, V. Open for lunch Sunday through Friday from 12:30 p.m. to 2:30 p.m. and for dinner daily from 6 p.m.*

Carambola

$$–$$$ Derricks   French/Caribbean/Asian

Dramatic lighting, alfresco dining on a terra-cotta terrace, and a cliffside setting overlooking the Caribbean (lit in the evenings) make this restaurant one of the island's most romantic. Carambola also serves some of the best food, with its dynamic menu of classic French and Caribbean cuisines — and a shot of Asian to add to the intrigue. Start with a spicy crab tart served with hollandaise sauce on a bed of sweet pepper coulis. For an entree, try mahimahi fillet broiled with Dijon mustard sauce, or sliced duck breast with a wild mushroom fumet served with stuffed tomatoes and potatoes au gratin. A selection of savory vegetarian dishes is offered, as are such Asian-influenced meals as the spicy Thai pork tenderloin. Just when you think you can't eat another bite, they'll finish you off with a wonderfully light *citron gateau* (lime mousse on a pool of lemon coulis). The impressive wine list features mostly French vintages.

Save your shorts — and your embarrassment — by breaking out your nicest resort wear here.

Derricks, St. James. ☎ *246-432-0832. Reservations required. Main courses: $22–$50. AE, MC, V. Open for dinner from 6 p.m. to 11 p.m. Closed Sundays.*

The Cliff

$$$ St. James   International/Caribbean

Our top choice for romance is this dramatically positioned, open-air restaurant, built atop a 10-foot coral cliff adjacent to the Coconut Creek Hotel. Its four-level dining area is crafted out of coral stone and terra-cotta tiles. The mastery of Chef Paul Owens has created one of the finest dining establishments in Barbados. Imaginative art accents the tiered dining terrace, and every candlelit table has a view of the sea. Despite the fact that the owners don't consider it exclusive, posh, or even particularly formal, it has attracted Prince Andrew and other renowned guests of the nearby upscale hotels. Despite all this, no one will mind if you wear well-tailored shorts; the place really is surprisingly low-key.

The artistry extends to the innovative menu, which offers excellent cuts of prime meat and fresh fish, creatively presented with nouvelle accents and accompanied by the freshest of local vegetables. Menu items include grilled snapper drizzled in three types of coriander sauce (cream-based, oil-based, and vinaigrette style), accompanied with garlic-infused mashed potatoes and Thai-style curried shrimp. When available, sushi is presented as a starter, complete with wasabi and portions of fresh local tuna, scallops, and snapper. As you dine, watch for manta rays, which glide through the illuminated waters below. The seas are usually calm enough to spot them, and a sighting is considered a sign of good luck. Don't skip dessert, which falls in the *sinful* category.

Derricks, St. James. ☎ *246-432-1922. Reservations required in winter. Main courses: $27–$37.50. AE, DC, MC. V. Open nightly for dinner from 6:30 p.m.*

David's Place

$$–$$$ Worthing   Bajan

Owner-operators David and Darla Trotman promise that in their restaurant you'll sample "Bajan dining at its best." They deliver on that promise (and at reasonable prices, too) in this small Bajan cottage. You won't notice the busy, South Coast main road location, thanks to the sounds of semi-classical music and the gently lapping waves of St. Lawrence Bay against the pilings of the open-air deck. The specialties — local flying fish,

Arawak pepper-pot stew, curried shrimp — and other entrees, including a vegetarian platter, come with homemade cheddar cheese bread. Desserts are equally good. Here, at last, is a restaurant that offers that old drugstore favorite of the 1940s and 1950s: a banana split. Or you might opt instead for the coconut cream pie or the carrot cake in rum sauce. David's has an extensive wine list.

St. Lawrence Main Road, Worthing, Christ Church. ☎ *246-435-9755. Reservations recommended. Main courses: $13–$30. AE, DISC, MC, V. Open for dinner Tuesday through Sunday from 6 p.m. to 10 p.m.*

Edgewater Inn

$ **Bathsheba** **Eclectic**

Tucked into a rainforest, Edgewater Inn's restaurant overlooks Bathsheba's famed Soup Bowl beach. Enjoy a cool drink and the wonderful view while sitting at hand-carved mahogany tables and chairs. Choose from sandwiches, salads, French-bread pizzas, or traditional Bajan dishes for a filling lunch. The best treat at the dessert buffet is a help-yourself frozen-yogurt machine. Dinners are also served here, but it's mostly inn guests who partake.

Bathsheba, St. Joseph. ☎ *246-433-9900. Main courses: $6–$15. AE, MC, V. Open daily for lunch from noon to 3 p.m. and dinner from 6:30 p.m. to 9:30 p.m.*

The Emerald Palm

$$$ **St. James** **International**

This coral stone-and-tile country house on Barbados's fashionable West Coast is in a tropical garden dotted with a trio of gazebos. After passing under an arbor, you'll be invited to order a drink, served on one of the flowered banquettes that fill various parts of the house. Chef David Jones whips out zesty dishes packed with international and island flavors. Begin with a spicy cucumber soup or a succulent version of Caribbean fish soup with fresh peppers before moving on to main courses. Specialties include dishes such as roast red snapper in coconut juice with local baby spinach. For a real taste of Barbados, try the roasted lobster with caramelized pears in a champagne and vanilla sauce.

Porters, St. James (two miles north of Holetown). ☎ *246-422-4116. Reservations required. Main courses $20–$40. AE, MC, V. Open for dinner Monday through Saturday.*

Ile de France

$$ **Holetown** **Classic French**

Place yourself in the capable hands of French Chef Michel and his charming wife/hostess Martine Gramaglia, who handle the kitchen and dining room with an enviable *savoir faire*. The atmosphere is charming and traditional. Ingredients are either obtained fresh on Barbados or flown in from France or Martinique. Specialties might include escargots de Bourgogne, a flavorful fish soup with lobster, foie gras with sauterne, or a marinade of three fish (the exact composition of this dish depends on the catch of the day). Other dishes include rack of lamb, shrimp, and roast lobster. For dessert, try the tarte tatin, crème brûlée, or banana terrine.

In the Settlers' Beach Hotel, Holetown, St. James (eight miles north of Bridgetown). ☎ *246-422-3245. Reservations recommended. Main courses $16–$37.50. MC, V. Open daily from 8 a.m. to 10 p.m.*

Luigi's Restaurant

$–$$ St. Lawrence Gap   Italian

Since 1963, this open-air trattoria has operated in a Greenland-white building built as a private house. The feeling is contemporary, airy, and comfortable. Pizzas are offered as appetizers, along with more classic choices such as a half-dozen escargots or a Caesar salad (when available). Many pastas are available in half-orders as starters. The baked pastas (a creamy lasagna, for one) are delectable. Other dishes include the fresh fish or veal special of the day. For dessert, try the zabaglione and one of the wide selections of coffee, ranging from Italian to Russian or Turkish.

Dover Woods, St. Lawrence Gap, Christ Church. ☎ *246-428-9218. Reservations required. Main courses: $11.50–$24.50. MC, V. Open for dinner nightly from 6 p.m.*

Mango's by the Sea

$$ Speightstown   International

This romantic hideaway, overlooking lapping waves, made a splash when it opened in quiet Speightstown, which in general had missed the boat when it came to fine dining. Montréal couple Gail and Pierre Spenard buy the catch of the day directly from the fishermen's boats and employ a light touch with the seasonings, preferring to let the fresh flavor of the fish speak for itself. You may be tempted to OD on lobster: Both the lobster bisque and grilled Caribbean lobster with lime butter and white wine are standouts. Appetizers might be anything from an intriguing green peppercorn pate to pumpkin soup. If you're not in a fish mood, opt for the 8-ounce tenderloin steak — always cooked to perfection — or the fall-off-the-bone barbecued baby back ribs. Finish the meal with a passion fruit cheesecake or a star fruit torte. After 10 p.m., cigar aficionados make their selection from a collection of Cubans from Pierre's humidor and puff away at the bar or their tables. It's also one of the few Caribbean restaurants to have a wine cellar.

2 West End, Queen Street, Speightstown, St. Peter. ☎ *246-422-0704. Reservations recommended. Main courses $14–$32. MC, V. Open for dinner Sunday through Friday from 6 p.m. Closed the month of June.*

Nico's Champagne Wine Bar & Restaurant

$–$$ Derrick's   International

This good-value, informal bistro, inspired by the wine bars of London, is set on the landward side of a road that bisects some of the most expensive residential real estate on Barbados (the west coast). *Gourmet* praised its signature dish, a grilled local lobster caught only off the island's east coast. Housed in a nineteenth-century building that once served as headquarters for a thriving plantation, it does a thriving business from its air-conditioned bar area where a dozen wines are sold by the glass. Meals are served at tables protected with a shed-style roof in the garden out back. Trust us: Try the deep-fried Camembert with passion fruit sauce.

Derrick's, St. James. ☎ 246-432-6386. Reservations recommended. Lunch main courses $9–$14; dinner main courses $12–$36. AE, DISC, MC, V. Open Monday through Saturday from 11:30 a.m. to 9:30 p.m.

Olives Bar & Bistro

$$–$$$ Holetown   Mediterannean/Caribbean

In 1994, owner-chef Larry Rogers and his wife Michelle turned a colorful old Bajan-style house into a delightful restaurant. The street-level, air-conditioned dining room (where no smoking is allowed) spills out from its original coral-stone walls and scrubbed-pine floorboards into a pleasant garden. Mediterranean and Caribbean flavors enliven gourmet pizzas and salads. Special dishes on the menu might include tasty Swiss-style *rösti* potatoes (shredded and fried like a pancake) with smoked salmon and sour cream, and fresh seafood served on a roasted garlic creamed potato with grilled ratatouille vegetables. The upstairs bar scene — dubbed "Olives" — has become a lively, popular spot.

2nd Street, Holetown, St. James. ☎ 246-432-2112. Reservations required in winter. Main courses: $14–$33. AE, MC, V. Open for light fare Monday through Friday from 8:30 a.m. to 4 p.m.; dinner nightly from 6:30 p.m. to 10 p.m.

Pisces

$$–$$$ St. Lawrence Gap   Bajan

This beautiful old favorite offers alfresco dining at the water's edge. The contemporary decor is accented with hanging tropical plants and twinkling white lights that reflect on the water. The menu focuses on Caribbean seafood. Start with the split pea or pumpkin soup. Flying fish, dolphinfish, kingfish, crab, shrimp, prawns, and lobster are prepared here in every way, from charbroiled to sauteed. Specialties include conch strips in tempura, tropical gazpacho, panfried fillets of flying fish with a toasted almond crust and light mango-citrus sauce, and pepper-encrusted tuna with fresh papaya and balsamic vinaigrette. Whatever your selection, the herbs that flavor it and the accompanying vegetables come from the chef's own garden. The homemade rum-raisin ice cream is delicious.

From Bridgetown, take Hwy. 7 south for about four miles, then turn right at the sign toward St. Lawrence Gap. St. Lawrence Gap, Christ Church. ☎ 246-435-6564. Reservations recommended. Main courses: $14–$38. AE, DC, MC, V. Open for dinner nightly from 6:30 p.m. to 9:30 p.m.

Ragamuffins

$$ Holetown Caribbean

The only restaurant on Barbados within an authentic chattel house, Ragamuffins is funky, lively, and affordable. Leave any pretension at the door. The menu offers seafood, perfectly broiled T-bone steaks, West Indian curries, and vegetarian dishes like Bajan stir-fried vegetables with noodles. Dine inside or out. The kitchen is within sight of the bar — a popular meeting spot most evenings. It's casual and fun for the family, and the food is delicious. Still, you'll need reservations, because it's tiny.

1st Street, Holetown, St. James. ☎ 246-432-1295. E-mail: raga@caribsurf.com. *Main courses: $14–$33. AE, MC, V. Open for dinner Sunday through Friday from 7:30 p.m. to 9:30 p.m.*

The Ship Inn

$$$–$$$$ St. Lawrence Gap English pub/Bajan

South of Bridgetown between Rockley Beach and Worthling, the Ship Inn is a traditional English-style pub with an attractive, rustic decor of nautical memorabilia. Atmosphere and fun are the prime draws. Many guests come for a game of darts and to listen to the live music presented nightly by some of the island's top bands. The Ship Inn serves substantial bar food, such as homemade steak-and-kidney pie, shepherd's pie, and chicken, shrimp, and fish dishes. For more formal dining, visit the **Captain's Carvery,** where you can have your fill of succulent cuts of prime roasts on a nighttime buffet table, as well as an array of traditional Bajan food (flying fish fillets, for example).

St. Lawrence Gap, Christ Church. ☎ 246-435-6961. Reservations recommended for the Captain's Carvery only. Main courses $8–$14.50; all-you-can-eat Carvery meal $12 at lunch, $21 at dinner, plus $9 for appetizer and dessert. AE, DC, MC, V. Open Sunday through Friday for lunch from 12:15 p.m. to 3 p.m. and for dinner from 6 p.m. to 2 a.m.

Sunbury Plantation House

$–$$$ St. Philip Eclectic

In the Courtyard Restaurant, on a patio surrounded by beautiful gardens, luncheon is served to visitors as part of the house tour (see Chapter 15). The buffet includes chicken and fish, salads, rice and peas, and steamed local vegetables. Sandwiches and other à la carte items are available, too. Trifle, pastries, and ice cream are dessert choices.

Within the elegant plantation house, up to 20 people can be seated at the 200-year-old dining table for a private, five-course dinner, with wine. After-dinner liqueurs are served in the drawing room. Dinner reservations must be made well in advance.

Off Hwy. 5, near Six Cross Roads, St. Philip. ☎ 246-423-6270. Reservations essential. Main courses: lunch $5–$13; buffet lunch with house tour $20; buffet lunch without house tour $15.65; fixed-price 5-course dinner $60. AE, MC, V. Luncheon served during house tour. Dinner served by special arrangement only.

The Terrace Restaurant at Cobblers Cove
$$$$ St. Peter   British Haute

This English country house on a beach is one of only three restaurant/
hotels in the Caribbean to receive the *Relais & Chateaux* designation (recognizing excellent small hotels with top-notch restaurants). This elegant
yet casual restaurant's open-air terrace allows sea breezes to waft
through. Young English chef John Hardwick turns out his bold new take
on English fare with a hint of the Caribbean. Panfried swordfish with
fennel and orange salad, gratte potatoes, and citrus glaze; or panfried
barracuda with scallop and crab tortellini sauce are standouts.

On Tuesday evening, there's a barbecue buffet, and on Sunday a special
curry lunch with steel pan music (in winter only). On Tuesday, Thursday,
and Saturday nights, a duo playing sax and guitar entertain.

If you have special dietary needs, this energetic cheery chef does back
flips to please his guests.

Cobblers Cove, St. Peter. ☎ *246-422-2291. Fax: 256-422-1460. E-mail:*
cobblers@caribsurf.com. Reservations recommended. Main courses:
$23–$32. AE, MC, V. Open for breakfast, lunch, and dinner. Closed July 1 through
October 15.

T.G.I. Boomers
$–$$ St. Lawrence Gap   American/Bajan

Four miles south of Bridgetown near Rockley Beach along Highway 7,
T.G.I. Boomers offers some of the best bargain meals on the island. An
American/Bajan operation, it has an active bar and a row of tables where
food is served, usually along with frothy pastel-colored drinks. The cook
prepares a special catch of the day, and the fish is served with soup or
salad, rice or baked potato, and a vegetable. You can always count on
seafood, steaks, and hamburgers. For lunch, try a daily Bajan special or
a jumbo sandwich. Most folks come here for a belt-busting good time
with tried-and-true dishes that never go out of favor. Sample one of the
16-ounce daiquiris, but only if you're not driving.

St. Lawrence Gap, Christ Church. ☎ *246-428-8439. Breakfast $5.50–$7.50; lunch*
specials $4–$11.50; main courses $12–$23; Sunday buffet $12.50. AE, MC, V. Open
daily from 8 a.m. to 10 p.m.

Waterfront Cafe
$$ Bridgetown   International

In a turn-of-the-century warehouse originally built to store bananas and
freeze fish, this marina-side cafe serves international fare with a strong
emphasis on Bajan specialties. Facing the busy harbor in Bridgetown,
this friendly bistro is the perfect place to enjoy a drink, snack, or meal —
and to people-watch. Locals and tourists gather at outdoor cafe tables
for sandwiches, salads, fish, pasta, pepper-pot stew, and tasty Bajan
snacks such as *buljol*, fish cakes, or plantation pork (plantains stuffed

with spicy minced pork). The panfried flying fish sandwich is especially popular. In the evening, from the brick and mirrored interior, you can gaze through the arched windows while you savor creole cuisine, enjoy cool trade winds, and listen to live jazz. Live steel pan music is presented along with a Bajan buffet featured on Tuesday from 7 to 9 p.m. If you want to see the Dixieland bands on Thursday nights, you need to make reservations about a week in advance. On Fridays, you get Latin Jazz.

The Careenage, Bridgetown, St. Michael. ☎ 246-427-0093. Main courses: $12–$18. AE, DC, MC, V. Open Monday through Saturday from 10 a.m to 10 p.m.

Chapter 15

Hitting the Beach and Other Fun Things to Do

. . . .

In This Chapter

▶ Soaking up the sun on Barbados's top beaches

▶ Diving into fun with watersports

▶ Satisfying the landlubber: Activities, shopping, nightlife, and the arts

▶ Planning some super side trips

. . . .

*B*ecause both of us have recently discovered that our Irish and Scottish ancestors immigrated to Barbados before entering the U.S., we must confess that we've suddenly developed a soft spot for this island where polo and cricket are considered great fun. We're a bit more inclined now to overlook the fact that it's overdeveloped, crowded, and geared to the package tour groups from Canada and the United Kingdom who are perfectly happy to spend their entire holidays at their respective resorts.

The mood on Barbados, which is the easternmost island of the Lesser Antilles and juts out into the Atlantic, is unmistakably civilized. Despite more than three decades of independence from Great Britain, Barbados still exudes a British air of formality — so much so that we have personally felt a little stifled there at times.

Bajans (as these islanders are called) do cut loose when it comes to rum. Bajans are extremely proud of the locally made rums, and several little dives called "rum shops" around the island serve rum at all hours. In fact, Barbados claims that it has more than 1,200 rum shops, which are simple bars where mostly men congregate.

What else can you do on this island besides play polo and drink rum? Plenty. In this chapter, we guide you toward Barbados's best beaches and activities.

Hitting the Beaches

When it comes to beaches, Barbados has a great selection; if you love nothing better than hanging out on the beach, this island is a good pick. Barbados has more than 70 miles of coastline. We discuss some of our favorites in this section.

East coast

One bright morning during one of our visits, we set out in a rental car (reminding each other to drive on the left) to explore this coral island. While the west coast of the island boasts white-sand beaches and calm, turquoise Caribbean water, we headed toward the crashing waves of the Atlantic pounding the east and craggy north coast. Our first stop: windswept **Bathsheba/Cattlewash,** where magnificent boulders frame crashing waves, to watch the sunrise. We were surprised to find a gaggle of surfers already there to catch the waves.

Bajans ride the waves here almost daily. (Barbados is the location of the Independence Classic Surfing Championships, which are held each November.) If you decide to try surfing, be sure to get advice on where to enter the water.

On the east coast, you'll see miles of untouched beach along the island's wildest, hilliest, and most beautiful stretch of coast. But swimming at Bathsheba or along the Atlantic coast can be extremely dangerous, so you may want to stick to sightseeing in these areas and save your swimsuit for the south or west coast beaches.

South coast

South coast beaches, where you'll find medium waves, generally draw a young, energetic crowd. The beaches are consistently broad with white powdery sand; the reef-protected waters are crystal clear and safe for swimming and snorkeling.

Accra Beach in Rockley is popular — lots of people, activity, food, and drink are nearby. Rental equipment is available here for snorkeling and other watersports. You'll even find a parking lot at the beach. This spot is good for bodysurfing and body watching.

Casuarina Beach at the Casuarina Beach Hotel (east end of St. Lawrence Gap area) is a big, wide breezy beach with a fair amount of surf. Public access is available from Maxwell Coast Road.

Needham's Point and its lighthouse are at the south end of Carlisle Bay, just outside Bridgetown. One of the island's best beaches, Needham's Point is crowded with local people on weekends and holidays. The Carlisle Bay Centre has changing rooms and showers to accommodate cruise ship passengers spending a day at the beach.

In Worthing, **Sandy Beach** has shallow, calm waters and a picturesque lagoon. It's an ideal location for families and offers beach activities on weekends. You'll find parking on the main road and plenty of places nearby to buy food or drink.

If you're in the mood for a picnic, we recommend the lovely cove at **Bottom Bay,** north of Sam Lord's Castle. Follow the steps down the cliff to a strip of white sand lined by coconut palms and washed by an aquamarine sea. You'll even find a cave to explore. It's out of the way and not near restaurants, so bring your own goodies.

Silver Rock Beach, close to the southernmost tip of the island, has a beautiful expanse of white-sand beach with a stiff breeze that attracts windsurfers who use Silver Rock Hotel as their base.

West coast

If you want the calm, magnificently clear Caribbean, head for the west coast, where you'll find stunning coves and sandy beaches. Here you can find excellent watersports and swimming. The water is so smooth (especially early in the morning) that you can water-ski here.

Nicknamed the **"Gold Coast,"** an almost unbroken chain of beaches forms the coastline between Speightstown (in the north) and Bridgetown. Elegant private homes and luxury hotels line this stretch.

The beaches aren't crowded, but they aren't private either. Vendors come by with armloads of goods, such as handmade baskets, hats, dolls, jewelry, and even original paintings. You may also be approached by private boat owners who offer to take you waterskiing, parasailing, or snorkeling. You won't find concession stands, but hotels welcome nonguests for terrace lunches as long as you have a decent cover-up with you. Picnic items can be purchased at supermarkets in Holetown.

You can park on the main road and walk to **Mullins Beach,** just south of Speightstown at Mullins Bay. Its glassy clear waters are ideal for swimming and snorkeling. **Mullins Restaurant (☎ 246-422-1878)** serves snacks, meals, and drinks. At the southern end of the beach, you'll find a good picnic area.

Pretty **Paynes Bay,** south of Holetown, has a number of luxury hotels and plenty of beach to match. Parking areas and public access are available opposite the Coach House Pub. Grab a bite to eat and liquid refreshments at **Bombas Beach Bar.**

Finding Water Fun for Everyone

Barbados hasn't become known among divers, and there's a reason. Fishing is still big business around this island, and you rarely see any large fish on its reefs. But if you're a beginning diver who wants to get in a few dives between rounds of golf, you'll likely enjoy the experience. Visibility is generally around 80–90 feet, but during the rainy season from June to January, it may be much less than that.

Locating dive sites

More than two dozen dive sites, several with shallow wrecks, are concentrated along the west coast between Maycocks Bay and Bridgetown and off the south coast as far as St. Lawrence Gap. Certified divers can explore barrier reefs and the wrecks, which have been covered with soft corals, sea fans, and huge barrel sponges. More than 50 varieties of fish populate these waters, too.

The most popular dive site is at **Dottin's Reef** off Holetown. It's a gorgeous reef festooned with sea fans, gorgonians, and brain coral. You can see schooling fish, parrotfish, snappers, barracuda, and a few turtles starting at depths of 65 feet. South of Dottin's Reef is the *Stavronikita,* a 356-foot Greek freighter that lies about 135 feet under water; it's often crowded with tourist divers, but it's a good wreck to explore. You'll see hundreds of butterfly fish darting around its mast. Virtually every part of the ship is accessible, but its depth will likely dissuade less experienced divers.

Renting underwater gear

A one-tank dive on this island runs about $55; a two-tank dive costs about $90. All gear is supplied, and you can purchase multi-dive packages. Gear for snorkeling can be rented for a small charge from most hotels. Snorkelers can usually accompany dive trips for $20–$25 for a one- or two-hour trip.

The **Dive Shop, Ltd.** (Aquatic Gap near Bay Street, St. Michael; ☎ 800-348-3756 or 246-426-9947; e-mail hardive@caribnet.net; Internet www.barbados.org/diving/diveshop/diveshop.html) is the oldest dive shop on Barbados and teaches all levels of certification.

On the west coast, **Hightide Watersports** (Coral Reef Club, St. James; ☎ 800-513-5763 or 246-432-0931; fax 246-432-0931; e-mail hightide@ sunbeach.net; Internet www.divehightide.com) specializes in small groups. Hightide offers one- and two-tank dives, night reef/wreck/drift dives, the full range of PADI instruction, and free transportation. It also has a custom-built 30-foot dive boat.

In an effort to conserve the magnificent sea turtles that were once plentiful around the island, local authorities launched the **Barbados Sea Turtle Project** in 1987. There's a 24-hour hotline that you can call to report any nesting activity: ☎ **246-230-0142.**

Taking a ride under the sea

Atlantis Submarines (Shallow Draught, Bridgetown; ☎ 246-436-8929) offers enormously popular mini-submarine voyages good for families with youngsters and those who are curious about what's under the sea but don't want to dive or snorkel. You have two choices on Barbados:

  ✔ The 48-passenger, 65-foot *Atlantis III* gives you a 45-minute tour (for $80 a pop) of wrecks and reefs as deep as 150 feet. Special nighttime dives, using high-power searchlights, are spectacular.

  ✔ Children enjoy the *Atlantis SEATREC* (Sea Tracking and Reef Exploration Craft), which essentially lets you experience the same views you'd get snorkeling without getting wet. The 46-passenger vessel has large viewing windows six feet below the surface, where you view the underwater marine life on a near-shore reef from the air-conditioned craft.

If you even think that you might be claustrophobic, don't try this little adventure.

Waterskiing the Caribbean

We recommend waterskiing early in the day, because the waters can get a little rough in the afternoons. Many hotels on the west and south coasts of the island offer waterskiing, sometimes at no additional cost. If your hotel doesn't provide this service and you're staying on the west coast, try **Blue Reef Watersports** at the Royal Pavilion hotel in St. James (Porters; ☎ 246-422-4444).

Private speedboat owners troll for business along the St. James and Christ Church waterfront, but you water-ski at your own risk with these operators.

Riding the wind

Barbados is one of the top spots in the world for windsurfing and is part of the World Cup Windsurfing circuit. If you want to try your hand, here are the best operators on the island:

  ✔ **Mistral Windsurfing School** is at Grand Barbados Beach Resort in Carlisle Bay, south of Bridgetown (Aquatic Gap, St. Michael; ☎ 246-426-4000).

  ✔ **Silver Rock Windsurfing Club** is at Silver Rock Hotel (Silver Sands Beach, Christ Church; ☎ 246-428-2866).

Winds are strongest between November and April and at the island's southern tip, which is where the Barbados Windsurfing Championships are held in mid-January. Boards and equipment are often free of charge for guests at the larger hotels, and you might even get lessons kicked in as part of your package.

Telling fish tales

Half- or full-day fishing charter trips are available for serious deep-sea fishers looking for billfish or for those who prefer angling in calm, coastal waters where wahoo, barracuda, and other small fish reside. Charter fishing trips depart from the Careenage in Bridgetown.

You're in good hands with captain and owner Winston "The Colonel" White, who has been plying the waters around Barbados for more than a quarter of a century. His *Billfisher II* (Bridge House, Cavans Lane, the Careenage, Bridgetown; ☎ 246-431-0741) is a 40-foot Pacemaker that accommodates up to six people. Half-day charters get you drinks (rum, beer, and soft drinks) and sandwiches. Full-day charters include a full lunch, and the confident captain even guarantees fish. You can keep everything you catch, and the crew will clean and cook your catch for you at day's end.

The affable captain will match you with other people who would like to share the cost of the charter.

The *Blue Jay* (St. James; ☎ 246-429-2326) is a 45-foot, fully equipped Sports-Fisherman with a huge cockpit and four fishing chairs. The fishing party is limited to four, guaranteeing that everyone gets to cast his line. Captain "Callie" Elton's crew knows the waters where the bigger game fish frolic. You may hook into such game fish as blue marlin, sailfish, barracuda, and kingfish. Each person fishing can invite a guest free of charge. Drinks and snacks are provided.

Sailing away

Party boats depart from the Careenage or Bridgetown Harbour area for lunchtime snorkeling or cocktail-hour sunset cruises. Prices are around $50–$55 per person. Catamaran cruises are available on *Limbo Lady* (☎ 246-420-5418), *Tiami* (☎ 246-430-0900), and *Tropical Dreamer* (☎ 246-427-7245). *Secret Love* (☎ 246-432-1972), a 41-foot Morgan sailboat, offers daily lunchtime or evening snorkel cruises.

The red-sailed *Jolly Roger* "pirate" ship (☎ 246-436-6424) runs lunch-and-snorkeling sailing cruises (with complimentary rum punches) along the west coast. Four- and five-hour daytime cruises along the west coast on the 100-foot motor vessel *Harbour Master* (☎ 246-430-0900) stop in Holetown and land at beaches along the way; evening cruises add a buffet dinner and entertainment. Day or night, you can view the briny deep from the ship's onboard 34-seat semi-submersible.

Exercising On-Land Options

If your sea legs need a break from all that fun in and on the water, check out some of the options you'll find on dry land.

Duffer's delight

Bajans love golf, but until recently the island didn't make itself too welcoming to outsiders looking to play a game. In 1998, only two 18-hole golf courses were on the island, and only one — Sandy Lane — was open to tourists. All that's changed.

By 2001, Barbados will have three new 18-hole championship courses. Greens fees range from $12.50 for 9 holes at Club Rockley to $145 for 18 holes at Royal Westmoreland Golf Club. During low season, prices can fall by almost half.

In July 2000, the redesigned and reconstructed **Barbados Golf Club** (Durants, Christ Church; ☎ 246-434-2121; fax 256-418-3131; e-mail bgc@caribsurf.com; Internet www.barbadosgolfclub.com) on the south coast opened as Barbados's first public championship golf course. The 6,905-yard, par-72 course, designed by respected architect Ron Kirby, has been approved and sanctioned to host the PGA Seniors Tournament in 2002. Greens fees for 18 holes are $99 plus $13 for a cart and $20 for Callaway club rentals. A three-day unlimited golf pass during high season is $225.

The **Royal Westmoreland Golf Club** (St. James; ☎ 246-422-4653) has a world-class Robert Trent Jones, Jr., 18-hole championship course that meanders through the 500-acre Westmoreland Sugar Estate. Greens fees include use of an electric cart; equipment rental is available. To play at this exclusive course, you have to stay at a hotel with access privileges (such as Cobblers Cove, Coral Reef Club, Glitter Bay, Royal Pavilion, or Turtle Beach).

Almond Beach Village (St. Peter; ☎ 246-422-4900), on the northwest corner of the island, has a 9-hole, par-3 executive course for guest use only. No greens fees are charged, and clubs are provided.

Club Rockley Barbados (Rockley, Christ Church; ☎ 246-435-7873), on the southeast coast near Sam Lord's Castle, has a challenging 9-hole course that can be played as 18 from varying tee positions. This course is open to the public daily, and trolleys and clubs can be rented inexpensively.

The prestigious **Sandy Lane Golf Club** (St. James; ☎ 246-432-4653) underwent a dramatic redesign by renowned course architect Tom Fazio and reopened in December 1999. Eventually, Sandy Lane will boast 45 holes with two 18-hole championship courses, both designed by Fazio.

Taking a hike

Hilly but not mountainous, the northern interior and east coast of Barbados are good for hikers who aren't looking for an Iron Man kind of workout. The **Barbados National Trust** (Wildey House, Wildey, St. Michael; ☎ 246-426-2421) sponsors free 5-mile (8-km) walks year-round on Sundays from 6 a.m. to about 9:30 a.m. and from 3:30 to 6 p.m. The Trust also leads monthly moonlight hikes.

For the more fit, the Trust sponsors a three-hour trek through the **Arbib Nature & Heritage Trail,** which won *Islands* magazine's 1999 Ecotourism Award. You must book a spot for this walk by 3 p.m. the day before you want to go. Hikes take place on Wednesday, Thursday, and Saturday starting at 9 a.m. and 2:30 p.m. The fee for adults is $15 and for children is $7.50.

Horseback riding

To get a good sense of the island, we recommend horseback riding through the hilly north country of Barbados or along the beach. Equestrian tours can accommodate any level of experience. Advance reservations are recommended. The **Caribbean International Riding Center** (Auburn, St. Joseph; ☎ 246-422-7433 or 246-420-1246) offers one- and two-hour rides through the countryside of the Scotland District and longer treks that continue on to Morgan Lewis beach on the Atlantic coast. Prices range from $40 for a one-hour trail ride to $82.50 for a 2½-hour trek; transportation to and from your hotel is included.

Tennis and squash

Most hotels have tennis courts that can be reserved day and night. Bring your proper tennis whites. On the west coast, public tennis courts are available for free on a first-come, first-served basis at **Folkestone Park** (Holetown; ☎ 246-422-2314). On the south coast, **National Tennis Centre** (Sir Garfield Sobers Sports Complex, Wildey, St. Michael; ☎ 246-437-6010) charges $12 per hour and requires reservations.

On the south coast, guests can play squash at **Accra Beach Hotel and Resort** (Rockley, Christ Church; ☎ 246-435-8920). At **Club Rockley Barbados** (Rockley, Christ Church; ☎ 246-435-7880), nonguests can reserve air-conditioned courts for $10 per hour.

Watching from the Sidelines

Barbados's spectator sports include several thoroughly British options.

Cricket

Not Jiminy Cricket — just plain cricket. Barbados is mad for the game, which has a season from May to late December. International test matches are played from January to April. Newspapers give the details of time and place. Tickets to cricket matches at Kensington Oval, Bridgetown, range from $5 to $25. For information, call the **Barbados Cricket Association** (☎ **246-436-1397**).

Horse racing

Horse races take place on alternate Saturdays, from January to March and May to December, at the **Garrison Savannah** (☎ **246-426-3980;** e-mail barturf@sunbeach.net; Internet barbadosturfclub.com) in Christ Church, about 3 miles (5 km) south of Bridgetown. Like the horse events in the other parts of the world, the races are really a social happening. The annual **Cockspur Cup** is run in early March. The track opens at 1:30 p.m. on race days, and admission is $5.

Polo

If you've never experienced a polo match, here's a great opportunity. And if you're an old hand, you'll be in enthusiastic company watching a match in Barbados. Polo matches here are much more casual than at other places, so spectators are more than welcome. Matches are played at the **Barbados Polo Club** in Holders Hill, St. James (☎ **246-427-0022**) on Wednesdays and Saturdays from October through April.

Touring Historic Sites

To encourage you to tour the island's many historic sites, the Barbados National Trust has designed the **Heritage Passport,** a free pass to some of Barbados's most popular attractions and historic sites, including **Gun Hill Signal Station.** When the holder pays full admission to visit some attractions, the passport will be stamped to validate free admission to other sights. Passports are free and can be picked up at displays in supermarkets, shops, hotels, and restaurants.

Every Wednesday afternoon from mid-January through mid-April, the Trust offers a bus tour of historic great houses and private homes open for public viewing, including Tyrol Cot Heritage Village (St. Michael); St. Nicholas Abbey (St. Peter); Francia Plantation, Drax Hall, and Brighton Great House (St. George); Villa Nova (St. John); and Sam Lord's Castle and Sunbury Plantation House (St. Philip). The cost is $18 per person, which includes transportation to and from your hotel. (If you wish to visit the homes on your own, they're open on those Wednesday afternoons from 2:30 to 5:30 p.m.; entrance fees at each range from $1.25 to $5.)

History-rich Barbados has much to offer to those interested in the past. Thanks to the British influence, it also boasts some of the Caribbean's finest gardens. Here are our favorite picks to get a flavor for both aspects of Barbados:

✔ **Barbados Wildlife Reserve:** Home to herons, land turtles, a kangaroo, screeching peacocks, lots of green monkeys, geese, brilliantly colored parrots, and a friendly otter, this lovely reserve has a giant walk-in aviary and natural-history exhibits. Across from Farley Hill, St. Peter. ☎ **246-422-8826.** $10. Open daily from 10 a.m. to 5 p.m.

✔ **Farley Hill:** At this national park in northern St. Peter, across the road from the Barbados Wildlife Reserve, the imposing ruins of a plantation great house are surrounded by gardens, lawns, an avenue of towering royal palms, and gigantic mahogany, whitewood, and casuarina trees. Behind the estate, you'll see Barbados's Scotland District (so named for its rugged landscape), which hikers can also explore. St. Peter. $1.50 per car; walkers free. Open daily 8:30 a.m. to 6 p.m.

✔ **Folkestone Marine Park & Visitor Centre:** At this park north of Holetown, a museum explains Barbados's marine life. It also has an underwater snorkeling trail around Dottin's Reef. A glass-bottom boat ride allows youngsters and nonswimmers to get a good look, too, at a barge sunk in shallow water teeming with reef fish. Church Pt., Holetown, St. James. ☎ **246-422-2314.** Admission 60¢ (the boat ride costs extra). Open weekdays from 9 a.m. to 5 p.m.

✔ **Andromeda Gardens:** We spent an entire afternoon here, admiring the fascinating collection of unusual and beautiful plant specimens from around the world. You get the sense that a loving and thoughtful hand carefully cultivated the six acres of gardens nestled among streams, ponds, and rocky outcroppings overlooking the sea above the Bathsheba coastline. The orchid collection is especially beautiful. The **Hibiscus Café** serves snacks and drinks, and a **Best of Barbados** gift shop is on the property. Bathsheba, St. Joseph. ☎ **246-433-9384.** Adults $6; children $3. Open daily from 9 a.m. to 5 p.m.

✔ **Flower Forest:** Walk amidst the fragrant flowering bushes, cannas, ginger lilies, puffball trees, and more than a hundred other species of tropical flora. A ½-mile (1-km) path winds through the 50 acres of grounds. This site has a restaurant, a gift shop, and a beautiful view of Mt. Hillaby. Richmond Plantation, Hwy. 2, St. Joseph. ☎ **246-433-8152.** Adults $7; children $3.50. Open daily from 9 a.m. to 5 p.m.

✔ **Gun Hill Signal Station:** The 360-degree view from windswept Gun Hill, built in 1818 at 700 feet above sea level, was what made this location of strategic importance to the 19th-century British army. Today, it's a cool place to get the best view on the island. St. George. ☎ **246-429-1358.** $5.00. Open Monday through Saturday from 9 a.m. to 5 p.m.

✔ **Harrison's Cave:** This limestone cavern, complete with stalactites, stalagmites, subterranean streams, and a 40-foot waterfall, is a rarity in the Caribbean and one of Barbados's most popular attractions. The 45-minute tours are made by electric tram and fill up fast. Reserve a spot ahead of time. Hard hats are provided, but the only thing that might hit you is dripping water. Hwy. 2, St. Thomas. ☎ 246-438-6640. $7.50. Open daily from 9 a.m. to 6 p.m.; the last tour starts at 4 p.m.

✔ **Sam Lord's Castle:** The Regency house built by the buccaneer Sam Lord is considered by many to be the finest mansion in Barbados. Built in 1820 and now part of a resort, the rooms are furnished with fine mahogany furniture and gilt mirrors that Sam Lord is reputed to have pillaged from passing ships. The pirate supposedly lured ships onto Barbados's treacherous reefs by hanging lanterns in palm trees to simulate harbor lights. Long Bay, St. Philip. ☎ 246-423-7350. Admission $5; resort guests free. Open daily from 10 a.m. to 4 p.m.

Sizing Up the Shopping Scene

Bridgetown's **Broad Street** is the primary shopping area in the capital. You'll see lots of signs advertising dutyfree goods. If you want to buy any of the luxury items, you'll need to show your passport and airline ticket. We aren't big shoppers, but the upscale offerings here reminded us of Bermuda.

Cave Shephard and **Harrison's** are the largest department stores, with huge selections of dutyfree merchandise; branches of these stores are located at the Cruise Ship Terminal, the airport, and in large hotels.

Try **Colours of De Caribbean** (the Careenage, Bridgetown; ☎ 246-436-8522) for original hand-painted and batik clothing; imported cottons, linens, and silks for day and evening; and handmade jewelry. We found an interesting Picasso-esque handpainted throw pillow cover there for Echo's mom.

At **Sunny Shoes, Inc.** (Cave Shephard, Broad St., Bridgetown; ☎ 246-431-2121), concessionaire DeCourcey Clarke will make a pair of women's strap sandals while you wait — in any color(s) you wish — for about $30.

Check out the new **Cruise Ship Terminal** shopping arcade, where passengers can buy both dutyfree and Barbadian-made merchandise at more than 30 boutiques and a dozen vendor carts and stalls.

Our idea of a fun shopping excursion was sampling Barbados's famed liquid gold — rum — after a fun tour of the **Mount Gay Rum Factory** (☎ 246-425-8757). The Factory is a quick drive outside of Bridgetown, and we picked up a smattering of the island's history there. Island music was blaring over the loudspeaker while a gleeful bartender enjoyed pouring samples from Barbados's oldest distillery.

Courting St. Lucia's island charm

Many travelers split their vacations between Barbados and St. Lucia, an often-overlooked, easily accessible gem that yields one surprise after another: a steamy volcano, secluded waterfalls, dramatic mountain vistas, lush rain forest preserves, and even private mineral baths used by Napoleon's muse Josephine, who grew up on one of the island's plantations.

St. Lucia is rougher around the edges than neighboring prim and proper Barbados; it's much more akin in spirit to Jamaica, which has an equally colorful past. You can expect to see more of the real Caribbean here than on any of the other islands in this book.

The crowning glory of St. Lucia (pronounced *LOO-sha*) are the Pitons, postcard-perfect twin volcanic peaks rising majestically out of the sea near the tiny fishing village of Soufriére. In this area, you'll find a trio of our personal favorite resorts for romance Caribbean-style:

✔ **Anse Chastanet:** This small boutique resort boasts gourmet food, stunning views, and great snorkeling/diving just off its dark-sand, quarter-mile-long crescent of a beach. Invest in one of the premium or deluxe octagonal rooms (numbers 7 and 14) that feel like deluxe treehouses for adults, and you're in for a slice of heaven. Eco, romance, and dive packages are available.

✔ P.O. Box 7000, Soufrière, St. Lucia. ☎ **800-223-1108,** reservations for divers 888-GO-LUCIA or 758-459-7000. Fax: 758-459-7700. E-mail: ansechastanet@candw.lc. Internet: www.ansechastanet.com. Rack rates: $415–$695 includes mandatory MAP. AE, DC, MC, V.

✔ **Jalousie Hilton Resort & Spa:** Snuggled between St. Lucia's signature twin landmarks, the Pitons, this 325-acre resort overlooking Jalousie Bay has been designated a rain forest nature sanctuary by the St. Lucia Naturalist's Society. Built on the remains of an eighteenth-century sugar plantation, it has 102 bright and air-conditioned 550-square-foot cottages with huge bathrooms and private plunge pools. You can select from honeymoon, tennis, scuba, spa, cooking, and other packages.

✔ 5 miles from Soufrière on Anse des Pitons St. (P.O. Box 251), Soufrière, St. Lucia. ☎ **800-445-8667,** 888-744-5256, or 758-459-7666. Fax: 758-459-7667. E-mail: jhr_sales&mkt@candw.lc. Internet: www.jalousie-hilton.com. EP, MAP, and FAP. Rack rates: $475 Sugar Mill Room; $500 Villa; $600 Villa Suite. AE, DISC, DC, MC, O, V.

✔ **Ladera Resort:** This sophisticated stunner has just a few rooms, each with some of the better views in the Caribbean and private plunge pools or Jacuzzis. The on-site restaurant is one of our favorites in the Caribbean, too. Romance and wedding packages are available.

✔ Above the Pitons, 2 miles south of town, P.O. Box 225, Soufrière, St. Lucia. ☎ **800-738-4752** or 758-459-7323. Fax: 800-404-1841 or 758-459-5156. E-mail: Ladera@candw.lc. Internet: www.Ladera-StLucia.com. Rack rates: Suites from $345; luxury villa with pool $725. AE, MC, V.

For information on St. Lucia, contact the St. Lucia Tourist Board, **888-4-STLUCIA,** 800-456-3984, or 212-867-2950; e-mail: slutour@candw.lc; Internet: www.stlucia.org.

Locating Local Craft Shops

Typical Bajan crafts are pottery, woven floor mats and placemats, hand-printed fabrics, dolls, needlecraft, shellwork, wood carvings, baskets and straw items, and artwork.

You can find good examples of these types of items at the **Barbados Museum Annual Craft Fair** held each December and at major festivals such as **Crop Over, Oistins Fish Festival,** and the **Holetown Festival.**

Our top pick takes a little driving, and you'll have to keep a sharp eye to find the sign pointing to **Earthworks** (Edgehill Heights 2, St. Thomas, Barbados; ☎ **246-425-0223;** fax 246-425-3224; e-mail earthworks@ caribsurf.com; Internet www.earthwork-pottery.com). Earthworks is a family-owned pottery shop in the hilly countryside. Here you'll find stacks of colorful pottery from a complete dinner service to one-of-a-kind art pieces. If you're looking for a bargain, ask to be pointed to the seconds shelves. We spent about an hour watching the potters work. The shop is open Monday through Friday from 9 a.m. to 5 p.m. and Saturday from 9 a.m. to 1 p.m.

Fairfield Pottery & Gallery (North of Bridgetown, St. Michael; ☎ **246-424-3800**) is in an old syrup-boiling house. Each piece of pottery is handcrafted from local clay and individually painted. Call for a tour; items are for sale on-site and in island gift shops.

Pelican Village (Harbour Road; ☎ **246-426-4391**) is a cluster of open-air shops where local craftspeople are at work. Leather goods, coconut-shell accessories, mahogany items, and grass rugs and mats are good buys. Within the chattel houses at **Tyrol Cot Heritage Village** (Codrington Hill, St. Michael; ☎ **246-424-2074**), you can watch local artisans make hand-painted figurines, straw baskets, clothing, paintings, and pottery.

Did Someone Say "Party"?

Just a quarter of a century after Barbados was settled in 1627, Bridgetown already had more than 100 bars. That tradition continues today. We've never seen an island with this many watering holes in the Caribbean. Barbados averages 12 per square mile. In other words, you won't have a problem finding a happy hour.

Bajans might keep a stiff upper lip by day, but at night, this island has one of the most rollicking party scenes in the Caribbean. You can choose your poison at beach bars, pubs, wine bars, sports bars, jazz clubs, reggae clubs, discos, floorshows, nightclubs, Latin parties, karaoke bars, cinemas, live theatre, and even at the opera.

When the sun goes down, folks go *limin'* (hanging out) in Barbados. The nightclubs open around 9:30 p.m., but the action doesn't really heat up until at least 11 p.m. The live bands and DJs at the clubs may party till 3 a.m. Although Barbados isn't known for crime, we still urge you to exercise caution, especially if you're out late after the wallop of a few Planter's Punches has settled in.

Take a cab back to your resort if you've had much to drink, because the roads on Barbados are narrow and dark.

Baku Beach (Holetown, St. James; ☎ **246-432-BAKU**) and its sister nightclub the **Casbah** are currently the hot spots on Barbados. The trendy crowd at Baku, open nightly from 6:30 p.m., consists of locals and tourists alike. Some of the hottest bands on the island perform at its cocktail bar. The Casbah, open nightly from 10 p.m. to 3 a.m., resembles a New York City lounge with a DJ spinning tunes all night.

Women usually wear dresses or skirts, although nice pants are fine too. Men can be found in khaki pants, collared shirts, and dress shoes.

The Gap, or St. Lawrence Gap, situated on the south coast in the Worthing Area, has long had a reputation as the place for late-night limin'. Its "hip strip" boasts a mind-boggling 40 bars, pubs, clubs, and restaurants. **Café Sol** (St. Lawrence Gap, Christ Church; ☎ **246-435-9531**) has a wraparound terrace with a great view of the St. Lawrence Gap strip. Margaritas (rubbed with sugar, not salt) will fortify you for the late-night complimentary Spanish dance lessons. One of the best-known nightspots is the **Ship Inn** (St. Lawrence Gap, Christ Church; ☎ **246-435-6961**), a friendly pub with live local bands every night for dancing.

On the south coast, the hot spot is **The Boatyard** (Bay Street on Carlisle Bay five minutes from Bridgetown; ☎ **246-436-2622**). It has a pub atmosphere with both a DJ and live band music. From happy hours (twice daily: 3 to 6 p.m. and 10 to 11 p.m.) until the wee hours, you'll find locals and visitors mingling. Fridays are especially thumping with a DJ spinning tunes in between a live band's sets.

The **Rusty Pelican** (the Careenage, Bridgetown, St. Michael; ☎ **246-436-7778**) overlooks the bustling waterfront activity of the Careenage and features an easy listening guitarist. **Upstairs at Olives** (Holetown, St. James; ☎ **246-432-2112**) is a sophisticated watering hole that's open late.

Harbour Lights (Marine Villa, Bay St., Bridgetown, St. Michael; ☎ **246-436-7225**; e-mail harbourlights@sunbeach.net; Internet www.funbarbados.com) claims to be the "home of the party animal," and its popular beachfront location does draw the crowds who dance under the stars to live reggae and soca music. It has three large bars and a late night BBQ grill on the beach. Monday night, the entertainment is beach limbo and fire-eating with a beachside BBQ. Wednesdays and Fridays, your drinks are on the house from 9:30 a.m. to 3 p.m. after you've paid a $12.50 entry fee. On Sunday nights, this is party central on an island known for getting down.

Part V
The British Virgin Islands

The 5th Wave   By Rich Tennant

FEW MOMENTS IN SAILING COMPARE IN MAJESTY TO THE SHRINERS SUNSET REGATTA.

In this part . . .

Sailors love these peaceful, sparsely populated islands; if you're looking for a true getaway, you'll love them, too. We describe the best of the islands' accommodations and explain how to reach them by air and by sea.

While seafood is the specialty on the BVIs, we offer recommendations for the best spots to experience a wide variety of cuisine. Finally, we give you the lowdown on the best ways to spend your time on the BVIs, including how to plan some island-hopping trips.

Chapter 16

The Lowdown on the British Virgin Islands' Hotel Scene

. . . .

In This Chapter

▶ Sizing up hotel locations

▶ Focusing on top hotel picks

. . . .

*I*f you know anything about the British Virgin Islands, you probably know that they're a favorite with sailors. But the truth is that you can be a complete know-nothing about sailing and still fall in love with these idyllic islands. We did.

The British Virgin Islands attract an entertaining mix of humanity. During Happy Hour at your hotel bar, you may very well find yourself swapping sailor yarns with a dot com millionaire or European royalty.

These sparsely populated islands — only 14 of the 50 are inhabited — are dotted with small inns, cottages, villas, and casually elegant boutique resorts, including many of our favorite Caribbean resorts. What you won't find here are gargantuan mega-resorts with rah-rah activity directors. More than half of the "rooms" available in the BVIs are actually on the many boats found plying the peaceful waters here.

Figuring Out Where You Want to Stay

Unlike most of the other islands you've read about in this book, many of the exquisite resorts in the British Virgin Islands aren't necessarily right on a beach. You won't find broad strands of powdery, sugar-white beach lined with hotels like on Aruba, Barbados, Puerto Rico, or Jamaica. With the notable exception of flat-as-a-johnny-cake Anegada, which has an amazing stretch of beach but a barebones hotel scene, these are hilly, volcanic islands. Many hotels and resorts are nestled high above the water to make the most of some of the Caribbean's grandest views.

But don't cross the BVIs off your list just because you can't step out of your hotel room and onto the beach. If you do, you'll miss out on one of the Caribbean's premier getaway destinations. (Besides, all of our accommodation choices are within easy reach of some of our favorite beaches — see Chapter 19.)

The bulk of our accommodation choices are concentrated on **Tortola,** the most populated island and the site of the capital, and verdant and hilly **Virgin Gorda.**

The remaining hotels, resorts, and inns that we've highlighted are on islands that run the gamut from Gilligan's Island to Fantasy Island. Some are small, ultra-exclusive resorts that occupy an entire island; others are as primitive as can be.

Jost Van Dyke boasts a village of picturesque wooden houses on a sandy beach that transports you to the Caribbean of yesteryear. We think the word *quaint* is overused in guidebooks, but it applies to this spot.

Conserving Cash

Because many of our favorite hotels here are on the small side, they often get booked quickly during high season (January 4 to April 14). Also, many require a minimum stay of seven nights during holiday season (December 15 to January 3). However, if you're willing to go during the summer months, you can get great bargains on your accommodations. And you'll likely have even more places practically all to yourself.

Many places on the resort islands have all-inclusive rates but only because it's expensive and often not easy to get to a different restaurant.

Private villas can be booked through **Virgin Gorda Villa Rentals Ltd.** (P.O. Box 63, The Valley, Virgin Gorda, BVIs; ☎ **800-848-7081** or 284-495-7421; fax 284-495-7367; e-mail leverick@surfbvi.com; Internet www.VirginGordaBVI.com). Maid service, cooks, and staff are easily arranged. Efficiencies start at $833 a week in the winter.

The BVIs' Best Accommodations

The rack rates listed are in U.S. dollars and are for a standard double room during high season (mid-December to mid-April), unless otherwise noted. Lower rates are often available during the off-season and shoulder season; see Chapter 2 for more information on travel seasons.

Biras Creek
$$$$$ Virgin Gorda

Accessible only by boat, this remote, 33-room resort perched on a ridge between two hills on a 140-acre peninsula is one of our top five most romantic resorts in the Caribbean. Our favorite suite is situated on the rocky Atlantic Ocean side (perfect for shell collecting, but don't go barefoot), where you'll be lulled to sleep by the sound of crashing waves. It was private enough that one night we fell asleep in each other's arms on the terrace after watching stars shoot across the midnight blue skies. The roomy, outdoor shower is set up so that even the most modest will be comfortable making good use of it.

The British Virgin Islands' Hotels

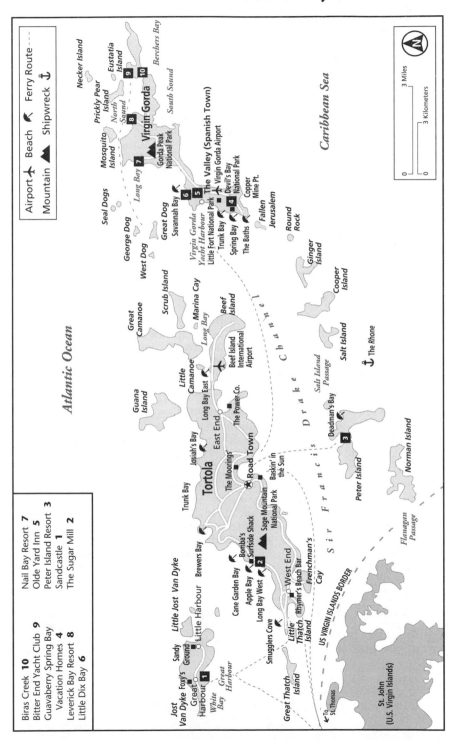

Biras Creek **10**
Bitter End Yacht Club **9**
Guavaberry Spring Bay Vacation Homes **4**
Leverick Bay Resort **8**
Little Dix Bay **6**

Nail Bay Resort **7**
Olde Yard Inn **5**
Peter Island Resort **3**
Sandcastle **1**
The Sugar Mill **2**

Airport ✈ Beach ☀ Ferry Route ---
Mountain ▲ Shipwreck ⚓

Atlantic Ocean

Caribbean Sea

N

3 Miles
3 Kilometers

Necker Island
Eustatia Island
Prickly Pear Island
Mosquito Island
Berchers Bay
North Sound
South Sound
Virgin Gorda
Gorda Peak National Park
Seal Dogs
George Dog
Great Dog
West Dog
Long Bay
Savannah Bay
The Valley (Spanish Town)
Virgin Gorda Airport
Devil's Bay National Park
Copper Mine Pt.
Virgin Gorda Yacht Harbour
Little Fort National Park
Trunk Bay
Spring Bay
The Baths
Fallen Jerusalem
Round Rock
Ginger Island
Cooper Island
Salt Island
The Rhone
Scrub Island
Marina Cay
Beef Island
Beef Island International Airport
Great Camanoe
Little Camanoe
Long Bay
Long Bay East
The Power Co.
Guana Island
Josiah's Bay
East End
Trunk Bay
The Moorings
Road Town
Baskin' in the Sun
Tortola
Brewers Bay
Cane Garden Bay
Apple Bay
Bomba's Surfside Shack
Sage Mountain National Park
Long Bay West
West End
Frenchman's Cay
Rhymer's Beach Bar
Smugglers Cove
Little Thatch Island
Great Thatch Island
US VIRGIN ISLANDS BORDER
St. John (U.S. Virgin Islands)
To St. Thomas
Little Jost Van Dyke
Sandy Ground
Foxy's
Little Harbour
Jost Van Dyke
White Bay
Great Harbour
Deadman's Bay
Peter Island
Norman Island
Flanagan Passage
Salt Island Passage
Drake Channel
Sir Francis
Atlantic Ocean

The resort boasts miles of scenic trails, a freshwater seaside pool, a small private beach with a large shelter where barbecue lunch is served, and a salt pond bird sanctuary. Snorkeling fins, windsurfing equipment, sailboats, and motor dinghies are available for guest use, and bicycles are parked outside each suite. A French chef produces delicious meals served in an open-air, hilltop stone restaurant with stunning sea views. Biras Creek is one of only half a dozen Caribbean restaurants to have a wine cellar.

Bottom line: great food, hip décor, and nature galore. The resort was recently inducted into the exclusive *Relais & Chateaux,* which recognizes the world's best small hotels with notable restaurants on site. It is one of only four in the Caribbean to attain that honor. Kids are welcome only in the summer, but we'd only recommend it for older children.

North Sound, Virgin Gorda, (P.O. Box 54), BVI. ☎ *800-223-1108 or 284-494-3553. Fax: 284-494-3557. E-mail:* biras@surfbvi.com. *Internet:* www.biras.com. *Rack rates: Garden Suite $425–$650, Ocean Suite $525–$750, Grand Suite $625–$850, Villa $725–$950. Rates include all meals. AE, MC, V.*

Bitter End Yacht Club
$$$$$ Virgin Gorda

Consistently on the list of the Caribbean's best resorts, this casual, rustic resort, only reachable by sea, has been a favorite with sailors, windsurfers, and divers (because of a dramatic wreck and gorgeous reefs nearby) for 25 years. Bitter End is comprised of a collection of 95 villas and suites — some beachside, and some dotting the lush hillsides overlooking the North Sound (a protected, deep water harbor). For the ultimate in luxurious privacy, you can charter a Freedom 30 live-aboard yacht (100 watercrafts are available for guests). Using Bitter End as a home base, you can explore nearby islands. The most secluded and scenic beachfront digs have king-size beds, giant showers, and a wraparound veranda strung with a hammock for two.

You won't want for entertainment here. This resort boasts three glittering beaches stretched along a mile dotted with covered lounge chairs and hammocks. (That's the one area where the Bitter End beats out Biras Creek, which we prefer on all other counts.) A steel pan band plays most nights, and active types will love the fitness course with a jogging track and 16 exercise stations. The accommodations and restaurants got a much-needed overhaul, but you'll definitely want to book dinner at neighboring Biras Creek one night.

Family packages often offer essentially two connecting rooms for the price of one. The rate for children age 12 and under is $50 a night when they stay in their parents' room; for children 13 and up the rate is $100 a night. With stays of five nights or more, a Sailing 101 course is included.

North Sound, Virgin Gorda (P.O. Box 46), BVI. ☎ *800-872-2392 or 284-494-2746. Fax: 284-494-4756. E-mail:* binfo@beyc.com. *Internet:* www.beyc.com. *Rack rates: $500–$700 double or suite. Rates include all meals. Packages available. AE, MC, V.*

Guavaberry Spring Bay Vacation Homes

$$$ Virgin Gorda

These white-roofed, redwood hexagonal houses, nestled amid huge boulders and billows of brilliantly hued tropical flowers, are within walking distance of Virgin Gorda's top natural attraction, The Baths. You'll feel like you're in a treehouse, and the owners, Tina and Ludwig Goschler, are kind hosts. Louvered windows are open to the breezes, and the tile floors stay cool. The terrace overlooks the Sir Francis Drake Channel. Each home has one to two bedrooms, a living room with a kitchen/dining area, a private bath, a kitchenette, an open sun deck, and daily maid service. A quick walk brings you to Spring Bay, a gold sand beach with crystal-clear waters. A commissary is on-site, or you can shop for food at the Virgin Gorda Yacht Harbour, about a mile away.

Spring Bay, Virgin Gorda (P.O. Box 20), BVI. ☎ *284-495-5227. Fax: 284-495-5283. E-mail:* gsbhomes@surfbvi.com. *Internet:* www.guavaberryspringbay. com. *Rack rates: $168–$235 one- or two-bedroom home. No credit cards.*

Leverick Bay Resort

$$ Virgin Gorda

This resort offers a colorful collection of 14 spacious hillside rooms, each with marvelous sea views overlooking a small marina. The small pool is a nice spot to cool off if you don't want to make the five-minute walk to the patch of sand the hotel calls a beach. (The volleyball court takes up most of it.) A spa has been added (☎ 284-495-7375) featuring body treatments, massage, manicures, and pedicures. Each room has a refrigerator, coffeemaker, safe, and private balcony. This modest property is a good choice for the independent traveler who wants a good-value base from which to explore.

The Valley, Virgin Gorda (P.O. Box 63), BVI. ☎ *800-848-7081 or 284-495-7421. Fax: 284-495-7367. E-mail:* leverick@surfbvi.com. *Internet:* www. VirginGordaBVI.com. *Rack rates: $149 double. AE, MC, V.*

Little Dix Bay

$$$$$ Virgin Gorda

Set on a fabulous crescent strand of white-sand beach, nestled amid the lush hills of Virgin Gorda, is the elegant Little Dix Bay, a resort designed by Laurance Rockefeller in 1964 to make the most of its natural surroundings while catering to the rich.

The mood at this gracious and upscale 500-acre retreat is peaceful and unhurried. There's no pool or TV, but its 98 rooms recently got AC, telephones, and refrigerators — much to the consternation of the loyal clientele. Rates include waterskiing, snorkeling gear and lessons, water taxis to nearby beaches, sunfish sailboats, kayaks, nightly movies, biking trails, tennis courts, fitness center, afternoon tea, and, of course, your daily *New York Times* fax.

Little Dix is positioned on one of the best beaches in the BVI, and it even has a fleet of boats ready to sail you to a private beach. The clientele tend to be older couples during high season. This resort is the sort of place where ladies will always want to have their most chic beach cover-up close at hand. Honeymooners and families flock here during the summer when rates drop dramatically. We find the setting absolutely romantic and the service excellent without being obnoxious. Housekeeping comes twice a day. The room décor is genteel Caribbean and fabulous, dah-ling. Grab your tennis racquet and your wallet. The transfer from Tortola's Beef Island, for instance, is not included. You'll fork over $65 per person for Little Dix's private launch.

Thanks to the general manager's wife, Little Dix also boasts the poshest kids' program that we've seen in the Caribbean, called Children's Grove. A miniaturized pirate's paradise has been created for wee ones — complete with pirate garb for dress-up play. Children are now welcome year-round at Little Dix, and there's no additional charge for those under age 16 staying in their parents' room. During summer, you can get a second room for your kids at a 50% discount.

*P.O. Box 70, Virgin Gorda, BVI. ☎ **888-ROSEWOOD** or 284-495-555. Fax: 284-495-5661. Internet:* www.rosewood-hotels.com *or* www.littledixbay.com. *Rack rates: $450–$600 double. AE, MC, V.*

Nail Bay Resort
$$$ Virgin Gorda

Nestled beneath Gorda Peak National Park is lovely Nail Bay Resort. Located on the site of a 19th-century sugar plantation, the enclave is comprised of luxurious rooms, apartments, and two-to-five bedroom villas, all with sweeping views of the stunning Caribbean below. All have CD/cassette/radios, TV/VCRs, fridges, microwaves, toaster ovens, coffeemakers, and either king or two twin beds; a few have espresso machines.

Facilities include pools replete with a waterfall and swim-up bar (a rarity in the laid-back BVIs), a tennis court, and bocce and croquet lawns. Three crescent beaches are within easy walking distance of the 147-acre estate. If you don't want to cook, a chef will come to your villa and prepare meals. Ask about the package deals.

*P.O. Box 69, Virgin Gorda, BVI. ☎ **800-871-3551** or 284-494-8000. Fax: 284-495-5875. E-mail:* info@nailbay.com. *Internet:* www.nailbay.com. *Rack rates: $125–$425 double, apartment, or villa. Packages available. AE, DISC, MC, V.*

Olde Yard Inn
$$–$$$ Virgin Gorda

If you like B&Bs, this charming inn is a great choice. It's a mile from the airport, on a hilltop in the midst of a beautiful garden overlooking Virgin Gorda's Handsome Bay. The comfortable rooms have simple island furniture, tile floors, and roomy baths. Some are air-conditioned. A beautiful pool, Jacuzzi, open-air health club, and poolside bar keep guests busy. The nearest beach is one mile away, but the helpful staff happily arranges sails and complimentary transport to the surf. Or you can walk it in 20 minutes. The guests here come for the beautiful surroundings. The owners also pride themselves on the library — open to guests — with one of the largest private collections of books in the Caribbean.

P.O. Box 26, Virgin Gorda, BVI. ☎ *800-653-9273 or 284-495-5544. Fax: 284-495-5986. E-mail:* oldeyar@surfbvi.com. *Internet:* www.travelxn.com/oldeyard. **Rack rates:** *$145–$245 double. AE, MC, V.*

Peter Island Resort

$$$$$ **Peter Island**

If you tire of the BVIs' pristine waters in your yacht, drop anchor at Peter Island, one of *Condé Nast Traveler's* "Best Places to Stay in the World." This 1,800-acre, 52-room boutique escape lets couples snorkel in secluded coves or cast-off on the resort's sailing yacht. Honeymoon, the most intimate of the five beaches necklacing the island, offers two lounge chairs beneath a thatch hut. At White Bay Beach, you can order up a custom-made gourmet picnic lunch complete with fine linens, china, and flatware.

The cuisine can be disappointing, however, but your courses are all accompanied by a choice of fine champagne, wine, cognac, or armagnac. At press time, the resort was tinkering with the menus. If you somehow manage to get tired of sunning, sailing, or napping in palm-sheltered hammocks, you can hike the Loop, a dramatic bluff on the island's south side. You won't feel entirely cut off from civilization, though, not with the resort's satellite television, the *New York Times* by fax at breakfast, telephones, and, of course, the Internet.

Peter Island, BVI. ☎ *800-346-4451, 800-323-7500, or 284-495-2000. Internet:* www.peterisland.com. *Rack rates: $705–$970 two-bedroom villa. Rates include transfers to island and all meals. AE, MC, V.*

Sandcastle

$$$ **Jost Van Dyke**

Phones and televisions are nonexistent at this tiny inn with hexagonal cottages set in lush gardens — and radios and hair dryers are discouraged! Tucked along the sugary White Bay Beach, this six-room hotel is a great escape. Indeed, it just got electricity in 1996. If you manage to roll out of your hammock, you can sign up for an array of activities. There's also a small fun restaurant on-site called **The Soggy Dollar Bar** (see Chapter 18).

White Bay, Jost Van Dyke, BVI. ☎ *284-495-9888. Fax: 284-495-9999. E-mail:* sandcastle@candwbvi.net. *Internet:* www.sandcastle-bvi.com. *Rack rates: $170–$220 double. EP, MAP. AE, MC, V.*

The Sugar Mill

$$$–$$$$ Tortola

The Sugar Mill is a cottage colony that sweeps down the lush hillside on the north side of Tortola to a small private beach with snorkeling off shore. You can see Bomba's Beach Shack, a funky little bar, down the road, and at certain times of the year you'll also see surfers. This 360-year-old sugar plantation has been a sweet success for its owners/managers, who also run the extremely popular, award-winning restaurant of the same name (see Chapter 17). If you don't want to make the walk down to the beach, no worries: Just take a plunge in the circular pool. The 20 units range from studio apartments to suites; all have kitchenettes and private terraces with sweeping views. Snorkeling equipment is free.

*Apple Bay, Tortola (P.O. Box 425, Road Town), BVI. ☎ **800-462-8834** or 284-495-4355. Fax: 284-495-4696. E-mail:* sugmill@surfbvi.com. *Internet:* www.sugarmillhotels.com. *Rack rates: $180–$585 double. AE, V, MC. No children under 11 from December 21 to April 15. Closed August to September.*

Chapter 17

Settling into the British Virgin Islands

. . . .

In This Chapter

▶ Knowing what to expect when you arrive

▶ Getting around the islands

▶ Discovering the British Virgin Islands from A to Z

. . . .

Most visitors to the British Virgin Islands connect through San Juan, Puerto Rico (a 30-minute flight) or make a brief stop on St. Thomas, in the nearby U.S. Virgin Islands (see Part V), and then continue on to the BVIs either by plane or regularly scheduled ferry.

Arriving in the BVIs by Plane

Tortola's **Beef Island Airport** (☎ **284-494-3701** or BVI Customs 284-495-2235) is the main airport serving the BVIs. This small airport, which is undergoing a $53 million expansion, currently has the feel of a sleepy outpost — scruffy but easy to negotiate. Several of the hotels have welcome desks in the terminal to smooth your way, but don't expect a tourist board office or ATM. The airport is connected to Tortola by **Queen Elizabeth Bridge,** a one-laner with half a calabash gourd for all-comers to drop in their 50¢ toll on the honor system. With the new construction, which includes the bridge, that calabash will likely be a quaint memory soon.

Your vacation can run more smoothly if you fax your flight arrival information to your resort well in advance and request a confirmation detailing transportation to the resort — especially if your accommodations are on an island other than Tortola. If you take your resort's suggestion, transfer costs (usually by regularly scheduled ferry) are often included in your final hotel bill. You'll just sign vouchers along the way.

Going through passport control and customs is slow in the BVIs. The officials are efficient and welcoming, but they're also thorough.

Arriving in the BVIs by Boat

You can also travel to the BVIs from the U.S. Virgin Islands by public ferry. Ferries connect St. Thomas and St. John with Road Town and West End on Tortola. Generally, ferry service starts at 6:15 a.m. with scattered departures throughout the day until 5:30 p.m. Fares are about $25 one-way or $45 round-trip. Because schedules change frequently, consider calling ahead to get up-to-date information, or enlist your hotel's help in making advance arrangements.

Following are the main BVI ferry operators:

- ✔ **Native Son, Inc.** (☎ **284-495-4617**) connects St. Thomas (Red Hook) and St. John to Road Town and West End, Tortola daily.

- ✔ **Smith's Ferry Services** (☎ **284-494-4454** or 284-495-2355) operates daily to connect St. Thomas (Red Hook) and St. John to Road Town and West End, Tortola. Also connects Tortola to Virgin Gorda.

- ✔ **Inter-Island Boat Services** (☎ **284-495-4166**) connects St. John (Cruz Bay) and West End, Tortola daily.

The ferries that run between the USVIs and the BVIs travel along the Sir Francis Drake Channel. The channel can be somewhat rough at times, but the ferries that ply those waters are so large that they are relatively stable. If you're worried, bring Dramamine (or your preferred seasickness remedy), and take it half an hour before you board.

 If you plan to take a day trip from the BVIs to the U.S. Virgin Islands, which are within sight of the BVIs, be sure to bring your ID with you. You won't be allowed back onto the BVIs without it. Customs and immigrations booths are located at the ferry docks on Tortola, Virgin Gorda, and Jost Van Dyke, and you'll need to show your passport or other documents there. In BVI waters, your boat might encounter Port Authority officials who can ask to see your passport at any time.

Getting from the Airport to Your Final Destination

Getting to your final destination is usually the toughest part of a trip to the BVIs, because many of the islands are accessible only by boat or puddle jumpers. But don't assume that travel between islands is terribly complicated. Once you arrive in the BVIs, you can relax with the reality that the islands are in close proximity to one another.

By car

The government has banned renting cars at the Beef Island Airport, so driving yourself to a resort on Tortola is not an option. You'll have to take one of the many cabs or the open-air shuttle. Numerous cabs congregate out front when you exit customs. The locals are friendly and helpful, always happy to point the way if you're feeling confused.

By taxi

One of the best taxi drivers we've had in the Caribbean — the most knowledgeable, nicest, and most courteous — operates on Tortola. He's James Pickering, the young proprietor of the unfortunately named **Deadman's Taxi Service.** (Let him tell you the story behind the name.) Call ☎ **284-495-2216** at the airport; cellular 284-496-7979 or 284-496-6555.

The 20-minute ride from the airport to **Road Town** costs $18. The more riders who crowd in, the more the price goes down per person. So if you're pinching pennies, be patient while your cabby tries to round up more folks.

By ferry

If you're headed to **Virgin Gorda** from the airport, you'll board an open-air courtesy bus with a gaily covered awning and travel past a grungy-looking area to Trellis Bay to catch the **North Sound Express Ferry** (☎ **284-495-2138** or 284-495-2261). (You could walk this route if you didn't have luggage.) This small, high-speed ferry drops you either at Bitter End or Biras Creek's dock. Along the way, you get a great view of these gorgeous islands — notice how Virgin Gorda really does look like a fat lady reclining in the fantastically blue waters. The islanders on board are happy to give impromptu explanations of what you're seeing.

The North Sound Express Ferry departs promptly at 6:15 a.m., 10:30 a.m., 3:30 p.m., 5:30 p.m., and 7:15 p.m.; it costs $20 each way and takes about 45 minutes. Reservations are required. If you arrive after 7:15 p.m., you can still get to Virgin Gorda, but you have to arrange in advance and fork over a $30 surcharge per person.

If you're going to **Spanish Town** or a resort nearby in Virgin Gorda, take a cab to Road Town's ferry dock and catch **Smith's Ferry Services** (☎ **284-495-4495**) or **Speedy's** (☎ **284-495-5240**) for the half-hour ride, which costs $20.

By plane

If your final destination is an island other than Tortola or Virgin Gorda, you can take a small puddle jumper or sea plane for a quick flight.

If you don't mind tiny planes and want to skip the ferry ride, try one of the following airlines:

- ✔ **Clair Aero Services** (☎ **284-495-2271**) has scheduled flights from Tortola to Anegada on Monday, Wednesday, Friday, and Sunday.

- ✔ **Cape Air** (☎ **800-352-0714** or 284-495-2100; Internet www.flycapeair.com) has hourly service between Tortola, San Juan, and St. Thomas.

- ✔ **Air Sunshine** (☎ **800-327-8900** or 284-495-8900) takes you from Tortola to miniscule Virgin Gorda Airport, which closes at dusk. The trip's so brief you'll barely have time to fasten your seatbelt.

- ✔ Once on Virgin Gorda, **Mahogany Taxi Service** (☎ **284-495-5469**) or **Potter's Taxi** (☎ **284-495-5329** or 284-495-5960) meets you at the airport for the 10-minute, $20 roller-coaster ride to the North Sound, where your hotel's launch will pick you up and quickly ferry you across a small bay.

Getting Around the BVIs

Going from island to island in the BVIs is so commonplace that many locals live on one island and commute via ferry daily to their jobs or schools. You're likely to see fellow vacationers who start to look familiar as you roam from island to island, too.

By ferry

With boatloads of islands to explore, your best bet is to travel by sea. Boats are often the cheapest and easiest mode of transportation. Take advantage of the excellent public ferries that connect the BVIs as well as St. John and St. Thomas. The ferries are clean and comfortable; you'll probably encounter mostly locals and a few tourists on board. For a list of the major ferry operators, see the "Arriving in the BVIs by Boat" section.

Timing is everything in the BVIs. Double-check ferry schedules, and plan to arrive about 10 minutes early to get your pick of seats. When you call for the schedule, confirm the proper pickup point so that you can be ready and waiting for the ferry's arrival. The ferries here run like clockwork, so save yourself stress and allow ample time to get from Point A to Point B. If you're the classic wait-till-the-last-minute type who thrives on cutting everything close, the BVIs will cure you of that habit. See the previous section for names of ferries and contact information.

Little Dix Bay and several of the private island resorts provide their own ferry service for guests, too, so make sure to check with your hotel.

If you miss the boat, hiring a private water taxi or charter can be an extremely expensive proposition. Think ten times the going rate of the ferry for the same route — depending on the mood of the boat's owner.

On foot

We feel fine about walking anywhere in the BVIs — something we unfortunately can't say about every Caribbean island.

Part of the fun of the BVIs is hiking the lush islands (with the exception of Anegada, which is flat and desert-like). You can amble around these islands safely, but there's really not much to see, except for extremely limited shopping in Road Town. For suggestions, see "Taking a Hike" in Chapter 19.

By taxi

Rates are officially set by the government and nonnegotiable. On Tortola, you can find taxis at the airport and at the ferry docks in Road Town and West End. Most taxis offer island tours starting at $45 for three hours. Get your hotel to make the arrangements, or contact the **BVI Taxi Association** (☎ **284-495-1982** or 494-2322). Besides our friend James, whom we mentioned earlier in the chapter, you could also contact **Style's Taxi Service** (☎ **284-494-2260**) or **Turtle Dove Taxi Service** (☎ **284-494-6274**).

Open-air safari trucks with benches in the back (popular on St. John and St. Croix) and roomy vans are starting to become popular for group tours. If you don't mind sharing with strangers, you can get a low-cost island tour this way. Contact the **BVI Taxi Association** (☎ **284-495-1982** or 284-494-2322) for good operators.

By car

We don't recommend renting a car in the BVIs if you're planning on island-hopping. It's a big pain and expensive, and you're more likely to spend most of your time on the beach or plying the peaceful waters by boat anyway. When we want to explore, we find it much simpler to get a taxi driver guide for one morning, because there isn't that much to see anyway — even in Road Town, the capital.

Near Road Town's massive marina, you'll encounter the BVIs' only real traffic mess. Rush-hour traffic foul-ups in the early mornings and late afternoons, as well as the two-to-three times a week when the cruise ships are in, can have you at a standstill for 20 minutes or more.

If you think you'll go stir-crazy without your own wheels, or if you're staying in a villa on Tortola, go ahead and get a car. Villas or out-of-the-way hotels sometimes include rental cars in their packages. Some hotels have rentals on-site, or the hotel will arrange to have the car waiting for you.

You'll have to show your valid driver's license and shell out $10 to get a temporary BVI license. You're also going to have to pay at least $50 a day. Taking the car with you if you want to island-hop is pricey, too, and it's illegal to take a car from the BVIs to the USVIs.

Unless you get written confirmation in advance, don't count on your car being there for you when you arrive — especially in high season. You're best bet is to stick with U.S. rental firms, which are easier to deal with if a problem pops up. On Tortola your choices are

- **Avis** (☎ **800-331-1212** or 284-494-3322)
- **Budget** (☎ **800-527-0700** or 284-494-2639)
- **Hertz** (☎ **800-654-3131** or 284-495-4405)
- **National** (☎ **800-227-7368** or 284-494-3197)

Don't forget to drive on the left — the British way — but your steering wheel will be on the left, just like home. Confusing, huh?

By motorcycle or bicycle

Because of the steep hills, you'd have to be a pretty serious biker to tool around Tortola, but some folks do it. You can get mountain bikes and helmets for about $20 a day at **Boardsailing BVI** (☎ **284-495-2447**) at Nanny Cay and Trellis Bay; and **Last Stop Sports** (☎ **284-494-0564;** Internet www.laststopsports.com) at Nanny Cay near Road Town on Tortola. Last Stop also arranges bike/hike excursions.

You can get motor scooters for about $30 a day at **DJ's Scooter Rentals** (☎ **284-494-5071**) in Road Town.

Quick Concierge

ATMs

ATMs are available on Tortola and Virgin Gorda only. On Tortola, head to **Banco Popular** (☎ 284-494-2117) on Main St. next to the customs office in Road Town, and at **Chase Manhattan Bank** (☎ 284-494-2662).

Baby-sitters

Hotels will happily make arrangements. Sitters cost $8 an hour and up.

Banks

Barclays (☎ 284-494-2171) in Road Town. You get the best exchange rates at banks. Hours vary but are typically Monday to Thursday 8 a.m. to 4:30 p.m. and Friday until 5:30 p.m.

Currency Exchange

Sorry old chap, the U.S. dollar is the official currency of the BVIs. You'll have no problem spending your greenbacks.

Doctors

Check with your resort for a referral; serious emergencies may require an airlift to St. Thomas or San Juan. Divers will be comforted to know a decompression tank is in nearby St. Thomas.

Emergencies

For fire, police, and ambulance, dial ☎ **999** or ☎ **911.**

Festivals

April's **Spring Regatta** is a sailor's dream; the two-week BVI Emancipation Festival starts at the end of July and goes into August; in December the best local fungi bands compete at the Scratch/Fungi Band Fiesta on Tortola.

Hospitals

Peebles Hospital (☎ 284-494-3497) is on Porter Road in Road Town, Tortola. It's the only hospital in the BVIs.

Hurricanes

The season swirls from June to November (September is trickiest).

Information

The **British Virgin Islands Tourist Board** office is above the FedEx office on the AKARA Building's second floor in Wickham's Cay in Road Town (☎ 800-835-8530 from the U.S. or 284-494-3134). You can also e-mail bvitourb@caribsurf.com with specific questions about the BVIs. The official Web site is www.bviwelcome.com. On the island, pick up the latest copy of *The British Virgin Islands Welcome Tourist Guide,* published bi-monthly. For extra credit, you can read *Treasure Island* by Robert Lewis Stevenson, supposedly based on the BVIs' Norman Island.

Language

English is the official language.

Maps

The colorful pocket-sized map published by the tourist board is everywhere — and it's free: at the airport, by the ferry docks, at your hotel, and in gifts shops.

Newspapers/Magazines

The more deluxe resorts offer the *New York Times* by fax. Otherwise, you'll be hard pressed to find either the *Times* or *USA Today.* The best way to stay connected: Most hotels — if they have televisions — offer CNN.

Pharmacies

J. R. O'Neal Drugstore is at 80 Main St. in Road Town, Tortola (☎ 284-494-2292).

Police

Dial ☎ **999** or ☎ **911** for emergencies.

Post Office

Where else? Main Street in Road Town, Tortola (☎ 284-494-3701, ext. 4996). Hours are Monday through Friday 8:30 a.m. to 4 p.m. and Saturday 9 a.m. to noon. Fun fact: There are no zip codes in the BVIs.

Safety
Take normal precautions in town, but crime is extremely rare on these islands. You can walk about freely, but don't do goofy things like leave valuables wrapped in your towel on the beach or dangle your camera behind you while you look at the shops along the waterfront. There are still a few hotels that don't even have locks on their doors.

Taxes
Room tax costs 7%; departure tax is $10 by air and $5 by sea (not included in the price of your ticket).

Taxis
Call the **BVI Taxi Association** (☎ 284-494-2875, 284-494-2322, or 284-495-2378).

Telephone
To reach the BVIs directly, dial 1+284, then the seven-digit local number. You can now make a credit card call from the BVIs by dialing 111 from any phone and following the recorded instructions on completing your call. To dial North America and in the Caribbean, dial 1+area code+number. Dial 011+country code+number for Europe.

At your resort, dial your hotel operator and get exact instructions on how to dial direct using your calling card. We once spent almost an hour trying to use our calling card, only to find out the long-distance service hadn't been turned on in our room. Plus, the instructions vary all over the place, so ask.

Time
Zone Atlantic Standard time year-round, which means that the BVIs are an hour ahead of Eastern Standard Time during fall and winter when the U.S. goes on daylight savings time.

Tipping
Restaurant service calls for 10%–15%, if not already included in your tab; $1 per bag for bellhops, and $1 a day for maid service. No tip required for taxi drivers unless they go beyond the call of duty.

Weather and Surf Reports
The Web site www.caribwx.com has updated reports three times a day. The British Virgin Islands receive little annual rainfall. The temperature ranges from 75 to 85 degrees F, and a steady trade wind keeps the temperature comfortable.

Chapter 18

Dining in the British Virgin Islands

● ●

In This Chapter

▶ Sampling the local cuisine

▶ Locating the islands' best restaurants

● ●

Seafood is by far the biggest treat in the British Virgin Islands. The crystal clear Caribbean waters and the deep Atlantic yield treasures such as fresh grouper and the famed Anegada lobster, sweeter than the well-known Maine lobster. Even though this group of islands has begun to attract some of the hot young European chefs, eager to cut their teeth on the New World cuisine of the Caribbean, most restaurants keep menus fairly straightforward. They focus on the natural deliciousness of the catch itself, without fancy garnish.

Although these little islands are definitely British, formality doesn't rule when it comes to dining. Casual is the dress code of choice at almost all the nicer resort restaurants, not to mention at the funky little beach shacks that boast no phones and no addresses and are accessible only by boat.

Because many items have to be imported, prices are high, though not quite as pricey as Barbados.

Relishing a Taste of the Islands

In the BVIs, bring your sense of adventure — and some cash, because many places don't take credit cards. Part of the fun here is making your own discoveries — finding those little treasures like **Mrs. Scatliffe's** famous baked chicken in coconut served with her own garden vegetables. You can find this treasure on the second-floor terrace of Mrs. Scatliffe's home, a yellow-and-white building across from Carrot Bay in

Road Town. (☎ **284-495-4556;** lunch Monday through Friday; dinner nightly 7 to 9 p.m.; reservations essential; curries $20–$27.) A lively fungi band performs some evenings. Another delight is the **Sandcastle** (☎ **284-497-9888**) on Jost Van Dyke, a candlelit beachside restaurant where four-course delights like duck à l'orange and stuffed grouper regularly make the menu. (See our complete review of Sandcastle later in the chapter.)

Of course, fresh seafood seasoned with local herbs is frequently part of the menu on these islands. You'll also find spicy West Indian cooking, with curries of every description, at small, locally owned places all around.

The British Virgin Islands' Best Restaurants

Geography limits dining choices in the BVIs somewhat, because many of the BVIs are accessible only by boat or small plane. If you plan to stay put on one island, you're likely to select an all-inclusive plan at your resort (see Chapter 16 for details). If you happen to visit the British Virgin Islands as part of an island-hopping adventure, you can check out the hot spots we recommend in the A-to-Z list below.

The upscale resorts typically employ European-trained chefs who could match whisks with just about any good chef out there. Guests return year after year, in part because the food is so top-notch. (We'd venture so far as to say cutting edge.) The cuisine at Virgin Gorda's **Biras Creek** and **Little Dix Bay,** as well as at **The Sugar Mill,** is particularly spectacular. The fine dining restaurants at all three are open to outside guests. (An added bonus: The view at Biras Creek from its stone and wood open-air "castle" is one of the island's most heavenly.) Finally, the venerable **Bitter End Yacht Club** has given its dining operations a sorely needed update. We have sampled the Sunday Brunch at its new **Clubhouse,** and it was quite the spread: grilled swordfish, smoked ham, salads, and steamed vegetables. (See Chapter 16 for reviews of these resorts.)

If you're on a boat, you can still make reservations at many of the restaurants in the BVIs by contacting them via radio on VHF (very high frequency) Channel 16. Ask the captain to call ahead for you.

Bing's Drop Inn Bar
$$ Tortola   Local

Do drop in at this low-key watering hole popular with locals as an after-hours dance spot. Conch fritters and spicy fish stew are the specialties of the house. A good spot if hunger strikes late in the day.

Fat Hog's Bay, East End. ☎ *284-495-2627. Main courses: $10–$20. AE, MC, V. Open for dinner Tuesday through Sunday from 7 p.m.*

The British Virgin Islands' Restaurants

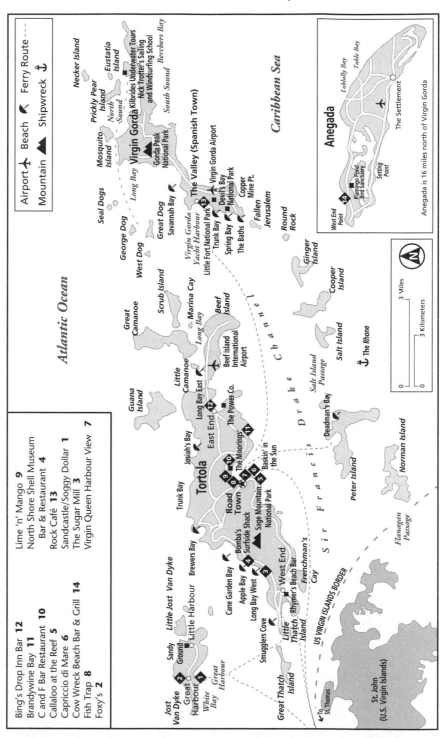

Bing's Drop Inn Bar **12**
Brandywine Bay **11**
C and F Bar Restaurant **10**
Callaloo at the Reef **5**
Capriccio di Mare **6**
Cow Wreck Beach Bar & Grill **14**
Foxy's **2**

Lime 'n' Mango **9**
North Shore Shell Museum
Bar & Restaurant **4**
Rock Café **13**
Sandcastle/Soggy Dollar **1**
The Sugar Mill **3**
Virgin Queen Harbour View **7**

Brandywine Bay

$$$$ **Tortola** **Tuscan**

For a special evening, drive ten minutes east of Road Town to this hillside home on a peninsula overlooking Sir Francis Drake Channel. Chef-owner David Pugliese's skill with Tuscan cooking has won wide praise from foodie magazines like *Bon Appetit*. He uses lots of homegrown herbs and vegetables on a menu that changes daily (based on what's freshest). A favorite starter is his homemade mozzarella. From simply grilled fish with herbs to an elaborately sauced roast duckling, you can't go wrong here. The topper? The presentation is picture-perfect — Pugliese was a former fashion photographer — and everything's served on a beautiful terrace overlooking the channel. An excellent wine list and *tiramisu* for dessert make for a memorable evening.

Just outside of Road Town on Sir Francis Drake Highway, Brandywine Bay. ☎ *284-495-2301. Reservations recommended. Main courses: $20–$28. AE, MC, V. Open for dinner Monday through Saturday from 6:30 p.m. Closed August through October.*

C and F Bar Restaurant

$$–$$$ **Tortola** **West Indian**

Crowds cluster at this casual favorite near The Moorings (see Chapter 19 for description) for Chef Clarence's zesty island-style barbecued chicken, fish and ribs, fresh local fish prepared to your request, or spicy curried conch or lobsters. The food is worth the short wait you'll sometimes have for a table. The hardest thing about coming here? Choosing between key lime pie (the real stuff — not that icky green imitation) and carrot cake for dessert.

Purcell Estate. ☎ *284-494-4941. Reservations not necessary. Main courses: $12–$17. AE, MC, V. Open for dinner nightly from 6:30 p.m. to 11 p.m.*

Callaloo at the Reef

$$$$ **Tortola** **Contemporary Caribbean**

This elegant waterfront restaurant overlooking a small lagoon on the outskirts of Road Town at Prospect Reef offers an excellent, five-course Caribbean dinner with a creative menu changing nightly. For example, you might select scallops sautéed in honey and spice topped with ginger wine zabaglione, pumpkin and seafood bisque, tomato and grilled peppers in caramelized onion vinegar, oven-baked snapper with callaloo on a passion butter sauce and, finally, coconut bread pudding with caramel sauce. All entrees are accompanied by island sides like green gungo peas and rice, bread fruit gratin, saffron rice, or yam and potato mash. This place has a good and extensive wine list.

Waterfront Drive, Road Town. ☎ *284-494-3311. Reservations recommended. Main courses: $35 (price-fixed, five-course). AE, DISC, MC, V. Open daily from 7 a.m to 3 p.m. and from 6:30 p.m. to 11 p.m.*

Capriccio di Mare

$–$$ Tortola Italian

The owners of the well-regarded Brandywine Bay restaurant (see review earlier in this chapter) also operate this informal Italian-style *trattoria* where you can sit outside on the sidewalk across from the ferry dock in Road Town and nibble pastries while you sip your morning cappuccino. Look forward to perfectly cooked, homemade pasta dishes, robust sandwiches, and generous salads here. You can also get picnic fixings for your own private feast at the beach.

Waterfront Drive, Road Town. ☎ *284-494-5369. Reservations not necessary. Main courses: $6–$16. No credit cards. Open: Monday through Saturday from 8 a.m. to 9 p.m. Closed Sunday.*

Cow Wreck Beach Bar & Grill

$$$ Anegada West Indian

This funky, family-owned and managed little spot is a fun place to hang out on Anegada, one of the most laid-back islands we've found in the Caribbean. Open-air and sheltered from the sun by a straw roof, this eatery serves lunch and dinner on picnic tables in view of the Atlantic Ocean and a wide, white-coral sand beach. Sun-bleached conch shells border the paths. You can snorkel while you wait for lunch. (Once, scoping life beneath the water's surface, Kevin got so busy looking at the lobsters in a cage waiting for their turn in the pot that he failed to notice the barracuda bunched together, eyeing him as well as the lobster.) Luncheon fare includes salad, rice, or potatoes alongside trigger fish, lobster, or sandwiches. For dinner, your choices are similar.

Lower Cow Wreck Beach, Anegada. ☎ *284-495-8047 or VHF Channel 16. Main courses: $16–$35. Reservations necessary for dinner. Open for lunch from 10 a.m. to 3 p.m. daily. Dinner seatings are between 6 p.m. and 7 p.m. daily, unless there are no reservations, in which case the restaurants closes.*

Fish Trap

$$–$$$ Tortola International

If all that sun and sea has helped you work up an appetite, you can get hearty meals at a good value at the open air Fish Trap, which features barbecues on Saturdays and Sunday nights. During the week, local fish, conch fritters, burritos, lobster, teriyaki chicken, and burgers dominate the eclectic menu.

Columbus Centre, Wickham's Cay. ☎ *284-494-3026. Main courses: $12–$20. AE, MC, V. Open for lunch Monday through Friday from 11:30 a.m. to 3 p.m. and Saturday from 11:30 a.m. to 2 p.m. Open for dinner from 6:30 p.m. to 11 p.m. nightly.*

Foxy's

$$$ Jost Van Dyke West Indian

Foxy presides over a continual party at his famed beach bar — an institution with the yachting crowd. This popular point of food and fun has also become known over the last 30 years as *the* hot spot to ring in the New Year in the Caribbean. Munch on grilled meat or seafood and relax with a rum concoction while you listen to the strains of calypso, reggae, or soca. At lunch time, *rotis* (flat African bread stuffed with curried fillings) and burgers are a popular choice. If you want to eat dinner here, you must make reservations by 5 p.m. or you'll miss out. Dinner nightly features filet mignon and Calypso Caribbean lobster. Bands play every Thursday, Friday, and Saturday night, and barbecue is the specialty on weekends.

Great Harbour. ☎ 284-495-9258 or VHF Channel 16. Main courses: $11–$28. AE, MC, V. Reservations required for dinner. Open daily for lunch from noon to 2:30 p.m. and dinner from 6:30 p.m. to 9 p.m., but you must reserve by 5 p.m. The bar is open from 9:30 a.m. until "everybody goes home."

Lime 'n' Mango

$$$ Tortola International

If there's a politicos' hangout in the BVIs, this Road Town gathering place is it. We're not sure why BVI residents seem to be fascinated with Mexican food, but you'll find the odd combination of Caribbean dishes and Mexican on this menu — like many others throughout these islands. The giant fish taco is stuffed with a half-pound of red snapper marinated in lime and served with all the fixings. The coconut shrimp is tasty, too. The dinner menu features Anegada conch sauteed in butter, baby back ribs, and New York strip steak. Wines by the glass are a reasonable (for the Caribbean) $4; the restaurant has a modest but decent wine list.

Road Town, Treasure Isle Hotel, Tortola. ☎ 284-494-2501. Reservations strongly recommended. Main courses: $12.50–$25. AE, MC, V. Open daily for breakfast from 7:30 to 10 a.m.; lunch from noon to 2:30 p.m.; and dinner from 7 p.m.

North Shore Shell Museum Bar & Restaurant

$$$ Tortola West Indian

This concrete-block, two-story building doesn't look like much at first glance, but it's one of those quirky finds that we love so much, we almost don't want to share. But, hey, we get paid to tell all our secrets. The "museum," and we use the word loosely, is on the bottom floor with hand-painted signs. It reminds us of American folk artist Howard Finster's place. The Shell Museum's proprietor cheerily serves as museum guide, host, bartender, waiter, chef, and busboy. After dinner, he organized us all into an impromptu fungi band — giving each guest a noisemaker — er, instrument. We had a ball, plus a terrific West Indian meal of grilled lobster, made even better by our kindly host with the most.

Carrot Bay, North Shore, Tortola. ☎ 284-495-4714 or VHF Ch 16. Reservations rec-
ommended at dinner. Main courses: $14–$25. AE, MC, V. Open for breakfast from
8 a.m. to 10 a.m., for lunch from 10:30 a.m. to 3 p.m., for Happy Hour from 4 p.m. to
6 p.m., and for dinner from 6 p.m. to 9 p.m.

Rock Cafe

$$$$ **Virgin Gorda**   **Italian/Caribbean**

What a surprise. We expected some island take on the ubiquitous Hard
Rock Café. Instead, we were escorted through the bar area out the back
door into a theatrical setting amidst the boulders like the ones at the
Baths, sheltered by a pair of 400-year-old cotton trees. Recessed lighting
and boardwalks add to the appeal. Few diners opt for the air-conditioned
dining room — the outside atmosphere's too inviting. The owners regularly circulate among the guests.

We recommend the chicken piccata and red snapper in a tangy marinade.
The restaurant has a nice and reasonably priced wine list featuring
Californian, Italian, and French vintages, plus a good selection of spe-
cialty drinks served in its bar upstairs — from classic martinis to
Caribbean coolers (island juices, Mount Gay rum, strawberries, and
coconut with a touch of cream).

The Valley. ☎ 284-495-5482 or VHF Channel 16. Reservations strongly recom-
mended. Main courses: $12.50–$25. AE, MC, V. Open for dinner nightly from 4 p.m.
to midnight. Special Tequila bar upstairs.

Sandcastle-Soggy Dollar

$$$ **Jost Van Dyke**   **West Indian**

Corporate escapees Debby Pearse and Bruce Donnath came to run this
small resort in 1996. Until then, the only access to the bar-restaurant was
via a small dinghy, and invariably guests took a dunk up to their waists,
thus the name. By day, flying fish sandwiches, rotis, and jumbo burgers
keep guests sated at the unassuming open-air spot. Bartender K.C.
Chinnery, whose grandfather was a practitioner of bush medicine, mixes
a mean painkiller. On Sunday afternoons Ruben Chinnery's calypso and
reggae tunes draw charter yachts to the small beach. By night at the
beachfront dining room, you're treated to linen-and-silver-set tables by
candlelight and a four-course affair accompanied by homemade bread.

White Bay, Jost Van Dyke at Sandcastle Resort. ☎ 284-497-9888 or VHF Channel
16. Reservations for dinner must be made by 4 p.m. for 7 p.m. seating. Main courses:
$32. MC, V. Open daily for a bar lunch from 11 a.m. to 4 p.m. and for dinner at 7 p.m
(one seating).

The Sugar Mill

$$$$ Tortola Caribbean/New World

Have you ever wished those food critics would put down their laptops and pick up their sauteeing pans and launch their own restaurant if it's all so easy? Former *Bon Appetit* columnists Jefferson and Jinx Morgan did just that when they bought The Sugar Mill, a 360-year-old former plantation in Apple Bay, which they subsequently transformed into the BVIs' most atmospheric inn and restaurant. Candles cast a golden glow on the thick walls of ballast stone and coral of what was a former rum distillery, and fine examples of colorful Haitian art decorate the walls.

The handful of menu offerings rotates nightly and includes wine pairings recommended by wine connoisseur Jeff. The West Indian influence is evident, but the experimental duo doesn't stop there. Standouts are the Cajun oyster étouffée, grilled mahimahi in banana leaves with a peppery Creole sauce, and Jamaican jerk pork roast with pineapple chipolte sauce. The liberally used vegetables and herbs are *primo,* thanks to the Mill's extensive garden. The mango and pineapple mousse or Creole banana crepes are a sweet and scrumptious ending note.

Apple Bay. ☎ 284-495-4355. Reservations required. Main courses: $21–$32. AE, MC, V. Open for dinner nightly from 7 p.m. Lunch is served daily at the Islands beach bar from noon to 2 p.m.

Virgin Queen Harbour View

$ Tortola Pizza/British pub grub

Sailors gather at the Virgin Queen, across the street from Ed Wheatley's Harbour View Marina, to throw darts, quaff beer, and devour the Queen's pizza, a thick-crusted pie some call the Caribbean's best. The other draw is the English pub and West Indian fare: bangers and mash, saltfish, and shepherd's pie.

Fleming Street, Road Town. ☎ 284-494-2310. Main courses: $8–$12. No credit cards. Open daily from 11a.m. to midnight. Closed Sundays.

Chapter 19

Hitting the Beach and Other Fun Things to Do

● ●

In This Chapter

▶ Soaking up the sun on the BVIs' top beaches

▶ Diving into fun with watersports

▶ Satisfying the landlubber: Activities and nightlife

● ●

*I*n this chapter, we help chart the course for an unforgettable trip through some of our favorite islands of the Caribbean. Sailors come here to cruise the small bays and hidden coves, but non-sailors will find plenty to enjoy.

These laid-back islands are verdant, though not jungly like Jamaica. There's not much to see on tours, but if you love nature and the sea, you'll never be bored. Besides, the best part of the BVIs is skipping from one small island to the next, because they are so close. If you do feel the need for more civilization, you can always take a quick day trip over to the USVIs by ferry or seaplane.

 Note that we haven't included anyone's address here, as the postal system in the BVIs is notoriously slow. Rely on the phone or e-mail to make a connection, or you might be home from your vacation before you get a reply.

Hitting the Beaches

The British Virgin Islands appeal to the escapist in all of us. You know, that nomadic spirit that dreams of finding an increasingly rare treasure: a glistening, flaxen strand of beach with no footprints.

You can easily live that fantasy in the BVIs. You won't encounter crowds on the golden and white-sand beaches ringing this collection of 50 small islands and cays. Well, except for maybe an extended family of iguanas sunning themselves. Whatever you're looking for in a beach paradise, you can find it in the BVIs.

We'd be hard-pressed to name our favorite beaches in the BVIs. We can give you some cool spots to check out, though. Keep in mind that in these laid-back islands, almost all beaches are public. Nudity is strongly discouraged. In fact, bare bathing is against the law, although we've never seen any naked tourists being hauled away in cuffs.

Even the poshest resorts typically don't mind if you homestead a spot on their beach. At Necker Island, though, where people such as the late Princess Diana found a place to escape camera lenses, gentlemen meet you on the beach and ask you politely to snorkel elsewhere.

If you want a glimpse of the high life but don't want to shell out the big bucks, **Deadman's Bay,** Peter Island Resort's idyllic palm-fringed beach, can be reached by boat or ferry from Road Town.

On Tortola

If you're looking for a beach party, you can find one on Tortola island's **Apple Bay** beach, home of **Bomba's Surfside Shack** (☎ **284-495-4148**), whose construction is purely flotsam and jetsam *de jour.* You'll find hand-painted exhortations to have fun — as if you need them amid the rollicking mix of reggae and surfers. Lethal Bomba Punch will have you dancing barefoot in the sand all night long. By day, Bomba's Surfside Shack might not look like much, but the legendary Full Moon Parties bring raucous revelers. Local bands usually play on Sunday and Wednesday nights.

Snorkelers enjoy **Smuggler's Cove,** a small sand beach at the western tip, as well as **Brewer's Bay,** which has two beach bars and a campground. The gently curving beach at **Cane Garden Bay** offers more facilities than most: watersports, restaurants, bars, and shops. Smuggler's is also a popular anchorage.

One of the most dramatic beaches in the BVIs is **Josiah's Bay** on Tortola's East End. If you want a wide, palm-fringed beach in that area, try **Elizabeth Beach.**

On Virgin Gorda

Virgin Gorda can lay claim to the BVIs' signature beach and features the islands' most photographed site, **The Baths.** At this site, granite boulders — some as big as cars — form a series of spectacular pools and grottoes, which flood with sea water. It *is* magnificent, but the problem is that everyone knows it. Go early in the morning before the cruise ships and charters from St. John and St. Thomas start rolling in. Or wait and head out late in the day. We suggest that you don't miss this unique spot. Nobody can figure out how on earth the magnificent boulders got here in the first place, and you can lose yourself snorkeling and swimming among them.

If you think you'd like to take a dip, plan to spend at least two hours here. Children love climbing around these rocks, but they do get slick. Even on the path coming down, you have to watch your step.

Top of the Baths, an outdoor terrace restaurant surveying the view, is okay for a drink, but don't be surprised if you sense that the staff has seen more than its share of cruise shippers. You'll find a few small gift shops, which sell Caribbean crafts and tacky T-shirts.

You may want to snorkel at The Baths, just for the experience. However, because of the steady stream of visitors, this tourist attraction isn't the sort of place we'd choose for a full morning or afternoon of lounging.

Better snorkeling can be found just north at **Spring Bay,** a white-sand beach with crystal-clear waters. For more privacy and even wider beaches, head to **Little Trunk** and **Valley Trunk Bay,** reachable by a rough path from Spring Bay or via boat.

Mango Bay Resort's **Mahoe Bay** boasts some of the most vivid blue waters we've seen anywhere in the Caribbean. On the north end, the beaches of the **Bitter End Yacht Club** (see Chapter 16) have great facilities and every kind of watersport rental you can imagine.

Shellcombers will like untamed **Bercher's Bay Beach** on the Atlantic side, which is accessible via footpaths from both **Biras Creek** and **Bitter End Yacht Club** (see Chapter 16). Expect to be sprinkled with salt spray here. You'll find well-worn chunks of coral and beautiful shells among the rocks.

On Jost Van Dyke

Tiny Jost Van Dyke (four miles square), north of Tortola's West End, was once the hideaway of a pirate. **Great Harbour** and **White Bay** are gorgeous beaches. Thanks to Jost's (pronounced with a "y," rhyming with ghost) popularity with the yachting crowd, small bars and cafes line the beaches. The most famous is **Foxy's** (see Chapter 18), where the charismatic owner greets guests with little musical ditties he makes up on the fly. It's known as *the* spot for New Year's Eve in the Caribbean, and this unassuming little bar attracts celebrities, millionaires, and friendly locals year-round. The last time we were there, Jimmy Buffett, the Beach Boys, and Clint Black all swung by to play a few tunes.

On Anegada

The entire island of Anegada boasts the beauty of bleached coral sand and the surround-sight of a coral reef. Anegada is flat and a mere 28 feet above sea level. (It's so low that even though Anegada is about the size of Manhattan, you can't see it from the surrounding islands.)

Anegada reminds us of Gilligan's Island; the mood is jovial, and everything's a little worn and sunbleached, but nobody cares.

If you fantasize about having fresh lobster for breakfast, lunch, and dinner, head to **Big Bamboo,** a beach bar at the gorgeous **Loblolly Bay.** Hammocks are handy for naps.

Another fun spot is the **Cow Wreck Bar and Grill** on **Lower Cow Wreck Beach.** This is a great place to watch the sun go down and then have Anegada lobster at the source for dinner. (See Chapter 18 for dining details.) We, of course, had to ask about the bar's name. Seems that about a hundred years ago, a ship carrying cow bones — which were going to be used to make buttons — hit the reef and spilled its contents. For years, cow bones washed ashore.

Finding Water Fun for Everyone

The water is a major attraction in the BVIs. You can spend practically your entire vacation either on or in the crystalline waters. Whether skimming across the surface in a watercraft or getting wet while enjoying a personal encounter with the islands' natural wonders, you're bound for an experience that's colorful and fun.

Sailing away

The BVIs' many sheltered moorings allow you to reach someplace neat and refreshing without making long overnight sails. And the way the islands are clustered helps cut down on the wave action. With minimal currents and well-marked reefs and shoals, these placid waters keep you out of trouble in your travels. Plus, you're always within sight of land in the BVI chain.

Whether you're a first-time sailor who needs to hire a captain and crew or an old salt comfortable sailing bareboat and hauling your own anchor, the BVIs have a wealth of possibilities for chartering a craft. An excellent Web site to check for more information is www.britishvirginislands.com/divebvi.

Just off Virgin Gorda, the **North Sound's** calm waters are a prime place to learn to sail or windsurf. Lots of people do both at **Nick Trotter's Sailing and Windsurfing School,** which offers advanced and beginners' courses at the **Bitter End Yacht Club,** North Sound, Virgin Gorda (☎ **800-872-2392** or 284-494-2745; fax 284-494-4756). You can also charter boats at this popular sailor's resort. All guests are entitled to a free Sailing 101 course (see Chapter 16).

The granddaddy of the sailing scene is **The Moorings** (☎ **800-535-7829** or 888-724-5273; fax 813-530-9747; Internet www.moorings.com), which has a flagship base on the protected side of Tortola in Road Town. It has 18 crewed yachts and 150 bareboats (including 32- to 50-foot sloops and catamarans). Bareboats run $2,660 to $7,070 a week; crewed yachts cost $8,988 to $18,200 for six people per week.

Catamaran Charters (Village Cay Marina, Road Town; ☎ 284-495-6661) charters catamarans with or without captains. **BVI Yacht Charters** (Inner Harbour Marina, Road Town; ☎ 284-494-4289) has 38- to 51-foot sailboats for charter.

Windjammer's 208-foot, three-masted barkentine *Flying Cloud* specializes in 6- and 13-day sails through the BVIs. The price ranges from $1,750 to $2,350. You can contact this company at ☎ 800-327-2601; fax 305-674-1219; or Internet www.windjammer.com.

Paddling your own kayak

We think that seeing the Virgin Islands via a sea kayak is quite cool — and a lot less pricey than hiring a yacht. A typical itinerary starts at Peter Island, goes to Norman Island, Tortola, Jost Van Dyke, and then ends in St. John. A five-day trip costs $945 per person. Book with **Arawak Expeditions** (Internet www.arawak-exp.com) through **American Wilderness Experience, Inc.** (☎ 800-444-0099).

Exploring the deep blue sea

The BVIs, which have two dozen established dive sites, are well known among scuba divers for their colorful coral formations, abundant marine life, and wreck diving. (Before doppler weather reports, hurricanes could sweep in with no warning, smashing ships.) The nearly translucent waters make for great visibility, and the rock formations give you plenty of nooks and crannies to explore.

The other piece of good news is that the size of the island chain enables you to see a wide range of sites all within a 35-mile stretch. Even so-called "remote" dive sites here are only a half-hour boat ride from Virgin Gorda or Tortola.

But while the coral reefs here are in much better shape than those in the U.S. Virgin Islands (which handle far more cruise ship day-trippers and visitors), we wouldn't recommend coming to the BVIs solely for a dive vacation. The BVIs are more notable as a yachter's paradise. For diving, we recommend Grand Cayman (see Chapter 23) or Bonaire, next to Aruba (see Chapter 11).

The most popular dive site by far is the **RMS Rhone,** a 310-foot royal mail steamer that sank in 1867. The ship's four parts rest at depths from 15 to 75 feet and are so well preserved that scenes from *The Deep* were filmed here. Our dive experience with **Kilbrides Underwater Tours** (see description later in this section) was greatly enhanced by the knowledgeable dive briefing that covered the history of the ship and explained the tragedy. Just be prepared: You'll have lots of company at this site.

Because the waters are so clear, half the dive sites are good for snorkelers, too. Snorkelers can even see some of the Rhone, because its rudder is in shallow water about 15 feet below the surface.

Another favorite dive site is the four caves at **Norman Island** (one is suitable for snorkelers), the setting for Robert Louis Stevenson's *Treasure Island*. At nearby **Angelfish Reef,** you can usually see graceful eagle rays and schools of angelfish.

Snorkeling around the BVIs is incredible, and sadly, we aren't able to say that about all the Caribbean. You'll see plenty of brilliantly colored, stoplight parrot fish (one of our favorites and a sign of healthy reefs). Most dive operators and resorts have snorkeling gear on hand and provide free instruction. The **Bitter End Yacht Club** (North Sound, Virgin Gorda; ☎ 800-872-2392) is near prime snorkeling sites and rents gear to nonguests.

If the seas are a little choppy while you're snorkeling in one area, you can simply move to the next cove or sail on a few moments till you find calmer waters. During the summer, the waters are usually at their calmest, but watch out for your partner anyway. Because the waters are so calm and what's underneath the surface can be so mesmerizing, you can lose track of each other.

The BVIs have a dozen land-based dive operators, and twice as many dive operators whose guests live aboard. Well-regarded **Baskin' in the Sun** (Prospect Reef, Tortola; ☎ 800-233-7938 or 284-494-2858; fax 284-494-4303; e-mail baskindive@aol.com; Internet www.dive-baskin.com) charges $60 for a one-tank dive, $80 for a two-tank dive, and $25 for a snorkel trip. Its programs emphasize reef ecology, with both beginning and advanced diving courses available. Daily trips leave promptly at 8:30 a.m. Ask for top-notch divemaster Randy Kiel.

PADI five-star **Dive B.V.I. Ltd.** (☎ 800-848-7078 or 284-495-5513; fax 284-495-5347; e-mail dbvi@caribsurf.com) operates out of Leverick Bay, Virgin Gorda Yacht Harbour, Peter Island, and Marina Cay. Owner Joe Giacinto has been diving the BVIs for more than three decades. He charges $85 for a two-tank dive.

We got our history lesson on the *RMS Rhone* wreck from **Kilbrides Underwater Tours** (Bitter End Yacht Club; ☎ 800-932-4286 or 284-495-9638; e-mail sunscuba@surfbvi.com; Internet www.come.to/bvi), which takes divers to 50 different sites and offers resort dive courses and PADI certification. Rates are $60 for a one-tank dive and $80 for a two-tank dive.

Underwater Safaris at The Moorings, Tortola, and Cooper Island (☎ 284-494-3535 or 284-494-3965) offers resort and advanced diving courses and day and night dives. Rates are $55 for a one-tank dive, $80 for two tanks, and $95 for a resort course.

Reeling in the big one

Some whoppers (and we don't mean burgers) have come out of these waters, and now tournaments take place each year to compete for the biggest bluefish, shark, and wahoo. If you want to have some reel fun, try **Blue Ocean Adventures** (Road Town, Tortola; ☎ 284-494-2872), which charges $400 for a half-day charter, or try the **Bitter End Yacht Club** (see contact information in the previous section). For a special treat, ask if your resort's chef will prepare your catch for you, too. Most will happily accommodate your request.

For a challenge, you could try *bonefishing* (fishing for small but fiesty catches in the salt-water flats). This is a popular sport, but be warned: These fish are skittish — one wrong move can send the school fleeing. Try your hand at snagging these elusive critters on **Anegada. Anegada Reef Hotel** (☎ 284-495-8002) can arrange it for you.

Taking a Hike

For such a small land mass, the BVIs certainly have their share of national parks. You can hike **Little Fort National Park,** the site of a wildlife sanctuary and an old Spanish fort with partially intact stone walls, or **Devil's Bay National Park,** one of several pristine parks given by the Rockefellers to the BVI government in the 1960s. The hills around the Virgin Gorda's **Gorda Peak National Park** have well-marked nature trails that reward you with jaw-dropping views. You can also explore the remains of a primeval rain forest in **Sage Mountain National Park,** which contains the British Virgin Islands' highest point (at 1,780 feet). This small national park west of Road Town on Tortola has three trails leading up to the summit, where you can have a picnic with panoramic views of Peter, Salt, Cooper, and Ginger islands and Jost Van Dyke and Sandy Cay.

Contact the British Virgin Islands Tourist Board for more information. The office is above the FedEx office on the AKARA Building's second floor in Wickham's Cay in Road Town (☎ 800-835-8530 or 284-494-3134; e-mail bvitourb@caribsurf.com; Internet www.bviwelcome.com).

No-Shopping Zone

If shopping's your bag, you've picked the wrong islands. Homemade jams, spices, Pusser's Rum, and guava berry liqueur are about the best you can do here. The small shops are *not* dutyfree, and bargaining is not the norm here, either. For better shopping options, head to Charlotte Amalie on St. Thomas in the U.S. Virgin Islands, which you can visit on a day trip.

Living It Up after the Sun Goes Down

You have to really search hard to find nightlife in the BVIs. Your best bet is to visit funky little beach bars like **Soggy Dollar** (☎ 284-495-9888) at White Bay, Jost Van Dyke. (See Chapter 18 for a full description.) Soggy Dollar has a clothesline strung out front where you can dry your paper money. Why, you may ask? Guests frequently get caught by sea swells and wind up in waist-deep water. On Sundays, Ruben Chinnery plays calypso and reggae.

Foxy's (see Chapter 18) is another famed watering hole in these parts, and **Rhymer's Beach Bar** on Tortola's West End (☎ 284-495-4639) has made a name for itself, too. At these little bars you can hear *soca* (a combination of calypso, soul, and reggae) plus indigenous music such as *fungi* — music played by scratch bands that use objects such as washtubs, gourds, and bottles (and no, not mushrooms) as instruments. Check the weekly *Limin' Times* (*limin'* means hanging out) for current entertainment schedules.

The BVIs' Painkiller — made from local Pusser's Rum, orange and pineapple juice, and a touch of coconut crème — is the most popular libation. Taste the original at **Pusser's Road Town Pub** on Waterfront Dr. in Tortola (☎ 284-494-3897). This popular spot also serves British pub food like shepherd's pie and fish 'n' chips.

Happy Hour at many bars in the BVIs usually features 2-for-1 drinks as well as complimentary snacks. The hours usually run from 4 p.m. to 7 p.m.

Grand Cayman

The 5th Wave   By Rich Tennant

"Your serve is basically good, it's just
you're doing something funny right
at the very end."

In this part . . .

*I*f you've got your eye on this peaceful, laid-back diving mecca, we've got some tips for spotting the best accommodations and saving a penny or two during your stay. We show you how to navigate toward your destination and how to find your way around the island after you arrive.

You have a wide variety of dining options on Grand Cayman; we share the restaurants that top our list of favorites. Finally, we let you know some of the best ways to soak up fun and sun in, around, and under the water.

Chapter 20

The Lowdown on Grand Cayman's Hotel Scene

In This Chapter
▶ Sizing up hotel locations
▶ Focusing on top hotel picks

Grand Cayman is a curious place. Although tourism is huge here, and its famous Seven Mile Beach (like Aruba's hotel strip) features a lineup of every type of hotel and condo imaginable, the island still manages to exude a certain laid-back charm. Maybe that's because its residents by-and-large have the security of wealth — they're glad you're vacationing here, but nobody's desperate for your money. In fact, Grand Cayman's wealth isn't based just on tourism. It's built on banking, and with the prices you pay for the privilege of staying on this island (unless you get a great low season package or dive package), islanders may need to build more banks to hold all the dough rolling in.

This peaceful, safe, and upscale island takes all the work out of your vacation if you just want to hang at the beach or swim with the fishes. That's why it's become a favorite with honeymooners, cruise ship passengers, and seniors — despite warnings from previous tourists to "take half as many clothes as you think you'll need and twice as much money."

Families with young children have discovered that huge summer discounts make the cost of a week on this clean, safe island about the same as a week at Disney World. So if your kids can entertain themselves in the water, and if you'll be happy with a sanitized version of the Caribbean, Grand Cayman is a good choice. If we were going to Grand Cayman with our two sons, we'd go during Pirate's Week in October. (For more details, see "The Caribbean's Calendar of Special Events" in Chapter 2.)

Despite its British ways, Grand Cayman has veered toward being too Americanized for some tastes. In recent years, many fast-food chains, cutesy little boutiques in restored buildings in George Town (the capital), and homogenized timeshares have increased the Florida-come-to-the Caribbean look. You can find local color, thanks to some of the quirky artists who live on the island, but you've got to look for it.

You'll find about as broad a range of accommodations here — from big chains to condos, villas, and modest guesthouses — as on the much larger islands of Puerto Rico, Jamaica, and St. Thomas. In fact, the Cayman Islands (islanders hate to hear them called "the Caymans") have more than 2,000 hotel rooms and an equal number of units in condos (timeshares), guesthouses, and dive lodges. You'll see tons of "For Sale" signs on the island, and you'll probably be pitched to buy a timeshare at least once if you're on the island for more than a day.

What the Cayman Islands don't have is a predominance of mega all-inclusives. Although a few resorts offer this option, the European Plan (EP) and Modified American Plan (MAP) are more popular, as are the many dive packages. Traditionally, the islands have also lacked ultra deluxe, five-star resorts, but with The Ritz-Carlton, Grand Cayman, being built to the tune of $350 million, the tide will finally turn. Until it opens in May 2002, if you're looking for the lap of luxury, head to Barbados, Jamaica, St. Thomas, or Puerto Rico.

About a third of the one million visitors who come to Grand Cayman annually are here for the scuba diving, but Grand Cayman also gets loyalists (not to the Crown) who use their timeshares the same week year after year. Lots of retirees and couples visit, as do honeymooners, though we'd guess that these newlyweds tend to be on second or third marriages — just judging by age. You won't see many single people, and gays and lesbians are boycotting the island (see Chapter 4).

Before you spring for a dive package up front, make sure you know what you're buying with your bucks. Some dive operators are more geared toward experienced divers, whereas others are better suited to beginners.

During the summer months, when Grand Cayman's resorts offer big price breaks, many families tour the island. We've heard grousing from teens who are bored because of the dearth of nighttime activities. For families with young children, though, the gentle waters are ideal; your little wannabe mermaids and mermen won't be disappointed. Both Hyatt and Westin have strong children's programs.

Figuring Out Where You Want to Stay

As with Aruba, almost all 50 of Grand Cayman's hotels and condos are crowded along the island's famous Seven Mile Beach. Even if you go to the island for diving, you may want to be close to this lovely beach. From here, you have broad dining options; you can walk to town from many resorts.

Hard-core divers like to stay on the East End, near Grand Cayman's best diving. If you want to skip the crowds and Cayman Cowboys (as the dive operators who pack people in are derisively called), head to the much more secluded north side, which also offers good diving. A brand new option that opened in March 2000 on the North Sound is

The Grand Caymanian Beach Club & Resort (Safehaven/Crystal Harbor; ☎ **345-949-3100;** fax 345-949-3161; Internet www. grandcaymanian.ky), an all-suite property. It's the only resort on the North Sound and is near both Stingray City and Rum Point.

The Grand Caymanian Beach Club & Resort is owned by Gary and Theresa Foster. The Fosters' Caymanian roots date to a shipwreck in the 1700s, when a local girl rescued and subsequently married a man named Foster.

Divers who want more of an escape will do better on Cayman Brac or Little Cayman, which we describe at the end of this chapter. But if you think nightlife is limited on Grand Cayman, you'll be bored out of your wetsuit on those quiet islands.

Conserving Cash

Food is one of your bigger expenses when you vacation on Grand Cayman; restaurants here charge top dollar, compared with costs on other Caribbean islands. So that you don't have to eat out all the time, we recommend booking into a resort with a meal plan. But make sure that the resort has more than one good restaurant; otherwise, you'll be ready to mutiny by the time your stay is over.

If you don't mind making your own meals, you can save a bundle by renting one of this island's many condos or guesthouses with kitchens. You can easily spend as much on one dinner out on in Grand Cayman as it would take to stock up enough groceries for a week. Two well-stocked grocery stores are **Hurley's Supermarket** (in Red Bay just beyond the intersection of Crewe Road and South Sound Road), which has 30,000 square feet with a bakery, deli, and sandwich and salad bar, and **Fosters Food Fair** (The Strand on Seven Mile Beach and at the Airport).

Remember that you can't bring in any fresh fruit or vegetables from outside the island. Also, request an advance list from management detailing what's already stocked in the kitchen, so you don't waste precious suitcase room on basics (such as spices). You'll need a rental car to haul groceries if you decide to prepare food on your own.

Grand Cayman's Best Accommodations

Because Grand Cayman doesn't have a lot of rowdy nightlife, shopping, or even much sightseeing, you'll probably spend much of your time around the property in which you are staying. Therefore, the amenities and what your room, pool, and particular stretch of beach are like are very important.

Grand Cayman's Hotels

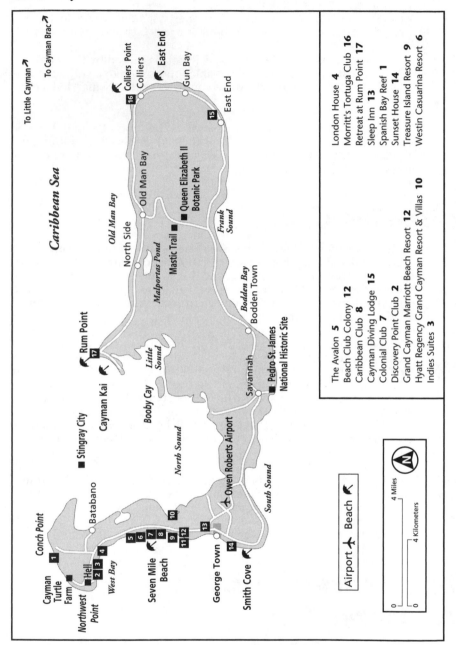

Caribbean Sea

To Little Cayman
To Cayman Brac

Colliers Point
Colliers **16**
East End
Gun Bay
East End **15**

Old Man Bay
North Side
Old Man Bay
Queen Elizabeth II Botanic Park
Mastic Trail
Frank Sound
Malportas Pond

Bodden Bay
Bodden Town

Rum Point **17**
Cayman Kai

Little Sound
Booby Cay
Savannah
Pedro St. James National Historic Site

Stingray City
Batabano

North Sound
Owen Roberts Airport
South Sound

Conch Point
Cayman Turtle Farm
Northwest Point
Hell **2 3**
West Bay **4**
1
5 6 7 8
11 12 **9**
Seven Mile Beach
10
13
George Town
14
Smith Cove

Airport ✈ Beach ☚

N

0 _____ 4 Miles
0 _____ 4 Kilometers

The Avalon **5**
Beach Club Colony **12**
Caribbean Club **8**
Cayman Diving Lodge **15**
Colonial Club **7**
Discovery Point Club **2**
Grand Cayman Marriott Beach Resort **12**
Hyatt Regency Grand Cayman Resort & Villas **10**
Indies Suites **3**

London House **4**
Morritt's Tortuga Club **16**
Retreat at Rum Point **17**
Sleep Inn **13**
Spanish Bay Reef **1**
Sunset House **14**
Treasure Island Resort **9**
Westin Casuarina Resort **6**

Guesthouses may be some distance from the beach and short on style and facilities, but in addition to being a good bargain, they're a great choice for families with older children. (With babies and toddlers, we'd stick to the hotels with established children's programs.) Some guesthouses have outdoor grills and picnic tables.

Most guesthouse owners do not accept personal checks or credit cards but do take reservations through the **Cayman Islands Reservation Service** (6100 Blue Lagoon Dr., Suite 150, Miami, FL 33126; ☎ **800-327-8777**). This service can also describe and book most condominiums and villas on the islands. **Cayman Villas** (☎ **800-235-5888** or 345-947-4144; fax 345-949-7471) and **Hospitality World Ltd.** (☎ **800-232-1034** or 345-949-3458; fax 345-1949-7054) are local agencies that make reservations.

The rack rates listed below are in U.S. dollars and are for a standard double room during high season (mid-December to mid-April), unless otherwise noted. Lower rates are often available during the off season and shoulder season; see Chapter 2 for more information on travel seasons.

The Avalon

$$$$ Seven Mile Beach

The Avalon graces prime real estate on Seven Mile Beach and is one of the better condo options on Grand Cayman. We like the oversized tub and separate shower in the spacious baths, as well as the tropical décor of the roomy units. This facility has daily maid service except on Tuesdays. The handsome property consists of 27 three-bedroom / three-bathroom units (15 of which can be rented). All are located right on the Caribbean.

Only a short distance from restaurants and a five-minute drive from George Town, the Avalon has style that's disappointingly rare on Grand Cayman. Each condo has a fully equipped open kitchen and a large, screened lanai overlooking the glorious beach. Fitness buffs will also like the tennis court, fitness center, swimming pool, and Jacuzzi.

West Bay Road (P.O. Box 31236), Grand Cayman, BWI. ☎ *345-945-4171. Fax: 345-945-4189. Rack rates: $600 for an apartment for four; $670 for an apartment for six. AE, MC, V.*

Beach Club Colony

$$$ Seven Mile Beach

Three miles north of George Town, the Beach Club — with its 41 rooms, built in the early 1960s — snagged one of the finer spots on Seven Mile Beach. Over the years, the Club has established a loyal following among divers, who return year after year.

Unfortunately, the cruise ship day-trippers have also discovered the strand of beach in front of the hotel. So on days when the ships are in, you'll wish you were somewhere else.

The center of activity is designed like a large colonial plantation villa with a formal Doric portico. A popular beach bar featuring Grand Cayman staples of calypso and rum draws both guests and outsiders. The resort has a dive shop on-site and offers all types of watersports.

Divers tend to like to spread out and typically spring for one of the tile-floored villas clustered amid coconut palms at the edge of the beach. If you stay in one of the bland units at the hotel, ask for an ocean view and a four-poster bed.

West Bay Road (P.O. Box 903G), Grand Cayman, BWI. ☎ *800-482-DIVE or 345-949-8100. Fax: 345-945-5167. Rack rates: $400–$500 double. Rates are all-inclusive. Children 6 and under stay free in parents' room; ages 7–17 $85 daily. Honeymoon and dive packages available. AE, MC, V.*

Caribbean Club

$$$–$$$$ Seven Mile Beach

If you like potluck dinners, you'll like the homey feel of this cluster of 18 one- and two-bedroom condos, six of which are right on lovely Seven Mile Beach. Each is individually owned, so you never know what you'll get when it comes to décor. The condos are set in tropical gardens and offer some seclusion. Nothing fancy, but pleasant. There's no pool, but the beach is terrific. Tennis courts are on-site. These condos are wheelchair accessible and draw a low-key crowd looking for a quiet, comfortable beachside escape. **Lantana's,** one of Grand Cayman's top restaurants, is on-site and serves Caribbean and American fare. (See our review in Chapter 22.)

Seven Mile Beach (P.O. Box 30499). ☎ *800-327-8777 or 345-945-4099. Fax: 345-945-4443. E-mail:* reservations@caribclub.com. *Internet:* www.caribclub.com. *Rack rates: $300–$440. Rates include MAP (two full meals daily). AE, MC, V. No children under age 11 are accepted during high season.*

Cayman Diving Lodge

$$ East End

If you care more about gazing at the creatures of the deep than eating them at fancy restaurants, you'll like this remote spot east of George Town (20 miles and a $49 cab ride from the airport). The rooms here are 30 feet from the water's edge. The pace is slow, like the Grand Cayman of 20 years ago.

The two-story lodge sits amidst tropical palms on a private coral-sand beach. A live, horseshoe-shaped coral barrier reef just offshore — about 4 to 10 feet deep and great for macro shots of the critters — means that the continually available diving and snorkeling equipment gets a good work-out. Three ample squares a day are served family-style, ensuring that the dive crowd gets refueled. (The menus are heavy on seafood.) The rather worn rooms, which have only showers, are no great shakes, but good service and housekeeping help make up for the lack of ambience. Internet and e-mail connections are recent additions to the in-room offerings.

Experienced divers gravitate to this small (14-room) family-owned and operated ultra-casual place, voted "Best Dive Operator" in the Caribbean for 1999 by the readers of *Rodale's Scuba Diving*. The resort owns two comfortably outfitted, 45-foot Garcia dive boats, employs ten PADI-certified instructors, and offers complete valet services for your dive gear, so you don't have to haul it around. Scuba trips include a daily two-tank morning dive of 3¾ hours. One-on-one instruction for noncertified novices is available, but the lodge is really much better for hard-core scuba enthusiasts.

East End (P.O. Box 11), Grand Cayman, BWI. ☎ 800-TLC-DIVE or 345-947-7555. Fax: 345-947-7560. E-mail: divelodge@aol.com. *Internet:* www.vsu.smdivelodge. com. *Rack rates: $594 double for three nights, $1,325 for seven nights. Rates are all-inclusive and include two-tank dives. AE, DISC, MC, V.*

Colonial Club

$$$$ Seven Mile Beach

Pretty-in-pink Colonial Club occupies a highly desirable stretch of Seven Mile Beach. Built in 1985, the main appeal of these 24 standard condos is the good upkeep and service of the neat-as-a-pin accommodations. The three-story building is conveniently located ten minutes from the airport and four miles north of George Town.

Your choices are units with two bedrooms and three bathrooms or units with three bedrooms and three bathrooms. Besides a pool, you have a tennis court (lit at night) and Jacuzzi at your disposal. One drawback: There's no on-site restaurant.

West Bay Rd. (P.O. Box 320W), Grand Cayman, BWI. ☎ 345-945-4660. Fax: 345-945-4839. Rack rates: $364–$416 apartment for two; $416–$468 apartment for three to four; $468–$520 apartment for four to five. Minimum stay five nights December 16 through April 15. AE, MC, V.

Discovery Point Club

$$$$ Seven Mile Beach

This secluded complex, at the far north end of Seven Mile Beach in West Bay (six miles from George Town), has a lovely beach and great snorkeling in the protected waters of nearby Cemetery Reef. If you're the independent type who wants to stay far off the beaten path, you're assured of a quiet spot here. There's no nightlife and no restaurant. You'll need to rent a car. But what you do get is a screened patio, coin laundry, tennis courts, a hot tub, and a pretty pool.

West Bay (Box 439) Grand Cayman, BWI. ☎ 800-327-8777 for reservations or 345-945-4724. Fax: 345-945-5051. Rack Rates: $220–$360 double. Kids 12 and under stay free April through December. AE, DC, MC, V.

Grand Cayman Marriott Beach Resort

$$$$–$$$$$ Seven Mile Beach

The oversized adjoining rooms draw families to this five-story property (recently awarded Four Diamonds) converted from a Radisson in 1997, just one mile from George Town. The airy, marble lobby opens onto a plant-filled courtyard. Views are either of the ocean or the garden court-yard. Keep in mind that you can have an "ocean view" without being ocean front — our room's view gave us a mere sliver of the water. Make sure to double-check when making reservations if a view is important to you. All rooms have large balconies, and most are perfectly angled to make the most of the promised seaside view. This big resort offers all the usual watersports through Red Sail Sports. It also has the island's largest conference center, as well as 309 rooms; predictably, it's popular for conventions.

Seven Mile Beach (Box 30371), Grand Cayman, BWI. ☎ 800-228-9290 or 345-949-0088. Fax: 345-949-0288. E-mail: marriott@candw.ky. *Rack rates: $341–$429 double. AE, DISC, DC, MC, V.*

Hyatt Regency Grand Cayman Resort & Villas

$$$$ Seven Mile Beach

Hugging one of the prime spots on famed Seven Mile Beach and housed in grand, low-slung British Colonial–style buildings amid beautifully land-scaped gardens, this Hyatt Regency radiates elegance. We agree with *Travel & Leisure* that the facility should be in the Top 25 Caribbean Hotels. Actually, we'd probably put it in our Top 10 for its great beach location, over-the-top watersports (the top-notch Red Sail Sports even caddies your gear for you), fantasy-inducing water oasis (seven pools, rooftop sundeck, a footbridge, and two swim-up gazebo bars), new full-service spa (the only one on Grand Cayman), two health clubs, and breathtaking **Britannia Golf Club** with a Jack Nicklaus–designed nine-hole course.

For lunch or dinner, **Hemingway's** on the beach offers a good vantage point to soak in the view and the low-key atmosphere. The children's pro-gram is top-notch, as is customary with Hyatt resorts we've visited. And under age 18, they stay free if they share a room with their parents.

Guests in the Regency Club are treated to VIP service, and now you can also rent a villa or one of the new beachfront suites (built to the tune of $15 million).

Most of the accommodations here are across the street from the beach. But a covered walkway equipped with an elevator on either side over the road eliminates any concern about making it across with a stroller or wheelchair. The resort is quite large, with 298 units.

West Bay Road (P.O. Box 1588), Grand Cayman, BWI. ☎ 800-55-HYATT or 345-949-1234. Fax: 345-949-8528. E-mail: hyatt@candw.ky *or Internet:* www.hyatt.com *or* www.britanniavillas.com. *Rack rates: $305–$510 double; $550 one-bedroom villa; $445–$565 two-bedroom villa. Additional fee for meal plans: AE, DC, MC, V.*

Indies Suites

$$$$ Seven Mile Beach

Grand Cayman's only all-suite hotel is attractive, comfortable, and right across from the beach at the quieter north end of Seven Mile Beach. The extra roomy suites appeal to divers who like to buddy up and spread out with lots of gear. Of course, the wide open space is also welcomed by families, who happily take advantage of the fact that children under age 12 stay free with their parents.

The 41 one- or two-bedroom suites, done in Caymanian pastels, come with a well-equipped, sleek kitchen, a dining-living room (with a sleeper sofa), a terrace, and a storeroom for dive gear. Indies' dive operation has modern boats, and preference is given to hotel guests. Novices get a free introductory course to scuba diving in the pool, which is designed for dive instruction. Continental buffet breakfast, maid service, a free sunset cruise once a week, and a live band that entertains in the lushly landscaped courtyard twice a week are nice extras. The lobby is fun, with vintage 1930s Fords on display.

Seven Mile Beach (P.O. Box 2070 GT), Grand Cayman, BWI. ☎ 800-654-3130 or 345-947-5025. Fax: 345-947-5024. E-mail: indiessuites@worldnet.att.net. *Rack rates: $299 $360 suite. Rates include continental breakfast. Children under age 12 stay free with their parents. AE, MC, V.*

London House

$$$$ Seven Mile Beach

This mission-style complex at Seven Mile Beach's more tranquil northern end is beautifully maintained. If you like apartment living, these spacious units with private patios or balconies overlooking the Caribbean will please you. Each of the 22 rooms boasts a rattan-and-tropical décor as well as oversized living and dining areas and a well-stocked kitchen. Ceiling fans supplement the air-conditioning, and, for an extra charge, daily maid service is available. The complex has its own seaside swimming pool, which has a stone barbecue that is often the centerpiece of house parties. Try to get a room away from the pool if you're bothered by noise.

Seven Mile Beach, Grand Cayman, BWI. ☎ 345-945-4060. Fax: 345-945-4087. Rack rates: $295–$335 one-bedroom apartment; $315–$375 two-bedroom apartment; $900 three-bedroom apartment. Extra person $20 per day. AE, MC, V.

Morritt's Tortuga Club

$$$–$$$$ East End

These plantation-style, three-story condos are about 30 feet from the water. The surrounding eight beachfront acres are on the idyllic East End, about 26 miles from the airport and known for some of Grand Cayman's best diving. Some people would say this location is isolated, and that's exactly what the clientele here is after. Nothing is within walking distance, unless you count the scuba diving, snorkeling, and windsurfing. A rental car is an absolute must.

Home to **Tortuga Divers,** which offers resort courses, and **Cayman Windsurfing,** which offers snorkeling and windsurfing and rents sailing craft and catamarans, this well-managed complex is perfect for athletic types eager to get the most from sun, sand, and surf in a laid-back atmosphere. The snorkeling off the dock here is terrific thanks to a protective outer reef about a quarter mile off shore.

One of the two pools has a swim-up bar and a waterfall. Each of the comfortably furnished one- and two-bedroom townhouses — most facing one of two pools — has a fully equipped kitchen, but many guests eat at the restaurant on-site. The next closest restaurant is about two miles away.

Another option is to go for dinner at **Miss Viveen's** (☎ 345-947-7435), a local about three miles from the resort in Gun Bay, who cooks Caymanian dishes for $6–$10 a person. Call ahead to reserve a spot on her covered patio.

Morritt's has a metered electricity charge, which averages about $50 extra for a week's stay (unless you do something silly like leave the sliding door open with the AC running).

East End (P.O. Box 496GT), Grand Cayman, BWI. ☎ *800-447-0309 or 345-947-7449. Fax: 345-947-7669. E-mail:* reservations@morritt's.com. *Internet:* www.morritt.com. *Rack rates: $175–$185 studio; $230–$255 one-bedroom apartment; $295–$350 two-bedroom apartment. Dive packages available. AE, DISC, MC, V.*

Retreat at Rum Point

$$$$–$$$$$ **North Side**

On the north central tip, you'll find a collection of villas and condos stationed along a narrow beach fringed with casuarina trees, far from the madding crowds swarming Seven Mile Beach. Up to six people can rent a two-bedroom villa here; a group of two or three will be comfortable in a one-bedroom unit. The décor is potluck, but the units are spacious and have washers and dryers.

Dive facilities are nearby, and divers love the superb offshore diving, including the famed North Wall. On-site you have a restaurant, bar, pool, sauna, tennis court, exercise room, and racquetball court.

A rental car is a must: The Retreat is a 35-minute drive from town or the airport.

North Side (Box 46), Grand Cayman, BWI. ☎ *345-945-9135. Fax: 345-945-9058. E-mail:* retrempt@candw.ky. *Internet:* www.retreatcondos.com. *Rack rates: $275–$420 double. AE, DISC, MC, V.*

Sleep Inn

$$$ Seven Mile Beach

Bargain-hunters and those who like to be in the middle of the action find Sleep Inn fits the bill on both counts. This two-story Choice Hotels affiliate is a quick stroll from Seven Mile Beach, George Town's duty-free shopping, and popular restaurants. It's also near the airport. Eight of the plain-Jane suites have kitchenettes. For the ultimate in convenience, the Dive Inn dive shop is here, as well as a tour agency and car and motorcycle rental offices. You get a complimentary breakfast buffet each morning.

Seven Mile Beach (P.O. Box 30111), Grand Cayman, BWI. ☎ *800-597-2995 or 345-949-9111. Fax: 345-949-6699. E-mail:* sleepinn@candw.ky. *Internet:* www.sleepinn.com/hotel *or* www.choicecaribbean.com. *Rack rates: $200–$210 double. AE, DISC, DC, MC, V.*

Spanish Bay Reef

$$$$ North West Bay

One of Grand Cayman's few all-inclusive resorts, Spanish Bay Reef is on a small sandy beach at the island's northwest tip. The reef out front has a steep drop-off, which make for superior diving and good snorkeling. The outdoor bar-dining area surrounds the pool and has views of the ocean; the indoor bar-dining area is spacious and made of coral-stone. Fishing charters are available.

North West Bay (P.O. Box 903), Grand Cayman, BWI. ☎ *800-327-8777 or 345-949-8100. Fax: 345-949-1842. Rack rates: High season $210–$355 double. Rates include meals, Jeep rental, bicycles, scuba/snorkel lessons, and snorkeling equipment. AE, MC, V.*

Sunset House

$$$ Seven Mile Beach

Low-key describes this diver's resort with Spartan rooms on the ironshore (sharp, hard, calcified black coral) south of George Town and about four miles from Seven Mile Beach. Some rooms have kitchenettes, and all have dataports and e-mail access. The congenial staff, a happening bar, and a terrific seafood restaurant match with the full-service dive operation (including six dive boats) to make this place extremely popular with scuba divers.

Sunset House has become a hangout for country music and MTV stars like Travis Tritt and Little Texas, who sometimes give impromptu concerts. Full dive services include free waterside lockers, two- and three-tank dives with its fleet of six dive boats, and use of the excellent Cathy Church's Underwater Photo Centre. (Church was inducted into the Women's Diving Hall of Fame in 2000 and is the best teacher on the island for underwater photography.)

Perhaps to make up for not being on the beach, the hotel has two pools (one right by the sea), plus a whirlpool. It's a 5-minute walk to a sandy beach and a 10-minute walk to George Town. All-inclusive dive packages are the way to go here with great rates via Cayman Airways and American.

South Church Street (P.O. Box 479), Grand Cayman, BWI. ☎ 888-854-4767 or 345-949-7111. Fax: 345-949-7101. E-mail: sunsethouse@sunsethouse.com. *Internet:* www.sunsethouse.com. *58 rooms. Rack rates: $165–$252 double; $720 double for three nights. Meal plans available for extra charge. AE, DISC, MC, V.*

Treasure Island Resort

$$$ Seven Mile Beach

This sprawling, five-story complex — a Ramada in a previous incarnation — is one of the largest resorts on the island and has good snorkeling right in front of its reef beach. However, recent weather has somewhat eroded this southern stretch of Seven Mile Beach, leaving guests to walk gingerly on its rocky strand. Just a few resorts up, the beach greatly improves.

The resort's strong suit? Above par entertainment six nights a week, shopping and good restaurants within walking distance, a plethora of activities, and a caring staff who tries hard. But in the looks department, we're talking late 1960s apartment building grim. We'd compare Treasure Island to a nice Day's Inn in the U.S. It is a good moderate pick for active types who are watching their budgets and plan to spend most of their time enjoying watersports or scuba diving. The 278 guestrooms, which are in need of a redo and sometimes have sloppy housekeeping, surround a courtyard with two large pools, a Jacuzzi, and a waterfall.

Consider yourself forewarned: the term "air-conditioning" is used loosely here. What we call air-conditioning and what Treasure Island calls it are two different animals. The rooms do have refrigerators so you can at least keep your sodas or beer cold.

269 West Bay Rd. (P.O. Box 1817), Grand Cayman, BWI. ☎ 800-203-0775 or 345-949-7777. Fax: 345-949-8672.Internet: www.treasureislandresort. net. *Rack rates: $220–$260 double. AE, DC, MC, V.*

Westin Casuarina Resort

$$$$$ Seven Mile Beach

Like the Hyatt, the low-slung Westin has 700 feet on palm-fringed Seven Mile Beach. This beautiful and large (343-room) British Caribbean-style resort occupies one of the better stretches of Seven Mile Beach. The staff is cheerful and energetic.

Like many other hotels on Grand Cayman, the Westin offers a plethora of watersports including the biggie, scuba diving, through Red Sail Sports. You'll also find a challenging 18-hole golf course across the street, and a salon and a spa. **Camp Scallywag** is available for kids ages 4 to 12. Bright, airy rooms with private balconies face either the Caribbean or the lovely gardens. This elegant resort is one of those places where the sea view is worth the extra money, so go for it. You'll thank us when you're watching the sunset from your balcony. Two free-form pools with a happening swim-up bar are fun hangouts, though cruise shippers sometimes try to crash the scene.

If you love nightlife, you aren't going to love the Westin. There is a comedy club across the street, but this resort is the kind of place where everybody goes to bed early. Oh, but what a bed it is! If you haven't slept in Westin's new Heavenly Bed (yes, the company gave its specially designed and manufactured mattress a name), you are in for a treat. We've slept in a lot of hotel rooms, but the double-pillow topped mattress with premium sheets here are amazing.

You can get breakfast on the cheap across the street at **Crocodile Rock Eats Café.** But on Sunday, splurge for the sumptuous breakfast buffet at the on-site **Ferdinand's.**

Seven Mile Beach Road (Box 30620), Grand Cayman, BWI. ☎ *800-WESTIN-1 or 345-945-3804. Internet:* www.westin.com. *Rack rates: $385 to $625 double. AE, MC, V.*

Chapter 21

Settling into Grand Cayman

In This Chapter
▶ Knowing what to expect when you arrive
▶ Getting around the island
▶ Discovering Grand Cayman from A to Z

*I*f you come to Grand Cayman expecting to encounter an upper-crust attitude to coincide with the island's reputation as an offshore banking mecca, you'll be pleasantly surprised. Despite its wealth and status as a British Overseas Dependent Territory — we know, even the designation sounds stuffy — Grand Cayman is relaxed and casual. In fact, Kevin says it reminds him of his tiny hometown in Georgia where you have to buy a car with an automatic transmission so you can have one hand free to wave to people.

The cost of living is about 20% higher in Grand Cayman than in the United States; one U.S. dollar is worth only about 80 Cayman cents. Nonetheless, many of the 31,000 islanders are wealthy, and they wear their millionaire status without any ostentation. If you run into any problem while on the island, the warm and friendly folks on Grand Cayman are happy to point you in the right direction.

Arriving in Grand Cayman

With more than 100 flights landing at Owen Roberts International Airport weekly — 70 direct flights from Miami alone — officials are adept at handling a continuous stream of visitors. This clean, modern airport with its good air-conditioning system is one of the more comfortable in the Caribbean. Even if you're coming in on a packed flight, you'll likely encounter few lines and barely feel that you're entering a foreign country.

The airport (☎ 345-949-5252 for information) is centrally located for points east and west. After you clear customs and gather luggage, you'll note stacks of free tourist information. Grab a copy of everything you see — especially useful is *Key to Cayman,* available at the airport, hotels, and shops. These giveaways often contain coupons for meals, attractions, and car rentals.

The customs of the Cayman Islands

Here are a few tips to help you fit in.

Language: The Caymanians will know that you've just arrived if you make either of two *faux pas*: mispronouncing Grand Cayman (it's pronounced *K-man*) or referring to it as "the Caymans." Islanders either say "The Cayman Islands," or "Cayman" but *never* "the Caymans."

Clothing: Even though this island is laid-back, you won't see women *sans* bathing suit tops or even women in string bikinis strolling the beach. No form of public nudity is tolerated. Even jokey T-shirts are suspect. One way islanders can tell who has come off the cruise ships is by observing the number of logo'ed tank tops in the group.

Etiquette: You'll hear older people's first names preceded by "Mr." or "Miss" (for example, Mr. Sam) as a sign of respect.

No cash? No problem. ATMs are everywhere. (What else would you expect on an island 22 miles long and 8 miles wide with more than 500 bank offices?) But you'd better look like you can afford your vacation when you arrive on Grand Cayman. Otherwise, you're likely to be questioned by customs officials to determine whether you've got the bank account to bankroll your fun on the island.

Flights going onto Cayman Brac land at Gerrard-Smith Airport; flights to Little Cayman land at Edward Bodden Airfield. Air service from Grand Cayman to Cayman Brac and Little Cayman is offered via **Cayman Airways** (☎ 800-422-9626 or 345-949-2311) and **Island Air** (☎ 345-949-5252). Island Air recently introduced a same-day excursion "Day Trip Fare," which lets you visit either sister island for $110 round-trip for adults and $89 for kids under 12.

The other way to travel to Grand Cayman is by ship. Most major cruise lines call in Grand Cayman, docking in George Town. However, the Cayman Islands limit cruise visitors to a maximum of 6,000 cruise passengers or three ships per day, whichever is greater. Tuesdays, Wednesdays, and Thursdays tend to be the busiest days.

Best-selling mystery writer and former jockey Dick Francis told us over drinks one afternoon that he fell in love with the island after taking a cruise through the Caribbean and docking here. He and his wife now make Grand Cayman their home.

Traveling from the Airport to Your Hotel

Check with your hotel ahead of time to see if it offers free van pickup at the airport. All arriving flights are met by taxis, which line up neatly, awaiting an agent to assign them to deplaning passengers.

Taxis are usually vans (capable of transporting divers and all their accompanying gear) or Toyota Corollas. Taxi rates are fixed, and you can get fare information from the dispatcher at the curb. Drivers are generally charming and happy to share island lore. Typical one-way fares from the airport to Seven Mile Beach range from $11.50 to $20, depending, of course, on which end of the beach you're travelling to.

Taxis are also readily available from all resorts and from the taxi stand at the cruise ship dock in George Town. A sign with current rates is posted at the dock.

Local minibuses run along main routes between 7 a.m. and 6 p.m. from George Town parallel to Seven Mile Beach. The fare is $2.

If you've rented a condo but not a car and you need provisions, have **McCurley's Tours** (☎ **345-947-9626**) pick you up at the airport. The driver will gladly take you by a grocery store en route.

If you rent a car, getting to your hotel from the airport should be easy on this flat island. The roads are well marked and in good shape, and your car rental agent can pencil in the route for you on the map. The major car rental companies all have offices in a plaza across from the airport terminal, where you can pick up and drop off vehicles.

Getting Around Grand Cayman

This island is one of the easiest in the Caribbean to navigate. The terrain is flat, and the easy-going locals are ready to help if by some weird happenstance you were to get lost. (We can't imagine such a thing on this island, but you never know.) For the most part, you'll be able to walk to wherever you want to go.

You may want to tour the island for a day; you won't need more than that for a complete tour. For that day, rent a car — unless it's really important to you to pick up local history and color from a taxi driver, who will gladly serve as a guide. If you tour by taxi, though, the tab will likely exceed what you'd pay for a one-day car rental.

On foot

If your accommodations are along Grand Cayman's Seven Mile Beach, your feet will get you where you need to go. You can walk to the shopping centers, restaurants, and entertainment spots along West Bay Road. George Town is small enough to see on foot.

By bicycle, moped, and motorcycle

Biking is popular on this flat, safe island where drivers tend to take it easy; bikes, mopeds, and motorcycles are good means to explore. When renting a motor scooter or bicycle, don't forget to wear sunscreen. Also remember to drive on the left. Bicycles ($10–$15 a day) and scooters ($25–$30 a day) can be rented from **Bicycles Cayman** (☎ 345-949-5572); **Cayman Cycle** (☎ 345-945-4021); **Eagles Nest** (☎ 345-949-4866), which specializes in renting Harley Davidson motorcycles; and **Soto Scooters** (☎ 345-945-4652). Some resorts also offer free bicycles.

By car

Grand Cayman is relatively flat and fairly easy to negotiate if you watch out for traffic. You'll have to pay for a $7 rental permit to drive any vehicle on the island. You can get a permit from either the rental agent or the central police station in George Town if you have a valid driver's license. You must have a credit card and be at least 21 years of age — 25 with some companies — to rent a car.

Rates range from $35 to $75 a day; remember to use coupons and ask about special promotions. Gas prices at press time were about $2.50 for an "imperial" gallon, which is slightly more than a U.S. gallon. Car rental companies include **Ace Hertz** (☎ 800-654-3131 or 345-949-2280), **Budget** (☎ 800-472-3325 or 345-949-5605), **Cico Avis** (☎ 800-331-1212 or 345-949-2468), **Coconut** (☎ 800-262-6687 or 345-949-4377), **Economy** (☎ 345-949-9550), **Soto's 4X4** (☎ 345-945-2424), and **Thrifty** (☎ 800- 367-2277 or 345-949-6640).

Most firms have a range of models, from compacts to Jeeps to minibuses. Divers who are staying a bit farther afield and have gear to haul will definitely need a larger vehicle; we suggest a Jeep or van with plenty of sprawl room. Whatever kind of car you choose, you're sure to encounter lots of other people who have rented the exact same model. Put something in your car window, so that you'll be able to distinguish your car easily. Otherwise, you may find yourself staring at a sea of small, white, four-door Toyotas the way we did one morning when we came out of our hotel.

Everyone drives on the left side of the road, and the steering wheel is on the right, so when pulling out into traffic, look to your right. The car's setup may be slightly different in other ways, too. The local joke is to watch out for tourists with their windshield wipers on, because they're about to make a turn.

Once you get away from the airport, traffic thins out and driving is simple. You can't get lost, because you'll travel Grand Cayman's one main road, a route that offers a few little offshoots. George Town has several one-way streets marked with international signs. Ask the rental agent to show you what the signs look like. If you're behind a bus that stops to let off passengers, be sure to stop or else you may run over a fellow traveler: The exit doors swing out into traffic. Always watch for pedestrians; Grand Cayman attracts visitors from around the world, and you never know what the pedestrian rules are on their home turf.

Ask whether your speedometer is in kilometers per hour or miles per hour. They are often in kilometers, but the speed signs (circles with 25, 30, 40, or 50) are posted in miles per hour.

Quick Concierge

ATMs

Automatic Teller Machines are available universally on this bank-riddled island.

Baby-sitters

Hotels can readily help you arrange baby-sitting, but don't wait until the last minute. Expect to pay at least $7 an hour. Unemployment on the island is low, so plan in advance.

Banks

The principal banks are Barclays Bank, Cayman National Bank, Royal Bank of Canada, Bank of Nova Scotia, Canadian Imperial Bank of Commerce, and Washington International Bank.

Business Hours

Shops in George Town are open weekdays from 9 a.m. to 5 p.m. and Saturdays from 10 a.m. to 2 p.m.; in outer shopping plazas, shops are open daily from 10 a.m. to 5 p.m. Shops are usually closed Sundays except in hotels. Bank hours are Monday through Thursday 9 a.m. to 2:30 p.m. and Friday 9 a.m. to 1 p.m. and 2:30 to 4:30 p.m.

Credit Cards

Major credit cards are widely accepted.

Currency Exchange

Although the U.S. dollar is accepted everywhere, you'll save money if you go to the bank and exchange U.S. dollars for Cayman Island (CI) dollars, worth about US$1.20 at press time. The Cayman dollar is divided into a hundred cents with coins of 1¢, 5¢, 10¢, and 25¢ and notes of $1, $5, $10, $25, $50, and $100 (no $20 bills). Prices are often quoted in Cayman dollars, so it's best to ask. All prices quoted in this book are in U.S. dollars, unless otherwise noted.

Doctors

Healthcare on the island is excellent. Ask your hotel concierge for a referral, or call **Cayman Medical and Surgical Centre's** new 24-hour physician referral hotline at ☎ 345-949-8150.

Electricity

Electricity is the same in the Cayman Islands as it is in the United States (110-volt, 60 cycle).

Emergencies

For an ambulance, call ☎ **911** or **555**. For a hospital, call ☎ **911**.

Hospital

The new $150 million **Cayman Islands Hospital** (☎ 345-949-8600) in George Town on Hospital Road has a state-of-the-art accident and emergency unit, staffed 24 hours a day. **George Town Hospital** (Hospital Road, George Town; ☎ 345-949-4234 or 555) has a two-man double-lock hyperbaric chamber; it's manned on a 24-hour on-call basis by trained staff from the Cayman Islands Divers chapter of the British Sub Aqua Club, and it's supervised by a doctor trained to treat diving injuries.

Information

The main office of the **Department of Tourism** is in the Pavilion (Cricket Square and Elgin Avenue, P.O. Box 67; ☎ 345-949-0623 or 345-914-1270; fax 345-949-4053; Internet www.caymanislands.ky). You can find information booths at the airport (☎ 345-949-2635), at the Cruise Landing at Spotts when cruise ships are in port during rough seas, or in the kiosk at the cruise ship dock in George Town (☎ 345-949-8342). Grand Cayman also maintains an islands-wide tourist hot line (☎ 345-949-8989).

You can contact the **Tourist Information and Activities Service** (☎ 345-949-6598 or 345-945-6222) day or night for complete tourist information and free assistance in booking island transportation, tours, charters, cruises, and other activities.

Internet Access

See Magazines/Newspapers below.

Language

English is the official language, and it is spoken with a distinctive brogue that reflects Caymanians' Welsh, Scottish, and English heritage. For example, "three" is pronounced "tree"; "pepper" is "pep-ah"; and Cayman is "*K*-man."

Magazines/Newspapers

Dickens Literary & Internet Café (Galleria Plaza, West Bay Road, ☎ 345-945-9195) is a great place to see international newspapers, check your e-mail, and surf the net. You can also get light snacks, bagels, and muffins here, as well as your morning cappuccino or fruit smoothie.

Maps

You can pick up a good map at any tourist information kiosk or at the hotels.

Pharmacies

Island Pharmacy (☎ 345-949-8987) is in West Shore Centre on Seven Mile Beach. It's open daily.

Police

In an emergency, call ☎ **911.**

Post Office

Post offices are generally open weekdays from 8:30 a.m. to 3:30 p.m. and Saturday from 8:30 to 11:30 a.m. Beautiful stamps are available at the General Post Office in downtown George Town and at the philatelic office in West Shore Plaza. If you are addressing a letter to the Cayman Islands, include "BWI" (British West Indies) at the bottom of the envelope. Note that the islands don't use zip codes.

Safety

This island doesn't suffer from the crime that plagues some other Caribbean islands. You can walk wherever you like. Nonetheless, don't tempt fate: Don't leave valuables in plain sight in rental cars, be sure to lock your hotel room when you leave, and don't leave valuables unattended on the beach.

Frankly, Caymanians are more concerned about you breaking the law than they are about islanders infringing on someone's property or person. Locals strictly observe and enforce laws that prohibit collecting or disturbing endangered animal, marine, and plant life and historical artifacts found throughout the islands and surrounding marine parks. Simply put, take only pictures, and please don't stand on the coral reefs because that kills them.

Penalties for importing drugs and firearms and possession of controlled substances include large fines and prison terms.

Poisonous plants on the island include the maiden plum, the lady hair, and the manchineel tree. If in doubt, don't touch. The leaves and apple-like fruit of the manchineel are poisonous to touch and should be avoided; even raindrops falling from them can cause painful blisters.

As for sharks, we were assured that they don't hang around the popular dive sites; they generally prefer deeper water. However, at Stingray City, an 8½-foot hammerhead swam right underneath Kevin.

Taxes

All accommodations add a 10% government tax, and you'll encounter a departure tax of $10 when you leave the island. Otherwise, there is no tax on goods or services. But most hotels and restaurants tack on a 10%–15% service charge to your bill.

Telephone

For international dialing to Cayman, the area code is 345 (changed from 809). To call outside, dial 0+1+area code and number. You can call anywhere, anytime, through the cable and wireless system and local operators. To make local calls, dial the seven-digit number.

To place credit card calls, dial 110. **AT&T USA Direct** (☎ 800-872-2881) and **MCI Direct** (☎ 800-624-1000) can be used from any public phone and most hotels.

Time Zone

The islands are on Atlantic Standard Time, one hour ahead of EST.

Tipping

At large hotels, a service charge is generally included and can be anywhere from 6%–15%; smaller establishments and some villas and condos leave tipping up to you. Although tipping is customary at restaurants, note that some automatically include 15% on the bill, so check the tab carefully. Taxi drivers expect a 10%–15% tip.

Water

Water is safe to drink, but please conserve for the island's sake.

Weather and Surf Reports

Check out the following Web sites: www. 2gobeach.com/hurr.htm or www.weather.com.

Chapter 22

Dining in Grand Cayman

- -

In This Chapter

▶ Sampling the local cuisine

▶ Locating the island's best restaurants

- -

*I*n culinary schools, students are sometimes asked to create a meal with a box of miscellaneous ingredients — in a limited amount of time. Many days, chefs on Grand Cayman are forced to perform that same drill. The small coral island doesn't produce much in the way of fresh fruits and vegetables. About the only fruit around here is *las frutas del mar:* fish, conch, lobster, turtle (farmed on the island), octopus, and squid.

Although the local ingredients may be limited, your restaurant choices aren't. Like Aruba, this small island boasts a surprising number of restaurants — about 120 all told — featuring everything from Caribbean classic to New World, Thai, Asian, and American cuisine.

Using what they have on hand, Caymanian cooks have created their own distinctive cuisine, which prominently features a version of conch fritters, spicy pepperpot soup, Cayman patties (filled with lobster, chicken or other meat, or vegetables), fish "rundown" (fresh catches simmered in coconut milk), and the national dish of turtle stew. (Turtle is farmed here, so you don't have to feel guilty about eating it.) Local lobster is in season from summer's end until January.

 Dining out on Grand Cayman can put a serious dent in your budget, so consider whether some sort of meal plan at your hotel would make sense for you. It's easy to blow $20 or more per person at breakfast. To cut costs, many people bring their own groceries from home or buy them on the island and cook for themselves in their condos. Refer to Chapter 6 for budget tips.

 Despite the high prices and British influence, you won't have to spend money on fancy duds for dinner. Casual attire is suitable at most places.

Grand Cayman's Best Restaurants

Almond Tree

$$–$$$ George Town   Seafood

Conch is king at this eatery, which combines South Seas architecture from the isle of Yap with bones, skulls, and bric-a-brac from Africa, South America, and the Pacific. It's a casual place, surrounded by lush tropical trees and romantically lit with tiki torches at night. Especially recommended are Chef Ella May Terry's turtle steak and lobster tail. Almond Tree is also known for its exotic rum-based drink, the Hurricane, which packs almost as much of a wallop as its namesake.

North Church Street between George Town and West Bay. ☎ *345-949-2893. Main courses: $13–$26. AE, DISC, MC, V. Open for lunch October 1 through April 15; open for dinner year-round. Closed Tuesdays.*

Benjamin's Roof

$$–$$$ George Town   American

This casual restaurant, set on the upper floor of a shopping center, is decorated like the interior of a greenhouse. The cheery staff serves food and strong drinks to the accompaniment of live piano music and a singer/guitarist playing island favorites such as the tunes of Bob Marley. Swiss Chef Arnold Hanni's specialties are blackened alligator tail with Cajun spices, lobster bisque, a mixed seafood grill, Austrian-style Wiener schnitzel, lobster fettuccine, and grilled lamb with herbs. Catch a price break with the early bird menu, available from 3:00 p.m. to 5:30 p.m.; this place is one of the few in town that offers such a deal. The menu features kids' meals, which are less spicy than the regular fare.

Coconut Place off West Bay Road. ☎ *345-945-4080. Reservations recommended. Main courses: $12–$30. AE, MC, V. Open daily from 3:00 p.m. to 10:30 p.m.*

Captain Bryan's by the Sea

$$ George Town   English pub grub/Caribbean

This whimsical pub, situated in a low-slung cottage with a verandah in vivid shades of pink, blue, and yellow, has a loyal clientele. One side is a campy British pub with real English pub fare, soccer playing on the TV, and dartboards lining one wall. The other side is a Caribbean-inspired dining room that opens to a view of the harbor. For lunch, try the Caesar salad topped with marinated conch. Follow that with the West Indian sundae (vanilla ice cream with banana fritters and rum-raisin sauce).

The best time to try the Captain's fare is either for breakfast — they make terrific huevos rancheros, strangely enough — or for the rollicking happy hour (5:00 p.m. to 6:30 p.m.) with its great beer selection. This is one of the few restaurants in George Town open Sundays for lunch.

Grand Cayman's Restaurants

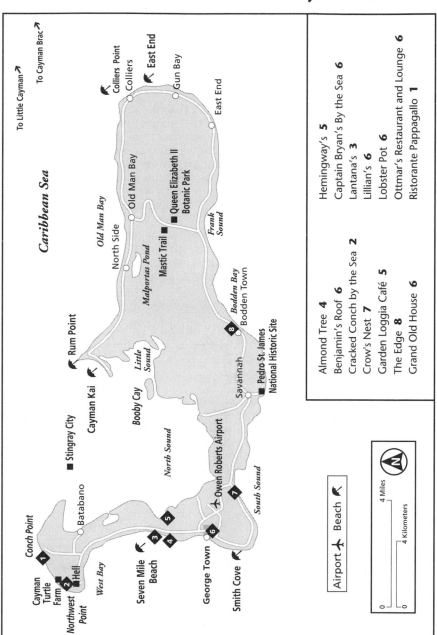

Hemingway's **5**
Captain Bryan's By the Sea **6**
Lantana's **3**
Lillian's **6**
Lobster Pot **6**
Ottmar's Restaurant and Lounge **6**
Ristorante Pappagallo **1**

Almond Tree **4**
Benjamin's Roof **6**
Cracked Conch by the Sea **2**
Crow's Nest **7**
Garden Loggia Café **5**
The Edge **8**
Grand Old House **6**

Caribbean Sea

To Little Cayman ↗
To Cayman Brac ↗
East End
Colliers Point
Colliers
Gun Bay
East End

Queen Elizabeth II
Botanic Park

Old Man Bay
Old Man Bay
North Side
Mastic Trail
Frank Sound

Rum Point
Malportus Pond
Bodden Bay
Bodden Town

Cayman Kai
Little Sound
Booby Cay
Savannah
Pedro St. James
National Historic Site

Stingray City
North Sound
Owen Roberts Airport

Batabano
Conch Point
South Sound

Cayman Turtle Farm
Hell
West Bay
Seven Mile Beach
George Town
Smith Cove

Northwest Point

Airport ✈ Beach ☚

N

4 Miles
4 Kilometers

North Church Street. ☎ *345-949-6163. Reservations recommended in winter. Main courses: $10–$21. AE, MC, V. Open for breakfast, lunch, and dinner daily. Bar open till midnight.*

Cracked Conch by the Sea

$$–$$$ North Coast   Seafood

Owner Susie Soto, wife of Grand Cayman diving pioneer Bob Soto, decorated this fun island landmark with nautical antiques like scuba gear and shipwreck finds. The plank floors came from the wreckage of a pirate ship, and the mirrors incorporate the rescued original shutters and doors of an old Cayman house. The expansive terrace is a great place to sit and watch the sunset. Specialties here include spicy Cayman-style snapper, turtle steak, and conch prepared every which way — cracked conch (tenderized and pan-fried), conch fritters, and conch chowder. If you're really hungry, spring for the Fisherman's platter. The Sunday buffet is a divine array of island-style curries and jerk meats.

Kids love this place, and the restaurant has a children's menu with preferred mainstays.

857 Northwest Point Road, near Turtle Bay Farm. ☎ *345-945-5217. Main courses: $12–$30. AE, DISC, MC, V. Open for lunch and dinner daily.*

Crow's Nest

$$–$$$ South Sound   Local

A 15-minute drive south of George Town, the Crow's Nest is tucked away in a rustic West Indian Creole cottage that sits right on the beach and is shrouded by flowering shrubs. From here, you have a wonderful view of Sand Cay Island; bring your snorkeling gear in case you want to take a closer look after lunch. For the best breezes, sit on the fishnet-draped terrace. If it's too warm for your taste, opt for the air-conditioned interior.

The shark du jour and fiery coconut shrimp with pineapple plum sauce are standouts. The Crow's Nest also offers inexpensive salads, nice stir-fries and pastas, and a children's menu. The key lime mousse was recently featured in *Bon Appetit.*

104 South Sound Road. ☎ *345-949-9366. Fax 345-949-6649. Main courses: $14–$24. AE, MC, V. Open for lunch Monday through Saturday and dinner daily.*

The Edge

$$$–$$$$ Bodden Town   Seafood

This rustic spot on the "edge" of the Caribbean, in what was the island's first capital, offers spanking fresh seafood supplied by local fishermen. We recommend the surf and turf and the yellowfin tuna steak. All entrees come with generous servings of fried bread, side salad, vegetables, rice and beans, plantains, and red potatoes. Take a stroll through historic Bodden Town, which got its name in 1773 from the many members of the Bodden family living there, before dinner or order takeout and have your own private picnic.

Bodden Town, a half-hour drive from Geroge Town (a $27 taxi ride). ☎ *345-947-2140. Reservations accepted. Main courses: $15–$30. AE, MC, V. Open for breakfast, lunch, and dinner daily.*

Garden Loggia Café

$$$ Seven Mile Beach Continental

This cafe at the Hyatt has a beautifully landscaped courtyard and is one of our favorite breakfast spots. If you eat inside, you'll be surrounded by soothing pastels and the coolness of ceiling fans and marble-top tables. The don't-miss event is Sunday champagne brunch, which features a generous salad buffet, international cheeses, spicy lobster soup, seafood quiche, Belgian waffles, and custom-made omelets. If that's not enough, you can also choose from roast beef with Yorkshire pudding, lamb's leg, black pepper chicken, veal, or pan-fried fish. The dessert choices are too numerous to mention — suffice it to say you won't go away unsatisfied. It also features a Caribbean-style spread on Tuesday evening.

Be sure to reserve a place at the Sunday brunch trough as far in advance as possible.

West Bay Road. ☎ *345-949-1234. Reservations essential. Main courses: $13.50 daily breakfast buffet; Tuesday dinner show $50. AE, DISC, DC, MC, V. Open daily from 7 a.m. to noon; Sunday brunch from 11 a.m. to 3 p.m.; Tuesday dinner and show from 6:30 p.m. to 9 p.m.*

Grand Old House

$$$–$$$$ George Town Caribbean/New World

This restaurant, set in a former plantation house built in the early 1900s, lives up to its lofty name. Chef Mathai has cooked for presidents and royalty. The menu here is the kind that gives its offerings lengthy descriptions — for example, the "terrine of wild boar and pheasant, served with cumberland sauce and garnished with orange segments." Try saying that mouthful fast!

Among the spicier appetizers is fried coconut shrimps with mustard apricot sauce ($8.95). On the milder side are entrees such as lobster tail "the Chef's Way" (dipped in egg batter and sautéed with shallots, mushrooms, tomatoes, and beurre blanc, $28.50) and pan-fried duck flamed in Cointreau ($18.95). The oceanside gazebos, surrounded by palms and cooled by ceiling fans, are refreshing; and you'll get stellar live entertainment every night except Sundays.

648 South Church Street. ☎ *345-949-9333. Dinner reservations essential. Main courses: $19–$29. AE, MC, V. Open for lunch Monday through Friday and dinner daily. Closed Sundays from May 15 through November 15.*

Hemingway's

$$–$$$ Seven Mile Beach   Nouvelle Caribbean

Sea views and breezes draw diners to this classy open-air restaurant that features a patio facing Seven Mile Beach. We love this romantic place, especially in the evenings under the stars with candles flickering on the tables and a classical guitarist serenading diners. Starters include spiny lobster tabouleh with fresh coriander and ginger lemongrass infusion, and seared ahi napoleon with crispy gyoza skins and wasabi lime aïoli (a Japanese-inspired dish). Try the pan-fried snapper on Peruvian blue mashed potatoes with Caribbean-spiced vinaigrette. Portions are large and service is superb.

If you want a tropical drink, try the Seven Mile Meltdown, with dark rum, peach schnapps, pineapple juice, and fresh coconut. Or try the Papa Doble, a daiquiri fashioned like those Hemingway preferred in Havana.

West Bay Road, on the beach in the Hyatt complex. ☎ *345-945-5700. Reservations recommended. Main courses: $20–$50. AE, CB, DISC, DC, MC, V. Open for lunch and dinner daily.*

Lantana's

$$–$$$ Seven Mile Beach   Contemporary American

Located at the Caribbean Club in the heart of Seven Mile Beach, this restaurant has garnered acclaim from *Gourmet* and *Bon Appetit.* However, the award-winning chef recently departed, so we can't promise the kitchen will be the same when you visit. Recent favorites include the chili-spiced squash bisque with garlic matchstick croutons and the rock lobster and lump crab cakes with marinated greens and fiery jerk mayo. The Caribbean seafood paella with broiled lobster, jumbo shrimp, scallops, and blackened dolphin is also a standout. Casual yet romantic, the two-story, air-conditioned restaurant is decorated with painted wooden fish, potted plants, and teak furniture.

Wine lovers take note: This restaurant has one of the more extensive wine lists on Grand Cayman.

West Bay Road, near the Strand Shopping Plaza. ☎ *345-945-5595. Reservations essential. Main courses: $18–$36. AE, MC, V. Open for dinner daily.*

Lillian's

$ George Town   Caribbean/Spanish

Traditional island and Spanish dishes are the specialties at this modest diner, packed with locals during lunchtime. Ask Miss Lillian about her "Fish Tea," which is actually a soup and billed as an aphrodisiac. We don't want to speculate about what's in it. Daily specials include barbecue ribs, meat loaf, and fish rundown — a stew made with fish, plantain, cassava, sweet potato, and breadfruit in a white sauce.

Christian Plaza, near the airport, on North Sound Road. ☎ *345-949-2178. Main courses: $8–$14. No credit cards. Open Monday through Saturday for lunch.*

Lobster Pot

$–$$$ George Town   Seafood

Lobster Pot is one of the island's older restaurants and has the feel of an English pub. At 6:30 nightly, the tarpons are fed in the lit waters, which is a fun show for kids as well as adults. The extensive menu includes both continental dishes and Caribbean specialties like conch chowder and lobster Cayman style. Kids feel welcome here, but it's a bustling spot with quick table turnover and lots of noise. If you want dessert, go for the island rum cake.

Arrive at this cozy restaurant in time to enjoy a frozen banana daiquiri and the terrific sunset view from the second-story terrace.

North Church Street. ☎ *345-949-2736. Main courses: $14–$31. AE, MC, V. Open for lunch Monday through Friday and dinner daily.*

Ottmar's Restaurant and Lounge

$$–$$$ George Town   French/International

Styled after a West Indian greathouse with peach walls, mahogany furniture, glass chandeliers, and a trickling fountain, Ottmar's is named for its German-born chef/owner. If you're looking for a quiet, romantic spot where you'll hear the whisper of a quartet playing Mozart rather than the roar of the surf, this is a good bet.

Favorites on the international menu include bouillabaisse, chicken breast Oscar (topped with crab, asparagus, and hollandaise), and French pepper steak (flamed in cognac and doused with green peppercorn sauce and crème fraiche). The wine list is excellent, and Chef Ottmar is happy to help you with your selection.

Grand Pavilion Commercial Centre, West Bay Road. ☎ *345-945-5879 or 345-916-2332. Reservations essential. Main courses: $14–$32. AE, MC, V. Open for lunch and dinner daily. Happy hour Friday from 5:30 p.m. to 7:30 p.m. on the Waterfall Terrace.*

Ristorante Pappagallo

$$–$$$ Conch Point   Northern Italian/Seafood

One of the island's more memorable restaurants lies on a 14-acre bird sanctuary overlooking a natural lagoon, 15 minutes north of George Town. Its designers incorporated Caymanian and Aztec weaving techniques in its thatched roof. Glass doors, black marble, and polished brass combine a kind of Edwardian opulence with a Tahitian décor, but it works. Chattering macaws in cages deliver lively background music.

For these prices, the food didn't bowl us over, but the setting made up for it. We'd recommend the black tagliolini with lobster sauce, fresh crab ravioli with asparagus sauce, lobster in brandy sauce, or the Italian-style veal and chicken dishes.

Barkers, near the northern terminus of West Bay Road and Spanish Cove, 8 miles north of George Town. ☎ *345-949-1119. Reservations required. Main courses: $20–$38. AE, MC, V. Open for dinner daily.*

Chapter 23

Hitting the Beach and Other Fun Things to Do

*I*f Grand Cayman is your vacation pick, we're assuming you love the water the way we do. And when it comes to activities centered around (and in) the sea, Grand Cayman makes a great choice.

Besides scuba diving, Grand Cayman is noted for other watersports like windsurfing and deep sea fishing, as well as for superb golf and decent shopping. In this chapter, we help make sure that you don't miss a thing Grand Cayman has to offer, and we take away any remaining stress factors. Hassle-free fun is what we're going for, and we're sure that's what you're seeking, too.

Heading for the Sand and Surf

Grand Cayman's Seven Mile Beach — one of the Caribbean's finer bands of sand — begins north of George Town, the capital. This famed stretch, which is actually only 5½ miles long (but who's counting?), boasts sparkling white sands edged by casuarina pines and a variety of palms. Toward the southern end, the landscape becomes quite rocky. Low-rise deluxe resorts, condos, and small hotels are strung along the beach, much like Aruba's immensely popular but crowded Palm Beach.

The surf is that milky teal color that invites you to loll on a raft. You don't have to worry about being swept out to sea either. The wave action along this beach mirrors the calm of the island, and the bath-warm water barely laps at your ankles.

Thankfully, you don't have to be a guest at a particular hotel to use the beach, and you're welcome to use the facilities at any spot. The Hyatt gets understandably persnickety about nonguests overtaking its pools and beach chairs. And Hyatt security can spot nonguests a mile away. (For starters, you won't have the plush Hyatt-issued blue beach towel tucked under your arm.) We somehow managed to stay below security's radar, but a Ralph Cramden lookalike sporting blue zinc oxide on his nose and a "Will Work for Beer" tank top was immediately tossed.

Be discreet if you're not a registered guest and you decide to venture beyond a hotel's beach bar or rest room facilities. We wouldn't recommend trying to use the pool at a place where you're not staying; however, if you eat lunch at the hotel restaurant, that's your meal ticket to splash in the pool if you like.

About the only time Seven Mile Beach gets crowded is when the cruise ships dock; no more than 6,000 passengers are allowed per day, but that's still a lot of folks. You'll never see the crush of people you find on the most popular beaches in Puerto Rico or Aruba. You also don't have to worry about vendors asking to braid your hair or inviting you to toss out the toll for cheap jewelry and tie-dyed T-shirts like in Jamaica or Puerto Rico. And panhandling is outlawed, so forget about being hassled. In fact, Grand Cayman, with one of the lower crime rates in this hemisphere, is among the few islands where we could actually visualize ourselves napping on the beach without worrying about what would be gone when we woke up. Of course, the annoying buzz of jet skis plying the waters off Seven Mile Beach makes snoozing unlikely, but we can dream.

The rockier beaches on the east and north coasts, a good 20- to 30-minute drive, are protected by an offshore barrier reef and offer good snorkeling. They are much less congested, and their reefs are in better shape than Seven Mile Beach, which has suffered from its popularity. On the southwest coast you can find small sandy beaches, but they're better for sunning than snorkeling because blankets of ribbon-like turtle grass have proliferated in the water.

Having Fun in and on the Water

What they lack in nightlife, the Cayman Islands make up for in watersports. The diving, fishing, swimming, and waterskiing are among the finest in the Caribbean.

Observing some underwater rules

- ✔ **Look, but don't touch.** Coral reefs are extremely sensitive, and some coral grows less than an inch per year. Breakage by careless divers can take decades for Mother Nature to repair. Please don't bump, stand on, break, or even touch the coral.

- ✔ **Don't feed the fish (or the stingrays).** We know you'll see other people doing it, but marine research has demonstrated that feeding by humans is doing serious damage to the fish population by throwing off the delicate balance of the coral reefs. Besides, you might wind up with a "stingray hickey." These graceful, buttery soft creatures vacuum the food out of your hands (their mouths are in the middle bottom part of their bodies), and sometimes the suction can be uncomfortable.

Diving right in

First things first. Grand Cayman, ringed by glorious coral reefs teeming with marine life, has earned its reputation as a world-class diving destination. Underwater visibility often exceeds 100 feet in these crystalline teal waters where you can indulge your Jacques Cousteau fantasies at more than 130 sites — everything from wall dives and wreck dives to cave dives, coral garden dives, and shore dives. The island has won kudos from every diver's publication and is the Caribbean's premier dive spot. (We must admit, though, that we adore Bonaire, which is less developed; see Chapter 11.)

Grand Cayman's diving is literally a mountaintop experience. The coral island sits at the top of an underwater mountain, the side of which — known as the Cayman Wall — plummets straight down for 500 feet before becoming a steep slope falling away for 6,000 feet and eventually plunging 23,000 feet to the ocean floor.

We'd heard rumors that Grand Cayman isn't what it used to be and that the popular dive sites have been overrun. So off we went to check it out ourselves. We're happy to report that you can still find gorgeous corals, diverse marine life, and great wall diving, but if you want more pristine diving, you need to go to the east or north of the island. Sadly, the diving hordes have damaged the corals, particularly to the west of the island.

Yes, divers seem to be everywhere. When a tiny island has more than 60 dive operators, what do you expect? But thanks to the good practices of the ultra-professional operators and vigorous conservation efforts, the diving experience here rates a definite thumbs up. (The Grand Cayman operators make sure divers' professed expertise really is up to snuff and that a diver has a current card from one of the national diving schools. We've been on islands where dive operators didn't even ask about those things.)

If something does go wrong during a dive, the island has a decompression chamber; most cases of decompression sickness (or "the bends") can be successfully treated locally (see Chapter 21).

Taking a scuba course

If you've never tried scuba diving, Grand Cayman is a great place to get your feet wet. You can take a "resort" or introductory course in the morning and make your virgin dive that afternoon. You won't have to worry about strong currents, and the (usually) patient dive instructors are used to dealing with beginners. A resort course allows you to sample the sport (which is expensive) without committing to the much more costly and lengthy process of getting certified.

One resort course designed to teach the fundamentals of scuba to beginners who already know how to swim costs $99. It requires a full day: The morning is spent doing some classroom work and learning skills in the pool; the afternoon incorporates a one-tank dive. All necessary equipment is included. Contact **Bob Soto's Diving Ltd.** (☎ **800-BOB-SOTO** or 345-949-2022) or **Red Sail** (☎ **877-RED-SAIL** or 345-945-5966) at Treasure Island Resort. For more information on these companies, see the following section.

If you aren't in good physical shape, or if you have a great deal of anxiety about the prospect of being under the sea, we wouldn't recommend a resort course. Unless you're the type who catches on quickly, you'll feel pushed, and we wouldn't want a bad initial experience to sour you on a great sport. If you have any sort of medical condition that might preclude you from diving, such as high blood pressure, frequent ear infections, or sinusitis, you'll need to obtain clearance from a doctor on-island who specializes in dive medicine. The dive shop will give you a referral.

If you're interested in becoming a certified diver, we strongly urge you to do all your course work at home. Otherwise, you may be certifiable after you realize how much precious beach and dive time you have to waste so close and yet so far from the Caribbean. Your local YMCA probably teaches a certification course with necessary pool work, then you can simply do your check-out dives in Grand Cayman and get official.

Reviewing recommended operators

Although most dive operators on Grand Cayman are excellent, you'll sometimes run into "cowboys." These "cattle boat" operators go out with disproportionate numbers of divers to instructors. Before you book, inquire about the maximum numbers of divers on a given trip. You'll have a better time with a smaller group where you get more personalized service and help with the heavy gear (called *valet service*) — especially if you're a beginning diver. Plus, smaller groups create less stress and damage to the reef.

Established in 1957, the best-known dive operation in the Cayman Islands is **Bob Soto's Diving Ltd.** (P.O. Box 1801, Grand Cayman; ☎ **800-BOB-SOTO** or 345-949-2022; fax 345-949-8731; e-mail: bobsotos@candw.ky). Known as the father of diving on Grand Cayman, Soto vividly recalls walking up and down the beaches trying to hustle up hotel guests willing to fork over a few bucks to dive. It was a primitive business in those days — empty fire extinguishers filled with air and lashed together served as tanks — and the hotel owners used to chase Soto away. He laughs, "They were afraid I'd kill their guests."

Ironically, today the island owes half its economy to Soto's vision. Now owned by Ron Kipp, Bob Soto's Diving, Ltd., runs full-service dive shops known for service and safety at four locations: Treasure Island Resort (see Chapter 20), the SCUBA Centre at The Lobster Pot; Soto's

Coconut in the Coconut Place Shopping Centre; and Soto's Water Emporium at the Strand shopping complex. You'll notice the name Soto plastered on many businesses on the island.

Certified divers can choose from a wide range of one-tank ($40) and two-tank ($60) boat dives daily on the west, north, and south walls, plus shore diving from the SCUBA Centre. A full certification course costs $375. Nondivers can take advantage of daily snorkel trips ($25), including tours of Stingray City.

Red Sail Sports (☎ **877-RED-SAIL** or 345-945-5966; Internet www. redsail.com) has locations at the Hyatt Regency Grand Cayman (☎ **345-949-8745**), Westin Casuarina (☎ **345-949-8732**), and the Marriott Grand Cayman (☎ **345-949-6343**). Red Sail is generally well-regarded and maintains an up-to-date and well-equipped watersports facility. We had a great time learning to dive with this outfit, but we've also heard quite a few complaints from more experienced divers about a blasé attitude from the staff. Toward the middle of the week when the cruise ships are in town, their boats tend to get crowded with cruise ship passengers visiting Grand Cayman for the day.

Red Sail Sports offers beginners' scuba diving as well as excursions for the experienced, including Nitrox tanks (which allow you to dive deeper and stay down longer) and certification to use Nitrox. A full certification course, requiring a minimum of five days, costs $440. A two-tank morning dive includes exploration of two different dive sites at depths ranging from 50 to 100 feet and costs $50 to $66. (Nitrox tanks are an additional $5.) A bonus: Red Sail Sports' diving operation is accessible for travelers with disabilities.

Red Sail was also selected to introduce the new Supplied Air Snorkel for Youth (SASY), a customized SCUBA unit for children as young as 4. (Previously, children under age 12 weren't allowed to SCUBA.)

FISHEYE (☎ **800-887-8569;** Internet www.fisheye.com) has established a Web site that's a great resource on diving as well as for summer and fall bargains on dive vacation packages and specials. You can register online to receive its e-mail newsletter with late-breaking specials and updates.

Small operator **Ocean Frontiers** (P.O. Box 30433 SMB, East End, Grand Cayman; ☎ **800-544-6576** or 345-947-7500; fax 435-947-7600; e-mail oceanf@candw.ky; Internet www.oceanfrontiers.com) is another top choice. Its dive masters and instructors are widely praised for being friendly, professional, and exceptionally customer-oriented. Book early, though, because Ocean Frontiers' comfortable boat only takes 12 divers per dive.

A good choice if you want to dive with experienced divers as well as newbies is **Peter Milburn's Dive Cayman Ltd.** (P.O. Box 596 GT, Grand Cayman; ☎ **345-945-5770;** fax 345-945-5786; e-mail pmilburn@ candw.ky). The congenial owner, who relies on word-of-mouth, will send you to sites that divers at both ends of the experience spectrum can enjoy. He limits dive groups to six, so reserve in advance. Try to get dive master Scotty Shoemaker, who will regale you with humorous island tales.

Dive rates

Here's what you can generally expect to pay for dives:

- ✔ Morning two-tank dive: US$70

- ✔ Night dive: US$60 (including lights)

- ✔ Stingray City dive: US$50

- ✔ Stingray City snorkel: US$30

- ✔ Resort course and dive: US$99

- ✔ Open water check-out (with referral letter): US$85

- ✔ Equipment rental (BCD and regulator): US$15; discount on weekly rentals

Peeking into an underwater world

What if you're not a diver? Snorkeling on Grand Cayman allows you to see much of the same scenery thanks to the incredible clarity of the water. Popular spots where you can snorkel right off the beach include the West Bay Cemetery Reef, Smith's Cove, and Eden Rock.

The snorkeling is excellent off the north coast. Many fish have taken to the Russian warship that was scuttled offshore from the now-defunct Buccaneer's Inn. (Look for the beautiful queen angelfish that make their home between two of the guns.)

All the dive operators listed in the previous section offer snorkeling trips, but one of our favorites is **Captain Marvin's Tropic Sea & Sea Tours** (☎ **800-550-6288,** ext. 3451 or 345-945-4590; fax 345-945-5673; e-mail: CAPTMVN@candw.ky). Captain Marvin Ebank, age 85, is still operating an all-day snorkel tour of the North Shore for $45 a person, taking guests out on his 40-passenger *Miss Jackie* every day except Sunday. The boat leaves at 9 a.m. for Conch Point, where you can see live queen conch (pronounced "conk" — as in what you'll get on the head if you try to remove any of these shells). The second stop is at a colorful shallow barrier reef. Lunch is Caymanian fare on Kaibo Beach. After lunch, it's full speed ahead to Stingray City, with a final stop at Coral Gardens.

Swimming with the stingrays

If you book a tour to Stingray City, which is two miles east of Grand Cayman's northwestern tip, forget walking shoes — you'll need your swimsuit. At this unusual underwater attraction (accessible via an easy dive in the 12-foot waters of North Sound or by snorkeling across the surface), you'll see hordes of graceful creatures. (We're talking stingrays, not tourists.) We absolutely love this dive. It's surreal to see all these beautiful creatures flitting about.

In the mid 1980s, when local fishers cleaned their catches and dumped the leftovers overboard, they noticed swarms of stingrays (which usually eat marine crabs) feeding on the debris, a phenomenon that quickly attracted local divers and marine zoologists. Today, between 30 and 50 relatively tame stingrays hover for daily handouts of squid from increasing hordes of snorkelers and scuba enthusiasts.

Treasure Island Divers (☎ 800-872-7552 or 345-949-4456) charges divers $45 and snorkelers $25 to visit this unusual attraction. The trip starts Monday, Wednesday, Friday, and Sunday at 1:30 p.m.

During the summer, Capt. Sterlin Ebanks of **Stingray City Tours** (call ☎ **345-949-9200,** ext. 71, and ask for the "Summer Special") gives half off the three-hour Stingray City snorkel trip, which stops at Stingray City, Coral Garden, and the shallow barrier reef. For $17.85, you get snorkeling equipment, refreshments, and a free pickup from Seven Mile Beach. Trips depart daily at 10 a.m. and 1:30 p.m. You must reserve in advance and pay cash to get this price.

Don't worry. The name stingray doesn't mean they'll sting you when you touch them. They do have prongs on their tails, but the only way to get stung is to stomp on a prong (which would be extremely difficult) or grab it. When these velvety creatures float over you looking for a handout, the sensation is something akin to being kissed by a vacuum cleaner. You'll see other people feeding them, but we don't recommend doing so.

Enjoying the Waves without Getting Wet

If you're yearning for a peek under the sea but don't want to dive, you still have plenty of options. **Atlantis XI** on Goring Avenue (☎ **800-253-0493** or 345-949-7700) is a $3 million submersible that's 65 feet long, weighs 80 tons, and was built to carry 48 passengers. You can view the reefs and colorful tropical fish through the 26 two-foot-wide windows as the vessel cruises at a depth of 100 feet through a coral garden maze. *Atlantis XI* dives Monday through Saturday; reservations are recommended 24 hours in advance.

You have two options when boarding the *Atlantis XI:*

- ✔ **Atlantis Odyssey** features such high-tech extras as divers communicating with submarine passengers by wireless underwater phone. This 45-minute dive costs $82.

- ✔ **Atlantis Expedition** lets you see the famous Cayman Wall, lasts 55 minutes, and costs $72 for adults, $49 for ages 13 to 18, and $36 for kids 4 to 12; no children under age 4 allowed.

Seaworld Explorer, which costs $35, is a semi-submarine that introduces viewers to the marine life of Grand Cayman. Children 4 to 12 are charged $19; younger children are free.

Telling fish tales

Sport fishers come to Grand Cayman from all over the world for a chance at reeling in one of the big ones: tuna, wahoo, and marlin. Most hotels can make arrangements for charter boats; experienced guides are also available. The Hyatt Regency Grand Cayman on West Bay Road (☎ **800-255-6425** or 345-947-5966) offers deep sea fishing excursions in search of tuna, wahoo, and marlin on a variety of air-conditioned vessels with an experienced crew from either **Just Fishin'** or **Bayside Watersports.** Half-day tours depart at 7 a.m. and 1 p.m. and cost $600; full-day tours cost $800. The fee can be split among as few as four or as many as ten people.

Navigating the waves

The best-known waterskiing outfitter is **Red Sail Sports** in the Hyatt Regency Cayman on West Bay Road (☎ **345-945-5966**). Water-skiing outings can be arranged for $75 per hour, with the cost divided among several skiers. Parasailing, which yields a great view of George Town, is offered for $50 per ride. Other outfitters are found at the **Westin Casuarina** (☎ **345-949-8732**), **Rum Point** (☎ **345-947-9203**), and the **Marriott Grand Cayman Beach Resort** (☎ **345-949-6343**), charging comparable prices.

Speed freaks looking for some thrills will be glad to know that jet skiing is allowed off Seven Mile Beach, where you can skip over the surf at more than 30 mph. You'll be several yards off shore. After a quick lesson in operating the watercraft and a review of some safety tips, you'll be on your way. We personally don't like these things, and we'd like to see them eliminated from rental options, particularly in a spot known for its reefs. Many islands have banned jet skis because of the damage they wreak on the reefs, not to mention the noise they produce. Check with your resort's front desk for the nearest watersports operator offering jet skiing — if you must.

Some jet skiers ignore swimmers and divers in the area and come too close — we know you won't be that careless.

If you prefer a gentler approach to the waves, you can glide quietly along the water enjoying the warm Cayman breezes from your rented sailboat. Anchor in a shallow spot and snorkel or swim to cool off. Red Sail Sports rents 16-foot Prindle catamarans for $28 per hour, depending on the time of day.

Living It Up on Dry Land

The underwater delights are the main attraction on Grand Cayman, but sea-based exploration only scratches the surface of available activities on this island. Check out a few other options for your vacation pleasure.

Teeing off

Grand Cayman offers an unusual golf experience at the **Britannia Golf Club** (☎ **345-949-8020**), next to the Hyatt Regency on West Bay Road. The course, the first of its kind in the world, was designed by Jack Nicklaus. It incorporates three different courses in one: a 9-hole championship layout, an 18-hole executive setup, and an 18-hole Cayman course. The last was designed for play with the Cayman ball, which goes about half the distance of a regulation ball.

The Britannia's greens fees run $50 to $80 in season, $40 to $65 off-season, depending on the configuration of the course you intend to play. Cart rentals go for $15 to $25; club rentals, $25. Hyatt guests receive a discounted rate and can reserve 48 hours in advance; the Britannia accepts reservations from everyone else no earlier than 24 hours ahead.

Exploring George Town

The good news on Grand Cayman is that you can feel safe walking anywhere on the island. The bad news? You won't have much to look at in your wanderings. The tiny capital of George Town can easily be explored in an afternoon. About the most exciting thing here is the post office on Edward Street where you can buy Cayman Islands' beautiful and highly collectible stamps.

Built in 1833, the **Cayman Islands National Museum** (☎ 345-949-8368) at Harbour Drive was used as a courthouse, a jail (now the gift shop), a post office, and a dance hall before reopening in 1990 as a museum. It's small but interesting with good displays and videos that illustrate local geology, flora, fauna, and island history. Admission is $5, and it's open weekdays from 9 a.m. to 5 p.m. and Saturday from 10 a.m. to 4 p.m.

Pick up a walking-tour map of George Town at the museum gift shop before leaving.

Going to Hell and back

Hell really does exist on Grand Cayman. And we don't mean being caught on a dive boat on a rough day without Dramamine. On Grand Cayman, Hell is a surreal craggy landscape at the far northwest end of West Bay Beach Road about a half-hour from George Town. Once you've reached Hell, that's the end of the line — er, road, we mean. The area got that nickname in the 1930s thanks to the otherworldly rock formation of dolomite and limestone. Caymanians, always looking for a business opportunity, turned the natural sculpture into a tourist attraction. If you want to thrill your friends back home, the postmaster will stamp your postcard with "Hell, Grand Cayman" — a certain hit with those who envied your travel plans.

You'll only want to spend 15 minutes tops in Hell. There's not much to do, and the biggest excitement is getting the postmarked proof that you've been there.

Ivan Farrington, the proprietor of the Devil's Hangout Gift Shop, dresses up like the demon himself. He'll crack lots of jokes — "It's a hell of a town, isn't it? But it's hotter than hell here" — about the place while you're buying your postcards. He'll also tell you where to go when you leave.

The **Cayman Turtle Farm** (☎ 345-949-3894), also on Northwest Point near Hell, is the only green sea turtle farm of its kind in the world. With some 250,000 visitors annually, it's the most popular land-based tourist attraction in the Cayman Islands. We saw turtles ranging in size from smaller than our hand to larger than the floats that people loll on at Seven Mile Beach.

Once the Cayman Islands' surrounding waters were teeming with turtles. (Columbus called the islands *Las Tortugas* because of them.) Today, these creatures have dwindled alarmingly in numbers; the green sea turtle is an endangered species.

The turtle farm has a twofold purpose: to provide the local market with edible turtle meat and to replenish the waters with hatchling and yearling turtles. You can sample turtle dishes at the farm's snack bar and restaurant, but we couldn't get past the endangered idea to take a taste. You cannot bring turtle products back into the United States. The turtle farm is open daily from 8:30 a.m. to 5 p.m. Admission is $6 for adults, $3 for children 6 to 12, and free for children 5 and under.

Enjoying a dose of local history

At the end of a quiet, mango and mahogany tree-shaded road in Savannah, Grand Cayman, high atop a limestone bluff, lies one of the Caribbean's most spectacular historic restorations. The **Pedro St. James Historic Site** (Savannah, ☎ 345-947-3329) is an historically accurate reconstruction of a 1780 Great House, which was the birthplace of democracy on the Cayman Islands and its first national landmark. The visitor's center offers a 20-minute film that gives a zippy overview of the Cayman Islands' 200-year history. It's a 20-minute ride from George Town. Hours are 8:30 a.m. to 5 p.m. daily. Admission is $8 for adults, $4 for children 6 to 12 years old, and free for children under 6.

The beautifully restored gardens on the grounds have become a popular place for weddings and vow renewals.

Communing with the wildlife

For a terrific walk, do it up royally at **Queen Elizabeth II Botanic Park** (☎ **345-947-9462** or 345-947-3558; for information call 345-947-7873 or e-mail guthrie@candw.ky) at Frank Sound Road on the North Side, about a 45-minute drive from George Town. The short trail (less than a mile long) slices through 60 acres of wetland, swamp, dry thicket, mahogany trees, orchids, and bromeliads. The trail is easy enough for children, and you could easily see it all in under an hour. You may spend two hours if you want to meander through the Heritage Garden and other new additions.

Time your visit for early in the day when the animals are more active. You'll probably see hickatees, the freshwater turtles found only on the Caymans and in Cuba. Occasionally you'll spot the rare Grand Cayman parrot or the anole lizard with its cobalt-blue throat pouch. Even rarer is the endangered blue iguana, but you can see 40 of them here. Your best chance to see them in motion is from 8:30 to 10:30 a.m. on a sunny day.

The park is open daily from 9 a.m. to 5:30 p.m.; guests are admitted until 4:30 p.m. Admission is CI$5 (US$6.25) for adults, CI$2.50 (US$3.15) for children, and free for children 5 and under.

A new visitor's center has opened in the botanic park, offering changing exhibitions, a good gift shop, and a canteen for food and refreshments. We like the new **Heritage Garden** with its restoration of a traditional early nineteenth-century Caymanian home, garden, and farm, and its floral garden with 2½ acres of flowering plants and traditionally grown fruit trees (mango, breadfruit, tamarind, plum, cherry, and ackee). Around the small lake you'll find many birds.

If you're more athletic and an eco-hound to boot, don't miss one of Grand Cayman's newer attractions: the **Mastic Trail** (west of Frank Sound Road, a 45-minute drive from George Town). This restored 200-year-old footpath winds through a 2-million-year-old woodland area leading to the North Sound. *Islands* magazine gave this site one of its top eco-preservation awards. Named for the majestic mastic tree, the rugged two-mile trail showcases the reserve's natural attractions, including a native mangrove swamp, traditional agriculture, and an ancient woodland area, home to the largest variety of native plant and animal life found in the Cayman Islands.

The hike is not recommended for children under 6, the elderly, or persons with physical disabilities. Wear comfortable, sturdy shoes and carry water and insect repellent. For reservations, call ☎ **345-945-6588** Monday through Friday.

For $50 per person, you can take a guided tour of Mastic Trail that includes transportation and cold soft drinks. For more information and reservations, call ☎ **345-949-1996;** fax 345-949-7494, or write Mastic Trail, P.O. Box 31116 Seven Mile Beach, Grand Cayman. Two-and-a-half-hour guided tours, limited to eight participants, are offered Monday through Friday at 8:30 a.m. and at 3 p.m. and on Saturday at 8:30 a.m.

Shopping Your Way through Grand Cayman

The dutyfree shopping in George Town encompasses the types of luxury items that you'll also see in the USVI: silver, china, crystal, Irish linen, and British woolen goods. Unfortunately, you'll also run into such local crafts as black coral jewelry. (We're disappointed to see this sold, especially on an island that relies on pristine corals to entice visitors.)

 The prices on many items are not that much better than in the United States. Our advice is to comparison shop before you come so you'll know if you're truly being offered a deal. Don't purchase turtle products or any shells. They cannot be brought into the United States.

We recommend the following shops:

- ✔ **Artifacts Ltd** (☎ 345-949-2442) on Harbour Drive, across from the cruise ship dock in George Town, is managed by Charles Adams, one of the country's philatelic experts. This is the premier outlet for antique stamps issued by the Caymanian government. Stamps range in price from 17¢ to $900, and the inventory includes the rare War Tax Stamp issued during World War II. Other items for sale are antique Dutch and Spanish coins unearthed from underwater shipwrecks, as well as antique prints and maps.

- ✔ **The Jewelry Centre** (☎ 345-949-0070) on Fort Street in George Town has the largest selection of jewelry on the island. Located in a two-story building, it encompasses six departments specializing in loose or set diamonds, gold (sold as chains or as ornaments, including coins found in shipwrecks offshore), and *caymanite,* the pinkish-brown striated rock found only on the Cayman Islands.

- ✔ **Kennedy Gallery** (☎ 345-949-8077) in West Shore Centre in George Town specializes in watercolors by local artists like Joanne Sibley, whose work we admire, as well as copies and originals of works by the establishment's founder, Robert Kennedy. Paintings range from $15 to as much as $7,000.

Longing for Some Nightlife

Okay, okay. You gotta understand. Divers expend a lot of energy on their sport, plus some of them would rather see nature's nighttime light show on the coral reefs than hang out in a disco. That means if you're looking for a cranking nightlife, you're on the wrong island.

Barhopping is about as crazy as it gets here, particularly during happy hour (usually from 5 p.m. to 7 p.m.). Watching the sunset and trying to see the mysterious green flash that people say they see on the horizon right at the moment the sun sizzles into the sea is the big entertainment. For other options, look at the freebie magazine *What's Hot* or check the Friday edition of the *Caymanian Compass.*

You can count on a fun crowd of locals and visitors at the **Cracked Conch** (☎ 345-945-5217) on West Bay Road near Turtle Farm. This place offers karaoke, classic dive films, and a great happy hour with hors d'oeuvres Tuesday through Friday evenings.

Sports nuts who can't live without ESPN head to the **Lone Star Bar & Grill** (☎ 345-945-5175) on West Bay Road. There, they can see sports events simultaneously on 15 different TV screens and sip lime and strawberry margaritas. Mondays and Thursdays are fajita nights — all-you-can-eat affairs. Tuesday is all-you-can-eat lobster night, virtually unheard of in the Caribbean.

Sharkey's (☎ 345-947-5366), in the Falls Shopping Centre, Seven Mile Beach, is a popular disco and bar filled with rock-and-roll memorabilia from the 1950s.

Coconuts Comedy Club (☎ 345-945-4444) sets up shop at different venues along the main drag and draws comedy acts — some surprisingly well-known — from all over the world. After the show, you can entertain yourself (and the audience) with karaoke — if you must.

Part VII
Jamaica

The 5th Wave   By Rich Tennant

JAMAICA'S ESCALATOR FALLS

In this part . . .

*J*amaica has something for everyone, from the seasoned traveler to the first-timer in the Caribbean. We weed through the vast array of accommodation choices to highlight our favorites. We show you how to get to the island and how to safely explore it after you arrive.

The cuisine on this island has a kick; we list some of our favorite spots to experience the fiery variety of local fare. Finally, whether you're looking for watersports or all-night parties, we show you how to make the most of your time on Jamaica.

Chapter 24

The Lowdown on Jamaica's Hotel Scene

In This Chapter

▶ Sizing up hotel locations

▶ Focusing on top hotel picks

*B*ased on the sheer breadth of its accommodations, Jamaica stands in a class by itself in the Caribbean. Whether you're a first-timer to the Caribbean or a been-there-done-everything traveler, a honey-mooner or part of a family on the go, Jamaica offers almost an endless array of choices. You can stay in a funky shack on the beach, a no-holds-barred all-inclusive resort, a posh ultra-exclusive resort, an inti-mate boutique hotel, a gorgeous villa, a family-run joint, or any type of chain from Comfort Inn & Suites to the sparkling new Ritz-Carlton.

We've noticed that visitors' feelings about the Caribbean's fourth largest island are directly connected to where they stay, probably because most tourists tend to settle in and stick close to their resorts. A bathing suit and a bed sheet (for Toga Night) may be all you need to fit in at hedonistic Negril, but if you book into a cushy, Old Jamaica–style resort on the outskirts of Montego Bay, you'll do well to break out your tropical best. So choosing the right place for your needs takes on major importance when you're visiting Jamaica. In this chapter, we explain the different characters of the main resort areas, help you sift through our favorites places to stay, and offer suggestions for other popular digs to consider.

Figuring Out Where You Want to Stay

Most of Jamaica's resorts are congregated along the beaches of and around Montego Bay, Negril, and Ocho Rios/Runaway Bay. A few worth considering are a bit far afield, but they are so special that we've included them in our recommendations later in this chapter. How do you know which part of the island fits your vacation dreams the most perfectly? Read on.

Romantic bargains

Competition for the honeymoon, anniversary, and romance market is hotly contested among the many all-inclusives on this island, so you can expect quite a few freebies that you likely won't get on most other islands. For example, SuperClubs Resorts announced at the end of 1999 that any couple honeymooning, celebrating an anniversary, or renewing vows and staying six nights at its resorts would get the seventh night free. Meanwhile, through January 31, 2001, honeymooners staying in a premium room or higher for six nights or more at any Sandals resort get a free set of china.

Couples who get married at SuperClubs now get 50% off a seven-night stay for a return five-year anniversary trip.

Montego Bay

Montego Bay, the most cosmopolitan of Jamaica's resort towns, is ground zero for the party crowd. Situated on the lush and hilly north-western coast, Mo Bay — as it's called by locals and those who've been on the island for more than five minutes — is the second largest city in Jamaica. Mo Bay got its start in tourism back in the 1940s when the wealthy crowd discovered Doctor's Cave Beach (see Chapter 27).

Thanks to years of a steady diet of marketing in the United States, Mo Bay is one of the best known spots in the Caribbean. Architecturally speaking, it doesn't hold a tiki torch to other harbor towns like Puerto Rico's beautiful Old San Juan or St. Thomas's historic Charlotte Amalie. But when the sun goes down and the neon lights up the night, Mo Bay's main strip throbs.

On the fringes in either direction just outside Mo Bay's sprawl, some of Jamaica's finest resorts discreetly host Hollywood's elite, British royalty, and anybody else who has the cash to get beyond the cloistered gates.

Mo Bay is a sort of microcosm of Jamaica, in that it reflects the problem the entire island struggles with: how to put on a happy face for tourists when poverty and crime are tugging at your sleeve. Most visitors to Jamaica land at the Mo Bay airport, so this area gets the first shot at making an impression. You'll quickly understand why your package tour to stay at one of the many hotels crowding along the strip is so cheap. Nonetheless, Mo Bay continues to be popular, because a seven-minute drive from the airport gets you to fine beaches, good shopping, and a pepper pot of locals and tourists mixing it up for a good time. College kids have begun to descend here for spring break, especially during the first few weeks of March.

ISLAND SPICE

Culture clash

Quick! What's the most exotic and far-flung honeymoon dream for many Japanese couples? Jamaica, mon. Many Japanese are fascinated with the late Bob Marley and reggae music. When the yen was at an all-time high, so many Japanese tourists were making the 30-hour pilgrimage that several north coast luxury hotels had staff members who were fluent in Japanese.

Negril

Meet Mo Bay's younger, wilder, prettier sister, Negril. This once sleepy fishing village on the island's western tip only started getting attention in the late 1960s when flower children from Canada and the U.S. adopted it as a groovy outpost. Then, it had no phones, no electricity, and a readily available supply of marijuana (or *ganja,* as those who smoked it called the stuff).

Today, sophisticated all-inclusive resorts, such as Swept Away, Grand Lido Negril, and Sandals Negril, draw a better-heeled and less rowdy crowd from all over the globe to Negril's three well-protected bays: Long Bay, Bloody Bay (now called Negril Harbour), and Orange Bay.

Negril has a dual personality. On the eastern fringe of Seven Mile Beach, which you pass on the road from Mo Bay as you enter town, you'll see most of the all-inclusives. Seven Mile Beach is action-packed with exhibitionists, watersport operators, vendors, and ganja peddlers all vying for attention. The quieter West End is a cluster of local restaurants, boutique hotels, and cottages tucked along the shaded limestone cliffs, which are honeycombed with caves.

Runaway development threatened to overtake Negril a few years ago. The water supply couldn't match the burgeoning demand; the drug peddlers and vendors grew so bold that many visitors fled, vowing never to return; and the roads got really bad.

But when we last visited Negril, the craft markets had been more neatly organized and the vendors were more low key. We didn't notice any problems with water pressure at our hotel. Echo felt comfortable enough to walk around the West End with some girlfriends — minus a male presence to fend off local men. The roads were slightly better. But most reassuringly, the funky spirit of the little village remained.

Recently, spring breakers discovered Negril. About 3,000 college kids descend upon the tiny town during March.

Runaway Bay/Ocho Rios/Port Antonio

We've lumped these north coast resorts together, because distance, like time, doesn't mean a whole lot on Jamaica. You may be told that a certain resort is in Ocho Rios when it's actually well outside of town. If you're traveling from Mo Bay via car, van, or bus, Runaway Bay is the first of the major resort areas that you'll hit. Several major all-inclusives are in this area.

Better known is Ocho Rios, which is nicknamed Ochi (pronounced *oh-chee*). *Ocho Rios* is a Spanish phrase meaning *eight rivers* — another Caribbean misnomer. We've never counted that many rivers here, but this north coast resort town, a good two-hour drive east of Montego Bay, is surrounded by the lush beauty that most people associate with the Caribbean.

It's hard to believe that Ocho Rios, which is now Jamaica's cruise ship capital, was once a small banana and fishing port. Its bay is dominated on one side by a decrepit-looking bauxite loading terminal. On the other side, a congested hotel district fronts the beaches; the Jamaica Grande Renaissance, Jamaica's largest hotel, holds center court. This sprawling resort town is where most visitors stay when they come for Ocho Rios's annual jazz festival.

Ochi is a busy port town, but the brilliant greens of the surrounding hills hint at the glorious gardens, waterfalls, and other treasures to be seen if you know where to look. A few hotels are tucked into the hill-sides — one of our favorite little secrets is renting the inexpensive apartment above the small museum in the heart of the enchanting **Coyaba Gardens** (☎ 876-974-6235). But the cushy all-inclusives and venerable favorite **Jamaica Inn** lie on the outskirts.

In the 1940s, Ochi and neighboring Port Antonio, which is even more jungle-like, became favorites of a glamorous crowd led by the likes of Sir Noel Coward, who hosted a parade of international guests, and Ian Fleming, creator of *James Bond*. Coward maintained a modest estate called Firefly, while Fleming built one called Goldeneye. Jamaican Chris Blackwell, founder of Island Records and the owner of a collection of boutique hotels called Island Outposts, bought both places and restored them in homage to Coward and Fleming. Now the houses are once again welcoming the rich and famous. (See our accommodation reviews later in the chapter for details on staying at Goldeneye.)

Small boutique resorts are the norm in and around Port Antonio, which is much more reflective of the Jamaica of yesteryear. Unfortunately, 20% occupancy rates have also become the norm of late in Port Antonio. Several of the hotels in the area have suffered from a lack of guests and have fallen into disrepair. Many guidebooks are still touting place as "charming" that would send us screaming into the night. Stick with our recommendations.

All-inclusives: Altogether successful

The fast-growing all-inclusive concept (see Chapter 3 for an in-depth explanation) was popularized by Jamaican Butch Stewart in 1981. Stewart, who incidentally also owns Air Jamaica, launched his first couples-only Sandals that year, and he continues to gain converts to the concept. Stewart now has 13 Sandals and Beaches resorts in the Caribbean, with the majority concentrated on Jamaica. SuperClubs, which encompasses Grand Lido Resorts, Hedonism, and Breezes resorts, is another Jamaican-based collection of all-inclusives.

Jamaica's Best Hotels

The rates listed in this section are in U.S. dollars and are for a standard double room during high season (mid-December to mid-April), unless otherwise noted. Lower rates are often available during the off season and shoulder season; see Chapter 2 for more information on travel seasons. Many hotels in Jamaica require a two- or three-day minimum stay. Please note that most of the rates are for all-inclusive plans, so the prices appear inflated. We've noted both these things in the following reviews.

Jamaica is one of those islands where you should never go for the published rack rate. You can *always* do better. Packages and special deals abound. If you don't want to stick to the big all-inclusives, one of the best travel agencies specializing in great hotel deals is **Changes in L'Attitudes** (☎ 800-330-8272). Its Web site, www.changes.com, is fast loading and informative, and it puts you in a good mood just surfing it.

For villas in Montego Bay, Ocho Rios, and Port Antonio, contact **Elegant Resorts International** (P.O. Box 80, Montego Bay, Jamaica; ☎ 800-237-3237 or 876-953-9150; fax 876-953-9563).

Beaches Negril

$$$$$ **Negril**

Beaches is part of Sandals, and when Sandals overbooks, the overflow is sent here. Beaches welcomes everybody — singles, couples, and families with children of all ages — but it's hard to be all things to all vacationers. This resort will marry you and take care of you on your honeymoon, but we don't recommend it for that occasion — unless you're on your second marriage and have kids in tow. It's hard to feel romantic when the pools and restaurants are overflowing with tots and teens.

Understandably, however, families flock to this well-landscaped, 20-acre resort at Long Bay fronting a wide strand of Negril's Seven Mile Beach. We thoroughly enjoyed ourselves here. More importantly, our kids had a blast with the Sega Centre, kids' pool, and Kids Kamp.

One of this resort's large free-form pools, adjacent to the main dining area and visible from the grand open-air lobby, has the feel of a town square: Everyone seems to congregate there, amicably chatting while the children happily splash away. We also like the spa housed in Jamaican-style wooden cottages, and the open-air workout facilities with top-notch equipment. Both are somewhat removed from the noisy kids' area.

The 225 rooms come in nine categories. They are all well air-conditioned and have ceiling fans, in-room safes, and king-size beds. Amenities include an amphitheater for nightly happenings, five restaurants, beach bandstand, disco, several bars, a beauty salon, two freshwater pools, three whirlpools, and a toddlers' pool. Available watersports are scuba diving, waterskiing, paddle boating, snorkeling, and windsurfing. The resort also offers tennis, beach volleyball, and board games.

Beaches Inn (P.O. Box 44, Negril, ☎ **876-957-5100**; fax: 876-957-5229), on Seven Mile Beach and formerly the Poinciana Resort, is the bargain secret for families. You can stay here for much less, but still have full access to the pricier Beaches Negril.

Norman Manley Blvd., Negril. ☎ ***800-726-3257.*** *Fax: 305-284-1336. E-mail:* beachesnegril@cwjamaica.com. *Internet:* www.beaches.com. *Rack rates: $480–$620 double. Rates are all-inclusive. Children under age 2 are free; kids ages 3 to 15 stay for $70 a night. AE, MC, V.*

The Caves

$$$$$ Negril

Cloistered on ten acres of the cliffs near Negril Lighthouse on the edge of town, these colorful wooden, thatched-roof cottages make the most of their fantastic location and cater to ultra-hip jet-setters like U2's Bono and supermodel Naomi Campbell.

Our favorite cottage, Sunshine, has a roomy bed in an upstairs loft that's open to the Caribbean breezes. Hand-carved furniture, original art, outdoor showers, king-sized beds with candles set all around, CD/cassette players, and a discreet staff make for a terrific experience. You won't find air-conditioning or a beach, but a web of grottos and stairs lead to a saltwater pool, sauna, hot tub, and sundecks overlooking the milky teal water below. You can climb down a ladder and slip into the sea for a swim over a coral reef with good snorkeling. Braver souls can take the plunge from Hopper's Hop (named for actor Dennis Hopper) where the aquamarine water below is 30 feet deep. At night, the dramatically lit sea caves below the resort are a fun place for snuggling.

Aveda spa treatments are given in an open-air gazebo. Stellar, authentic Jamaican cuisine is served throughout the day at a casual thatched-roof hut that's the gathering place in the middle of the property.

If you aren't on a rock star's budget, you can get some of the same vibes down the street at the Rockhouse (see our review later in this section) for less than half the price. You'll sacrifice the artsy details and seclusion of this place, and, of course, you'll blow your chance of making the pages of *InStyle*.

Lighthouse Road, Negril. ☎ *800-OUTPOST or 305-531-8800. E-mail:* reservations@ islandpost.com. *Internet:* www.islandoutpost.com. *Rack rates: $375 one-bedroom unit; $825 two-bedroom/two-bathroom unit. No children under age 16. AE, MC, V.*

Coyaba Beach Resort & Club

$$$–$$$$ Montego Bay

If the generic all-inclusive concept holds no appeal for you, we highly recommend this lovely 50-room resort. Just a 10-minute ride east of the Mo Bay airport, this resort is in the midst of a quiet stretch of beach populated by elegant resorts far from the craziness of downtown Mo Bay. (Okay, it's only 10 miles away, but it feels like another world.)

One of our favorite features of Coyaba, besides the fact that everything proceeds at a relaxed pace, is the fishing dock with a cabana at the end that juts out into the placid bay. But what sets Coyaba apart is how thoroughly the needs of families are ingrained in the culture here. You don't pay extra for cribs or use of the kids video library. Babysitters — who, your hosts assure you, are "kid-tested by Ericka and Jamie" — charge just $5 an hour.

Coyaba is one of the newer resorts on the island (having opened in August 1994) and one of the best maintained in Jamaica. Although families are welcome, the resort also manages to strike just the right note in the romance department. Its honeymoon package ($1,800 in the summer/$2,700 in the winter for eight days and seven nights per couple) is a standout. It features a private candlelit dinner for two, a two-hour horseback ride through the countryside, and a day's tour with a driver and picnic lunch.

Guestrooms are located in plantation-style, tiled-roof, butter-yellow buildings. Besides air conditioning, guestrooms have ceiling fans, satellite TV, and French doors leading to oversized private balconies overlooking the well-manicured courtyard and the private white-sand beach edging the sea beyond. The 24 deluxe oceanview rooms — the most expensive — are large and have mahogany four-poster king-size beds, dining alcoves with windows, and sitting areas.

Resort facilities include two stylishly decorated restaurants, a bar, a fitness gazebo, and a tennis court. (We especially like the free tennis clinics with visiting pros.) It also boasts a piano bar, volleyball, croquet, and bocce, as well as massage services.

Norman Manley Blvd., Little River (P.O. Box 88), Montego Bay. ☎ *800-237-3237 or 876-953-9150. Fax: 876-953-2244. E-mail:* coyaba@n5.com.jm. *Internet:* www.coyabajamaica.com. *Rack rates: $420 double. Meal plans available at additional cost. Three-night minimum stay required in winter. Kids ages 12 and under stay and eat free in parents' room. AE, MC, V.*

Jamaica's Hotels

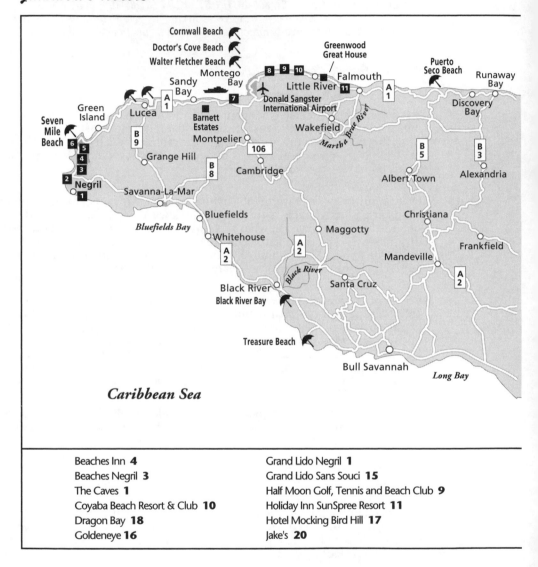

Cornwall Beach
Doctor's Cove Beach
Walter Fletcher Beach
Montego Bay
Sandy Bay
Greenwood Great House
Falmouth
Puerto Seco Beach
Runaway Bay

8 9 10
Little River
11
Donald Sangster International Airport
Green Island
Lucea
Seven Mile Beach
A 1
B 9
Barnett Estates
Montpelier
106
Wakefield
Discovery Bay
Martha Brae River
A 1
B 5
B 3
6 5
4
3
Grange Hill
B 8
Cambridge
Albert Town
Alexandria
2 Negril
1
Savanna-La-Mar
Christiana
Bluefields
Bluefields Bay
Whitehouse
Maggotty
Mandeville
Frankfield
A 2
A 2
Black River
Santa Cruz
A 2
Black River
Black River Bay
Treasure Beach
Bull Savannah
Long Bay

Caribbean Sea

Beaches Inn **4**	Grand Lido Negril **1**
Beaches Negril **3**	Grand Lido Sans Souci **15**
The Caves **1**	Half Moon Golf, Tennis and Beach Club **9**
Coyaba Beach Resort & Club **10**	Holiday Inn SunSpree Resort **11**
Dragon Bay **18**	Hotel Mocking Bird Hill **17**
Goldeneye **16**	Jake's **20**

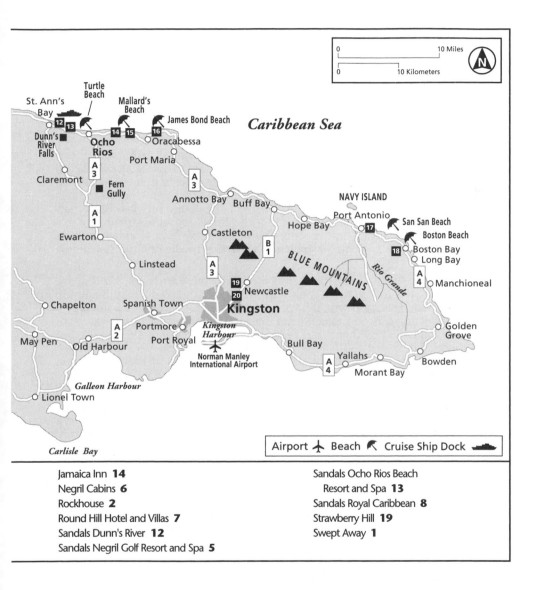

Jamaica Inn **14**
Negril Cabins **6**
Rockhouse **2**
Round Hill Hotel and Villas **7**
Sandals Dunn's River **12**
Sandals Negril Golf Resort and Spa **5**

Sandals Ocho Rios Beach
Resort and Spa **13**
Sandals Royal Caribbean **8**
Strawberry Hill **19**
Swept Away **1**

Goldeneye

$$$$$ Oracabessa

Ian Fleming built this simple house in 1946 and created the world's favorite spy, James Bond, here in 1952. Fleming, who wintered in Jamaica each year, wrote 14 of his 007 novels at a desk in his bedroom. You may recognize the name of this estate if you're a James Bond fan.

During the estate's heyday, Noel Coward (whose estate Firefly is now owned and managed by the same company as Goldeneye) was a frequent guest, as were Elizabeth Taylor, Errol Flynn, Truman Capote, and Evelyn Waugh. By 1998, Jamaican music mogul Chris Blackwell restored the property to its original dignity.

Goldeneye, which is set on a bluff overlooking a small cove, seems surprisingly simple at first glance. But then you start to notice all the playful touches. The main house is outfitted with oversized Indonesian bamboo couches, four-poster beds, batik fabrics, and African art. A media room is equipped with a complete collection of James Bond movies. Bath "gardens" have been added near each of the three bedrooms, giving guests outdoor showering and bathing options. (One has a clawfoot tub, imported from London, whimsically set in the middle of a rock garden.)

Unless you opt to rent the main house (as Pierce Brosnan, Jim Carrey, Martha Stewart, Quincy Jones, and Jamaica native son Harry Belafonte have done recently), you'll have to settle for one of the open-air bungalows set adjacent to a magnificent, blissfully private beach that has great snorkeling just offshore. But regardless of where you stay, friendly but discreet personal staff will be assigned to you to make sure that you get your fill of authentic Jamaican food and drink, including Blackwell's rum concoction called the "Goldeneye."

If you don't want to be shaken like one of Bond's favorite martinis during the two-hour ride from Montego Bay, you can always take the resort's private plane to a small airport called Boscobel, about eight minutes from Goldeneye. Or you can charter a helicopter and land on the property in Bond style. Fleming would approve.

Oracabessa, St. Mary's, Jamaica. ☎ *800-688-7678 or 876-974-3354. Fax: 876-975-3679. E-mail:* reservations@islandoutpost.com. *Internet:* www. islandoutpost.com. *Rack rates: $650 for a two-bedroom bungalow. Ian Fleming's three-bedroom house (which accommodates up to eight) is $3,000. Rates are all-inclusive. AE, MC, V.*

Dragon Bay

$$$ Port Antonio

Even if you don't remember that Tom Cruise trifle of a movie *Cocktail*, which was filmed here, Dragon Bay makes for a memorable hideaway in the foothills of the Blue Mountains around Port Antonio. This quiet collection of Colonial-style villas, which sits on a shimmering turquoise bay sheltered by deep green mountains and rimmed by a sandy beach, has also had a starring role in *Club Paradise* and the remake of *Lord of the Flies*.

Part of Elegant Resorts International, these one- to three-bedroom villas are an excellent value and occupy a prime spot in the heart of Jamaica's most picturesque countryside. Please note that only the deluxe suites have air-conditioning throughout; the bedrooms are air-conditioned in the other units. All units, newly refurbished, have king-size beds, and some suites have full kitchens.

The glorious setting makes the food here — a combo of Jamaican and European fare — worth a visit even if you aren't a guest. But thanks to Mr. Nicole Kidman, the most notable spot is the Tom Cruise Bar, adjacent to the beautiful beach. Order the Jungle Juice and relax.

Like most resorts, Dragon Bay offers a host of packages. We especially like Dragon Bay's new stress relief package, which is perfect for this relaxing setting. Don't worry though: If you want action, you can swim, scuba dive (with lessons), snorkel, sail, kayak, or hike the trails.

Couples should splurge on the Penthouse, on the top floor of the main building, which offers a grand view of this pristine cove.

Dragon Bay (P.O. Box 176), Port Antonio. ☎ ***877-677-3724*** *or 876-993-3281. Fax: 876-993-3284. E-mail:* reservations@dragonbay.com. *Internet:* www.dragonbay.com. *Rack rates: $220 one-bedroom suite; $330 two-bedroom suite. MAP (2 meals daily) costs $40 extra per person per day; an all-inclusive meal plan costs $80 extra per person per day. Ask about special packages. AE, MC, V.*

Grand Lido Negril

$$$$ Negril

In the last few years, both *Conde Nast Traveler*'s and *Travel & Leisure*'s readers have consistently ranked this classy all-inclusive, occupying a beautiful spot on Negril's Bloody Bay, as one of the Caribbean's best. We (almost) wholeheartedly agree. Set on 22 acres, the Mediterranean-style property, another link in the SuperClubs chain, bowls over guests with a dramatic entrance.

Recently, though, that entrance has been snarled at check-in with guests experiencing an uneven welcome. Part of the problem may lie with three general managers rotating through the property in 18 months and the accompanying staff turmoil. The bottom line: Some guests have been left to cool their heels for the afternoon because their rooms "weren't ready yet." Their luggage was nowhere in sight, so they couldn't even swim in the beckoning pool. Worse, no apologies were forthcoming. First impressions count, folks.

However, we're inclined to forgive these lapses — assuming they were just momentary hiccups — given the luxurious digs, all boasting fine sea views and all running parallel to the white-sand strand on famed Seven Mile Beach. The oceanview rooms that are closest to the water are on the nude beach side. You don't have to be in the buff to stay in these rooms, but you might get more of a view than you'd counted on. Be forewarned, however, that specific room requests seem to bog down the already slow check-in process even more.

Room service operates 24 hours. The clubhouse offers Jacuzzis, music, and (get this) laser karaoke at the piano bar. A spa has recently been added that features air-conditioned treatment rooms encircling a plunge pool and two massage gazebos by the sea, as well as a full salon. Grand Lido has an extensive 24-hour, air-conditioned fitness center, perfectly positioned for a sweeping vista of Bloody Bay. An evening sail aboard the resort's classic 147-foot yacht, a wedding gift from Ari Onassis to Monaco's Princess Grace and Prince Rainier, is a must.

Be prepared that the so-called express check out that is supposed to save you time at the airport can wind up lopping off an hour and a half out of your last day, too.

Negril Bloody Bay (P.O. Box 88), Negril. ☎ *800-467-8737 in the U.S., 800-553-4320 in Canada, or 876-957-5010. Fax: 876-957-5517. E-mail:* glnsales@cwjamaica.com. *Internet:* www.superclubs.com. *Rack rates: $360–$590 per person double occupancy. Rates are all-inclusive. Children under 16 are not allowed. AE, MC, V.*

Grand Lido Sans Souci

$$$$$ Ocho Rios

We didn't think we'd find an all-inclusive that could sweep us off our feet, but this beauty sure did. Charlie's Spa puts Grand Lido Sans Souci ahead of the competition. Treatments — one daily is included in the price — are done in three open-air gazebos on a cliff with dramatic views of the azure waters below. One of the most romantic treatments is the couple's massage.

Rooms are located in pretty-in-pink colonial buildings tucked into gentle hills covered with jungle-like, tropical growth. The setup yields a feeling of seclusion even when the resort is fully booked. Indeed, Grand Lido was completely filled during our stays, yet we never felt like one of the masses, nor were we forced to duke it out for a chaise lounge. If you want to splurge, go for the Roger Moore suite, which has a wide terrace on the top floor of the building overlooking the lovely main beach. Strolling musicians boost the romance factor.

The air-conditioned gym with floor-to-ceiling glass walls overlooking the calm Caribbean boasts one of the best views we've seen reserved for the hard-body crowd. Many resorts have gyms, but they're often stuck off in a corner, scarcely used. This one is positioned so that you want to be there. Besides, you can't miss it, so if the lure of the drop-dead gorgeous view doesn't get you, the guilt will. If you want to take a class, you can do that, too, at the open-air aerobics pavilion.

At one end of the property, a wide, white-sand beach beckons, and a newer section of rooms is located just steps away from the beach. (For our money, we prefer the more secluded rooms above the spa area.) Beyond the main beach is a small *au natural* section if you can't stand tan lines, and a lovely pond encircled by a good jogging trail.

The other notable attractions at this resort are the food and entertainment. Casanova (see Chapter 26) is well worth a visit, even if you're not staying at the resort; the lunch spread is bountiful as well as tasty. When the dancing on the terrace starts at other resorts, we're sometimes tempted to run for cover and put in our earplugs. Not so here. Management finds appealing local talents who know how to get the crowd — which spans a wide age range, from mid-20s to late 50s — on its feet.

On Rte. A3 (P.O. Box 103), Ocho Rios. ☎ *800-467-8737 or 876-994-1353. Fax: 876-994-1544. E-mail:* sslido@cwjamaica.com. *Internet:* www.superclubs.com. *Rack rates: $355 one-bedroom, $530 penthouse per person double occupancy. Rates are all-inclusive. Children under 16 are not allowed. AE, DC, MC, V.*

Half Moon Golf, Tennis and Beach Club

$$$$$ Montego Bay

Seven miles east of Montego Bay (and a universe away), Half Moon sprawls over 400 acres with 418 guestrooms, suites, and villas. The resort has a jaw-dropping 52 swimming pools, 13 tennis courts, a croquet lawn, and an equestrian center, to name just a few of our favorite things. Its fantastic, mile-long crescent-shaped beach (hence the name Half Moon) draws a loyal following, which includes everyone from sitting U.S. presidents to royalty to movie stars. Its excellent sport facilities (the legendary golf course was designed by Robert Trent Jones, Sr.) add to the appeal. For many years, about a third of the guests hailed from Europe, another third from the U.S., and another third from Japan. Lately, though, about 70% of the clientele is from the U.S.

Queen Anne and Chippendale reproductions and Oriental rugs blend appealingly with bright Caribbean colors in the airy and luxurious villas — many of which have private pools. The oceanview rooms are older, but we think they're a steal, because you'll be just steps from one of our favorite palm-lined beaches.

You get the same over-the-top service at this resort without some of the accompanying stuffiness of that grand dame, Round Hill, on the opposite side of town (see our review later in this section). One of Jamaica's most upscale shopping malls, with more than 40 stores, is on the grounds.

Montego Bay's busy nightlife is an easy taxi ride away — if you have any energy left after making the most of this terrific property, which has garnered AAA's Four-Diamond Award annually since 1978, as well as numerous kudos for being an environmental leader among Caribbean hotels. We love the fact that many of the fruits and vegetables used in the three fine dining restaurants are grown on the resort's 26-acre nature preserve.

The children's activity center for ages 3 to 10 features a swimming pool, a duck pond, sandboxes, thatched-roof playhouses, swings, a horseshoe court, and tennis courts. Activities here range from putting to planting trees, and from donkey rides to sandcastle building.

Rose Hall. ☎ *800-626-0592, 800-237-3237, or 876-953-2211. Fax: 876-953-2731. E-mail:* reservations@halfmoonclub.com. *Internet:* www.halfmoon.com.jm. *Rack rates: $195–$595 double. Weekly villa rates (sleeping up to eight) $19,650 and $20,580. Meal plans are available. Wedding and honeymoon packages available. AE, MC, V.*

Holiday Inn SunSpree Resort

$–$$ Montego Bay

Thanks to a $13 million redo in 1998, this resort (on 12 handsomely landscaped acres fronting a half-mile of beach) has been transformed into one of the best deals in Montego Bay. If you want the all-inclusive option without the walloping price tag, this resort is a great pick, especially for families with children.

This is Jamaica's second-largest resort, with 516 rooms. The pool area has a good children's section with a wading area and splashing fountains; and there's the Kidspree Centre for children from 6 months through the teens. The nursery is open from 9 a.m. to 9 p.m., or you can get a private nanny at a cost of $30 per child per day. Each additional child (up to three per nanny) runs another $5 a day.

The Holiday Inn SunSpree is near several ritzier resorts in one of the prettiest parts on Mo Bay, just 10 minutes from the airport. The friendly and efficient staff makes you feel like you're staying with an old family friend. (Just one caveat: Check-in can be slow at times.) Security is tight, and you don't have to worry about being hassled on the beach here or about walking around the property at any time. Housekeeping here is excellent, too.

The busy complex boasts nightly entertainment, a sports bar with a big-screen TV, golf at nearby Ironshore Golf Course, an electronic gaming parlor, a disco, a fitness center with Nautilus equipment, four lighted tennis courts, a watersports center, a 12-person Jacuzzi, and basketball and volleyball courts. The restaurants have improved greatly in the last few years; you get a good variety of choices, as well as more traditional Jamaican favorites, in ample servings.

Montego Bay (P.O. Box 480), Rose Hall. ☎ *800-HOLIDAY or 876-953-2485. Fax: 876-953-2840. Rack rates: $80 double (room only); $150 double (all-inclusive). AE, MC, V.*

Hotel Mocking Bird Hill

$$ Port Antonio

Just 10 rooms in the foothills of the Blue Mountains, surrounded by a wild tangle of tropical gardens and overlooking Port Antonio and the Caribbean, Mocking Bird Hill is lovingly run in European-style by owners Barbara Walker and Shireen Aga. The duo has found a niche, targeting environmentally sensitive travelers who appreciate the finer things in life.

Some of the rooms have air-conditioning, but ceiling fans were sufficient for us; you sometimes even need the blankets to ward off the mountain chill. The water is solar-heated, and handcrafted furniture is made from bamboo rather than hardwoods. Meals are made with local produce in Mille Fleurs (see our review in Chapter 24), and the manager, Barbara, displays her sculptures along with works of local artists in Gallery Carriacou on-site. You'll also find locally produced toiletries and stationery sets in the tasteful blue and white rooms. What you won't find are phones, TVs, or smokers. Lovely Frenchman's Cove beach is five minutes away, but most of the guests here prefer the pool, the hammocks strung on most terraces, or the many eco-tours offered.

If you aren't a dog-lover, book at Dragon Bay instead. The owners' large dogs are given full run of the hotel (and restaurant), which some guests may find disconcerting.

East of Port Antonio on North Coast Hwy. (P.O. Box 254), Port Antonio. ☎ *876-993-7267 or 876-993-7134. Fax: 876-993-7133. E-mail:* mockbrd@cwjamaica.com. *Internet:* www.mockingbirdhill.com. *EP. Rack rates: $120–$160 double. AE, MC, V.*

Jake's

$–$$$ Treasure Beach

The heliport is the only clue that Jake's has registered on the radar of the hip international jet set. Otherwise, you could easily imagine that you'd stumbled onto some hippie outpost circa 1960 when you first see this whimsical assemblage of 10 cottages by the beach. Each melds the artistry (influenced by the Caribbean, Morocco, America's Southwest, and Cape Dutch) of Sally Henzell, who co-owns this fun retreat with her son, Jason, a former investment banker.

If you want a rustic getaway — no phones, TV, or air-conditioning — Jake's is a good choice. Modern conveniences include coffeemakers, mini-bars, and CD players in each unit. Outdoor showers come with each room. Abalone, a romantic Moroccan-style adobe villa on the fringe of the property, would be our pick for a honeymoon hideout.

Jake's is set on a tranquil beach on Jamaica's undeveloped south coast. The main entertainments here are taking a dip in the small shell-and-colored-sea-glass encrusted pool, snorkeling, fishing with the locals, and touring the nearby Black River savannah area and Lover's Leap. The excellent Jamaican chef attracts locals and guests to the open-air restaurant, which quickly acquires a party atmosphere as the evening wears on.

If you can't take the heat, pass on Jake's, which is in the arid part of Jamaica, where the mosquito nets, though lovely, aren't just decoration.

Treasure Beach, Calabash Bay P.A., Saint Elizabeth. ☎ *800-OUTPOST or 305-531-8800. Fax: 876-965-0552. E-mail:* jakes@cwjamaica.com. *Internet:* www.islandoutpost.com. *Rack rates: $75–$95 one-bedroom, $150 suite, $245 two-bedroom, $325 three-bedroom villa. AE, MC, V.*

Jamaica Inn

$$$$$ Ocho Rios

Sometimes legends are a letdown when you finally see them. We get nervous when we see words like *venerable* and read lengthy lists of famous but long dead guests. But this gracious and elegant 45-room Wedgewood blue inn, set in waterfront gardens on a peaceful byway east of Ocho Rios, deserves every accolade and far exceeded our expectations. First opened in the early 1950s, it became known as a haven for famous guests seeking privacy in its spacious, airy rooms decorated with antiques. Churchill stayed here, as did T.S. Eliot. Noel Coward often tickled the ivories in the lounge, and movie stars like Marilyn Monroe and Elizabeth Taylor would drop by for an evening.

Classically Caribbean, secluded, and yet conveniently located, the Jamaica Inn is only 10 minutes away from the bustling port. The resort offers easy access to the area's plantation tours, Saturday polo matches at historic Drax Hall Polo Club, jumping lessons and trail rides at Chukka Cove equestrian center, golf on the par-71 Sandals Golf and Country Club, and torch-lit canoe rides.

However, we tend to stick with the inn's old-money guests, wandering the quiet grounds and enjoying the white-sand, ultra-private beach edged by glorious flower gardens. Jamaica Inn's airy suites have private verandahs that are complete living rooms, boasting a spectacular view of the beach and the Caribbean. Niceties include Crabtree and Evelyn amenities, hairdryers, recently installed "natural" lighting in each bathroom, and cotton robes with the Jamaica Inn logo. And for guests who can't take a holiday from their workout, Jamaica Inn's exercise room features state-of-the-art Life Fitness equipment — the Lifecycle bike, stairclimber, and treadmill. Its restaurant has been featured on the cover of *Gourmet*. (See our review in Chapter 26.)

The Clearwater Suite — adjacent to the property, on a bluff overlooking the sea — is a new option. This three-bedroom villa has a luxurious full-sized, broad-terraced pool and can accommodate up to six. You'll have a staff of three at your disposal here.

Main St. (P.O. Box 1), Ocho Rios. ☎ 800-837-4608 or 876-974-2514. Fax: 800-404-1841. Internet: www.jamaicainn.com. *Rack rates: $450–$525 double (including all meals). AE, MC, V.*

Negril Cabins

$$–$$$ Negril

Europeans, especially Italians, have eagerly adopted this great 90-room escape that features simple wood cabins on stilts tucked away at ground zero amidst a riot of royal palms, bull thatch, mango trees, and tropical flowers. Each cabin has a small balcony, and some are air-conditioned. A one-minute walk across the road takes you to the beach on Bloody Bay. Each timber cottage includes a balcony and ceiling fan; superiors and suites are air-conditioned.

The caring staff is continually making additions to this terrific family-owned bargain. The simple food — mainly fresh seafood and fruit — is abundant and tasty in the Coconut Palm's open pavilion. The open-air piano bar has become a favorite gathering place. Children under 12 stay free in parents' room. And a good kids' playground is on the beach.

If you buy the romance package, you get a free bottle of wine every day that it rains.

Norman Manley Blvd. (P.O. Box 118), Negril. ☎ *800-382-3444 or 876-957-5350. Fax: 876-957-5381. E-mail:* negrilcabins@cwjamaica.com. *Internet:* www.negril-cabins.com. *Rack rates: $145 to $310 double. AE, MC, V.*

Rockhouse

$$ Negril

A few years ago, the Rockhouse was purchased by a group of Australian friends intent on making it a stylish and fun retreat for their cool friends. Think of it as the Caves without the attitude (see our review earlier in this section) — and without the hefty bill at the end of your stay.

The owners have succeeded. The result is our favorite boutique hotel in Negril. The rooms (in timbers and stone with windows that allow uncluttered sea views) are perched on a dramatic cliff above the caves overlooking Pristine Cove. Some have romantic outdoor showers. The four-poster, queen-sized beds, the dressers, and the bedside tables are all made of local woods. The cottages sit in tropical gardens created by the sure hand of a landscaper who knows how to get the most out of the wild environment. The rooms along the water have no air-conditioning, but the open-air design lets you make the most of the cooling sea breezes and ceiling fans. If you have to have air-conditioning, opt for a studio in the gardens.

The best rooms are on the far end of the property, nearest the sea. The infinity pool built into the rocky cliff looks like it falls into the sea below. It's one of the most dramatic around. Plus, at night, the bar and excellent restaurant (see Chapter 26) attract a young, fun clientele — hip but without pretense.

West End Rd. (P.O. Box 24), Negril. ☎ *876-957-4373. Fax: 876-957-4373. Internet:* www.rockhouse.com. *16 rooms, 12 villas. Rack rates: $139 for studios and $215 for villas. AE, MC, V.*

Round Hill Hotel & Villas

$$$$–$$$$$ Montego Bay

If you like the pomp and circumstance of colonial Jamaica with British-style service, Round Hill, occupying a 98-acre peninsula next to the sea and 10 miles west of Montego Bay, is the classic retreat. During high season, villas are reserved months — even years — in advance. Guests are chauffeured around the perfectly clipped property in golf carts, because heaven forbid you should break a sweat. Round Hill is the sort of place where you never sweat — you perspire.

Comprised of 29 two- to four-bedroom villas (most with their own pools and all privately owned) and a 36-room, two-story hotel called Pineapple House, Round Hill draws an older, moneyed crowd that enjoys the white glove service. (You may opt for an all-inclusive plan here, but the staff steadily reminds you that tipping is not only allowed but expected. We found that annoying at times. Bring plenty of small bills.)

When you rent a villa, you get your own housekeeper, gardener, and breakfast cook whose mission each day is to serve up your eggs exactly the way you want. Although the grounds and beach are lovely, you never know what you'll get inside the villas. Ours was supposedly owned by an English Duchess, but the uninviting twin beds made us think of Lucy and Desi's days on 1950s TV. And the incredibly shabby furnishings hardly inspired romance. We couldn't help but think the poor duchess was either missing the good taste gene, or she'd inherited the place in the 1960s and then forgotten all about it. But we've been assured that the homeowner's association is aware of the problem and has since gently reminded its members that everything must be "fresh."

Later, when we danced under the stars on the terrace to the strains of the orchestra, we could understand how Round Hill enchanted Jackie and JFK, who spent part of their honeymoon here. Next, we reclined for a while on two chaise lounges by our pool. (Well, it was ours during our stay.) We took note of how the moon settled as if on cue above the main Georgian-style building, and how the lovely crescent beach below twinkled with tiki torches.

Manager Josef Forstmayr, who makes you feel welcome, has done a stellar job of quietly making changes that appeal to the new traveler without alienating the long-time clientele. His latest improvement is bringing a new spa called Bunty's Cottage (French products from Decleor, a pioneer in aromatherapy) to the mix.

Rt. A1, Hanover Parish, Montego Bay. ☎ *800-972-2159 or 876-956-7050. Fax: 876-956-7505. E-mail:* resround@cwjamaica.com. *Internet:* www.rounhilljamaica.com. *Rack rates: Villa suites with pool $700; Pineapple House $240, double. A variety of packages are available, including one that lets bride and groom stay free if 15 or more rooms are booked for friends and relatives. The Round Hill Rendezvous ($4,950 low season/$8,150 high season for seven nights) is especially romantic. Inquire about meal plans and all-inclusive rates. AE, DC, MC, V.*

Sandals Dunn's River Golf Resort and Spa

$$$$$ Ocho Rios

Set on 25 tropical acres fronting a North Coast beach near Ocho Rios, this couples-only resort is among the chain's best with professional yet welcoming service. The open-air, Italian palazzo-style lobby with marble columns and Oriental carpets scattered about is your first clue. Spacious guestrooms in the Mediterranean-style buildings come in seven categories and are generally pleasant and comfortable. Gourmet restaurants include Windies, Ristorante d'Amore, and Tappanyaki.

You'll also get the use of a full-service spa and daily complimentary golf clinics on the resort's championship 18-hole, par-71 course. This resort claims to have Jamaica's largest pool area; we forgot to bring our measuring tape, but it is gorgeous. For the price, you also get all watersports and a free trip to Dunn's River Falls. A free shuttle runs from the resort to Sandals Ocho Rios and the golf course. **Note:** All Sandals properties are open to heterosexual couples only.

Mammee Bay, along Rte. A3 (P.O. Box 51), Ocho Rios. ☎ 800-SANDALS in the U.S. and Canada, or 876-972-1610. Fax: 876-972-1611. E-mail: sdrinet@cwjamaica.com. *Internet:* www.sandals.com. *Rack rates start at $270 per person a night. Three-night minimum stay required. Rates are all-inclusive. AE, MC, V.*

Sandals Negril Beach Resort & Spa

$$$$$ Negril

We have a soft spot for this resort, which occupies some 13 acres of prime beachfront along sparkling Seven Mile Beach, a short drive east of Negril's center on the main highway leading in from Montego Bay. Echo's sister honeymooned here, and our neighbors (both originally from the Caribbean) love this resort so much that they meet here annually with a group of friends.

Typical clientele here are young honeymooners who have never been to the Caribbean and those who want an absolute no-hassle, reliable place. Be forewarned, though, that you may run into a few of the guests of rowdy Hedonism II next door, where nudity is the norm (along with wild and raunchy beach games).

Norman Manley Blvd. (Box 12), Negril. ☎ 888-SANDALS in the U.S. and Canada, or 876-957-5216. Fax: 876-957-5338. E-mail: sng@cwjamaica.com. *Internet:* www.sandals.com. *Rack rates start at $290 per person a night. Three-night minimum stay required. Rates are all-inclusive, including airport transfers. AE, MC, V.*

Sandals Royal Caribbean

$$$$$ Montego Bay

Okay, here's the crown jewel of the Sandals empire. Built around a Georgian-style great house on 17 acres near Montego Bay, this popular all-inclusive has all the bells and whistles. It is known for packing in folks determined to have a good time without ever having to leave the complex. Here you get continental breakfast in bed and afternoon tea.

You have a choice of four restaurants — including the Bali Hai, which is on Sandals Cay, a private offshore island — plus four bars, three pools, three tennis courts, a good health club, all watersports, organized activities, and entertainment. This resort is suited to couples who want guaranteed, hassle-free fun in the sun. Shopaholics also enjoy the heavy concentration of stores in Montego Bay.

Mahoe Bay, North Coast Hwy. (Box 167), Montego Bay. ☎ **888-SANDALS** *or 876-953-2231. Fax: 876-953-2788. E-mail:* sr.is@cwjamaica.com. *Internet:* www.sandals.com. *Rack rates: $260–$300 per person a night. Seven nights for a couple starts at $3,060. AE, MC, V.*

Strawberry Hill

$$$$–$$$$$ Irish Town, Blue Mountains

Our biggest surprise came in the form of this resort built on the site of an eighteenth-century coffee plantation in nineteenth-century Jamaican style. Set in gloriously restored botanical gardens, the 12 whitewashed, Georgian-style wooden cottages display carved fretwork, excellent Jamaican art, and plantation furnishings. Who needs a beach when you've got panoramic views at 3,100 feet in the Blue Mountains?

Owned by Chris Blackwell, founder of Island Records (which launched Bob Marley and U2), Strawberry Hill pampers you with an Aveda Concept Spa — the Caribbean's first — and one of the island's best restaurants showcasing New Jamaican cuisine. (See Chapter 26 for our review.) Its guest list reads like *People* magazine, from Kate Moss to Sting. Strawberry Hill has earned AAA's Four-Diamond Award.

Honeymooners flock to Birds Hill, a 1,500-square-foot house on the outpost of the property that has a private terrace perfect for breakfast and an outdoor Jacuzzi shrouded by lush tropical flowers. The living area features a large kitchen and living room. French doors lead to a spacious balcony that runs the cottage's entire length. The four-poster, canopied mahogany bed, hand-carved on the property, comes with a goose down comforter and heated mattress pad to ward of the mountain chill. (Honeymooners have asked to buy the beds so frequently that the resort now sells them.) Extras include CD players with a selection of CDs, coffee and tea makers, large writing desks, cordless telephones with answering machines, plush bathrobes, umbrellas, beach towels, hairdryers, refrigerators stocked with drinks, electronic safes, Aveda personal care products, and TV/VCRs.

Car transfers from Norman Manley International Airport to Strawberry Hill are $30 one way for two passengers. Helicopter transfers from the airport to Strawberry Hill are $600 one way for up to four passengers.

New Castle Rd., Irish Town, St. Andrew. ☎ **800-OUTPOST** *or 876-944-8400. Fax: 876-944-8401. E-mail:* reservations@islandoutpost.com. *Internet:* www.islandoutpost.com. *Rack rates: $280–$595 for 12 Georgian-style cottages ranging from studios to three-bedroom suites.*

ROMANCE

Swept Away

$$$$ Negril

This gorgeous, couples-only, all-inclusive resort has built an excellent reputation as a tranquil, romantic place for those active types more interested is sipping fresh carrot juice than a piña colada. Bodies beautiful abound at Swept Away, which occupies a prime half-mile stretch of Negril's famed Seven Mile Beach.

The verandah suites, housed in 26 two-story villas each with private, plant-shrouded terraces, make you feel secluded even when the resort is completely booked (which is most of the time). Rooms are tastefully decorated in minimalist style with Mexican tile floors, white canvas sailcloth upholstery, and clay lamp sconces. The centerpiece to this gem lies across the road: ten acres of an adult playground with an excellent health club, a lap pool, and ten tennis courts. It's one of the Caribbean's most extensive sports complexes. Nonguests can get a day pass.

Norman Manley Blvd., Long Bay (P.O. Box 77), Negril. ☎ **800-545-7937** *in the U.S. and Canada, or 876-957-4061. Fax: 876-957-4060. Internet:* www.sweptaway.com. *Rates: $1,500–$1,875 per couple. Rates are for three nights and are all-inclusive, including airport transfers. AE, DC, MC, V.*

Chapter 25

Settling into Jamaica

· ·

In This Chapter

▶ Knowing what to expect when you arrive

▶ Getting around the island

▶ Discovering Jamaica from A to Z

· ·

*J*amaica is undeniably a ravishing beauty, boasting mountains that soar to 7,500 feet (higher than any in the eastern half of North America) and 160 rivers laced with cascading waterfalls, not to mention fabulous white and black sand beaches as well as tropical rain forests. If we squint our eyes, the flat southern coast reminds us of the African savanna. And if we ignore the palm trees, Jamaica's rolling green hills look like the south of England.

The Jamaican people stand out, too. Predominantly of African descent (about 95% of the 2.5 million population), many Jamaicans also claim Chinese, East Indian, Middle Eastern, or European ancestry and every combination thereof. We've found Jamaicans to be some of the warmest, funniest people in the Caribbean. They are fiercely proud and opinioned on normally taboo topics in other cultures, like politics and religion.

Obviously, Jamaica, which celebrates 40 years of independence from Great Britain in 2002, has captivated us. We even painted our office in colors meant to transport us to one of our favorite little Jamaican resorts, **Jake's** (see Chapter 24).

While we're comfortable with this island's promise of excitement and expression, many visitors find Jamaica a shock to their systems. Although it's wildly vibrant and beautiful, Jamaica can also be plain wild. Much of its population is extremely impoverished, and things that we take for granted are sometimes not available in Jamaica.

 Schedules certainly aren't sacred here. Most workers travel on foot an hour or more just to get to work, and much of the country still operates on a paper ledger system rather than by computer. These are a couple of reasons why "island time" is a bit different from the pace we're used to. Jamaicans joke about the pace; when someone tells you, "Soon come," that can mean anything from "I'll be there in five minutes" to "forget it."

Bring your appetite for adventure and be prepared to dive into a whole different world. If you can get into the groove, you're likely to have a wonderful time.

Arriving in Montego Bay or Kingston

When you come to Jamaica, you'll most likely fly into **Donald Sangster International Airport** (☎ 876-952-3124), about two miles east of Montego Bay. It's the most efficient point of entry for those heading to Ocho Rios, Runaway Bay, Negril or, of course, Mo Bay, where virtually all the major resorts are located. **Norman Manley International Airport** (☎ 876-924-8235) in Kingston is best for visitors headed to Strawberry Hill in Irish Town in the Blue Mountains or the small resorts in Port Antonio.

Landing in Mo Bay

The Mo Bay airport is the product of upgrades over the last several years, but you still deplane on the tarmac and walk in the heat to the terminal. Once inside, you walk down a wide, overly air-conditioned hallway and join the throngs waiting to go through Customs and Immigration. The lines move efficiently, except during the summer when hordes of Jamaican nationals come home for vacation.

Your warm welcome at this airport will include a serenade of island favorites, courtesy of a small group of entertainers in Jamaican dress. You'll also see a Jamaica Tourist Board counter where you can grab some material about the island to peruse while you wait your turn in line. (You'll also find coupons for attractions, rental cars, and more inside the free magazines.) The longest we've ever had to wait was about 20 minutes.

Immediately after you go through Customs and Immigration, you'll see a currency exchange office, where you can get Jamaican dollars. If you're carrying U.S. currency, we suggest holding onto it; U.S. money is widely accepted and even preferred by many. But if you want or need to get local currency, you can expect a slightly better rate of exchange here than at your hotel or the banks. Exchanging money at banks — whether it be dollar-for-dollar or as a credit card transaction — is often a lengthy ordeal, so it's best to deal with the issue immediately. You can find ATM machines at the airport, but they are almost always out of order or out of cash, so don't count on them.

If you checked luggage, you'll wait for it. We find that collecting luggage adds at least an additional 15 minutes or so and sometimes as much as 45 minutes. Once you get your luggage, keep a close eye on it, because theft can be a problem.

Flying into Kingston

 Security is extremely tight at the Kingston airport. We advise tourists to avoid flying into or out of that airport if possible. Our last trip, we were both pulled aside by security after passing through three checks. We were patted down bodily, which was not a fun way to end a trip.

The airport lies about 11 miles southeast of the capital city. When you exit customs in Kingston, you'll see a taxi information booth on the left and beyond that a counter for **Island Car Rentals,** the most reputable local rental agency, and the **JUTA** (Jamaica Union of Travelers Association) taxi office. Again, keep an eye on your luggage at all times.

Traveling from the Airport to Your Accommodations

After you get your luggage in Mo Bay, you'll walk through doors leading to an open area where you'll make your way to ground transportation. The larger hotels and resorts usually include the lift as part of your package. If you're supposed to have a ride arranged, look for a driver holding a sign with your name or your resort's name, or go to the kiosk for your particular resort.

The all-inclusives, like Sandals, have their own large buses and vans. SuperClubs arrivals are contracted out, so you may be on a bus or a van. The attendant for the properties will have a list of all the arrivals due in at the same time as you, and you won't roll until everyone has been accounted for. Baggage handlers will hoist your luggage onto the bus or into the van. Tip them $1 per bag and watch to be sure that all your property makes it on. This process for all passengers can take another 20 to 30 minutes.

 If you need to arrange your own transport or pick up a rental car, deal only with official representatives. Do not accept help with your luggage from anyone whom you cannot identify as an airport baggage handler, and do not accept a ride from someone who approaches you.

By taxi

If your hotel isn't handling your transportation, we strongly urge you to get into only special taxis and buses operated by **JUTA,** the Jamaica Union of Travelers Association (☎ **876-952-0813;** fax 876-952-5355). All such vehicles will have the union's emblem on the side. Their prices are controlled, and any local JUTA office will supply a list of rates. These vehicles are clean, air-conditioned, and up to the standards you expect in the U.S. or Europe.

Only taxis with red license plates, issued by the Jamaica Tourist Board, with the initials PPV (public passenger vehicle) are properly insured and licensed to carry fee-paying passengers. To secure a lift, go to the airport taxi dispatcher, who will have a clipboard and be located near a dispatch booth. Tell the dispatcher your destination, and he or she will tell you the fare and arrange your ride.

Do not wander beyond the ground transportation dispatch area. Kevin once went in search of bottled water after a particularly long flight. Immediately outside the main terminal area, he became aware that some characters lurking nearby were sizing him up. He was also approached by drug dealers as soon as he entered the men's bathroom while we were waiting for our group to gather for the ride in the resort's van.

By air

If you want to skip the notoriously wild drive to the resorts outside of Montego Bay, you could catch a flight on **Air Jamaica Express.** Reservations are handled by **Air Jamaica** (☎ **800-523-5585,** Internet www.airjamaica.com; 876-952-4300 in Mo Bay; 876-922-4661 in Kingston; 876-957-4210 in Negril; and 876-974-2566 in Ocho Rios). We suggest you reserve before you leave home through a travel agent or through Air Jamaica to secure a seat, because the planes are small. Be sure to reconfirm your departing flight a full 72 hours in advance.

Air Jamaica Express offers more than 50 scheduled flights daily, covering all the major resort areas: Montego Bay, Kingston, Negril, Ocho Rios, and Port Antonio. The flights themselves are brief (about 20–30 minutes in the air) and provide a gorgeous view of the dramatic coastline. The fare from Montego Bay to Negril is $116 round-trip, $58 one-way. The airport is small, so you won't have trouble locating the departure gate.

Charter service between Mo Bay, Ocho Rios, Port Antonio, and Negril is also available via **Jamaica AirLink** (☎ **877-359-5465** in the U.S. or 876-940-7747). You let the airline know when you are coming in, and a representative will meet you, help you with your luggage, and guide you to your plane. At the time this book went to press, four people (in one party or collected as a party by the dispatcher) could ride from Mo Bay to Negril for $60 per person or $85 per person from Mo Bay to Ocho Rios.

By bus

You can take a bus to Negril or Ocho Rios. The fare is $20 a person for the two-hour trip to Negril's Seven Mile Beach area; $25 for the hotels along the West End's cliffs. We recommend **Tour Wise** (☎ **876-979-1027**), which has a desk in the transportation hall at the Montego Bay airport just outside the passenger arrival hall, or **Caribic Vacations** (☎ **876-953-9874**) in Montego Bay. The bus will drop you off at your final destination.

Negril is a mere 60 miles from the Montego Bay airport. We always heard that Negril was a wild spot for free spirits. The spot got crazy for us early in our trip. Our bus ride from Montego Bay was a white-knuckle adventure, as we whizzed along the scenic coast, passing slower traffic on curves and up hills. Apparently, our driver embraced the notion that if you're the biggest on the road, you automatically have the right of way. Thanks to continual road "improvements," you can count on at least a two-hour trip — especially if the cows decide to come out into traffic for a rousing game of chicken with the buses and cars.

Traveling the roadways in Jamaica can be a religious experience. For half the trip to Negril, the woman in front of us was looking out the window, clawing her husband's arm and muttering repeatedly, "Oh, my God, oh, my God, Tom. Tom, we're passing again." At the halfway point, we stopped for a bathroom break. Tom got back on the bus and handed his wife two Red Stripe beers. "Here," he said. "Drink these and stop looking out the window."

By car

Another way to get to your resort is to rent a car for the two-hour drive to either Ocho Rios (about 75 miles) or Negril (about 65 miles), but we don't recommend it, especially if you're a first-timer on Jamaica. Here are some of the reasons why:

- Bad roads
- Bad drivers
- Bad characters
- Bad directions
- Bad vibes

Although Jamaica has dozens of car rental companies (several with airport branches), rentals can be difficult to arrange once you've arrived. Make reservations and send a deposit before your trip, and get a confirmation number or receipt to present to the person at the counter.

Even then, you may still find that no cars are available. And getting pugnacious doesn't help with Jamaican service people. One gentleman began screaming when he was told there was no car available for him. The woman at the counter left him cooling his heels while she chatted on the phone for several minutes. After she hung up, he asked, "What did your boss say?" "My boss?" she said. "Dat weren't my boss." She shrugged and called the next person in line, leaving the unhappy customer gaping at her.

Getting Around Jamaica

Driving on Jamaica can be an adventure — and not always a good one. Luckily, you have many other options when it comes to transportation to island hot spots.

By taxi

Jamaica's taxis have no meters, so agree on a price before you get in. JUTA is the largest taxi franchise and has offices in all resort areas. (For more information, see the "Traveling from the Airport to Your Accommodations" section earlier in this chapter.)

JUTA rates are per vehicle, not per passenger, and 25% is added to the rate between midnight and 5 a.m.

 If you do get in a cab that isn't approved by JUTA, drivers — called "robots" by locals — will often stop to pick up other passengers, and soon you'll find yourself sharing a ride with three or four strangers. We've also found that such vans rarely have seatbelts or air-conditioning.

JUTA drivers handle nearly all ground transportation, and some offer sightseeing tours. (Prices for a one-day tour run about $50 to $100 plus tip.) Your hotel concierge can arrange a taxi. If you're going to a restaurant, always call ahead and ask if the restaurant provides complimentary transport. If you do get a taxi, your driver will often ask if you want him or her to come back and pick you up. We've found those arrangements work well. The drivers are happy to have the guaranteed business, and we know we're assured to be in the care and vehicle of someone we already know.

In a pinch, you can flag down a taxi on the street, but you're better off having the restaurant or resort that you're visiting call a cab for you in advance. A typical one-way fare from Montego Bay to Ocho Rios is $50 to $60. Drivers will negotiate sometimes, especially if you agree to let them come back and pick you up for the return trip.

 If a quote sounds really outrageous to you, make other arrangements. We discovered that the concierges and tour desk personnel at some of the all-inclusives apparently have worked out deals with certain drivers. You'll be quoted an inflated rate, and the person who steered the business to the driver will get a kickback.

On foot

If you want to explore the resort towns on foot, you'll be fine if you stick to the main drags where you find shopping and restaurants. Use common street sense, and you can walk around the following places without a problem:

 ✓ Mo Bay's hip strip, where you'll find lots of restaurants, clubs, shopping, and beaches.

✔ Ochi's shopping district, near where the cruise ships unload their passengers.

✔ Negril's Seven Mile Beach or West End.

These areas are well-populated by tourists. Just don't stop to talk to strangers or pull out money to buy anything on the street. Jamaica reminds us of New York City. You're fine on most streets, as long as you project confidence and keep moving. But take a wrong turn, and you can quickly get into trouble.

If you do venture to Kingston, we would not recommend walking the streets. The U.S. State Department has a traveler's advisory issued for that city.

Wherever you are, be aware of your surroundings at all times and don't walk around alone — especially if you're a woman. Jamaican men apparently have heard about the book and movie *How Stella Got Her Groove Back* (the story of an author who falls in love with a young Jamaican man while she's on vacation). You'll get lots of offers if you're walking unaccompanied. Just say no, firmly but politely, and stride on.

By bus

You may be tempted to ride the local buses, because they're cheap (a few dollars for most places) and offer frequent service between Kingston, Mo Bay, and other major destinations. However, resist the temptation. Local buses are so slow, stiflingly hot, and rife with pickpockets that even the locals aren't using them much anymore. Tourists rarely attempt to use this form of transportation — with good reason. Schedule information (although the buses rarely follow one) and route information are available at bus stops (usually near the main markets) or from the bus driver.

By car

Jamaica beckons, with its considerable charms, but for the reasons we already mentioned, we don't recommend renting a car to explore it. Accidents and petty theft make damage to the rental car highly probable, and even if you're used to the British style of driving on the left, you still practically need the driving skills of James Bond to stay out of trouble. Avis pulled its offices out of Jamaica entirely in 1998.

If you still want to rent wheels after all our Heads Ups, here's the scoop. You must be at least 21 years old to rent a car (at least 25 years old at most agencies) and have a valid driver's license (from any country) and credit card. You may be required to post a security deposit of several hundred dollars on your credit card before taking possession of your car; ask about a required security when you make the reservation. Your security, of course, will be refunded when you turn in the car in good order.

Toyota Corollas and Suzuki Sidekicks are the most popular rentals. Rates average $50 to $120 a day, but on top of that several agencies also insist that you carry their pricey insurance (as much as $50 a day), even if your home auto insurance covers rentals. You'll also get socked with a 15% government tax on your car rental. If you need a baby seat or anything special, be sure to ask when you reserve.

Check your insurance policy carefully, because international car rentals are sometimes excluded. Also make sure that the rental agent goes over the exterior and inside of your car — with you in attendance — before you hit the road. Any previous damage should be noted to relieve you of responsibility for scratches, dents, or upholstery tears when you return

A few tour operators offer good fly-drive packages that include rental cars. If you are determined to have your own wheels, consider that route to conserve funds.

Again, hiring a guide at a daily rate for sightseeing works out much cheaper. Plus, you'll be with someone who knows where the enormous potholes are; where school children tend to congregate right by the road; where persnickety farm animals tend to be on the loose, grazing with their hindquarters occupying half the lane; and where construction goes on for miles and years with no end in sight.

Because disputes often break out about whether you've actually reserved a car during seasons when they get snapped up quickly, we strongly recommend booking through a familiar company before you leave your home country and insisting on a confirmation number. Several agencies offer free delivery and pickup of your vehicle to your hotel or villa.

Budget International (☎ **800-472-3325** or 876-952-3838 at the Montego Bay Airport, or 876-924-8762 in Kingston) is a good choice; with Budget, a daily collision-damage waiver costs another $15 and is mandatory.

Other U.S.-based operators on Jamaica include:

- **Dollar International** (☎ **800-800-4000** in the U.S.).
- **Hertz International,** which operates branches at both airports. (☎ **800-654-3001** in the U.S.; reservations ☎ 876-952-4250; fax 876-952-8064; Mo Bay's Donald Sangster airport 876-979-0438; or Kingston's Norman Manley airport 876-924-8028).
- **Thrifty Car Rental** (opposite the Mo Bay airport at ☎ **876-952-5825** or 876-952-5826; fax 876-952-2679).
- **Kernwel International** (☎ **800-678-0678**).

Local car rental companies include:

- **Island Car Rentals** (☎ **876-952-5771** in Montego Bay; 876-926-5991 in Kingston).

✔ **Jamaica Car Rental** (☎ **876-952-5586** in Montego Bay; 876-974-2505 in Ocho Rios).

✔ **Prospective Car Rentals** (☎ **876-952-0112** in Mo Bay; 876-957-3584 in Negril; and 876-974-8050 in Ocho Rios).

✔ **United Car Rentals** (☎ **876-952-3077** in Montego Bay).

✔ **Vernon's Car & Jeep Rental** (☎ **876-957-4354** in Negril or fax 876-957-4057), which has convertible Jeeps.

Depending on road conditions, driving time for the 50 miles from Montego Bay to Negril is 1¼ hours. The work on the much-ballyhooed new highway has once again screeched to a halt, and the road now isn't expected to be complete until late in 2001. "Soon come," as they say. From Montego Bay to Ocho Rios, expect a minimum drive of 1¼ hours; from Ocho Rios to Port Antonio, 2 hours; and from Ocho Rios to Kingston, 2 hours. Be especially cautious at night. Speed limits in town are 30 mph, and they are 50 mph outside towns. Speed traps are common. Our driver got stopped twice one evening trying to get us to a restaurant outside of Ocho Rios.

Gas stations are open daily, but few accept credit cards. Most require Jamaican dollars. Gas costs roughly $2.50 a gallon and is measured in the Imperial gallon (a British unit of measure that is 25% larger than a U.S. gallon).

By bicycle, moped, and motorcycle

Most hotels' concierge or tour desks can arrange the rental of bicycles, mopeds, and motorcycles. Daily rates run from about $45 for a moped to $70 (helmets and locks included) for a Honda 550. Deposits of $100 to $300 or more are required. However, we highly recommend that you *don't* rent a moped or motorcycle, because of Jamaica's status as the country with the third highest accident rate in the world combined with the hassle-factor of fending off aggressive vendors and drug dealers at traffic lights.

If you ignore our advice, at least check on your medical insurance before you leave and have proper identification handy in case you land at a healthcare facility (see Chapter 7).

Mountain biking has become particularly popular around Negril, Port Antonio, and the rural Treasure Beach area where traffic and other hazards aren't as pronounced. You'll need your valid driver's license to rent anything motorized.

Following are some rental operators, all licensed by the Jamaica Tourist Board:

✔ **Montego Honda-Bike Rentals** (21 Gloucester Avenue; ☎ **876-952-4984**) rents Honda scooters for $30 to $35 a day (24 hours) plus a $300 deposit. Bikes cost $35 a day, plus a $200 deposit. Deposits are refundable if the vehicles are returned in good shape.

✔ **Kryss Bike Rental Ltd.** (39 Gloucester Avenue, Mo Bay; ☎ 876-940-0476) specializes in Hondas, Suzukis, and Yamahas from 200–600cc and offers free pickup and delivery.

✔ **Tykes Bike Rental & Tours** (West End Road near Rick's Café and at the Visitors Information office in Negril; ☎ 876-957-0388) offers free pickup and drop-off service.

Quick Concierge

ATMs

Few ATM machines in Jamaica accept U.S. bank cards, although cash advances can be made using credit cards. Currency from the machines, of course, is Jamaican dollars.

Baby-sitters

Most charge about $7 an hour for one child. Sitters are easily arranged, and we've found that the caregivers on Jamaica are among the best in the Caribbean. If you stay out late, though, please tip extra and ask how the sitter plans to get home.

Banks

You can find branches of the **Bank of Nova Scotia** at the following addresses throughout the island: Sam Sharpe Square, Montego Bay (☎ 876-952-4440); Main St., Ocho Rios (☎ 876-974-2081); Negril Square, Negril (☎ 876-957-3040); 35 King St., Kingston (☎ 876-922-1420).

Banks islandwide are open Monday to Thursday from 9 a.m. to 2 p.m. and Friday from 9 a.m. to 4 p.m. A few are open on Saturday morning. Be aware, however, that the banks don't have computers, and you're likely to encounter at least a half-hour wait in line. Many hotels and resorts offer currency exchange.

Credit Cards

Major credit cards are widely accepted. MasterCard and VISA are the most popular, followed by American Express. Some places also accept Discover and Diners Club.

Currency Exchange

The unit of currency on Jamaica is the Jamaican dollar, represented by the same symbol as the U.S. dollar ($). Both U.S. and Jamaican currencies are widely accepted. Always clarify which currency is being quoted. There is no fixed rate of exchange for the Jamaican dollar. At press time, the exchange rate was about $41 Jamaican to $1 U.S.

Jamaican currency is issued in banknotes of J$10, J$20, J$50, J$100, and J$500. Coins are available in denominations of 5¢, 10¢, 25¢, 50¢, J$1, and J$5. We recommend carrying small change in Jamaican or U.S. dollars for tips, beach fees, and other incidentals.

Bank of Jamaica exchange bureaus are located at both international airports (Montego Bay and Kingston), at cruise ship terminals, and in most hotels. Immigration cards, needed for bank transactions and currency exchange, are given to visitors at the airport arrivals desks. It is illegal to exchange currency outside of the banking system.

Customs

We cannot emphasize strongly enough that you'd have to be crazy to use or try to transport illegal drugs in Jamaica. On almost every trip we see at least a few people pulled aside by customs officials. Drug-sniffing police dogs are stationed at the airport, and on one recent trip we went through *two* checkpoints where the Jamaican officials were hand-checking carry-ons.

Doctors

Hotels have doctors on call. If you need any particular medicine or treatment, bring evidence, such as a letter from your own physician.

Electricity

Most places have the standard 110 volts AC (60 cycles), same as the United States. However, a few establishments operate on 220 volts AC (50 cycles). If your hotel is on a different current from your U.S.-made appliance, ask for a transformer and adapter.

Emergencies

To report a fire or call an ambulance, dial ☎ **110.** For the police and air rescue, dial ☎ **119.**

Festivals

The biggest festival is **Carnival,** an event filled with music and dancing in the streets. It's held in Kingston, Ocho Rios, and Mo Bay every April and in Negril every May. The first week of August, music lovers stream to the island for **Reggae Sumfest.** Anglers come to Port Antonio to compete in the annual **Blue Marlin Tournament,** usually held in October.

Hospitals

For dire situations, seek help in Puerto Rico or Miami. **St. Ann's Bay Hospital,** St. Ann's Bay (☎ 876-972-0150) has a hyperbaric chamber for scuba diving emergencies. In Kingston, the **University Hospital** is at Mona (☎ 876-927-1620); in Montego Bay, the **Cornwall Regional Hospital** is at Mount Salem (☎ 876-952-5100 or 876-952-6683); and in Port Antonio, the **Port Antonio General Hospital** is at Naylor's Hill (☎ 876-993-2646). Negril only has minor-emergency clinics.

Homework

Read one of the late Ian Fleming's 14 James Bond novels written at his Jamaican second home, Goldeneye.

Information

You'll find the **Jamaica Tourist Board** offices at the international airports and at 2 St. Lucia Ave., Kingston (☎ 876-929-9200); Cornwall Beach, St. James, Montego Bay (☎ 876-952-4425); Shop no. 29, Coral Seas Plaza, Negril, Westmoreland (☎ 876-957-4243); in the Ocean Village Shopping Centre, Ocho Rios, St. Ann (☎ 876-974-2582); in City Centre Plaza, Port Antonio (☎ 876-993-3051); and in Hendriks Building, 2 High St., Black River (☎ 876-965-2074).

Before you visit, you can contact the Jamaica Tourist Board at 801 Second Avenue, 20th Floor, New York, NY 10017 (☎ 800-233-4582 or 212-856-9727; fax 212-856-9655).

Language

The official language of Jamaica is English. However, among themselves islanders usually speak *patois,* a distinctive and lyrical blend of English, Spanish, and myriad African languages. An example of patois is *me diyah* (I'm here; pronounced *mee de-ya*). If someone asks how your vacation is going, just say "irie" (pronounced *eye-ree*), which means "great."

Nudity

Nude bathing is allowed at a number of hotels, clubs, and beaches (especially in Negril), but only where signs indicate that swimsuits are optional. Elsewhere, English sensibilities prevail, and the law does not even allow topless sunbathing.

Maps

Good maps are widely available at the airport, tourist information offices, and resorts.

Newspapers and Magazines

Resort gift shops carry a decent selection, including *USA Today,* and many resorts offer *The New York Times* via fax at no charge. However, serious news junkies will find the cover price on foreign magazines and newspapers extremely inflated.

Pharmacies

In Montego Bay, **Rosehall Village Pharmacy**, Shop 22, Half Moon Bay (☎ 876-953-2399; fax 876-953-2287; open 9 a.m. to 7p.m.); in Ocho Rios, **Great House Pharmacy**, Brown's Plaza (☎ 876-974-2352); and in Kingston, **Moodie's Pharmacy**, in the New Kingston Shopping Centre (☎ 876-926-4174). Prescriptions are accepted by local pharmacies only if they're issued by a Jamaican doctor.

Police

For the police and air rescue, dial ☎ **119.** In Negril, dial ☎ 876-957-4268.

Post Office

Jamaica issues gorgeous stamps. The **Montego Bay** post office (☎ 876-952-7389) is at 122 Barnett Street and is open weekdays 8 a.m. to 5 p.m. As you leave Negril Square, the post office is on the Lighthouse Road.

Safety

Most hotels, resorts, and even some villas have private security guards, so you probably won't run into any problems. However, beaches are public, so if you go for a stroll, you can expect to be approached by people selling everything from wood carvings and shells to drugs and sex to tours of the "real Jamaica." Safeguard your valuables and never leave them unattended on a beach. Likewise, never leave luggage or other valuables in a car or in the trunk. The U.S. State Department has issued a travel advisory about crime rates in Kingston, so don't go walking around alone at night. Caution is also advisable in many north coast tourist areas, especially remote houses and isolated villas that can't afford security.

Drugs (including marijuana) are illegal, and imprisonment is the penalty for possession. Also, you may well be buying *ganja* from a police informant, many of whom target tourists so that they aren't turning on their hometown buddies. Don't smoke pot openly in public, no matter who you see doing it. You may be the one who gets caught. Above all, don't even consider bringing marijuana back into the United States. Drug-sniffing dogs are stationed at the Jamaican airports, and they will check your luggage. U.S. Customs agents pay keen attention to all those arriving from Jamaica, and they easily catch and arrest those who try to take that sort of souvenir home.

Shopping Hours

Hours vary widely, but as a general rule most establishments are open Monday to Friday from 8:30 a.m. to 4:30 or 5 p.m. Some shops are open on Saturday until noon.

Taxes

Jamaica now charges a general consumption tax of 15% on all goods and services, which includes car rentals and telephone calls. Additionally, the government imposes a 6.25% tax on hotel rooms. You'll also encounter a J$1,000 ($27 U.S.) departure tax at the airport, payable in either Jamaican dollars or in its equivalent in U.S. dollars. Do not count on getting the cash at the airport, because few ATMs accept U.S. bank cards, and the machines are often out of money or service.

Telephone

To call direct from the United States, dial the area code 876, then the local number. Likewise to call the U.S., you simply dial the area code and number. But the best idea is to call collect. Otherwise, you'll pay about $3 a minute plus hefty surcharges, including the 15% general consumption tax. To make on-island calls, simply dial the six-digit phone number. Coin-operated phones are rare. If you need to make many calls outside of your hotel, purchase a World-Talk card at the post office or other outlets advertising it. Local and international calls made with these cards are cheaper than operator-assisted calls.

Time Zone

Jamaica is on Eastern Standard Time year-round; it does not observe daylight saving time. So, when the United States is on daylight saving time, it's 6 a.m. in Miami when it's 5 a.m. in Mo Bay.

Tipping

Tipping is customary. Generally, hotels and restaurants expect 10% or 15%, and the same goes for tour guides and drivers. Some places add a service charge to the bill. Tipping is not allowed in the all-inclusive hotels. But on our last day, we discreetly tip those staff members who went out of their way to make our stay pleasant.

Water

Water is safe to drink island-wide, because it's filtered and chlorinated. But, as always, you're more prudent to drink bottled water if it's available. Negril has had problems with water shortages.

Weather and Surf Reports

The local newspaper is the most reliable source.

Chapter 26

Dining in Jamaica

● ●

In This Chapter

▶ Sampling the local cuisine

▶ Locating the island's best restaurants

● ●

*T*he character of Jamaica is reflected in its fiery cuisine. Some people just can't take it, and others fall passionately in love with the place and its palate-tantalizing specialties. We're in the second category. We love the island's spicy and exotic foods, capable of sending shock waves of heat rolling over our taste buds.

In particular, we crave the excitement of sampling new tastes in Jamaica, as well as the opportunity to pick up two of our favorite items while we're on the island: Pickapeppa Sauce and famed Blue Mountain coffee. The first is a spicy brown pepper sauce that locals often carry around with them to liven up their food. We've adopted that habit. As for the coffee, we agree with that worldly James Bond character, who declared that the coffee grown in the fertile soil of the gorgeous Blue Mountains must be the world's finest.

Exploring the Local Flavor

Jamaica's most famous contribution to the food world is its jerk pork — the island's version of barbecue. This way of cooking has a long and tangled history, involving everybody from Peruvian Indians to escaped African slaves called "Maroons." A paste of Scotch bonnet peppers, rum, pimento berries (also known as allspice), garlic, and other herbs covers the pork. (Purists cook a whole pig.) The meat then cooks slowly over a coal fire.

 The best jerk comes from tiny stalls on **Boston Beach** near Port Antonio, where vendors line up next to their barbecue pits, which issue smoke and marvelous smells for the pleasure of passersby. They'll hand you your order straight from the grill, wrapped in a little foil with a piece of *bammy* (the Jamaican bread similar in texture to cornbread and made from the cassava root). You'll see jerk pork, chicken, and fish on menus from the tiniest shack to white-table affairs serving nouvelle Jamaican cuisine.

Rastafarian cooking has spawned its own cuisine, called *I-tal,* which accents natural ingredients. Rastafarianism is a religion practiced on Jamaica and popularized by the late Bob Marley. Rastas don't drink alcohol, eat meat, or use salt, but their vegetarian dishes are fantastic. A good place to try this cuisine is the **Hungry Lion** in Negril.

Another popular dish that's cheap and tasty is traditional rice and peas, also known as "coat of arms," which is similar to the *moros y christianos* of Spanish-speaking islands: white rice cooked with red kidney beans, coconut milk, scallions, and seasonings. This dish is often paired with curried goat, which was introduced by indentured laborers from India.

The island's most famous soup — the fiery pepper pot originated by the Taino Indians — is a peppery (of course) mixture of salt pork, salt beef, okra, and the island green known as *callaloo*, which reminds us of a cross between spinach and turnip greens. Jamaican patties (sweetly spicy meat pies) are another point of pride, and you can find them at any small bakery.

Dressing for dinner in Jamaica is usually casual chic (or just casual at many local hangouts). A few exceptions exist at the top resorts, some of which require semiformal wear in the evening during high season. Jamaica Inn and Round Hill are two examples.

The venerable Jamaica Inn, playground to luminaries like Noël Coward and Elizabeth Taylor back in the 1950s and 1960s, only bowed to the move toward casual dress for the millenium. The resort actually sent out notices to the press, alerting them to the policy change that jackets would be required only after 7 p.m. for gentleman during high season and that they could lose their ties entirely.

At most of the nicer resorts, you'll usually see men in collared shirts with nice slacks during the evening and women in pretty sundresses. (Bring a shawl or sweater, though, because restaurants that have air-conditioning usually set the controls for overkill.)

Jamaica's Best Restaurants

On Jamaica, most guests simply take an all-inclusive plan and never venture out to a restaurant. The food has been vastly improved lately at many of the all-inclusives; most offerings are not quite gourmet, but we'd certainly put most of the food operations in the category of a strong three-star. Sometimes you catch a glimmer of a four-star on the horizon — with a bit of polish and innovation.

The availability of good food at the all-inclusives, combined with the perception that going outside the gates of a resort isn't necessarily a good idea, has effectively put a chill over the dining scene in Jamaica. We're sorry to see this happen, because some of our absolute best dining experiences in the Caribbean have been on Jamaica. But the truth is that many restaurants are hurting for business. Prices have gone up, which means tourists are even less likely to take in the local charm. It's a vicious cycle.

If you plan to stay at an all-inclusive, reserve at least one night off-property to experience something new. Also, make reservations a day or so in advance; because business has been off, restaurants' hours may be irregular, so calling ahead is a must. During high season, you should make reservations shortly after you arrive in order to secure your spot at any of the more popular restaurants.

Most restaurants outside the resorts in Mo Bay and Ocho Rios will provide complimentary transportation. Ask when you make your reservations. Otherwise, a taxi ride can get mighty expensive.

A good option in Negril is to go right where the West End meets with Seven Mile Beach. Vendors and fishermen often set up shop here. One afternoon, we got a couple of grilled lobsters, plus generous sides and two rum punches, for about $20 from one of the fishermen.

Sandals, which has six resorts on the island, has a dine-around program that gives you access to any of its 23 restaurants on Jamaica.

Almond Tree

$$$$ Ocho Rios   Jamaican/International

This small inn, with an almond tree growing through its roof, is tucked into a cliff overlooking the Caribbean. It features unique swinging chairs in its bar area, a popular meeting place for guests. The menu is expansive, but the last time we were there, the food quality had dropped off. However, like Rick's in Negril, this place is a traditional stop-off in Ocho Rios. The Rolling Stones's Keith Richards, who maintains a house in Ocho Rios, drops by sometimes. The pumpkin soup is silky and well spiced. You never know who might be tinkling the ivories at the inn's piano bar after dinner.

83 Main St., Ocho Rios. ☎ *876-974-2813. Reservations essential. Main courses: $12–$26. AE, DC, MC, V. Open daily from noon to 2:30 p.m. and 6 p.m. to 9:30 p.m.*

The Casanova

$$$$ Ocho Rios   International

The suave Casanova is one of the most elegant spots along the north coast, a super choice when you feel like dressing up. The dining room is surprisingly romantic in an Old World Rome kind of way. Meals are included for guests of Grand Lido Sans Souci (see Chapter 24), but nonguests who purchase a nonresident pass can also dine here and be entertained as well — with drinks included. Jazz or other strains from the local talent waft in from the terrace under the stars, where a young crowd gathers to dance in the late evenings. Salads, vegetarian dishes, and soups are made fresh daily. Typical dishes include smoked chicken breast in a continental berry sauce as an appetizer, or a small vegetable mousse with a fontina cheese sauce. For your main course, try roast Cornish hen with citrus and mild spice. Desserts are sumptuous. You can also sample one of the house's four special coffees.

In the Grand Lido Sans Souci. Along Rte. A3, 3 miles east of Ocho Rios. ☎ 876-994-1353. Reservations required. Nonresident evening pass of $95 per person includes dinner and drinks (including alcohol). Tuesday and Friday evenings there is a beach buffet, entertainment, and drinks. AE, DC, MC, V. Open daily from 6:30 p.m. to 9:30 p.m.

Cosmo's Seafood Restaurant and Bar

$$ Negril Seafood

Owner-character Cosmo Brown rules his roost on the East End beach, specializing in all manner of seafood. He's a wizard with conch (which can be chewy and tasteless in unskilled hands), whether stewed, curried, or in a soup. You can also order grilled Caribbean lobster when it's in season. Cosmo's place is a good spot to try Jamaica's version of grilled or baked *escovitch* (a Spanish-influenced fish dish, well-marinated in spices). Cosmo's is situated in an informal, thatched-roof hut on a sparsely populated East End beach. You have to pay a few dollars for the entrance fee to the beach.

Norman Manley Blvd., Negril. ☎ 876-957-4330. No reservations. Main courses: $7–$15. AE, MC, V. Open daily from 11 a.m. to 10 p.m.

Evita's

$$$ Ocho Rios Italian

Italian restaurateur Eva Myers has no trouble drawing in pasta lovers and others craving Italian food to this 1860s-era gingerbread house perched over Mallard's Bay. Myers, a lively blonde who loves chatting up her guests, infuses a sense of fun into her menu, which features more than 30 kinds of homemade pastas from lasagna rastafarian to Viagra pasta (a concoction that includes oysters). Myers grows her own herbs, which are generously blended into these excellent dishes.

Request the table for two on the edge of the balcony for one of our favorite restaurant views in the Caribbean. The scene is gorgeous at sunset, when the lights of Ocho Rios filter up from the city below. Until Toscannini came along (see our review later in this section), we didn't think Italian food in the Caribbean could get any better than this. Half orders of pasta are available, and kids under age 12 eat for half price.

Mantalent Inn, Eden Bower Rd, Ocho Rios. ☎ 876-974-2333. Reservations recommended. Main courses: lunch $8–$24; dinner $10–$24. AE, MC, V. Open daily from 11 a.m. to 11 p.m.

The Gap Café

$$ Blue Mountains Jamaican

A visit to The Gap Café, located on a former mule path to Newcastle and built in the late 1930s, is a journey to another Jamaica — one where a fireplace may be glowing all year round (understandable at this elevation of 4,200 feet). Gloria Palomino welcomes guests to sip fresh-brewed, aged Blue Mountain coffee — trust us, it's heavenly — and savor some of the best pastries on the island, served at lunch and at high tea on Sundays. Lunch is a simple affair: bammy, chicken breast stuffed with callaloo, or rasta pasta with vegetables. Native guavas are used in the cheesecake, and soursop and passion fruit are used in cakes and mousses.

The Café, a cozy, flower-filled charmer decked out in tones of maroon and blue, offers a few tables on a terrace, overlooking the misty, wild flower-dotted mountainside. Hummingbirds busily flit around, attracted by feeders and agapanthus lilies and other flowers that surround the small café. The gift shop on premises carries island coffee, food products, and a few crafts, but prices are usually higher than you could find elsewhere.

Hardwar Gap, Blue Mountains. ☎ 876-997-3032. Reservations recommended. Main courses: lunch $12–$15; dinner $17–$22. AE, MC, V. Open daily from 10 a.m. to 9 p.m.

Hungry Lion

$$ Negril   I-tal

The verdant, colorful setting at this 40-seat popular restaurant is accentuated by the bar, which was handpainted by the owner using bright flowers and tropical birds as inspiration. This restaurant was created because owners, who are also partners in The Caves resort in Negril (see Chapter 24) and who moved here more than two decades ago, wanted good food for their own eight children to eat. The couple adopted many of the rules of Rastafarianism in their cooking. I-tal cuisine uses all natural ingredients — no salt and no dairy. Only in the late 1990s did they break down and add chicken to the menu. The offerings change nightly, according to which fish and other ingredients are the freshest. Coconut milk is a recipe mainstay. If you dine outside by the fish pond, you'll be surrounded by a greenhouse of flowering plants. Inside, the dining room is a living canvas. Come here for a taste of Jamaican cuisine at its freshest in Negril's hippest restaurant.

West End Rd., Negril. ☎ 876-957-4486. Main courses: $8–$20. AE, MC, V. Open daily from 5 p.m. to 10:30 p.m.

Jamaica Inn

$$$$ Ocho Rios   Euro-Nouvelle Caribbean

Jamaican-born chef Wilbert Mathison prepares beautiful meals that match the romantic setting of the dining terrace at Jamaica Inn. Rave reviews aren't new to him, and he has even made the cover of *Gourmet* magazine. Start with his Jamaican jerk sushi, then move to the chilled potato and leek soup. For the main dish, go with the fillet of snapper satiated with spinach and mushrooms, wrapped in phyllo dough and baked. Afterward, choose from the ample desserts, or you can end with Jamaican coffee and a piece of homemade fudge. The flavors are not overpowering, and if you expect spicy heat, you're likely to leave disappointed. Nonetheless, we're captivated by this classic and beautiful restaurant. After dinner, couples dance under the starlight and the warm glow of lamplights, or they slip off to the loggia — an open gallery — where the sound of the waves competes with the quartet who softly plays reggae classics.

Jamaica's Restaurants

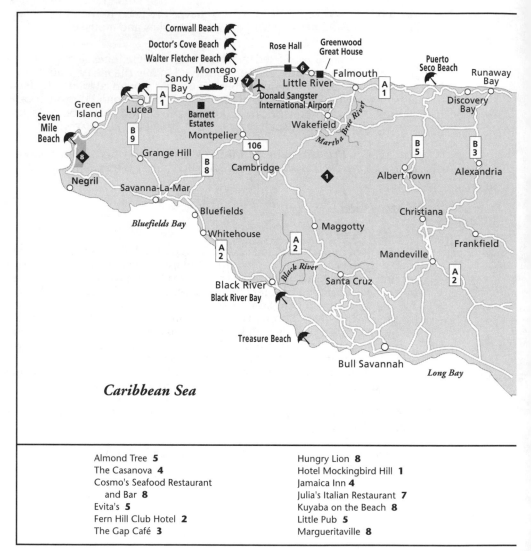

Almond Tree **5**
The Casanova **4**
Cosmo's Seafood Restaurant
   and Bar **8**
Evita's **5**
Fern Hill Club Hotel **2**
The Gap Café **3**

Hungry Lion **8**
Hotel Mockingbird Hill **1**
Jamaica Inn **4**
Julia's Italian Restaurant **7**
Kuyaba on the Beach **8**
Little Pub **5**
Margueritaville **8**

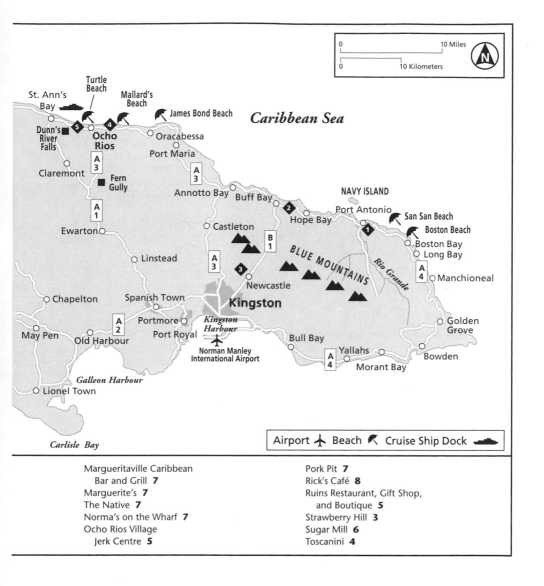

0   10 Miles

0   10 Kilometers

Turtle Beach
St. Ann's Bay
Mallard's Beach
James Bond Beach
Caribbean Sea
Dunn's River Falls
Ocho Rios
Oracabessa
Port Maria
Claremont
Fern Gully
Annotto Bay
Buff Bay
NAVY ISLAND
Port Antonio
San San Beach
Hope Bay
Boston Beach
Ewarton
Castleton
Boston Bay
Long Bay
Linstead
BLUE MOUNTAINS
Rio Grande
Manchioneal
Chapelton
Spanish Town
Newcastle
Kingston
Portmore
Kingston Harbour
Port Royal
Golden Grove
May Pen
Old Harbour
Norman Manley International Airport
Bull Bay
Yallahs
Bowden
Morant Bay
Galleon Harbour
Lionel Town

Carlisle Bay

Airport ✈ Beach 🅺 Cruise Ship Dock 🚢

Marguaritaville Caribbean Bar and Grill **7**
Marguerite's **7**
The Native **7**
Norma's on the Wharf **7**
Ocho Rios Village Jerk Centre **5**

Pork Pit **7**
Rick's Café **8**
Ruins Restaurant, Gift Shop, and Boutique **5**
Strawberry Hill **3**
Sugar Mill **6**
Toscanini **4**

North Coast Highway, just east of Ocho Rios. ☎ *876-974-2514. E-mail:* jaminn@cwjamaica.com. *Jacket and tie requested. Main courses: lunch $10–$15; dinner $40 (fixed price) per person. AE, MC, V. Open daily from noon to 2 p.m. and 7 p.m. to 9 p.m.*

Julia's Italian Restaurant

$$$$ Montego Bay Italian

Although Julia's take on Italian is no match for Toscannini or Evita's (see our reviews in this section), this Mo Bay restaurant with a stunning view from the hills high above the city has become popular with romantics. You can choose from an à la carte menu or order a five-course prix-fixe meal that includes homemade soups and pastas; entrées of fish, chicken, and veal; and good desserts. If you go to Julia's, you may not be bowled over by the food, but the view will make up for any shortfalls.

Bogue Hill. ☎ *876-952-1772. Reservations essential. Fixed-price dinner $33–$45 per person. AE, MC, V. Open daily from 5:30 p.m. to 10:30 p.m. Private van transportation provided upon request.*

Kuyaba on the Beach

$$ Negril Eclectic

For great service and good food, stop in at this thatch-roofed, brightly colored restaurant on the West End. The menu features a mix of kingfish steak, grilled lamb with sautéed mushrooms, and several pasta dishes. By day, you can snag a chaise lounge and hang out at the small beach. It's become especially popular with Europeans, who seem to have a knack for finding good value when it comes to dining. Go early on a busy night, because this place gets deservedly crowded.

Norman Manley Blvd., Negril. ☎ *876-957-4318. Main courses $10.95–$19.95. Burgers, sandwiches, and salads $5.75–$7.95. AE, MC, V. Open daily from 7 a.m. to 11 p.m.*

Little Pub

$$ Ocho Rios Jamaican/International/Italian

Something happens here every night, from Jamaican revues to cabaret to reggae bands. The place also has a bustling sports bar and an energetic Caribbean review several nights a week. Jamaican standards (jerk or curried chicken, baked crab, sautéed snapper) accompany surf and turf, lobster thermidor, pasta primavera, seafood stir-fry, crepe suzette, and bananas flambé. Burgers and other standard pub fare are also available. A fun, casual evening out.

59 Main St. Ocho Rios. ☎ *876-974-2324. Reservations recommended. Main courses: $13.50–$28.50. AE, MC, V. Open daily from 7 a.m. to 1 a.m.*

Margueritaville

$$$ Negril American/International

We were expecting a tacky operation, but this place on Seven Mile Beach adds a nice dimension to Negril. A sibling of the popular spot in Mo Bay with the same name, it's a sports bar, disco, beach club, and restaurant. You'll also find an art gallery, a gift shop, a five-star PADI dive shop, volleyball and basketball courts, and changing rooms so that you can slip out of your wet bathing suit.

Lobster is the house specialty, but we recommend the less expensive fish platters. As the name promises, the restaurant and bar offer more than 50 different kinds of margaritas. Go with a group on a night when a band is playing, and you're guaranteed fun.

Norman Manley Blvd., Negril. ☎ *876-957-4467. Main courses: $7.75–$25.95; burgers and sandwiches $5–$8. AE, MC, V. Open daily from 9 a.m. to 11 p.m.*

Margueritaville Caribbean Bar and Grill

$$$ Montego Bay Eclectic

This brightly painted bar-restaurant has quickly become the No. 1 nightspot in Mo Bay. It even has a slide that connects it with the water. The casual menu is centered on burgers, chicken sandwiches, tuna melts, pizza, and the like, but the food is beside the point.

Gloucester Ave., Montego Bay. ☎ *876-952-4777. Main courses: $8–$20. AE, MC, V. Open all day and into the night.*

Marguerites

$$$ Montego Bay Seafood

At this romantic pierside dining room located on the popular strip in MoBay, flambé is the operative word. Lobster, shrimp, fish, and several desserts are prepared in dancing flames as you sip an exotic cocktail. You can also order a classic caesar salad for preparation at your table.

Gloucester Ave, Montego Bay. ☎ *876-952-4777. Reservations essential. Main courses: $18–$25. AE, MC, V. Open from 6 p.m. to 10 p.m.*

Norma's on the Wharf

$$$$ Reading New Jamaican

Jamaica's finest restaurant, this historical dockside beauty is the creation of Norma Shirley, Jamaica's most famous chef, who launched Jamaican nouvelle cuisine. (She's often called the Caribbean's Julia Child, but she hates that comparison.) The tables on the wharf are peppered with influential Jamaicans and visiting celebrities at this 300-year-old warehouse. Shirley, who owned a restaurant in New York, utilizes the rich bounty of the region to spectacular effect; the menu, which changes daily, often includes red snapper in thyme and scotch bonnet caper sauce or grilled deviled crab backs.

The restaurant is located on the opposite side of the hip strip on the road to Negril. Shirley's newest venture, Norma's on the Terrace in Kingston, was recently named one of the "60 Best Restaurants in the World" by *Condé Nast Traveler.* We haven't had a chance to try it yet, but we're heading there soon.

10 minutes west of Mo Bay in Reading. ☎ *876-979-2745. Dinner reservations essential. MC, V. Main courses: $26–$34. Open Thursday through Sunday from noon to 2:30 p.m. and from 7:30 p.m. to 10:30 p.m.*

Ocho Rios Village Jerk Centre

$ Ocho Rios   Jamaican

This blue-canopied, open-air restaurant doles out frosty Red Stripe beer and Tings (a local lime-flavored soft drink) with fiery jerk pork, chicken, or seafood. We came here with our boys and whiled away an hour watching the Reggae Boyz (Jamaica's soccer team) on the telly while the locals cheered them on. You'll see locals hanging out, playing dominoes, and talking politics (a popular topic in Jamaica) here. At lunch when the cruise ships are in, you might have a long wait.

Da-Costa Drive. ☎ *876-974-2549. Jerk pork $3 for a quarter-pound, $11 per one-pound. Whole jerk chicken $14. MC, V. Open daily from 10 a.m. to 11 p.m.*

Pork Pit

$ Montego Bay   Jamaican

If we've had a long day of traveling, we head to this pitstop in Mo Bay, where we were first introduced to fiery jerk pork on the casual picnic benches open to the sea breezes. Common accompaniments include local cornbread (called *festival*), yams, rice and peas, and Red Stripe beer. Located five minutes from the airport, Pork Pit is a popular stop for hungry travelers headed to points beyond, like Negril.

Gloucester Avenue, a half-mile past the brewery and Walter Fletcher Beach, Montego Bay. ☎ *876-952-1046. Main courses: $3–$10. Open daily from 11a.m. to 11 p.m.*

Restaurant Mille Fleurs

$$$ Port Antonio   Nouvelle Tropical Caribbean

The Jamaican chef here boasts feature billing in *Gourmet* magazine. Many of the tasty vegetables and herbs used in the cuisine are grown on the grounds of this tiny hotel, which has garnered much praise for its eco-friendly ways. His starters were melt-in-your-mouth tastes, exploding with flavor. Each night you get a wide range of choices for your main course, and the restaurant always has plenty of vegetarian selections. Plus, all the jams, pastas, and breads are homemade. We especially liked the olive bread, and the herbed butters.

The bar area, decorated with wicker and floral accents, offers dramatic views of the Blue Mountains, as well as the Caribbean. The scent of night jasmine perfumes the air. This is a perfect setting for a nightcap or a great place to pop the question.

In Hotel Mocking Bird Hill, East of Port Antonio on North Coast Hwy., Port Antonio. ☎ *876-993-7267 or 876 993 7134. Fax 876-993-7133. E-mail:* mockbrd@cwjamaica. com. *Internet:* www.hotelmockingbirdhill.com. *Reservations a must. Main courses: $12–$31. AE, MC, V. Open daily from 7:30 a.m. to 10 p.m.*

Rick's Café

$$ Negril   Seafood/Steaks

This famous bar-restaurant-hangout is a place to be seen. The main draw is copped from the famed La Quebrada divers in Acapulco. Locals and visitors plunge some 25 feet into the deep teal Caribbean Sea from the coral cliffs. Just before sunset, crowds of the young, tanned, and buffed pack the palm-fronded terrace for the sunsets extraordinaire that have made this place famous. But unless you're chomping at the bit to waste money on overpriced, overcooked American fare, dine elsewhere.

West End Road, Negril. ☎ *876-957-4335. Reservations not accepted for parties of fewer than 6. Main courses: $11–$28. MC, V. Open daily from noon to 10 p.m.*

Ruins Restaurant, Gift Shop, and Boutique

$$$ Ocho Rios   Chinese/International/Jamaican

This establishment's lovely setting on the edge of Ocho Rios lures crowds of tourists. In 1831, a British entrepreneur constructed a sugar mill on the site, using the powerful stream to drive his water wheels. Today, all that remains is a jumble of ruins, hence the restaurant's name. After you cross a covered bridge, you'll feel a million miles from the hustle of Ocho Rios. The gardens and sounds of the water rushing from the cascades are soothing. A wooden deck serves as stage for a scattering of tables.

Our enchantment with this place quickly faded, however, when we were told that item after item on the menu was unavailable. We couldn't even get jerk chicken, and the staff was unapologetic. If you're hot and tired from shopping nearby, stop in for a drink, but don't stay for dinner.

Turtle River, DaCosta Drive. ☎ *876-974-2442. Reservations recommended. Main courses: $13–$37. AE, DC, MC, V. Open Monday through Saturday from noon to 2:30 p.m.; daily from 6 p.m. to 9:30 p.m.*

Strawberry Hill

$$$$ Blue Mountains   Jamaican

The spectacular setting alone would be enough to merit a trip up the mountain to this fabulous place, which draws a sophisticated crowd of Kingston's intellegensia and the music world. The bar area includes a crackling fire in the fireplace, unusual walls that took workmen weeks to finish, and clay masks by a Kingston artist. Book a table right at sunset and watch the twinkling lights of Kingston below. You can dine on the second-floor, wraparound verandah, where an English garden stands on one side and the city and the mountain slope appears on the other. Or on a chilly night, dine at a table in the greathouse, which has soaring ceilings with custom made, wrought iron chandeliers. Black-and-white photos of music greats decorate the walls, reminding you of owner Chris Blackwell's musical connections.

James Palmer, the native Jamaican chef, has become renowned for his new Jamaican cuisine. He uses native specialties to conjure up his own creations, such as Irish Town potato cakes with passion fruit sauce and mango relish, and grilled jumbo shrimp brushed with Jamaican rum and molasses on a bed of pineapple-papaya salsa. Crème caramel with a dash of Grand Marnier provides a perfect end to the meal. Sunday brunch has become a hot ticket. Service comes at a leisurely pace, but when you're sitting this close to heaven, relax and enjoy.

Irish Town. ☎ 876-944-8400. Main courses: lunch $18–$24; dinner $18–$27. DC, MC, V. Open from noon to 4 p.m. and from 6 p.m. to 10 p.m.

Sugar Mill

$$$–$$$$ Montego Bay   New Jamaican/European

Chef Alex Radakovitz of Austria dishes out New Jamaican and European cuisine in historic Rose Hall. Its romantic terrace, sheltered by large trees, overlooks the ocean and the golf course of the Half Moon Club, which is across the road. The emphasis here is on creative use of Jamaican ingredients with an international flair. Marlin, a specialty catch of the area, is often smoked and served with pasta. Even if you're just passing through, come for a look at an antique sugar wheel. Romantics should request a private table out by the waterfall.

7 miles (11 km) east of Mo Bay, Rose Hall. ☎ 876-953-2228. Dinner reservations essential. Main courses: $14–$39. AE, MC, V. Open from noon to 2:30 p.m. and from 7 p.m. to 10 p.m.

Toscanini

$$$$ Harmony Hall   Italian

Housed in a handsomely restored Methodist nineteenth-century mansion, Toscanini is expertly run by a young couple, Emanuele and Lella Giulivi, and her brother Pierluigi (P.G.), all from Parma, Italy. P.G.'s skills as a chef combined with his exuberant charm serve this place well. An excellent but pricey wine list (Emanuele is a *sommelier,* or wine steward) pushes this wonderful surprise to a level rarely attained in the Caribbean.

The marriage of traditional Italian cuisine and fresh tropical produce and spices is worth the expense of a cab to get here. Try the marinated marlin appetizer. The homemade pastas are scrumptious, as is the seafood. If Caribbean lobster is in season, have it shelled and tossed with basil vinaigrette. For dessert, try the traditional tiramisu, or indulge with a dark chocolate truffle with Appleton Special Jamaica Rum. Reserve a candlelit table for two on the small terrace, away from the bar. Or if you go for lunch, wander through the Art Gallery and Craft Shop, which features good works by Jamaican artists.

Harmony Hall (P.O. Box 192), four miles east of Ocho Rios on the Oracabessa main road. ☎ *876-975-4785. Internet:* www.harmonyhall.com. *Main courses: $18–$34. Open daily from noon to 2:30 p.m. and Tuesday through Sunday from 7 p.m. to 10:30 p.m.*

Chapter 27

Hitting the Beach and Other Fun Things to Do

. . . .

In This Chapter

▶ Soaking up the sun on Jamaica's top beaches

▶ Diving into fun with watersports

▶ Satisfying the landlubber: Activities, shopping, and nightlife

. . . .

*1*f you can shift into the groove of Jamaica, you may be attracted to this surprising place the same way the *doctor bird* is attracted to the jade vine. Your romance with the island may even begin the first time you catch a glimpse of this streamer-tailed hummingbird, Jamaica's national bird, flitting among the vine's iridescent blooms. The flowers — and the bird's aerial dance among them — are so exquisite and exotic that you may wonder if your eyes are deceiving you.

Thanks to its varied coastline, Jamaica delivers many amazing sights, especially in its collection of beaches. The island boasts practically every imaginable watersport and some of the best golf courses in the West Indies, as well as outdoor activities like river rafting, mountain hiking, and serious biking. And of course, around Montego Bay, Negril, and Ocho Rios, you can count on a party going on if you're so inclined. Disc jockeys set up huge speakers and blast throbbing rhythms of reggae, rock steady, and other Jamaican favorites.

In this chapter, we touch on the reasons that we've fallen in love with this wild child of the Caribbean. Jamaica's cultural and natural beauty are much more than skin-deep, but unfortunately, we only have room to scratch the surface.

The culture club

Jamaica's cultural life — its reggae music, distinctive art, and fiery cuisine — is as rich as most of its population is poor. When you're in Jamaica, you quickly realize that it's a pepper pot of cultures; its people (95% of whom trace their ancestry to Africa) are a heady mix of other Caribbean islands, Great Britain, the Middle East, India, China, Germany, Portugal, and South America. But you may well feel a palpable racial tension and hostility, the legacy of slavery and colonization. We've never run into a problem, but at times we've had an uneasy feeling. We don't want you to be overly concerned about crime. Indeed, most of the potential trouble is concentrated in the capital of Kingston, which you won't find in our recommendations. We urge you to get out and see this island, which is one of the more physically attractive and diverse in the Caribbean. But if you are new to the islands, we strongly suggest that you limit your adventures to those you can do with a guide recommended by your hotel — and stick close.

Heading for the Beaches

Take your pick: Jamaica has 200 miles (325 km) of beaches, some of them relatively deserted. In reality, though, the sand you're most likely to see will be the strip in front of your resort. Luckily, this island's beach hotels and resorts live up to their promise. We can't think of any accommodations that left us disappointed with the beach. The beaches we've highlighted in this section are public; some require an entry fee of a couple of dollars.

If you plan to center your vacation around beach activities, you'll probably want to spend it in Negril, which has the fine, white-sand Seven Mile Beach. Like Aruba's Palm Beach, this popular strand is lined with resorts — most all-inclusives — and sunbathers, strollers, vendors, and watersports lovers crowd the landscape. A few resorts have designated small patches of their properties as clothing-optional. Fellow travelers may ask if you're staying on the nude or prude side.

In fact, one of Negril's main attractions is the X-rated and aptly named Booby Cay, a tiny islet off the Negril coast. Once featured in the Walt Disney film *20,000 Leagues Under the Sea*, and formerly a favorite picnic spot for locals, this picturesque little atoll is now overrun by nudists from Hedonism II, a sprawling all-inclusive geared to singles. (We heard that the guest ratio is four men to every woman.) If you go, bring mirrored sunglasses and suntan lotion with a protection factor of 30 or higher, and leave the kids at home.

Speaking of kids, they tend to ask some awkward questions in Negril. You can follow our example and be blissfully naive about the kind of activity some of your fellow sojourners are seeking. Our first time in Negril, we brought our sons Caleb, then age 4, and Connor, 18 months. One day when we were out tooling around on a catamaran, Caleb suddenly piped up and said, "Daddy, what's that naked man doing on that boat?" We laughed and said, "What naked man?" "The one standing on the boat behind you," he replied. We turned just in time to see a badly burned fellow wearing nothing but his spare tire commanding his tiny Sunfish with his spinnaker hanging out.

To find a beach off the main tourist routes where you won't be regularly pitched by vendors eager to sell you wood carvings, conch shells, or *ganja* (otherwise known as pot), head for Jamaica's unexploited south-west coast. **Bluefields Beach** near Savanna-La-Mar (or, just Sav-La-Mar to locals), south of Negril, and **Crane Beach** at Black River are both pretty and remain undiscovered by the masses.

Another of our favorites is **Treasure Beach,** near a quaint fishing village. If you arrive in the early morning, stop by the **TransLove Café,** a funky throwback to the 1960s hippie culture, where the owner/waitress sings Supremes' hits while she pours your coffee and serves you an omelette. You can spend the day lazing in the sun, snorkeling, or fishing in the tranquil coves. For a few dollars, local fishermen will gladly take you out on the water. In the evening, have dinner outdoors at **Jake's** (see Chapter 24) and then join the odd collection of locals and jet-setters who sidle up to the bar and dance in the moonlight. Treasure Beach is the new Negril, laid-back and peaceful — for the moment.

In Montego Bay, you can find several good beaches. We were surprised that several are right in town, along the hip strip. If you want to mingle with the locals, head to **Cornwall Beach** (☎ 876-952-3463), a lively beach along the main drag where you can easily get food and drink as well as make use of a watersports concession and dressing cabanas. The five-mile-long **Doctor's Cave Beach** on Gloucester Avenue (☎ 876-952-2566) helped launch Mo Bay as a resort in the 1940s and now often looks like Daytona Beach during spring break. Dressing rooms, chairs, umbrellas, and rafts are available from 8:30 a.m. to 5:30 p.m. daily. Admission to both beaches is $2 for adults and $1 for children ages 12 and under. Expect to be approached by several vendors throughout the day.

Walter Fletcher Beach, in the heart of Mo Bay (☎ 876-952-5783), is noted for its tranquil waters, which makes it a particular favorite for families with children. The beach offers protection from the surf on a windy day, plus unusually fine swimming. A lifeguard is on duty, and you have changing rooms and a decent restaurant at your disposal. The beach is open daily from 9 a.m. to 10 p.m., with an admission charge of $2 for adults and $1 for children.

If you want to get away from the main drag and are willing to pay for the privilege, we recommend **Rose Hall Beach Club** (☎ 876-953-2323), lying on the main road 11 miles east of Mo Bay. It's set on half a mile of secure, secluded white-sand beach with crystal-clear water. This excel-lently equipped club offers a full restaurant, two beach bars, a covered pavilion, an open-air dance area, showers, rest rooms, and changing facilities, plus beach volleyball courts, various beach games, and a full watersports activities program, as well as live entertainment. Admission fees are $8 for adults and $5 for children. The club is open daily from 10 a.m. to 6 p.m.

In Ocho Rios, **Mallards Beach** has become too popular for our tastes because it attracts the many cruise ship passengers who stop in Ochi. A better choice is **Turtle Beach,** a white sandy beach stretching behind the Renaissance Jamaica Grande. It's the busiest beach in Ocho Rios because the islanders come to swim here.

James Bond Beach, east of Ocho Rios in the quaint village of Oracabessa, is popular because of the live reggae performances on its bandstand.

Romantic **Frenchman's Cove Beach** in Port Antonio attracts couples and families to its white-sand beach, a shoreline that features a fresh-water stream. Non-hotel guests pay a fee of $3 to enjoy the sand and surf here. But you'll be undisturbed by vendors, and waiters in long pants and long sleeves sell drinks and snacks from a tent. You'll feel like you've entered a time warp.

Taking the Plunge with Water Fun

Sadly, Jamaica's once glorious coral reefs have been heavily damaged by overfishing and careless boaters. Many of the reefs are dead. We don't really think scuba diving is worth the expense and time here (though some resorts include it as part of your package). You'll see few mature reef fish. Locals snatch sea fans and pretty shells out of the water to sell to tourists.

However, if you're determined to dive, you can. You'll need to show a C-card as evidence of your training and certification. The following operators are licensed by the tourist board and offer certification courses, dive trips, and snorkel gear rentals:

- ✔ The **Negril Scuba Centre** (Negril Beach Club Hotel and Hotel Sam Sara on Norman Manley Boulevard; ☎ 800-818-2963 or 876-957-9641), is the most modern, best-equipped scuba facility in Negril. Beginner's dive lessons are offered daily, as well as multiple-dive packages for certified divers. Full scuba certifications and specialty courses are also available. A resort course, designed for first-time divers with basic swimming abilities, includes all instruction, equipment, a lecture on water and diving safety, and one open-water dive. It begins at 10 a.m. daily and ends at 2 p.m. The price is $75. A one-tank dive costs $30 per dive plus $20 for equipment rental. More economical is a two-tank dive, which includes lunch; you must complete your dive in one day. It costs $55, plus the (optional) $20 rental of all equipment. This organization is PADI-registered, although it accepts all recognized certification cards. It specializes in night dives and has been in business for almost two decades.

- ✔ Another good choice in Negril is **Scuba World,** a PADI-approved five-star dive shop located at Orange Bay (☎ 876-957-6290). It's open daily from 8 a.m. to 5 p.m. and offers a four-day certification course for $350. A resort course for beginners costs $70, and a one-tank dive for certified divers costs $30, plus $20 for the rental of the necessary equipment. A two-tank dive costs $55, plus $10 for equipment rental.

In Negril, the best area for snorkeling is off the cliffs in the West End. On our last visit, we saw stingrays, rock beauties, sergeant majors, and several parrot fish on the reef at a depth of about 10 to 15 feet. You can find dozens of shops along West End Road, where you can rent snorkeling equipment at fairly modest prices.

Runaway Bay and Ocho Rios offers decent snorkeling, too. The reef fish seem to be making a slight comeback, and on recent visits we were surprised at the variety of marine life we saw. Although some reefs are accessible from the shore, you can avoid the boats and beach activity if you take a short boat ride to the better reefs further off shore. Try **Resort Divers Shop,** Main Street, Turtle Beach (☎ 876-974-6632). The skilled staff here can hook you up for dive trips or snorkeling. A boat leaving daily at 1 p.m. goes to Paradise Reef, where tropical fish are plentiful. Resort Divers also provides sports fishing jaunts as well as scuba diving certification and equipment, and also offers sailing lessons and equipment.

If you're going to Port Antonio, snorkel with **Lady Godiva's Dive Shop** in Dragon Bay (☎ 876-993-8988), seven miles from Port Antonio. Lady Godiva offers two excursions daily to San San Bay, a colorful reef off Monkey Island, for $10 per person. Snorkeling equipment costs $9 for a full day's rental. Dive prices on the island range from $40–$60 per person.

Enjoying the Water without Getting Wet

Jamaica is known for its plethora of waterfalls and rivers, great for exploring. You don't have to be a big waterbuff to enjoy them.

Rolling down the river on a raft

One of the more unique ways to enjoy the water in Jamaica is to take one of its famed river raft rides, popularized by the late Errol Flynn — the dashing, womanizing actor who used to challenge his friends to raft races.

Here's how it works: A raftsman will pole you down the Rio Grande (yes, Jamaica has a Rio Grande, too), an 8-mile-long (13 km), swift, green waterway from Berrydale to Rafter's Rest. You can pack a picnic lunch for the three-hour trip, and eat it on the raft or on the riverbank. Wherever you lunch, a vendor of Red Stripe beer will appear at your elbow. A restaurant, bar, and several souvenir shops are at Rafter's Rest.

The following companies arrange rafting trips:

- ✔ **Attractions Limited**, Rafter's Restaurant, St. Margaret's Bay (☎ 876-993-5778), provides a fully insured driver who will take you in your rented car to the starting point at Grants Level or Berrydale, where you board your raft. The rafts, some 33 feet long and only 4 feet wide, are propelled by stout bamboo poles. The raised double seat about two-thirds of the way back accommodates two passengers. The skipper stands in the front, trousers rolled up to his knees, the water washing his feet, and guides the craft down the lively river, between steep hills covered with coconut palms, banana plantations, and flowers, through limestone cliffs pitted with caves, past the "Tunnel of Love" (a narrow cleft in the rocks), then on to wider, gentler water. Trips last two to three hours and are offered from 8 a.m. to 4 p.m. daily at a cost of $40 per raft, which is suitable for two people. The trip ends at the Rafter's Restaurant, where you collect your car, which has been returned by the driver.

- ✔ **Martha Brae River Rafting** (Claude Clarke Ave., Montego Bay, ☎ 876-952-0889) leads trips down the Martha Brae River, about 25 miles (40 km) from most hotels in Mo Bay. The cost is just under $42 per person for the one-and-a-half-hour river run.

- ✔ **Mountain Valley Rafting** (Lethe, ☎ 876-956-4920) runs trips down the River Lethe, approximately 12 miles (19 km) southwest of Mo Bay. The hour-long trip is about $45 per raft (two per raft) and takes you through unspoiled hill country. You can also book through your hotel tour desk.

- ✔ If you're staying in Negril or on the South Coast, we recommend the **South Coast Safaris** (1 Crane Road, ☎ 876-965-2513) where you can take a boat ride up Jamaica's largest river, navigated through mangrove swamps in Savanna country. You'll see egrets and other water birds, as well as Jamaica's crocodiles. We thought it was fun, but when the guide waved a dead chicken in the water to lure the big guys out for a snack, the crocs were a little too close for comfort. The two-hour safari costs $15 per person.

Also in that area, you should also check out the **Y.S. Falls** (☎ 876-997-6055); a *jitney* (small bus) will drop you near the falls. It's a great place to play in the cool waters and have a picnic. The site is not nearly as touristy as the famed Dunn's River Falls. The admission cost is $10.

Dunn's River Falls, in Ocho Rios, are Jamaica's most photographed destination. Although you have to run the gauntlet of vendors hawking "I Survived the Falls" T-shirts, we still recommend the dramatically beautiful natural wonder. These 600-foot, icy cold waterfalls cascade over rock steps winding down to the Caribbean. They can be climbed, but to do so you'll need to form a human chain, led by a guide (who will expect a tip at the end). Don a swimsuit and take tennis shoes that you don't mind getting soaked.

Itinerary tips

If you're staying in Port Antonio, reserve a day for a guided excursion to the Blue Mountains. You'll find at least three days' worth of activity around Mo Bay. If you're staying in Mo Bay, you may want to head up the road to Ocho Rios and Runaway Bay. If you're based in Ocho Rios, be sure to visit Dunn's River Falls, Coyaba Gardens, and Fern Gully; you may also want to stop by Firefly or Port Antonio. If Negril is your hub, take in the south shore, including Treasure Beach, Y. S. Falls, and the Black River.

The rocks are very slippery, and the climb isn't suitable for those who are easily winded. Children age 6 or older can handle it. Do not attempt this climb with a toddler in your arms. (We've seen it, folks, or we wouldn't say it.) If you want to do more than take a quick gander at the falls, you'll need to set aside an hour or more for your visit. They're located off A-l, between St. Ann's and Ocho Rios. Call ☎ **876-974-2857** for information. Admission is $6. Open daily from 9 a.m. to 5 p.m.

On the day you see Dunn's River, take a side trip along Route A3 to drive through **Fern Gully,** a four-mile road covering what was originally a riverbed through the mountains, where more than 600 types of ferns have been found. Our guide said it used to be so shady that drivers had to turn on their headlights in the daytime. That was before a hurricane in 1988 destroyed some of the vegetation. The gully is still beautiful, and artists offering carved-wood souvenirs and baskets live in the nooks and crannies. Ask to make a stop at a roadside stall, where the proprietor will take you on a nature walk (for $10) into the rain forest.

Angling off the island

Northern Jamaican waters are world-renowned for their game fish, including blue and white marlin, sailfish, tarpon, and barracuda. Port Antonio makes deep sea fishing headlines with its annual **Blue Marlin Tournament.** Licenses aren't required, and you can arrange to charter a boat at your hotel. A boat (with captain, crew, and equipment) that accommodates four to six passengers costs about $400 for a half day.

Sticking to Dry Land

If you're athletic, you're in luck, because you can find lots of fun — and adrenaline-boosting — pursuits on Jamaica.

Riding high on horseback

Horseback riding is available on three scenic trails at **Prospect Plantation** on Route A3, 3 miles east of Ocho Rios in St. Ann (☎ 876-994-1058). The rides vary from 60 to 120-plus minutes. Advance booking of one hour is necessary to reserve horses. Tours cost $12 for adults and are free for children 12 and under. A one-hour horseback ride costs $20. Tours leave Monday to Saturday at 10:30 a.m., 2 p.m., and 3:30 p.m.; Sunday at 11 a.m., 1:30 p.m., and 3 p.m. On your leisurely ride through the scenic beauty of Prospect, you'll readily see why this section of Jamaica is called "the garden parish of the island." You can view the many trees planted by such visitors as Sir Winston Churchill, Dr. Henry Kissinger, Charlie Chaplin, Pierre Trudeau, and Sir Noel Coward.

Chukka Cove Farm (☎ 876-972-2506) near Ocho Rios offers hour-long trail rides ($30) and three-hour beach rides ($55). During in-season weekends, this is the place for polo. You can also saddle up at the **Rocky Point Riding Stables at Half Moon** (☎ 876-953-2286), which is just east of the Half Moon Club in Mo Bay.

Exploring the rain forest in an ATV

One of our better moves during one of our Jamaican holiday, was booking a trip with **Wilderness Resort,** St. Mary (☎ 876-974-5189), which is located in the countryside about 45 minutes from Ocho Rios and charges $100 per person. We spent half an hour fishing and then went for a guided ATV tour through the hills. Driving through mud puddles in the rain forest caused squeals of delight from our son Caleb.

Eventually, we rounded a corner to see a stone bridge that was constructed by the Spanish during their stay on the island. The bridge leads to one of the cool lagoons for which Jamaica is famed. The children happily cooled off with a swim while we dangled our feet in the water and waved to the local kids in their school uniforms who were arriving home. When we got back, a simple meal of fried fish (our catches), bammy, and french fries was waiting.

Linking up with a round of golf

Golfers appreciate both the beauty and the challenges offered by Jamaica's courses, and the game has deep roots here. Some of the courses were established more than 100 years ago.

Caddies are mandatory throughout the island, and rates are $12 to $25, but you'll get extra entertainment: They carry your golf bag and clubs balanced sideways on their heads.

Some of the best courses are in Mo Bay. The following are our favorites:

- ✔ The **Half Moon Golf, Tennis, and Beach Club,** 7 miles (11 km) east of Mo Bay (☎ 876-953-3105), has a Robert Trent Jones–designed 18-hole course, which is the home of the Red Stripe Pro Am. Greens fees are $55 for guests, $110 for nonguests.

- ✔ **Ironshore,** 3 miles (5 km) east of the airport (☎ 876-953-2800), is an 18-hole, links-style course. The greens fee is $50.

- ✔ **Tryall Golf, Tennis, and Beach Club,** 15 miles (24 km) west of Mo Bay on North Coast Hwy. (☎ 876-956-5681), has an 18-hole championship course on the site of a nineteenth-century sugar plantation. Greens fees run $40 to $60 for guests, $100 for nonguests.

- ✔ **Wyndham Rose Hall**, 4 miles (6½ km) east of the airport on North Coast Hwy. (☎ 876-953-2650), hosts several invitational tournaments. Fees run $70 for guests, $80 for nonguests.

- ✔ Ocho Rios has the **Sandals Golf and Country Club,** 2 miles (3 km) east of Ocho Rios (☎ 876-975-0119), whose adjacent 18-hole course is 700 feet above sea level. The greens fee is $70 for nonguests.

- ✔ **Breezes Golf and Beach Resort,** North Coast Hwy., Kingston (☎ 876-973-7319), is an 18-hole course that has hosted many championship events. The greens fee is $80 for nonguests; guests play for free.

- ✔ **Grand Lido Braco,** in Runaway Bay, Trelawny, between Duncans and Rio Buena (☎ 876-954-0000), is a 9-hole course with lush vegetation. Call for fee information.

- ✔ Great golf, rolling hills, and a "liquor mobile" go hand in hand at the 18-hole **Negril Hills Golf Club,** east of Negril on Sheffield Rd. (☎ 876-957-4638). The greens fee is $58.

Having a ball with tennis or squash

Many hotels have tennis facilities that are free to their guests, and some will allow nonguests to play for a fee. Court fees generally run $5 to $8 per hour for nonguests; lessons start at $12 an hour. Here's a sampling:

- ✔ **Half Moon Golf, Tennis, and Beach Club,** 7 miles (11 km) east of Mo Bay (☎ 876-953-2211), has 13 Laykold tennis courts (7 lit for night play) along with a pro and a pro shop.

- ✔ **Tryall Golf, Tennis, and Beach Club,** 15 miles (24 km) west of Mo Bay on North Coast Hwy. (☎ 876-956-5660), has nine courts.

✔ **Ciboney, Ocho Rios,** Main St., Ocho Rios (☎ 876-974-1027), has a pro and six lighted courts (three clay and three hard).

✔ **Grand Lido Sans Souci,** North Coast Hwy., 2 miles (3 km) east of Ocho Rios (☎ 876-974-2353), has two lighted courts and a pro.

✔ **Sandals Dunn's River Golf Resort and Spa,** North Coast Hwy. (☎ 876-972-1610), has two courts lit for night play and a pro.

✔ **Breezes Golf and Beach Resort,** North Coast Hwy., Runaway Bay (☎ 876-973-2436), has four courts.

✔ **Sandals Montego Bay,** Kent Ave., Mo Bay (☎ 876-952-5510), has four courts lit for night play and a tennis pro.

✔ In Negril, you'll find five hard courts and five clay courts, all lit for night play, at **Swept Away Negril,** Norman Manley Blvd. (☎ 876-957-4040).

Climbing every mountain

Jamaica has some of the most varied and unusual topography in the Caribbean, including a 7,500-foot mountain range laced with rough rivers, streams, and waterfalls.

Hiking in the Blue Mountains is magnificent. You'll come across sweeping fields of wildflowers, and with a guide, you can visit the famous Blue Mountain coffee plantations. On one of our more memorable treks, we finished the two-hour hike with steaming cups of coffee sweetened with wildflower honey harvested on the estate.

You can book with Kingston's best-known specialists in eco-sensitive tours, **Sunventure Tours,** 30 Balmoral Ave., Kingston 10 (☎ 876-960-6685). The staff here can always arrange an individualized tour for you and your party, but it also has a roster of mainstream offerings.

We recommend **Valley Hikes** (Port Antonio, ☎ 876-993-3881) for excellent guided tours in the Blue Mountain/John Crow Mountain National Park and Rio Grande Valley. Our favorite stop was at the home of Maroon herbalist Iveylyn Harris, who can be contacted through Valley Hikes. The energetic woman entertains with the tales of Maroon history and culture. She also does traditional herbal baths with herbs from her garden ($30) and massage ($50). With advance notice, she'll also make lunch ($10).

Going to the birds

Many bird-watchers flock (excuse the pun) here for the chance to see the *verrain hummingbird* — the second smallest bird in the world, larger only than Cuba's bee hummingbird. Also of interest is the Jamaican *tody,* which nests underground. The island's 27 unique species of feathered wonders are spectacular advertisements for the special colors of Jamaica.

A great place to spot birds is the **Rocklands Feeding Station,** Anchovy, south of Montego Bay (☎ 876-952-2009). It costs about $8 for the morning. In Mandeville, tours of the bird sanctuary at **Marshall's Penn Great House** (☎ 876-962-7979) are led by owner Robert Sutton, one of Jamaica's leading ornithologists. Tours are arranged by appointment only; a full-day tour costs $100 for as many as three people.

Exploring the Island's Past

Jamaica's colonial past is preserved in some of its fabulous great houses. Here are our picks:

- ✔ In the 1700s, **Rose Hall,** east of Montego Bay and across the highway from Rose Hall resorts (☎ 876-953-2323), may well have been the greatest of great houses in the West Indies. Visitors today are enthralled by the legend surrounding its second mistress: Annie Palmer murdered three husbands and a *busha* (plantation overseer) who was her lover. The story is told in a novel that's sold everywhere in Jamaica: *The White Witch of Rose Hall.* Admission $15. Open daily 9 a.m. to 6 p.m.

- ✔ **Greenwood Great House** is located 15 miles (24 km) east of Montego Bay (☎ 876-953-1077). The Barrett family, from which the English poet Elizabeth Barrett Browning was descended, once owned all the land from Rose Hall to Falmouth, and they built Greenwood and several other great houses on it. Highlights of Greenwood include oil paintings of the Barretts, china made for the family by Wedgwood, a library filled with rare books from as early as 1697, fine antique furniture, and a collection of exotic musical instruments. Admission $10. Open daily 9 a.m. to 6 p.m.

Checking Out Some Don't-Miss Sites

Exploring the natural beauty as well as the art and culture of Jamaica is one of our favorite things in the Caribbean. Here are some of our top picks.

Situated a mile from the center of Ocho Rios, at an elevation of 420 feet, the **Coyaba River Garden and Museum** (☎ 876-974-6235) stands on the grounds of the former Shaw Park plantation. The word *coyaba* comes from the Arawak name for paradise, and this small but beautiful garden lives up to its name. Proprietess Toni Allen will gladly talk to you about the native flora. The tiny but intriguing museum boasts a collection of artifacts from the Arawak, Spanish, and English settlements in the area. The gardens and museum open at 8:30 a.m. and close at 5 p.m. seven days a week. Admission is $4.50 for ages 13 and up, free for children 12 and under. Plan to spend about an hour here. A small on-site snack bar helps keep you cool and refreshed during your sightseeing stay.

Jamaica serves up a slice of frozen time with **Firefly** (☎ 876-997-7201), the home of Sir Nöel Coward. The restored house, located in St. Mary, 20 miles east of Ocho Rios and above Oracabessa, is more or less as it was on the day Sir Nöel died in 1973. His Hawaiian print shirts still hang in the closet of his austere bedroom, with its mahogany four-poster bed. The library contains a collection of his books, and the living room is warm and comfortable, with big armchairs and two grand pianos (where he composed several famous tunes). You can visit any day of the week from 8:30 a.m. to 5:30 p.m. The price of admission is $10.

If you wouldn't mind stumbling on a great place to experience art — to look at, to take to your tummy, and to satisfy your refined tastes in souvenir-shopping — seek out **Harmony Hall** (☎ 876-975-4222), built near the end of the nineteenth century as the centerpiece of a sugar plantation. The resident restaurant, **Toscanini,** is among our top choices for a memorable taste of Jamaica (see Chapter 26 for details about this most inspiring dining experience). **The Garden Café** is open the same hours as Toscanini — 10 a.m. to 10 p.m., seven days a week. Among the featured gift items available in the Art Gallery and Craft Shop are works by some of Jamaica's best artists, as well as Sharon McConnell's Starfish Oils, which contain natural additives harvested in Jamaica and smell heavenly. The gallery shop also carries the "Reggae to Wear" line of sportswear, designed and made on Jamaica. Admission to the Art Gallery and Craft Shop is free.

To Market, to Market

Jamaica offers lots of great local crafts and goods that are worthy of your gift-giving consideration. We find the craft markets of Negril much less pressured than several years ago, and you can find a good range of price and products there. Ocho Rios is too crowded for our comfort. We like dealing with the craftspeople around Fern Gully, too.

Here's a thing or three you might want to bring back with you — all dutyfree:

- ✔ Jamaican rum
- ✔ Tia Maria, Jamaica's world-famous coffee liqueur
- ✔ Blue Mountain coffee
- ✔ Hot sauces
- ✔ Wood carvings
- ✔ Fine handmade Macanudo cigars

Although Montego Bay and Ocho Rios (with seven shopping plazas) are famous for dutyfree shopping, we studiously avoid the throngs that crowd these places. We've also found through much comparison that the gift shops at the Mo Bay airport actually have reasonable prices on items like rum, coffee, and even crafts. You won't do much better in the craft markets.

Gallery of West Indian Art (Round Hill, Montego Bay; ☎ 876-952-4547) is the place to find Jamaican and Haitian paintings. A corner of the gallery is devoted to hand-turned pottery (some painted) and beautifully carved and painted birds and animals.

Looking for Limin' and Nightlife

Jamaica supports a lively community of musicians. Reggae, popularized by the late Bob Marley and the Wailers and performed today by Ziggy Marley, Jimmy Tosh (the late Peter Tosh's son), Gregory Isaacs, Third World, Jimmy Cliff, and many others, is its most famous contribution to the music world.

For the most part, the liveliest late-night happenings throughout Jamaica are in the major resort hotels. Some of the all-inclusives offer a dinner and disco pass from about $95. Pick up a copy of *The Daily Gleaner, The Jamaica Observer,* or *The Star* (available at newsstands throughout the island) for listings on who's playing when and where.

The principal club in Ocho Rios is **Jamaica'N Me Crazy,** Renaissance Jamaica Grande, Main St. (☎ 876-974-2201). The place usually hosts a packed crowd.

The place to be in Mo Bay on Friday night after 10 p.m. is **Pier 1,** Howard Cooke Blvd., opposite the straw market (☎ 876-952-2452). **Margueritaville** (☎ 876-952-4777) on the hip strip has also steadily become ground zero for the party crowd. It's a giant sports bar that turns into a music and dance scene late in the evenings.

In Negril, you'll find the best music and an eclectic crowd of locals and in-the-know tourists at **Alfred's Ocean Palace,** Norman Manley Blvd. (☎ 876-957-4735). It has a dance area set up on a beach and a stage for live reggae (Tuesday, Wednesday, and weekend nights). On Mondays and Thursdays, there's live jazz.

Part VIII
Puerto Rico

The 5th Wave By Rich Tennant

"Oh quit looking so uncomfortable. It's the
Caribbean! No one wears a cape and formal
wear in the Caribbean."

In this part . . .

*P*uerto Rico is a big island, and the range of accommodations available is stunning. We try to keep things simple by narrowing down our recommendations to the best of the best. While this island is one of the easier to access in the Caribbean, we share tips for ensuring a smooth arrival and for planning some successful sightseeing.

From cutting-edge preparations to simple down-home meals, we point you toward the best dining options on Puerto Rico. Finally, we give you ideas for how to spend your time on the island, from lounging at the beach to exploring the beauty of Old San Juan.

Chapter 28

The Lowdown on Puerto Rico's Hotel Scene

Sparkling high-rises, soft-sand beaches, stunning nature reserves — you'll find it all in Puerto Rico. You want glitzy casinos? No problemo. How about charming seaside villages with modest country inns? Ditto. Want history? You can stay in an old convent. The range of accommodations is impressive.

In this chapter, we tell you about our favorite Puerto Rican hotels and resorts, and we put them in context to help you choose the best one for your vacation.

Figuring Out Where You Want to Stay

Puerto Rico is big — 100 miles long by 35 miles wide — and you have tons of lodging choices on this island. We try to keep your options simple in this chapter.

Most hotels in Puerto Rico operate on the European Plan (or EP — see Chapter 6), although larger establishments offer other meal plans. All-inclusive packages haven't quite taken hold on Puerto Rico, and we're glad. It's not the kind of island where you want to just stay at one resort the whole time.

San Juan: A tale of two cities

Think of San Juan as two towns: one old, one new. **Old San Juan** is seven square blocks of living history, a World Heritage Site graced with sixteenth-, seventeenth-, and eighteenth-century buildings and fortifications in which people go about twenty-first-century daily life. Of all the Caribbean capitals, it's our favorite because of its beauty, its thriving art scene, and — thank goodness — the absence of tacky T-shirt shops clogging every corner. One of our favorite hotels in all of the Caribbean — the El Convento — is found here, too.

Most of our picks, though, are in **Condado** or **Isla Verde,** both just a short hop from the airport. These neighborhoods, which cater primarily to the gambling crowd and to cruise passengers in port for a day or so, are strung along the Atlantic shore due east of Old San Juan's peninsula. This area reminds us of Waikiki Beach in Hawaii, with high-rise after monolithic 1960s high-rise interspersed with resorts commanding nice stretches of beach. What makes this newer San Juan scene fun is the party atmosphere and the people-watching.

Most of the big hotels have casinos; gambling is big in San Juan. Don't expect the frenzy of Las Vegas, though. For one reason, liquor isn't served free of charge for gamblers in casinos here.

Elsewhere on the island

Outside San Juan, particularly on the east coast, you can find self-contained luxury resorts that cover hundreds of acres. In the west, southwest, and south — as well as on the islands of **Vieques** and **Culebra** — lodging is primarily in smaller inns, villas, and condominiums for short-term rentals.

Here, government-sponsored *paradores* are a popular option. Some paradores are rural inns, some offer no-frills apartments, and some are large hotels. But all must meet certain standards, such as proximity to an attraction or beach. Most have a small restaurant that serves local cuisine. Paradores are great bargains (prices range from $50–$125 for a double room), but they can get noisy on weekends when local families descend for mini-vacations. You can make reservations for all paradores by contacting the tourist board's **Paradores of Puerto Rico,** Box 4435, Old San Juan, PR 00902 (☎ **800-443-0266** in North America, 787-721-2884 in San Juan, and 800-981-7575 elsewhere in Puerto Rico).

In hotels outside of San Juan, rates don't often include airport transfers. Be sure to ask when you book.

Renting a Villa or Condo

If you're traveling with several people, villas and condominiums can be fun and affordable options. Here are some contacts to make if you want to investigate this lodging choice:

   ✔ For rate information about higher-end properties in San Juan's Isla Verde area, contact **Condo World,** 4230 Orchard Lake Rd., Suite 5, Orchard Lake, MI 48323 (☎ **800-521-2980;** fax 248-683-5076).

✔ For information on some 200 properties in Condado and Isla Verde, contact **Puerto Rico Vacation Apartments,** Marabella del Caribe Oeste S-5, Isla Verde, San Juan, PR 00979 (☎ **800-266-3639** or 787-727-1591; fax 787-268-3604).

✔ For weekly and monthly rentals in Rincon, contact **Island West Properties,** Rte. 413, Km 1.3, Box 700, Rincon, PR 00677 (☎ **787-823-2323;** fax 787-823-3254).

✔ For properties on Vieques, try either **Connections,** Box 358, Esperanza, Vieques, PR 00765 (☎ **787-741-0023**) or **Acacia Apartments,** Box 1211, Esperanza, Vieques, PR 00765 (☎ **787-741-1856**).

Puerto Rico's Best Hotels

The rack rates listed in this section are in U.S. dollars and are for a standard double room during high season (mid-December to mid-April). Rates are lower during the off-season and shoulder season; see Chapter 2 for advice on when to go. Purchasing a package tour is another way to save money on accommodations; see Chapter 5 for details.

Copamarina Beach Resort

$$$ Guanica

This south coast resort is a dream come true for watersports and nature freaks. Set on 18 acres between the Caribbean Sea and the Guanica Dry Forest, it is in a UNESCO-designated world biosphere reserve, home to more than 100 species of birds. The dive center here also rents kayaks, paddle boats, and snorkel gear. The pools (one with a Jacuzzi and a new one for kids) are surrounded by the open-air reception area, manicured lawns, and the building wings.

The bay bottom on this section of beach is covered in seaweed, but secluded beaches with clear water are just a few minutes' drive down the road. The spotless rooms — much improved since a $5.5-million renovation — have small terraces with water views and either one queen-size or two double beds. The **Coastal Cuisine** dining room also got a facelift; while there, try Chef Wilo Benet's red snapper. Scuba packages are available, or you can arrange a snorkeling excursion to Gilligan's Island, an offshore key ($3 for the ride). This resort also has two bars, two tennis courts, and volleyball. Bicycles are available for rental.

Rte. 333, Km 6.5, Cana Gorda (Box 805), Guanica, PR 00653. ☎ *800-468-4553 (direct to hotel) or 787-821-0505. Fax: 787-821-0070. Internet:* www.copamarina.com. *Rack rates: $155–$180 double. AE, MC, V. EP.*

Puerto Rico's Hotels

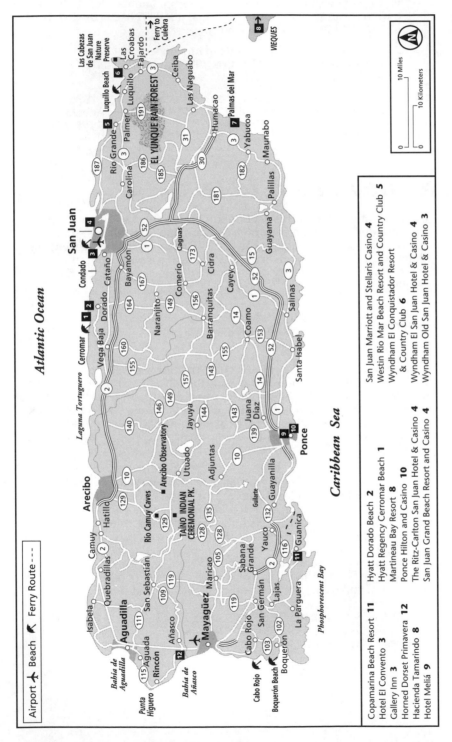

Airport ✈ Beach ↙ Ferry Route - - -

Atlantic Ocean

San Juan

Arecibo

Aguadilla

Mayagüez

Ponce

Caribbean Sea

EL YUNQUE RAIN FOREST

Las Cabezas de San Juan Nature Preserve

Ferry to Culebra

VIEQUES

Phosphorescent Bay

10 Miles

10 Kilometers

Copamarina Beach Resort **11**
Hotel El Convento **3**
Gallery Inn **3**
Horned Dorset Primavera **12**
Hacienda Tamarindo **8**
Hotel Meliá **9**

Hyatt Dorado Beach **2**
Hyatt Regency Cerromar Beach **1**
Martineau Bay Resort **8**
Ponce Hilton and Casino **10**
The Ritz-Carlton San Juan Hotel & Casino **4**
San Juan Grand Beach Resort and Casino **4**

San Juan Marriott and Stellaris Casino **4**
Westin Rio Mar Beach Resort and Country Club **5**
Wyndham El Conquistador Resort
& Country Club **6**
Wyndham El San Juan Hotel & Casino **4**
Wyndham Old San Juan Hotel & Casino **3**

Hotel El Convento

$$$$ Old San Juan

This intimate, elegant hotel in the heart of Old San Juan transports you to the days of Spain's conquest of the New World. Formerly a convent constructed in 1636 by royal decree and converted to a hotel by the Woolworth family in 1963, it was finally reborn in its current luxury form in 1997, replete with a Spanish courtyard and splashing fountain.

The 59 rooms are unique and delightful, with mahogany antiques and hand-crafted Spanish furnishings and tiles. Bright paint and stencils adorn the walls. The rooftop plunge pool and Jacuzzi have glorious views of dramatic Old San Juan and its harbor. Pop diva/actress Jennifer Lopez stays here when she's in town.

In the evenings, savor a martini at the **El Picoteo Tapas Bar** — artsy and discreet — before heading out for a late dinner at one of the city's many ultra-hip restaurants. The street side **Café Bohemio** is a great spot for lunch or a quick coffee. You get three restaurants, two bars, in-room safes, mini-bars, an exercise room, shops, a library, and parking (for a fee).

100 Cristo Street, Old San Juan, PR 00901. ☎ *800-468-2779 or 787-723-9020. Fax: 787-721-2877. E-mail:* elconvento@aol.com. *Internet:* www.elconvento.com. *Rack rates: rooms $195–$380 double; suites $550–$1,200. AE, DISC, DC, MC, V.*

Gallery Inn

$$$–$$$$ Old San Juan

Owners Jan D'Esopo and Manuco Gandia transformed this rambling, classically Spanish house — one of the city's oldest residences — into an inn of "bohemian opulence," as some describe it. It's full of comforts and quirky details: winding, uneven stairs; balconies; a music room with a Steinway grand piano; and nooks in which to curl up with a good book. The lush courtyard gardens, where Jan's pet macaws and cockatoos hang out, reach for the sunlight. Several rooms have whirlpool baths, but none has a TV.

From the rooftop deck, the spectacular panorama is of El Morro and San Cristobal forts and the Atlantic ocean. **Galeria San Juan,** a small gallery and studio, displays various pieces by Jan D'Esopo, Bruno Lucchesi, and others. The inn has no sign in front, so tell your taxi driver it's on the corner of Calles Norzagaray and San Justo.

204–206 Calle Norzagaray, Old San Juan, PR 00901. ☎ *787-722-1808. Fax 787-724-7360. Rack rates: $195–$300 double, includes continental breakfast. AE, MC, V. CP.*

Horned Dorset Primavera

$$$$ Rincón

This handsome Spanish colonial-style resort is tucked away amid lush landscaping overlooking the sea. It's geared to the high-powered exec who wants to get away and relax, rest, and relax some more. No cell phones here, folks; the only sounds that you're likely to hear as you lounge on the long, secluded beach are the crash of the surf and an occasional squawk from Pompidou, the enormous *guacamayo* (parrot) in the lounge.

Suites have balconies and are exquisitely furnished with antiques, including mahogany four-poster beds, dressers, and nightstands. Casa Escondida, where you'll find the most exclusive accommodations, has eight rooms — four with their own plunge pools and hot tubs — and is designed as a turn-of-the-century Puerto Rican hacienda, with tile or wood floors, mahogany furnishings, terraces overlooking the ocean, and black marble baths. The rooms have no radios, TVs, or phones. The **Horned Dorset Primavera** restaurant is popular with locals (see our review in Chapter 30). Parents take note: Kids under 12 are not permitted.

Rte. 429, Km 3 (Box 1132), Rincón, PR 00677. ☎ *787-823-4030 or 787-823-4050. Fax: 787-823-5580. Rack rates: $280–$650 double. AE, MC, V. EP, MAP.*

Hacienda Tamarindo

$$–$$$ Vieques

Owners Burr and Linda Vail left Vermont to build this extraordinary hotel, which has a huge tamarind tree right in the middle and sweeping Caribbean views from its windswept hilltop location. Rooms are individually decorated but have such details as mahogany louvered doors and terra-cotta tile floors. Some rooms have terraces, and half the rooms have air-conditioning. Those that aren't air-conditioned face the trade winds. All have ceiling fans and are furnished with eclectic art and antiques shipped from Vermont. A full breakfast is served on the second-floor terrace. You can walk down the hill to the **Inn on the Blue Horizon** for dinner. Box lunches are available on request. (Children under 12 won't feel comfortable here; it's best to leave the kids at home.)

Rte. 996, Km 4.5 (Box 1569), Vieques, PR 00765. ☎ *787-741-8525. Fax: 787-741-3215. Rack rate: $140 double. AE, MC, V. CP.*

Hotel Melia

$–$$ Ponce

Set in the heart of Ponce and facing the Parque de Bombas and the Ponce Cathedral, this family-owned hotel provides a wonderful, low-key base for exploring the marvelous turn-of-the-century architecture, museums, and landmarks of downtown. The lobby has an Old World feel, with high ceilings, blue-and-beige tile floors, and well-worn but charming decor. The bland rooms are dated, but ask for one of the six rooms with balconies that overlook the park. Breakfast is served on the rooftop terrace, which offers pretty views of the city and mountains.

2 Calle Cristina (Box 1431), Ponce, PR 00733. ☎ *787-842-0260 or 787-842-0060. Fax: 787-841-3602. Rack rates: $75–$95 double. AE, MC, V. CP.*

Hyatt Dorado Beach

$$$$ Dorado

Located on a 1,000-acre estate 22 miles west of San Juan and shared with its sister property, the Hyatt Regency Cerromar Beach, this deluxe operation aims to please — and succeeds. Accommodations are in the Oceanview Houses, 14 two-story buildings (no taller than the coconut trees). Spacious and romantic with plantation furnishings and terra-cotta tiles, each room has a balcony or terrace, mini-bar, cable TV, and marble bath. Two- or three-bedroom *casitas* (bungalows) line the fairway.

Recreational options here are the best on the island: two 18-hole golf courses designed by Robert Trent Jones, Sr.; a clubhouse; two pools (one Olympic-sized); a spa and fitness center with aerobics classes; eight tennis courts; oceanside inline skating and jogging trails; a windsurfing school; and a private beach with watersports. Dining options range from four formal restaurants to the casual beach bar to theme night minglers; the food is high priced and sometimes mediocre.

A shuttle bus takes you to the casino and other facilities (including two more golf courses) at the neighboring Hyatt Regency Cerromar Beach. If you're torn between the two properties, keep in mind that the Dorado has nicer rooms and a better beach and appeals to an older crowd, while the Cerromar has a better pool, a younger clientele, and a renowned children's program. Upper-level rooms in the Oceanview Houses have a vista of the two beaches. The only drawback to this resort is the service, which can be less than attentive.

Rte. 693, Km 10.8 (Box 1351), Dorado, PR 00646. ☎ 800-55-HYATT or 787-796-1234. Fax: 787-796-2022 or 787-796-6560. Rack rates: $205–$1,785. AE, DISC, DC, MC, V. EP, MAP (compulsory in season).

Hyatt Regency Cerromar Beach

$$$$–$$$$$ Dorado

The sister property to the Hyatt Dorado Beach shares the same 1,000 acres. This plush resort was voted one of the world's best family resorts by 30,000 travel agents. Guestrooms are decorated in an island theme and have mini-bars, spacious baths, and balconies. The hotel boasts of having the world's largest riverpool (1,776 feet), complete with whirlpools, a Jacuzzi grotto, a swim-up bar, 14 waterfalls, five separate swimming areas, and an impressive three-story waterslide. Or you can settle for its Olympic-size pool. A rain forest is on the property, along with 220 varieties of orchids.

Guests stay busy at the spa, which offers aerobics and water aerobics classes, morning tennis clinics on 14 tennis courts, waterskiing and lit snorkeling at the beach, a windsurfing school, supervised children's activities, bicycle and jogging trails, nature walks, water volleyball, basketball, and 36 holes of golf on courses designed by Robert Trent Jones, Sr. This resort is excellent all the way. The clientele are mainly business travelers and families.

Rte. 693, Km 11.8 (Box 1351), Dorado, PR 00646. ☎ ***800-233-1234*** *or 787-796-1234. Fax: 787-796-4647. Internet:* www.hyatt.com. *Rack rates: $205–$435. AE, DISC, DC, MC, V. EP, MAP optional.*

Ponce Hilton and Casino

$$$ Ponce

The biggest resort on the island's south coast — a cream-and-turquoise complex on 80 acres of landscaped gardens — is completely self-contained and caters to a corporate clientele. Nonetheless, if you don't mind the "nametag" ambiance, you'll find good facilities here. It has a casino, a shopping arcade, a pool, access to a public beach, and a disco with pool tables and live music on weekends. Although (like most Hiltons) the lobby has all the warmth of an airline terminal, the large guestrooms are attractive enough; they're decorated in sky blue, teal, and peach with modern rattan. All have balconies. A drawback is the hotel's location — a 10-minute cab ride from town.

Rd. 14, Santiago Avenue (Box 7419), Ponce, PR 00732. ☎ ***800-445-8667*** *or 787-259-7676. Fax: 787-259-7674. Rack rate: $210 double. AE, DISC, MC, V. EP.*

San Juan Grand Beach Resort and Casino

$$$$ Isla Verde

In place of the former Sands Hotel stands the sparkling San Juan Grand, which opened under new management in late 1998 after $12 million in renovations. The 16-story monolith sits on one of the city's most popular beaches. The theme of understated luxury carries from the large cream-and-brown-tiled lobby (with its blue sky ceiling motif) to the spacious rooms, decorated in somber brown and green hues. Suites of the Plaza Club (which has 24-hour snacks on hand and a private concierge) overlook the pool area, but the views from the standard rooms — either over the ocean or toward the city and the San Jose Lagoon — are almost as nice. Off the lobby is a mammoth casino overlooking tropical gardens and the pool area.

On-site restaurants include the steak emporium **Ruth's Chris Steak House; Momoyama** for Japanese cuisine; and the **Grand Market Cafe,** with deli favorites that you can eat on the spot or have packed for a beach picnic. Besides five restaurants, you get two bars, in-room safes, no-smoking rooms, a pool, a hot tub, an exercise room, a spa, boating, the beach, shops, the casino, and children's programs.

187 Avenue (Box 6676), Isla Verde, PR 00914. ☎ ***800-544-3008*** *or 787-791-6100. Fax: 787-255-2510. Rack rates: $325–$475 double. AE, DISC, MC, V. EP.*

San Juan Marriott and Stellaris Casino

$$$$ Condado, San Juan

This Marriott, which rose from the ashes of the burned-out Dupont Plaza in 1995, unapologetically caters to the business crowd. It's on a terrific beach and has live entertainment in the lobby on the weekends. If you get a package here, you'll be in a good location and have Marriott's reliability. Restaurants include the awarding-winning **Tuscany** for northern Italian cuisine and the more casual **La Vista,** which is open 24 hours and popular for dining alfresco. The pool area is large, and so is the hotel's spa-gym. As prime a spot as it occupies, this hotel has yet to find its island personality.

1309 Avenue, Ashford, San Juan, PR 00907. ☎ **800-228-9290** *or 787-722-7000. Fax: 787-722-6800. Rack rates: $285–$405 double. AE, DISC, DC, MC, V.*

The Ritz-Carlton San Juan Hotel & Casino

$$$$$ **Isla Verde**

Opening right before Christmas in 1997, the Ritz-Carlton immediately became one of the most spectacular deluxe hotels in Puerto Rico. This beachfront hotel lies only 15 minutes from the airport on eight acres of prime ocean-view property. (Don't worry: The construction means you won't notice plane noise.) Appealing to both business travelers and vacationers, it is a trailblazer in tropical elegance. Artwork from established local artists reflects the Caribbean flavor and Hispanic culture of the island. Soft tones and pale colors are complemented by wrought-iron chandeliers and tropical plants, and beveled and leaded glass is featured throughout the building to capture views of the ocean.

A selection of guestrooms is specifically designed to meet the needs of guests with disabilities. The preferred accommodations are in the upper floor Ritz-Carlton Club, which has the added benefit of a private lounge and personal concierge staff, accessed by a key-activated elevator. A total of 46 guestrooms and suites are in this private-seeming club.

The 12,000-square foot spa here, the largest and most sophisticated of its kind on Puerto Rico, offers panoramic ocean views. The elegant marble and stone bilevel building is also the setting for yoga, aerobics, aqua-aerobics, and other fitness activities. Upstairs are 11 treatment rooms that offer facials, massages, manicures, pedicures, hydrotherapy, and body wraps, among other treatments.

6961 Avenue of the Governors, Isla Verde, San Juan, PR 00979. ☎ **800-241-3333** *or 787-253-1700. Fax: 787-253-0700. Internet:* www.ritzcarlton.com. *Rack rates: $400–$475 double; from $950 suite. AE, DC, MC, V.*

Westin Rio Mar Beach Resort and Country Club

$$$–$$$$$ **Rio Grande**

This property represents Puerto Rico's first to be built from scratch in 15 years. It opened in August 1996 and marked Westin's first foray into the Caribbean. The seven-story hotel is situated on 481 lush acres hemmed in by a one-mile beach on the island's northeast coast and the Caribbean National Forest.

Guestrooms come in six categories, all including private balconies or patios, voice mail, electronic security locks, in-room safes, 24-hour room service, ice, cable TV, and mini-bars. A concierge level has added amenities on the seventh floor. Facilities at the $178-million property include 11 restaurants and lounges, a Las Vegas-style casino, a 35,000-square-foot clubhouse, 13 tennis courts and a tennis clubhouse, a fitness center and spa, and a business center. Activities include 36 holes of golf (at Tom and George Fazio's Rio Mar Ocean Course, and River Course by Greg Norman) and watersports (especially scuba diving and deep sea fishing). A children's program ($40 a day per child) and baby-sitting ($5 an hour) are available. A thoroughbred track is also nearby.

Avoid suites 5099 and 5101 — the balconies overlook the hotel's noisy air-conditioning ducts.

6000 Rio Mar Blvd. (Box 6100), Rio Grande, PR 00745. ☎ 800-WESTIN-1 or 787-888-6000. Fax: 787-888-6600. Internet: www.westinriomar.com. *Rack rates: $205–$475 double. AE, DISC, DC, MC, V. EP, MAP.*

Wyndham El Conquistador Resort & Country Club

$$$$$ Fajardo

This $250-million enclave crowns a cliff, overlooking the Caribbean on one side and the Atlantic on the other, and consists of a main hotel and three villages occupying 500 acres. Guestrooms are decked out with three phones, two TVs, VCRs, stereos, and refrigerators; 88 suites and 176 one- to three-bedroom casitas offer more room and special amenities. You can also get star treatment by opting for "Club Conquistador," which gives you private check-in, all-day snacks, free continental breakfast, and access to a private bar.

The resort opened in 1993 and is one of the Caribbean's largest. It boasts a casino, six pools, seven tennis courts, a pro shop, a health spa, 16 restaurants and 4 bars, and watersports. Among the gee-whiz attractions is the 6,700-yard, par-72 Arthur Hills' golf course, recognized as one of the Caribbean's finest. Other especially appealing elements are an art collection worth a million dollars; a 100-acre private island 10 minutes away where you can spend the day snorkeling, windsurfing, and diving; a 32-slip marina; and 22 retail shops. Lately, complaints have bubbled up about the service and the blandness of the food. Golfers have nothing but kudos for this incredible resort, but watersports buffs may have a better time where the beach is more handy.

1000 Avenue El Conquistador (Box 70001), Fajardo, PR 00738. ☎ 800-468-8365 (direct to hotel), 800-WYNDHAM, or 787-863-1000. Fax: 787-863-6500. Rack rates: $395–$595 double. AE, DISC, DC, MC, V. EP, MAP.

Wyndham El San Juan Hotel & Casino

$$$$–$$$$$ Isla Verde

When the Rat Pack was in town, they stayed in this opulent resort, sprawled on one of Puerto Rico's finest beaches. The eye-popping grand lobby, splendorous with carved mahogany ceilings and a chandelier as big as an old Cadillac, sets the stage for a continual fiesta. In one corner is a 12-piece Cuban band. Off to the side is a snazzy casino. A Las Vegas-style showroom is within earshot, as is San Juan's hottest disco. And that's not even the whole scene!

Even if you're stuck on a layover, take a five-minute cab ride over here; the lobby spectacle affords some of the best people-watching in the Caribbean. An $80-million redo has brought this terrific resort one of our favorite pools — it's Olympic-size; has whirlpools, a waterfall, and a swim-up bar; and fronts the 700-foot beach.

The hotel's 56 new suites are roomy and feature showers for two and Jacuzzi tubs in spacious bathrooms, as well as handsome Caribbean furnishings. The suites also have a more private pool in a gated area. All rooms have VCRs, CD players, mini-bars, three multi-line phones, fax/modem, and voice mail. Excellent shopping is available on-site, as well as eight bars and the island's most popular disco. (Teens were clamoring in their prom dresses when we were there last.) Six fine dining options — from southwestern to northern Italian to Chinese — include some of San Juan's finest restaurants. (See Chapter 30 for our review.)

Avenue Isla Verde (Box 2872), Isla Verde, San Juan, PR 00902. ☎ *800-468-2818, 800-WYNDHAM, or 787-791-1000. Fax: 787-791-0390. Rack rates: $395–$545 double. AE, CB, DC, MC, V. EP, MAP.*

Wyndham Old San Juan Hotel & Casino

$$$ Old San Juan

The gleaming Wyndham has a triangular structure that subtly echoes the cruise ships docked nearby yet also has classic neo-Spanish Colonial lines. The lobby, adjacent to the casino, shines with multihued tiles and mahogany. Each standard room — decorated with honey-color rugs, floral prints, and light woods — has a two-line phone, cable TV, a coffee-maker, and a hair dryer. Spacious suites also have sitting rooms, extra TVs, and mini-bars. On the ninth floor, you'll find a small patio, swimming pool, and whirlpool bath. The seventh-floor concierge level provides hassle-free check-ins and continental breakfasts.

100 Calle Brumbaugh 00901. ☎ *787-721-5100 or 800-WYNDHAM. Rack rates: $150–$350 double. Fax: 787-721-1111. AE, DISC, DC, MC, V. EP.*

Chapter 29

Settling into Puerto Rico

• •

In This Chapter

▶ Knowing what to expect when you arrive

▶ Getting around the island

▶ Discovering Puerto Rico from A to Z

• •

*Y*ou can scarcely ask for an island easier and cheaper to get to in the Caribbean than Puerto Rico, which is the gateway island to the region. You'll know that you're not in Kansas anymore — though still in a U.S. territory — from the moment you touch down on this island, which is about half the size of New Jersey and two hours by plane from Miami, Florida. You'll feel at least 1,000 miles away (which you are!) when you hear Spanish being spoken all around you.

Arriving in Puerto Rico

The **Luis Muñoz Marin International Airport** (☎ 787-791-4670), east of downtown San Juan, is one of the easiest and cheapest destinations to reach in the Caribbean. It's also the Caribbean's premier airport — clean, safe, spacious, and modern. It reminds us somewhat of the Miami airport with its tropical flair.

Luis Muñoz Marin International Airport is the Caribbean hub for American Airlines, which has nonstop flights from New York, Newark, Miami, and many other North American cities. American has 82 daily departures, serving 21 Caribbean destinations. Several other major airlines serve the Caribbean from this airport, too. Both Delta and TWA are negotiating to increase their presence at press time. That means it's also the busiest Caribbean airport, so expect bustling crowds.

If you are a U.S. citizen or resident, you don't have to go through Customs and Immigration at the airport, because Puerto Rico is a U.S. territory. Just follow the signs to ground transportation. U.S. citizens do not need a passport to visit Puerto Rico.

If you're worn out from traveling and have a layover at this airport, get the kinks in your neck, back, and shoulders worked out at **Diamond Point International Massage** (☎ 787-253-3063). You'll find it near gates 4 and 5; the cost is $1 per minute. If you want a foot massage, you can pay $20 for a 15-minute session. For the same cost, you can get 15 minutes of aromatherapy treatment. MC and V accepted; open seven days a week from 9 a.m. to 6 p.m.

If you're traveling with kids and have some time to kill (and quarters to spend), let them burn off some energy at the video arcade, which has games featuring X-Men, Cruisin' USA, and Marvel Superheroes. It has a change machine, if you need one.

Puerto Rico is an hour ahead of Miami, except when the U.S. goes on daylight saving time. (When that happens, Puerto Rico and Miami are on the same time.) Don't forget to consider whether you're losing an hour when you land here.

As soon as you arrive in Puerto Rico, grab several of the island's terrific materials for tourists. For some odd reason, we find it difficult to research this island on the Web. However, after you're on the island, you'll find a wealth of information (and great coupons that you'll want in hand if you've rented a car).

One of the better discount programs is the Fun and Savings Program ($50 per person), which offers up to $3,400 worth of savings for everything from restaurants, car rentals, hotels, shows, sightseeing tours, and more. You can sign up for it at the airport, or you can find information at hotels. For information, call ☎ **800-866-STAR** or 787-723-3135 or check the Web site www.prtourism.com.

Getting from the Airport to Your Hotel

If you're not traveling on a package deal that includes transfers to your hotel, you'll see lots of options after landing at the San Juan airport.

By taxi

Taxis are plentiful in the tourist areas, and you can expect about the same fares as you'd find in most U.S. cities. Go to the uniformed and badged official at the taxi stand, where you'll find lines of taxis waiting for a fare. Tell the official your destination, and you get a slip with your fare written on it, which you then present to your driver. Fixed rates apply only from the airport. Otherwise, most taxis are metered.

The major company at the airport is **Taxi Turísticos,** which charges set rates based on zones, so the fare depends on the destination. To Isla Verde, the fare is $8; to Condado, it's $12; to Old San Juan, it's $16.

If you're carrying more than two pieces of luggage, you'll pay an additional 50 cents per bag and another dollar for use of the trunk.

Bracero Limousine Ltd. (☎ 787-253-1133) offers minivan transport from the airport to various neighborhoods of San Juan for prices that are lower than for similar routings offered by taxis. Whenever eight to ten passengers can be accumulated, the fare for transport (with luggage) to any hotel in Isla Verde is $2.50 per person; to Condado, $3 per person; and to Old San Juan, $3.50 per person.

By car

Car rentals are easily handled at the airport, too. You'll find that all the major U.S. companies have rental desks in the ground transportation hall adjacent to baggage claim. For more information on car rentals, see the next section.

If you need a wheelchair-accessible van, you can get such a vehicle via **Wheelchair Getaway** (☎ **800-868-8028**).

Moving around Puerto Rico

Puerto Rico offers a variety of ways to make touring the island easy and enjoyable. Your preferred method may depend on how much time and money you're willing to spend.

By car

If you're staying in San Juan, you can get around on foot or by bus, taxi, and hotel shuttle, but if you venture out on the island, you should definitely rent a car.

Roads in Puerto Rico are generally good and well-marked, until you get out in the more rural areas. There, many exits just read *salida* (which means "exit"), with no indication of what town you'll be accessing. Some car-rental agencies give you a free island map when you pick up your car, but these maps lack detail and are usually out of date. Be sure to get a good map (see the "Quick Concierge" section later in this chapter) — one that's as detailed and up to date as possible.

Getting lost can be half the fun on Puerto Rico. If it happens to you, just pull off and ask locals for help. Almost everyone is bilingual, so you shouldn't have a problem communicating.

A valid driver's license from your country of origin can be used in Puerto Rico for three months. All major U.S. car rental agencies are represented on the island, including **Avis** (☎ **800-874-3556** or 787-791-2500); **Budget** (☎ **800-527-0700** or 787-791-3685); **Dollar** (☎ **800-800-4000** or 787-791-5500); **Hertz** (☎ **800-654-3030** or 787-791-0840); **National** (☎ **787-791-1805**), and **Thrifty** (☎ **787-253-2525**). Local rental companies, sometimes less expensive, include **L & M Car Rental** (☎ **800-654-3030** or 787-791-1160) and **Tropical** (☎ **877-791-2820** or 787-791-2820).

Rental rates can start as low as $30 per day (plus insurance), with unlimited mileage. Discounts are offered for long-term rentals, and insurance can be waived for those who rent with American Express or certain gold credit cards. (Be sure to check with your credit card company before renting.) Look for discount coupons in tourist magazines. Some discounts are offered for AAA membership or 72-hour advance bookings.

Most car rentals have shuttle service to or from the airport and the pickup point.

You may go *loco* with all the mixed signage: Speed limits are posted in miles per hour, but distances are listed in kilometers. Gas is sold per liter and priced accordingly. Note that many service stations in the central mountains don't take credit cards.

By taxi

Taxi Turisticos, which are painted white and bear the company's logo on the doors, is the major company in the tourist areas. It charges set rates based on zones, so your cost will depend on your destination. These taxis run from the airport or the cruise ship piers to Isla Verde, Condado/Ocean Park, and Old San Juan, with rates ranging from $6–$16.

Metered cabs authorized by the **Public Service Commission** (☎ 787-756-1919) have a minimum charge of $3 and an initial $1 to get rolling. After that, you're charged 10¢ for every additional ⅓ mile or every 45 seconds of waiting time. You'll also pay 50¢ for every suitcase. Be sure that the driver starts the meter. You can also call **Major Taxicabs** (☎ 787-723-2460) in San Juan and **Ponce Taxi** (☎ 787-840-0088) in Ponce.

Taxis are lined up outside the entrances to most hotels, and if not, a staff member can almost always call one for you. But if you would like to arrange a taxi on your own, call the **Rochdale Radio Taxi** (☎ 787-721-1900).

On foot

If you stay in one of the major tourist areas, you can easily tool around on foot — especially in Old San Juan, which is a walking city. If you get tired, you can always hop on Old San Juan's free trolley (which is described later in this section).

You can go on a self-guided walking tour; look for tour outlines in a copy of *Que Pasa,* available at all tourist offices and hotels. If you want to go deeper, hire a tour guide from **Colonial Adventure** (201 Recinto Sur; ☎ 787-729-0114). The company offers a variety of informative walking tours; rates range from $16–$22 per person.

By bus

The **Metropolitan Bus Authority** (☎ 787-729-1512) operates *guaguas* (buses) that thread through San Juan. The fare is 25¢ on a regular bus and 50¢ on a Metrobus. Depending on the route, the buses run in exclusive lanes on major thoroughfares, stopping at magenta, orange, and white signs marked PARADA or PARADA DE GUAGUAS. The main terminals are Covadunga parking lot and Plaza de Colón in Old San Juan, and Capetillo Terminal in Río Piedras, next to the central business district. Buses are comfortably air-conditioned, but sometimes they are crowded and don't always run on schedule. We'd only use them if our funds were exceptionally tight.

Publicos (public cars), with yellow license plates ending in "P" or "PD," scoot to towns throughout the island, stopping in each town's main plaza. These 17-passenger vans operate primarily during the day, with routes and fares fixed by the Public Service Commission. In San Juan, the main terminals are at the airport and at Plaza Colón on the waterfront in Old San Juan.

Information about publico routes between San Juan and Mayagüez is available from **Linea Sultana,** Calle Esteban González 898, Urbanización Santa Rita, Rio Piedras (☎ 787-765-9377). Information about publico routes between San Juan and Ponce is available from **Choferes Unidos de Ponce,** Terminal de Carros Publicos, Calle Vive in Ponce (☎ 787-764-0540) or **Linea Boricua** (☎ 787-765-1908).

If you want to deviate from the predetermined routes, you'll pay more by waving down a publico than if you wait for a publico beside the main highway. Fares from San Juan to Mayaguez run $16–$30; from San Juan to Ponce, $15–$25. Although prices are admittedly low, the routes are slow, with frequent stops, an often erratic routing, and lots of inconvenience.

By trolley

If your feet fail you in Old San Juan, climb aboard the free open-air trolleys that rumble and roller-coast through the narrow streets. Departures are from the Covadonga parking lot in the southeastern corner of the city. The trolleys cover two routes: up to Plaza de Armas, and a northern route to El Morro. Passengers can get on and off at any stop.

By ferry

The **Ferry de Cataño** (☎ 787-788-1155) crosses San Juan Bay between Old San Juan (Pier 2) and costs a mere 50¢ one-way. It runs every half hour from 6 a.m. to 10 p.m. The 400-passenger ferries of the **Fajardo Port Authority** (☎ 787-863-0705), which carry cargo as well as passengers, make the 90-minute trip between Fajardo and Vieques three times daily ($2 one-way). They make the 90-minute run from Fajardo to Culebra twice a day on weekdays and twice (with three runs from Culebra to Fajardo) on weekends ($2.50 one-way).

Quick Concierge

ATMs
These machines are called ATH on Puerto Rico, but they operate the same as ATMs and are widely available on the island. You'll find one at the airport near Gate 4.

Baby-sitters
Expect to pay $7 and up per hour.

Banks
Most major U.S., Canadian, and European banks have branches in San Juan and are open weekdays from 8:30 a.m. to 2:30 p.m. and Saturday from 9:45 a.m. to noon.

Credit Cards
All major credit cards are widely accepted on the island.

Currency Exchange
Puerto Rico, as a commonwealth of the United States, uses the U.S. dollar as its official currency.

Departure Tax
Airport departure tax is included in the price of your ticket.

Doctors
Puerto Rico has an excellent healthcare system. Ask your hotel for a referral if necessary.

Electricity
Puerto Rico uses a 110-volt AC (60-cycle) electrical system, the same as in North America. European guests who have traveling appliances that use other systems can call ahead to confirm that their hotel has adapters and converters.

Emergencies
Ambulance, police, and fire: ☎ **911.**

Hospitals
If you need hospital care, contact one of the following: **Ashford Presbyterian Community Hospital** (1451 Av. Ashford, Condado, San Juan; ☎ 787-721-2160); **Bella Vista Hospital** (Cerro las Mesas, Mayagüez; ☎ 787-834-6000 or 787-834-2350); the clinic **Eastern Medical Associates** (267 Av. Valero, Fajardo; ☎ 787-863-0669), and **San Juan Health Centre** (200 Av. de Diego, San Juan; ☎ 787-725-0202).

Homework
Listen to native son Ricky Martin's latest release.

Information
Contact the **Puerto Rico Tourism Company** (Box 902-3960, Old San Juan Station, San Juan, PR 00902-3960; ☎ 800-223-6530, from the United States, or 787-721-2400; Internet: www.prtourism.com). Other branches are located at: 3575 W. Cahuenga Blvd., Suite 560, Los Angeles, CA 90068; ☎ 213-874-5991; and 901 Ponce de León Blvd., Suite 601, Coral Gables, FL 33134; ☎ 305-445-9112.

Government and tourism-company information offices are also found at **Luis Muñoz Marín International Airport** in Isla Verde (☎ 787-791-1014 or 787-791-2551); La Casita (☎ 787-722-1709); at **Plaza Darsenas** near Pier 1 in Old San Juan (open until 8 p.m. Monday through Wednesday and Saturday); and at **La Playita la Condado,** the small public beach at the Condado Plaza Hotel.

Further out on the island, information offices are in Ponce (Fox Delicias Mall, 2nd floor, Plaza Las Delicias; ☎ 787-840-5695); Aguadilla (Rafael Hernández Airport; ☎ 787-890-3315); Cabo Rojo (Rte. 100, Km 13.7; ☎ 787-851-7070), and in many towns' city halls on the main plaza. Offices are usually open weekdays from 8 a.m. to noon and from 1 to 4:30 p.m.

Language
Puerto Rico's official language is Spanish. Although English is widely spoken, you'll probably want to take a Spanish phrase book with you, especially if you plan to travel beyond San Juan.

Maps

On Puerto Rico, the **Puerto Rico Tourism Company** (Paseo de la Princesa, Old San Juan, PR 00901; ☎ 787-721-2400) is an excellent source for maps and printed tourist materials. Be sure to pick up a free copy of *Qué Pasa* and *Bienvenidos,* the official visitors' guide.

Newspapers/Magazines

Getting publications from all over the world is easy on this island. You'll find excellent newsstands at the airport. The *San Juan Star* comes out daily in English and Spanish.

Pharmacies

The most common and easily found pharmacies are **Puerto Rico Drug Company** (157 Call San Francisco, Old San Juan; ☎ 787-725-2202) and **Walgreens** (1330 Av. Ashford, Condado, San Juan; ☎ 787-725-1510). Walgreens operates more than 30 pharmacies on the island. Condado has one that is open 24 hours a day (☎ 787-725-1510).

Police

For assistance with a police emergency, ☎ 911.

Post Office

Post offices in major Puerto Rican cities offer Express Mail next-day service to the U.S. mainland and to Puerto Rican destinations.

Major post office branches are located at 153 Calle Fortaleza in Old San Juan, 163 Avendia Fernandez Juncos in San Juan, 60 Calle McKinley in Mayagüez, and 102 Calle Garrido Morales in Fajardo. Post offices are open weekdays from 7:30 a.m. to 4:30 p.m. and Saturday from 8 a.m. to noon.

Safety

San Juan, like any other big city, has its share of crime, so guard your wallet or purse on the city streets. Puerto Rico's beaches are open to the public, and muggings can occur at night even on the beaches of the posh Condado and Isla Verde tourist hotels. Although you certainly can, and should, explore the city and its beaches, use common sense. Don't leave anything unattended on the beach. Leave your valuables in the hotel safe, and stick to the fenced-in beach areas of your hotel. Always lock your car and stash valuables and luggage out of sight. Avoid deserted beaches at night. Surfers have had several problems with gear being stolen from rental cars.

Store hours

Street shops are open Monday through Saturday from 9 a.m. to 6 p.m. (9 a.m. to 9 p.m. during Christmas holidays). Mall stores tend to stay open later, until 8 or 9 p.m. in most cases.

Taxes

Some hotels automatically add a 10%–15% service charge to your bill. Check ahead to confirm whether this charge is built into the room rate or will be tacked on at checkout. Some smaller hotels might charge extra (as much as $5 per day) for the use of air-conditioning, called an "energy tax." The government tax on rooms is 9% (11% in hotels with casinos and 7% on paradores). As with service charges, you'll need to confirm whether or not the tax is built into the room rate.

Telephone

Puerto Rico's area code is 787 — for North Americans, dialing Puerto Rico is the same as dialing another state in the U.S. or a Canadian province. When making a call on the island, just dial the seven-digit number.

Time Zone

Puerto Rico is in Atlantic Standard Time, one hour ahead of Eastern Standard Time and the same as Eastern Daylight Time. For the current time of day, call ☎ 787-728-9696.

Tipping

Tips are expected, and appreciated, by restaurant waitstaff (15%–18% if a service charge isn't included), hotel porters ($1 per bag), maids ($1–$2 per day), and taxi drivers (10%–15%).

Water

Tap water is generally fine on the island; just avoid drinking it after storms (when the drinking-water supply might become mixed with sewage). Thoroughly wash or peel produce that you buy in markets before eating it.

Weather Reports

Log on to the Caribbean Weather Man at the Web site www.caribwx.com/cyclone.html or listen to Radio WOSO (1030 AM), an English-speaking radio station.

Chapter 30

Dining in Puerto Rico

· ·

In This Chapter

▶ Sampling the local cuisine

▶ Saving money on meals

▶ Locating the island's best restaurants

· ·

*I*f eating well is a key part of your vacation, you'll love Puerto Rico. Old San Juan is known as a haven for cutting-edge chefs who win rave reviews from food enthusiasts. But you can also linger over a simple down-home meal that fuses the best of Puerto Rico's Spanish and Caribbean heritage.

If you want to splurge on one of Puerto Rico's many chic restaurants, remember that this is an island where appearance matters. Ladies should pack high heels and an attitude; gents should bring their finest resort wear. You won't be shut out of a restaurant because you don't look the part, but the right dress and approach will help to determine how you're treated. Wherever you go, make reservations during the busy season (mid-November through April).

In most of the other dining chapters, we concentrate our recommendations on restaurants outside of hotels. However, Puerto Ricans love to dress up and dine out, and the scene at the over-the-top weekend extravaganza that happens at their beloved El San Juan every week, which has numerous terrific restaurants, has trained the locals to expect great cuisine from the hotels.

Enjoying a Taste of Puerto Rico

Puerto Rican cuisine involves many local vegetables. Plantains are prepared several ways: They are fried while still green to make savory *tostones;* baked when ripe to make sweet *amarillos;* and shaved into chips. Rice and beans with tostones or amarillos are basic accompaniments to every dish.

Locals cook white rice with *habichuelas* (red beans) and saffron; brown rice with *gandules* (pigeon peas); and *morro* (black rice) with *frijoles negros* (black beans). *Sofrito* — a puree of garlic, onion, sweet pepper, coriander, oregano, and tomato — is used as a base for practically everything. Beef, chicken, pork, and seafood are rubbed with *adobo,* a garlic-oregano marinade, before cooking. *Arroz con pollo* (chicken with rice), *sancocho* (beef and tuber soup), *asopao* (a soupy rice gumbo with chicken or seafood), and *encebollado* (steak smothered in onions) are all typical plates.

Favorite snacks are *empanadillas* (fried turnovers stuffed with either meat or vegetables), *surrullitos* (cheese-stuffed corn sticks), *alcapurias* (stuffed green-banana croquettes), and *bacalaitos* (codfish fritters). Local *pan de agua* is an excellent French-loaf bread, best hot out of the oven.

Local desserts include *flan* (custards blanketed with caramel), puddings, and fruit paste served with native white cheese. We love the strong Puerto Rican coffee, but we need to tone it down *con leche* (with hot milk).

If you want great food for little *dinero,* look for *comidas criollas* (traditional Caribbean-Creole meals). *Mesones gastronomicos* are restaurants designated as such by the Puerto Rico Tourism Company for preserving island culinary traditions and maintaining high standards. You have your choice of more than 40 of these restaurants island-wide.

Puerto Rico's Best Restaurants

Any one of the following restaurants will give you a taste of the best the island has to offer.

Ajili-Mójili

$$$ **Condado**   **Puerto Rican/Creole**

Chef Mariano Ortiz elevates *comida criolla,* the starchy, sometimes greasy cuisine that developed on the island a century ago, to an art form. The popular restaurant, in a modern building across from the Convention Center, is owned by Jose and Rafael Benitez. But look for artfully crumbling brick walls you'd expect in Old San Juan and a bar that evokes something right out of a colony of Spain a century ago, and you'll be in the right place.

If you want to learn about what *mamacita* cooked, come here and let the staff explain these tasty dishes to you. A few examples: *mofongos* (green plantains stuffed with veal, chicken, shrimp, or pork); *arroz con pollo* (stewed chicken with saffron rice); *medallones de cerdo encebollado* (pork loin sauteed with onions); and *lechon asado con maposteado* (roast pork with rice and beans). Have an ice-cold bottle of Medalla, or another local beer.

1052 Av. Ashford (at the corner of Calle Joffre). ☎ *787-725-9195. Reservations required. Main courses: $16–$34. AE, MC, V. Open for lunch Sunday through Friday and dinner nightly.*

Restaurants in Old San Juan

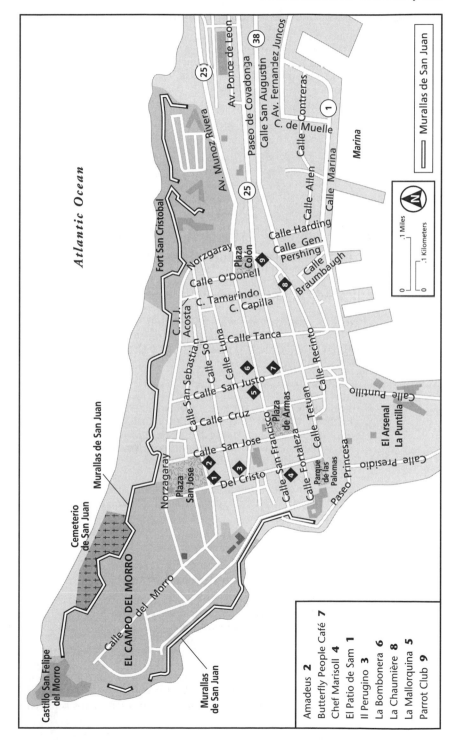

Amadeus **2**
Butterfly People Café **7**
Chef Marisoll **4**
El Patio de Sam **1**
Il Perugino **3**
La Bombonera **6**
La Chaumière **8**
La Mallorquina **5**
Parrot Club **9**

Amadeus

$$–$$$ Old San Juan   Contemporary Puerto Rican

Head straight through the outside passage to the romantic dining room in the back of the restaurant, where you'll find printed tablecloths, candles, and exposed brick. Among the appetizers is an excellent plantain mousse with shrimp. Escargots, cheese ravioli with a goat-cheese-and-walnut sauce, and Cajun-grilled mahimahi are a few of the delectable entrees. For a main course, try the chicken breast with escargots and mushrooms.

106 Calle San Sebastian. ☎ *787-722-8635. Reservations recommended. Main courses: $7–$22. AE, MC, V. Open for lunch and dinner Tuesday through Sunday and for dinner only on Monday.*

Back Street Hong Kong

$$$$ Isla Verde   Mandarin/Szechuan/Hunan

This landmark restaurant — one of half a dozen in the ever-popular El San Juan — consistently gets high marks for its Chinese cuisine. We haven't come across another place in the Caribbean that approaches this fantastical setting. To enter, you walk down a re-creation of a backwater street in Hong Kong. Disassembled from its original home at the 1964 New York World's Fair, the set was rebuilt here with the original design intact. Beneath a soaring redwood ceiling, you'll enjoy pineapple fried rice served in a juicy island pineapple, or a Dragon and Phoenix (lobster mixed with shrimp).

We enjoyed the food, and the service was grand, but Back Street wasn't our favorite restaurant at the hotel. (See our review of La Piccola Fontana in this section.) Still, this definitely satisfied our yen and dim sum, and we're extremely picky about Chinese food — spoiled as we've become by a favorite New York Szechuan restaurant around the block when we lived in the city B.C. (Before Children).

In the El San Juan Hotel & Casino, Isla Verde Ave. ☎ *787-791-1000. Reservations recommended. Main courses: $16.50–$31.50. AE, MC, V. Open daily for dinner at 5:30 p.m.*

Butterfly People Café

$$ Old San Juan   Continental/American

This restaurant's appeal has less to do with the food than with the unique setting. Here, next to the world's largest gallery devoted to butterflies, you can dine on the second floor of a restored mansion and overlook a courtyard. The cuisine is tropical, light European fare made with fresh ingredients. Go for the zesty gazpacho and maybe follow with a slice of quiche. A full bar offers tropical specialties such as piña coladas, fresh-squeezed orange juice, and Fantasias — a frappé of seven fresh fruits. Except for a gallery in New York City, we've never encountered any other place like this, where the walls are decorated with butterflies.

Calle Fortaleza 152. ☎ 787-723-2432. Main courses: $4.50–$10. AE, DC, MC, V. Open Monday through Saturday from 10 a.m. to 6 p.m.

Chef Marisoll

$$$$ Old San Juan Continental

We were lured into Chef Marisoll by the dramatic arrangement of tables in a palm-studded courtyard overhung with ornate balconies; more tables were tucked into high-ceilinged rooms on either side. After making our reservation a day in advance, we were even more intrigued to learn that Chef Marisoll Hernández is one of the top chefs in Puerto Rico — one of the few women to achieve that acclaim.

We were escorted to a table with dark wood furnishings and colorful, eye-catching art on the walls. When the first dish arrived, we decided that Chef must have been the art buyer, too. Her dishes were works of art, almost too pretty to eat. Starters were a butternut squash soup with crisp ginger and smoked lobster tails over a seaweed salad. Our main course was fillet of halibut with roasted elephant garlic and sun-dried tomatoes in a cream sauce. For dessert, try Chef Marisoll's specialty — creme caramel. The one thing that marred our evening slightly was the uneven service; at the prices we were paying, we expected perfection.

202 Calle Cristo. ☎ 787-725-7454. Reservations required. Main courses: $24–$30. AE, MC, V. Dinner from 7 p.m. to 10:30 p.m. Closed Mondays. Lunch served Thursday through Saturday from noon to 2:30 p.m.

El Patio de Sam

$$–$$$ Old San Juan Eclectic

A warm dark-wood and faux-brick interior and a wide selection of beers make Sam's a popular late-night hangout. The menu is mostly steaks and seafood, with a few native dishes mixed in. Try the Samuel's Special pizza, with mozzarella, tomato sauce, beef, pepperoni, and black olives; it feeds two or three. The flan here melts in your mouth. Sam's has live entertainment from Monday through Saturday, with a guitarist playing Spanish music some nights and a classical pianist performing other nights.

102 Calle San Sebastian. Across from the Iglesia de San José ☎ 787-723-1149. Main courses: $17.50–$22. AE, DISC, DC, MC, V. From 11 a.m. to 11 p.m. daily.

Horned Dorset Primavera

$$$$–$$$$$ Rincón French

This restaurant, tucked away on the west coast of the island in the posh Horned Dorset Primavera hotel, is where foodies head when they want to get out of Old San Juan. Owners Harold Davies and Kingsley Wratten take their dining room seriously. Tropical accents appear here and there, but the cuisine is heavily Cordon Bleu–influenced: Filet mignon in a mushroom sauce, grilled squab in a black currant sauce, and grilled fish du jour are staples here. A five-course, prix-fixe menu is available for $56 per person. This restaurant helped the hotel achieve one of only a handful of Relais & Chateaux designations awarded in all of the Caribbean.

Rte. 429, Km 3, Rincón. ☎ **787-823-4030** *or 787-823-4050. Main courses: $56–$88. AE, MC, V. Open for dinner from 7 p.m. to 9:30 p.m. nightly.*

Il Perugino

$$$–$$$$ Old San Juan   Italian

The best Italian restaurant in Old San Juan, this small, intimate eatery set in a 200-year-old townhouse stresses attentive service and delicious Italian cuisine. The entire setting is painted in shades of ochre and umber reminiscent of Perugia, the homeland of owner/chef Franco Seccarelli. He does a beautiful carpaccio of scallops and a perfectly marinated fresh salmon. Another good dish: "black pasta" with crayfish and baby eels. Daily specials sometimes add variety to the menu. Don't miss the tiramisu, a killer dessert. A choice from the excellent wine cellar, housed in the former cistern, completes the experience.

105 Calle Cristo. ☎ **787-722-5481.** *Main courses: $18–$31. MC, V. Open daily for dinner from 6:30 p.m. to 11p.m. Call for reservations after 4 p.m.*

La Bombonera

$ Old San Juan   Café

This landmark restaurant, with its ornate streetside facade, was established in 1902 and is known for its strong Puerto Rican coffee and excellent pastries. We spent an afternoon here, people-watching and enjoying the atmosphere. If your grandmother was Puerto Rican, this food is what you'd get at her house: flavorful chicken soup, peas and rice, and sweet plantains. Full breakfasts are served until 11 a.m. It's a favorite Sunday-morning gathering place.

259 Calle San Francisco. ☎ **787-722-0658.** *Main courses: under $15. AE, MC, V. Open for breakfast, lunch, and dinner daily from 7:30 a.m. to 8:15 p.m.*

La Chaumiére

$$$$ Old San Juan   French

Behind the famous Tapla Theater, this restaurant with a cafélike decor has a loyal following drawn to its classic cuisine. The menu thrills Francophiles, who feast on the country paté and then follow with a rack of baby lamb Provençale. Two old standbys, veal Oscar and oysters Rockefeller, are given new life in this flowery setting.

Calle Tetuán 367. ☎ **787-722-3330.** *Reservations recommended. Main courses: $21.50–$32.50. AE, DC, MC, V. Open for dinner Monday through Saturday from 6 p.m. to 9 p.m. Closed July through August.*

La Mallorquina

$$–$$$ Old San Juan   Latin

The food here is basic Puerto Rican and Spanish fare (such as *paella,* the famous saffron rice dish). The decor consists of peach walls and whirring ceiling fans, and the staff is neatly attired and friendly. But the atmosphere itself recommends this spot. La Mallorquina dates from 1848 and, hence, is considered Puerto Rico's oldest restaurant.

207 Calle San Justo. ☎ 787-722-3261. Main courses: $15–$35. AE, MC, V. Open for lunch and dinner daily from 11:30 a.m. to 10 p.m. Closed Sundays.

La Piccola Fontana

$$$$ Isla Verde   Northern Italian

What a surprise! We weren't expecting our experience at the El San Juan to involve an Italian restaurant, but this formal place serving classic northern Italian cuisine blew us away. Dining is an event here, but the delectable food is unpretentious and served in an endearing fashion — almost as if the waitstaff knows you came with somewhat low expectations. We'd been put on guard by the two neo-Palladian dining rooms whose frescoed walls, painted by a visiting French artist a few years ago, depict Italy's ruins and landscapes.

Menu items range from the appealingly straightforward and simple (such as grilled fillets of fish or grilled veal chops) to such elaborate dishes as tortellini San Daniele (made with veal, prosciutto, cream, and sage) or linguine scogliere (with shrimps, clams, and other seafood). Scallopine of veal is delicious with lemon and white wine sauce, and grilled medallions of filet mignon are served with braised arugula, Parmesan cheese, and balsamic vinegar. Now *that's* Italian.

In the El San Juan Hotel & Casino, 6063 Av. Isla Verde Ave. ☎ 787-791-0966. Reservations required. Main courses: $17–$35. AE, MC, V. Open daily for dinner from 6 p.m. to 10 p.m.

Parrot Club

$$$ Old San Juan   Contemporary Puerto Rican

Currently, the red-hot restaurant (and beautiful people's second home) in Old San Juan is this deservedly crowded bistro and bar serving a Nuevo Latino cuisine. Chef Roberto Trevino skillfully blends traditional Puerto Rican cookery with Spanish, Taíno, and African influences, then accents with rich, contemporary touches. The gorgeous setting elevates the experience further — the restaurant is housed in a circa-1902 building that once served as a hair-tonic factory, in a neighborhood known as SOFO (South of Fortaleza Street). In the lushly landscaped courtyard, seating for at least 200 is scattered amid potted ferns, palms, and orchids. Live music, classic Cuban, wild salsa, or Latino jazz, is the norm every night of the week, as well as during the popular Sunday brunches.

We adore Trevino's concoctions, such as fresh fish ceviche nuevo latino and Parrot Club crabcakes caribeños. For a main course, try seared pork medallions with sweet plantain chorizo or sugar-cured lamb on skewers with Israeli cous-cous. Menu items are purely based on updated interpretations of old-fashioned Puerto Rican specialties. Everybody's favorite drink is a "parrot passion" that's made from lemon-flavored rum, triple sec, oranges, and passion fruit. The owners of this place, Emilio Figueroa and his wife Gigi Zafero, learned their restaurant-keeping craft well, thanks to stints in places as diverse as Spain, Key West, Miami, and New Orleans.

363 Calle Fortaleza. ☎ 787-725-7370. Reservations not accepted. Lunch main courses $8.50–$13; brunch main courses $13.50–$17; dinner main courses $16–$24. AE, MC, V. Open for lunch and dinner daily. Closed Mondays and for two weeks in July.

Chapter 31

Hitting the Beach and Other Fun Things to Do

. . . .

In This Chapter

▶ Soaking up the sun on Puerto Rico's top beaches

▶ Diving into fun with watersports

▶ Satisfying the landlubber: Activities, shopping, and nightlife

▶ Planning some super side trips

. . . .

*I*n this chapter, we hit the high points of the most diverse destination in the Caribbean: Puerto Rico. From the glorious art scene of the beautifully restored Spanish Colonial city of Old San Juan to dramatic rain forests, gargantuan caves, 18 golf courses, and beaches boasting activities from whale watching to surfing, Puerto Rico is like the most lavish buffets on the cruise ships that make San Juan the Caribbean's busiest port. If you can't find something you like on Puerto Rico, you aren't really hungry for a good time.

On our whirlwind tour, we give you the lay of the land (and sea) of Puerto Rico's beaches, followed by a guide to watersports galore, from diving to deep sea fishing. We give you the scoop on Puerto Rico's passion for horses, hiking, spelunking, and just about anything to do with sports. We wind up with a look at Puerto Rico's rollicking fiesta of a nightlife scene, a tempest and trendsetter among all the islands in this book. Finally, we island-hop Puerto Rican–style, exploring Puerto Rico's Spanish Virgins.

Spending a Day (or More) at the Beach

Much of the action on Puerto Rico revolves around its excellent beaches, which are well appreciated by locals as well as tourists. On some Caribbean islands, you'll see only a handful of islanders on any given day at the beach. Puerto Ricans relish their sand and surf, flocking to the waterfront to enjoy the warmth and beauty of the place they call home. With almost 300 miles of shoreline, you'll see everything from blanket-to-blanket beach fiestas on city beaches to white-sand crescents so far removed that the locals haven't even given them names.

The continental shelf, which surrounds Puerto Rico on three sides, gives this island an abundance of coral reefs, caves, sea walls, and trenches ideal for scuba diving and snorkeling.

By law, all Puerto Rican *playas* (beaches) are open to the public. The government runs 13 *balnearios* (public beaches), which have dressing rooms, lifeguards, guarded parking, police, and in some cases, cafeterias, gazebos, picnic tables, playgrounds, and camping facilities. Admission is free, but parking is $2. Most balnearios are open from 9 a.m. to 5 p.m. Tuesday through Sunday. When a holiday falls on a Monday, they are open on the holiday and closed the following day. For more information, you can contact the **Department of Recreation and Sports** (☎ 787-722-1551 or 787-724-2500).

Sometimes, residents as well as visitors forget that trash cans serve a purpose in life. At the end of a day of picnicking, families occasionally leave evidence of their fun behind — on the ground, just waiting for the lift of a tropical breeze. The government has been campaigning to make people more sensitive to the problem, but awareness seems to require ongoing reminders.

Puerto Ricans love the beach. So if you plan to hit the sand on the weekend or a holiday, go early to beat traffic and stake a good spot.

You can get off the plane and be on the beach in 15 minutes at **Condado/Isla Verde,** white-sand stretches dominated by high-rise resort hotels. This area made us think of Miami Beach (the buildings) meshed with Negril's Seven Mile Beach (the people, with a Spanish twist, of course). Set near San Juan, the most lively of these is **Carolina Beach,** punctuated with tall coconut palms and jammed with city folk mingling with resort guests. Boom boxes blare, young women dare with their barely-theres, and vendors happily sell colorful *pareos* (island wraps), anklets, T-shirts, and cheap eats. You can find plenty of places to rent watersports equipment around, too.

Ocean Park, a residential neighborhood just east of the Condado, is home to San Juan's prettiest beach. The waters off this wide, one-mile-long (1½ km) stretch of fine golden sand are often choppy, but you can still swim. On weekends, local college students rule the popular strand. It's also one of two beaches that are popular with the gay community. (The other is in front of the Atlantic Beach Hotel.)

The polar opposite of these city beaches is on scenic Route 115, where you'll find Punta Higuero near Rincón, the site of the World Surfing Championship in 1968. Skilled surfers flock here in winter, when the water is rough and challenging. Locals boast that the best diving and snorkeling in Puerto Rico (and some even say the Caribbean) is off the Rincón coast, particularly around the island of Desecheo, a federal wildlife preserve. Whale-watching is another draw for this town; endangered humpback whales winter off the coast from December through February.

Only 30 miles east of San Juan (Highway 3 at km-marker 35.4 near the town of Luquillo) lies one of Puerto Rico's finer beaches: crescent-shaped **Playa Luquillo,** nicknamed the "Sun Capital." It boasts calm blue waters fringed by coconut groves and palms. Once a flourishing coconut plantation, the site provides changing rooms, lockers, showers, picnic tables, tent sites, and stands that sell savory Puerto Rican delicacies. Coral reefs protect its crystal-clear lagoon from the Atlantic waters, making it an ideal place to swim. This beach is one of the island's largest and best-known strips of sand, so you can expect lots of company on the weekends.

Luquillo has a unique wheelchair-accessible program called *Mar Sin Barreras* or "sea without barriers," which allows physically challenged people to bask in the warm ocean waters. For more information, call ☎ 787-889-4329.

Fajardo's **Seven Seas** (Route 987), an elongated strip of hard-packed sand east of Luquillo, is always popular with sun-worshippers. It has precious little shade. If you want to picnic, the beach has tables as well as tent and trailer sites. Snorkeling, scuba diving, and boat rentals are nearby.

Dorado Beach, Cerromar Beach, and **Palmas del Mar** are the chief centers for those who crave golf, tennis, and excellent beaches. San Juan's hotels on the Condado/Isla Verde coast also offer a full array of watersports.

The beautiful **Playa Flamenco** is on the north shore of **Culebra** Island. The 3-mile-long (5 km) crescent has shade trees, picnic tables, and rest rooms and is popular on weekends with day-trippers from Fajardo, which is a springboard for the many little cays dotting the area. In winter, storms in the Atlantic often create great waves for bodysurfing. **Playa Soni,** on the eastern end of Culebra, is a wide strand of sparkling white sand on a protected bay with calm waters. The views of the islets of Culebrita, Cayo Norte, and St. Thomas are stunning. Bring lots of water and an umbrella to cope with a lack of facilities and shade. **Playa Sombé** (Sun Bay; Route 997), a white-sand beach on Vieques Island, has shade trees, picnic tables, and tent sites and offers snorkeling and scuba diving concessions. Boat rentals are nearby. If you really want to skip the hordes, go to the oft-deserted beaches on U.S. Navy land: **Green Beach** for snorkeling, **Red Beach** for sunbathing, or **Blue Beach** for shellcombing. The little-known **Guanica's Cana Gorda** is a tucked-away beach with only a subtle clue that anyone has been here before — palm fronds dotting the sandscape.

Whetting Your Appetite for Water Fun

The crystal-clear Caribbean may inspire you to dive right in and cool off in refreshing waters during your stay in Puerto Rico.

Diving Puerto Rican waters

You're not likely to find Puerto Rico at the top of a diver's list of favorite spots among the Caribbean islands. For one thing, all the fishing in its waters means that you won't see many larger fish. However, both hard and soft corals are still abundant and in good to great shape at many sites. The island's many caves, mangrove swamps that serve as fish nurseries, and two bioluminescent bays for night dives all offer rich prospects for diving adventure.

Check out your dive operator thoroughly. Reaching some of the better sites requires a lengthy boat trip. Some operators have acquired a reputation for trying to pawn off more accessible sites with little marine life when a little more effort would transport divers to pristine reefs with far more action. Plus, you don't want to be on an old boat spewing fumes if you have to travel far. Seasickness is no fun anytime — especially when you're paying the toll for an island experience that you want to remember with some fondness.

You can also find some fairly pristine sites from Puerto Rico's offshore islands. Popular among divers is tiny **Desecheo Island,** about 15 miles (24 km) off the coast of Rincón in the west. The rocky ocean floor around the base of the islet is full of coral and tropical fish, as well as several rock terraces and caverns. **The Cracks,** just off the coast from **Humacao** in the east, are large fissures in the reef in which fish and other marine life feed. The whimsically named **Magical Mystery Tour,** known for its maze of tunnels and shimmering coral, lies in depths of 40 feet off **Culebra** (18 miles from Fajardo) in the northwest. To the east, popular dive sites off Fajardo range from 25–70 feet in depth and feature lots of hard corals as well as a good variety of marine life.

You can locate package deals combining accommodations with daily diving trips. Escorted half-day dives range from $45–$90 for one- and two-tank dives, including all equipment. Packages, which include lunch and other extras, start at $60. Plan to pay at least double for a night dive. Snorkeling excursions, which include transportation (most often a sailboat filled with snorkelers), equipment rental, and sometimes lunch, start at $40. Snorkel equipment rents at beaches for about $5–$7.

Snorkeling and scuba diving instruction and equipment rentals are available at **Boquerón Dive Shop** (Main St., Boquerón; ☎ 787-851-2155); **Caribbean School of Aquatics** (San Juan Bay Marina; ☎ 787-728-6606); **Taíno Divers** (Rincón; ☎ 787-823-6429; Internet: www.tainodivers.com); **Descheco Dive Shop** (Rincón; ☎ 888-823-0390 or 787-823-0390); and **Dive Copamarina** (Copamarina Beach Resort, Rte. 333, Km 6.5, Guánica; ☎ 787-821-6009).

You can become disoriented in even the most easily accessible caverns. (**Shacks Beach** is a good example.) Never dive or snorkel alone. Put yourself in the hands of a good guide who can help you explore underwater labyrinths.

A family of manatees (called sea cows) often grazes near **Jobos Beach.** Ask operators about swimming with them. Just remember: Look, but don't touch. We admit we're tempted, too. How often do you get a chance to pet what looks like an 800-pound puppy?

Advanced divers who are comfortable with boat dives should try **Parguera Divers Training Center** (Posada Par La Mar, Rte. 304, La Parguera; ☎ **787-899-4171**). Divemaster Efra Figueroa has been diving the walls for three decades and knows every crevice of the wall diving. Figueroa and assistant Angel Rovira put a premium on customer service, and they make sure that repeat guests don't repeat sites. Under their watchful eyes, you'll likely see nurse sharks, Atlantic spadefish, queen angelfish, and more.

Boarding the surf

When storms roll down from the northern Atlantic, nothing breaks their swells until they meet Rincón, resulting in gnarly waves as high as 20 feet from November through April. The best surfing beaches are along the Atlantic coastline from **Borinquén Point** south to **Rincón,** where you'll find several surf shops, including **West Coast Surf Shop** (2 E. Muñoz Rivera St., Rincón; ☎ **787-823-3935**). But the reefs and rocks here mean that this Surf City is better for the truly experienced. Rank beginners might meet the phrase "Knock yourself out" head-on. Novices can check out **Aviones** in Piñones east of San Juan, **La Concha** beaches in San Juan, and **Casa de Pesca** in Arecibo, all summer surfing spots that have nearby surf shops.

Spending Time on the Water without Getting Wet

If you can't imagine a trip to the Caribbean without seafaring experience as part of the picture, check out the ways you can take to the water — without jumping in.

Wandering the water's surface

Puerto Rico is great for sailors. The island's eastern ports lie within an hour or two of the Icacos and Palomino cays. Farther east are the islands of Culebra and Vieques, and beyond lies the archipelago of the Lesser Antilles. Navigating is simple, since you can see land during the day. Marinas and charter boats are found all around the island, but the biggest concentration is in the vicinity of Fajardo. Catamarans, known for their stability, are especially popular. A typical charter starts from 9:30 a.m. for a leisurely sail to Icacos. (Prices start at $50 a person; many operators will arrange your transportation to Fajardo if you're staying in San Juan.)

Ocean kayaking along lagoons and through mangrove channels has become increasingly popular in Puerto Rico.

Virtually all the resort hotels on San Juan's Condado and Isla Verde strips rent paddleboats, Sunfish, Windsurfers, and kayaks. The waves here can be strong, but the constant wind makes for good sailing. In San Juan, contact the **Condado Plaza Hotel and Casino Water-sports Center** (999 Ay. Ashford; ☎ **787-721-1000,** ext. 1361) or the **Wyndham El San Juan Hotel & Casino Watersports Center** (Av. Isla Verde; ☎ **787-791-1000**). Boating and sailing trips of all kinds are offered by **Caribbean School of Aquatics** (San Juan Bay Marina; ☎ **787-728-6606**) and **Castillo Watersports** (ESJ Towers, Isla Verde; ☎ **787-791-6195** or 787-725-7970).

Outside of San Juan, **Iguana Water Sports** (Westin Rio Mar Beach Resort and Country Club, 6000 Rio Mar Blvd., Rio Grande; ☎ **787-888-6000**) has a particularly good selection of small boats. Sailing instruction is available at the **Palmas Sailing Center** (Doral Resort at Palmas del Mar, Rte. 906, Humacao; ☎ **787-852-6000**). **East Wind II Catamaran** (Fajardo; ☎ **787-860-3434**) can fix you up with a catamaran, mate.

If oddities interest you, make plans to visit the fishing village of La Parguera, an area of simple seafood restaurants, mangrove cays, and small islands, south of San German at the end of Route 304, off Route 116. It is an excellent scuba diving area, but the main attraction is **Phosphorescent Bay.** Boats tour the bay, where microscopic *dinoflagellates* (marine plankton) light up like Christmas trees when disturbed by any kind of movement. The phenomenon can be seen only on moonless nights. Boats leave for the hour-long trip nightly from dusk until midnight, depending on demand, and the trip costs $5 per person. You can also rent or charter a small boat to explore the numerous cays.

Hooking the big one

Known as "Blue Marlin Alley," Puerto Rico wears its fish stories with pride and proof. Puerto Rico's Annual Billfish Tournament is the world's largest consecutively held competition of its kind. Puerto Rico's rich waters are home to game fish such as blue and white marlin (most prevalent in late summer), wahoo, dorado (best in November to early April), yellow and blackfin tuna, and barracuda. Catches off the island's shores have set more than 30 world records. Boats range from 34–61 feet in length. Half-day (four hours in the morning or four hours in the afternoon), full-day, split charters, and big- and small-game fishing can be arranged through **Benitez Deep-Sea Fishing** (Club Nautico de San Juan, San Juan; ☎ **787-723-2292**; fax: 787-725-4344). Other options include **Castillo Watersports** (Isla Verde; ☎ **787-791-6195**).

Outside of San Juan, try **Parguera Fishing Charters** (La Parguera; ☎ **787-899-4698** or cellular 787-382-4698) and **Tropical Fishing Charters** (Av. El Conquistador, Fajardo; ☎ **787-860-8551** or 787-759-1255).

Charter prices include food and drink; find out exactly what the host provides on board to be sure that what the captain considers lunch is enough to satisfy your appetite. Otherwise, you may want to bring a few additional snacks. Fishing excursions don't involve any extra taxes or licenses.

Enjoying the Day (and Night) on Dry Land

Puerto Rico's spectacular landscape begs for closer inspection, and you can take in the view from a variety of perspectives.

Heading to the greens

For golf lovers, Puerto Rico is paradise. In recent years, the island has hosted the LPGA tour and the Hyatt PGA Matchplay Challenge. You can pick from 18 courses on the island, 14 of which are championship links designed by the best-known names: Greg Norman; Robert Trent Jones, Sr.; George Fazio; Arthur Hills; Greg Player; and, of course, home-island hero Chi Chi Rodriguez. Call ahead for details on reserving tee times. Hours vary, and several hotel courses limit their players to guests only (or at least give preference to guests). Greens fees start at about $25 and go up as high as $114.

The island's newest courses are **Dorado del Mar** (☎ 787-796-3065), and **Flamboyan** at the Doral Resort at Palmas del Mar (Rte. 906, Humacao; ☎ 787-852-6000). The Flamboyan, a Rees Jones creation, is classic, elegant, and beautiful. The view from the twelfth hole is breathtaking, and the thirteenth hole is a showstopper. If you can't get a tee time on this course, try the property's older but revitalized Gary Player–designed Palmas course, or book time at the immense driving range.

Just 19 miles from San Juan, the **Westin Rio Mar Beach Resort and Country Club** (6000 Rio Mar Blvd., Rio Grande; ☎ 787-888-6000) has two world-class courses. Greg Norman designed the River Course, while George Fazio designed the famous Ocean Course. Both are sandwiched between the ocean and the foot of El Yunque, the only tropical rain forest in the U.S. National Forest system.

Four attractive Robert Trent Jones–designed 18-hole courses are shared by the **Hyatt Dorado Beach** and the **Hyatt Regency Cerromar Beach** hotels (Rte. 693, Km 10.8 and Km 11.8, Dorado; ☎ 787-796-1234, ext. 3238 or 3016). Some of Chi Chi's favorite holes are on these courses.

Engaging in a game of tennis

If you want to use courts at a property where you aren't a guest, call in advance for information about reservations and fees. Your best bet for playing tennis in the San Juan area are the 17 lighted courts at

San Juan Central Municipal Park (Calle Cerra, exit on Rte. 2; ☎ 787-722-1646). Fees run $3 per hour from 8 a.m. to 6 p.m. and $4 per hour from 6 p.m. to 10 p.m. Two tennis courts are available at the **Condodo Plaza Hotel and Casino** (999 Av. Ashford; ☎ 787-721-1000). Fees for nonguests range from $10–$20 per hour.

Other island-based tennis facilities include the following:

- ✔ Seven courts at the **Hyatt Dorado Beach** (Rte. 693, Km 10.8, Dorado; ☎ 787-796-1234).

- ✔ Eight courts at the **Hyatt Regency Cerromar Beach** (Rte. 693, Km 11.8, Dorado; ☎ 787-796-1234).

- ✔ Four courts at the **Ponce Hilton and Casino** (Rte. 14, 1150 Av. Caribe, Ponce; ☎ 787-259-7676).

- ✔ Thirteen courts at the **Westin Rio Mar Resort and Country Club** (6000 Rio Mar Blvd., Rio Grande; ☎ 787-888-6000).

- ✔ Twenty courts at **Doral Resort at Palmas del Mar** (Rte. 906, Humacao; ☎ 787-852-6000).

Rooting for the home team

When it comes to baseball, Puerto Ricans reach a fever pitch. If you have any fans in your family, consider taking in a ballgame on the island that's given birth to such greats as Roberto Clemente; Roberto and Sandy Alomar of the Cleveland Indians; and their father, Sandy Alomar, a former league player and coach of the San Diego Padres. The island's season runs from October through February. Stadiums are in San Juan, Santurce, Ponce, Caguas, Arecibo, and Mayaguez; the teams also play once or twice in Aguadilla. Contact the **Puerto Rico Tourism Company** (☎ 800-223-6530) for details or call **Professional Baseball of Puerto Rico** (☎ 787-765-6285).

Hiking the island

Trails lace the 28,000 acres of the Caribbean National Forest known as **El Yunque,** which is 45 minutes from San Juan (El Portal Tropical Forest Center, Highway 3 then right on Rte. 191; ☎ 787-888-1810 or 787-888-1880). This is the only tropical rain forest in the U.S. National Park system and is named a Biosphere Reserve by the United Nations.

Named after the good Indian spirit Yukiyú, the rain forest is verdant with feathery ferns, thick ropelike vines, white tuberoses and ginger, miniature orchids, and some 240 species of trees. (El Toro, the highest peak in the forest, is 3,532 feet.) El Yunque is also a bird sanctuary and the home of the rare Puerto Rican parrot. Millions of inch-long *coquis,* Puerto Rico's indigenous tree frogs, serenade you as you hike. Each year, the forest's rugged slopes shed up to 200 inches of rain. So bring good hiking shoes and a lightweight rain slicker if you plan to hike. Picnic shelters are set amid the flora, and observation towers reward the adventurous.

El Portal Tropical Forest Center features displays that explain El Yunque and tropical forests around the world. A theater holds shows in English and Spanish. The visitor's center for the forest is open daily from 7:30 a.m. to 5 p.m. (6 p.m. on weekends). El Portal has a $3 entry fee.

For more information, you can contact the Department of Natural Resources (☎ 787-724-3724) and the U.S. Forest Service (☎ 787-766-5335). We suggest planning a full day of exploring this magnificent preserve, and if you have kids along, you'll find plenty of easy trails for them to tackle.

Most San Juan hotels have a tour desk that can make arrangements for you to hike the forests. All-day tours ($25–$45) can include a trip to Ponce, a day at El Comandante Racetrack, or a combined tour of the city and E1 Yunque rain forest. Leading tour operators include **Gray Line of Puerto Rico** (☎ 787-727-8080), **Normandie Tours, Inc.** (☎ 787-722-6308), **Rico Suntours** (☎ 787-722-2080 or 787-722-6090), **Tropix Wellness Tours** (☎ 787-268-2173), and **United Tour Guides** (☎ 787-725-7605 or 787-723-5578).

Horsing around

Going to the tracks is another passion on Puerto Rico. Thoroughbred races are run year-round at **El Comandante Racetrack** (Rte. 3, Km 15.3, Canovanas; ☎ 787-876-2450), about 20 minutes east of San Juan. On race days — Wednesday, Friday, and Sunday — the dining rooms are open from 12:30 p.m. to 6 p.m. Post time is 2:30 p.m.

If you've fantasized about galloping through an island landscape, now's your chance. Puerto Rico's famous and unique paso fino horses, with their distinct gait, are often used for riding. **Hacienda Carabali** (Rte. 992, Km 4, Luquillo; ☎ 787-889-5820 or 787-889-4954) offers beach riding and rain forest trail rides. **Gaby's World** (Rte. 127, Km 5.1, Yauco; ☎ 787-856-0381) offers riding through the trails of its 200-acre ranch, as well as playgrounds and a restaurant. Beach and trail rides can be arranged for all skill levels at **Doral Resort at Palmas del Mar Equestrian Center** (Rte. 906, Humacao; ☎ 787-852-6000).

Pedaling around Puerto Rico

In general, bikers should pass up the opportunity to take to the streets if they are vacationing in San Juan or Old San Juan. The traffic is too heavy and the automobile fumes too thick. However, in the country-side, particularly along the southern coast, biking is a great way to get around. The broad beach at Boqueron makes for easy wheeling. In the southwest, you can rent bikes at **Boqueron Balnearios** (Dept. of Recreation and Sports, Rte. 101, Boqueron; ☎ 787-722-1551 or 787-722-1771), the **Copamarina Beach Resort** (Rte. 333, Km 6.5, Carla Gorda, Gufinica; ☎ 787-821-0505), and the **Ponce Hilton** (Rte. 14, 1150 Av. Caribe, Ponce; ☎ 787-259-7676). In the Dorado area on the north coast, you can rent bikes from the **Hyatt Dorado Beach** (Rte. 693, Km 10.8; ☎ 787-796-1234) or the **Hyatt Regency Cerromar Beach** (Rte. 693, Km 11.8; ☎ 787-796-1234).

Going on a shopping spree

San Juan isn't a free port, so you won't find bargains on electronics and perfumes. But what you will find, especially in Old San Juan, are beautiful locally made crafts, antiques, and art. We aren't big shoppers, but we found enough to keep us intrigued for a full day. For guidance, contact the **Puerto Rico Tourism Company's Artisan Center** (☎ 787-721-2400) or the **Fomento Crafts Project** (☎ 787-758-4747, ext. 2291).

Popular items include *santos* (small handcarved figures of saints or religious scenes), hand-rolled cigars, handmade mundillo lace from Aguadilla, *veijigantes* (colorful masks made of papier-maché and coconut husks and used during Carnival and local festivals) from Loiza, and fancy men's shirts called *guayaberas.* Also, some folks swear that Puerto Rican rum is the best in the world, but we're not rum experts, so you'll have to decide for yourself.

Old San Juan is full of shops, especially on Cristo, Fortaleza, and San Francisco Streets. The stores are all within walking distance of each other, and trolleys are plentiful. Check out these unique spots:

- ✔ **DMR Gallery** (204 Calle Luna, Old San Juan; ☎ 787- 722-4181) has handmade furniture by artist Nick Quijano.

- ✔ **Galeria Gotay** (212 Calle San Francisco, Old San Juan; ☎ 787-722-5726) carries contemporary art.

- ✔ **Galeria San Juan** (Gallery Inn, 204-206 Calle Norzagaray, Old San Juan; ☎ 787-722-1808) offers sculptures by artist Jan D'Esopo.

- ✔ The **Haitian Gallery** (367 Calle Fortaleza, Old San Juan; ☎ 787-725-0986) carries Puerto Rican crafts and a selection of folksy, often inexpensive paintings from around the Caribbean.

- ✔ The **Instituto de Cultura Puertorriquena** (98 Calle Norzagaray, Old San Juan; ☎ 787-721-6866), in the Dominican Convent on the north side of the old city, features baskets, masks, the famous cuatro guitars, santos, books and tapes, and Indian artifacts.

- ✔ **Puerto Rican Arts & Crafts** (204 Calle Fortaleza, Old San Juan; ☎ 787-725-5596) has one-of-a-kind buys.

Living la vida loca

Wherever you find *sanjuaneros* (San Juan's residents), you'll find a party going on. Puerto Ricans love their social life, and tops on their lists are dancing and dressing up. Ladies should bring their killer heels (just watch the ballast stone streets), and gentlemen should prepare to show up decked out, too.

Like New York, the whirling club scene of San Juan can be tough to keep up with. *Que Pasa,* the official visitor's guide, has current listings of the happenings in San Juan and out on the island. Also, pick up a copy of the *San Juan Star, Quick City Guide,* or *Bienvenidos,* and check with the local tourist offices and the concierge at your hotel to find out what's doing.

Fridays and Saturdays are big nights in San Juan, so dress to party. Bars are usually casual, but if you go out in jeans, sneakers, and a T-shirt, you'll probably be refused entry at most nightclubs or discos, unless you look like a model. You have to be stylish in this town.

Old San Juan's cobblestone streets are closed to auto traffic on Friday and Saturday nights, making the area perfect for a romantic stroll. If you're looking for more action, walk to **Calle San Sebastian,** lined with trendy bars and restaurants where you'll see lines of people waiting to get through the doors. Outside of San Juan, nightlife is hard to come by beyond the resorts.

If you're staying at an upscale hotel, ask the concierge if he or she can reserve a good table at the most happening spots; otherwise, you're likely to be left standing outside the gilded doors. Remember, though, the hottest action doesn't start until around 10 p.m.

Open nightly till the wee hours, the multilevel **Club Lazer** (251 Calle Cruz; ☎ 787-725-7581) has a landscaped roof deck overlooking San Juan and attracts a youthful crowd and cruise shippers looking for action; Saturday is Ladies Night.

Eros (1257 Av. Ponce de Leon, Santurce, San Juan; ☎ 787-722-1390) plays terrific dance music and is popular with the gay community. **La Fiesta Lounge** (Condado Plaza Hotel and Casino, 999 Av. Ashford, San Juan; ☎ 787-721-1000) sizzles with steamy Latin shows. A dressy crowd heads for the dance music, live performances, record parties, and fashion shows at **Club Martini's** (187 Av. Isla Verde, Isla Verde; ☎ 787-791-6100, ext. 356) on Thursday, Friday, and Saturday nights. Friday is disco night.

The place to see and be seen is the lobby of the **El San Juan Hotel & Casino,** where you can even find couples doing the merengue to live Latin bands. (A ten-member Cuban band was rocking when we were there last). The hotel's **Babylon** (☎ 787-791-2781) is the hot ticket for Puerto Ricans, but the dress is decidedly upscale so make sure you look the part.

By law, all casinos are in hotels, primarily in San Juan. The government keeps a close eye on them. Dress for the larger casinos tends to be on the formal side, and the atmosphere is refined. The law permits casinos to operate from noon to 4 a.m., but individual casinos set their own hours within that time frame. In addition to slot machines, typical games include blackjack, roulette, craps, Caribbean stud poker (a five-card stud game), and *pai gow* poker (a combination of American poker and the ancient Chinese game of *pai gow*, which employs cards and dice). Hotels that house casinos have live entertainment most week-ends, restaurants, and bars; players can usually buy drinks in the casino. The minimum age is 18.

Among the San Juan hotels that have casinos are Condado Plaza Hotel, San Juan Grand Beach Resort, San Juan Marriott, Wyndham El San Juan Hotel, and Wyndham Old San Juan Hotel. Elsewhere on the island, there are casinos at the Ponce Hilton and Casino, Wyndham El Conquistador Resort & Country Club, the Hyatt Dorado Beach and Hyatt Regency Cerromar, the Westin Rio Mar Beach Resort and Country Club, and the Doral Resort at Palmas del Mar. We prefer the casino at the Wyndham El San Juan, because you can hit the club scene if you get bored at the tables.

Exploring Old San Juan

The crown jewel of Puerto Rico is Old San Juan, the most beautiful city in the Caribbean. The original city, founded in 1521, contains carefully preserved examples of sixteenth- and seventeenth-century Spanish colonial architecture and is the oldest capital city under the U.S. flag. More than 400 buildings show off the grandeur of complete restoration. Graceful wrought-iron balconies, with lush hanging plants, extend over narrow streets paved with *adoquines* (blue-gray stones originally used as ballast for Spanish ships). Once completely surrounded by protective walls, the old city now stands partially enclosed by original structures that date from 1633.

Designated a U.S. National Historic Zone in 1950, Old San Juan is one of those rarities for the U.S.: a city rich with history and character without being marred by tacky souvenir shops and cutesy restorations. Our favorite place for strolling, Old San Juan is easy to navigate because it's laid out pretty much on a grid, like Washington, D.C., or New York City. As we wandered down the streets and in and out of terrific galleries, antique shops, and little cafes, we felt relaxed and transported to Spain.

History and art buffs will want to soak in the entire area, which requires about three days of exploring, because so many museums and old buildings compete for your attention. You may want to set aside extra time to see **El Morro** and **Fort San Cristobal,** especially if you're an aficionado of military history. UNESCO has designated each fortress a World Heritage Site; each is also a National Historic Site. Both are administered by the National Park Service; you can take one of its tours or wander on your own.

Here are some highlights of Old San Juan:

> ✔ **Casa Blanca.** The original structure on this site, not far from the ramparts of El Morro, was a frame house built in 1521 as a home for Ponce de Leon. But de Leon died in Cuba, never having lived in the house. Casa Blanca was almost destroyed by a hurricane in 1523, after which his son-in-law had the present masonry home built. His descendants occupied the house for 250 years. From the end of the Spanish-American War in 1898 to 1966, Casa Blanca was the home of the U.S. Army commander in Puerto Rico. A museum

Attractions In Old San Juan

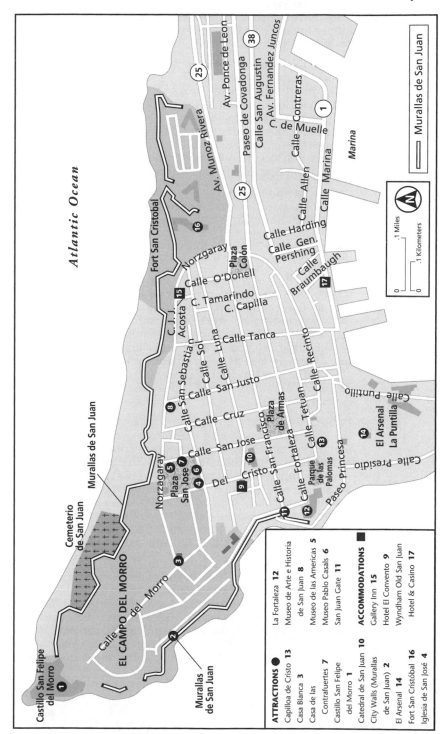

Atlantic Ocean

Marina

Murallas de San Juan

.1 Miles

.1 Kilometers

Av. Ponce de Leon

Paseo de Covadonga

Calle San Augustín

Av. Fernandez Juncos

Calle Contreras

C. de Muelle

Calle Allen

Calle Marina

C. Braumbaugh

Calle Harding

Calle Gen. Pershing

Calle O'Donell

C. Tamarindo

C. Capilla

C.T.J.

Acosta

Av. Munoz Rivera

Fort San Cristóbal

Norzgaray

Plaza Colón

Calle Sol

Calle San Sebastian

Calle Luna

Calle Tanca

Calle San Justo

Calle Cruz

Calle San Jose

Calle San Francisco

Plaza de Armas

Calle Recinto

Calle Tetuan

Calle Fortaleza

Parque de Palomas

Del Cristo

Calle Puntilla

Calle Presidio

El Arsenal

La Puntilla

Paseo Princesa

Cemeterio de San Juan

EL CAMPO DEL MORRO

Calle del Morro

Murallas de San Juan

Norzgaray

Plaza

San Jose

Castillo San Felipe del Morro

Murallas de San Juan

ATTRACTIONS ●
Capilloa de Cristo **13**
Casa Blanca **3**
Casa de las Contrafuertes **7**
Castillo San Felipe del Morro **1**
Catedral de San Juan **10**
City Walls (Murallas de San Juan) **2**
El Arsenal **14**
Fort San Cristóbal **16**
Iglesia de San José **4**

La Fortaleza **12**
Museo de Arte e Historia de San Juan **8**
Museo de las Americas **5**
Museo Pablo Casals **6**
San Juan Gate **11**

ACCOMMODATIONS ■
Gallery Inn **15**
Hotel El Convento **9**
Wyndham Old San Juan Hotel & Casino **17**

devoted to archaeology is on the second floor. The lush surrounding garden, cooled by spraying fountains, is a tranquil spot for a restorative pause. 1 Calle San Sebastian; ☎ 787-725-5584. Admission is $2. Open Tuesday through Saturday from 9 a.m. to noon and 1 p.m to 3:45 p.m.

✔ **Catedral de San Juan.** The Catholic shrine of Puerto Rico had humble beginnings in the early 1520s as a thatch-topped, wooden structure. Hurricane winds tore off the thatch and destroyed the church. Reconstruction in 1540 added a graceful circular staircase and vaulted Gothic ceilings, but most of the restoration work was done in the nineteenth century. The remains of Ponce de Leon are in a marble tomb here. 153 Calle Cristo; ☎ 787-722-0861. Open weekdays 8:30 a.m. to 4 p.m. Masses held Saturday at 7 p.m., Sunday at 9 a.m. and 11 a.m., and weekdays at 12:15 p.m.

✔ **Centro Nacional de Artes Populares y Artesanias.** Run by the Institute of Puerto Rican Culture, the Popular Arts and Crafts Center is in a colonial building next to the Casa del Libro and is a superb repository of island crafts, some of which are for sale. 253 Calle Cristo; ☎ 787-722-0621. Admission is free. Open Monday through Saturday from 9 a.m. to 5 p.m.

✔ **Convento de los Dominicos.** Built by Dominican friars in 1523, this convent often served as a shelter during Carib Indian attacks and, more recently, as headquarters for the Antilles command of the U.S. Army. Now home to the Institute of Puerto Rican Culture, the beautifully restored building contains an ornate eighteenth-century altar, religious manuscripts, artifacts, and art. The institute also maintains a bookshop here and occasionally holds classical concerts on the premises. 98 Calle Norzagaray. ☎ 787-721-6866. Admission is free. Open Monday through Saturday from 9 a.m. to 5 p.m.

✔ **La Fortaleza.** Sitting on a hill overlooking the harbor, La Fortaleza, the Western Hemisphere's oldest executive mansion in continuous use and official residence of the governor of Puerto Rico, was built as a fortress. The original primitive structure, constructed in 1540, has seen numerous changes over the past four centuries, resulting in the present collection of marble and mahogany, medieval towers, and stained-glass galleries. You can join a guided tour, conducted every hour on the hour in English and on the half hour in Spanish. Calla Recinto Oeste. ☎ 787-721-7000, ext. 2211; 787-721-7000, ext. 2211 or 2358. Admission is free. Open weekdays from 9 a.m. to 4 p.m.

✔ **Fuerte San Filipe del Morro.** On a rocky promontory on the northwestern tip of the Old City in El Morro stands an imposing fortress built by the Spaniards between 1540 and 1783. Rising 140 feet above the sea, the massive six-level fortress covers enough territory to accommodate a nine-hole golf course. El Morro is a labyrinth of dungeons, ramps and barracks, turrets, towers, and tunnels. Built to protect the port, the fortress has a commanding view of the harbor. Its small, air-conditioned museum traces the history of the site. Tours and a video show are available in English. On the broad expanse of lawn, you'll see people flying kites and playing Frisbee in the cool of day as the sun sets. Calle Norzagaray; ☎ **787-729-6960.** Admission is $2. Open daily from 9 a.m. to 5 p.m.

✔ **Museo de Arte y Historia de San Juan.** A bustling marketplace in 1855, this handsome building is now the modern San Juan Museum of Art and History. You'll find exhibits of Puerto Rican art and audiovisual shows that present the island's history. Concerts and other cultural events take place in the huge courtyard. Calla Norzagaray at Calle MacArthur; ☎ **787-724-1875.** Admission is free. Open Tuesday through Sunday from 10 a.m. to 4 p.m.

✔ **Museo Pablo Casals.** The Pablo Casals Museum contains memorabilia of the famed cellist, who made his home in Puerto Rico for the last 16 years of his life. Manuscripts, photographs, and his favorite cellos are on display, in addition to recordings and videotapes of Casals Festival concerts (the latter shown on request), 101 Calle San Sebastian, Plaza de San Jose; ☎ **787-723-9185.** Admission is $1. Open Tuesday through Saturday from 9:30 a.m. to 5:30 p.m.

✔ **San Cristobal.** This eighteenth-century fortress guarded the city from land attacks. Even larger than El Morro, San Cristobal was known in the seventeenth and eighteenth centuries as the Gibraltar of the West Indies. Calle Norzagaray; ☎ **787-729-6960.** Admission is $2. Open daily 9 a.m. to 5 p.m.

Exploring the Rest of the Island

Western Puerto Rico's 3,500 square miles (9,100 square km) is a lot of land to explore. Renting a car makes sense. Most of the roads are excellent. However, routes through the mountains are tangled and not always well-marked; buy a good road map.

Families can bank on fun and education when they visit **Parque Zoologico de Mayaguez,** a 45-acre tropical compound that's home to exotic animals from around the world. Rte. 108 at Barrio Miradero. ☎ **787-834-8110.** Admission is $3; parking $1. Open Wednesday through Sunday from 9 a.m. to 4 p.m.

Fifty miles (80 km) west of Mayaguez, in the turbulent shark-infested Mona Passage, lies **Mona Island.** Nicknamed the Galapagos of the Caribbean, Mona's population includes many endangered and unique indigenous species; the marine and bird life is breathtaking. The coastline is rimmed with imposing limestone cliffs that reach up to 200 feet. Some say that the precipices hold buried treasure. Of great archaeological value are the perfectly preserved Taino hieroglyphs and rock paintings here. You can access the island only via private plane or boat. The pristine beaches offer limited camping facilities. Call the **Department of Natural Resources** (☎ **787-723-1616** or 787-721-5495) for information and camping reservations.

If E.T. phones home, the scientists at **Observatorio de Arecibo** will catch the call. Some of the coolest scenes of James Bond's movies were filmed here, as well as the Jodie Foster film *Contact*. The town of Arecibo is home to one of the world's largest radar-radio telescopes, the size of 13 football fields. A 20-acre dish, with a 600-ton suspended platform hovering over it, sits in a 565-foot-deep sinkhole. (*Karst fields,* an alien landscape of collapsed limestone sinkholes, are the prevalent geology throughout this part of the island.) You can take a self-guided tour of the observatory, where groundbreaking work in astronomy, including SETI (the search for extraterrestrial intelligence), continues with scientists from Cornell University and the National Science Foundation.

Allow a half-day to tour this site — especially if you have budding astronomers in your family. This facility is part of the National Astronomy and Ionosphere Center of Cornell University. Rte. 625. ☎ **787-878-2612**. Admission is $3.50. Open Wednesday through Friday from noon to 4 p.m., weekends 9 a.m. to 4 p.m.

The 300-acre **Río Camuy Cave Park** reserve contains one of the world's most massive cave networks. The first tour takes you on a tram down through dense tropical vegetation to the cave entrance, where you continue on foot over underground trails, ramps, and bridges. The caves, sinkholes, and subterranean streams are all spectacular (the world's second-largest underground river runs through here), but this trip isn't for the claustrophobic. The second tour transports you via trolley to the edge of the 400-foot-deep Tres Pueblos sinkhole where the river flows to the sea. Be sure to call ahead; the tours allow only a limited number of people, and they are deservedly popular. Normally, caves don't interest us, but this one is worth the trek. Tours change slightly in the off-season. Rte. 129, Km 18.9. ☎ **787-898-3100** or 787-756-5555. Admission is $10; parking $2. Open Tuesday through Sunday from 8 a.m. to 3:45 p.m.

The area that is now the Caguana Indian Ceremonial Park — **Parque Ceremonial Indigena de Caguana** — was used 800 years ago by the Taino tribes for recreation and worship. Mountains surround a 13-acre site planted with royal palms and guava. According to Spanish historians, the Tainos played a game similar to soccer, and in this park, you can see ten of their courts, or *bateyes,* now bordered by cobbled walkways. You can also see stone monoliths — some with colorful petroglyphs — and visit a small museum and souvenir shop. Rte. 111, Km 12.3; ☎ **787-894-7325.** Admission is free. Open daily from 9 a.m. to 4:30 p.m.

If your appetite for travel includes full servings of rich history, plan to take in the charm of **Ponce.** From San German, Route 2 traverses splendid peaks and valleys; pastel houses cling to steep, green hillsides. The Cordillera Central mountains run parallel to Route 2 here and provide a stunning backdrop. East of Yauco, the road dips and sweeps right along the Caribbean and into Ponce.

Ponce's special character stems from a combination of neoclassical, Ponce Creole, and Art Deco styles. The tiny streets lined with wrought-iron balconies are reminiscent of New Orleans's French Quarter. Stop in and pick up information about this seaside city at the columned **Casa Armstrong-Poventud,** the home of the Institute of Puerto Rican Culture and a tourist information office, open weekdays 8 a.m. to noon and 1 to 4:30 p.m. (Use the side entrance.) Stroll around the Plaza Las Delicias, with its India-laurel fig trees, graceful fountains, gardens, and park benches. View the Catedral de Nuestra Senora de Guadelupe (Our Lady of Guadelupe Cathedral; masses are held daily) and walk down Calles Isabel and Christina to see turn-of-the-century wooden houses with wrought-iron balconies.

At the **Centro Ceremonial Indigena de Tibes** (Tibes Indian Ceremonial Center), you'll find pre-Taino ruins and burials dating from A.D. 300 to A.D. 700. Some archaeologists, noting the symmetrical arrangement of stone pillars, surmise the cemetery may have been of great religious significance. The complex includes a detailed re-creation of a Taino village and a museum. Rte. 503, Km 2.2. Ponce; ☎ **787-840-2255** or 787-840-5685. Admission is $2. Open Tuesday through Sunday from 9 a.m. to 4 p.m.

Most of Puerto Rico's natural habitats — mangrove swamps, coral reefs, beaches, and a dry forest — are rolled into **Reserva Natural las Cabezas de San Juan's** 316 acres. The only habitat missing is a rain forest. Nineteenth-century El Faro, one of the island's older lighthouses, is restored and still functioning; its first floor contains a small nature center that has an aquarium and other exhibits. The reserve is open, by reservation only, to the public Friday through Sunday and to tour groups Wednesday and Thursday. Tours are available on request (in advance, by phone) three times a day — in Spanish at 9:30 a.m., 10:30 a.m., and 2 p.m.; in English at 2 p.m. Rte. 987, Km 5.8. ☎ **787-722-5882** or 787-860-2560. Admission $5.

Venturing to Other Islands

Culebra, an island off Puerto Rico's east coast, has lovely white-sand beaches, coral reefs, and a wildlife refuge. In the sleepy town of Dewey (called "town" by everyone on the island) on Culebra's southwestern side, check the visitor information center at city hall (☎ 787-742-3291) for boat, bike, or car rentals. Don't miss the very pretty **Playa Flamenco,** 3 miles (5 km) north of town, or **Playa Soni** on the island's eastern end.

Vieques, located off Puerto Rico's east coast, claims fame for its **Playa Sombé** (see "Spending a Day (or More) at the Beach" earlier in this chapter), a gorgeous stretch of sand with picnic facilities and shade trees. Red and Blue beaches, on the U.S. Marine-Camp Garcia base (open to the public 6 a.m. to 6 p.m.), are superb for snorkeling and privacy. **Bahia Mosquito** (Mosquito Bay) is best experienced on moonless nights, when millions of bioluminescent organisms glow when disturbed — an amazing experience akin to being caught in a cloud of fireflies. The U.S. Navy owns 70% of Vieques, which ensures that the

natural environment will remain unspoiled. The deserted beaches —
Green, Red, Blue, Navia, and Media Luna — are among the Caribbean's
loveliest; you may even see a wild paso fine horse galloping in the surf.
The visitor information center (☎ 787-741-5000) is in the fishing village of Esperanza.

Both Vieques and Culebra, parched in contrast to the lush eastern end
of Puerto Rico, are havens for colorful expatriates escaping the rat race
stateside. We love these laid-back, fun, funky, and unspoiled islands,
the kind of getaway that's fast disappearing to the pinch of ongoing
development.

Part IX
The U.S. Virgin Islands

The 5th Wave   By Rich Tennant

"Don't worry, they may be called
St. Martin, St. John, and St. Lucia,
but you're not required to act like
one while you're there."

In this part . . .

Whether your destination is St. Thomas, St. Croix, or St. John, and whether your taste runs toward chain resorts or private villas, we list the best accommodation choices available. We show you how to travel to and among the islands by air and by sea.

Local seafood takes center stage in USVI restaurants, and we guide you toward the best dining options for your budget. Finally, we offer suggestions for ways to while away your days in paradise, from snorkeling to shopping for local crafts.

Chapter 32

The Lowdown on the U.S. Virgin Islands' Hotel Scene

*I*n the U.S. Virgin Islands (USVIs), you can find as many different kinds of accommodations as swimsuit fashions. Like Puerto Rico and Jamaica, the USVIs have everything from gorgeous villas to simple guesthouses. The islands also have familiar chains — from the Best Western to more upscale choices like Marriott, Westin, and The Ritz-Carlton.

In this chapter, we give you an overview of our favorite places to stay in the USVIs, as well as a list of other options just in case our picks are fully booked at the time you want to travel. You may encounter a full house with popular properties like the deluxe Caneel Bay Resort and the award-winning eco-friendly campgrounds, both on St. John, and The Ritz-Carlton, St. Thomas, during the busy winter season. The much-in-demand campgrounds often stay booked as much as a year in advance.

Highly developed St. Thomas supports a mind-boggling number of rooms, many of them timeshares. If you like atmospheric bed-and-breakfast inns, you can find a few on St. Thomas and St. Croix. Eco-hounds delight in St. John.

Figuring Out Where You Want to Stay

You can expect the densest concentration of hotels and timeshares east and north of **Charlotte Amalie,** the capital of St. Thomas. Several smaller properties are in this area—ideal if you plan to get out and mingle with the locals. You'll be within walking distance of Frenchtown. If you just want a clean room to return to after a day of exploring or beach-bumming, consider staying in town, where you can find inexpensive lodgings that will meet your standards of convenience and tidiness.

On St. John, a few new villas have sprung up in the hills above **Cinnamon Bay.** Most of the villas and resorts on St. John, though, are near **Cruz Bay.** On St. Croix, some of the hotels are near the waterfront in **Christiansted,** but most of our recommendations are out of town on wonderful beaches.

Not all of our picks are on a beach, but all have access to some of the best beaches in the Caribbean. We alert you in our reviews if a place isn't on a beach.

Conserving Cash

The all-inclusive plan has landed in the USVIs but has yet to be widely embraced. You'll typically have MAP or EP options (see Chapter 3 for details). Several resorts offer terrific package deals; wedding and honeymoon packages are especially generous. Several also extend great values for families, particularly during the summer.

Families often stay at an East End condominium complex on St. Thomas. Although condos are somewhat pricey (winter rates average $240 per night for a two-bedroom unit, which usually sleeps six), the accommodations have full kitchens. You can save money by cooking for yourself — especially if you bring your own nonperishable foodstuffs and pick up the rest of what you need in the new mega-stores that are now open on St. Thomas.

Most food in the USVIs is imported, so your restaurant bills will be fairly pricey, though not swoon-inducing like Barbados or Aruba.

You can arrange villa or condo rentals on St. Thomas through agents, including the following:

- ✔ **Calypso Realty,** P.O. Box 12178, St. Thomas, USVI 00801 (☎ **800-747-4858** or 340-774-1620; Internet www.calypsorealty.com).

- ✔ **McLaughlin-Anderson Villas,** 100 Blackbeard's Hill, Suite 3, St. Thomas, USVI 00802 (☎ **800-537-6246** or 340-776-0635).

Both specialize in luxury-end properties. Write for brochures with photos of the properties they represent. Some residences are suitable for travelers with disabilities.

Plan to rent a car because most of the villas are up in the hills. (Few are at the beach.) Villa managers usually pick you up at the dock, arrange for your rental car, and answer your questions when you arrive as well as during your stay.

To rent a luxury villa or condo on St. John, contact one of the following rental agents:

✔ **Caribbean Villas & Resorts,** P.O. Box 458, St. John, USVI 00831 (☎ **800-338-0987,** 207-871-1129, or 340-776-6152; fax 340-779-4044; Internet: www.caribbeanvilla.com).

✔ **Catered To, Inc.,** P.O. Box 704, St. John, USVI 00830 (☎ **800-424-6641;** 340-776-6641; fax 340-693-8191; e-mail cateredto@islands.vi; Internet www.cateredto.com).

✔ **Destination St. John,** P.O. Box 8306, St. John, USVI 00831 (☎ **800-562-1901** or 340-779-4647; Internet www.destinationstjohn.com).

✔ **Private Homes for Private Vacations,** Mamey Peak, St. John, USVI 00830 (☎ **340-776-6876;** Internet www.privatehomesvi.com).

✔ **Vacation Homes,** P.O. Box 272, St. John, USVI 00831 (☎ **340-776-6094;** fax 340-693-8455; Internet www.vacationstjohn.com).

✔ **Windspree,** 6-2-1A Estate Carolina, St. John, USVI 00830 (☎ **340-693-5423;** fax 340-693-5623).

For villas or condos on St. Croix, contact one of the following:

✔ **Island Villas** (☎ **800-626-4512** or 340-773-8821; Internet www.stcroixislandvillas.com).

✔ **Rent A Villa** (☎ **800-533-6863;** Internet www.rentavilla vacations.com).

✔ **Richards & Ayer Associates** (☎ **340-772-0420** — can call collect; Internet www.ayervirginislands.com).

✔ **Teague Bay Properties** (☎ **800-237-1959** or 340-773-4850; Internet www.teaguebayproperties.com) does short-term and long-term rentals.

Room rates on St. Croix tend to be big bargains in the summer months, which is a slower season. Many properties offer family, honeymoon, and dive packages that are also big money-savers.

The USVI-based Internet site www.caribbeanchannel.com recently announced the launch of two new Web pages featuring information about "Hotels & Resorts" and "Inns & Small Hotels" in the territory and throughout the Caribbean.

The USVIs' Best Accommodations

The rack rates listed in this section are in U.S. dollars and are for a standard double room during high season (mid-December to mid-April), unless otherwise noted. Lower rates are often available during the off-season and shoulder season; see Chapter 2 for information on travel seasons.

St. Thomas's Hotels

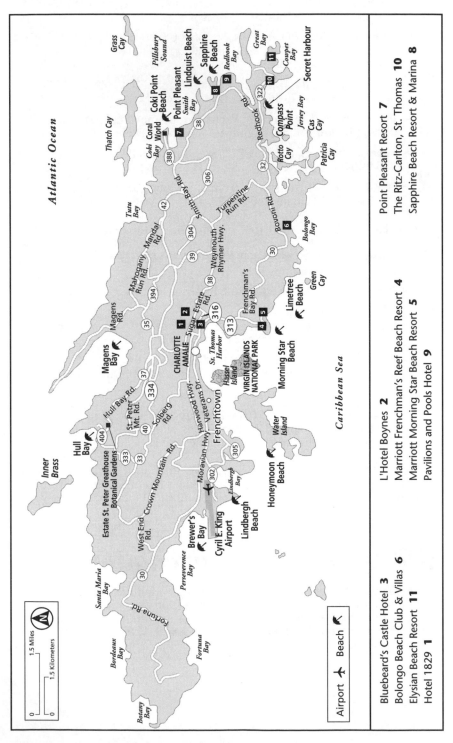

Bluebeard's Castle Hotel **3**
Bolongo Beach Club & Villas **6**
Elysian Beach Resort **11**
Hotel 1829 **1**

L'Hotel Boynes **2**
Marriott Frenchman's Reef Beach Resort **4**
Marriott Morning Star Beach Resort **5**
Pavilions and Pools Hotel **9**

Point Pleasant Resort **7**
The Ritz-Carlton, St. Thomas **10**
Sapphire Beach Resort & Marina **8**

Airport ✈   Beach

Bluebeard's Castle Hotel

$$$ Charlotte Amalie, St. Thomas

If you like great views and proximity to good shopping and great restaurants, this castle, a red-tile roof complex with recently redone rooms, is a good pick. All rooms have terraces. There's a small pool, two tennis courts, and three restaurants. (We haven't heard great things, so we haven't tried them.) The hotel is a short ride from the shops of Charlotte Amalie and Havensight Mall and offers free transportation to Magens Bay Beach and to town. Service is sometimes uneven.

Bluebeard's Hill (P.O. Box 7480), St. Thomas, USVI 00801. ☎ *800-524-6599 or 340-774-1600. Fax: 340-774-5134. Rack rates: $235–$399; for MAP (two meals daily) add $50 per person per night. Additional person $30 extra. AE, DC, MC, V.*

Bolongo Bay Beach Club & Villas

$$$$ South Shore, St. Thomas

This straightforward, 75-room, beachfront resort works well for families and is a good choice if you want a no-fuss, no-muss vacation. It also includes the 20-room Bolongo Villas next door and the six-room Bolongo Bayside Inn across the street. The best part is Bolongo's beautiful white-sand, palm-encircled beach.

The resort opened in 1974 but has stayed fresh. It has a nice feel and is family-owned and operated by Dick and Joyce Doumeng, long-time hoteliers on St. Thomas. All rooms — whether they're one of the mini-suites or a one- or two-bedroom unit — have efficiency kitchens and balconies and are just steps from a 1,000-foot strand of white sand. The resort, known for its friendly staff, offers a choice of all-inclusive or semi-inclusive plans, which means you can pay less if you opt for fewer activities. The all-inclusive rate covers all meals and drinks, the use of tennis courts, and many watersports activities — including an all-day sail and half-day snorkel trip on one of the resort's yachts. The all-inclusive plan requires a minimum three-night stay.

There are two restaurants and bars, three pools (including one with a swim-up bar), two tennis courts, a large health club with free weights and lots of gear, a dive shop, and a dock. Guests often play volleyball on the beach. Snorkeling, windsurfing, boating, jet skiing, and baby-sitting services are available at an extra charge.

Kids age 12 and under stay free year-round and eat free during the summer.

7150 Bolongo, St. Thomas, USVI 00802. ☎ *800-524-4746 or 340-775-1800 (both direct to the hotel). Fax: 340-775-3208. E-mail:* bolongobeach@worldnet.att.net. *Internet:* www.bolongo.com. *Rack rates: $325–$460. AE, DISC, DC, MC, V.*

St. Croix's Hotels

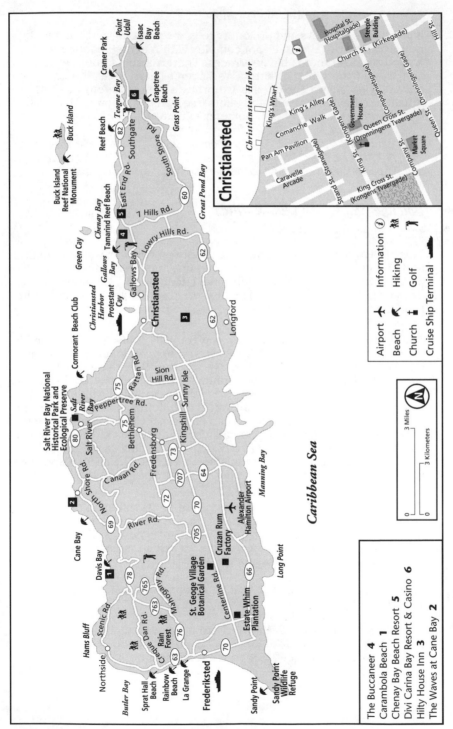

Caribbean Sea

Christiansted

The Buccaneer **4**
Carambola Beach **1**
Chenay Bay Beach Resort **5**
Divi Carina Bay Resort & Casino **6**
Hilty House Inn **3**
The Waves at Cane Bay **2**

Airport ✈   Information ℹ
Beach ⚓   Hiking
Church ♦   Golf
Cruise Ship Terminal

3 Miles
3 Kilometers

Point Udall
Isaac Bay Beach
Cramer Park
Grapetree Beach
Teague Bay
Grass Point
Reef Beach
Southgate
Buck Island
Buck Island National Monument
Buck Island Reef National Monument
82
Reef Beach
60
Great Pond Bay
East End Rd.
South Shore Rd.
7 Hills Rd.
Chenay Bay
Tamarind Reef Beach
Lowry Hills Rd.
Green Cay
62
Gallows Bay
Gallows Bay
Longford
Christiansted
Christiansted Harbor
Protestant Cay
Cormorant Beach Club
62
Sion Hill Rd.
Rattan Rd.
Salt River Bay National Historical Park and Ecological Preserve
75
Salt River Bay
Salt River
Peppertree Rd.
Sunny Isle
80
Salt River Rd.
75
Bethlehem
Fredensborg
Kingshill
73
North Shore Rd.
Canaan Rd.
707
64
Manning Bay
72
70
Cane Bay
69
River Rd.
705
Alexander Hamilton Airport
Cruzan Rum Factory
Davis Bay
78
765
Long Point
66
Hams Bluff
Scenic Rd.
Mahogany Rd.
Centerline Rd.
St. Geoge Village Botanical Garden
Estate Whim Plantation
763
Creque Dan Rd.
Rain Forest
76
70
Northside
Butler Bay
Sprat Hall Beach
Rainbow Beach
La Grange
63
Frederiksted
Sandy Point
Sandy Point Wildlife Refuge

Christiansted

Christiansted Harbor

Hospital St. (Hospitalgade)
Steeple Building
Church St. (Kirkegade)
Hill St.
King's Wharf
King's Alley
Comanche Walk
Pan Am Pavilion
Caravelle Arcade
Government House
Queen Cross St. (Dronningens Tvaergade)
King St. (Kongens Gade)
Strand St. (Strandgade)
Queen St. (Dronningens Gade)
Company St.
Market Square
King Cross St. (Kongens Tvaergade)

The Buccaneer

$$$$$ East End, St. Croix

We debated over highlighting this outstanding resort for romance or its kid-friendliness. We decided on both because the resort is one of the few we've seen successfully handle both markets. We're particularly impressed with its excellent educational programs for kids, studying the natural beauty of St. Croix. On the grounds of a former 340-acre sugar plantation, this family-owned and operated resort, which celebrated its fiftieth anniversary in 1998, boasts three sandy beaches; one of our favorite swimming pools in the Caribbean; an 18-hole golf course; a championship tennis facility with eight courts; and more activities than you can shake a shak-shak at.

A palm tree-lined drive leads to an imposing pink Danish Colonial structure atop a hill. Shops, restaurants, and other guest quarters dot the rolling, manicured lawns. The ambience and decor are Mediterranean-meets-Caribbean, with tile floors, four-poster beds, massive wardrobes of pale wood, pastel fabrics, spacious marble baths, and local works of art. Manager Elizabeth Armstrong, whose Dutch family owns this elegant place, is an excellent hotelier who makes guests feel welcome.

Many couples marry at this elegant property. The new Doubloon rooms right on the water are especially romantic.

Rte. 82 (P.O. Box 25200), Gallows Bay, St. Croix, USVI 00824. ☎ 800-255-3881 or 340-773-2100. Fax: 340-773-6665. Internet: www.thebuccaneer.com. *Rack rates: $250–$600. BP. Rates include full breakfast. AE, DISC, DC, MC, V.*

Caneel Bay Resort

$$$$$ Caneel Bay, St. John

A private boat fetches you from the dock at St. Thomas and ferries you to another time and place. Built by Laurance Rockefeller in 1952 on a 170-acre peninsula, Caneel Bay, now well-run by Rosewood Hotels & Resorts, remains a cherished retreat of the old-money set. With seven spectacular (and we don't use that word lightly) beaches and some of St. John's better restaurants, this resort may hold you in its glorious grasp, making you hesitate to venture outside the confines of paradise. Of the luxury digs in the USVIs, this one is our pick, edging out The Ritz-Carlton because Caneel Bay puts you more in touch with the Caribbean experience.

The reasonably priced rooms near the tennis courts are actually more spacious than the higher-price, beachfront rooms. Yet they still have the rock-lined showers and well-loved antiques that elevate them above the cookie-cutter blandness of many Caribbean resorts. Who cares if you have to walk a few more feet to the beach? Air-conditioning is a recent addition, but you really don't need it in these peaceful rooms open to tropical breezes. Cottage 7, which Rockefeller favored, stays continually booked. The attentive staff makes sure that you take full advantage of the 3 restaurants, 11 tennis courts, dive shop, windsurfing, boating, and children's program.

Children are welcome at Caneel Bay year-round, but if you're debating between here and Little Dix Bay (see Chapter 16 on the British Virgin Islands' hotel scene), the latter has better children's facilities.

Caneel Bay has recently introduced three new packages: Explore (for active, energetic travelers), Allure (for romantics), and Unwind (for Type A's looking to de-stress).

Rte. 20 (P.O. Box 720), Cruz Bay, St. John, USVI 00831. ☎ *800-928-8889 or 340-776-6111. Fax: 340-693-8280. Internet:* www.caneelbay.com. *Rack rates: $400–$750 double; $950 cottage. EP. AE, MC, V.*

Carambola Beach Resorts

$$$$ North Shore, St. Croix

Like Little Dix Bay and Caneel, this resort was originally built by the Rockefellers. It boasts a marvelously set-apart locale, a great beach, and rustic chic appeal. However, over the years, it's been treated as a stepchild and is still trying to sort out its audience. The 26 two-story, red-roof villas (including one that's wheelchair-accessible) are connected by lovely, lush arcades strung along the seaside. They have terra-cotta floors, ceramic lamps, and mahogany ceilings and furnishings. We enjoyed the rocking chairs on screened-in porches, and we loved being lulled to sleep by the sound of surf at night. Each room has a huge bath (shower only). The large pools and hammocks strategically strung between the ancient seagrapes invite lounging. The two-bedroom suite, with its 3-foot-thick plantation walls and large patio, is ideal for families. The on-site picnics offered by the **Carambola Beach Club** open-air restaurant have a sophisticated, contemporary menu.

Golfers can enjoy the 18-hole award-winning championship golf course designed by Robert Trent Jones. Carambola Golf Course has been called the "best in the Caribbean." GOLF Magazine awarded the resort/course a gold medal as one of the finest golf resorts in the world, and Golf Digest gave the resort/course a four-star rating.

However, when we were there, the service wasn't perfect. The resort staff seemed befuddled by the few arrivals trying to check in. The restaurants have improved, thanks to a new chef. We'd call this a diamond in the rough. If you can get a good package deal and are willing to put up with less than stellar service, go for it.

Rte. 80 (P.O. Box 3031), Kingshill, St. Croix, USVI 00851. ☎ *888-316-9648 or 340-778-3800. Fax: 340-778-1682. Internet:* www.sunterra.com *Rack rates: $275–$370 for one- to two-bedroom cottage. AE, DISC, DC, MC, V.*

Chenay Bay Beach Resort

$$$–$$$$ East End, St. Croix

The sheltered, calm location on one of our favorite beaches for families, combined with complimentary tennis and watersports equipment (including kayaks), make this casual resort a real find. Set on 30 acres of a former sugar plantation, spacious but basic cottages have ceramic-tile floors, bright peach or yellow walls, front porches, rattan furnishings, and kitchenettes with microwaves and coffeemakers. Gravel paths connect the terraced gray-and-white wood cottages with the shore, where you find a large L-shape pool, a picnic area, and a casual restaurant. The hotel offers an inexpensive day camp, "Cruzan Kidz," for children 4 to 12. Children ages 18 and under share accommodations with their parents free of charge.

Rte. 82 (P.O. Box 24600), Christiansted, St. Croix, USVI 00824. ☎ *800-548-4457 or 340-773-2918. Fax: 340-773-6665. E-mail:* chenaybay1@worldnet.att.net. *Internet:* www.chenaybay.com. *Rack rates: $236–$380 cottage for one or two. EP. AE, MC, V.*

Cinnamon Bay Campgrounds

$$ St. John

Camping here puts you in the national park, surrounded by jungle and at the edge of the excellent Cinnamon Bay Beach. The unlockable, concrete cottages have electric lights, and the tents have propane lanterns. Both come with propane camping stoves, coolers, cooking gear, and linens. Bring your own tent and supplies for the bare sites (a steal at $25 a night), which, like the cottages and tents, have a grill and a picnic table. The showers (on the cool side) and flush toilets, as well as a restaurant and a small store, are a trek down the hill. Hiking, snorkeling, swimming, and evening environmental or history programs are free and at your doorstep. Call for reservations because spaces for the winter months fill up as much as a year in advance.

Rte. 20 (P.O. Box 720), Cruz Bay, St. John, USVI 00831. ☎ *800-539-9998 or 340-776-6330. Fax: 340-776-6458. Rack rates: $125 beachfront; $105 cottage; $80 tent; $25 bare site. AE, MC, V.*

Divi Carina Bay Resort and Casino

$$$$ Christiansted, St. Croix

The Divi Carina Bay is St. Croix's newest resort, offering the discerning traveler a unique vacation environment. Guests find a high standard of personalized service and attention to detail. The distinct décor merges the flair of today's European design with the comfort of casual chic. Ideal for those guests with multiple expectations from their trip, Divi Carina offers a comprehensive array of amenities: a spectacular beach, the Divi Carina Bay Casino, a selection of dining options, lighted tennis courts, and varied watersports. All rooms have air-conditioning, satellite TV, VCR, telephone with dataport and voice mail system, in-room safes, wet bar, mini-refrigerator, and plush robes.

The **Starlite Bar and Grill,** the resort's signature restaurant, features fine dining. The **Dockside Café & Deli** offers a casual, market-style setting for breakfast, lunch, light snacks, and dinner with indoor and outdoor seating in the pool area.

St. John's Hotels

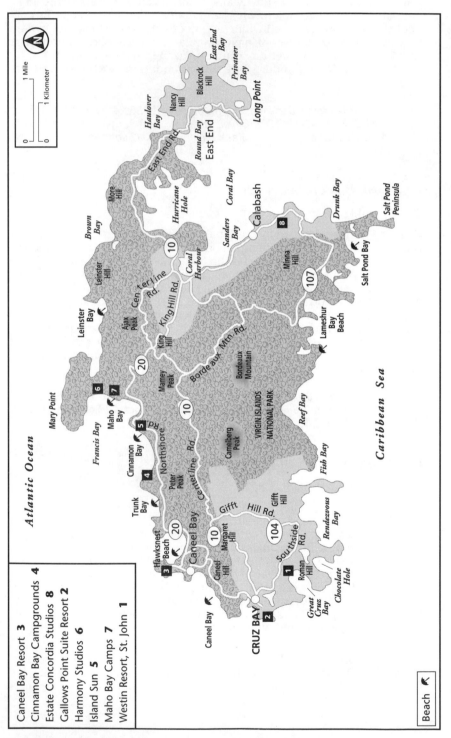

Caneel Bay Resort **3**
Cinnamon Bay Campgrounds **4**
Estate Concordia Studios **8**
Gallows Point Suite Resort **2**
Harmony Studios **6**
Island Sun **5**
Maho Bay Camps **7**
Westin Resort, St. John **1**

Divi Carina Bay is the home of the USVIs' first casino. The 10,000-square-foot casino features 275 slot machines and 12 gaming tables.

25 Estate Turner Hole, St. Croix, USVI 00822. ☎ **888-464-3484** *or 340-773-9700. Fax: 340-773-6802. Internet:* www.divicarina.com. *Rack rates: $225–$400 double. AE, MC, V.*

Elysian Beach Resort

$$$ Cowpet Bay, St. Thomas

The coral-color villas here sit along the hillside, all the way to the edge of Cowpet Bay. Decorations in muted tropical floral prints carry the Caribbean mood out to each villa's private terrace. Some accommodations have full kitchens. Activity centers on a kidney-shape pool with a waterfall and thatched-roof pool bar.

6800 Estate Nazareth (P.O. Box 51), Red Hook, St. Thomas, USVI 00802. ☎ **800-753-2554** *or 340-775-1000. Fax: 340-776-0910. Rack rates: $275 double. EP. AE, MC, V.*

Estate Concordia Studios

$$ St. John

These environmentally correct studios and duplexes offer some of St. John's premier vistas from 51 oceanfront acres of remote Salt Pond Bay, 45 minutes from Cruz Bay. They're the latest brainchild of Stanley Selengut, the developer of Maho Bay Camps and Harmony Studios (see upcoming reviews). The spacious units can sleep five or six adults comfortably. They're constructed of recycled materials, and energy for all appliances (even the ice-makers) is wind- and solar-generated. Next door are five eco-tents — upscale camping structures made of environmentally friendly materials and equipped with solar power and composting toilets.

20-27 Estate Concordia, Coral Bay, St. John, USVI 00830. ☎ **800-392-9004**, *340-693-5855, or 212-861-6210 in New York City. Fax: 340-693-5960. Rack rates: $135–$190 studio for two; $95 eco-tent for two. Additional person $25 extra. MC, V.*

Gallows Point Suite Resort

$$$ Cruz Bay, St. John

These soft-gray buildings with peaked roofs and shuttered windows are clustered on a peninsula south of the Cruz Bay ferry dock. If you want to stay on St. John but don't want a villa or the more expensive Westin or Caneel Bay, Gallows Point is a great value. The garden apartments have kitchens and sky-lighted, plant-filled showers that are big enough for frolicking. The upper-level apartments have loft bedrooms and better views. Only the first-floor units are air-conditioned. The harborside villas get better trade winds, but they're also noisier. The entranceway is bridged by **Ellington's** restaurant, which serves good contemporary cuisine. Ask about generous homeymoon packages. These ultra-spacious and airy condos are a terrific choice for families or a small group of friends, too.

Gallows Point (P.O. Box 58), Cruz Bay, St. John, USVI 00831. ☎ *800-323-7229 or 340-776-6434. Fax: 340-776-6520. Internet:* www.gallowspointresort.com. *Rack rates: $160–$380 apartment. AE, DC, MC, V.*

Harmony Studios

$$ Maho Bay, St. John

Nestled in the tree-covered hills adjacent to the Maho Bay Camps is another of Stanley Selengut's award-winning eco-tourism resorts. The spacious two-story units have the usual amenities — decks, sliding glass doors, living-dining areas, and great views. What makes this place unusual are the materials used to build it. Though you can't tell when you look at them, the carpets are made of recycled milk cartons and the pristine white walls are old newspapers enjoying new life. Energy for the low-wattage appliances is generated entirely by the wind and the sun. Each unit has a laptop computer programmed to monitor energy consumption. Tile floors, undyed cotton linens, and South American handicrafts create a decor that seems in keeping with the ideals. A watersports outfitter can help gear you up for snorkeling at the lovely beach.

Maho Bay (P.O. Box 310), Cruz Bay, St. John, USVI 00831. ☎ *800-392-9004, 340-776-6240, or 212-472-9453 (in New York City). Fax: 340-776-6504. Internet:* www. harmonystudios.com. *Rack rates: $165–$195 studio for two. Additional person $25 extra. Seven-night minimum stay in winter. MC, DISC, V.*

Hilty House Inn

$$ Christiansted, St. Croix

For an alternative to beach and in-town lodgings, try this tranquil hilltop bed-and-breakfast. Built on the ruins of an eighteenth-century rum factory, the Hilty House has the feel of a Florentine villa. The couple who opened its doors as a bed-and-breakfast are genuinely caring. You can escape to a patio and while away an afternoon in sun or shade by the large, beautifully tiled pool. The comfortable great room is handsomely furnished and invites curling up with a good book. A prix-fixe dinner is served on Monday to guests and locals (reservations essential). However, we have to admit that in all of our Caribbean ramblings, this lovely house is one place where we missed air-conditioning. Because the inn is not on the beach, the ceiling fans simply aren't enough at times. You'll also need a rental car so you can tool around the rest of the island.

Queste Verde Rd. (P.O. Box 26077), Gallows Bay, St. Croix, USVI 00824. ☎ *340-773-2594. Fax: 340-773-2594. E-mail:* hiltyhouse@worldnet.att.net. *Rack rates: $120 double-occupancy house; $145 cottage. No credit cards.*

Hotel 1829

$$ Charlotte Amalie, St. Thomas

What a find. This Spanish-style, family-owned inn built by a French sea captain for his bride has sprawled to six levels interlaced with lovely gardens. The inn, now a National Historic Site, boasts fabulous views of

Charlotte Amalie, which is second only to Old San Juan as the Caribbean's most beautiful city. You won't have elevators to rely on, but if you don't mind the stairs and narrow pathways, you'll find rooms with character-adding elements like old brick walls and antique Colonial furnishings. Some visitors may find them too small, but to us, the setting makes up for it.

A new museum at the top of the property shows colonial life on St. Thomas amidst riotous gardens. The second-floor botanical gardens and open-air champagne bar make a romantic spot for sunset viewing before you indulge in dinner at the gourmet Hotel 1829 restaurant. Hotel 1829 counts phones and VCRs in its list of in-room amenities. There's a tiny, tiny pool for cooling off, and the shops of Charlotte Amalie are just a stroll down the steep hill away.

This is not a good pick if you have children or are physically challenged in any way.

Kongens Gade (P.O. Box 1567), St. Thomas, USVI 00804. ☎ *800-524-2002 or 340-776-1829. Fax: 340-776-4313. Internet:* www.hotel1829.com. *Rack rates: $90–$180 double. Rates include continental breakfast. AE, DISC, MC, V.*

Island Sun

$$$$ Estate Catherineberg, St. John

Sitting high atop St. John in the heart of the national park, Island Sun offers some of the Caribbean's most exquisite, breathtaking views. Island Sun is set among a small group of private homes, 800 feet above **Cinnamon Bay.** Nestled among lush tropical flowers and fragrant bay trees, each home has four bedrooms that feature king-size beds and private baths. Each home also has a deck or balcony, fully equipped kitchen, ceiling fans, 25-foot swimming pool, hot tub, secluded outdoor shower, grill, telescope, washer/dryer, telephone, fax, TV, VCR, stereo, and a stock of games, books, videos, and CDs. Of the villas we've seen on St. John, this one was our favorite.

Estate Catherineberg, P.O. Box 272, St. John, USVI 00831. ☎ *340-776-6094. Fax: 340-693-8455. Rack rates: $5,900 per week. AE, MC, V.*

L'Hotel Boynes

$$ Charlotte Amalie, St. Thomas

On a hill just above the harbor and the Hotel 1829, this intimate inn (owned by a West Indian gent formerly employed by Frenchman's Reef) stands like a monument to a time gone by. Each room in the 200-year-old stone and ballast-brick building, high on Governor's Hill, has its own character — ranging from the sophisticated Red Room, with its mahogany four-poster bed and Persian carpets, to the fanciful Whimsy Room, where the bed is built into an old Danish oven. This terrific inn has attracted a following in the upscale African-American community. It has a small pool, but the attraction here is the character of the place. Guests traditionally take cocktails on the terrace, watching spectacular sunsets. On the weekends, guests can enjoy live piano music, poetry readings, and mingling with the local working crowd. The inn provides free transportation to Magens Bay.

Blackbeard's Hill, St. Thomas, USVI 00801. ☎ *800-377-2905 or 340-774-5511. Fax: 340-774-8509. Internet:* www.hotelboynes.vi. *Rack rates: $135–$195 double. AE, MC, V.*

Maho Bay Camps

$$ St. John

Eight miles (13 km) from Cruz Bay, Maho Bay is a lush hillside community of 114 rustic structures and a world-acclaimed eco-resort with great views of the Caribbean. The 16-x-16-foot tents (wooden platforms protected from the elements by canvas and screening) are linked by wooden stairs, ramps, and walkways — some of them elevated — so that you can trek around camp and down to the beach without disturbing the terrain. The tents sleep as many as four people and have beds, tables and chairs, electric lamps, propane stoves, coolers, kitchenware, and cutlery. Though all the units are surrounded by tropical greenery, some have spectacular views of the Caribbean. The beach is good for snorkeling, kayaking, windsurfing, and sailing. The camp has the chummy feel of a retreat, making it popular, so book at least a year in advance.

Maho Bay (P.O. Box 310), Cruz Bay, St. John, USVI 00831. ☎ *800-392-9004, 340-776-6240, or 212-472-9453. Fax: 340-776-6504. Internet:* www.maho.org. *Rack rates: $105–$115 double. MC, DISC, V.*

Marriott Frenchman's Reef Beach Resort

$$$$ South Shore, St. Thomas

Sprawling, luxurious, and on a prime harbor promontory east of Charlotte Amalie, this full-service 408-room superhotel and its smaller neighbor, Morning Star, were renovated extensively in 1998. Each of the 88 suites has a glorious ocean or harbor view; 21 are loft-style, with a spiral staircase that takes you to your bed where you can watch the cruise ships roll in and out. Rooms also have ice-makers, a nice touch, but they can be noisy in the middle of the night. Frenchman's Reef's fabulous Jacuzzis on the rocks overlooking the harbor almost give the resort the edge with us. However, the decor and feel of this resort are still too businesslike to make you feel like it's a true Caribbean getaway. You have a better shot of getting that "I'm on vacation" sense at the 96-room Morning Star.

Guests at either resort can work out at the **Reef Health Club & Spa,** which offers state-of-the-art cardiovascular and strength training equipment, therapeutic massages, and skin care therapies. Dining is alfresco on American or gourmet Caribbean fare, or oceanfront at the **Tavern on the Beach;** there's also a lavish buffet, served overlooking the sparkling lights of Charlotte Amalie and the harbor. Live entertainment and dancing, scheduled activities for all ages, and a shuttle boat to town make having fun easy.

Both Marriott resorts offer wedding packages, from the "Tropical Wedding," which includes the basic ceremony for $550, to the "Royal Wedding," with all the bells and whistles, including flowers, photographer, cake, champagne, video, live music, sunset cruise, and more for $1,439.

Estate Bakkeroe (P.O. Box 7100), St. Thomas, USVI 00801. ☎ *800-524-2000 or 340-776-8500. Fax: 340-715-6191. Internet:* www.marriott.vi. *Rack rates: $350–$395 double. AE, DISC, DC, MC, V.*

Marriott Morning Star Beach Resort

$$$$ Flamboyant Point, St. Thomas

Both the public areas and the plush accommodations here are among the most outstanding on the island. The resort stands on the landscaped flatlands near the beach of Marriott's well-known Frenchman's Reef. Rooms are elegantly turned out in Caribbean chic in buildings nestled surfside along the fine white sand of Morning Star Beach. Each of the five buildings contains between 16 and 24 units, all having rattan furniture and views of the garden, the beach, or the lights of Charlotte Amalie. Guests can enjoy the amenities, restaurants, and attractions of the larger hotel nearby yet escape to the privacy of this more exclusive enclave.

Caesar's Ristorante, located on beautiful Morning Star Beach, serves Italian and Mediterranean fare for lunch and dinner.

The Frenchman's Reef provides the Morning Star Beach resort with its baby-sitting, valet, and room services.

Guests can take advantage of two giant swimming pools, four tennis courts, watersports — including parasailing — a dive shop, a Jacuzzi, and one of the island's finer private beaches.

At Frenchman's Reef Beach Resort, Flamboyant Point, Charlotte Amalie, P.O. Box 7100, St. Thomas, USVI 00801. ☎ *800-524-2000 or 340-776-8500. Fax: 340-776-3054. Internet:* www.marriott.vi. *Rack rates: $350–$450 double; for MAP (two meals daily), add $73 per person per night. AE, DC, MC, V.*

Pavilions and Pools Hotel

$$$ Estate Smith Bay, St. Thomas

Popular with honeymooners, this resort, seven miles east of Charlotte Amalie, is a string of tastefully rebuilt and furnished condominium units.

After check-in, you follow a wooden pathway to your villa, where you enter your own private world complete with a private swimming pool encircled by a deck and plenty of tropical greenery. Each villa has floor-to-ceiling glass doors, an individually styled bedroom, and a roomy outdoor shower. The resort adjoins **Sapphire Bay,** which boasts one of the island's best beaches and watersports concessions.

A small bar and barbecue area sit against a wall on the reception terrace, where the hotel hosts rum parties and cookouts. Informal, simple meals are served nightly, and occasionally a musician or singer entertains. Free snorkeling gear is offered. Honeymoon packages are available.

6400 Estate Smith Bay, St. Thomas, USVI 00802. ☎ *800-524-2001 or 340-775-6110. Fax: 340-775-6110. Internet:* www.pavilionsandpools.com. *Rack rates: $250–$275 double. CP. Rates include continental breakfast in winter only.*

Point Pleasant Resort

$$$$ St. Thomas

This private, unique resort sits on **Water Bay,** on the northeastern tip of St. Thomas, just a five-minute walk from lovely Stouffer's Beach but far-removed from the bustle of Charlotte Amalie. The 95 villa-style suites are rented when their owners are not in residence. From your living room gallery, you look out on the islands of Tortola, St. John, and Jost Van Dyke. The complex sits on a 15-acre nature preserve lush with flowering shrubbery, century plants, and frangipani trees. Waiting for your discovery are secluded nature trails, old rock formations, and lookout points. Some of the villas have kitchens, and the furnishings are light and airy, mostly with rattan and floral fabrics.

The restaurant, **Agavé Terrace,** one of the finest on the island, offers three meals a day. The cuisine, featuring seafood, is a blend of nouvelle American dishes with Caribbean specialties. Locals entertain several nights a week.

Guests (age 25 or older with a valid driver's license) can reserve a car for one of three four-hour blocks a day for a $20 charge, based on availability. There's also a free dining and shopping shuttle daily. Three freshwater swimming pools, lit tennis courts, snorkeling equipment, and Sunfish sailboats round out the offerings.

6600 Estate Smith Bay #4, St. Thomas, USVI 00802. ☎ *800-777-1700 or 340-775-7200. Fax: 340-776-5694. Internet:* www.pointpleasantresort.com. *Rack rates: $270–380 double; $525 two-bedroom villa. Packages available for families, honeymoons, and anniversaries. AE, DC, DISC, MC, V.*

The Ritz-Carlton, St. Thomas

$$$$ Charlotte Amalie, St. Thomas

When you walk into the grand welcoming area here, with all the crystal, marble, and finery, you might think you've suddenly landed in Venice — for good reason. This grand property was originally built by an Italian hotel company. Guestrooms, in six buildings that fan out from the main villa, are spacious and tropically furnished. Each has a good view of the bay facing St. John. The Ritz has given the place its own special brand of treatment, and the results show in this deluxe Caribbean property. The few complaints that we've heard whispered by other guests indicate that you don't quite capture the Caribbean rhythm here. The atmosphere is a little too buttoned up.

The marvelous suites at the end of the property with the best views, though, do give in to the prime Caribbean setting and get into the groove with plantation-style furnishings and wooden hurricane windows that crank open to let in the tropical breezes. A multilingual staff and 24-hour room service enhance the sophisticated atmosphere. The exercise room is on the small side, and the air-conditioning definitely wasn't working when we last visited.

The resort offers generous and surprisingly well priced honeymoon packages which include treats like a sunset cruise.

6900 Great Bay Estate, St. Thomas, USVI 00802. ☎ ***800-241-3333*** *or 340-775-3333. Fax: 340-775-4444. Internet:* www.ritzcarlton.com. *Rack rates: $325–$575 double. AE, DISC, DC, MC, V.*

Sapphire Beach Resort & Marina

$$$$ Charlotte Amalie, St. Thomas

You can easily see the British Virgin Islands from this casually elegant MeriStar resort on one of St. Thomas's prettiest beaches, which boasts good snorkeling. This place has found a spot in the heart of the yachties who love St. Thomas. You can nap while swinging in one of the hammocks strung between the palm trees in the front yard of your unit. But don't try it on Sunday, when the place rocks with a beach party. All units have fully equipped kitchens, phones, and satellite TV. The beach boasts good snorkeling. Children may join the Kids Klub, where 4- to 12-year-olds can enjoy such supervised activities as sandcastle building, arts and crafts, and sing-alongs.

Rte. 36, Smith Bay Rd. (P.O. Box 8088), St. Thomas, USVI 00801. ☎ ***800-524-2090*** *or 340-775-6100. Fax: 340-775-2403. Internet:* www.usvi.net/hotel/sapphire. *Rack Rates: $295–$440 suite for two. Children 18 years old and under stay free in parents' room; children under 12 eat free as well. Add $70 per person per night for MAP (two meals daily). Wedding packages available. AE, MC, V.*

The Waves at Cane Bay

$$–$$$ East End, St. Croix

Lapping waves lull you to sleep at this isolated inn well-run by Suzanne and Kevin Ryan, avid divers who tapped this spot as their dream. Although the beach is rocky, **Cane Bay Beach** is next door, and the world-famous **Cane Bay Reef** is just 100 yards offshore (divers take note). You can also sunbathe on a small patch of sand beside the unusual pool, carved from the coral along the shore. Waves crash dramatically over its side, creating a foamy whirlpool on blustery days. Two peach and mint-green buildings house enormous balconied guestrooms done in soothing creams and accented with homey touches like well-worn books and shells collected by the Ryans' children. All have kitchens or kitchenettes, but not all have air-conditioning.

Rte. 80 (P.O. Box 1749), Kingsbill, St. Croix, USVI 00851. ☎ ***800-545-0603*** *or 340-778-1805. Fax: 340-778-4945. Internet:* www.thewavesatcanebay.com. *Rack rates: $140–$195 double. AE, MC, V.*

Westin Resort, St. John

$$$$$ **Great Cruz Bay, St. John**

Spread out over 47 acres adjacent to **Great Cruz Bay,** the Westin is one of two luxe choices on St. John. It has lushly planted gardens, a large pool, and a good beach where you can swim or sail. If you want to get out and about, taxi jaunts into Cruz Bay are a breeze. Rooms recently underwent the Starwood treatment, meaning they were redone in Caribbean chic. Ultra-comfy beds (we've tried to duplicate the set-up at home), which have deservedly become the signature of these hotels, have been installed. Many rooms have excellent views of the Caribbean, and all have computer ports for those who just *have* to keep in touch with the world. As we've noted at several corporate resorts, the staff, especially in the restaurants, could use some additional training in service with a smile. However, the dramatic fine dining restaurant **Coccoloba** delivers on the promise of its tasteful decor with equally tasty dishes. Younger guests will appreciate the children's program. If we were arranging a reunion of family or friends, this resort would be our pick as the place.

Guests at the Westin Vacation Club, a condominium complex located across the street, enjoy all the hotel amenities. At your disposal are three restaurants, a masseuse, six tennis courts, an exercise room, a beach, a dive shop, snorkeling, windsurfing, boating, fishing, and shops. Physically challenged guests might find the grounds too sprawling and hilly for their comfort.

Rte. 104 (P.O. Box 8310), Great Cruz Bay, St. John, USVI 00831. ☎ *800-808-5020 or 340-693-8000. Fax: 340-693-4500. E-mail:* stjon@westin.com. *Internet:* www.westin.com. *Rack rates: from $440 double. AE, DISC, DC, MC, V.*

Chapter 33

Settling into the U.S. Virgin Islands

. . . .

In This Chapter

▶ Knowing what to expect when you arrive

▶ Getting around the islands

▶ Discovering the USVIs from A to Z

. . . .

*W*hether you come by air or by sea, the United States Virgin Islands (USVIs) are among the easier destinations to connect with in the Caribbean. Many airlines have direct flights to both St. Thomas and St. Croix, and many cruise ships have these islands in their schedules. Most visitors arrive on St. Thomas, and then either take a ferry to St. John or a plane to St. Croix, if either is their final destination.

Arriving in St. Thomas

If you fly to the 32-square-mile island of St. Thomas, you land at its western end at **Cyril E. King Airport** (☎ **340-774-5100**), a modest but busy airport that serves flights continuing on to St. Croix as well as the British Virgin Islands.

One advantage to visiting the USVIs is the abundance of nonstop and connecting flights that can whisk you away to the beach in three to four hours from most eastern United States departures — especially since you won't be slowed by going through U.S. customs. You'll breeze right through to pick up your luggage and follow the signs to ground transportation. Pick up a copy of the excellent *What To Do: St. Thomas & St. John*, a terrific tourist magazine, which contains several coupons and all the latest happenings on the islands.

Getting from the Airport to Your Hotel

Because most visitors arrive on St. Thomas, this section guides you either directly to your hotel or to means for making your way to your next destination.

By taxi

Most hotels on St. Thomas don't have airport shuttles, but taxi vans at the airport are plentiful. A trip from the airport to Charlotte Amalie, St. Thomas's glorious capital city on the harbor, takes about 20 minutes unless there is heavy traffic, which often occurs in the mornings and late afternoons. From the airport, fees (set by the Virgin Island Taxi Commission) for two or more people sharing a cab are $14 to The Ritz-Carlton, $12 to Renaissance Grand Beach Resort, $10 to Marriott Frenchman's Reef, and $7 to Bluebeard's Castle. Expect to be charged 50¢ per bag and to pay a higher fee if you're riding alone. During rush hour, the trip to East End resorts can take up to 40 minutes, but a half-hour trip is typical.

By car

Many of the big North American car rental chains have offices at the airport in St. Thomas, and competition with local agencies is stiff. You can usually get a good deal with one of the larger companies like Avis, Budget, Hertz, or National. A mid-size car for a week's rental was running about $320 at press time.

All four companies offer cars with automatic transmission and air-conditioning. During the summer, many packages include a rental car for a day or two. Some villas also include a rental car in the price, too.

To be on the safe side, we recommend getting collision-damage insurance, which usually costs an extra $13 to $14 per day. But be aware that even with this insurance, you could still get hit with a whopping deductible. The Hertz deductible is the full value of the car; at Avis it's $250; and Budget has no deductible.

Always drive on the left. We know that's weird because these islands are U.S. territories, but this custom is a throwback to the USVIs' colonial past. The speed limit is 20 mph in town and 35 mph outside town. Take extra caution when driving in St. Thomas, especially at night. Many roads are narrow, curvy, and poorly lit.

Traveling Inland from the Docks

Virtually every type of ship and major cruise line calls at St. Thomas. Many of the ships that call at St. Thomas also call in St. John or offer an excursion to that island. Only a few ships call at St. Croix. On St. Thomas, taxi vans line up along Havensight and Crown Bay docks when a cruise ship pulls in. If you booked a shore tour, the operator will lead you to a designated vehicle.

Otherwise, there are plenty of air-conditioned vans and open-air safari buses to take you to Charlotte Amalie or the beach. The cab fare from Havensight to Charlotte Amalie is $4; you can, however, walk to town in about 30 minutes (1½ miles or 2½ km) along the beautiful waterfront.

From Crown Bay to town, the taxi fare is $3 per person whether you travel solo or you share; it's a one-mile (1½ km) walk, but the route passes along a busy highway. Transportation from Havensight to Magens Bay for swimming is $6.50 per person ($4 per person if you share a ride).

In St. Croix, taxis greet arriving cruise ships at the Frederiksted pier. All the shops are just a short walk away, and you can swim off the beach in Frederiksted, where you'll actually find some decent snorkeling. Most ship passengers visit Christiansted on a tour. A taxi to Christiansted will cost $20 for one to two people.

Some cruise ships stop at St. John to let passengers disembark for a day. The main town of Cruz Bay is near the ship terminal. If you want to swim, the famous Trunk Bay is a $7.50 taxi ride (for two) from town.

Getting Around the USVIs

These islands are easy to navigate. The businesses and residents are accustomed to handling tourists, so if you're confused, just ask for directions or other information.

By ferry

If you're heading to St. John, you'll fly into St. Thomas and take a taxi to either the dock at Charlotte Amalie or Red Hook, where you'll catch a ferry to Cruz Bay, St. John. The ferry from Charlotte Amalie makes the 45-minute trip several times a day and costs $7 a person.

Red Hook is a funky little community where you can grab a soda and fish patty from a vendor while you wait. The ferry runs at 6:30 and 7:30 a.m., then on the hour starting at 8 a.m. till midnight. The 20-minute trip costs $3 per person. We recommend getting a seat on top and toward the front where you can take in the view.

Ferries are also a great way to travel around the islands; you can pick up service between St. Thomas and St. John and their neighbors, the BVIs.

Ferries to Cruz Bay, St. John, leave St. Thomas from either the Charlotte Amalie waterfront west of the U.S. Coast Guard dock or from Red Hook. From Charlotte Amalie, ferries depart at 9 and 11 a.m. and 1, 3, 4, and 5:30 p.m. (To Charlotte Amalie from Cruz Bay, they leave at 7:15, 9:15, and 11:15 a.m. and at 1:15, 2:15, and 3:45 p.m.) The one-way fare for the 45-minute ride is $7 for adults, $3 for children. From Red Hook, the ferries to Cruz Bay leave at 6:30 and 7:30 a.m. Starting at 8 a.m., they leave hourly until midnight. (Returning from Cruz Bay, they leave hourly starting at 6 a.m. until 11 p.m.) The 15- to 20-minute ferry ride is $3 one-way for adults, $1 for children under 12. Schedules vary; for the most up-to-date departure times, contact your hotel travel desk or check in with the ferry services.

There's daily service between either Charlotte Amalie or Red Hook on St. Thomas, and West End or Road Town on Tortola (BVI), by either **Smith's Ferry** (☎ 340-775-7292) or **Native Son, Inc.** (☎ 340-774-8685). Smith's Ferry also runs to Virgin Gorda (BVI). The times and days the ferries run change, so it's best to call for schedules once you're on the islands. The fare is $22 one-way or $40 round-trip. The trip from Charlotte Amalie to West End takes between 45 minutes and an hour. To Road Town, the trip takes up to 1½ hours. From Red Hook to Road Town, the trip is only half an hour. The twice-weekly, 2½ hour trip from Charlotte Amalie to Virgin Gorda costs $28 one-way and $40 round-trip. There's also daily service between Cruz Bay, St. John, and West End, Tortola, aboard the **Sundance** (☎ 340-776-6597). The half-hour one-way trip costs $21.

Reefer (☎ 340-776-8500, ext. 445) is the name of both brightly colored 26-passenger skiffs that run between the Charlotte Amalie waterfront and Marriott Frenchman's Reef Beach Resort daily every hour from 9 a.m. to 4 p.m., returning from the Reef from 9:30 a.m. until 4:30 p.m. (See Chapter 32 for more information on the resort.) The skiffs are a good way to beat the traffic to Morning Star Beach, which adjoins the Reef. A ride on a skiff costs about the same as a taxi fare. Plus, you get a great view of the harbor as you travel. The captain of the *Reefer* may also be persuaded to drop you at Yacht Haven, but check first. The fare is $4 each way, and the trip takes about 15 minutes.

You'll need to present proof of citizenship upon entering the BVIs; a passport is best, but a birth certificate or voter's registration card with a photo ID will suffice.

By plane

If your final destination is not St. Thomas, following are some common carriers who fly to other nearby islands:

- ✔ **American Eagle** (☎ 340-778-2000) offers frequent flights daily from St. Thomas to St. Croix's Henry E. Rohlsen Airport.

- ✔ **LIAT** (☎ 340-774-2313) has service from St. Thomas and St. Croix to Caribbean islands to the south.

- ✔ **Cape Air** (☎ 800-352-0714; Internet www.flycapeair.com) offers hourly air service to St. Croix and Tortola (BVI).

- ✔ The **Seaborne Seaplane** (☎ 340-773-6442), which you catch from a terminal on the waterfront across from Charlotte Amalie's main drag, also flies between St. Thomas and St. Croix several times daily as well as to Tortola (BVI). A round-trip ticket to St. Croix costs $120 and to Tortola costs $80. One child can fly free per accompanying adult.

You'd be wise to make reservations for the seaplane and check your luggage early. It has a strict weight limit of 40 pounds of luggage per passenger. Your luggage may be on the next flight if you don't check in early; we learned that the hard way. We found the plane really handy and fun, though. The 20-minute flight to St. Croix is pretty, and you're dropped off right at the dock, a five-minute walk from Christiansted. If you do get caught waiting for your luggage, you can wander around and look at the neat little shops or grab a bite at one of the waterfront restaurants there.

On foot

All three islands have nice towns for strolling. If you're content with your hotel's beach, you can do fine exploring the main areas downtown by foot. The *St. Thomas–St. John Vacation Handbook,* available free at hotels and tourist centers, has an excellent self-guided walking tour of Charlotte Amalie on St. Thomas. The St. Thomas Historical Trust has published a self-guided tour of the historic district; it's available in book and souvenir shops for $1.95.

St. Croix Heritage Tours (Box 7937, Sunny Isle, 00823; ☎ 340-778-6997) leads walks through the historic towns of Christiansted and Frederiksted, detailing the history of the people and the buildings. Custom tours that cover the island are also available.

By public transportation

St. Thomas's 20 deluxe, mainland-size buses make public transportation a comfortable but slow way to get from east and west to Charlotte Amalie and back. (Service to the north is limited.) Buses run about every 30 minutes from stops that are clearly marked with VITRAN signs. Fares are $1 between outlying areas and town and 75¢ in town.

Privately owned taxi vans crisscross St. Croix regularly, providing reliable service between Frederiksted and Christiansted along Route 70. This inexpensive ($1.50 one way) mode of transportation is favored by locals, but the many stops on the 20-mile (32-km) drive between the two main towns make the ride slow. The public VITRAN buses aren't the quickest way to get around the island, but they're comfortable and affordable. The fare is $1 between Christiansted to Frederiksted or to places in between.

On St. John, modern VITRAN buses run from the Cruz Bay ferry dock through Coral Bay to the far eastern end of the island at Salt Pond, making numerous stops in between. The fare is $1 to any point.

By taxi

USVI taxis don't have meters, but you needn't worry about fare-gouging if you check a list of standard rates to popular destinations. Drivers are required by law to carry the rate lists, and the lists are often posted in hotel and airport lobbies and printed in free tourist periodicals, such as *St. Thomas This Week* and *St. Croix This Week.*

Settle on the fare before you start out. Fares are per person, not per destination, but drivers taking multiple fares (which often happens, especially from the airport) will charge you a lower rate than if you're in the cab alone.

On St. Thomas, taxis of all shapes and sizes are available at various ferry, shopping, resort, and airport areas, and they also respond to phone calls. Try one of the following:

   ✔ **Islander Taxi** (☎ 340-774-4077)

   ✔ **The VI Taxi Association** (☎ 340-774-4550)

   ✔ **East End Taxi** (☎ 340-775-6974)

Taxi stands are located in Charlotte Amalie across from Emancipation Garden (in front of Little Switzerland, behind the post office) and along the waterfront. But you probably won't have to look for a stand, because taxis are plentiful and routinely cruise the streets, looking for fares. Walking down Main Street, you'll be asked regularly: "Back to ship?"

On St. Croix, taxis (generally station wagons or minivans) are a phone call away from most hotels and are available in downtown Christiansted, at the Alexander Hamilton Airport, and at the Frederiksted pier during cruise ship arrivals. Try the **St. Croix Taxi Association** (☎340-778-1088) at the airport and **Antilles Taxi Service** (☎ 340-773-5020) or **Cruxan Taxi and Tours** (☎ 340-773-6388) in Christiansted.

On St. John, taxis meet ferries arriving in Cruz Bay. Most drivers use vans or open-air safari buses. You'll find them congregated at the dock and at hotel parking lots. You can also hail them anywhere on the road. You're likely to travel with other tourists en route to their destinations. On this tiny island, you may find it difficult to get taxis to respond to a phone call. If you need one to pick you up at your rental villa, ask the villa manager for suggestions on whom to call or arrange a ride in advance. If the person doesn't show up within 15 minutes of the appointed time, put in a call. Drivers on St. John can be somewhat unreliable.

By car

If you want to explore much, especially on St. Thomas and St. Croix, we recommend renting a car. On St. John, a car is a good idea if you're staying in a villa some distance from Cruz Bay. Otherwise, we suggest hiring a driver for a day or two of touring.

Any U.S. driver's license is good for 90 days on the USVIs, as are valid driver's licenses from other countries. The minimum age for drivers is 18, although many agencies won't rent to anyone under the age of 25.

Driving is on the left side of the road (although your steering wheel will be on the left side of the car). The law requires *everyone* in a car to wear seat belts. Many of the roads are narrow, and the islands are dotted with hills, so there's ample reason to put safety first.

Even at a sedate speed of 20 mph, driving can be an adventure. For example, you may find yourself in a stick-shift Jeep slogging behind a slow tourist-packed safari bus at a steep hairpin turn. Give a little beep at blind turns; there are some lu-lus on St. John.

Note that the general speed limit on these islands is only 25 mph to 35 mph, which will seem fast enough for you on most roads. If you don't think you'll need to lock up your valuables, a Jeep or open-air Suzuki with four-wheel-drive will make it easier to navigate pot-holed dirt side roads and to get up slick hills when it rains. We consider four-wheel-drive a necessity on St. John. All main roads are paved. Expect to pay top prices for gasoline.

All the islands have garages that will tow broken-down vehicles, but always call the rental company first. If your car requires extensive repairs because of a mechanical failure, a new one will be sent to replace it.

Driving on St. Thomas

Traffic on St. Thomas sometimes crawls along like a sea turtle on dry land, especially in Charlotte Amalie at rush hour (from 7 to 9 a.m. and 4:30 to 6 p.m.). Cars often line up bumper-to-bumper along the waterfront.

If you need to get from an East End resort to the airport during these times, use the alternate route (starting from the East End, Route 38 to 42 to 40 to 33) that goes up the mountain and then drops you back onto Veteran's Highway. If you plan to explore by car, be sure to pick up the *2000 Road Map St. Thomas – St. John* that includes the route numbers *and* the names of the roads that are used by locals. It's available anywhere you find maps and guidebooks.

You can rent a car on St. Thomas from

- ✔ **Budget** (☎ **800-626-4516** or 340-776-5774)
- ✔ **Cowpet Rent-a-Car** (☎ **340-775-7376**)
- ✔ **Dependable Car Rental** (☎ **800-522-3076** or 340-774-2253)
- ✔ **Discount** (☎ **340-776-4858**)
- ✔ **Sun Island Car Rental** (☎ **340-774-3333**)

Driving on St. Croix

Unlike St. Thomas and St. John, where narrow roads wind through hillsides, St. Croix is relatively flat, and it even has a four-lane highway. The speed limit on the Melvin H. Evans Highway is 55 mph and ranges from 35 mph to 40 mph elsewhere. Roads are often unmarked, but locals are friendly on this rural island and will put you back on the right route.

Occasionally, all the rental companies run out of cars at once. To avoid disappointment, make your reservations early. Call one of the following:

- ✔ **Avis** (☎ **800-331-1084** or 340-778-9355)
- ✔ **Budget** (☎ **888-227-3359** or 340-778-9636)
- ✔ **Olympic** (☎ **888-878-4227** or 340-773-2208)
- ✔ **Thrifty** (☎ **800-367-2277** or 340-773-7200)

Driving on St. John

Use caution on St. John. The terrain is extremely hilly, the roads winding, and the blind curves numerous. You may suddenly come upon a huge safari bus careening around a corner, or a couple of hikers strolling along the side of the road. Major roads are well paved, but once you get off a specific route, dirt roads filled with potholes are common. For such driving, a four-wheel-drive vehicle is your best bet.

At the height of the winter season, it may be tough to find a car. Reserve well in advance to ensure that you get the vehicle of your choice. Call one of the following:

- ✔ **Cool Breeze** (☎ **340-776-6588**)
- ✔ **Delbert Hill Taxi Rental Service** (☎ **340-776-6637**)
- ✔ **Denzil Clyne** (☎ **340-776-6715**)
- ✔ **St. John Car Rental** (☎ **340-776-6103**)
- ✔ **Spencer's Jeep** (☎ **888-776-6628** or 340-693-8784)

By helicopter

Air Center Helicopters (☎ **340-775-7335**), on the Charlotte Amalie waterfront (next to Tortola Wharf) on St. Thomas, has 25-minute island tours priced at $125 per trip per person (two-person minimum). You can also arrange longer flights that loop over to the neighboring BVIs, as well as photography tours. **Seaborne Seaplane Adventures** (5305 Long Bay Rd., ☎ **340-777-1227**) offers narrated "flightseeing" tours of the USVIs and the BVIs from its Havensight base on Sr. Thomas. The 40-minute "Round-the-Island" tour is $94 per person.

Quick Concierge

ATMs

On St. Thomas, the branch of **First Bank** (☎ 340-776-9494) near Market Square and the waterfront locations (☎ 340-693-2777) and **Chase Manhattan Bank** (☎ 340-775-7777) have automatic teller machines. On St. Croix, contact **Banco Popular** (☎ 340-693-2777) or **Chase Manhattan Bank** (☎ 340-775-7777) for information on branch and ATM locations. On St. John, **Chase Manhattan Bank** (☎ 340-775-7777) has the island's only ATM machine.

Baby-sitters

You can find sitters easily, but try to reserve 24 hours in advance. Expect to pay $7 or more per hour.

Banks

Bank hours are generally Monday through Thursday from 9 a.m. to 3 p.m. and Friday 9 a.m. to 5 p.m. A handful have Saturday hours (9 a.m. to noon). Walk-up windows open at 8:30 a.m. on weekdays.

Credit Cards

Credit cards are widely accepted in the USVIs. VISA and MasterCard are the cards of choice at most local businesses, although American Express and, to a lesser extent, Diners Club are also popular.

Currency Exchange

The U.S. dollar is used throughout the territory, as well as in the neighboring BVIs. All major credit cards and traveler's checks are generally accepted.

Doctors

On St. Croix, a good local doctor is Dr. Frank Bishop, **Sunny Isle Medical Center** (☎ 340-778-0069). On St. Thomas, **Doctors-on-Duty** (Vitraco Park, ☎ 340-776-7996) in Charlotte Amalie is a reliable medical facility. On St. John, contact **St. John Myrah Keating Smith Community Health Clinic** (28 Sussanaberg; ☎ 340-693-8900).

Emergencies

On all USVIs, call ☎ **911** for ambulance, fire, and police.

Hospitals

St. Thomas Hospital (☎ 340-776-8311) has a recompression chamber. On St. Croix, outside Christiansted there's the **Gov. Juan F. Luis Hospital and Health Center** (6 Diamond Ruby, north of Sunny Isle Shopping Center on Rte. 79; ☎ 340-778-6311). You can also try the **Frederiksted Health Center** (516 Strand St.; ☎ 340-772-1992). On St. John, visit the **Myrah Keating Smith Community Health Center** (Rte. 10, about 7 minutes east of Cruz Bay; ☎ 340-693-8900).

Homework

Read Herman Wouk's *Don't Stop the Carnival.*

Information

Before you visit the island, contact the **USVI Division of Tourism** at #1 Tolbod Gade, St. Thomas, VI 00802 (☎ 800-372-USVI or 212-332-2222; fax 212-332-2223; Internet www.usvi.net).

On St. Thomas, the USVI Division of Tourism has an office in Charlotte Amalie (Box 6400, Charlotte Amalie 00804; ☎ 800-372-8784 or 340-774-8784). You'll also find a visitors center in downtown Charlotte Amalie and a cruise ship welcome center at Havensight Mall. The **National Park Service** has a visitors center across the harbor from the ferry dock at Red Hook.

On St. Croix, the USVI Division of Tourism has offices at 53A Company Street in Christiansted (Box 4538, Christiansted 00822; ☎ 340-773-0495) and on the pier in Frederiksted (Strand St., Frederiksted 00840; ☎ 340-772-0357).

On St. John, there's a branch of the USVI Department of Tourism (Box 200, Cruz Bay 00830; ☎ 340-776-6450) in the compound between Sparky's and the U.S. Post Office in Cruz Bay. The **National Park Service** (Box 710, 00831; ☎ 340-776-6201) also has a visitors center at the Creek in Cruz Bay.

Language

English is the official language, though island residents often speak it with a lilting Creole accent, so you might not recognize certain words at first.

Maps

If you plan to do extensive touring of the island, purchase *The Official Road Map of the U.S. Virgin Islands*, available at island bookstores and free at the Christiansted office of the Department of Tourism.

St. Thomas This Week, distributed free by the visitors center and usually on cruise ships stopping on St. Thomas, contains a great two-page map with a clear, easy-to-follow street plan of Charlotte Amalie, plus the locations of important landmarks and all of Charlotte Amalie's leading shops.

The **St. John Tourist Office** (☎ 340-776-6450) is located near the Battery, a 1735 fort that is a short walk from where the ferry from St. Thomas docks. You'll find plenty of travel information here, including a free map of Cruz Bay and the entire island that pinpoints all the main attractions. Hours are Monday through Friday from 8 a.m. to noon and 1 to 5 p.m.

St. Croix This Week, which is distributed free to cruise ship passengers and air passengers, has detailed maps of Christiansted, Frederiksted, and the entire island, pinpointing individual attractions, hotels, shops, and restaurants.

Newspapers/Magazines

Copies of U.S. mainland newspapers, such as *The New York Times, USA Today,* and *The Miami Herald,* arrive daily in St. Thomas and are sold at hotels and newsstands. The latest copies of *Time* and *Newsweek* are also for sale. *St. Thomas Daily News* covers local, national, and international events. Pick up *Virgin Islands Playground* and *St. Thomas This Week;* both are packed with visitor information and are distributed free all over the island.

Newspapers such as *The Miami Herald* are flown into St. Croix, which also has its own newspaper, *St. Croix Avis. Time* and *Newsweek* are widely sold as well. Your best source for local information is *St. Croix This Week,* which is distributed free by the tourist offices.

On St. John, copies of U.S. mainland newspapers arrive daily and are for sale at Mongoose Junction, Caneel Bay, and Hyatt. The latest copies of *Time* and *Newsweek* are also for sale. Complimentary copies of *What to Do: St. Thomas/St. John* contain many helpful hints, although this publication is a commercial mouthpiece. It is the official guidebook of the St. Thomas and St. John Hotel Association and is available at the tourist office and at various hotels.

Pharmacies

On St. Thomas, **Havensight Pharmacy** (☎ 340-776-1235) in the Havensight Mall is open daily from 9 a.m. to 9 p.m. **Kmart** (☎ 340-777-3854) operates a pharmacy inside the Tutu Park Mall; it's open from 8 a.m. to 9 p.m. **Sunrise Pharmacy** (☎ 340-775-6600), in Red Hook, is open daily from 9 a.m. to 7 p.m.

On St. Croix, although most drugstores are open daily from 8 a.m. to 8 p.m., off-season hours may vary; call ahead to confirm times. **Kmart** (☎ 340-692-2622) operates a pharmacy at its Sunshine Mall store. **People's Drug Store, Inc.,** has two branches: on the Christiansted Wharf (☎ 340-778-7355) and at the Sunny Isle Shopping Center (☎ 340-778-5537), just a few miles west of Christiansted on Route 70. In Frederiksted, try **D&D Apothecary Hall** (501 Queen St.; ☎ 340-772-1890).

On St. John, the **St. John Drug Center** (☎ 340-776-6353) is in the Boulon shopping center, up Centerline Road in Cruz Bay. It's open Monday through Saturday from 9 a.m. to 5 p.m.

Post Office
Hours may vary slightly from branch to branch and island to island, but they are generally 7:30–8 a.m. to 4–5:30 p.m. weekdays and 7:30–8 a.m. to noon–2:30 Saturday.

The main U.S. Post Office on St. Thomas is near the hospital, with branches in Charlotte Amalie, Frenchtown, Havensight, and Tutu Mall. There's a post office at Christiansted, Frederiksted, Gallows Bay, and Sunny Isle on St. Croix, and one at Cruz Bay on St. John.

Safety
Vacationers tend to assume that normal precautions aren't necessary in paradise. They are. Though there isn't quite as much crime here as in large U.S. mainland cities, it does exist. To be safe, stick to well-lighted streets at night, and use the same kind of street sense that you would in any unfamiliar territory. (Don't wander the back alleys of Charlotte Amalie after five rum punches, for example.)

If you plan to carry things around, rent a car — not a Jeep — and lock possessions in the trunk. Keep your rental car locked wherever you park. Don't leave cameras, purses, and other valuables lying on the beach while you snorkel for an hour (or even for a minute), whether you're on the deserted beaches of St. John or the more crowded Magens and Coki beaches on St. Thomas. St. Croix has several remote beaches outside of Frederiksted and on the Fast End; it's best to visit them with a group rather than on your own.

Shops
In St. Thomas, stores on Main Street in Charlotte Amalie are open weekdays and Saturday from 9 a.m. to 5 p.m. Shop hours at Havensight Mall (next to the cruise ships dock) are the same, though some sometimes stay open until 9 p.m. on Friday, depending on how many cruise ships are at the dock. You may also find some shops open on Sunday if a lot of cruise ships are in port. Hotel shops are usually open evenings, as well.

St. Croix shop hours are usually Monday through Saturday 9 a.m. to 5 p.m., but you'll find some shops in Christiansted open in the evening. On St. John, store hours run from 9 or 10 a.m. to 5 or 6 p.m. Wharfside Village and Mongoose Junction shops in Cruz Bay are often open into the evening.

Telephone
The area code for all of the USVIs is 340, and you can dial direct to and from the mainland as well as to and from Australia, Canada, New Zealand, and the United Kingdom. Local calls from a public phone cost 25¢ for five minutes.

On St. John, the place to go for telephone or message needs is **Connections** (Cruz Bay; ☎ 340-776-6922; Coral Bay; ☎ 340-779-4994).

Time Zone

The USVIs are on Atlantic Time, which places the islands one hour ahead of Eastern Standard Time. However, during daylight saving time, the USVIs and the East Coast are on the same clock.

Tipping

Many hotels add a 10% to 15% service charge to cover the room maid and other staff. However, some hotels may use part of that money to fund their operations, passing on only a portion of it to the staff. Check with your maid or bellman to determine the hotel's policy. If you discover you need to tip, give bellmen and porters 50¢ to $1 per bag and maids $1 or $2 per day. Special errands or requests of hotel staff always require an additional tip. At restaurants, bartenders and waiters expect a 10% to 15% tip, but always check your tab to see whether or not service is included. Taxi drivers get a 15% tip.

Water

There is ample water for showers and bathing in the Virgin Islands, but please conserve. Many visitors drink the local tap water with no harmful aftereffects. To be prudent, especially if you have a delicate stomach, stick with bottled water.

Weather & Surf Reports

All three islands receive both cable and commercial TV stations. Radio weather reports can be heard at 8:30 a.m. and 7:30 p.m. on 99.5 FM.

Chapter 34

Dining in the U.S. Virgin Islands

. . . .

In This Chapter

▶ Sampling the local cuisine

▶ Saving money on meals

▶ Locating the island's best restaurants

. . . .

*Y*ou can find good restaurants on St. Thomas, St. John, and St. Croix, whether you're looking for simple and cheap local food or a more sophisticated dining experience with experimental dishes whipped out by professional chefs. The USVI's dining scene attracts some of the best chefs and waitstaffs the U.S. has to offer, because these beautiful islands offer plenty in return.

Even hotel restaurants are rolling out the culinary carpet for guests, recognizing the role that food plays in the total vacation experience that today's traveler expects.

At all but the plain restaurants serving simple local fare, you can count on forking over a pirate's small fortune for the price of your meal. Generally speaking, you won't be disappointed with the flavorful and inventive fare. Think of the outlay as the toll for having a nice meal out in your own hometown. Now add in the stunning views and tropical surroundings that you probably don't find back home. Takes some of the bite out of the fact that main courses hover at around $20 and up, doesn't it?

Enjoying a Taste of the U.S. Virgin Islands

Particularly good bets here are fresh local fruit and local seafood like wahoo, mahimahi, and conch.

If you want a light meal of local food, order a *johnnycake* (a cornbread/ flour treat), a *pate* (small pastry filled with meat or fish), or a thick slice of *dumb bread* (a dense round loaf often cut into triangles and filled with cheddar cheese) from any of the mobile food vans you see around the islands.

For a "belonger" experience (as locals call themselves), stop at a local restaurant for goat stew, leg of lamb with guava, curry chicken, or fried pork chops. Local cooks pile on the sides, so dining is akin to eating at a "meat-'n'-three" in the Southern U.S.

Seven flags have flown over St. Croix, and you can detect the legacy of each in its restaurants. Italian, French, Danish, and American dishes are all commonly served, and you'll often see a creative fusion of these cuisines on the same menu.

St. John, where a disproportionate number of residents claim the job of artist on their tax forms, attracts creative types when it comes to chefs, too. Here you can find something tasty no matter what your budget, whether you're staying at **Caneel Bay** (where men may be required to wear a jacket at dinner) or sampling the casual in-town eateries of **Cruz Bay.**

Dining in the USVI is relaxed and informal; few restaurants require a jacket and tie. But while shorts and a tank top may not get you tossed out of a better restaurant, you may find yourself seated at a dark corner table. Men should wear slacks and a shirt with buttons. Women should wear a nice sundress or pants outfit in the evenings.

Eating Out without Breaking the Bank

 For quick and cheap lunches, try the West Indian food stands in **Cruz Bay Park** and across from the post office. The cooks prepare fried chicken legs, pates (meat- and fish-filled pastries), and *kallaloo* (a greens, onion, and crabmeat soup).

If your accommodations have a kitchen and you plan to cook, you can find most of your back-home staples in St. Thomas's supermarkets. But you'll pay about 20% more than you would in the United States. Try shopping at one of the big new superstores on St. Thomas or St. Croix to get better prices on basics, especially if you're staying for a week or more. Shopping on St. Thomas for St. John is more likely to yield a bargain — or at least a reasonable price; you can haul the groceries with you on the ferry.

The U.S. Virgin Islands' Best Restaurants

When you visit one of the U.S. Virgin Islands, you're likely to stay put, perhaps popping over to one of the other islands for a day or so. We arranged our dining favorites to reflect the ways you're most likely to experience the USVI — island by island. We start with St. Thomas; it has the widest selection. Next up is St. Croix, which has some nice up-and-comers. We wind up with St. John, where you'll find a surprisingly sophisticated scene.

On St. Thomas

Here's what you can expect to find to feed your appetite for a variety of fare on this 32-square-mile island.

Agavé Terrace

$$$–$$$$ East End, St. Thomas   Seafood

Perched high above a steep and heavily forested hillside on the eastern tip of St. Thomas, this outstanding restaurant offers a sweeping panorama of St. John and the BVIs at night. Owners Greg and Daniela, a young couple, oversee this excellent spot, which serves inventive fresh fish prepared as steaks or fillets. The fare has gleaned six gold medals in Caribbean cooking competitions. Come early and have a drink at the **Lookout Lounge.** The house drink, Desmond Delight, is a combination of Midori, rum, pineapple juice, and a secret ingredient. The extensive wine list won a "Wine Spectator" award. A live steel drum band draws listeners Tuesday, Thursday, and Saturday nights.

Point Pleasant Resort, Smith Bay. ☎ 340-775-4142. Reservations recommended. Main courses: $17.50–$38. AE, MC, V. Open daily for dinner from 6 p.m. to 10 p.m.

Alexander's Café

$$$ Frenchtown, St. Thomas
Austrian/German with a touch of American Continental

Small, intimate Alexander's, west of town, has just 12 tables in an air-conditioned room with picture windows overlooking the harbor. The Teutonic dishes are the best on the island, especially when they involve seafood; a delectable conch schnitzel is served on occasion. This place is a favorite with people in the restaurant business on St. Thomas — always a sign of quality. Alexander is Austrian, and the schnitzels are delicious and reasonably priced. The pasta specials are especially good. Save room for strudel. Lunch features a variety of crepes, quiches, and a daily chef's special. At both lunch and dinner, you can choose from 10 to 13 different pasta dishes.

24A Honduras. ☎ 340-776-4211. Reservations essential. Main courses: $12–$24.95. AE, DISC, MC, V. Open for lunch and dinner daily except Sunday. Lunch from 11:30 a.m. to 5 p.m.; dinner from 5:30 p.m. to 10 p.m.

St. Thomas's Restaurants

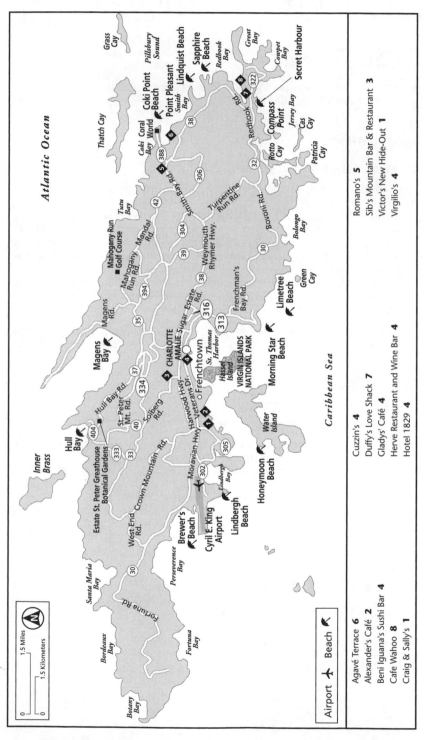

Airport ✈ Beach ☚

Agavé Terrace **6**
Alexander's Café **2**
Beni Iguana's Sushi Bar **4**
Cafe Wahoo **8**
Craig & Sally's **1**

Cuzzin's **4**
Duffy's Love Shack **7**
Gladys' Café **4**
Herve Restaurant and Wine Bar **4**
Hotel 1829 **4**

Romano's **5**
Sib's Mountain Bar & Restaurant **3**
Victor's New Hide-Out **1**
Virgilio's **4**

Banana Tree Grille

$$$ Charlotte Amalie   International Caribbean

After you wind your way through the historic Bluebeard's Castle, you find this open-air, cheery spot clinging to the hillside of Charlotte Amalie. The restaurant is one of our favorites in St. Thomas, and it sports one of the best views of this harborfront city. When you call for reservations, ask for a table as far to the edge of the multilevel terrace as possible. It's the sort of typically Caribbean place we've come to love: palm trees twined with tiny, twinkling lights, waiters in tropical shirts hoisting trays of equally tropical drinks overhead, candlelight, and views like a postcard. Here's the best part: The seafood is excellent and served in generous portions. We recommend the bacon-wrapped horseradish shrimp with mango glaze for a starter. For the main event, we loved the sugar cane coco-lacquered tuna and the coconut shrimp tempura served with yams. Plus, the homemade bread — *chiabatta*, crispy on the outside and soft on the inside, a specialty that comes with a roasted garlic and white bean spread — is a don't-miss.

Although we saw families there, and they are welcome, we'd leave the kiddoes at home and concentrate on romance at this restaurant.

Bluebeard's Castle, Charlotte Amalie. ☎ *340-776-4050. Reservations highly recommended. Main courses: $18–$45. AE, V, MC. Open Tuesday through Sunday from 6 p.m. to 9:30 p.m.*

Beni Iguana's Sushi Bar

$–$$ Charlotte Amalie, St. Thomas   Asian

Right in the heart of Charlotte Amalie is another fresh fish offering. This time it's sushi, served as "edible art" in a charming Danish courtyard setting. If you're not a sushi fan, try the tasty green-lipped mussels. Among the offerings are cucumber and avocado or scallop with scallion rolls, and tuna or salmon sashimi. A pictorial menu board makes ordering by the piece, plate, or combination platter much easier.

In the Grand Hotel Court, Veteran's Dr. ☎ *340-777-8744. Reservations recommended. Sushi $4.50–$6 per portion (two pieces); main courses $6–$13.75. AE, MC, V. Open daily for lunch from 11 a.m. to 3 p.m.; closed Sunday.*

Cafe Wahoo

$$–$$$$ East End, St. Thomas   Seafood

The chef/owner here gets first pick from the fishermen who bring their catches across the dock of Red Hook's American Yacht Harbor. Then he applies his Euro-Caribbean recipes for good results. His beautiful wife is the hostess at this casual open-air eatery. For starters, try the medallion of yellowfin tuna seviche marinated in lime, onion, and white wine.

Entrees include a grilled fillet of wahoo with pineapple and cucumber sauce and sea bass poached in spiced carrot essence and topped with caviar. Steak, poultry, and pasta lovers will find something to please on the menu, too.

Piccola Marina, Red Hook. ☎ *340-775-6350. Recommendations recommended year-round. AE, MC, V. Open for dinner nightly from 6 p.m. to 10 p.m.*

Craig & Sally's

$$–$$$ Frenchtown, St. Thomas   International

This long-time favorite with many locals has a daily changing menu with only a few staples, such as eggplant cheesecake with pinenut-garlic bread crumb crust as a starter. Boasting an extensive wine list with a dozen wines offered by the glass, this Frenchtown classic relies on the wine selections of husband Craig while Chef Sally Darash concentrates her skills in the kitchen. She whips out new ideas continually, but they usually have a Mediterranean, Asian, and Caribbean flair. Examples of her enterprising entrees include sauteed Chilean sea bass with mango barbecue glaze and fresh mango couscous; baked halibut in a Mexican mole sauce with rice and jalapeno jack-black bean quesadilla; or grilled pork loin atop linguine tossed with carrots, water chestnuts, zucchini, onions, ginger, and szechwan sauce, topped with fried wontons. Try her white-chocolate cheesecake for dessert.

22 Estate Honduras. ☎ *340-777-9949. Reservations recommended. Main courses: $15–$28. AE, MC, V. Open for lunch Wednesday through Friday from 11:30 to 2:30 p.m.; dinner Wednesday through Sunday from 5:30 p.m. to 9:30 p.m.*

Cuzzin's

$$ Charlotte Amalie, St. Thomas   Local Caribbean

This casual restaurant makes a great stop for a simple but hearty lunch of local fare. The 250-year-old yellow brick building near the main shopping district of Charlotte Amalie was once the family home of the owner's mother. Prints by Pissarro decorate the exposed brick walls. The friendly and attentive servers will patiently explain any unfamiliar items on the menu (like *sea moss* — a drink of milk, sugar, seaweed, and nutmeg). The fried fish with sides of sweet potato, *kallaloo* (a soup concoction), and rice and peas is excellent. Ask for the hot sauce, locally made, if you want to spice things up.

Historic district, #7 Backstreet. ☎ *340-777-4711. Reservations recommended. AE, MC, V. Open for lunch Monday through Saturday from 11 a.m. to 5 p.m. and dinner Tuesday through Saturday from 5 p.m. to 9:30 p.m.*

Duffy's Love Shack

$–$$$ East End, St. Thomas   Eclectic

This funky little institution near the Red Hook ferry has a second location on St. John. Its claim to fame is that the couples who eventually became the Mamas and the Papas sometimes camped out on St. John, and they would come over to sing for the original owner. Their act became so popular that they decided to form their famous group.

Floating bubbles emanate from this zany eatery, which has lime-green shutters, throbbing rock music, and delicious chicken super nachos to attract you. Staking the establishment's reputation of being the "ultimate tropical drink shack," bartenders shake up such exotic concoctions as the Love Shack Volcano — a 50-ounce flaming extravaganza. Try the assortment of Great White Bites, blackened shark, tequila shrimp, or Jamaican jerk nachos. Thursday nights feature theme parties complete with prizes and giveaways.

Red Hook Plaza parking lot. ☎ *340-779-2080. No credit cards. Open daily from 11:30 a.m. to 2 a.m.*

Gladys' Café

$$–$$$ Charlotte Amalie, St. Thomas   Caribbean/Creole

For great local food right in the heart of town, head to Gladys's table. She'll greet you warmly and leave you all smiles once you've tasted her conch in butter sauce, saltfish and dumplings, or hearty red bean soup. While you're here, pick up some of her special hot sauce for $6 a bottle.

Royal Dane Mall. ☎ *340-774-6604. AE, DC, MC, V. Open Monday through Saturday for breakfast from 6:30 a.m. to 11 a.m. and lunch from 11 a.m. to 4:30 p.m. Sunday for breakfast from 8 a.m. to 11 a.m. and lunch from 11 a.m. to 2 p.m. on Sunday. No dinner service.*

Hervé Restaurant and Wine Bar

$$$–$$$$ Charlotte Amalie, St. Thomas
Continental/American/Caribbean

Next door to **Hotel 1829** (see the next entry), this restaurant offers a great view of the harbor. French-trained Hervé Chassin's long career on St. Thomas has resulted in a creative menu featuring Caribbean and contemporary French and American cuisine. Candlelight flickers on the century-old black-and-white photos of St. Thomas. Tables are impeccably set with linen, silver, and fine crystal. Start with crispy conch fritters served with a spicy-sweet mango chutney. Then choose from such entrees as fresh tuna encrusted with sesame seeds or succulent roast duck with a ginger and tamarind sauce. Finish with the creamy mango cheesecake.

Government Hill. ☎ *340-777-9703. Reservations necessary. Main courses: $17.75–$24.75. AE, MC, V. Open Monday through Thursday for lunch from 11:30 a.m. to 2:30 p.m.; dinner nightly except Wednesday from 6 p.m. to 9:30 p.m.*

Hotel 1829

$$$–$$$$ Charlotte Amalie, St. Thomas   Continental

Before dinner, have a drink in the cozy, darkly atmospheric bar, which will prompt you to wonder who has lingered in this special place before you discovered it. Candlelight flickers on the stone walls and on the pink table linens at this Government Hill terrace restaurant. The menu is extensive, including Caribbean rock lobster and rack of lamb, and the award-winning wine list is equally vast, featuring 325 varieties — 15 available by the glass.

Many items, including a warm spinach salad, are prepared tableside. The restaurant is justly famous for its dessert soufflés: chocolate, Grand Marnier, raspberry, or coconut, to name a few.

Kongens Gade (at the east end of Main St.). ☎ 340-776-1829. Reservations essential but not accepted more than one day in advance. Main courses: $19.50–$32.50; fixed-price dinner $28.50. AE, DISC, MC, V. Open for dinner from 6 p.m. to 9:30 p.m.; closed Sundays.

Romano's

$$$–$$$$ East End, St. Thomas   Northern Italian

Near Coral World, inside a rambling, old stucco house with exposed brick walls, we found a restaurant serving superb Northern Italian cuisine. Owner Tony hasn't advertised since the restaurant opened in 1988 — word-of-mouth sends diners packing in for his pastas. He likes to play with your food, introducing fun twists to classic Italian cuisine. The wine racks are well-stocked, too.

97 Smith Bay. ☎ 340-775-0045. Reservations essential. Main courses: $22.95–$26.95; pastas $15.95–$18.95. MC, V. Open for dinner Monday through Saturday from 6 p.m. to 10 p.m; closed Sunday. Closed August and one week in April for the annual Carnival celebration.

Sib's Mountain Bar and Restaurant

$$ Northside, St. Thomas   U.S. All-American

Here you can find inexpensive barbecued ribs and chicken, along with a rollicking good time. Live music plays, except when there's a football game on. Kids of all ages can doodle on the paper tablecloths with the colorful crayons left on every table.

Mafolie Hill. ☎ 340-774-8967. AE, MC, V. Dinner daily from 5 p.m. to 11 p.m.

Victor's New Hide-Out

$$–$$$ Frenchtown, St. Thomas   Caribbean/Creole

The landmark restaurant, sandwiched between Nisky Shopping Center and the airport, overlooks Water Island. Its colorful owner, Victor Sydney, hailing from the tiny Caribbean island of Montserrat, has attracted celebrities for decades with his Caribbean cooking. If you're driving, call for directions. Otherwise, take a taxi. Local food — steamed fish, marinated pork chops, and lobster — and local music liven up the casual and friendly West Indian atmosphere. The large, airy restaurant serves fresh lobster prepared Montserrat style (in a creamy sauce) or grilled in the shell. For dessert, try Victor's apple pie.

Sub Base. ☎ 340-776-9379. Reservations recommended. Main courses: $9.95–$29.95. AE, MC, V. Open Monday through Saturday for lunch from 11:30 a.m. to 3:30 p.m. and dinner 5:30 p.m. to 9:45 p.m. No lunch on Sunday.

Virgilio's

$$$–$$$$ Charlotte Amalie, St. Thomas   Northern Italian

Owner Virgilio de Mare has established himself as the Don of Northern Italian cuisine on St. Thomas with more than 40 homemade pastas and superb sauces. He's created an elegant hideaway with two-story brick walls decorated with eclectic art. His lobster ravioli is scrumptious.

18 Dronningens Gade (entrance on a narrow alleyway running between Main St. and Back St.). ☎ *340-776-4920. Reservations essential. Main courses: $8.95–$19.95. AE, MC. V. Open Monday through Saturday for lunch from 11:30 a.m. to 3 p.m. and dinner 6 p.m. to 10 p.m.*

On St. Croix

The largest of the U.S. Virgin Islands, St. Croix dishes out rich dining opportunities.

Blue Moon

$$$ Fredricksted, St. Croix   Eclectic

We like this small, waterfront bistro, advertised on a sign made Haitian-style from an old oil drum. Painted in bright Caribbean colors, this spot is popular for its live jazz on Friday night. Like many restaurants on St. Croix, its eclectic and ever-changing menu draws on Asian, Cajun, and local flavors. Try the seafood chowder as an appetizer, the roasted vegetables and shrimp over linguine as an entree, and the almond joy sundae for dessert.

17 Strand St. ☎ *340-772-2222. Main courses: $14–$18.50. AE, DISC, MC, V. Open Tuesday through Saturday for lunch from 11:30 a.m. to 2 p.m. and dinner from 6 p.m. to 10 p.m.; Sunday brunch from 11 a.m. to 2 p.m. Closed July to August.*

Bombay Club

$$–$$$ Christiansted, St. Croix   Eclectic

This bar, with its cool, exposed stone walls, is a favorite expatriate hangout. In the dim light, after a couple of rum punches, you'll think you see a pirate in the corner. If you want food to go along with your liquid supper, go for the heavenly stuffed crabs with roast garlic herb sauce.

5A King St. ☎ *340-773-1838. Reservations recommended. Main courses: $10–$18. MC, V. Open Monday through Friday for lunch from 11:30 a.m. to 4 p.m. and dinner daily from 5:30 p.m. to 10 p.m.*

St. Croix's Restaurants

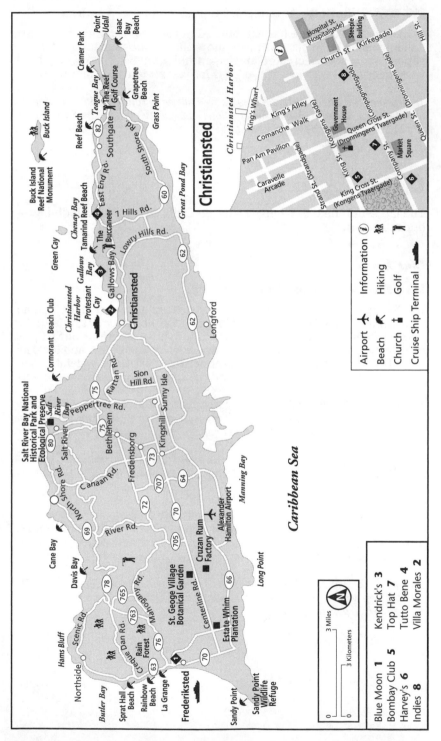

Harvey's

$ Christiansted, St. Croix   Caribbean/Creole

This local spot has been turned into a shrine to home-island basketball hero Tim Duncan of the San Antonio Spurs. Larger-than-life-sized murals loom over the plain dining room with 12 tables. If you've got a jones for great local fare, this place will sate you with goat stew and tender whelks (similar to mussels) in butter, served with heaping helpings of rice, fungi, and vegetables. Daily specials are listed on the blackboard. Genial owner Sarah Harvey takes great pride in her kitchen, bustling out from behind the stove to chat and urge you to eat up.

11B Company St. ☎ 340-773-3433. Main courses: $7–$10. No credit cards. Lunch daily from 11:30 a.m. to 4 p.m. Closed Sunday.

Indies

$$$–$$$$ Christiansted, St. Croix   Caribbean/Creole

Tiny lights add a soft glow to this open-air courtyard where palms gently rustle overhead in the tropic breeze. The Caribbean has infused and inspired the daily-changing menu of owners/chefs Eric Zolner and Steve Hendren. The duo has positioned it to make the most of St. Croix's freshest fish, fruit and vegetables. Indulge in dolphinfish baked in coconut milk, ginger, tomato, and spicy peppers. Great for a Friday or Saturday evening under the stars when the strains of live jazz sooth.

55–56 Company St. ☎ 340-692-9440. Reservations recommended. Main courses: $16–$21. AE, DISC, MC, V. Open daily for lunch from 11:30 a.m. to 2:30 p.m. and dinner from 6 p.m. to 9:30 p.m.

Kendricks

$$$$ Gallows Bay, St. Croix   French Contemporary

For several years, Kendricks, decorated with island antiques, has been known as the island's most in-tune restaurant. A recent move to Gallows Bay hasn't changed this open-air restaurant's status. Now you not only come across inventive cuisine, which merited a write-up in *Bon Appetit;* you also gain the pure joy of a view of Christiansted Harbor. Try the warm chipolte pepper with garlic and onion soup. Move on to the house specialty: pecan-crusted roast pork loin with ginger mayonnaise.

12 Chandlers Wharf, Gallows Bay. ☎ 340-773-9199. Reservations required. Main courses: $14–$26. AE, MC, V. Open nightly for dinner from 6 p.m. to 10 p.m.

Top Hat

$$$$ Christiansted, St. Croix   Continental

Although the Danes ruled St. Croix for many years, this restaurant is the only one focusing on Danish specialties these days. Since 1970, the owners have turned out dishes like crisp roast duck stuffed with apples and prunes, *frikadeller* (savory meatballs in a tangy cocktail sauce), fried Camembert with lingonberries, and smoked eel. The signature dessert is a rum ice cream-filled chocolate windmill with blades that turn.

52 Company St., ☎ *340-773-2346. Reservations recommended. Main courses: $20–$34; all include access to a salad bar. AE, DISC, MC, V. Open Monday through Saturday for dinner from 6 p.m. to 10 p.m. Closed May through August.*

Tutto Bene

$$$–$$$$ Christiansted, St. Croix   Italian

Don't let Tutto Bene's looks fool you. Although it may remind you more of Mexico than of Italy, owners Smokey and Kelly Odum have conjured up a taste of mamma's homey Italian fare. The daily menu reads well on hanging mirrors. It includes items like seafood Genoveses with mussels, clams, and shrimp in a white-wine pesto over linguine, or a veal chop with sundried tomatoes.

2 Company St. ☎ *340-773-5229. Reservations accepted only for parties of six or more. Main courses: $14.95–$24.95. AE, DISC, MC, V. Open nightly for dinner from 5 p.m. to 10 p.m.*

Villa Morales

$ Fredricksted, St.Croix   Caribbean/Creole

Locals come to this family-run spot for the food and the dancing (in the cavernous back room). The kitchen turns out such well-prepared Cruzan and Spanish dishes as goat stew and baked chicken, all served with heaping helpings of fungi (the island version of polenta or grits), rice, and vegetables. Specialities include *Arroz con Pollo con habituelas* (chicken and rice with beans), saltfish with green bananas, and salmon balls (similar to salmon croquettes).

Plot 82C (off Rte. 70). Estate Whim. ☎ *340-772-0556. Reservations essential. DISC, MC, V. Open Thursday through Saturday for lunch and dinner from 10 a.m. to 10 p.m.*

On St. John

Treats for the eyes and palate await on St. John Island, an expanse of 20 square miles that is far from diminutive in its tasty offerings.

Asolare

$$$–$$$$ Cruz Bay, St. John   Asian

From the moment we stepped into this cloud-kissing spot, we knew we were in for a treat. Reserve a table at Asolare, which means "leisurely passing the time," on a night when you can linger and linger and linger. Your table on the balcony looks down on Cruz Bay and takes in one of the grandest views in the Caribbean. The inventive magician of a chef, Carlos Beccar Varela, makes full use of his knowledge of contemporary Asian fusion, veering more into fiery Thai flavors. Come early and relax over drinks while you enjoy the sunset over the harbor. His presentation is beautiful.

Start with a crab summer roll (a variation on the spring roll theme) with tamarind peanut sauce, or spicey tuna tartare. Entrees include such delights as salmon rolled in Szechuan spices with a *wasabi* (spicy green mustard similar to horseradish) and passion fruit cream sauce. The chocolate pyramid, a luscious cake with homemade ice cream melting in the middle, is worth every calorie.

Caneel Hill. ☎ 340-779-4747. Reservations required. Main courses: $20–$29. AE, MC, V. Open daily for dinner from 5:30 p.m. to 10 p.m.

Equator

$$$–$$$$ St. John Caribbean/Latin/Thai

Even if the food weren't fantastic (and we enjoyed every last bite), we'd recommend Equator for its setting alone. This jewel is tucked behind the tower of an eighteenth-century sugar mill. A flight of stairs leads to a monumental circular dining room. The wraparound veranda shares sweeping views of Caneel Bay's lovely grounds, which were replanted with 1,000 trees after Hurricane Marilyn's tour of damage in 1995. The restaurant features a giant poinciana — known to islanders as "woman's tongue tree" — in its central dining area.

The daring cuisine, a romp through equatorial cuisines around the globe, largely works. The teriyaki tuna comes with a pickled lobster roll and tempura vegetables. The pepper-cured tandoori lamb with Egyptian-style couscous is another tasty winner, as is the wok-fried catfish with Polynesian ponzu and fried rice.

In the Caneel Bay Hotel. ☎ 340-776-6111. Reservations required. Main courses: $12–$27. AE, MC, V. Open daily for dinner in the winter. During off-season, open Wednesday, Thursday, and Sunday for dinner from 6 p.m. to 9:30 p.m.

Fish Trap

$$$ Cruz Bay, St. John Eclectic

The rooms and terraces here open to the breezes and buzz with a mix of locals and visitors. Chef Aaron Willis conjures up such tasty appetizers as conch fritters and Fish Trap chowder (a creamy soup tinged with tomato; fresh fish, lobster, conch, or snapper; white wine; paprika; and secret spices). Come for good seafood in a laid-back St. John atmosphere.

Downtown, next to Our Lady of Mount Carmel Church. ☎ 340-693-9994. Reservations not accepted unless parties include six or more. Main courses: $7.95–$22.95. AE, DISC, MC, V. Open Tuesday through Sunday for dinner from 6 p.m. to 9:30 p.m.

St. John's Restaurants

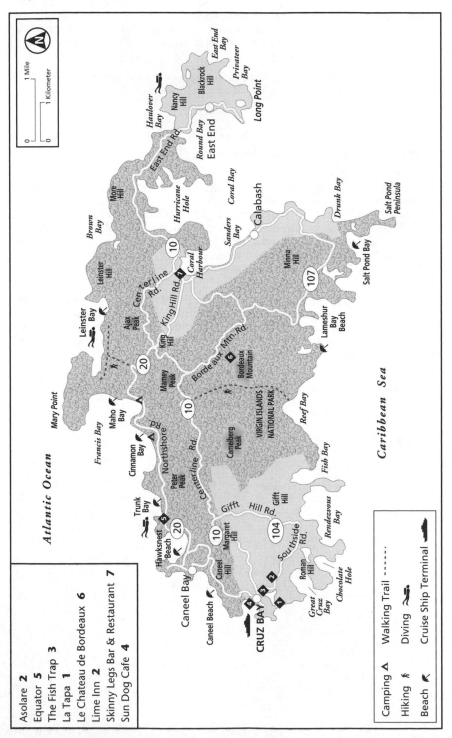

Asolare **2**
Equator **5**
The Fish Trap **3**
La Tapa **1**
Le Chateau de Bordeaux **6**
Lime Inn **2**
Skinny Legs Bar & Restaurant **7**
Sun Dog Cafe **4**

Camping ⚑   Walking Trail ------
Hiking 🚶   Diving 🤿
Beach 🏖   Cruise Ship Terminal ⚓

La Tapa

$$–$$$ Cruz Bay, St. John   Eclectic

Locals congregate here to feast on *tapas* (hors d'oeuvres) and sip sangria. Although street side tables let you watch the world go by, they're a little noisy. Request a spot inside for a quiet, cozy, bistro-like atmosphere. Owner Alex Ewald dishes up a changing menu of delicious soups, tapas as lighter fare for dinner, and yummy desserts. The buffalo mozzarella served with tomatoes and basil, crusty breads, and spicy chutney are made in her own tiny kitchen.

Across from Scotia Bank on an unnamed street that heads inland from Red Hook ferry dock. ☎ 340-693-7755. AE, MC, V. "Tapas hours" Monday through Friday from 3:30 p.m. to 6:30 p.m. Open for dinner Monday through Saturday from 6 p.m. to 10 p.m.

ROMANCE

Le Chateau de Bordeaux

$$$–$$$$ Bordeaux Mountain, St. John   Contemporary

If you've ever imagined supping in a tree house, you'll feel right at home in this rustic yet ultra-romantic spot graced with wrought-iron chandeliers, fine lace tablecloths, and Victorian antiques. Given a choice, we'd skirt the air-conditioned dining room and head for the terrace. After all, you are on one of St. John's highest peaks. The innovative preparations appeal equally to eye and palate. Start with the chicken crawfish gumbo. Segue into rosemary-perfumed rack of lamb with a honey-Dijon-nut crust in a shallot-and-port-wine sauce, or salmon poached with white wine and capers and served on a bed of pasta. The game dishes are usually excellent. The comprehensive, moderately priced wine list is predictably strong on Bordeaux reds.

*Junction 10, Centerline Rd. ☎ **340-776-6611**. Reservations recommended. Main courses: $18–$28. AE, MC, V. Open Monday through Saturday with two seatings, 5:30 p.m. to 6:30 p.m. and 7:30 p.m. to 8:45 p.m. Closed Sunday and Monday in summer.*

Lime Inn

$$$ Cruz Bay, St. John   Contemporary

This charming open-air restaurant in Cruz Bay offers gargantuan and excellent seafood salads in a congenial atmosphere with fantastic service. We ordered the lobster special, which was perfectly prepared and delicious, still tender despite its stint on the grill. The menu also features shrimp and steak dishes and such specials as sautéed chicken with artichoke hearts in lemon sauce. On Wednesday night, feast on all-you-can-eat shrimp. Prime rib is the specialty every Saturday night.

*Downtown, east of Chase Manhattan Bank. ☎ **340-776-6425**. Lunch $7–$15; dinner $12–$20. AE, MC, V. Open Monday through Friday for lunch from 11:30 a.m. to 3 p.m. and Monday through Saturday for dinner from 5:30 p.m. to 10 p.m.*

Skinny Legs Bar and Restaurant

$ Coral Bay, St. John   American

Sailors who live aboard boats anchored just off shore and long-time residents alike swap tales over fish sandwiches and burgers at this funky and fun watering hole. If owners Doug Sica and Mo Chabuz are around, take a gander at their gams. You'll see where the restaurant got its name.

Rte. 107 (near the Coral Bay dinghy dock). ☎ **340-779-4982.** *Main courses: $6– $15. No credit cards. Open daily for lunch and dinner from 11 a.m. to 10 p.m.*

Sun Dog Cafe

$–$$ Cruz Bay, St. John   Eclectic

Stop in for a light lunch at this small restaurant tucked into a courtyard in the upstairs of the Mongoose Junction shopping center. Munch on the white artichoke pizza with roasted garlic, artichoke hearts, mozzarella cheese, and capers. The Jamaican jerk chicken sub and the three-cheese quesadilla are also good choices.

Mongoose Junction shopping center. ☎ **340-693-8340.** *Main courses: $4.75–$11. No credit cards. Open daily for lunch from 11 a.m. to 6 p.m.*

Chapter 35

Hitting the Beach and Other Fun Things to Do

....

In This Chapter

▶ Soaking up the sun on USVIs' top beaches

▶ Diving into fun with watersports

▶ Satisfying the landlubber: Activities, shopping, and nightlife

▶ Planning some super side trips

....

*B*illed as an "American Paradise," the U.S. Virgin Islands (USVIs) deliver a vacation experience as rich and rewarding as any Caribbean getaway. Each lively island in the USVI, though certainly showing its connection to the United States, has its own exotic flavor. You're sure to feel the warm welcome of the culturally diverse people who make their homes in the islands, 1,000 miles south of the southernmost tip of the U.S. mainland.

St. Thomas, which has one of the Caribbean's loveliest harbor cities, Charlotte Amalie, is the best known of the three main islands. It's the second busiest cruise port in the Caribbean. Cruise shippers love the shopping just off the waterfront in the old colonial harbor city.

Just a short ferry ride away from St. Thomas lies our favorite of the trio of USVIs: **St. John.** Two-thirds national park, this beautiful little island has a funky, collegial feel to it.

The close runner-up for us is **St. Croix,** which has been overlooked by many tourists. It has two historic towns with beautiful Dutch architecture to explore, and it's a rural island with many working farms where you can get a good sense of the old Caribbean.

All three islands have fantastic beaches. Each is so different from the others that we strongly recommend splitting your time between at least two. If you've got a longer trip planned, hit all three and decide for yourself which is your favorite.

Hitting the Beaches

Following is a brief sketch of what you'll find on each island and our recommendations for the best beaches to visit.

On St. Thomas

All 44 St. Thomas beaches are open to the public, although you can only reach some of them by walking through a resort. Hotel guests frequently have access to lounge chairs and floats that are off-limits to nonguests. For this reason, you may feel more comfortable at a beach not associated with a resort, like stunningly beautiful **Magens Bay** (Route 35 and 42; the beach charges a $3 entrance fee; 25¢ per child under 12; open 8 a.m. to 6 p.m.), known for its heart-shaped shoreline and crystal-clear waters ideal for snorkeling around the rocks. Lined with lush green palms and equipped with showers and changing rooms, this beach is a good place to spend a whole day. The **Virgin Island Eco-Tours** (☎ 340-779-2155) has a new kayak tour that launches from this beach.

Arrive early on weekends and holidays, because Magens Bay gets crowded. There's also an outdoor bar, bathhouses, a nature trail (unmarked and often overgrown), and a snack bar. East of the beach is **Udder Delight** (☎ 340-777-6050), a one-room shop of the St. Thomas Dairies that serves a USVI tradition — a milk shake with a splash of Cruzan rum. Kids can enjoy virgin shakes, with a touch of soursop, mango, or banana flavoring.

Coki Beach, next to Coral World (turn north off Route 38), is a popular snorkeling spot for cruise ship passengers and a favorite for beginning scuba divers. It is also a good place to dash in for a swim or just do some people-watching from shore. The extras here include a bathroom, a food stand, a place to rent snorkel gear, and a great view of Thatch Cay and Leeward Passage.

Hull Bay beach, on the north shore (Route 37), faces Inner and Outer Brass cays and attracts fishermen and beachcombers. With its rougher Atlantic surf and relative isolation, Hull Bay is one of the best surfing spots on the island.

Morning Star Beach, close to Charlotte Amalie, is where many young locals bodysurf, play volleyball, or sailboard. The pretty curve of beach is adjacent to Marriott's Frenchman's Reef and fronts Marriott's Morningstar resort; you can find good beachside restaurants at the latter. Snorkeling is decent near the rocks when the current doesn't affect visibility. But the popular things to do here are waverunners and windsurfing.

Sapphire Beach has a fine view of St. John. The snorkeling is excellent at the reef to the right or east, near Prettyklip Point. Sapphire Beach Resort has a dive shop that rents watersports gear.

Secret Harbour's condo resort doesn't at all detract from the attractiveness of its covelike beach. Not only is this East End spot pretty, it also has superb snorkeling — head out to the left, near the rocks — and is the best place to snorkel at night.

On St. Croix

A visit to **Buck Island National Reef Monument,** part of the U.S. National Park system, is a must on any trip to St. Croix. The desert-like isle's beach is beautiful, but its finest treasures are those you can see when you plop off the boat and adjust your mask, snorkel, and flippers. President Kennedy declared it a marine park after a snorkeling trip here.

The waters aren't always gentle at **Cane Bay,** a breezy north shore beach, but it's perfect for a getaway. Plus, you've got great scuba diving and snorkeling. You'll see elkhorn and brain corals, and less than 200 yards out is the drop-off called Cane Bay Wall.

Isaac Bay is an East End beach almost impossible to reach without a four-wheel-drive vehicle, but it's worth the effort. You'll find secluded sands for sunbathing, calm waters for swimming, and a barrier reef for snorkeling. You can also get here via footpaths from Jacks Bay.

Small but attractive **Tamarind Reef Beach** is located east of Christiansted. Both Green Cay and Buck Island offer an arresting view. The snorkeling is good.

On St. John

If you want a great beach vacation, you'll find it on St. John. The beaches along the north shore are all within the 11,560 acre national park. Some are more developed than others, and all are crowded on weekends, holidays, and in high season, but by and large they're still pristine. Beaches along the south and eastern shores are still quiet and isolated.

Caneel Bay is a catch-all name for seven white-sand beaches on the north shore, six of which can be reached only by water if you aren't a guest at the Caneel Bay Resort. (Access to beaches is a civil right in the USVIs, but access to land that leads to the beaches is not.) The seventh, **Caneel Beach,** is open to the public and easy to reach from the main entrance of the resort; ask for directions at the gatehouse.

Cinnamon Bay is a long, sandy beach that faces beautiful cays and abuts the greens of a national park campground. The facilities are open to the public and include showers, toilets, a commissary, and a restaurant. You can rent watersports equipment here. That's a good thing, because Cinnamon Bay has some excellent snorkeling off the point to the right — far superior to Trunk Bay, which is still recommended in most guidebooks. You might spot sea turtles and small sharks, as well as good-sized parrot fish and triggerfish.

The Cinnamon Bay hiking trail begins across the road from the beach parking lot; the ruins of a sugar mill mark the trailhead. It takes about an hour to complete. The level nature trail, which features signs along the side that identify the flora, loops through the woods and passes an old Danish cemetery, while a steeper trail starts where the road bends past the ruins and heads straight up the hill.

Sea-grape trees line narrow **Hawksnest Beach,** which features rest rooms, cooking grills, and a covered shed for picnicking. It's the closest beach to town, so it's often crowded.

Popular **Maho Bay** beach is below the Maho Bay Camps — a wonderful hillside enclave of tents. The campground offers informal talks and slide and film presentations on nature, environmentally friendly living, and whatever else crosses the manager's mind. In spring, jazz and jungle harmonize during an outdoor music series.

Trunk Bay is St. John's most photographed beach and also the preferred spot for beginning snorkelers because of its marked underwater trail. Unfortunately, so many people have abused the trail that you'll rarely see any of the marine life that the signs highlight. On our most recent visit, we saw only a few small stoplight parrot fish, a lone grouper, and a handful of other small reef fish.

Cruise ship passengers interested in snorkeling for a day come to Trunk Bay, so if you're looking for seclusion, check cruise schedules in *St. Thomas This Week* before heading here. Crowded or not, this looker is a good place for sunning, swimming, and hanging out. It's one of the best-equipped beach operations we've seen. Because of the top-notch facilities and calm waters, Trunk Bay is great for families.

Soaking Up Some Water Fun

If you want to get your feet wet with cool Caribbean-style underwater exploration, consider the possibilities on the USVIs.

On St. Thomas

Dive sites around St. Thomas feature wrecks such as the **Cartanser Sr.,** a 35-foot-deep, beautifully encrusted, World War II cargo ship, and the **General Rogers,** a 65-foot-deep Coast Guard cutter with a gigantic resident barracuda.

Reef dives offer hidden caves and archways at **Cow and Calf Rocks,** coral-covered pinnacles at **Frenchcap,** and tunnels where you can explore undersea from the Caribbean to the Atlantic at **Thatch Cay, Grass Cay,** and **Congo Cay.** Many resorts and charter yachts offer dive packages. A one-tank dive starts at $40; two-tank dives are $55 or more. There are plenty of snorkeling possibilities, too. Nick Aquilar's *At-A-Glance Snorkeler's Guide To St. Thomas,* available at local souvenir shops, describes 15 idyllic spots in detail.

Aqua Action (6501 Red Hook Plaza; ☎ 340-775-6285) is a full-service, PADI, five-star dive shop that offers all levels of instruction at Secret Harbour Beach Resort. Owner Carl Moore, a certified instructor for the Handicap Scuba Association, teaches scuba to physically disabled visitors. **Chris Sawyer Diving Center** (☎ 800-882-2965 or 340-775-7320), at Compass Point Marina, is a PADI five-star outfit that specializes in dives to the 310-foot-long **RMS Rhyne** in the BVIs. (Don't forget your passport and your C-card if you take this trip.) This center also has a NAUI certification center that offers instruction up to "dive master."

Because the waters around the USVIs are so clear, you can get a view of the reefs without getting your hair wet. For an aerial view, parasailers sit in a harness attached to a parachute that lifts off from the boat deck until they're sailing up in the air. **Caribbean Parasail and Watersports** (6501 Red Hook Plaza; ☎ 340-775-9360) makes parasailing pickups from every beachfront resort on St. Thomas. It also rents such water toys as jet skis, kayaks, and floating battery-powered chairs.

Try your luck clipping through the seas around St. Thomas on a surfboard with a sail. Most beachfront resorts rent windsurf gear and offer one-hour lessons for about $50. One of the island's best known independent outfits is **West Indies Windsurfing** (Vessup Beach, No. 9 Nazareth; ☎ 340-775-6530).

On St. Croix

St. Croix has several excellent dive sites. At **Buck Island National Reef Monument,** a short boat ride from Christiansted or Green Cay Marina, you'll likely see lots of barracuda and stoplight parrot fish, which live up to their name.

You can dive right off the beach at **Cane Bay,** which has a spectacular drop-off. **Frederiksted Pier** is home to a colony of small seahorses, creatures seldom seen in the waters off the Virgin Islands.

At **Green Cay,** just outside Green Cay Marina in the East End, you'll see colorful fish swimming around the reefs and rocks. Two exceptional North Shore sites are **North Star** and **Salt River,** which you can reach only by boat. You can float downward through a canyon filled with colorful fish and coral.

The island's dive shops take you out for one- or two-tank dives. Plan to pay about $50 for a one-tank dive and $70 for a two-tank dive, including equipment and an underwater tour. **Anchor Dive Center** (Salt River Marina, Rte. 801; ☎ 800-532-3483 or 340-778-1522) explores the wall at Salt River Canyon from its base at Salt River Marina. It provides PADI certification. **Dive St. Croix** (☎ 800-523-3483 or 340-773-3434) takes divers to 35 different sites from its base on the Christiansted Wharf. It's the only operation that runs dives to Buck Island. **V.I. Divers Ltd.** (☎ 800-544-5911 or 340-773-6045) is near the water in the Pan Am Pavilion. It's a PADI five-star training facility and takes divers to their choice of 28 sites.

St. Croix's trade winds make windsurfing a breeze. You can also check in with Kevin and Suzanne Ryan, who operate a good dive operation from their hotel, The Waves at Cane Bay (see Chapter 36).

Most hotels rent windsurf and other watersports equipment to non-guests. **Tradewind-Surfing Inc.** (Hotel on the Cay; ☎ **340-773-7060**) offers Windsurfer rentals, sales, and rides; parasailing; and a wide range of watersports equipment, such as jet skis and kayaks.

On St. John

While just about every beach on St. John has nice snorkeling, we favor **Cinnamon Bay** and **Waterlemon Cay** at Leinster Bay. Otherwise, you'll need a boat to head out to the more remote snorkeling locations and the best scuba spots. Sign on with any of the island's watersports operators to take you to hot spots between St. John and St. Thomas, including the tunnels at **Thatch Cay,** the ledges at **Congo Cay,** and the wreck of the **General Rogers.** Dive off St. John at **Stephens Cay,** a short boat ride out of Cruz Bay, where fish swim around the reefs as you float downward. At **Devers Bay,** on St. John's south shore, fish dart about in colorful schools.

Count on paying $55 for a one-tank dive and $75 for a two-tank dive. Rates include equipment and a tour. **Cruz Bay Watersports** (☎ **340-776-6234**) has three locations: Cruz Bay; the Westin Resort; and Palm Plaza Shopping Center. Owners Marcus and Patty Johnston offer regular reef, wreck, and night dives and USVI and BVI snorkel tours. **Low Key Watersports** (☎ **340-693-8999**) at Wharfside Village offers PADI certification and resort courses, one- and two-tank dives, and specialty courses.

St. John's steady breezes and expert instruction make learning to windsurf a snap. Try **Cinnamon Bay Campground** (Rte. 20; ☎ **340-776-6330**), where rentals are available for $12–$15 per hour. Lessons are available right at the waterfront; just look for the windsurf boards and gear stacked up on the beach. The cost for a one-hour lesson is about $40.

Enjoying the Waves Without Getting Wet

Sailors, fisherpeople, and those who just plain love to hang out on the sea are in heaven around this trio of islands.

On St. Thomas

With well more than 100 vessels to choose from, St. Thomas is the charter boat mecca of the USVIs. You can go through a broker to book a private sailing vessel with a crew, or you can contact a charter company directly.

Island Yachts (6100 Red Hook Quarter, 18B; ☎ 800-524-2019 or 340-775-6666) is a charter boat company in Red Hook. **Nauti Nymph** (6501 Red Hook Plaza, Suite 201; ☎ 800-734-7345 or 340-775-5066) has a large selection of powerboats for rent. Rates range from $215 to $350 a day and include snorkel gear.

Fish dart, birds sing, and iguanas lounge in the dense mangrove swamps deep within a marine sanctuary on St. Thomas's southeast shore. **Virgin Islands Ecotours** (2 Estate Nadir on Rte. 32; ☎ 340-779-2155) offers 2½-hour, guided trips on two-man sit-atop ocean kayaks; there are stops for swimming and snorkeling. It also offers a new tour starting in Magens Bay (see the previous section, "Hitting the Beaches"). Many of the resorts on St. Thomas's eastern end have kayaks, too.

On St. Croix

You can sail to Buck Island aboard one of the island's charter boats. Most leave from the Christiansted waterfront or Green Cay Marina. The captain stops to allow you to snorkel at the eastern end of the island before dropping anchor off a gorgeous beach for a swim, a hike, and lunch.

Big Beard's Adventure Tours (☎ 340-773-4482) takes you on a catamaran, the *Renegade,* from the Christiansted Waterfront to Buck Island for snorkeling before dropping anchor at a private beach for a barbecue lunch. **Buck Island Charters'** (☎ 340-773-3161) trimaran *Teroro II* leaves Green Cay Marina for full- or half-day sails. Bring your own lunch.

On St. John

For a speedy trip in St. John to offshore cays and remote beaches, a power boat is a necessity. If you're boatless, book with one of the island's agents. Most day sails include lunch, beverages, and at least one stop to snorkel.

Connections (Cruz Bay, a block up from the ferry dock and catty-corner from Chase Manhattan Bank, ☎ 340-776-6922) pairs you with sailboats that suit you. **Ocean Runner** (☎ 340-693-8809), on the waterfront in Cruz Bay, rents one-and two-engine boats for fast trips around the island's seas. **Proper Yachts** (☎ 340-776-6256) books day sails and longer charters on its luxury yachts that depart from Caneel Bay Resort.

Poke around and explore St. John's crystal bays in a sea kayak. **Arawak Expeditions'** (☎ 800-238-8687 or 340-693-8312) professional guides use kayaks to ply coastal waters. Prices start at $40 for a half-day trip.

Telling Fish Tales

Several world records have been set in these waters, legendary locations for sportsfishing and catches of monumental proportions.

On St. Thomas

Fishing from St. Thomas is synonymous with blue marlin angling — especially from June through October. Four 1,000-pound-plus blue marlins, including three world records, have been caught on the famous **North Drop,** about 20 miles (32 km) north of St. Thomas. If you're not into marlin fishing, try hooking sailfish in the winter, dolphinfish (also called mahimahi) in spring, and wahoo in the fall.

To book a boat, contact the **Charter Boat Center** (6300 Red Hook Plaza; ☎ 800-866-5714 or 340-775-7990) or **Sapphire Beach Marina** (Sapphire Bay; ☎ 340-775-6100). Or, to find the trip that will best suit you, walk down the docks at either American Yacht Harbor or Sapphire Beach Marina and chat with the captains.

On St. Croix

In the past 25 years, some 25 world records — many for blue marlin — have been set in these waters. Sailfish, skipjack, bonito, tuna (allison, blackfin, and yellowfin), and wahoo are abundant.

Ruffian Enterprises (St. Croix Marina, Gallows Bay; ☎ 340-773-6011) will take you out on a 38-foot powerboat, the *Fantasy.*

On St. John

Well-kept sportfishing boats head out to the north drop (an area between the BVIs and the USVIs, known for great fishing) or troll along the inshore reefs. The captains usually provide bait, drinks, and lunch, but you'll need your hat and sunscreen. **American Yacht Harbor** (☎ 340-775-6454) offers sportfishing trips, and though it's based in Red Hook on St. Thomas, the operator will pick you up on St. John. **St. John World Class Anglers** (☎ 340-779-4281) offers light-tackle shore and offshore half- and full-day trips.

Exercising Other Onshore Options

If you need a change of pace after so much spectacular water adventure, try one of the following dry-land activities.

Duffer's delight

The USVIs offer several great options for practicing your swing.

On St. Thomas

When we were last in the BVIs, we met a group of fellows who were sailing around the isles but decided to take a break in the midst of their pirate adventure. They chartered helicopters to take them over to St. Thomas's **The Mahogany Run Golf Course** (Rte. 42; ☎ 340-777-5000). The course, favored by U.S. President Clinton for his vacation, is open daily and often hosts informal tournaments on weekends. A spectacular view of the BVIs and challenging three-hole "Devil's Triangle" attracts avid golfers to this Tom Fazio–designed, par-70, 18-hole course.

On St. Croix

St. Croix's courses welcome you with spectacular vistas and well-kept greens. Check with your hotel or the tourist board to determine when major celebrity tournaments will be held; there's often an opportunity to play with the pros. **The Buccaneer** (off Rte. 82 at Teague Bay, ☎ 340-773-2100) is an 18-hole course conveniently close to (east of) Christiansted. **The Reef Golf Course** (☎ 340-778-5638), in the northeastern part of the island, has nine holes. The spectacular course at **Carambola Beach Resort** (Rte. 80; ☎ 340-778-5638), in the remote and rural northwest valley, was designed by Robert Trent Jones.

Tennis (or squash) anyone?

Finding a place to break out your tennis whites is easy on these islands. But remember, the Caribbean sun is hot, so be sure to hit the courts before 10 a.m. or after 5 p.m. (Many of the courts are lighted.) Most hotels rent time to nonguests.

On St. Thomas

Several tennis facilities are available here. To make reservations, try one of the following:

- **Mahogany Run Tennis Club** (Rte. 42; ☎ 340-775-5000)
- **Marriott Frenchman's Reef Tennis Courts** (Estate Bakkeroe; ☎ 340-776-8500, ext. 444)
- **Renaissance Grand Beach Resort** (Smith Bay Rd.; ☎ 340-775-1510)
- **The Ritz-Carlton, St. Thomas** (6900 Great Bay Estate; ☎ 340-775-3333)
- **Sapphire Beach Resort** (Sapphire Bay; ☎ 340-775-6100, ext. 2131)

Two public courts are at Sub Base (next to the Water and Power Authority), open until 8 p.m. on a first-come, first-served basis.

On St. Croix

Tennis aficionados will be tempted to tuck into **The Buccaneer,** with its eight courts (two lighted), plus a pro and a full tennis pro shop (Rte. 82; ☎ 340-773-2100). You'll also find three lighted courts at **Club St. Croix** (Rte. 752, ☎ 340-773-4800) and four courts (two lighted) at the **Carambola Beach Resort** (Rte. 80; ☎ 340-778-3800).

On St. John

The **Westin Resort** (St. John 104; ☎ **340-693-8000**) has six lighted courts. Nonguests are welcome to play here for a fee of $15 an hour. The public courts, near the fire station in Cruz Bay, are lighted until 10 p.m. and are available on a first-come, first-served basis.

Using your pedal power: Bicycling

To really get a feeling for rural and flat St. Croix, let the pedals be your guide on a biking adventure. St. Thomas doesn't offer good biking options; St John's roads are extremely steep, and no one rents bikes here anymore.

On St. Croix

A bike tour to some of the island's top sites adds a new dimension to your vacation and helps you stay in shape. **St. Croix Bike and Tours** (Pier 69 Courtyard, Frederiksted; ☎ **340-772-2343** or 340-773-5004) offers two tours, both of which cost $35 and include bike, helmet, water bottles, and guide. One heads through historic Frederiksted before cycling on a fairly flat road to Hamm's Bluff. The second takes you up and through the rain forest.

Taking a gallop: Horseback riding

Try a truly unique view of the Caribbean from the saddle.

On St. Thomas

Half Moon Stables (☎ **340-777-6088**) offers hour-long guided rides along a secluded trail that winds through lush, green hills to a pebble-covered beach on the East End. Horses and ponies are available, and so are Western or English saddles. The cost is $45.

On St. Croix

At Sprat Hall, near Frederiksted, Jill Hurd runs **Paul and Jill's Equestrian Stables** (Rt. 58; ☎ **340-772-2880** or 340-772-2627). She'll take you clip-clopping through the rain forest (explaining the flora, fauna, and ruins on the way), along the coast, or on moonlit rides. Costs range from $50 to $75 for two-hour rides. She's a character whose family has long been on the island. You can mount up a horse or a donkey.

On St. John

Clipclop along the island's byways for a slower-pace tour of St. John. **Carolina Corral** (☎ **340-693-5778**) offers donkey and horseback rides as well as riding lessons. Rates start at $45 for a one-hour ride.

Taking a hike

Get a ground-level view of all the flora, fauna, and other attractions by strapping on your most comfortable shoes and setting out to explore. (St. Thomas doesn't rate high scores for cool hiking sites.)

On St. Croix

Although you can set off by yourself on a hike through a rain forest or along a shore, a guide will point out what's important and tell you why. The nonprofit **St. Croix Environmental Association** (Arawak Bldg., Suite 3, Gallows Bay, 00820; ☎ **340-773-1989**) offers hikes through several of the island's ecological treasures, including Estate Mt. Washington, Estate Caledonia in the rain forest, and Salt River. The hikes take nearly two hours and cost $20 per person.

On St. John

Although it's fun to go hiking with a Virgin Islands National Park guide, don't be afraid to strike out on your own. We found the trails easy to follow and more fun on our own. However, unless you're just wild about hiking, you can cover the most interesting trails in a day.

To find a hike that suits your ability, stop by the park's visitors center in Cruz Bay and pick up the free trail guide. The guides detail points of interest, dangers, trail lengths, and estimated hiking times.

 Although the park staff recommends pants to protect against thorns and insects, most people hike in shorts because pants are too hot. Wear sturdy shoes or hiking boots even if you're hiking to the beach. Don't forget to bring water and insect repellent, and coat yourself in waterproof sunscreen. Older kids will do fine on these relatively easy hikes, but we wouldn't recommend bringing along a child younger than age six.

The **Virgin Islands National Park** (☎ **340-776-6201**) maintains more than 20 trails on the north and south shores and offers guided hikes along popular routes. A full-day trip to Reef Bay is a must; it's an easy hike through lush and dry forest, past the ruins of an old plantation, and to a sugar factory adjacent to the beach. Take the public Vitran bus to the trailhead where you'll meet a ranger who will serve as your guide. The park provides a boat ride back to Cruz Bay for $14.50 to save you the walk back up the mountain. The schedule changes; call for times and reservations, which are essential.

Reef Bay Trail is one of the most interesting hikes on St. John, but unless you are a rugged individualist who wants a physical challenge (and that describes a lot of people who stay on St. John), you'll probably get the most out of the trip if you join a hike led by a park service ranger. A ranger can identify the trees and plants, fill you in on the history of the Reef Bay Plantation, and tell you about the petroglyphs on the rocks at the bottom of the trail.

Shopping Till You Drop

You may want to wave buy-buy to all the goodies in the USVIs marketplace — enough stuff to make all your friends back home happy that you included them in your souvenir sweep.

On St. Thomas

St. Thomas lives up to its self-described billing as a shopper's paradise. Monday and Saturday are usually the least crowded with cruise shippers, making it more pleasant to browse. Among the best buys are liquor, linens, imported china, crystal (most stores will ship it for you), and jewelry.

Whether you're a power shopper in a time crunch or (like us) someone who needs some handholding, invest 15 minutes in **Holly's Shop Talk,** an insider's guide to the best shops that are currently having sales and such. Holly Palm gives the brief but informative talk at the dock where the ferry from the Marriott comes in.

Local crafts include shell jewelry, carved calabash bowls, straw brooms, woven baskets, and dolls. Spice mixes, hot sauces, and tropical jams and jellies are other island products worth purchasing.

There's no sales tax in the USVIs, and shoppers can take advantage of the $1,200 dutyfree allowance per person. (Save your receipts.) Although you'll find the occasional sales clerk who will make a deal, haggling isn't typical, except at the vendor's plaza (see below).

Where to shop

The prime shopping area in Charlotte Amalie is between Post Office and Market squares; it consists of three parallel streets that run east-west — Waterfront Highway, Main Street, and Back Street — and the alleyways that connect them. Particularly attractive are the historic **Royal Dane Mall, A. H. Riise Alley,** and **International Plaza** — quaint alleys between Main Street and the Waterfront.

Vendors Plaza, on the waterfront side of Emancipation Gardens, is a an outdoor crafts market where you'll find handmade earrings, necklaces, and bracelets; straw baskets and knock-off handbags; T-shirts; fabrics; African artifacts; hairbraiding; and local foods.

East of town, **Tillett Gardens** (Estate Tutu; ☎ **340-775-1929**) is an oasis of artistic endeavor across from the Tutu Park Shopping Center. A changing group of craftspeople and artisans produce silk-screen fabrics, pottery, candles, watercolors, gold jewelry, stained glass, and other handicrafts.

Artistic creations

✔ **MAPes MONDe Limited.** Historic and contemporary prints, posters, and photo note cards depicting West Indian life are sold here. 37 Main St. at Riise's Alley; ☎ **888-774-3280** or 340-776-2303; Internet www.mapesmondo.com.

✔ **Mango Tango.** Works by popular local artists — originals, prints, and note cards — are displayed and sold here. There's a one-person show at least one weekend a month. You'll also find the island's largest humidor and a brand name cigar gallery. Al Cohen's Plaza, atop Raphune Hill, a half mile (¾ km) east of Charlotte Amalie; ☎ **340-777-3060.**

Handicrafts

✔ **Local Color.** Here St. John artist Sloop Jones exhibits colorful, hand-painted island designs on cool dresses, T shirts, and sweaters. You'll also find wearable art by other local artists; unique jewelry; sundresses, shorts, and shirts in bright Jams World-brand prints; and straw hats dipped in fuchsia, turquoise, and other tropical colors. Hibiscus Alley; ☎ 340-774-3727.

✔ **Down Island Traders.** These traders deal in hand-painted calabash bowls; finely printed Caribbean note cards; jams, jellies, spices, hot sauces, and herbs; herbal teas made of lemongrass, passion fruit, and mango; coffee from Jamaica; and a variety of handicrafts from throughout the Caribbean. Waterfront Hwy. at Post Office Alley; ☎ 340-776-4641.

✔ **Pampered Pirate.** This busy store carries island-made dolls, Christmas ornaments, prints, and paintings along with other gift items. 4 Norre Gade; ☎ 340-775-5450.

✔ **Mr. Tablecloth.** This island classic is better than it sounds from the dull name. The friendly staff here will help you choose from the floor-to-ceiling array of linens, from Tuscany lace tablecloths to Irish linen pillowcases. The prices will please you. 6–7 Main St.; ☎ 340-774-4343.

Foodstuffs

✔ **Cost-U-Less.** This store is a must for those staying in condos or villas. It sells everything from soup to nuts in giant sizes and case lots. The meat and seafood department has smaller family-size portions. One mile (1½ km) east of Charlotte Amalie on Route 38; ¼ mile/¾ km west of the Route 39 intersection; ☎ 340-777-3588.

✔ **Gourmet Gallery.** Visiting millionaires buy their caviar here. There's also an excellent and reasonably priced wine selection, as well as specialty ingredients for everything from tacos to curries to chow mein. A full-service deli offers imported meats and cheeses, and in-store prepared foods are perfect for a gourmet picnic. Crown Bay Marina; ☎ 340-776-8555. Havensight Mall; ☎ 340-774-4948.

Liquor and tobacco

✔ **H. Riise Liquors.** This shop offers a large selection of tobacco (including imported cigars), as well as cordials, wines, and other liquors (rare vintage cognacs, Armagnacs, ports, and Madeiras). It also stocks fruits soaked in brandy, as well as barware from England. 17 Main St., at Riise's Alley; ☎ 340-776-2303. Havensight Mall; ☎ 340-776-7713.

On St. Croix

Although St. Croix doesn't offer as many shopping opportunities as St. Thomas, the island does have an array of small stores with unique merchandise. In Christiansted, the best shopping areas are the **Pan Am Pavilion** and **Caravelle Arcade** off Strand Street, Kings Alley Walk, and King and Company streets. Stores are often closed on Sunday. Here are two of our favorites:

- ✔ **Caribbean Clothing Company.** This fashionable store features contemporary sportswear by top American designers. 41 Queen Cross St., Christiansted; ☎ **340-773-5012.**

- ✔ **From the Gecko.** Come here for the hippest clothes on St. Croix, from superb batik sarongs to hand-painted silk scarves. 1233 Queen Cross St., Christiansted; ☎ **340-778-9433.**

Foodstuffs

St. Croix offers excellent shopping at its stateside-style supermarkets. Try the open-air stands strung out along Route 70 for island produce. Supermarkets include the following:

- ✔ **Plaza Extra.** United Shopping Plaza, Rte. 70; ☎ **340-778-6240.**

- ✔ **Schooner Bay Market.** Rte. 82; ☎ **340-773-3232.**

- ✔ **Cost-U-Less** (a warehouse-style store with no membership fee). Rte. 70 across from the Sunshine Mall; ☎ **340-692-2220.**

Gifts

- ✔ **The Royal Poinciana.** You'll find island seasonings and hot sauces, West Indian crafts, bath gels, and herbal teas at this attractive shop. 1111 Strand St., Christiansted; ☎ **340-773-9892.**

- ✔ **Folk Art Traders.** Owners Patty and Charles Eitzen travel to Guyana as well as Haiti, Jamaica, and elsewhere in the Caribbean to find treasures for their shop. The baskets, ceramic masks, pottery, jewelry, and sculpture they find are unique examples of folk-art traditions. IB Queen Cross St. at Strand St., Christiansted; ☎ **340-773-1900.**

- ✔ **Sonya's.** Sonya Hough opened this store in 1964 to showcase her jewelry creations; now she runs it with her daughter, Diana. Sonya invented the Crucian hook bracelet. 1 Company St., Christiansted; ☎ **340-778-8605.**

Liquor

- ✔ **Cruzan Rum Distillery.** A tour of the company's rebuilt factory culminates in a tasting of its products, all sold here at bargain prices. West Airport Rd; ☎ **340-692-2280.**

✔ **Kmart.** We know it sounds wacky, but you get the best buys here. The two branches of this discount department store — a large one in the Sunshine Mall and a smaller one mid-island at Sunny Isle Shopping Center — carry a huge line of discount, dutyfree liquor. Sunshine Mall, Rte. 70, Frederiksted; ☎ **340-692-5848.** Sunny Isle Shopping Center, Rte. 70; ☎ **340-719-9191.**

On St. John

You'll find luxury items and handicrafts on St. John. The Cruz Bay shopping district runs from Wharfside Village (around the corner from the ferry dock) through the streets of town to North Shore Road and **Mongoose Junction,** an inviting shopping center with stonework walls. Our favorite shops include:

✔ **Coconut Coast Studios.** This waterside shop, a five-minute walk from Cruz Bay, showcases the work of Elaine Estern. She specializes in undersea scenes. Frank Bay; ☎ **340-776-6944.**

✔ **Bajo del Sol.** A cooperative gallery, Bajo del Sol features Aimee Trayser's expressionistic Caribbean scenes, Les Anderson's island scenes in oil, Kat Sowa's watercolors, and works by a handful of other artists. Mongoose Junction; ☎ **340-693-7070.**

Gifts

✔ **Bamboula.** Owner Jo Sterling travels the Caribbean and the world to find unusual housewares, rugs, bedspreads, accessories, shoes, and men's and women's clothes for this multicultural boutique. Mongoose Junction; ☎ **340-693-8699.**

✔ **Donald Schnell Pottery.** In addition to hand-thrown pottery, this place sells unique hand-blown glass, wind chimes, kaleidoscopes, fanciful fountains, and more (see Chapter 36, "Our Ten Favorite Caribbean Souvenirs"). Your purchases can be shipped worldwide. Mongoose Junction; Internet: www.DonaldSchnell.com; ☎ **800-253-7107** or 340-776-6420.

✔ **Free Bird Creations.** Head here for unique handcrafted jewelry — earrings, bracelets, pendants, and chains — as well as a good selection of waterproof watches great for your excursions to the beach. Wharfside Village; ☎ **340-693-8625.**

✔ **Pink Papaya.** This store is the home of longtime Virgin Islands resident M. L. Etre's well-known artwork plus a huge collection of one-of-a-kind gift items, including bright tablecloths, unusual trays, dinnerware, and unique tropical jewelry. Lemon Tree Mall, Cruz Bay; ☎ **340-693-8535.**

> ✔ **R&I Patton Goldsmiths.** Rudy and Irene Patton design most of the unique silver and gold jewelry in this shop. The rest comes from various jeweler friends of theirs. Sea fans (those large, lacy plants that sway with the ocean's currents) in filigreed silver, lapis set in long drops of gold, starfish and hibiscus pendants in silver or gold, and gold sand dollar–shaped charms and earrings are tempting choices. Mongoose Junction; ☎ **340-776-6548.**

Food

If you're renting a villa, condo, or cottage and doing your own cooking on St. John, there are several good places to shop for food; just be aware that prices are much higher than those at home. Try **Starfish Market**(☎ 340-779-4949) in the Boulon Center, **Marina Market** (☎ 340-779-4401) on Route 104, and **Tropicale** (☎ 340-693-7474), also on Route 104 in Palm Plaza.

Exploring the USVIs

These islands each have something very different, but all share a rich history. Here we hit the absolute high points.

St. Thomas

St. Thomas is only 13 miles (21 km) long and less than 4 miles (6½ km) wide, but it's an extremely hilly island. Even an 8- or 10-mile (13- or 16-km) trip could take several hours in a vehicle. Don't let that discourage you, though, because the ridge of mountains that runs from east to west through the middle and separates the Caribbean and Atlantic sides of the island has spectacular vistas and is a lot of fun to explore.

When exploring Charlotte Amalie, look beyond the pricey shops, T-shirt vendors, and crowds for a glimpse of the island's history.

> ✔ **Government House.** Built as an elegant residence in 1867, today Government House serves as the governor's office with the first floor open to the public. The staircases are made of native mahogany, as are the plaques hand-lettered in gold with the names of past governors. Brochures detailing the history of the building are available, but you may have to ask for them.
>
> In the reception room are two small paintings by Camille Pissarro, but unfortunately they are hard to appreciate because they're enclosed in frosted-glass cases. More interesting, and visible, is the large painting by an unknown artist that was found in Denmark: It depicts a romanticized version of St. Croix. Government Hill; ☎ **340-774-0001.** Admission is free. Open weekdays from 8 a.m. to 5 p.m.

- ✔ **Synagogue of Beracha Veshalom Vegmiluth Hasidim.** The synagogue's Hebrew name translates to the Congregation of Blessing, Peace, and Loving Deeds. The small building's white pillars contrast with rough stone walls, as does the rich mahogany of the pews and altar. The sand on the floor symbolizes the exodus from Egypt. Since the synagogue first opened its doors in 1833, it has held a weekly Sabbath service, making it the oldest synagogue building in continuous use under the American flag and the second oldest (after the one on Curaçao) in the Western Hemisphere. To the rear of the synagogue, the **Weibel Museum** showcases Jewish history on St. Thomas. 15 Crystal Gade; ☎ 340-774-4312. Open weekdays from 9 a.m. to 4 p.m.

Outside of Charlotte Amalie, check out the following:

- ✔ **Coral World Marine Park & Underwater Observatory.** This is the best marine park on the islands we cover in this book. The only thing close to it is the Seaquarium on Curaçao, but we give this one the edge because of Coral World's multi-level off-shore underwater observatory. It houses the Predator Tank, one of the world's largest coral reef tanks, and an aquarium with more than 20 portholes providing close-up views of Caribbean sealife. Our favorite exhibit was of the seahorses in different stages of development. Outside are several outdoor pools where you can touch starfish, pet a baby shark, feed stingrays, and view endangered sea turtles. Coki Point, turn north off Rte. 38 at sign approximately 20 minutes from Charlotte Amalie; ☎ 340-775-1555; Internet www.coralworldvi.com. Admission is $18; $9 for children 3–12. Open daily from 9 a.m. to 5 p.m. Expect to spend at least a few hours here, especially if you have kids.

- ✔ **Frenchtown.** If you want to check out local bars and good restaurants, head here. Turn south off Waterfront Hwy. at the U.S. Post Office.

- ✔ **Mountain Top.** Stop here for a banana daiquiri and spectacular views from the observation deck more than 1,500 feet above sea level. There are also shops that sell everything from Caribbean art to nautical antiques, ship models, and T-shirts. Head north off Rte. 33; look for signs.

- ✔ **Paradise Point Tramway.** Fly skyward in a gondola, similar to a ski lift, 700 feet up the hill to Paradise Point, an overlook with breathtaking views of Charlotte Amalie and the harbor. There are several shops, a bar, and a restaurant. A one-mile long nature trail leads to spectacular sights of St. Croix to the south. Wear sturdy shoes. Rte. 30 at Havensight; ☎ 340-774-9809. Admission is $12 round trip; $6 for ages 6–12; ages 5 and under free. Open daily from 7:30 a.m. to 4:30 p.m.

St. Croix

Christiansted is a historic, Danish-style town that has always served as St. Croix's commercial center. Spend the morning, when it's still cool, exploring the historic sites here. This two-hour endeavor won't tax your walking shoes and will leave you with energy to poke around the town's eclectic shops. Break for lunch at an open-air restaurant before spending as much time as you like shopping.

An easy drive (roads are flat and well marked) to St. Croix's eastern end takes you through some choice real estate. Ruins of old sugar estates dot the landscape. You can make the entire loop on the road that circles the island in about an hour, a good way to end the day. If you want to spend a full day exploring, you'll find some nice beaches and easy walks, with places to stop for lunch.

You can't get lost on St. Croix. All streets lead gently downhill to the water. Still, if you want some friendly advice, stop by the **Visitor's Center** (53A Company St.; ☎ **340-773-0495**) weekdays between 8 a.m. and 5 p.m. for maps and brochures.

Be sure to check out some of these sites on your trip to St. Croix:

✔ **Danish Customs House.** Built in 1830 on foundations that date from 1734, the Danish Customs House (near Ft. Christiansvaern) originally served as both a customs house and a post office. In 1926, it became the Christiansted Library, and it has been a National Park Service office since 1972. King St.

✔ **Government House.** One of the town's most elegant structures, the Government House was built as a home for a Danish merchant in 1747. Today it houses USVI government offices. If the building is open, slip into the peaceful inner courtyard to admire the pools and gardens. King St.; ☎ **340-713-9807.**

✔ **St. Croix Aquarium.** This small, nonprofit education center contains an ever-changing variety of local sea creatures. Allow a half hour for the guided tour of the 32 tanks conducted by marine biologists. Children are invited to explore the discovery room with its microscopes, interactive displays, and educational videos. They'll especially enjoy the touch tank, where they can feel starfish. 13 Caravelle Arcade, Christiansted; ☎ **340-773-8995.** Admission $4.50, $2 for children under 12. Open Tuesday through Saturday from 11 a.m. to 4 p.m.

✔ **Estate Whim Plantation Museum.** This lovingly restored estate, with a windmill, cook house, and other buildings, will give you a sense of what life was like on St. Croix's sugar plantations in the 1800s. The oval-shaped great house has high ceilings and antique furniture, décor, and utensils. The apothecary exhibit is the largest in all the West Indies. If you have kids, the grounds are the perfect place for them to stretch their legs while you browse in the museum gift shop. Rte. 70, Frederiksted; ☎ 340-772-0598. Admission $6. Open Monday through Saturday from 10 a.m. to 4 p.m.

✔ **Fredriksted.** The town is noted less for its Danish than for its Victorian architecture, which dates from after the slave uprising and the great fire of 1878. One long cruise ship pier juts into the sparkling sea. The former Customs House, now **The Visitor's Center** (Waterfront; ☎ 340-772-0357), right on the pier, was built in the late 1700s; the two-story gallery was added in the 1800s. Today, you can stop in weekdays from 8 a.m. to 5 p.m. and pick up brochures or view the exhibits on St. Croix. Waterfront; ☎ 340-772-2021. Admission is free.

✔ **St. Croix Leap.** This workshop sits in the heart of the rain forest, about a 15-minute drive from Frederiksted. It sells a wide range of articles, including mirrors, tables, bread boards, and mahogany jewelry boxes crafted by local artisans. Rte. 76; ☎ 340-772-0421.

✔ **St. George Village Botanical Gardens.** At this 17-acre estate, you'll find lush, fragrant flora amid the ruins of a nineteenth century sugarcane plantation village. There are miniature versions of each ecosystem on St. Croix, from a semiarid cactus grove to a verdant rain forest. Turn north off Rte. 70 at sign; Kingshill; ☎ 340-692-2874. Admission $5. Open Monday through Saturday from 9 a.m. to 4 p.m.; closed holidays.

St. John

Few residents remember the route numbers, which were instituted about five years ago, so have your map in hand if you stop to ask for directions. Bring along a swimsuit for stops at some of the most beautiful beaches in the world. Be advised that roads are narrow and sometimes steep, so don't expect to get anywhere in a hurry.

You'll find lunch spots at Cinnamon Bay and in Coral Bay, or you can do what the locals do — picnic. The grocery stores in Cruz Bay sell Styrofoam coolers for this purpose. If you plan to do a lot of touring, rent a car; taxis are reluctant to go anywhere until they have a full load of passengers. Although you may be tempted by an open-air Suzuki or Jeep, a conventional car can get you just about everywhere on the paved roads, and you'll be able to lock up your valuables. You may be able to share a van or open-air vehicle (called a safari bus) with other passengers on a tour of scenic mountain trails, secret coves, and eerie bush-covered ruins. Don't miss these favorite spots:

✔ **Annaberg Plantation.** In the eighteenth century, sugar plantations dotted the steep hills of the USVIs. Slaves and free Danes and Dutchmen harvested the cane that was used to create sugar, molasses, and rum for export. Built in the 1780s, the partially restored plantation at Leinster Bay was once an important sugar mill. Though there are no official visiting hours, the National Park Service has regular tours, and some well-informed taxi drivers will show you around. Occasionally you'll find a living-history demonstration — someone making johnnycake or weaving baskets. For information on tours and demonstrations, contact the **St. John National Park Service Visitor's Center.** Leinster Bay Rd; ☎ **340-776-6201.** Admission $4.

✔ **Bordeaux Mountain.** St. John's highest peak rises to 1,277 feet. Centerline Road passes near enough to the top to offer breathtaking views. Drive nearly to the end of the dirt road for spectacular views at Picture Point and for the trailhead of the hike downhill to Lameshur. Get a trail map from the park service before you start. Rte. 70.

✔ **Catherineberg Ruins.** This is a fine example of an eighteenth-century sugar and rum factory. In the 1733 slave revolt, Catherineberg served as headquarters for Amina warriors, a tribe of Africans captured into slavery. Rte. 70.

We Love the Nightlife

On any given night, you'll find steel pan orchestras, rock-and-roll bands, piano music, jazz, disco, and karaoke. Pick up a copy of the free, bright yellow *St. Thomas This Week* magazine when you arrive. (You'll see it at the airport, in stores, and in hotel lobbies.) The back pages list who's playing where. The Thursday edition of the *Daily News* carries complete listings for the upcoming weekend.

St. Thomas

✔ **Iggies.** Sing along karaoke style to the sounds of the surf or the latest hits at this beachside lounge. There's often a DJ on weekends, when a buffet barbecue precedes the 9 p.m. music fest. Dance inside, or kick up your heels under the stars. 50 Estate Bolongo; ☎ **340-775-1800.**

✔ **Andiamo at the Martini Café.** You'll find a piano bar nightly at this spot. 70 Honduras, Frenchtown; ☎ **340-776-7916.**

✔ **Agave Terrace.** Island-style steel pan bands play here on Tuesday, Thursday, and Saturday. Point Pleasant Resort, Smith Bay; ☎ **340-775-4142.**

St. Croix

Christiansted has a lively and casual club scene near the waterfront.

✔ **Cormorant.** On Thursday night during the winter season, this club at 4126 La Grande Princesse dishes up a West Indian buffet with a small local band. ☎ 340-778-8920.

✔ **Hotel on the Cay.** This spot has a West Indian buffet on Tuesday night in the winter season that features a broken-bottle dancer (a dancer who braves a carpet of broken bottles) and mocko jumbie characters (stilt-walkers in wild costumes). Protestant Cay, ☎ 340-773-2035.

✔ **Indies.** Easy jazz flows from the courtyard bar on Saturday evenings. 55–56 Company St.; ☎ 340-692-9440.

✔ **2 Plus 2 Disco.** DJs spin a great mix of calypso, soul, disco, and reggae; there's live music on weekends. 17 La Grande Princesse; ☎ 340-773-3710.

St. John

St. John isn't the place to go for glitter and all-night partying. Still, after-hours Cruz Bay can be a lively little village in which to dine, drink, dance, chat, or flirt. Notices posted on the bulletin board outside the Connections telephone center (up the street from the ferry dock in Cruz Bay) or listings in the island's two small newspapers (the *St. John Times* and *Tradewinds*) keep you apprised of special events, comedy nights, movies, and the like.

✔ **Ellington's.** After a sunset drink at this spot up the hill from Cruz Bay, you can stroll here and there in town; much is clustered around the small waterfront park. Gallows Point Suite Resort; ☎ 340-693-8490.

✔ **Caneel Bay Resort.** This spot outside of town usually has entertainment (generally of the quiet calypso variety) several nights a week in season. Rte. 20; ☎ 340-776-6111.

✔ **Fred's.** There's calypso and reggae on Wednesday and Friday. Cruz Bay; ☎ 340-776-6363.

✔ **Skinny Legs Bar and Restaurant.** Check out the action at this happening place at Coral Bay on the far side of the island. Rte. 107; ☎ 340-779-4982.

✔ **Woody's.** Young folks gather at this casual spot to mingle with locals. Its sidewalk tables provide a close-up view of Cruz Bay's action. Cruz Bay; ☎ 340-779-4625.

Taking a Side Trip

Visitors to St. Thomas and St. John are often intrigued by the neighboring British Virgin Islands. If your curiosity has been piqued, consider a side trip to these splendid isles. The most frequently visited BVIs are Tortola, Virgin Gorda, and Jost Van Dyke. If you decide to go, take along your passport or proof of citizenship. **Smith's Ferry Service (☎ 340-775-7592**) offers daily day trips to Tortola and Virgin Gorda, along with car rental packages, historic tours, horseback riding, and a two-island day trip every Saturday.

Part X
The Part of Tens

"Did you want to take the Schwinn bicycle dive, the Weber gas grill dive, or the Craftsman riding lawn mower dive?"

In this part . . .

We appeal to the shopper in you by listing our ten favorite souvenirs to bring home from the Caribbean. We also reveal the ten dishes that we crave the most whenever we're away from the islands too long. And finally, we show you the ten easiest ways to make certain that every islander you meet knows that you're a tourist.

Chapter 36

Our Ten Favorite Caribbean Souvenirs

• •

In This Chapter

▶ Shopping with smarts

▶ Finding the best products and deals

• •

*Y*ou'll want to bring back memories of your Caribbean vacation, and what better way to preserve the moment than by toting home some souvenirs from the islands. The problem we have with this practice is that many visitors' good taste evaporates as quickly as their cares in the Caribbean. How else can we explain the voluminous number of items with the name of the island emblazoned, stitched, or painted on virtually every hunk of cloth, wood, or plastic you could possibly imagine?

Truly annoying is the fact that hordes of people buy only dutyfree items made elsewhere in the world when they're in the Caribbean. These folks are so busy snapping up Irish linens and French perfume that they ignore some of the nifty island items. Making the situation worse is that so-called "dutyfree" has lost its luster and savings in the last several years, meaning it's more of an illusion than reality. Combine that observation with the airlines' crackdown on carry-ons, and the hassle of transporting items home really isn't worth it, unless you've done your homework and are absolutely sure you're getting a bargain or a unique find.

Every island has its own artists and craftspeople. We urge you to take a look. You're almost guaranteed a better buy in the markets than in the gift shops or from authorized vendors at resorts and at the airports. However, if you're the kind of person who can't say no, you won't enjoy the markets. In the markets, you're expected to haggle, but in shops with marked prices generally not. In the markets, expect to pick up items for about 30% less than the first offer you hear or see. Bring lots of small bills with you, because it's bad form to haggle down a vendor and then pull out a $100 bill and expect change.

We like to scope out what's available, and then come back to do business. What are our favorite items to shop for on the islands? Read on.

Aloe Products

The aloe plant grows extensively on Aruba, and you can find wonderful skin-care products and soaps manufactured from this natural plant. Aloe is also the key ingredient in several soothing sunburn remedies, handy items to have on hand when you're this close to the equator.

Coffee Beans

We learned a lot about coffee production by visiting a Blue Mountain coffee plantation. One important tip that we picked up: If you can smell the coffee through the bag, it's losing freshness. Coffee beans should be tightly sealed from air. Ever since James Bond declared Blue Mountain coffee the world's finest, Jamaica's coffee has become synonymous with good quality. However, we also discovered that much like wine producers, different coffee plantations produce different tasting beans depending on an array of factors — the soil, rainfall, mountain temperatures, and the handling and roasting of the beans once they've been plucked. The hot thing among coffee connoisseurs is aged coffees that are marked similarly to wine vintages.

Blue Mountain coffee is extremely expensive, unless, of course, you're on Jamaica. We always buy a few pounds of the pride and joy. The coffee is actually one of the few items sold at the airport at a reasonable price.

Another island with coffees worth buying is Puerto Rico. Puerto Rico produces a strong, aromatic coffee that was originally imported from the Dominican Republic. The best brand names from Puerto Rico are Café Crema, Café Rico, and Rioja. We must confess that we're lightweights and usually order ours *con leche* (with milk).

Gouda Cheese and Dutch Chocolates

The direct connection to the Netherlands that Aruba enjoys makes its buys on gouda cheeses and luscious Dutch chocolates too good to pass up. Enjoy the duty-free prospects.

Island Art

Serious collectors of art head to Puerto Rico and Jamaica for fine selections. **Old San Juan** is ground zero for a vibrant art scene, which highlights internationally known sculptors and painters. At **Round Hill Hotel & Villas** in Montego Bay, you'll find a small but excellent gallery that features Jamaican and Haitian artists.

Though the selection was out of our price range, we recommend **Galeria Botello** (208 Cristo St., Old San Juan; ☎ **787-723-9987;** fax 787-723-2879), where the works of Angel Botello Barros are displayed.

In Charlotte Amalie on St. Thomas, **MAPes MONDe** (Reese's Alley, ☎ 340-776-2886; also at Mongoose Junction on St. John, ☎ 340-779-4545) is owned by the son of St. Thomas's former governor. The shop features antique prints (some newly discovered) by native son Pissarro. We once watched a German couple consider plunking down the $38,000 asking price for one of them, recognizing its rarity. The famed impressionist recorded colonial life on the island before departing for France. The small shop also features several fine art prints of contemporary island artists as well as antique maps and books of the region.

Pottery

Several years ago, after a visit to New Mexico where Echo bought four large pieces of pottery (including a particularly beautiful but unwieldy and fragile raku piece), our family established a new rule: You buy it, you carry it. In the Caribbean, you'll find some artisans whose work is too tempting to pass up. The good news is that these places all gladly ship your picks.

Our favorite artisan is **Donald Schnell,** whose St. John studio is at Mongoose Junction (P.O. Box 349, Cruz Bay, St. John 00831; ☎ **800-253-7107** or 340-776-6420; fax 340-776-6920; e-mail Donald Schnell@csi.com; Internet www.DonaldSchnell.com.). The Michigan-born Schnell creates handcrafted ceramics imprinted with natural objects such as shells and ferns that give them a fossilized look. His works include water fountains, lights, planters, and windchimes. His unique designs decorate Richard Branson's Necker Island digs, Caneel Bay, and Biras Creek, all some of our favorite Caribbean resorts.

Another great spot is the **Earthworks** studio and shop at Edgehill Heights 2, St. Thomas, Barbados (☎ **246-425-0223;** fax 246-425-3224; e-mail earthworks@caribsurf.com; Internet www.earthwork pottery.com). The studio started as a teaching project in the 1970s to revive the tradition of pottery-making on the island. The pieces most commonly associated with Earthworks feature the blue and green hues of the Caribbean Sea. Mosaics decorate the walls and floors of the shop, and guests are left to mill about the studio where you can get a discount by buying at the source. Next door, several artisans display their works at **The Potter's House** (☎ **246-425-2890**), where you can also grab lunch.

In Negril, some of the craftspeople from the Rastafarian communes bring their handsome clay pots past **The Caves,** hoping to attract buyers' attention. Echo wound up buying a waist-high one with tropical designs etched into the sides for $18. A sympathetic flight attendant on Air Jamaica Express let her stow it, and it made it all the way home to Marietta, Georgia, where it shows off its freshly potted plants in front of our house. These days, we don't recommend trying to haul something that large and fragile on a plane.

Rum

If you're into spirits, the rums of the Caribbean allow you to bring a taste of the islands home. Several islands produce their own rums, including Barbados, St. Croix, Jamaica, and Puerto Rico. And rum-based drinks are everywhere as well: Puerto Rico claims ownership of the Pina Colada; the BVIs invented the Painkiller; and Barbados's Planter's Punch is famous. The oldest rum distillery still in operation is **Mount Gay** on Barbados, which has been in continual production since 1703. Of course, each island claims that it has the best rum. Puerto Rico alone produces more than two dozen different rums. If you visit a distillery, you'll often find a rum-tasting counter in the gift shop, much like a wine tasting if you were visiting a vineyard. Our recommendation is to sample a few and make your own pick.

Sarongs

You can purchase sarongs, or *parreos,* colorful pieces of cloth that you can use as beach cover-ups or evening wraps for overly air-conditioned Caribbean restaurants, at a good price on many islands. Some have batik designs; others display beautiful tropical scenes with birds, flowers, and fish. The best buys and most creative designs that we've found are on Aruba at a shop on **De Palm Island** (☎ **297-854-799**) and in St. John at a shop called **Flashbacks** (☎ **340-779-4277**) in Coral Bay, next to Skinny Legs, a local watering hole. We think Aruba offers such fabulous ones because it imports them from Indonesia, which was also once a Dutch colony, so its ties to that region are still strong. At the shop on St. John, handpainted sarongs could be had for $12. Some also came tucked into a matching handbag for $16 and $18.

They also make fantastic gifts. Similar sarongs in the U.S. are at least double the price, plus you don't find the breadth of choices.

Straw Hats

Don't doubt the fry-power of the Caribbean sun; you'll need a hat to protect you from the sizzle. Hats are inexpensive, and you can actually use them at home when you're gardening, watching your kids play soccer, or lounging by the pool reflecting on your Caribbean adventure. You can find decent woven hats at most any of the markets. You'll notice a variation of techniques from island-to-island. Or if you want to spend more and get a good quality hat, you can spring for a spiffy Panama straw hat in Old San Juan. We also found a wide-brimmed, finely woven hat that Echo loves in Oranjestad's main shopping area in Aruba.

Wood Carvings

We've seen incredible works on Jamaica and St. Croix. Most of the carvings are the creations of self-taught artists. Before you buy any wood carving, inspect it carefully for problems with worms or bugs. Also think about how the island art is going to look back home in Des Moines. That cool Rastafarian walking stick looks fine in Negril, but we can't think of too many houses in Atlanta where it would coordinate with the interior design.

On Jamaica, you can find great buys in the markets. We prefer shopping in the craft markets in **Negril,** or if you're near Ocho Rios, about 100 craftspeople live and work in **Fern Gully.** We really like the hummingbirds carved into birdfeeders from coconut shells.

In the middle of St. Croix near Frederiksted, you'll find an open-air shop called **St. Croix Life and Environmental Arts Project** (L.E.A.P.; ☎ **340-772-0421**), on Mahogany Road, that features wonderful furniture and decorative objects fashioned from naturally fallen island wood. The artisan will personalize your pick by carving the date or your name in a discreet spot. If you're interested in one of the pieces, we suggest going early in your trip and putting in your order. We have a beautiful coffee table in our living room made from mahogany from an old plantation.

If you fall in love with the beautiful island plantation furniture and Jamaican carved fretwork, Jamaica's **Strawberry Hill** at Newcastle Road, Irishtown, St. Andrew (☎ **876-944-8400;** fax 876-944-8408; e-mail strawberry@cwjamaica.com; Internet www.islandlife.com) has established its own furniture shop on-site, because so many guests wanted to buy the furniture at the resort. A bedside table is $330; a planter's chair $870; and a four-poster king-size bed (popular with honeymooners) is $3,600.

Chapter 37

Our Ten Favorite Local Caribbean Dishes

· ·

In This Chapter

▶ Finding local taste treats

▶ Revisiting recipes back home

· ·

*F*ood can be a big expense in the Caribbean, especially if you stick with familiar dishes that you recognize from home (because much of what you eat has to be imported). To us, one of the great pleasures of traveling is experimenting by trying foods with names that we've never even heard before. One great advantage of sampling local cuisine is that it's almost always the cheapest choice. Another is that your sense of adventure will be rewarded by delicious food and drink.

Ackee and Saltfish (Jamaica)

The first time we saw this dish, a favorite of Jamaicans for breakfast, we thought it looked a lot like scrambled eggs. Being from the U.S., we aren't used to eating fish for breakfast, so we were a little uneasy about the combination. But having the adventurous palates that we do, we decided to give ackee and saltfish a try — especially after we found out it's the national dish.

Ackee was a hit with both of us. It is actually a fruit, but Jamaicans tend to use it like a vegetable. When prepared, it does resemble scrambled eggs and tastes a lot like them, too, with a hint of nuttiness. We found out that it's not commonly shipped to other parts of the world, because the fruit must be eaten when it turns ripe. If you eat ackee at the wrong time, its seeds are poisonous.

Saltfish is a cod cured in salt, and it gives the dish just the right flavor. Over the years, we've been thrilled to find that Air Jamaica occasionally serves ackee and saltfish on its flights. Probably the best saltfish and ackee that we've ever had was prepared by a Jamaican chef at Jake's (see Chapter 26). You'll sometimes see this dish on the morning buffet at all-inclusive resorts, but you may need to request it a day ahead. It's also fairly commonly served on Grand Cayman.

Caribbean Lobster (Anegada, British Virgin Islands)

This small coral atoll is famous for the spiny Caribbean lobsters caught in its waters. You'll find lobster on every menu of every restaurant on the island. Our favorite place to sup on lobster in Anegada is the Cow Wreck Bar & Grill. If you want to try a Caribbean cholesterol jamboree diet — Kevin's invention — with lobster and butter at every meal, the British Virgin Islands are the place to do it. Don't try this at home.

Conch Fritters (Grand Cayman)

Pronounced *conk*, this edible mollusk resides in a beautiful shell with a pink interior that lines the yards of many houses on Grand Cayman. The meat is pounded out to tenderize it, or it's often served chopped up and made into tasty fritters. Conch has become so popular that it now suffers from overcollection. Therefore, on some islands, conch fritters, chowder, marinated, and stewed are no longer so common.

Our first meal in the Caribbean was conch. We'd come on our honeymoon to a small island on a Sunday where there were no restaurants. A few private homes served meals, and you were supposed to make reservations the day before you wanted to dine. We hadn't done that, and we were starving. Finally, the fellow who'd met us at the boat convinced one lady to take pity on us. She served us conch and cabbage floating in vinegar — our first official dinner as a married couple. We much prefer conch in fritters.

Flying Fish (Barbados)

These small, silvery fish, which look like they have wings when they leap out of the sea, are the national fish of Barbados and the main ingredient in several Bajan specialties. One memorable morning, we had flying fish for breakfast. Delicious!

Grouper Sandwich (Anywhere in the Caribbean)

You'll see grouper listed on almost every Caribbean menu that carries a catch-of-the-day selection. Grouper inhabit shallow to mid-range reefs. The meat is a white, sweet, mild-tasting fish. When fried in a nice batter, it's the main ingredient of Kevin's favorite sandwich.

Jerk Chicken (Jamaica)

Spicy jerk chicken has probably become the most widely known Caribbean dish. It originated in Jamaica and is a method of barbecuing using well-seasoned meat. It supposedly originated with the Maroons, escaped slaves who lived in the mountains. They would roast pork seasoned with scotch bonnet pepper, pimento seeds, thyme, and nutmeg over sizzling hot coals covered with the branches of pimento or allspice wood. Although pork was the original meat used, jerk chicken has become more popular, and it's what we prefer.

Besides jerk pork, grill men operating pits around Jamaica have added chicken, sausage, and fish to their repertoire. Port Antonio's Boston Beach is best known, but we'd skip it. Only a few pits remain open, and the quality has suffered for lack of competition. Instead, get a good taste at The Pork Pit in Montego Bay, the Ocho Rios Jerk Center, or the stalls by the beach in Negril.

Keshi Yena (Aruba)

This Dutch treat tastes better than it sounds. You take a wheel of gouda cheese, pack the hollowed out center with a spicy meat mixture of either chicken or beef, and then bake the whole concoction. This dish is especially popular at Christmas time. It's served at restaurants that serve traditional Aruban fare like Brisas del Mar and Papiamento (see Chapter 10).

Rice and Beans/Peas (Puerto Rico and Jamaica)

The Spanish influence on Puerto Rico is evident in the simple local fare. You can get a steamy plate of rice with either black or red beans for a few dollars. We like to order it with a side of sweet plantains, which are kin to the banana, but you can't eat them raw. (Try plantains baked or fried with a little brown sugar.)

On Jamaica, you'll often find a variation of this cheap but good dish. In that country, rice and peas (red kidney beans) are cooked with coconut milk, a ham bone or bacon, and spices. Rice and peas are served as a side dish to almost every traditional Jamaican meal.

Bringing Island Flavor Home with You

Although you aren't allowed to bring fresh fruit and vegetables from the islands through customs, you can bring spices and alcoholic beverages used in many recipes. Islanders are incredibly warm and generous people, so if you love a particular recipe, the chef generally will be quite flattered and glad to pass the secrets on if you ask.

If you fall in love with a particular type of cooking, pick up a recipe book while you're on the island. We've sometimes thought we'd wait and get the same book back home. Big mistake. Too many times, that terrific little cookbook isn't available in the U.S. Of the Caribbean cookbooks we've surveyed, we especially like *The Essential Caribbean Cookbook* (edited by Heather Thomas; published by Courage Books) and *The Culinaria Caribbean: A Culinary Discovery* (written by Rosemary Parkinson; published by Konemann).

Chapter 38

Ten Tip-offs That You're a First-Time Visitor to the Caribbean

---

In This Chapter

▶ Revealing our own island bloopers

▶ Standing out in the Caribbean crowd — glaringly

---

*1*n our travels to the Caribbean, we've seen people pull some pretty silly moves — usually because they didn't know any better. In this chapter, we fess up to a few of our own outstanding gaffes. We also share surefire ways to convince everyone around you that you've never been in the Caribbean before.

No matter how well-prepared you are for your visit, something quirky is bound to happen, because in the tropics nothing ever goes as planned. When we were at The Ritz-Carlton, St. Thomas, for example, we came in to get ready for a dinner at the extremely dressy dining room only to find that work crews had severed the water lines and electricity for the rooms. Naturally, we'd spent the day wind- and sun-kissed on a yacht. The salt spray and sand were still in evidence as we slipped into the restaurant, praying for a dark table that night.

At the Wyndham El San Juan, Echo settled into our chic new suite's whirlpool for a relaxing bath. The jets were in a fixed position, spraying up, quickly resulting in an inch of water all over the marble bathroom, and a scene like something out of a Lucille Ball TV show.

We've also had trips where the resort's infirmary knew our family by name — and reputation. We were the folks who seemed drawn to mishaps that required medical attention.

Invariably, we forget sunglasses, because we leave our house before daybreak in order to catch the first flight of the day. Our memory lapse means that we make a stop at a Miami Airport gift stand and pay dearly for a pair that we expect to stay in one piece for most of the trip. (If you buy a cheap pair, you'll spend your vacation peering through lenses that provide the clarity of a shower curtain at a cheap motel.) Only recently did we figure out that we could pick up shades at a better price in the dutyfree shop at the airport.

On more than one occasion, we've left home without sunscreen, only to discover that the island we were visiting was suffering from a shortage. Echo's fair complexion inspires her to joke that her strolls on the beach can spark a glare alert. So when we couldn't find any sunscreen at our resort on Aruba, Echo had to stay away from the rays — not easy when you're vacationing so close to the equator.

Forgetfulness is forgivable; the look-at-me-I'm-new-here stuff is a whole other matter. To help you avoid primary pitfalls, we offer ten clues to making it clear that you've never been in the Caribbean. (In other words, don't try these in someone else's homeland, kids.)

Note: Yes, we do know how to count, and we do realize we list only nine tips here. Relax! When you're in the Caribbean, you need to learn to go with the flow.

Share Your Grievances Loudly

We're always amazed at how insensitive some visitors can be. They sit at dinner or on a tour bus and loudly complain about a litany of things that displease them. Just because islanders speak English with a different accent doesn't mean they don't understand what you say. Get a grip, or do all of us a favor and stay home.

Refer to the Local People as "Natives"

On many islands, locals are deeply insulted by being referred to as "natives" or "boy" or "girl." Understand that slavery inflicted a deep pain, and respect is so important that the English word "respect" is actually used as a greeting on some islands. Show service people common courtesy.

Show service people common courtesy. We've seen visitors who do not even deem it necessary to offer a greeting in the morning. Even in an all-inclusive that says tipping isn't allowed, we always tip discreetly; the staff is not well paid, and good service merits notice. We left money for the maids daily and wound up with fresh flowers on our pillows every evening at turndown time.

Other small gestures mean a great deal. On some of the poorer islands, photographs are great gifts for islanders. If a staff member has gone above and beyond, you might ask to take his or her photo and then send the person a copy.

Go Everywhere in Just Your Swimsuit

Island dress is generally pretty modest, especially on the British and Dutch islands. The only women you see going topless on the islands tend to be from Europe. (Some of Jamaica's all-inclusive chains have small sections of their beaches set aside for au naturel sunbathing.) Topless sunbathing is generally frowned upon.

If you're going to the market or for a walk through town, for goodness sake, wear a cover-up, no matter how casual you think the island is. We've seen women in halters and men in tank tops and bikini swim-briefs looking around inside churches on the islands. Hello, is anybody home? If you wouldn't dream of parading around your own town in such as fashion, what makes you think the spectacle is okay in a completely unfamiliar place? Would you go to the Piggly Wiggly in your thong?

Hunt with Your Camera

People on vacation with their cameras can be as obnoxious and rude as those who indulge their road rage from the enclosed safety of their cars. We've seen tour buses disgorge and people practically shove their cameras in vendors' faces and click away. One of the more egregious moves we've witnessed — and unfortunately most common — is the random snapping of photos of school children without permission. Imagine how you'd feel if someone suddenly appeared at your child's bus stop and started photographing your kids.

Take a moment to become acquainted with the people who intrigued you enough to want to take their pictures. Always ask permission before you take a photograph. And if someone says no, move on. Remember that important word: Respect.

Bring Your Entire Wardrobe

No matter what we bring, it's invariably too much. A couple of the other common fashion faux pas are as follows:

- ✔ Wearing black in the sweltering heat of midday when you're on an island tour.
- ✔ Bringing only high heels and dainty little sandals, or cowboy boots and heavy hiking boots.

We saw both in the USVIs. One heavy gentleman showed up the first day on St. Croix sporting black jeans, a long-sleeve black shirt, and black cowboy boots. He was as wet with sweat as if he'd swam over from St. Thomas. On St. Thomas, one member of our tour group inexplicably brought strappy, high-heeled sandals for the shopping expedition through the cobblestone, hilly streets. But not to worry, she had four pairs along for the excursion, in case calamity struck. She teetered and tottered like a drunken sailor on leave.

Refuse to Wear Sunscreen

If you like pain and court danger, bare your tender skin to the Caribbean's sizzling rays, especially if your hair is thinning or you think that you'd look hip with your hair braided in cornrows.

On one island, we saw a gentleman who sported what appeared to be a tic-tac-toe design on his bald head. It seems that at the beginning of his vacation, he had his long hair braided into cornrows. Then after an afternoon of swilling rum on the beach, he fell asleep. His head got severely sunburned and was driving him crazy when he sobered up, so he decided to shave the entire mess.

Stick to Your Culinary Comfort Zone

Turn up your nose at any local food or drinks, because you've never heard of them. One couple we encountered in our travels ordered fried shrimp and french fries at virtually every meal. As long as you're out for some new experiences, why not sample a few new tastes as well?

Shop Till You Drop

And make sure that you drag home as many dutyfree European imports as your money — and customs — allow. Don't bother with the beautiful handwrought crafts of the islanders, some of them investing the age-old skills of their ancestors. If you must return with evidence of where you've been, buy a T-shirt or something plastic that has the name of the island stamped out in neon letters. (We can't hold our tonques in our cheeks any longer. Forget the cheesy souvenirs; go for authenticity in your purchases. You can find plenty of island genius waiting to be appreciated.)

Feed the Fish and Touch the Coral

In the past decade that we've been diving and snorkeling in the Caribbean, we've witnessed the serious pummeling taken by the fragile coral reefs. Sadly, many of the reefs around Jamaica have collapsed. St. John's once-glorious Trunk Bay, which has a marked snorkeling trail, has been loved to death. On our last visit, we were with two first-time snorkelers who were thrilled with the few fish we saw, but we knew the rich bounty that this site should suport, and it's now sadly lacking.

We've seen heads of brain coral where numbskulls couldn't resist carving their initials. Please don't touch anything, don't purchase shells from locals, and don't feed the marine life. Feeding bread and other foodstuffs may bring you a thrill, but studies show that any human interference messes with the fragile ecosystem on the reef.

One of our funny-but-sad adventures involved a man we'll call Captain Coral to protect the not-so-innocent. At St. Croix's Buck Island, which has a national underwater marine park, this fellow insisted that he didn't need fins and that he was an old salt when it came to snorkeling. The guide repeatedly emphasized to the group not to venture off the marked trail. Soon enough, the man was lagging well behind our group. At one point he drifted and wound up in an area where the coral reefs were just beneath the surface. After scraping his belly over the reef, he literally stood up on the coral, putting his hand over his eyes like he was surveying the horizon to get his bearings. We thought the guide was going to go into a seizure as he shouted for the man to get off the fragile community of coral.

Fare Game: Choosing an Airline

Travel Agency: _____ Phone: _____

Agent's Name: _____ Quoted Fare: _____

Departure Schedule & Flight Information

Airline: _____ Airport: _____

Flight #: _____ Date: _____ Time: _____ a.m./p.m.

Arrives in:_____ Time: _____ a.m./p.m.

Connecting Flight (if any)

Amount of time between flights: _____ hours/mins

Airline: _____ Airport: _____

Flight #: _____ Date: _____ Time: _____ a.m./p.m.

Arrives in:_____ Time: _____ a.m./p.m.

Return Trip Schedule & Flight Information

Airline: _____ Airport: _____

Flight #: _____ Date: _____ Time: _____ a.m./p.m.

Arrives in:_____ Time: _____ a.m./p.m.

Connecting Flight (if any)

Amount of time between flights: _____ hours/mins

Airline: _____ Airport: _____

Flight #: _____ Date: _____ Time: _____ a.m./p.m.

Arrives in:_____ Time: _____ a.m./p.m.

Notes

Fare Game: Choosing an Airline

Travel Agency: _____ Phone: _____

Agent's Name: _____ Quoted Fare: _____

Departure Schedule & Flight Information

Airline: _____ Airport: _____

Flight #: _____ Date: _____ Time: _____ a.m./p.m.

Arrives in:_____ Time: _____ a.m./p.m.

Connecting Flight (if any)

Amount of time between flights: _____ hours/mins

Airline: _____ Airport: _____

Flight #: _____ Date: _____ Time: _____ a.m./p.m.

Arrives in:_____ Time: _____ a.m./p.m.

Return Trip Schedule & Flight Information

Airline: _____ Airport: _____

Flight #: _____ Date: _____ Time: _____ a.m./p.m.

Arrives in:_____ Time: _____ a.m./p.m.

Connecting Flight (if any)

Amount of time between flights: _____ hours/mins

Airline: _____ Airport: _____

Flight #: _____ Date: _____ Time: _____ a.m./p.m.

Arrives in:_____ Time: _____ a.m./p.m.

Notes

Making Dollars and Sense of It

Expense	Amount
Airfare	
Car Rental	
Lodging	
Parking	
Breakfast	
Lunch	
Dinner	
Baby-sitting	
Attractions	
Transportation	
Souvenirs	
Tips	
Grand Total	

Notes

Making Dollars and Sense of It

Expense	Amount
Airfare	
Car Rental	
Lodging	
Parking	
Breakfast	
Lunch	
Dinner	
Baby-sitting	
Attractions	
Transportation	
Souvenirs	
Tips	
Grand Total	

Notes

Sweet Dreams: Choosing Your Hotel

Enter the hotels where you'd prefer to stay based on location and price. Then use the worksheet below to plan your itinerary.

Hotel	Location	Price per night

Sweet Dreams: Choosing Your Hotel

Enter the hotels where you'd prefer to stay based on location and price. Then use the worksheet below to plan your itinerary.

Hotel	Location	Price per night

Places to Go, People to See, Things to Do

Enter the attractions you most would like to see. Then use the worksheet below to plan your itinerary.

Attractions	Amount of time you expect to spend there	Best day and time to go

Places to Go, People to See, Things to Do

Enter the attractions you most would like to see. Then use the worksheet below to plan your itinerary.

Attractions	Amount of time you expect to spend there	Best day and time to go

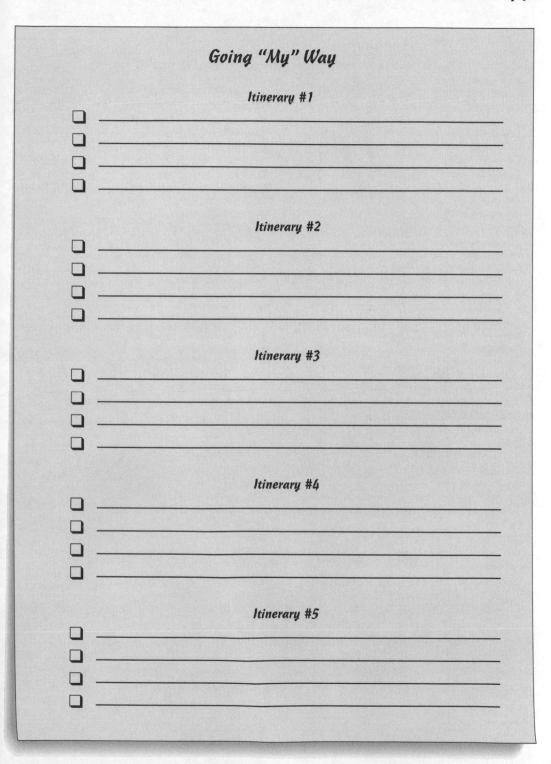

Going "My" Way

Itinerary #1

- ❏ _____
- ❏ _____
- ❏ _____
- ❏ _____

Itinerary #2

- ❏ _____
- ❏ _____
- ❏ _____
- ❏ _____

Itinerary #3

- ❏ _____
- ❏ _____
- ❏ _____
- ❏ _____

Itinerary #4

- ❏ _____
- ❏ _____
- ❏ _____
- ❏ _____

Itinerary #5

- ❏ _____
- ❏ _____
- ❏ _____
- ❏ _____

Itinerary #6

- ☐ _____
- ☐ _____
- ☐ _____
- ☐ _____

Itinerary #7

- ☐ _____
- ☐ _____
- ☐ _____
- ☐ _____

Itinerary #8

- ☐ _____
- ☐ _____
- ☐ _____
- ☐ _____

Itinerary #9

- ☐ _____
- ☐ _____
- ☐ _____
- ☐ _____

Itinerary #10

- ☐ _____
- ☐ _____
- ☐ _____
- ☐ _____

Menus & Venues

Enter the restaurants where you'd most like to dine. Then use the worksheet below to plan your itinerary.

Name	*Address/Phone*	*Cuisine/Price*

Menus & Venues

Enter the restaurants where you'd most like to dine. Then use the worksheet below to plan your itinerary.

Name	Address/Phone	Cuisine/Price

Notes

Notes

Index

• *U* •

Accommodations Index

Notes

··

_____

_____

_____

_____

_____

_____

_____

_____

_____

_____

_____

_____

_____

_____

_____

_____

_____

_____

_____

Notes

Discover Dummies Online!

The Dummies Web Site is your fun and friendly online resource for the latest information about *For Dummies*® books and your favorite topics. The Web site is the place to communicate with us, exchange ideas with other *For Dummies* readers, chat with authors, and have fun!

Ten Fun and Useful Things You Can Do at www.dummies.com

1. Win free *For Dummies* books and more!
2. Register your book and be entered in a prize drawing.
3. Meet your favorite authors through the IDG Books Worldwide Author Chat Series.
4. Exchange helpful information with other *For Dummies* readers.
5. Discover other great *For Dummies* books you must have!
6. Purchase Dummieswear® exclusively from our Web site.
7. Buy *For Dummies* books online.
8. Talk to us. Make comments, ask questions, get answers!
9. Download free software.
10. Find additional useful resources from authors.

Link directly to these ten fun and useful things at
http://www.dummies.com/10useful

For other technology titles from IDG Books Worldwide, go to
www.idgbooks.com

Not on the Web yet? It's easy to get started with *Dummies 101*®: *The Internet For Windows*® *98* or *The Internet For Dummies*® at local retailers everywhere.

Find other *For Dummies* books on these topics:
Business • Career • Databases • Food & Beverage • Games • Gardening • Graphics • Hardware
Health & Fitness • Internet and the World Wide Web • Networking • Office Suites
Operating Systems • Personal Finance • Pets • Programming • Recreation • Sports
Spreadsheets • Teacher Resources • Test Prep • Word Processing

IDG BOOKS WORLDWIDE BOOK REGISTRATION

Register This Book and Win!

We want to hear from you!

Visit **http://my2cents.dummies.com** to register this book and tell us how you liked it!

- ✔ Get entered in our monthly prize giveaway.

- ✔ Give us feedback about this book — tell us what you like best, what you like least, or maybe what you'd like to ask the author and us to change!

- ✔ Let us know any other *For Dummies*® topics that interest you.

Your feedback helps us determine what books to publish, tells us what coverage to add as we revise our books, and lets us know whether we're meeting your needs as a *For Dummies* reader. You're our most valuable resource, and what you have to say is important to us!

Not on the Web yet? It's easy to get started with *Dummies 101*®: *The Internet For Windows*® *98* or *The Internet For Dummies*®[3] at local retailers everywhere.

Or let us know what you think by sending us a letter at the following address:

For Dummies Book Registration
Dummies Press
10475 Crosspoint Blvd.
Indianapolis, IN 46256

BESTSELLING BOOK SERIES